JAVA
Distributed Objects

Bill McCarty and Luke Cassady-Dorion

A Division of Macmillan Computer Publishing
201 West 103rd St., Indianapolis, Indiana, 46290 USA

JAVA DISTRIBUTED OBJECTS

Copyright © 1999 by Sams

International Standard Book Number: 0-672-31537-8

Library of Congress Catalog Card Number: 98-86975

Printed in the United States of America

First Printing: December 1998

00   99   4   3

Trademarks

WARNING AND DISCLAIMER

EXECUTIVE EDITOR
Tim Ryan

DEVELOPMENT EDITOR
Gus Miklos

MANAGING EDITOR
Patrick Kanouse

PROJECT EDITOR
Carol L. Bowers

COPY EDITORS
Tonya Maddox
Bart Reed

INDEXER
Rebecca Salerno

PROOFREADER
Kim Cofer

TECHNICAL EDITOR
Mike Forsyth

SOFTWARE DEVELOPMENT SPECIALIST
Craig Atkins

INTERIOR DESIGN
Anne Jones

COVER DESIGN
Anne Jones

LAYOUT TECHNICIAN
Marcia Deboy

OVERVIEW

CONTENTS

APPENDIXES

FOREWORD

Every time I give a presentation somewhere in the world, I ask a simple question of the audience: "Raise your hand if your company is developing a distributed application." Depending on the type of audience, I might get from 10 percent to 90 percent of the audience to admit that they are taking on this difficult development task. The rest are wrong.

You see, every organization that features more than a single employee or a single computer—or needs to share information with another organization—is developing a distributed application. If they're not quite aware of that fact, then they are probably not designing their applications properly. They might end up with a "sneakernet," or they might find themselves with full-time personnel doing nothing but data file reformatting, or they might end up maintaining more server applications or application servers than necessary. Every organization builds distributed applications; that is, applications which mirror, reinforce, or enhance the workflow of the company and its relationships with buyers and suppliers. Because the purpose of an organization is to maximize the output of its employees by integrating their experience and abilities, the purpose of an Information Technology (IT) infrastructure is to maximize the output of its computing systems by integrating their data and functionality.

The complexity of distributed application development and integration—indeed, of any systems integration project—makes such projects difficult. The rapid pace of change in the computer industry makes it nigh impossible.

This tome helps alleviate this problem by gathering together, in one place, descriptions and examples of most of the relevant commercial solutions to distributed application integration problems. By recognizing the inherent and permanent heterogeneity of systems found in real IT shops today, this book provides a strong basis for making the tough choices between approaches based on the needs of the reader. An easy style with abundant examples makes it a pleasure to read, so I invite the reader to dive in without any more delay!

> Richard Mark Soley, Ph.D.
> Chairman and CEO
> Object Management Group, Inc.
> September 1998

ABOUT THE AUTHORS

Bill McCarty, Ph.D., is a professor of MIS and computer science at Azusa Pacific University. He has spent more than 20 years developing distributed computing applications, and seven years teaching advanced programming to graduate students. Dr. McCarty is also coauthor of the well-received *Object-Oriented Programming in Java*.

Luke Cassady-Dorion is a professional programmer with eight years of experience developing commercial distributed computing applications. He specializes in Java/CORBA programming.

Rick Hightower is a member of Intel's Enterprise Architecture Lab. He has a decade of experience writing software, from embedded systems to factory automation solutions. Rick's current work involves emerging solutions using middleware and component technologies, including Java and JavaBeans, COM, and CORBA. Rick wrote Chapter 20 of this book.

About the Technical Editor

Mike Forsyth, Technical Director, Calligrafix, graduated with a computer science degree from Heriot Watt University, Edinburgh, Scotland, and developed high speed free text retrieval systems. He is currently developing Java servlet and persistent store solutions using ObjectStore and Orbix in pan European Extranet projects.

ACKNOWLEDGMENTS

Luke Andrew Cassady-Dorion: As I sit looking over the hundreds of pages that form the tome you are now holding, I am finally able to catch my breath and think about everything that has gone into this book. Starting at ground zero, none of this could have come together without the work done by Bill McCarty, my co-author. Bill, you have put together an excellent collection of work; thank you. In addition, Tim Ryan, Gus Miklos, Jeff Taylor and the countless faces that I never see have worked day and night to help this project. To all of you, this could never have happened without your help; bravo. My family, who has always supported everything that I did (even when I dropped out of college and moved to California), your support means mountains to me. All of my friends, who understood when I said that I could not go out as I had to "work on my book," thank you, and the next round is on me. Finally, to all of the musicians, composers and authors who kept me company as I wrote this book. Maria Callas, Phillip Glass, Stephen Sondheim, Cole Porter, and Ayn Rand, your work has kept me sane during this long process. Finally, a word of advice to my readers: Enjoy this book, but know that the best computer programmers do come up for air. Make sure that there is always time in your life for fun, fiction, family, friends and—of course—really good food.

Bill McCarty: As with any book, a small army has had a hand in bringing about this book. Some of them I don't even know by name, but I owe each of them my thanks. I'm especially grateful for the work of my co-author, Luke, who wrote the CORBA material that forms the core of the book. I'm also grateful for the wise counsel and able assistance of my literary agent, Margot Maley of Waterside Productions, without whom this book wouldn't have been completed. I thank Tim Ryan of Macmillan Computer Publishing who graciously offered help when I needed it and who generously spent many hours helping us write a better book. Gus Miklos, our development editor, not only set straight many crooked constructions, but taught me much in the process. I envy his future students. My family patiently endured untold hardships during the writing of this book; I greatly appreciate their understanding, support, and love. My eternal thanks go to the Lord Jesus Christ, who paid the full price of my redemption from sin and called me to be His disciple and friend. To Him be all glory, and power, and honor now and forever.

TELL US WHAT YOU THINK!

As the reader of this book, you are our most important critic and commentator. We value your opinion and want to know what we're doing right, what we could do better, what areas you'd like to see us publish in, and any other words of wisdom you're willing to pass our way.

As the Executive Editor for the Java team at Macmillan Computer Publishing, I welcome your comments. You can fax, email, or write me directly to let me know what you did or didn't like about this book—as well as what we can do to make our books stronger.

Please note that I won't have time to help you with Java programming problems.

When you write, please be sure to include this book's title and author as well as your name and phone or fax number. I will carefully review your comments and share them with the author and editors who worked on the book.

Fax: 317-817-7070

Email: java@mcp.com

Mail: Tim Ryan, Executive Editor
           Java Team
           Macmillan Computer Publishing
           201 West 103rd Street
           Indianapolis, IN 46290 USA

INTRODUCTION

STRUCTURE OF THIS BOOK

Now that you are familiar with the aims of this book, let's explore its structure. This will help you map out your study of the book. As you'll discover, you may not need to read every chapter.

Part I: Basic Concepts

Distributed object technologies do not stand on their own. Instead, they depend on a set of related technologies that provide important services and facilities. You can't thoroughly understand distributed object technologies without a solid understanding of networks, sockets, and databases, for example. The purpose of Part I is to acquaint you with these related technologies and prepare you for the more advanced material in subsequent parts of this book.

Chapter 1, "Distributed Object Computing"

Chapter 1 sets the stage for the main topic of this book by introducing fundamental concepts and terms related to distributed objects. It also explains the structure of this book and provides some friendly advice intended to enhance your understanding and application of the material. Specifically, Chapter 1 covers what distributed object systems are; why objects should be distributed; which technologies facilitate the implementation of distributed object systems; which related technologies distributed objects draw upon; and who should read this book and how it should be used.

Chapter 2, "TCP/IP Networking"

Chapter 2 introduces the basic terms and concepts of TCP/IP networking, the technology of the Internet and Web. You'll learn how various protocols and Internet services work and how to perform simple TCP/IP troubleshooting.

Chapter 3, "Object-Oriented Analysis and Design"

Chapter 3 presents an overview of object-oriented analysis and design (OOA and OOD), including the Unified Modeling Language (UML), which is used in subsequent chapters to describe the structure of distributed object systems.

Chapter 4, "Distributed Architectures"

Chapter 4 presents an evolutionary perspective on distributed computing architectures. You'll learn the strengths and weaknesses of a variety of system architectures.

Chapter 5, "Design Patterns"

Chapter 5 provides an overview of the important and useful topic of design patterns, the themes that commonly appear in software designs. You'll learn how to describe and use patterns and learn about several especially useful patterns.

Chapter 6, "The Airline Reservation System Model"

Chapter 6 presents an example application that we refer to throughout subsequent chapters, in which we implement portions of the example application using a variety of technologies. The Airline Reservation System helps you see how technologies can be applied to real-world systems rather than the smaller pedagogical examples included in the explanatory chapters.

Part II: Java

Part II presents the Java language and APIs important to distributed object systems.

Chapter 7, "Java Overview"

Despite the impression conveyed by media hype, Java is not the only object-oriented language, nor is it the only language that you can use to build distributed object systems. Programmers have successfully built distributed systems using other languages, notably Smalltalk and C++. However, this book is unabashedly Java-centric. Here are some reasons for this choice:

- Java is an easy language to read and learn. Much of Java's syntax and semantics are based on C++, so C++ programmers can readily get the gist of a section of Java code. Moreover, Java omits some of the most gnarly features of C++, making Java programs generally simpler and clearer than their C++ counterparts.

- Java provides features that are important to the development of distributed object systems, such as thread programming, socket programming, object serialization, reusable components (Java Beans), a security API, and a SQL database API (JDBC). Although all these are available for C++, they are not a standard part of the language or its libraries. We'll briefly survey each of these features.

- Java bytecodes are portable, giving Java a real advantage over C++ in a heterogeneous network environment. Java's detractors decry the overhead implicit in the interpretation of bytecodes. But Java compiler technology has improved significantly over the last several years. Many expect that Java's execution speed will soon rival, and in some cases surpass, that of C++.

- Java is inexpensive. You don't need to purchase an expensive IDE to learn or use Java: You can run and modify the programs in this book using the freely available JDK. Of course, if you decide to spend a great deal of time writing Java programs and getting paid for doing so, an IDE is a wise investment.

- The last reason is the best one: Java is fun. One of the authors has been programming for almost three decades. But not since those first weeks writing Fortran code for the IBM 1130 has programming been as much fun as the last several years spent writing Java code. Having taught Java programming to dozens of students who've had the same experience, we can confidently predict that you too will enjoy Java.

For readers not familiar with Java, Chapter 7 presents enough of the Java language and APIs to enable most readers—especially those already fluent in C++—to understand, modify, and run the example programs in this book. If you find you'd prefer a more thorough explanation of Java, please consider *Object-Oriented Programming in Java*, by Gilbert and McCarty (Waite Group Press, 1997), which is designed to teach programming and software development as well as the Java language and APIs.

Chapter 8, "Java Threads"

Chapter 8 presents threads, an important topic for distributed object systems. The chapter deals not only with the syntax and semantics of Java's thread facilities, but also with several pitfalls of thread programming, including race conditions and deadlocks.

Chapter 9, "Java Serialization and Beans"

Chapter 9 presents two additional Java APIs: serialization and Beans. Serialization is important to creating persistent and portable objects, while beans are important to creating reusable software components.

Part III: Java's Networking and Enterprise APIs

Part III presents Java's networking and enterprise APIs. Distributed object systems use these APIs either directly or through the mediation of a distributed object technology.

Chapter 10, "Security"

Chapter 10 presents Java's security API, including ciphers and public key encryption systems.

Chapter 11, "Relational Databases and Structured Query Language (SQL)"

Chapter 11 presents the basics of relational database technology, including an overview of Structured Query Language (SQL).

Chapter 12, "Java Database Connectivity (JDBC)"

Chapter 12 presents the JDBC API, which facilitates access to SQL databases.

Chapter 13, "Sockets"

Chapter 13 explains socket programming and shows how to create clients and servers that exchange data using sockets.

Chapter 14, "Socket-Based Implementation of the Airline Reservation System"

Chapter 14 describes a socket-based implementation of a portion of the Airline Reservation System example presented in Chapter 6. Chapter 14 helps you place the explanations of Chapter 13 in a real-world context.

Chapter 15, "Remote Method Invocation (RMI)"

Chapter 15 presents RMI and shows how to create and access remote objects.

Chapter 16, "RMI-Based Implementation of the Airline Reservation System"

Chapter 16 describes an RMI-based implementation of a portion of the Airline Reservation System example presented in Chapter 6. Chapter 16 helps you place the explanations of Chapter 15 in a real-world context.

Chapter 17, "Java Help, Java Mail, and Other Java APIs"

Chapter 17 describes two more APIs of interest to developers of distributed object systems: Java Help and Java Mail. This chapter also surveys several Java APIs that are currently under development.

Part IV: Non-CORBA Approaches to Distributed Computing

Part IV describes three non-CORBA approaches to distributed computing: RMI, Java servlets, and DCOM.

Chapter 18, "Servlets and Common Gateway Interface (CGI)"

Chapter 18 presents Java servlets, which provide services to Web clients. The chapter also describes CGI and surveys the HTML statements necessary to build typical CGI forms for Web browsers.

Chapter 19, "Servlet-Based Implementation of the Airline Reservation System"

Chapter 19 describes a servlet-based implementation of a portion of the Airline Reservation System example presented in Chapter 6. Chapter 19 helps you place the explanations of Chapter 18 in a real-world context.

Chapter 20, "Distributed Component Object Model (DCOM)"

Chapter 20 describes Microsoft's DCOM and compares and contrasts it with other distributed object technologies.

Part V: The CORBA Approach to Distributed Computing

Part V presents CORBA and shows how to write Java clients and servers that interoperate using the CORBA object bus.

Chapter 21, "CORBA Overview"

Chapter 21 presents an overview of CORBA, the OMG, and the process whereby the OMG ratifies a specification.

Chapter 22, "CORBA Architecture"

Chapter 22 describes the CORBA software universe and shows you how CORBA describes objects in a language-independent fashion.

Chapter 23, "Survey of CORBA ORBs"

Chapter 23 surveys popular CORBA ORBs, related products, and development tools.

Chapter 24, "A CORBA Server"

Chapter 24 presents a simple CORBA server written in Java and explains its implementation in detail.

Chapter 25, "A CORBA Client"

Chapter 25 presents a simple CORBA client written in Java and explains its implementation in detail.

Chapter 26, "CORBA-Based Implementation of the Airline Reservation System"

Chapter 26 describes a CORBA-based implementation of a portion of the Airline Reservation System example presented in Chapter 6. Chapter 26 helps you place the explanations of Chapters 24 and 25 in a real-world context

Chapter 27, "Quick CORBA: CORBA Without IDL"

Chapter 27 presents Netscape's Caffeine and other technologies that let Java programmers create CORBA clients and servers without writing IDL.

Part VI: Advanced CORBA

Part VI describes advanced CORBA features, facilities, and services.

Chapter 28, "The Portable Object Adapter (POA)"

Chapter 28 discusses one area that is changing under CORBA 3.0. The Basic Object Adapter (BOA) is being replaced with the Portable Object Adapter (POA). Since the POA will eventually replace the BOA, this chapter prepares you for the upcoming change by first discussing problems inherent in the BOA, and then discussing how the POA solves these problems. The chapter concludes with the POA IDL and a collection of examples showing how Java applications use the POA.

Chapter 29, "Internet Inter-ORB Protocol (IIOP)"

Chapter 29 presents details of the Inter-ORB Protocol and demonstrates how it supports interoperation of CORBA products from multiple vendors.

Chapter 30, "The Naming Service"

Chapter 30 presents CORBA's naming service, which enables CORBA objects to locate and use remote objects.

Chapter 31, "The Event Service"

Chapter 31 presents CORBA's event service, which enables CORBA objects to reliably send and receive messages representing events.

Chapter 32, "Interface Repository, Dynamic Invocation, Introspection, and Reflection"

Chapter 32 presents the CORBA Interface Repository and Dynamic Invocation Interface (DII), which enable CORBA objects to discover and use new types (classes).

Chapter 33, "Other CORBA Facilities and Services"

Chapter 33 surveys other CORBA facilities and services that are less commonly available than those presented in previous chapters.

Part VII: Agent Technologies

Part VII presents software agents, which are objects that can migrate from network node to node.

Chapter 34, "Voyager Agent Technology"

Chapter 34 presents software agent technology, using ObjectSpace's Voyager as a reference technology.

Chapter 35, "Voyager-Based Implementation of the Airline Reservation System"

Chapter 35 describes a Voyager-based implementation of a portion of the Airline Reservation System example presented in Chapter 6. Chapter 35 helps you place the explanations of Chapter 34 in a real-world context.

Part VIII: Summary and References

Part VIII provides a summary of the book's contents, suggestions for further study, and handy references.

Chapter 36, "Summary"

Chapter 36 recaps the book's contents and offers suggestions for further study.

Appendixes

Appendix A, "Useful Resources"

Appendix A presents a bibliography of information useful to developers of distributed object systems.

Appendix B, "Quick References"

Appendix B presents quick references that summarize key information and APIs in handy form.

Appendix C, "How to Get the Most from the CD-ROM"

Appendix C provides a summary of the contents of the CD-ROM that accompanies this book. It also provides system requirements, installation instructions, and a general licensing agreement for the software on the CD-ROM. (Additional licensing terms may be required by the individual vendors on certain software.)

Who Should Read This Book?

This book is written for the intermediate to advanced reader. We assume that you've written enough programs to know your way around the tools of the trade, such as operating systems, editors, and command-line utilities. It's helpful if you've had some previous experience with Java. However, we provide an overview that will help you make sense of the Java example programs even if you haven't previously worked with Java.

We assume that you know about program variables, arrays, and files. It's helpful if your programming experience includes some work with an object-oriented language. But we provide some explanation of basic object-oriented programming along with our explanation of Java.

However, we don't assume that you're familiar with networks, object-oriented analysis and design, or Unified Modeling Language (UML). This book includes chapters that address each of these important topics.

We don't assume that your Java experience includes an understanding of advanced features such as threads, Java Beans, serialization, or security. We also don't assume that you're familiar with SQL or JDBC. Instead, we present all these topics.

So if you've got a solid understanding of programming, this book contains all you need to equip yourself to develop distributed object systems.

HOW TO USE THIS BOOK

A book can communicate ideas, but it cannot impart skills. Reading this book won't instantly make you a better programmer, nor a competent developer of distributed object systems. Experience is, in the end, the only teacher of skills.

Here's how to gain experience in an unfamiliar programming domain: You should run each of the example programs for yourself, studying them line by line until you thoroughly understand how they work. It's best to type them, rather than simply copy them from the CD-ROM. By doing so, you'll force yourself to notice and question everything. Lest you think this is mere idle advice, be assured that we apply this method ourselves. One of the authors learned UNIX system programming, X-Windows, and Java exactly this way. In the case of X-Windows he typed in, ran, and studied all the examples in three textbooks. The method requires time and patience, but it is quite effective.

After you've understood a program, you should modify it to perform new, but related, functions. Humans learn—or at least have the capacity to learn—from their mistakes. The more mistakes you make and recognize as such, the more you've learned. Here's a point to ponder: You won't make enough mistakes by merely reading this book. So get in front of your keyboard and make some mistakes. That's the way to learn.

BASIC CONCEPTS

PART

I

IN THIS PART

DISTRIBUTED OBJECT COMPUTING

IN THIS CHAPTER

Somewhat oddly, the principal purpose of a system of distributed objects is to better integrate an organization. By properly distributing pieces of software (objects) throughout the organization, the organization becomes more cohesive, more effective, and more efficient. As you might know from experience, the devil is in that important adverb *properly*. Experience shows that scattering software to the wind is likely to bring about disorder, ineffectiveness, and inefficiency.

This book aims to help you avoid such catastrophes, by introducing you to a comprehensive toolkit of technologies and methods for implementing distributed object systems. Our emphasis is on the Common Object Request Broker Architecture (CORBA) because, as we see it, it's the most powerful technology for building distributed object systems available today. But we don't give other options short shrift. We describe each technological option, present and explain simple examples showing how to use it, compare and contrast it with other technologies, and provide a larger example that demonstrates how to apply it to real-world-sized systems.

This chapter sets the stage for the play that follows, by introducing fundamental concepts and terms related to distributed objects. It also explains the structure of this book and provides some friendly advice intended to enhance your understanding and application of the material it presents. More specifically, in this chapter you learn:

- What distributed object systems are.

    Objects are software units that encapsulate data and behavior. Objects that reside outside the local host are called *remote objects*; systems that feature them are termed *distributed object systems*.

- Why objects should be distributed.

    The introduction to this chapter presents a brief business case for distributed object systems. However, the introduction doesn't explain how distributed object technologies actually support the business case by providing more effective and efficient computation. That explanation is the topic of the second section of this chapter.

- Which technologies facilitate the implementation of distributed object systems.

    Before the advent of the Web, people talked about the rapidity of technological change. Now, technology seems to change so rapidly that few dare talk about it, lest they suffer the social embarrassment of reporting old news. In the third section of this chapter, we'll give you a map that will help you navigate the forest of distributed object acronyms.

- Which related technologies distributed objects draw upon.

    Distributed objects didn't autonomously spring into existence, and they don't exist within a technological vacuum. Rather, they're a logical milestone in the progress of computing. In the fourth section of this chapter, we'll identify and describe the technological progenitors and cousins that make distributed objects what they are.

* Who should read this book and how it should be used.

Generally, this information is presented in the introduction of a book. However, we've observed that most software developers are impatient to read about technology and therefore skip book introductions. Because this information is important, we've put it in this chapter, where we hope you'll read it and follow its advice. For those who actually read introductions, we've included one in this book that contains an abridged version of this material. So, if you read the introduction, congratulations, and thanks. Be sure to read this section anyway, because it contains information not found in the introduction.

WHAT IS A DISTRIBUTED OBJECT SYSTEM?

Simply put, *distributed object computing* is the product of a marriage between two technologies: networking and object-oriented programming. Let's examine each of these technologies.

Distributed Systems

The word *distributed* in the term *distributed object system* connotes geographical separation or dispersal. A distributed system includes *nodes* that perform computations. A node may be a PC, a mainframe computer, or another sort of device. The nodes of a distributed system are scattered. You refer to the node you use as the *local node* and to other nodes as *remote nodes*. Of course, from the point of view of a user at another node, your node is the remote node and his is the local node.

Networks make distributed computing possible: You can't have a distributed system without a network that connects the nodes and allows them to exchange data. One of the great forces driving distributed systems forward is the Web, which you can think of as the largest distributed computing system in the world. Of course, the Web is a rather unique type of system. For example, it has no single purpose, no single designer, and no single maintainer. The Web is actually a federation of systems, a network of networks. A unique aspect of the Web is its popularity: A rapidly increasing proportion of computers connects to the Web and therefore—at least potentially—to one another.

Object-Oriented Systems

Of course, not every distributed system is "object oriented." However, mingling objects and distributed computing yields a synergistic result akin to that of mingling tomatoes and basil. You can have objects that aren't distributed, and you can distribute software that's not object oriented, just as can make pasta sauce with either tomatoes or basil. But, put the two together, and something marvelous happens.

In the case of software systems, that marvelous result is *standardization*. You've probably read many accounts that define object-oriented technology: What it is and how it differs from non–object-oriented technology. We've written a few of these, and almost all (some of our own included) make too much of too little. The real uniqueness of object-oriented technology can be summed up in a single word: *interface*.

An interface is a software affordance, like the knob on your front door, the steering wheel of your car, or a button on your television remote control. You manipulate and interact with an affordance to operate the device of which it is a part. Software interfaces work the same way. When you want to use the XYZ Alphabetic Sorter Object in your program, you don't need to know what's inside it, how it was made, or how it works. You only need to know its interface.

Our modern civilization rests on the notion of conveniences. If we had to understand electronics in order to watch TV or automotive engineering to drive to the supermarket, our lives would change radically. Yet, until object-oriented technology, the software world required programmers to surmount analogous obstacles.

If you're familiar with object-oriented technology, you may object to this simple—seemingly simplistic—explanation. "What of P-I-E (polymorphism, inheritance, and encapsulation)?" you might wish to protest. As we see it, these important properties are not ends in themselves but merely means—means intended to provide flexible, reliable, easy-to-use interfaces. In a nutshell, because of these properties, object-oriented programs provide more flexible, reliable, and easy-to-use interfaces than non–object-oriented systems.

These better interfaces, in turn, provide two useful properties: *interchangeability* and *interoperability*. Just as precision-machined components spurred an industrial revolution, interchangeable software components—made possible by high-quality object-oriented interfaces—have spurred a software revolution. You may not be aware that today's extensive markets for software components—spelling checkers, email widgets, and database interfaces, for example—did not exist even ten years ago. Today, using an Interactive Development Environment (IDE), you can drop a chart-drawing component into your program rather than write one yourself, saving you and your employer both time and trouble. If your needs are simple, it may not matter a great deal which chart-drawing component you choose to use. Any of the available choices will work in your program because their standardized interfaces make them interchangeable.

Standardized interfaces also promote *interoperability*, the ability of components to work together. Software components from different vendors can be plugged into an object bus, which lets the components exchange data. You can build entire systems from software components that have never previously been configured together. The components will interoperate successfully because their interfaces are standardized.

The case for the use of object-oriented systems could be further elaborated. If you're interested in the topic, you should consult any of the several books by Dr. Brad Cox, which are among the best on the subject.

WHY DISTRIBUTE OBJECTS?

So far, we've established that objects are "good" and that it's possible, by means of networking, to distribute them. However, the question remains: Why distribute them?

If your organization occupies a single location and has few computers, you probably don't need a distributed object system. However, in search of economies of scale and scope, many organizations have grown large, occupying many locations and owning many computers. These organizations can benefit from applying distributed object technologies.

To see these benefits, consider the polar opposite of a distributed system: a centralized system supported by a single mainframe computer, as illustrated in Figure 1.1. In this configuration, the mainframe computer does all the application processing, even though the remote systems may be PCs capable of executing millions of instructions per second. The remote systems act as mere data entry terminals.

As proponents of the client/server architecture have pointed out, several drawbacks attend this monolithic architecture:

- When the mainframe computer is unavailable, no processing can be performed anywhere.
- All data must be transported across the network to the central computer, which is the sole repository of data. This applies even if the data is needed only locally. The resulting volume of traffic requires greater network bandwidth than an architecture that stores data near the point of origin or probable need.
- The single mainframe computer is more costly to purchase and operate than an equivalently powerful set of smaller computers.

In contrast to the rigid "the mainframe does it all" policy that underlies a nondistributed system, distributed object systems take a more flexible approach: Perform the computation at the most cost-effective location. Of course, you can err by understanding the term *cost-effective* in too narrow a sense. We use the term as meaning the long-run total cost of building and operating a system, not merely such obvious and tangible initial costs as hardware.

FIGURE 1.1

A centralized system often uses resources inefficiently.

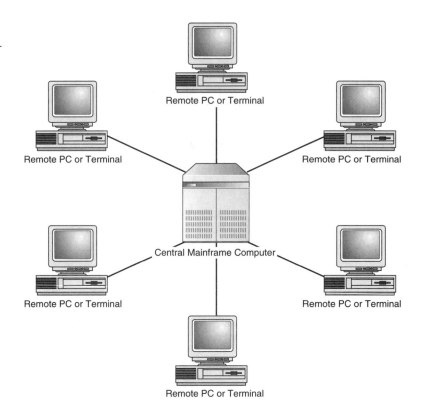

If your interest is technology rather than business, you may be put off by this mention of cost-effectiveness. Many books on distributed computing omit discussion of the reasons for distributing computation. Perhaps the reasons are so obvious that they go without saying. However, it's altogether too common for fans of technology to apply a technology just because it's the latest and "best." If distributed object systems are to have a future, software developers must build them intelligently. Only by bearing in mind the goals and needs of the organization can developers correctly decide which computations should be performed where. You'll learn more about computing architectures in Chapter 4, "Distributed Architectures."

DISTRIBUTED OBJECT TECHNOLOGIES

A distributed object technology aims at *location transparency*, thus making it just as easy to access and use an object on a remote node (called, logically enough, a *remote object*) as an object on a local node. Location transparency involves these functions:

- Locating and loading remote classes

- Locating remote objects and providing references to them
- Enabling remote method calls, including passing of remote objects as arguments and return values
- Notifying programs of network failures and other problems

The first three functions are familiar even to programmers of nondistributed systems. Nondistributed systems must be able to locate and load classes, obtain references to local objects, and perform local method calls. Handling nonlocal references is more complex than handling local references, but the distributed computing technology shoulders this burden, freeing the programmer to focus on the application. Let's consider each of these functions in more detail.

The first function, locating and loading remote classes, is needed by ordinary Java applets, which may contain references to classes that the browser must download from the host on which the applet resides. However, distributed object systems demand a somewhat more flexible capability that can locate and download classes from several hosts. Such a capability lets system developers store classes on whatever system can provide the classes most efficiently. Developers can even store classes on multiple systems, possibly providing improved system performance or availability.

The second function, locating and obtaining references to remote objects, requires some sort of catalog or database of objects and a server that provides access to the catalog. When your program needs a particular service, it can ask the catalog server to provide it with a reference to a suitable server object. Normally, object references are memory pointers or handles that reference entries within object tables. You can't simply send such a reference across a network, because it won't be valid at the destination node. At the least, remote references must encode their node of origin. Languages such as Java that support garbage collection of unused objects require mechanisms that can determine whether remote references to an object exist. An object must not be scrapped if it's in use by a remote node, even if it's not being used by the local node.

The third function, supporting method calls, requires mechanisms for obtaining a reference to the target method as well as mechanisms for transporting arguments and return values across the network. Because objects may contain other objects as components, much activity may be required to perform an apparently simple method call.

The fourth function, notifying programs of network failures, may be unfamiliar to you if you've programmed only nondistributed systems. You may even think that this function is unnecessary, but it serves an important purpose. Distributed computing differs from ordinary computing in several ways, so it's not always possible or even desirable to provide full location transparency. The fourth function is necessary so that the distributed system can notify programs when location transparency fails.

Consider the case of a nondistributed system running on a standalone computer. If the computer malfunctions, it can do no useful work and might as well be shut down. Distributed systems operate differently. If a single node of the network malfunctions, the other nodes can—and should—continue to operate. In a distributed environment, an attempt to reference an object may fail, yet such a failure need not entail shutting down the application. It may be more appropriate to simply advise the user that the requested object is not currently available. Such a fail-soft approach is less commonly helpful in standalone applications, where availability of objects is all or nothing.

Most approaches to distributed computing define special exceptions that are thrown when an attempt to reference a remote object fails. As you'll see in subsequent chapters, writing code to handle such exceptions is one of the greatest differences between programming distributed systems and nondistributed systems. Fortunately, due to help provided by distributed object technologies, this code is not difficult to write.

Now that you have a foundation for understanding distributed object technologies, let's survey some of the specific technologies you'll meet in subsequent chapters: Remote Method Invocation (RMI), Microsoft's Distributed Component Object Model (DCOM), the Common Object Request Broker Architecture (CORBA), and ObjectSpace's Voyager.

Remote Method Invocation (RMI)

Sun developed RMI as a Java-based approach to distributed computing. RMI provides a registry that lets programs obtain references to remote server objects and uses Java's serialization facility to transfer method arguments and return values across a network. Though it's Java-based, RMI is not necessarily Java only. By combining RMI with the Java Native-code Interface (JNI), you can interface C/C++ code with RMI, providing a bridge to non-Java legacy systems.

Moreover, Sun has announced a joint project with IBM that aims to develop technology that will let RMI interoperate with CORBA. Because RMI is implemented using pure Java and is part of the core Java package, no special software or drivers are needed to use RMI. However, Microsoft has announced that it does not plan to provide RMI as part of its implementation of Java, choosing instead to put the full weight of its considerable marketing muscle behind its own distributed object technology, DCOM.

Distributed Component Object Model (DCOM)

Microsoft's DCOM is an evolutionary development of Microsoft's ActiveX software component technology. DCOM lets you create server objects that can be remotely accessed by Visual Basic, C, and C++ programs. Visual J++ and Microsoft's Java Interactive Development Environment (IDE) let you write Java programs that access

DCOM objects. However, such programs will not currently run on non-Microsoft platforms. If other vendors choose to support DCOM, it may someday be possible to write portable Java programs that access DCOM servers.

Common Object Request Broker Architecture (CORBA)

The Object Management Group (OMG) is a consortium of over 800 companies that have jointly developed a set of specifications for technologies that support distributed object systems. CORBA specifies the functions and interfaces of an Object Request Broker (ORB), which acts as an object bus that allows remote objects to interact. Unlike RMI, CORBA is language-neutral. To use CORBA with a given programming language, you employ bindings that map the data types of the language to CORBA data types. CORBA bindings are available for COBOL, C, C++, and Java, among other languages.

Several vendors provide software that complies with CORBA. Because CORBA's interfaces are standard, you can build systems that include products from multiple vendors. However, the way you write a program to access an ORB does vary somewhat from vendor to vendor, so CORBA programs are not portable across platforms. Because CORBA implementations are widespread and relatively mature, this book focuses on CORBA. Moreover, you can explore CORBA without incurring significant cost: Sun freely distributes Java IDL, an ORB, with its Java Developer's Kit (JDK).

Missing from the CORBA bandwagon is Microsoft, which touts its own distributed object technology, DCOM, as superior to CORBA. However, Microsoft users find no shortage of support for CORBA among the vendors who offer CORBA products for use on Microsoft platforms.

Voyager

ObjectSpace offers a free software package called Voyager, which provides the ability to create and control Java-based software agents. *Agents* are mobile objects that can move from node to node. For example, an agent that requires access to a database may relocate itself to the node that hosts the database rather than cause a large volume of data to be transmitted across the network. The same agent may later relocate itself to the user's local node so that it can efficiently interact with the user.

Because Java byte codes are portable, Java offers unique developers of software agents unique advantages. Voyager makes it easy to explore software agent technology. Moreover, Voyager is no mere toy: Several companies have built sophisticated distributed object systems using Voyager.

FROM HERE

You've learned what distributed objects are and why distributed object systems are useful. You've learned about technologies important to the implementation of distributed systems, including RMI, DCOM, CORBA, and software agents. You've also learned about key enabling technologies such as Java and networking on the Web. The rest of this book builds on this chapter as its foundation.

TCP/IP NETWORKING

IN THIS CHAPTER

The pre-Columbian Indians known as the Inca, who lived along the Pacific coast of South America, knew the importance of communication. They linked an empire of about 12 million people with an elaborate system of roads. Two main north-south roads ran for about 2,250 miles, one along the coast and the other inland along the Andes mountains. The Inca roads featured many interconnecting links, as well as rock tunnels and vine suspension bridges. Runners could carry messages, represented by means of knotted strings, along these roads at the rate of 150 miles per day. Ironically, the Inca's effective transportation system made it much easier for the Spanish Conquistadors to conquer them.

In previous eras of computing, computers were mostly standalone devices; data communication was relatively limited. In contrast, the present era of computing is dominated by networks and networking. Just as the Inca road system permitted rapid delivery of information in the form of knotted strings, today's modern networks permit rapid delivery of digitally encoded packets of information.

Although there are a number of networking standards, the Transmission Control Protocol/Internet Protocol (TCP/IP) family of protocols has established itself as the most popular standard, connecting tens of millions of hosts of every imaginable manufacture and type. In this chapter you learn

- How the TCP/IP family of protocols is structured

  The TCP/IP protocols are arranged in four layers of increasing sophistication and power: the network access layer, the Internet layer, the transport layer, and the application layer.

- How the TCP/IP protocol moves data from one device to another

  TCP/IP forms data into packets and uses IP addresses to interrogate routers, which supply a route from the source to the destination.

- About the major TCP/IP services

  TCP/IP doesn't merely move data, it provides a rich variety of services to users, programmers, and network administrators.

- How to troubleshoot TCP/IP problems

  You don't need to be a TCP/IP guru to solve many common TCP/IP problems. You learn here how to use commonly available tools to diagnose TCP/IP problems.

TCP/IP PROTOCOL ARCHITECTURE

A *protocol* is nothing more than an agreed way of doing something. Diplomatic protocol, for example, avoids unintentional insult of dignitaries by rigidly fixing the sequence in which they are introduced to one another. In the world of computer networks, a communications protocol specifies how computers (or other devices) cooperate in exchanging messages. Some people refer to communications protocols as *handshaking*, which is an accurate, though metaphorical, picture of what's involved.

Diplomats often find it difficult to get disputing parties together to talk about and resolve their differences. In the hardware/software world, it seems even more difficult to introduce dissimilar computers to one another and get them to shake hands. As a consequence, communications protocols are vastly more complex than diplomatic protocols. As you'll see, a whole family of protocols is involved in simply moving a message from one computer to another.

In his book, *The Wealth of Nations*, the great economist Adam Smith argued in favor of core competencies. He believed that economic wealth is maximized when nations and individuals do only what they do best. Centuries later, modern corporations struggle to apply his advice as they decide which business functions should be maintained and which should be outsourced.

The TCP/IP protocols apply this wisdom: That's why they comprise a number of smaller protocols, rather than one enormous protocol. Each protocol has a specific role, leaving other considerations to its sibling protocols.

Unfortunately, there are so many TCP/IP protocols that the beginner is overwhelmed by their sheer number. To simplify understanding TCP/IP protocols, each protocol is commonly presented as belonging to one of four layers, as shown in Figure 2.1. Every protocol in a layer has a related function. The layers near the bottom of the hierarchy (network access and Internet) provide more primitive functions than those near the top of the hierarchy (transport and application). Typically, the bottom layers are relatively more concerned with technology than the top layers, which are concerned with user needs.

FIGURE 2.1

The four layers of the TCP/IP protocols form a pyramid.

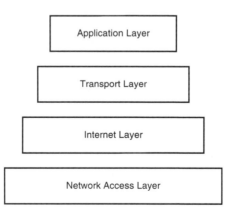

Application Layer

Transport Layer

Internet Layer

Network Access Layer

> **NOTE**
>
> If you're familiar with data communications, you may know the Open Systems Interconnect (OSI) Reference Model. This seven-layer model is presented in many textbooks and taught in many courses. However, its structure does not accurately match that of the TCP/IP protocols (or equally fairly, the structure of the TCP/IP protocols does not accurately match that of the OSI Reference Model). Consequently, this chapter ignores the OSI Reference Model, focusing instead on the four-layer model that better describes TCP/IP.

Let's examine each of the four layers of the TCP/IP protocols in detail. We'll start with the bottom layer and work our way up the pyramid.

Network Access Layer

The bottom layer of the TCP/IP protocol hierarchy is the network access layer. The functions it performs are so primitive—so close to the hardware level—that they're often transparent to the user. These functions include

- Restructuring data into a form suitable for network transmission
- Mapping logical addresses to physical device addresses

Networks often impose constraints on data they transmit. One of the network access layer's jobs is to restructure data so that it's acceptable to the network. Of course, it does this in a way that permits the data to be reconstituted into its original form at the destination.

Every device attached to a network has a *physical device address*. Some devices may have more than one address—a computer with multiple network cards, for example. Physical addresses are often cumbersome in form, consisting of a series of hexadecimal digits. Moreover, devices come and go; for example, a network interface card may fail and have to be replaced.

Programmers who write programs that must be revised whenever a device is replaced do not find many friends in the workplace. Therefore, programmers prefer to work with logical addresses rather than physical addresses. TCP/IP provides a logical address, known as an *IP address* or *IP number*, that uniquely identifies a network device. A network device can use a special TCP/IP protocol to discover its IP address when it is started. That way, programs can be insulated from changes in the hardware devices that compose the network.

The good news about the network access layer is that its functions are usually implemented in the network device's device driver. Neither users nor application programmers are typically much concerned with the workings of the network access layer. Of course, without the network access layer, the jobs of the Internet and other layers would be much more complicated.

Internet Layer

The Internet layer, which sits atop the network access layer, provides two main protocols: the Internet protocol (IP) and the Internet control message protocol (ICMP). All TCP/IP data flows through the network by means of the IP protocol; the ICMP protocol is used to control the flow of data.

The IP Protocol

Because the TCP/IP protocols are named, in part, for the IP protocol, you might correctly guess that the IP protocol performs some of the most important networking functions. For example, the IP protocol

- Standardizes the contents and format of the data packet, called a datagram, that is transmitted across the network
- Selects a suitable route for transmission of datagrams
- Fragments and reassembles datagrams as required by network constraints
- Passes data to an appropriate higher-level protocol

The IP protocol precedes every packet of data with five or six 32-bit words that specify, in a standard format, such information as the source and destination addresses of the packet, the length of the packet, and the TCP/IP protocol that will handle the data. By standardizing the location and format of this data, the IP protocol makes it possible to exchange messages between devices built by different manufacturers. The *open architecture* of TCP/IP is one of the reasons it is so popular, in contrast to the limited popularity of the several proprietary architectures promoted by vendors.

> **NOTE**
>
> An *open architecture* or *technology* is one developed and subscribed to by multiple vendors, such as Common Object Request Broker Architecture (CORBA), which is the product of the joint efforts of hundreds of companies. A proprietary architecture or technology is one developed and promoted by a single vendor, such as Microsoft's Distributed Object Component Model (DCOM) or Novell's IPX.

A central purpose of TCP/IP is to allow exchange of data among, not merely within, computer networks. To move data from one network to another, the two networks must somehow be connected. Typically, the connection takes the form of a device, called a *gateway*, that is attached to each network. The *hosts*, or *non-gateway devices*, of one network can exchange data with the hosts of the other network by means of the IP protocol, which routes the data through the common gateway (as shown in Figure 2.2).

FIGURE 2.2

The IP protocol routes information between networks.

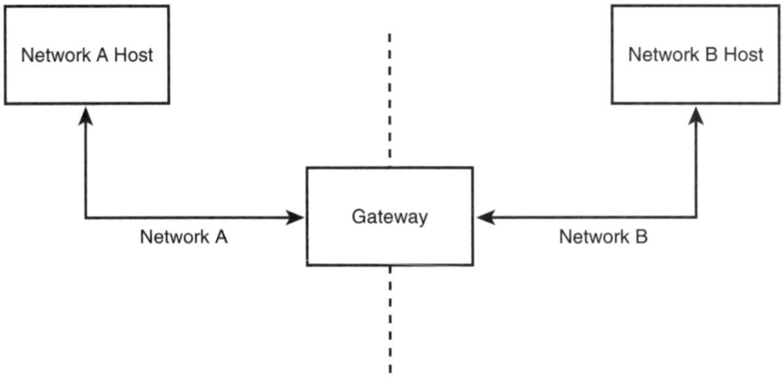

Hosts need not be connected via a single intermediate gateway. The IP protocol is capable of *multi-hop routing* (see Figure 2.3), which passes a packet through as many gateways as necessary in order to reach the destination system.

Another responsibility of the IP protocol is *packet fragmentation*. Networks typically impose an upper limit on the size of a transmitted packet, called the *maximum transmission unit* (MTU). The IP protocol hides this complexity by automatically fragmenting and reassembling datagrams so that the network MTU is never exceeded.

The IP protocol's final task is to pass received packets to the proper higher-level protocol. It relies on a protocol number stored in the packet to determine the protocol to which it should deliver the packet.

The IP protocol has two properties of particular interest. First, it is a *connectionless* or *stateless* protocol. To understand what this means, consider the opposite: a connection-oriented protocol. One example is the nurse who screens telephone calls directed to your physician. You explain the reason for your call and the nurse decides whether it's proper to interrupt the busy physician. You wait until finally you hear the reassuring, "Dr. Casey will speak to you now." Only then do you begin your dialog with the physician.

A connectionless protocol, on the other hand, imposes no screening. If your physician used a connectionless protocol, you could simply begin talking the moment the phone was answered. Of course, you might have dialed a wrong number; instead of your physician, you might have reached the local pizzeria, where the employees are puzzled and amused by your earnest questions regarding test results. To avoid mix-ups of this sort, the IP protocol depends upon other, higher-level protocols. In other words, the connectionless IP protocol alone won't prevent a connection to the wrong host or gateway.

FIGURE 2.3

Hosts can be connected via several intermediate gateways via IP protocol multi-hop routing.

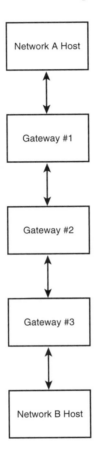

Second, the IP protocol is an *unreliable* protocol. This doesn't mean that data sent via the IP protocol may be received in corrupted form, only that the IP protocol itself doesn't verify that data has been transmitted correctly. Other, higher-level protocols are responsible for this important task. Because of the support the IP protocol receives from its sibling protocols, you can safely trust it with your most important data.

The ICMP Protocol

Like the IP protocol and the protocols of the network access layer, the ICMP protocol works behind the scenes to make networking as simple, reliable, and efficient as possible. The ICMP protocol has four main responsibilities:

- Ensure that source devices transmit slowly enough for destination devices and intermediate gateways to keep pace
- Detect attempts to reach unreachable destinations
- Dynamically re-route network traffic
- Provide an echo service used to verify operation of a remote system's IP protocol

When a network device, either a host or a gateway, finds that it cannot keep up with a source's flow of datagrams, it sends the source an ICMP message that instructs the source to temporarily stop sending datagrams. This helps avoid data overruns that would necessitate retransmission of data, which would reduce network efficiency.

The ICMP protocol also provides a special message that is sent to a host that attempts to send data to an unreachable host or port. (You learn about ports in this chapter's "Packets, Addresses, and Routing.") This message enables the sending host to deal with the error, rather than waiting indefinitely for a reply that will never come.

The ICMP protocol also enables dynamic re-routing of packets. For example, consider the networks shown in Figure 2.4. Two gateways join the networks, allowing data to flow from one network to the other through either gateway. The ICMP protocol provides a message that acts as a switch, telling hosts to use one gateway in preference to the other. This message, for example, can allow one gateway to take over when the other fails or is shut down for maintenance. The path from Host A to Host B has been dynamically re-routed through Gateway #2 due to the broken connection between Host A and Gateway #1.

Finally, the ICMP protocol provides a special echo message. When a host or gateway receives an echo message, it replies by sending the data packet back to the source host. This permits verification that the host or gateway is operational. The `ping` command, which you meet in this chapter's "Troubleshooting," relies upon this message.

Transport Layer

The transport layer sits atop the Internet layer. Like the Internet layer, the transport layer provides two main protocols: the transmission control protocol (TCP) and the user datagram protocol (UDP). Most network data is delivered by TCP. A few special applications benefit from the lower overhead provided by UDP.

Figure 2.4

Networks can provide multiple data paths by dynamic re-routing of packets.

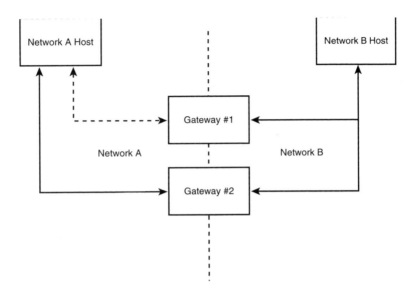

The TCP Protocol

As the name TCP/IP suggests, the TCP and IP protocols are at the center of TCP/IP networking. Recall that the IP protocol is an unreliable protocol that transmits data packets from one host to another. The TCP protocol builds on these basic functions by adding

- Error checking and re-transmission, so that data transmission is reliable
- Assembly of packets into a continuous stream of data in the proper sequence
- Delivery of data to the application program that processes it

The TCP protocol provides a sending host that periodically re-transmits a packet until it receives positive confirmation of delivery to the destination host. The receiving host uses a checksum within the packet to verify that the packet was received correctly. If so, it transmits an acknowledgment to the source host. If not, it simply discards the bad packet; the source host therefore re-transmits the packet when it fails to receive a timely acknowledgment.

Most programs view data as a continuous stream rather than packet-sized units of data. The TCP protocol takes responsibility for reconstituting packets into a stream. This is more difficult than it might sound because packets do not always follow a single path from source to destination. As you can see in Figure 2.5, packets may arrive at the destination out of sequence. The TCP protocol uses a sequence number in each packet to reassemble the packets in the original sequence.

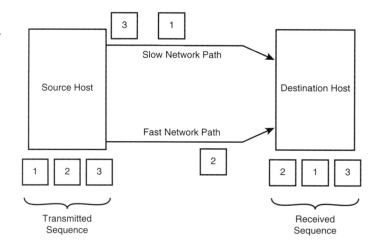

FIGURE 2.5

Data packets may arrive out of sequence and must be reassembled.

The TCP protocol delivers the data stream it assembles to an application program. An application listens for data on a port, which is designated by a number called the *port number*, which is carried within every datagram. The TCP protocol uses the port number to deliver the data stream. You learn more about ports in the "Ports and Sockets" section.

Every function exacts a price, however small, in overhead. Applications that do not require all the functions provided by the TCP protocol may use the UDP protocol, which has fewer functions and less overhead than the TCP protocol.

The UDP Protocol

Essentially, UDP provides the important port number that enables delivery of a packet to a particular application program. However, data transmission via UDP is unreliable and connectionless. This means that the application program must verify that packets were sent accurately and, if stream-oriented data are involved, reassemble them into proper sequence.

When small amounts of data are exchanged between network devices—that is, amounts less than the maximum size of a packet—the UDP protocol may present few programming difficulties, yet provide improved efficiency. For example, if messages strictly alternate between devices, following a query-response model in which one device transmits a packet and then the other transmits a response, packet sequence may not be an issue. In such a case, the capabilities of TCP are largely wasted.

In principle, UDP allows a system's designer to trade off performance under less than ideal conditions (where TCP shines) for performance under ideal conditions (where UDP shines). When network reliability is substandard, UDP performance may be no better, and perhaps worse, than that of TCP. As one wag put it, "UDP potentially combines the low performance of a connectionless protocol with the inefficiency of TCP."

Moreover, some network administrators who fear security breaches do not allow UDP packets to cross into their networks, allowing them only on the local, highly reliable network. Consequently, UDP remains a specialty protocol with limited application.

Application Layer

The uppermost layer of the TCP/IP family of protocols is the application layer, which includes every application program that uses data delivered by TCP/IP. Certain applications, such as mail and remote login, have become highly standardized. You learn about several standard applications in this chapter's "TCP/IP Services" section.

Other applications are highly specialized; the program used by a Web retailer to record your purchases and debit your account is an example. This is where the real action of distributed computing is taking place today. System designers and programmers are working to conceive and build entirely new sorts of applications using technologies like Java and mobile agents, which were not widely available even a few years ago.

PACKETS, ADDRESSES, AND ROUTING

In the last section you learned what the key TCP/IP protocols do. Now take a closer look at how TCP/IP works. This section's goal is not to make you a TCP/IP network administrator, but merely to give you a working knowledge of TCP/IP sufficient to develop network-capable software and to communicate with network administrators responsible for configuring the systems on which your programs run. By learning a bit more about the TCP/IP, you'll be a more effective system developer.

IP Addresses

Recall that the IP protocol provides every network device with a logical address, called an *IP address*, which is more convenient to use than the device's physical address. The IP addresses provided by the IP protocol take a very specific form: Each is a 32-bit number, commonly represented as a series of four 8-bit numbers (bytes), which range in value from 0 to 255. For example, 192.190.268.124 is a valid IP address.

The purpose of the IP address is to identify a network and a specific host on that network. However, the IP protocol uses four distinct schemes, known as *address classes*, to specify this information.

The value of the first of the four bytes that compose an IP address determines the form of the address:

- Class A addresses begin with a value less than 128. In a Class A address, the first byte specifies the network and the remaining three bytes specify the host. About 16 million hosts can exist on a single Class A network.

- Class B addresses begin with a value from 128 to 191. In a Class B address, the first two bytes specify the network and the remaining two bytes specify the host. About 65,000 hosts can exist on a single Class B network.

- Class C addresses begin with a value from 192 to 223. In a Class C address, the first three bytes specify the network and the remaining byte specifies the host. Only 254 hosts can exist on a single Class C network (hosts 0 and 255 are reserved).

IP addresses that begin with a value greater than 223 are used for special purposes, as are certain addresses beginning with 0 and 127.

As you can see, a Class A address enables you to specify a much larger network than a Class C address. Class A addresses are assigned to only the largest of organizations; smaller organizations must make do with Class C addresses, using several such addresses if they have more than 254 network hosts.

Routing

IP addresses are important because of their role in *routing*, finding a suitable path across which packets can be transmitted from a source host to a destination host. Every packet contains the destination host's IP address. Network hosts use the network part of the destination IP address to determine how to handle a packet. If the destination host is on the same network as the host, the host simply transmits the data packet via the local network. The destination host receives and processes the packet.

If the destination host is on a different network, the host transmits the packet to a gateway, which forwards the packet to the destination, possibly by way of several intermediate gateways. The host determines to which gateway it should send the packet by searching its *routing table*, which lists known networks and gateways that serve them. Generally, the routing table includes a default gateway used for destination hosts that are on unfamiliar networks. Internally, the default gateway is known by the special IP address 0.0.0.0. Other special IP addresses are 127.0.0.1, which is used as a synonym for the address of the host itself, and 127.0.0.0, which is used as a synonym for the local network.

The routing table does not provide enough information for a host to construct a complete route to the destination host. Instead, it determines only the next hop in the journey, relying on a downstream gateway to pick up where it left off.

Hosts can be configured to use *static routing*, in which the routing table is built when the host is booted, or *dynamic routing*, in which ICMP messages may update the routing table, supplying new routes or closing old ones. Typically, system administrators use static routing only for small, simple networks; larger, more complex networks are easier to manage using dynamic routing.

Ports and Sockets

Recall that the TCP protocol's final task is to hand the data stream to the proper application, identified by the port number contained in the packets that compose the data stream. Certain port numbers, so-called well-known port numbers (see Table 2.1), are normally reserved for standard applications.

TABLE 2.1 SOME REPRESENTATIVE WELL-KNOWN PORT NUMBERS AND THEIR ASSOCIATED APPLICATIONS

Port Number	Application
7	ECHO, which retransmits the received packet
21	FTP, which transfers files
23	Telnet, which provides a remote login
25	SMTP, which delivers mail messages
67	BOOTP, which provides configuration information at boot time
109	POP, which enables users to access mail boxes on remote systems

Port numbers are 16-bit numbers, providing for 65,536 possible ports. Although there are dozens of well-known ports, these are a fraction of the available ports. The remaining ports are dynamically allocated ports known as *sockets*. The combination of an IP address and a port number uniquely identifies a program, permitting it to be targeted for delivery of a network data stream.

Well-known ports and sockets are typically used together. For example, suppose a user on host 111.111.111.111 wants to access mail held on host 222.222.222.222. The user's program first dynamically acquires a socket on host 111.111.111.111. Assume that socket 3333 is assigned; the complete source address, including IP address and port number, is then 111.111.111.111.3333. Because the POP application uses well-known port 109, the destination address is 222.222.222.222.109. The user's program sends a packet to the destination address, a packet containing a request to connect to the POP application. The TCP/IP protocols pass the packet across the network and deliver it to the POP application.

The POP application considers the request and decides whether to allow the user to connect. Assuming it decides to allow the connection, it dynamically allocates a socket. Assume that socket 4444 is assigned. The two hosts now begin a conversation involving addresses 111.111.111.111.3333 and 222.222.222.222.4444. Port 109 is used only to initially contact the POP application. By allocating a socket specifically for the conversation between the hosts, port 109 is quickly made available to serve other users who want to request a connection. Other well-known applications respond similarly.

Hosts and Domains

Recalling the IP addresses of network hosts quickly grows tiring: Was the budget database on host 111.123.111.123 or 123.111.123.111? Fortunately, a standard TCP/IP service frees users and programmers from this chore. The Domain Name Service (DNS) translates from structured host names to IP addresses and vice versa.

The structured names supported by DNS take the form of words separated by periods. For example, one host familiar to many is the AltaVista Web search engine, known as `altavista.digital.com`. The components of this *fully qualified domain name* (FQDN) include the host name, `altavista`, and the domain name, `digital.com`. As the period indicates, the domain name itself is composed of two parts: the top-level domain, `com`, and the subdomain, `digital`.

There are six commonly used top-level domains in the U.S., as shown in Table 2.2. Outside the U.S., most nations use top-level domains that specify a host's nation of origin. For example, the top-level domain `ca` is used in Canada, and the top-level domain `uk` is used in the United Kingdom. However, there is no effective regulation of top-level domains, so alternative schemes are in use and continue to arise. For example, some host names within the U.S. use the domain `us`, following the style used by most other nations.

TABLE 2.2 COMMON TOP-LEVEL DOMAINS USED IN THE U.S.

Domain	Organization Type
com	Commercial organizations
edu	Educational institutions
gov	Government agencies
mil	Military organizations
net	Network support organizations and access providers
org	Non-profit organizations

Authority to establish domains is held by the Internet Resource Registries (IRR), which hold authority for specific geographic regions. In the U.S., InterNIC holds authority to assign IP addresses and establish domains.

Once an organization has registered a domain name with the appropriate IRR, the organization can create as many subdomains as desired. For example, a university might register the domain almamater.edu. It might then establish subdomains for various university departments, such as chemistry.almamater.edu and literature.almamater.edu. Hosts could then be assigned names within these domains. For example, hosts within the chemistry department might include benzene.chemistry.almamater.edu and hydroxyl.chemistry.almamater.edu; hosts within the literature department might include chaucer.literature.almamater.edu and steinbeck.literature.almamater.edu. Of course, the university might choose to forego the creation of subdomains (see Figure 2.6), particularly if it has few hosts. It might then use host names such as benzene.almamater.edu and chaucer.almamater.edu, which include no subdomain.

Of course, typing names of such length can become tiresome. Fortunately, DNS allows users to abbreviate host names by supplying omitted domain information on behalf of the user. For example, if a user of a host within the almamater.edu domain refers to a host named chaucer, DNS assumes that the user means chaucer.almamater.edu. Similarly, if a user within the ivywalls.edu domain refers to a host named chaucer, DNS takes the user to mean `chaucer.ivywalls.edu`. This convention makes it much easier to refer to hosts within one's domain, while preserving the possibility of addressing every host. For example, if the user within the ivywalls.edu domain wants to refer to the chaucer host within the almamater.edu domain, the user merely specifies the fully qualified domain name, chaucer.almamater.edu.

As you see, DNS is rather simple from the user's standpoint. On the other hand, it is somewhat more complex from the standpoint of the system administrator. The next section takes a more in-depth look at several TCP/IP application layer services, including DNS.

TCP/IP SERVICES

The popularity of TCP/IP is due in part to the fact that its bottom three protocol layers do their jobs well. However, much of the credit must go to the fourth layer, the application layer, which provides many useful functions that make network use and programming much more convenient.

This section surveys several representative services provided by the application layer of most TCP/IP implementations. It's necessary to say *most* because no law requires a vendor to include any of these services in its implementation. However, Adam Smith's "invisible hand" (the market) tends to reward those vendors who provide rich implementations of TCP/IP and punish those who do not. Of course, it's the consumer who decides whether a given implementation is rich or not, so it doesn't always follow that a popular operating system will support all, or even most, of these services—at least not right out of the box.

FIGURE 2.6

Domain and subdomain hierarchies.

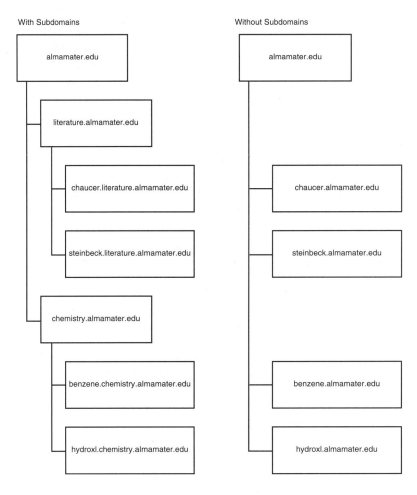

Consider Microsoft Windows 9x, one of the leading operating systems in terms of market share. Windows 9x is designed for personal use. Consequently, it can *access* most of these services, but it can *provide* only about half of them. For power users who want to provide the full range of TCP/IP services, Microsoft offers its flagship operating system, Windows NT. Because Windows NT is more expensive and more complex than Windows

9x, many Windows 9x users are reluctant to migrate to Windows NT, even though they wish their PC could provide some of the TCP/IP services that Windows 9x cannot.

Fortunately, another solution is available. Even though Microsoft has not included, for example, mail server protocols in Windows 9x, several shareware mail server packages are available. The same is true of most other application layer services, so even Windows 9x users can provide most application layer services, though they may need to hunt down and install special software in order to do so.

This section surveys the following application layer services:

- Domain Name Service (DNS)
- Telnet
- File Transfer Protocol (FTP)
- Mail (SMTP and POP)
- Hypertext Transfer Protocol (HTTP)
- Bootstrap (BOOTP and DHCP)
- File and Print Servers (NFS)
- Firewalls and Proxies

The point of this material is not to teach you how to install and configure these services. For that you can consult a book such as Timothy Parker's *TCP/IP Unleashed* (Sam's Publishing). This section provides enough information to help you identify services your applications may require and to communicate with network administrators responsible for installing and maintaining TCP/IP services.

Domain Name Service (DNS)

In the previous section you learned how DNS simplifies references to hosts by substituting host names for IP addresses and allowing use of abbreviated domain names. In this section you briefly consider how DNS works.

The main function of DNS is to map host names to IP addresses. DNS is, in effect, a large, distributed database with records residing in thousands of Internet hosts. No one host possesses a complete database that includes information on every host. Instead, DNS servers are arranged in a hierarchy. This structure makes DNS more efficient and more robust. Here's how:

When a new domain is established, a DNS server is designated for the domain, along with (at least) a second DNS server that acts as a backup. At all times, a domain's DNS server contains a complete record of the IP addresses and host names of hosts within its domain.

Hosts within the domain know the local DNS server's IP address. When a user specifies a host by name, the TCP/IP protocols contact the DNS server and determine the corresponding IP address, as you can see in Figure 2.7. The IP address is then incorporated within the outgoing packets as the destination address; the host name never appears in a packet.

FIGURE 2.7

Hosts contact the DNS server to look up destination IP addresses.

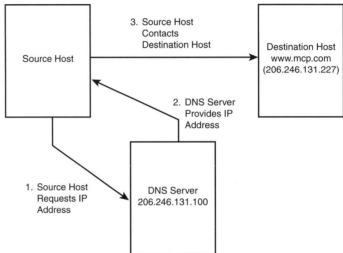

The situation is a little more involved when the destination host is outside the local network. In this case, the local DNS server does not contain a record identifying the remote host. Instead, the local DNS server contacts an upstream DNS server that may know a DNS server's IP address for the destination domain. If so, the upstream DNS server forwards the request to the designated DNS server (see Figure 2.8) for the destination domain.

If the upstream DNS server does not know where to find the needed record, it forwards the request to a DNS server further upstream. DNS servers are arranged in a hierarchy (see Figure 2.9); somewhere within that hierarchy is a description of any host. This find-or-forward process continues until the needed record is found or a root DNS server acknowledges that even it does not know the destination host. In that case, the reference fails and TCP/IP returns an error code to the requesting program. If you're using a Web browser, you may get the annoying "Cannot open the Internet site" message.

FIGURE 2.8

DNS servers forward unmatched requests to other DNS servers.

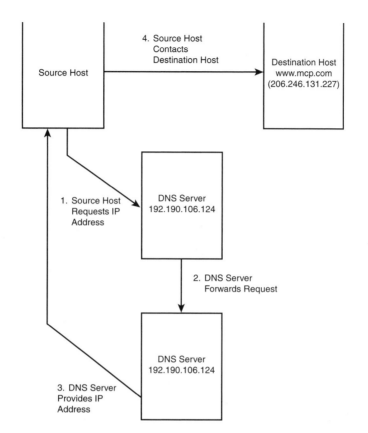

FIGURE 2.9

DNS servers form a hierarchy.

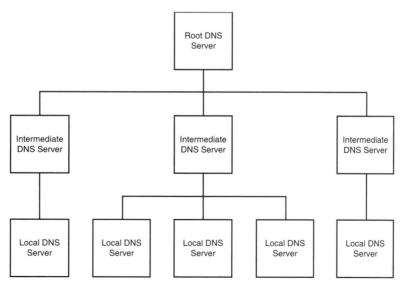

Remote Login (Telnet)

The Telnet protocol provides a simple but effective remote login facility. For example, a user working at home can connect via modem with a host that provides a Telnet server. By running a Telnet client on the home PC, the user can type commands to be executed by the remote host.

Telnet is a very popular application within the UNIX community; most UNIX hosts provide a Telnet server. However, Telnet is significantly less popular within the Microsoft Windows community. Most Windows PCs include a Telnet client because Microsoft includes one in its Windows operating systems. However, a standard installation of Windows NT does not include a Telnet server.

One reason for this seems to be Microsoft's emphasis on graphical user interfaces (GUIs). In contrast with the Windows GUI, the text-based, command-line interface of Telnet seems an anachronism. However, Telnet's text-based interface offers several advantages:

- Telnet requires very low communications bandwidth. Performance is adequate even under conditions of line noise that constrain connection rates to 2400 baud or less.

- Telnet is widely available on non-Microsoft systems.

- UNIX commands can be very powerful in the hands of a skilled user. The UNIX command shell is, in effect, a powerful programming language that enables quick and easy automation of repetitive tasks. The DOS command shell, by contrast, offers limited functionality.

- Most UNIX systems afford a text-based interface to every system function. Using Telnet, it's possible to reconfigure the kernel or network configuration of a system and restart the system remotely.

Microsoft does offer a beta implementation of Telnet for Windows NT and third parties have developed Telnet implementations available as shareware. You can establish a Telnet server even if your main sever runs a Microsoft operating system.

File Transfer Protocol (FTP)

One of the most widely used TCP/IP applications is File Transfer Protocol (FTP), which allows users to transfer files to and from network hosts. FTP is ubiquitous: Both UNIX and Microsoft operating systems include FTP clients and servers. Even popular Web browsers include built-in FTP clients.

A variety of FTP servers are available. Windows 9x sports an FTP server, although it is not installed by default. Shareware packages allow even Windows 3.1 users to provide FTP services.

FTP services can be provided in either of two modes: anonymous and non-anonymous. An FTP server configured for *anonymous access* allows any host to access its files. An FTP server configured for *non-anonymous access* requires users to provide a user ID and password before access is granted. An FTP server can be configured to allow anonymous access to some files and only non-anonymous access to others. Similarly, users and anonymous users can be allowed to download (read) files, upload (create) files, or both. Most servers allow access permissions to be set at the directory level, so some directories restrict access more stringently than others.

Although it's possible to download files using the HTTP protocol, FTP transmits files more efficiently. Therefore, FTP remains an important protocol, particularly for the transmission of large files.

Mail (SMTP and POP)

Email was one of the first Internet applications to reach public awareness. Today, it seems that everyone has an email address; some of us have several. Sending and receiving email has become a national pastime.

Mail involves two main protocols: SMTP is used to transfer email from one system to another. POP enables users to access mail boxes remotely.

As is true of most TCP/IP applications, mail involves a client program and a server program. Client programs are nearly universal; popular Web browsers include mail clients and there are several popular freeware mail clients.

Mail servers are less common. One reason for this is the complicated configuration options of the most popular UNIX mail server, sendmail. However, shareware mail servers are available even for Windows 3.1. Many of these trade off features for ease of configuration, making them quite simple to install and use.

Hypertext Transfer Protocol (HTTP)

The TCP/IP protocol that made the 1990s the decade of the Web is Hypertext Transfer Protocol (HTTP). HTTP, like other standard TCP/IP application layer protocols, is a relatively simple protocol that provides impressive capability.

HTTP was designed to solve the problem of providing access to large archives of documents represented using a variety of formats and encoding. The clever solution of Tim Berners-Lee was to design a simple protocol (HTTP) to transmit the data to a browser, a client program that knows how to deal with each of the various data formats and encoding. By putting most of the burden on the client, rather than the server, HTTP makes it easy to install and maintain the server.

The second innovation underlying the Web is the Universal Resource Locator (URL), which allows users to refer to documents on remote hosts. An URL (see Figure 2.10) consists of three parts:

- A protocol name, which identifies the protocol to be used to retrieve the document. The HTTP protocol is usually specified, but most browsers support other common protocols such as FTP and Telnet.
- The name of the host that contains the document.
- The file system path that identifies the document on the host.

FIGURE 2.10
An URL includes three main parts.

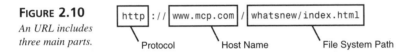

Because host names are unique and because file system paths are unique within a given host, URLs provide a simple way of uniquely identifying any document on the network. In effect, every document becomes part of one large document, whose chapters are designated by URLs. The resulting mega-document is called the *Web*.

The rest, as everyone knows, is history. Because Web (HTTP) servers are relatively easy to set up, many companies established them. Freeware and shareware Web servers are now available for every popular computing platform. Several companies, most notably Netscape and Microsoft, delivered browsers capable of handling a plethora of document types and formats. Soon, everyone, it seemed, was surfing the Web.

Bootstrap (BOOTP and DHCP)

Recall that one of the IP protocol's responsibilities is mapping logical addresses (IP addresses) both to and from physical addresses (device addresses). When you boot a host, it quickly discovers the manufacturer-assigned physical address of each network interface by probing the ROM of the network interface. A host's next task is to discover its user-assigned IP addresses.

The simplest approach is to give each host a fixed IP address. However, as pointed out earlier, this can present problems. For example, replacing a faulty network interface card may change the IP address assigned to a host.

TCP/IP provides two protocols that help system administrators apply a more flexible approach: BOOTP and DHCP. BOOTP and DHCP are widely implemented among UNIX systems; Microsoft Windows supports DHCP. Each allows a system administrator to build a table that maps physical addresses to IP numbers. A server process with access to the table runs on a host.

When a host starts, it runs a client process that sends a broadcast message to every host on its local network, inquiring what IP address it should use. A BOOTP or DHCP server that receives such a message searches its mapping table and sends a reply that tells the host its IP address.

In addition to this fixed method of assignment, DHCP allows a more sophisticated dynamic assignment of IP addresses that's particularly appropriate when computers are mobile. DHCP allows the system administrator to establish a block of IP numbers that forms a pool. When a host asks for an IP address, it's assigned an available address from the pool.

Of course, this dynamic method of IP address assignment is not suitable for hosts that run server processes because such hosts generally require fixed IP numbers; that way they can be readily contacted by clients. However, hosts that run client applications rather than servers are well served by this approach. An advantage of DHCP is that the pool need contain only enough IP addresses to accommodate the maximum number of simultaneously connected computers. This avoids the need to apply for, and maintain, a distinct IP number for every computer that might connect to the network. It's especially helpful for mobile computers that may connect to the network at various points, which would otherwise require that they be configured to somehow choose an IP address appropriate to the current connection point.

File and Print Servers (NFS)

Users can employ the FTP protocol to copy files from a server to their system, but it's often useful to be able to directly access a file rather than creating a copy. The Network File System (NFS) protocol provides this capability. Files on a system running an NFS server can appear as if they were local files of a host running an NFS client. Users can read and write such files using ordinary application programs. Files can even be shared, so that multiple users can access them simultaneously.

NFS also provides for sharing of printers. Rather than allocating a printer to each user, a cost-prohibitive approach for all but the cheapest and least capable printers, many users can share a single printer.

NFS is mainly found on UNIX systems, although third-party implementations of NFS for Microsoft operating systems exist. Microsoft supports its own set of network protocols that provide similar features—Server Message Block (SMB or Samba), for example. Several third-party implementations of SMB are available for UNIX systems, allowing integration of Microsoft and UNIX networks.

Firewalls and Proxies

One of the hazards of modern network life is the cracker. A *cracker* is anyone who attempts to access confidential data, alter restricted data, deny use of a computing resource, or otherwise hamper network operation. One tactic designed to thwart the cracker is the *firewall*, a filter intended to block traffic that might compromise the network. This brief discussion simply outlines the role of the firewall. To learn more about how firewalls work, see Sharp Amoroso's *PC Week Intranet and Internet Firewall Strategies* (Ziff-Davis Press).

The idea of a firewall is to prevent remote hosts from directly accessing servers on the local network. Instead, one host is designated as a *bastion host* (see Figure 2.11) that is visible to the outside world. When a remote host wants to access a service provided on the local network, it contacts the bastion host. The bastion host runs a *proxy* application that evaluates the request. If the proxy decides to allow the access, it forwards the request to the proper server within the local network. The server performs the requested service and sends a reply by way of the bastion host, rather than directly to the remote host. Essentially, all traffic flows through the bastion host, which acts as a drawbridge screening internal network resources from inappropriate outside access. Because all traffic flows through a single point, it's easier to monitor and control.

FIGURE 2.11

A firewall protects local hosts from unauthorized access.

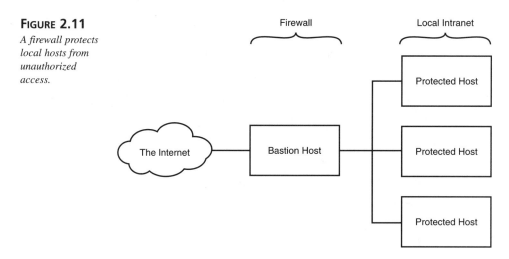

The bastion host often performs a similar service for requests originating within the local network, forwarding them to outside servers. By this means, remote hosts may remain unaware of the identities of hosts within the local network (other than the bastion host), making it difficult to compromise network security.

TROUBLESHOOTING

Now that you know what the TCP/IP protocols do when they're working properly, it's time to learn something about troubleshooting. That way, you can cope even when they're not working properly. Again, don't expect to become a networking guru by understanding and applying the information in this section. The goal is to help you pinpoint problem sources and show you how to collect information that may expedite your network administrator's response to your problem reports.

The `ping` Command

Both Windows 9x and UNIX, as well as most other operating systems, implement the `ping` command. As you recall, `ping` sends ECHO packets to a remote host, which responds by re-sending them to the source host. This works somewhat like the sonar system in *The Hunt for Red October*. When the source host receives a return `ping` it knows the remote host is operational. Moreover, it can make a crude estimate of network performance by timing the circuit from the source to the destination and back.

To use the `ping` command, you supply an argument, which can be a host name:

```
ping www.mcp.com
```

Alternatively, you can use an IP address:

```
ping 206.246.131.227
```

If the remote host is operational, you see something like this:

```
C:\WINDOWS>ping www.mcp.com

Pinging www.mcp.com [206.246.131.227] with 32 bytes of data:

Reply from 206.246.131.227: bytes=32 time=220ms TTL=230
Reply from 206.246.131.227: bytes=32 time=202ms TTL=231
Reply from 206.246.131.227: bytes=32 time=196ms TTL=231
Reply from 206.246.131.227: bytes=32 time=199ms TTL=231

C:\WINDOWS>
```

You can see from the output that it takes from 196 to 220 milliseconds for a packet to make the complete round trip. On a high-speed local area network you might see numbers in order of magnitude smaller than this.

If the host name is unknown, you get a message like this:

```
C:\WINDOWS>ping badhost.mcp.com
Bad IP address badhost.mcp.com.

C:\WINDOWS>
```

If you suspect that the host name may not be properly recorded in the DNS database (perhaps it's a new host, for example), you can try again using the IP address.

The traceroute Command

Suppose ping cannot find a route to the remote host. In that case, its output looks something like this:

```
C:\WINDOWS>ping 199.107.98.211

Pinging 199.107.98.211 with 32 bytes of data:

Reply from 134.24.95.73: Destination host unreachable.
Reply from 134.24.95.73: Destination host unreachable.
Request timed out.
Reply from 134.24.95.73: Destination host unreachable.

C:\WINDOWS>
```

Of course, the problem may lie with the remote host itself, or with any of the gateways between the local host and the remote host. The traceroute command, known to Windows 9x users by the abbreviated name tracert, helps you discover the location of the problem:

```
C:\WINDOWS>tracert 199.107.98.211

Tracing route to bmccarty.apu.edu [199.107.98.211]
over a maximum of 30 hops:

  1   114 ms    99 ms    99 ms  elay.hooked.net [206.80.11.2]
  2   108 ms   107 ms   119 ms  sgw1.la.hooked.net [206.80.11.1]
  3   118 ms   107 ms   127 ms  206.169.170.173
  4     *      750 ms   118 ms  ix-sf.bdr.hooked.net [206.80.17.3]
  5   125 ms   126 ms   118 ms  ix-pa-eth0.bdr.hooked.net [206.80.25.2]
  6   128 ms   116 ms   144 ms  fe2-0.sjc-bb3.cerf.net [134.24.23.1]
  7   143 ms   136 ms   124 ms  atm0-0-155M.sfo-bb2.cerf.net
➡[134.24.29.21]
  8   132 ms   123 ms  2215 ms  fe9-0-0.sfo-bb1.cerf.net [134.24.29.117]
  9   144 ms   123 ms   141 ms  atm10-0-155M.lax-bb1.cerf.net
➡[134.24.29.41]
 10   125 ms   134 ms   128 ms  fe0-0-0.lax-bb2.cerf.net [134.24.29.77]
 11   145 ms   142 ms   150 ms  azusa-la-smds.cerf.net [134.24.95.73]
 12  azusa-la-smds.cerf.net [134.24.95.73]
➡   reports: Destination host unreachable.

Trace complete.
```

The traceroute output includes one line for each intermediate gateway between the local host and the remote host. Notice how routing fails after the twelfth hop: azusa-la-smds.cerf.net reports that it does not know how to reach host 199.107.99.211. The problem, therefore, is not with any of the first 11 gateways, which successfully passed on the packet. Now you know where to focus your attention.

The netstat Command

Another useful command is netstat, which is something of a Swiss Army knife, providing many functions in one package. One of the most important of its functions is a report of TCP/IP statistics. The Windows 9x version of the command gives statistics for the IP protocol, the ICMP protocol, the TCP protocol, and the UDP protocol. To generate the statistics, simply type the following:

```
netstat -s
```

Here's an excerpt from a typical report, showing the TCP statistics:

```
TCP Statistics

    Active Opens                  = 200
    Passive Opens                 = 0
    Failed Connection Attempts    = 1
    Reset Connections             = 67
    Current Connections           = 1
    Segments Received             = 2188
    Segments Sent                 = 2223
    Segments Retransmitted        = 20
```

Notice that the report shows one failed connection attempt and 20 retransmissions out of over 2,000 segments sent—about a 1% error rate. These statistics apply to a dial-up modem connection. The error rate would normally be much lower over a local area network.

By using ping, traceroute, and netstat, you can collect important and helpful information concerning network performance—information that can help you and others quickly determine a point of failure. You'll find these commands very useful as you develop programs that operate over the network. They help you determine whether a failure is due to an error in your code or a problem with the network itself.

FROM HERE

As you've learned, TCP/IP is an important enabling technology: Distributed computing builds upon TCP/IP networking as its foundation.

The following chapters teach you more about networking and show you how networking fits into distributed computing:

- Chapter 4, "Distributed Architectures," shows how different ideas about networking determine the architecture, or shape, of an information system.

- Chapter 10, "Security," explains security risks that arise when computers are networked and presents the Java security model that attempts to control security risks.

- Chapter 13, "Sockets," shows how to write programs that communicate over a TCP/IP network.

OBJECT-ORIENTED ANALYSIS AND DESIGN

IN THIS CHAPTER

If you're a *Star Trek* fan, you're familiar with the transporter, an amazing device that can transport members of an orbiting starship's crew to the surface of a planet, or back again, in an instant. Series creator Gene Roddenberry once observed that the transporter's speed played a crucial role in the success of *Star Trek*. Without it, action-packed episodes would have devolved into tedium, owing to lengthy and boring shuttle trips from the Enterprise to whatever exotic planet lay below.

The operating principles of *Star Trek*'s transporter are simple, even if fantastic. It breaks objects (or beings) into their molecular components, transforms these components into energy that it temporarily stores in a pattern buffer, beams the energy to the designated location, and ultimately re-transforms the energy into a replica of the original object. The ship's surgeon, Dr. McCoy, is perhaps the wisest person on board the starship, because he alone expresses concern over the fact that his original molecules are forever lost, wondering what subtle differences may distinguish his replicated self from the original and what the cumulative effect of regularly scrambling his molecules may be.

Object-oriented analysis (OOA) and object-oriented design (OOD) work a little like *Star Trek*'s transporter. The process of analysis seeks to break a problem into small pieces (called *requirements*) so that it can be fully understood and readily communicated. The complementary process of design seeks to assemble a system that matches its requirements. Of course, the kind of matching performed in object-oriented design is different from that performed by the transporter system. The transporter seeks an exact match, a replica that duplicates every feature of the original. Object-oriented design instead seeks a complementary match of problem with solution. After all, users seldom have a desire to see their problems replicated (even if this is too often what actually occurs during system development).

This chapter teaches you how to perform object-oriented analysis and design and also introduces you to the basic tools of object-oriented analysis and design, which take the form of diagrams. In this chapter you learn

- How to use the object-oriented design process.

  The *object-oriented design process* defines a series of steps you can follow in analyzing and designing object-oriented systems. By following these steps, you can become a more efficient and effective object-oriented systems developer.

- How to use a problem summary paragraph to determine system requirements.

  The problem summary paragraph is the first product of the object-oriented analysis and design process. A well-written problem summary paragraph helps you quickly and accurately determine system requirements.

- How to identify classes and services by using Class-Responsibility-Collaboration (CRC) cards and use-cases.

CRC cards and use-cases are helpful and easy-to-use tools that assist you in identifying the classes you need and the services they provide.

- How to describe relationships by using Unified Modeling Language (UML), including inheritance diagrams and class diagrams.

  Unified Modeling Language appears poised to achieve the status of a de facto standard for representing design information. Its inheritance diagrams and class diagrams are generally more helpful to the developer than analysis-oriented CRC cards. *Inheritance diagrams* show parent-child relationships between classes. *Class diagrams* show the attributes and behaviors of classes.

INTRODUCING THE OBJECT-ORIENTED DESIGN PROCESS

Object-oriented analysis and object-oriented design have not been around for very long. Nevertheless, techniques (or *methodologies* as they're commonly called) for OOA and OOD have become legion. The 18–19th century clergyman-economist Thomas Malthus may have foreseen such circumstances when he observed that populations tend to outstrip food supplies. Although his predictions of worldwide famine failed to materialize during his lifetime, many in the twentieth century have become persuaded that his ideas are fundamentally sound.

In any case, we may now be witnessing the "Malthusian Effect" as it applies to OOA and OOD techniques, which now appear to be shrinking in number. The cause: Several originators of rival techniques have recently joined forces and begun developing the Unified Modeling Language (UML), which many expect will combine the best features of many popular OOA and OOD techniques.

The techniques described in this chapter loosely follow those of UML. Using the qualifier *loosely* is necessary because UML is not yet fully developed. Moreover, its potential status more resembles that of a *de facto* standard (one that reflects practice) rather than a *de jure* standard (one that reflects what some think should be done). Consequently, UML will doubtless continue to evolve even after it is initially published.

At the time of writing, the tools (diagrams) of UML have been described in several books, including Martin Fowler's *UML Distilled: Applying the Standard Modeling Language* (Addison-Wesley, 1997) and Pierre-Alain Muller's *Instant UML* (Wrox, 1997). However, the process underlying UML is to be the topic of a forthcoming book. Consequently, the process described in this chapter reflects common elements of existing analysis and design techniques, rather than the not-yet-published UML process.

The process, which is fully described in the following sections, consists of these steps:

1. Determine the requirements.
2. Identify the classes and the services they provide.
3. Describe the relationships.

Although the parts of the process are described as steps, you should not expect that these steps are typically performed one at a time, from first to last, without repetition or back-tracking. On the contrary, the nature of any problem-solving activity more closely resembles an exploration rather than a program. Problem solving is an iterative activity that much resembles what occurs when a psychologist drops a hungry rat into a cheese-baited maze. We may be relatively certain of the goals of the activity, but the means by which we achieve them are seldom clear at the outset. With hard work, persistence, and a little luck, they become progressively clearer as we near the goal. The trail blazed by the OOA/OOD processes more closely resemble that in the right panel of Figure 3.1 than that in the left.

Actually, once the analysis and design dichotomy breaks down, it's more usual to consider a single process that combines analysis and design. Rather than moving linearly from analysis to design, such a process cycles between analysis and design.

FIGURE 3.1

The actual path of OOA and OOD efforts is opportunistic.

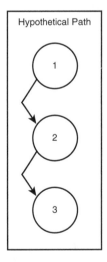
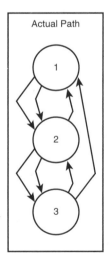

DETERMINING THE REQUIREMENTS

In Lewis Carroll's *Alice in Wonderland*, Alice naively asks the Cheshire Cat which path she should take. When the Cat asks Alice where she's going, she admits she doesn't know, prompting the Cat's famous rejoinder: "If you don't know where you are going, what difference does it make which path you take?"

Analysis and design are somewhat like Alice's journey. If your client doesn't know what the system should do, it doesn't matter what you ultimately deliver. Therefore, your first task in analysis and design is to figure out what the system should do, that is, what the requirements are. The formal name for this process is *requirements elicitation*.

Alas, there is no royal road to requirements elicitation. To see why this is so, consider that clients often do not know what they really want. Therefore, requirements elicitation often involves more than simply asking clients what they need. Often you must first help a client identify the real needs.

Requirements elicitation, therefore, is a communications-intensive process of learning and discovery for both the client and the software developer. It typically involves interviews, surveys, study of documents and existing systems, study of competitor's systems, and so on. The goal of requirements elicitation is an understanding that is

- Complete—The delivered system will satisfy only the identified requirements, so these must be as complete as possible.
- Consistent—The requirements should contain no contradictions.
- Correct—Perhaps it seems to go without saying that the requirements should be correct. However, achieving correctness is very difficult. For example, users may inadvertently (or even maliciously) provide you with incorrect information. You must keep the goal of correctness continuously in mind or risk failure.
- Clear—An understanding that is ambiguous is no understanding at all. The difficult work you devote to developing a complete, consistent, and correct understanding comes to naught if people interpret it differently because you've been unclear.
- Concise—Few people today enjoy novels as long as those popular during the Victorian era. Even fewer enjoy reading business documents of comparable length. The same phenomenon constrains the length of a business presentation. Unless your understanding can be communicated concisely, it won't be understood or acted upon.

Like other communications processes, the requirements elicitation process can be improved by developing a written record of what you discover along the way. The written record augments your limited recall of detail, helps bring others to a common understanding of the problem, and tends to increase the objectivity of the process. By documenting the requirements, you also make them portable. For example, they can be beamed across the country via email, so that people who can't be interviewed in person can nevertheless contribute their insights and expertise. A popular form for this record is the *problem summary paragraph*.

Writing the Problem Summary Paragraph

Many software developers see the completion of a problem summary paragraph as the first milestone on the journey to a completed system. But exactly how far down the road should that milestone be placed? Let's not push the term *paragraph*—no court has yet decreed that problem summaries of more than one paragraph violate the laws of any jurisdiction. If the system you're analyzing is a large one, you may exceed the budgeted single paragraph with complete impunity. The point of the word *paragraph* is to remind you that you should strive to be concise, but sacrificing completeness in order to be concise may not be the wisest course.

Perhaps now you begin to see why some organizations reward those involved in analysis and design better than those involved in implementation. Whether a section of code does, or does not, fulfill its purpose can be determined fairly easily and most qualified observers will agree with a carefully made determination. In contrast, the quality of system requirements is far more elusive. Improving one dimension of system requirements quality often diminishes the quality of one or more other dimensions. For example, it's difficult to be both complete and concise at the same time. Achieving completeness may require you to write more pages than many people are willing to read. If you try to cut corners, the clarity of your writing may suffer. You must bob and weave your way to quality, much like a pilot buzzing the Grand Canyon. Miss one turn and you're wall decoration for the marvelment of future tourists.

> **NOTE**
>
> If all this talk of failure depresses you, be encouraged. Recall that OOA/OOD is an iterative process. You shouldn't expect to get everything right at first, only eventually. Feedback is your ally. As long as your clients spend time reviewing and constructively criticizing your work products, your mutual understanding of the system will converge to reality over time.
>
> The biggest risk is that some organizational power figure, fearful of the march of time and mindful that time is money, will push to begin implementation even though the requirements are inadequately understood. It's like a mother giving birth who yields too early to the urge to push: The baby may be crushed by the pressure. There's a time to tough it out and a time to push. The trick is to know which should be done when. Try at the outset of a project to help the client understand this convergence principle, so that you can avoid a rush to implementation.

In the next section you begin a case study that gives you the opportunity to watch as a simple system is analyzed and designed. The case study begins with a problem summary paragraph. The design, including all the important UML diagrams, is complete by the end of the chapter.

Introducing Kvetch Net

In modern free enterprise, everyone is occasionally shortchanged. In response to every-day petty fraud, consumers fall into one of two categories: Some complain and some don't. In fact, some consumers are downright complaint-challenged. Others, however, elevate the mundane act of complaint to an art. These practitioners of *kvetch* (the Yiddish word for a complaint or an annoying complainer, pronounced *kuh-vetch*, with the accent on the last syllable) have a valuable service to offer their less adept fellow consumers. Kvetch Net, an Internet startup headquartered in New York, was founded to realize this vision, potentially benefiting consumers the world over.

You've been invited by Ms. Yenta Luftmensh, founder of Kvetch Net, to help her build the Web site that will serve her clients. Arriving early at her ostentatious downtown Manhattan headquarters, you spend the morning interviewing her about her information system needs. Ultimately, you determine that the Web site must support two transactions:

- A quote transaction, in which the user describes the sort of complaint needed and receives a price quotation
- A purchase transaction, in which the user approves the price, provides the required electronic funds, and receives the complaint via email

Based on the information supplied by Yenta, you develop the problem summary paragraph shown in Figure 3.2.

FIGURE 3.2

A problem summary paragraph identifies system requirements.

> The Kvetch System enables a client, who accesses Kvetch Net's Web site using a standard Web browser, to describe the sort of complaint required. The system selects a prefabricated complaint from its complaint database, one that closely matches the client's requirements. The system then proposes a price, which the client can accept or decline. To accept the price, the client simply authorizes an electronic fund transfer in the proper amount. The system responds by transmitting the selected complaint, which can be saved and modified by the client.

The rest of this chapter shows you how to develop the key diagrams that describe the required system. You start by learning how to use CRC cards to document classes and their services.

IDENTIFYING CLASSES AND THEIR SERVICES

Once you have a problem summary paragraph, you're ready to identify the classes and the services they provide. This is really quite easy.

First, activate the transporter. Second, put the problem statement on the transporter pad, slide the lever to the Activate position, and watch as the problem summary paragraph breaks into its component molecules.

Okay, unless you have a transporter, it isn't quite so simple—but, it's almost that easy. Here's what you do:

1. Underline the action phrases (verb phrases) that appear in the problem summary paragraph.

2. Draw a box around the phrases (noun phrases) that denote actors and objects of action that appear in the problem summary paragraph.

3. Study the actors that you circled in step 2, determining which of them should be represented as classes.

4. Study the actions that you underlined in step 1, deciding which of them are services provided by a class.

5. Record your findings as one or more CRC cards.

To get you started, Figure 3.3 shows the problem summary paragraph for the Kvetch System, with the actions and actors indicated. Next, you learn how to identify the classes.

FIGURE 3.3

The problem summary paragraph discloses candidate classes and services.

The Kvetch System enables a client, who accesses Kvetch Net's Web site using a standard Web browser, to describe the sort of complaint required. The system selects a prefabricated complaint from its complaint database, one that closely matches the client's requirements. The system then proposes a price, which the client can accept or decline. To accept the price, the client simply authorizes an electronic fund transfer in the proper amount. The system responds by transmitting the selected complaint, which can be saved and modified by the client.

Identifying Classes

To identify the classes, make a list of the problem summary paragraph phrases you circled. Table 3.1 shows such a table for the Kvetch System. Notice how *synonyms* (entries that mean the same thing, although they're expressed differently) have been removed.

For example, *Kvetch System* and *the system* refer to the same thing, so only *Kvetch System* (the more specific phrase) appears in the table.

TABLE 3.1   CANDIDATE CLASSES OF THE KVETCH SYSTEM

Candidate Class
amount
client
client's requirements
complaint
complaint database
electronic fund transfer
Kvetch System
price
Web browser
Web site

Now, further winnow the list by casting out these entries:

- Entries that do not need to be represented as objects or classes within the system
- Entries that represent attributes or characteristics of other entries

Admittedly, this task is tough. You don't really know at this point which entries need to be represented as classes. That's why OOA/OOD is iterative. You probably will make some mistakes at this point, but, as you proceed, your errors will become evident. When that happens, backtrack to this point, add the missing class or delete the unneeded class, and retrace your forward progress.

Perhaps the biggest difference between experienced analysts and inexperienced analysts is the number of false starts: Experienced analysts experience *more* false starts than inexperienced analysts, who tend to lock onto their early impressions, refusing to reconsider them even in the light of further information. Don't hesitate to backtrack: Backtracking is essential to quality work.

Table 3.2 shows the candidate classes of the Kvetch System after the winnowing cycle.

3

OBJECT-ORIENTED ANALYSIS AND DESIGN

TABLE 3.2 CANDIDATE CLASSES OF THE KVETCH SYSTEM

Candidate Class
client
client's requirements
complaint
complaint database
electronic fund transfer

The following candidates were discarded for the reasons given:

- Amount—It's really an attribute of the electronic fund transfer.
- Kvetch System—The system doesn't need to represent itself.
- Price—It's really an attribute of complaint selected by the system.
- Web browser—It's merely the means used by the client to access the system.
- Web site—It turns out to be roughly synonymous with the system.

Now that you've identified the classes, move on to identify the services they provide.

Identifying Services

You saw that the circled actors and objects (noun phrases) in the problem summary paragraph help you identify classes. The underlined actions (verb phrases) help you identify services. You may not be familiar with the term *services*, even if you know something about objects. Sometimes they're referred to as *behaviors*, *methods*, or *responsibilities*.

Among these alternatives, the term *services* is particularly apt because it places the emphasis on actions performed by an object on behalf of other objects. In addition to such public actions, most objects also have private actions, which do not concern us at this point. We prefer *services* because it emphasizes exactly those behaviors and methods that we seek.

A reason for preferring the term *services* over the term *responsibilities*, which also emphasizes public actions, is that *services* recalls the popular term *client-server*. The fundamental paradigm of client-server system is client objects requesting services of server objects, exactly the thing we seek to find mentioned in the problem summary paragraph. Table 3.3 shows the candidate services, which are the underlined phrases in the problem summary paragraph.

TABLE 3.3 CANDIDATE SERVICES OF THE KVETCH SYSTEM

Candidate Service
accept
accesses
authorizes
decline
describe
enables
matches
modified
proposes
required
responds
saved
selects
transmitting
using

Just as the list of candidate classes was winnowed, so now the list of candidate services is winnowed. Table 3.4 shows the winnowed list.

TABLE 3.4 REMAINING CANDIDATE SERVICES OF THE KVETCH SYSTEM

Candidate Service
authorizes
decline
describe
matches
proposes
selects
transmitting

Here are the reasons entries were deleted:

- *Accesses* and *using*—The phrase *accesses Kvetch Net's Web site using a standard Web browser* constrains the technology that is used to access the system, rather than specifying a requirement of the system.

- *Accept*—It can be treated as synonymous with *authorizes*.

- *Enables*—It describes a non-specific action of the entire system.

- *Modified* and *saved*—They specify actions of the client that do not concern the system.

- *Required*—It specifies the needs of the client rather than the actions of the client or system.

- *Responds*—It can be treated as synonymous with *transmitting*.

In all, about half of the candidate services were eliminated. This is good news because fewer services points to smaller classes that are more quickly and easily implemented. Let's move on to a discussion of CRC cards, which helps you pair classes with related services.

Using CRC Cards

Class-Responsibility-Collaboration (*CRC*) *cards* are one of the most useful tools during OOA/OOD. A CRC card is nothing more than an index card (for example, a 3×5 card) that records information about a class, including

- The name of the class
- A brief description of what the class represents
- The services provided by the class
- A list of class attributes

If you like, you can begin using CRC cards at the outset, rather than building lists of candidate classes and services. However, it's often easier to identify services and then match them with classes. Making lists first can make things go more smoothly.

Figure 3.4 shows a CRC card for the Kvetch System's complaint database. Notice that the class name and the names of services have been styled as Java identifiers; this makes it easier to code the class in Java.

Notice that the back of the CRC card includes a list of attributes. *Attributes* hold the characteristics of objects. For example, a simple `Ball` object might have attributes reflecting its color, diameter, weight, and rebound factor.

You may wonder how attributes are identified because you've seen no list of candidate attributes for the Kvetch System.

FIGURE 3.4

*A CRC card pre-
sents key informa-
tion about a class.*

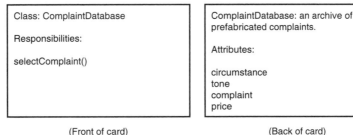

(Front of card)   (Back of card)

Attributes are seldom disclosed by the problem summary paragraph. Two attributes of the `ComplaintDatabase` class, `price` and `complaint`, appeared there. The remaining attributes, `circumstance` (is this a complaint about food or a complaint about rent?) and `tone` (should the complaint be calm or abusive?), are implicit in the phrase *matches the client's requirements* in the problem summary paragraph.

Perhaps a more complete problem summary paragraph would have mentioned them, but no problem summary paragraph is likely to mention all the attributes. That's another reason OOA/OOD is an iterative process. Recall the Lewis and Clark expedition that found a land route across the American territories to the Pacific coast. Despite the help of Indian guide Sacagawea, they merely found *a route*, not *the best route*. Don't expect to do better on your own first trip through a system.

You may also be wondering how the `selectComplaint` service shown on the CRC card came to be there, rather than on the CRC card of some other class. Determinations such as this involve a combination of problem insight, technical expertise, careful reflection, and luck. The essential function of the `ComplaintDatabase` class is to provide a complaint that matches the user's requirements. Therefore, the `selectComplaint` service is implicit in the essence of the class.

This is a good time for you to try your hand at making some CRC cards. Select one of the remaining candidate classes and make its CRC card. Do your best to identify the related services and attributes. You may discover a need for services that do not appear in the list of candidates: Feel free to add these. Similarly, feel free to disregard any listed services that don't seem to actually be needed. The same is true of classes: Add or delete classes as you see fit.

DESCRIBING RELATIONSHIPS

In the preceding section you learned how to identify services by studying the problem summary paragraph. In this section you learn an alternative technique that's especially helpful when systems are large or complex: the *use-case*. You also learn how to prepare two more UML diagrams: the *class diagram* and the *inheritance diagram*.

Developing Use-Cases

Identifying services from a problem summary paragraph and allocating them to classes by a combination of insight and intuition often works well, but the going gets tough when systems become large or complex. A helpful technique in these situations is the use-case and its accompanying collaboration diagram.

A use-case relates to a particular use of a system, a scenario or transaction, if you will. Consider the Kvetch System, which has the following use-cases:

- Client Requests Quote and Accepts
- Client Requests Quote and Declines

As the Kvetch System has been described, these two use-cases encompass all that it must, or can, do.

A collaboration diagram (see Figure 3.5) illustrates the classes and the sequence of actions involved in a use-case. For example, the "Client Requests Quote and Accepts" use-case has these actions:

1. `Client` sends requirements to the `ComplaintDatabase`, requesting that `ComplaintDatabase` select a complaint and provide a quotation.

2. `Client` sends an authorization to `FundTransfer`.

3. `FundTransfer` notifies `ComplaintDatabase` that payment has been received and authorizes `ComplaintDatabase` to transmit the complaint.

4. `Client` requests and receives the purchased complaint.

FIGURE 3.5

A collaboration diagram illustrates a use-case.

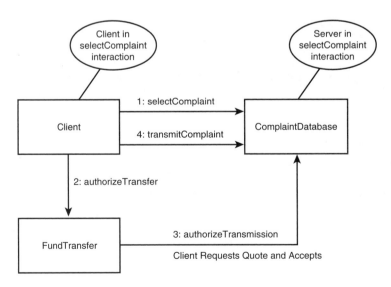

The collaboration diagram shows each of these four actions as a line joining the requestor (known as the *client*) and the requestee (known as the *server*). The arrowhead on each line points to the server, which performs the requested action. For example, consider action 1, the selectComplaint action; Client requests this action and the ComplaintDatabase performs it.

Generally, collaboration diagram actions have associated information flows. However, a collaboration diagram does not show these because the diagram would otherwise quickly become cluttered. This is an application of the principle of design abstraction, which is summed up in the aphorism "less is more." Human information processing capacity is limited; to avoid overwhelming the reader, UML diagrams present a limited amount of information. That's why there are several kinds of UML diagrams: Each presents a few aspects of the design, just enough to make its point. Taken together, a set of UML diagrams describes all the important aspects of the design.

A great way to prepare collaboration diagrams is to distribute CRC cards among the members of a team seated around a large table; then simulate each use-case as a series of conversations among the team members. Step through the requests one by one, having the team member who holds the CRC card for a class explain how that class will respond to the request. Often this will quickly disclose missing or unnecessary classes, services, data attributes, or use-case steps.

Developing Class Diagrams

CRC cards are handy during analysis but less handy during implementation. They tend to fall out of project notebooks, get out of order, and so on. Therefore, many developers transcribe information from CRC cards to class diagrams, which fit conveniently on standard-size sheets of paper and can be stored in a three-ring binder with the other diagrams and documents that pertain to a system. Moreover, as you'll see, class diagrams can record information pertaining to groups of classes, something that CRC cards cannot do.

Figure 3.6 shows a class diagram for the ComplaintDatabase class. Notice that the class diagram is divided by horizontal rules into three sections. The class name is shown in the top section, the attributes are listed in the middle section, and the services are listed in the bottom section.

Figure 3.6 lists one service, selectComplaint. Notice how the name of the service is followed by a pair of parentheses, which makes it clear that the name refers to a Java method, not a field.

FIGURE 3.6

A class diagram is a bit different from a CRC card.

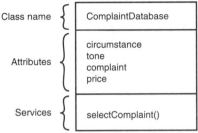

Some developers like to include more information on class diagrams, particularly as analysis and design progress and implementation nears. You can easily include type information in a class diagram by merely prefixing each attribute with its data type. For example, if you decide that price should be represented as a float, you could write either of these to specify the data type:

```
price:float
```

```
float price;
```

The former style is recommended for UML, but the latter has the virtue of more closely resembling Java.

Some developers like to also include default or initial values, describing attributes like this:

```
price:float = 0.0
```

UML provides a standard syntax for specifying visibility or access. You use a + to indicate public visibility, a # to indicate protected visibility, and a - to indicate private visibility. If price is a private field, its full UML description might be as follows:

```
- price:float = 0.0
```

UML also provides a syntax for more fully specifying the characteristics of services. The syntax closely resembles that of a standard Java method header. Here's an example of a fully specified service:

```
+ getComplaint(circumstance:int): float
```

This statement tells us that getComplaint is a public service that requires a single argument, an int that describes the client's circumstances. The service returns a float value.

Classes in OOA/OOD are often associated with one another. A class diagram can include multiple classes, with arrows that indicate associations between classes. Figure 3.7 shows a Kvetch System feature not previously discussed: the ability to track clients' purchases so that regular clients can be offered special terms or sent email catalogs describing new complaints Yenta has obtained. To support this feature, a `Purchase` class has been established. The line joining it to the `Client` class indicates that `Clients` and `Purchases` are related. The numbers to the right of the line show the *cardinalities* of the association, that is, the number of object instances that can participate in the association. The "1" indicates that each `Purchase` is associated with exactly one `Client`, whereas the "asterisk" indicates that a `Client` can be associated with zero, one, or more `Purchases`.

FIGURE 3.7

A class diagram can indicate associations.

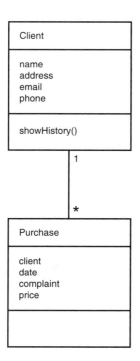

NOTE

If you're familiar with the entity-relationship diagrams used to model database relationships, you may correctly notice that class diagrams resemble them. However, don't push the superficial resemblance too far. Classes, which encapsulate data and behavior, are not the same as database tables, which merely contain data.

A class diagram can also indicate that a class extends another class. (If you're unfamiliar with extending classes by means of inheritance, you might like to look ahead to the section "Inheritance" in Chapter 7, "Java Overview.") Figure 3.8 shows an example. In the figure, the classes `LandlordComplaint` and `RestaurantComplaint` are subclasses of

`Complaint`, as indicated by the triangle that appears on the line joining them to the `Complaint` class.

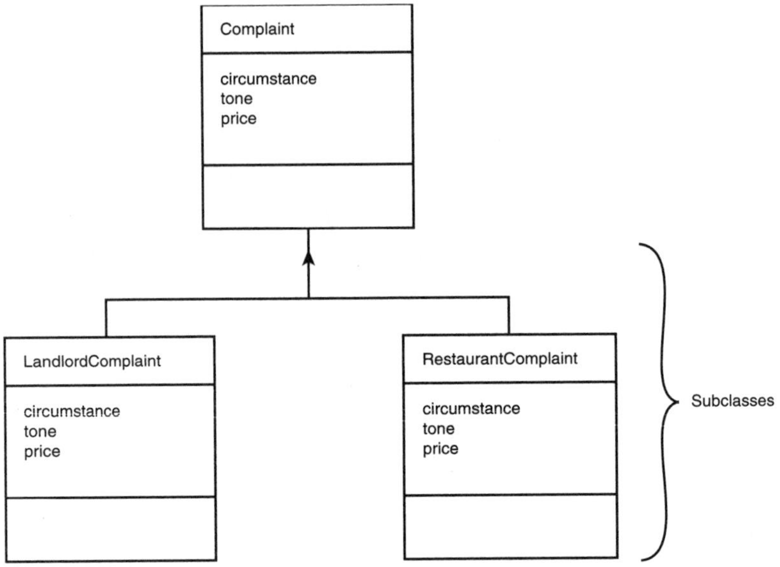

FIGURE 3.8

A class diagram can indicate inheritance.

FROM HERE

CRC cards, collaboration diagrams, and class diagrams can communicate a wealth of information about a system in an easy-to-understand, visual format. Whenever you create a system diagram, remember that your purpose is to communicate. Don't develop your own arcane and complicated system of notation when a standard notation such as UML will serve. Feel free, however, to rearrange things and break the rules once in a while in the interest of clarity.

Now that you've learned about object-oriented analysis and design, you're ready to develop your skills by applying its techniques to significant analysis and design problems. The following chapters give you that opportunity:

- Chapter 6, "The Airline Reservation System Model," uses object-oriented analysis and design to describe a simple distributed system. There you learn more about use-cases. You also learn about activity diagrams.

- Chapter 14, "Socket-Based Implementation of the Airline Reservation System," describes an implementation of the Airline Reservation System based on sockets.

- Chapter 16, "RMI-Based Implementation of the Airline Reservation System," describes an implementation of the Airline Reservation System based on Java's Remote Method Invocation (RMI) facility.

- Chapter 19, "Servlet-Based Implementation of the Airline Reservation System," describes an implementation of the Airline Reservation System based on Java servlets.

- Chapter 26, "CORBA-Based Implementation of the Airline Reservation System," describes an implementation of the Airline Reservation System based on Common Object Request Broker Architecture (CORBA).

- Chapter 35, "Voyager-Based Implementation of the Airline Reservation System," describes an implementation of the Airline Reservation System based on Voyager, a mobile agent technology.

3

**OBJECT-ORIENTED
ANALYSIS AND
DESIGN**

DISTRIBUTED ARCHITECTURES

IN THIS CHAPTER

Charles Darwin's 1859 book *The Origin of Species* inaugurated a conflict between science and religion that continues, at least in some circles, almost a century and a half later. Based on his five-year study of animal life in the Galapagos Islands off the Pacific Coast of South America, Darwin concluded that modern species had evolved from a few earlier species. To explain the evolution of species, he posited the existence of a mechanism he called *natural selection*.

Regardless of whether Darwin was correct in his understanding of animal species, his theory of natural selection helps us understand how information system architectures change. Just as the traits of a species are determined by its genes, the characteristics of an information system architecture are determined by the technologies it employs. Just as individuals of a species compete for scarce resources, information systems architects strive to find new ways of creating systems that cost less to build and operate, and are more effective in meeting user needs. The result is an evolutionary march of the sort Darwin believed operated to produce animal species.

This chapter introduces the elements of information system architectures and recapitulates major eras in the development of such architectures. Just as object-oriented programming builds upon the principles of structured programming, distributed object architectures build on the principles of their non–object-oriented forebears. By understanding non–object-oriented architectures and the forces that shaped them, you'll be prepared to understand not only the current styles of distributed object architectures presented in this chapter, but also those that have yet to be conceived.

In this chapter you learn

- How the management of user interface, data, and computation characterize an architecture.

  Technological change simultaneously presents new opportunities and changes user expectations. When user interface technology, data management technology, or computational technology change, computing architecture changes.

- How the mainframe and file-server architectures solved problems of their era and where they continue to be useful today.

  The venerable mainframe and file-server architectures were kings in their day. Despite a hoary reputation, they remain appropriate architectures for some modern systems.

- How client/server architectures led to more efficient and effective information systems.

  The 1990s client/server revolution gave users a higher return on their computing investments. You see how this was accomplished and how more modern architectures build on the lessons of client/server computing.

- How distributed object technologies such as object buses, mobile objects, and agents provide the information systems architect with exciting new options.

  After years of unfulfilled promises, distributed object technology now appears poised to become the dominant architecture. You'll see what this new technology offers and why information systems architects have begun to favor it over other technologies.

ARCHITECTURAL ELEMENTS

An *information system architecture* describes the way computers are used to meet organizational needs. For example, one very simple architecture consists of a standalone PC. This architecture might be suitable for a one-person professional office, for instance. A more elaborate architecture might consist of a minicomputer server connected via a high-speed LAN to dozens of PCs that run special application software under Microsoft Windows 9x.

NOTE

People generally use the terms *architecture* and *infrastructure* to refer to distinct aspects of an information system. *Architecture* refers to the technologies an information system uses and the way the technologies work together. *Infrastructure* sometimes refers to the specific components and types of components that realize an architecture; an IBM 3090 mainframe and Compaq PCs, for example. More often, however, *infrastructure* refers to the portfolio of information processing applications owned by an organization or the mode of organization of the information systems function (centralized, decentralized, and so on).

Even from these brief descriptions, you can see that an information systems architecture has several kinds of components including physical components, such as servers and PCs, and logical components, such as application programs. Let's examine each of these kinds of components in detail. This will lay a foundation for the subsequent discussion of architectures.

Network Components

A very simple non-networked information system can consist of a single component—the PC. However, a networked system like the one in Figure 4.1 always has at least three components:

- A *client*
- A *server*
- The *network* itself

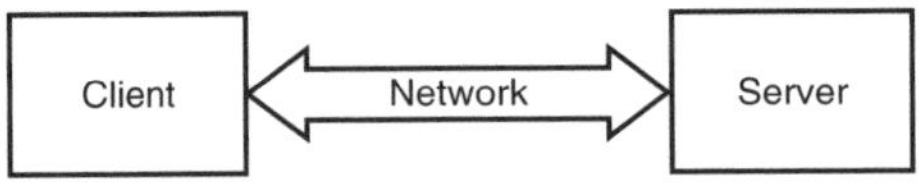

FIGURE 4.1

An information systems architecture has three components.

The user operates the client, which is used to initiate requests. Clients include PCs, video terminals, bank ATMs, and so on. The purpose of the client is to provide a user interface.

The server holds resources, such as data or programs, needed to satisfy client requests. Servers may be mainframe computers, minicomputers, or even PCs. From the architectural perspective, the size or power of the server doesn't matter. What does matter is that the server responds to client requests. Of course, the size and power of a server are important characteristics of an information system design: The more powerful the server, the more clients it can handle, but a server that serves only one client is nonetheless a server. The architectural perspective is a very high-level perspective, much like the view of a city you'd experience when flying in an airplane at an altitude of 50,000 feet. The architectural perspective draws your attention to a few prominent characteristics of a system that experience has shown to be important and relatively long-lived. It also helps you ignore details that don't much matter and would otherwise tend to get in the way of your thinking. After you've determined the architecture of a system, you must decide how to realize the architecture. It is then that matters of size and power become relevant. The network joins the client to the server. Client requests flow across the network to the server and server responses flow across the network to the client. A network can be a dial-up modem connection, a 100Mbps Ethernet, or any other means of connecting computers. As with servers, the capability of the network doesn't matter from the standpoint of architecture. What does matter is the network's role as a channel between client and server.

Just as modern househusbands reverse traditional family roles, clients and servers too can reverse their usual roles. Consider the situation shown in Figure 4.2. In Transaction #1, computer A acts as the client and computer B is the server. In Transaction #2, B acts as a client and C is the server. Therefore, computer B can be both a client and server as needed for a given situation.

FIGURE 4.2

Clients and servers can reverse roles as needed.

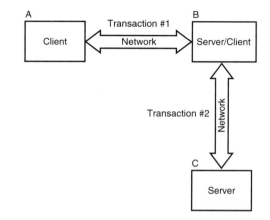

The key idea distinguishing a client from a server is usually that the client acts on behalf of a human user. The distinction can be hard to draw when each of a pair of cooperating computers is operated by a user. For example, if two users are talking via Internet phone software, which is the client and which is the server? And what about the situation in which pre-programmed computers communicate entirely without human intervention?

In such cases, *client* and *server* become roles (in a logical sense) rather than physical devices. Just as in the more usual case, the client initiates an interaction and the server responds.

An information system architecture can be better characterized in terms of its logical components rather than its physical components. Although the logical components are harder to see than the physical components, they're more central to the purpose of an information system. For example, a system can be implemented using any of several competing graphical user interfaces (GUIs). Which particular GUI is chosen is not much more important than the state of origin of lumber used to construct a home. Just as the size and strength of building components—rather than their origin—are the real concerns of a residential architect, the characteristics of the GUI—rather than its identity—are the real concerns of an information system architect.

Information system architectures differ in terms of the technology used to provide their logical components. Some of the most important components of an information system architecture are

- User interface
- Data management
- Computation

User Interfaces

Because it's the part of the system nearest the user, a system's user interface is some-times called the *front end*. In fact, from the limited perspective of the user, the user inter-face is the system. A typical modern user interface might consist of a keyboard, a video display, and a mouse. Alternatively, a system might employ a more specialized or exotic user-interface technology, such as a power glove. Some day we may even have futuristic thought-controlled interfaces such as that of the fictional Soviet fighter plane stolen by Clint Eastwood in the movie *Firefox*.

Three main user-interface technologies are used today:

- Dumb terminals
- X-terminals
- PCs

In addition, some expect a fourth technology to soon capture a significant share of the user-interface market: network computers.

Let's examine each of these technologies.

Introduced into widespread use in the 1960s, dumb terminals were one of the earliest user-interface technologies. Prior to dumb terminals, ordinary folk were not computer users: The privilege of access to expensive mainframes was the special prerogative of professional computer programmers and operators. Instead, users communicated with computers by filling out paper forms, the contents of which were transcribed by key-punch operators onto punched cards that were fed into the computer in batches. Typically hours or days elapsed before a user's transaction was processed. Computer output, too, was paper bound, taking the form of massive reports that were often out of date by the time they were distributed.

The early *dumb terminal* was nothing more than a keyboard and a monochrome text-only video display connected via a simple network to a mainframe server. Nevertheless, this humble device brought about a computing revolution. No longer was data passed through several hands, batched into the computer, and processed into reports. Instead, for the first time, users could submit transactions that the computer processed in *real-time*, that is, while the user waited. Results could be displayed on the video screen rather than on reports, which required much time to print and distribute. However, dumb terminals were not simple to operate: Users had to spend days or weeks in training in order to learn how to use them.

The early 1980s saw PCs transition from hobbyists' toys to business tools. At first they offered an interface little different from that of the dumb terminal, but PCs soon sported high-resolution color displays. These enabled development of GUIs that featured lines and simulated buttons, making the PC somewhat more *user-friendly* than the dumb terminal.

The Apple Macintosh and Microsoft's Windows operating system further improved the PC user interface by adding a computer mouse, which permitted the user to perform simple, common operations without typing. This opened PC use to a much wider audience. Businesses began to purchase PCs rather than dumb terminals because the higher cost of the PC was offset by its greater ease of use and consequently lower training costs.

However, replacing a dumb terminal with a PC did not automatically afford a GUI. Application programs had to be changed to support the new user interface technology. This proved to be costly and time consuming. One of the most thorny issues in information system management during the 1980s and 1990s was the struggle to improve the user interface of so-called *legacy systems* built during the era of dumb terminals.

The 1990s saw a specialization of GUIs as Web browsers. Browsers became a common tool for interacting with computers and networks. These easy-to-use programs allowed even novice computer users to access data from a variety of sources via a consistent user interface.

Manufacturers of non-PC user-interface devices did not willingly cede the market to the PC. The 1980s saw the advent of the *X-terminal*, which provided a graphical user interface comparable to that of the PC, but at lower cost. X-terminals were, and remain today, popular within the UNIX community. However, the strategic advantage of X-terminals, their low cost, was undercut by the falling price of general-purpose PCs. The capability of a PC to function, via emulation software, as an X-terminal further cut into the market potential of X-terminals. For just a few dollars more than an X-terminal, one could purchase a PC that ran standard PC applications, such as word processing, as well as an X-terminal emulator.

The 1990s brought the *network computer*, which combined the low cost of an X-terminal with the capability to run standard PC applications. At the time of this writing, the market success of the network computer remained at issue. However, the continued fall of PC prices seemed to be hampering their widespread acceptance.

Table 4.1 summarizes the characteristics of general-purpose user-interface technologies.

4

DISTRIBUTED ARCHITECTURES

TABLE 4.1   CHARACTERISTICS OF GENERAL-PURPOSE USER INTERFACE
TECHNOLOGIES

Technology	Characteristics
Dumb terminals	Low hardware cost
	High training cost
	Keyboard input
	Text-based output
Windows-based PCs	Medium-to-high hardware cost
	Low training cost
	Keyboard and mouse input
	Text and graphical output
	Run standard PC software
X-terminals	Medium hardware cost
	Medium training cost
	Keyboard and mouse input
	Text and graphical output
Network computers	Medium hardware cost
	Low training cost
	Keyboard and mouse input
	Text and graphical output
	Run standard PC software (with assistance of appropriate server)

Data Management

By definition, information systems involve storage and retrieval of data. Therefore, the technology used to manage data is a second important logical component of an information systems architecture. Modern systems generally employ relational databases as their data management technology.

Just as a system's user interface is known as its front end, a system's data management functions are known as its *back end* because they're invisible to the user. Not that *invisible* implies *unimportant*; data management is at the heart of the essential purpose of an information system: processing and storing data.

Two main data management technologies are in use today:

- Flat files
- Relational databases

In addition, a third data management technology is vying for a significant market share: object-oriented databases.

Let's examine each of these technologies.

So-called *flat files* are the ordinary sort of files processed by application programs. Flat files may be an appropriate technology for simple, standalone applications. However, flat files suffer from two deficiencies:

- A flat file does not include *meta data* that describes its contents and format.
- A flat file does not provide a way to relate records in one file with those in another.

The result is that application programs must contain descriptions of the flat files they use and of the relationships between them. As more and more programs are written, changing the format of a file or revising its relationships with other files becomes laborious and expensive.

Relational databases overcome these limitations. A relational database includes a *schema*, which describes the contents of the database. Moreover, relational databases allow relationships between files (*tables* in relational database parlance) to be specified and automatically maintained. This provides applications with an important property known as *data independence*. Many sorts of changes to the structure of the relational database can be made without requiring changes to application programs. For example, it's typically possible to add fields to relational tables or add tables to a relational database without affecting existing applications. This significantly lowers costs of database operation and maintenance.

Relational databases also facilitate sharing of data by multiple concurrent users. Without the special protection they provide, update transactions can "collide," resulting in corrupted data. Flat files require one-user-at-a-time access to data or elaborate (and error-prone) application programming to avoid data corruption.

Relational databases also generally support Structured Query Language (SQL), a standardized language for definition, access, manipulation, and control of data within relational databases. Because many vendors have provided SQL support for their relational databases and because SQL is standardized, programmers can write applications for one host platform and later cost-effectively port them to a different host platform rather than rewrite them. Chapter 11, "Relational Databases and Structured Query Language (SQL)," presents these concepts in more detail.

One limitation of relational databases is that they provide only limited support for objects. Most relational databases support the BLOB (Binary Large Object) data type, which can hold a persistent external representation of an object's attributes. An object can therefore be stored in a relational database. For example, you can store a Java String in a database as a BLOB item, but the BLOB item holds only the values of the fields of the String—its text characters. The .class file that defines the behaviors of the String class must be stored outside the database so that the Java virtual machine can access it. Essentially, BLOBs are handy for storing objects, but not classes. They're not fully object-oriented.

These sorts of capabilities are provided by *object-oriented databases*, which are becoming more widely used. One problem hindering acceptance of object-oriented databases is the present lack of an accepted standard. The American National Standards Institute (ANSI) and the International Standards Organization (ISO) have been working for some years on a revised version of the *SQL Standard* that supports objects known as SQL-3. However, the standard has not yet been finalized and implementations of the standard are not yet widely available.

To further complicate matters, the Object Data Management Group (ODMG) has proposed a standard that differs from the SQL-3 draft in important ways. For example, the ODMG standard does not attempt backward compatibility with SQL-2. On the other hand, several vendors (for example, Ardent Software and Poet Software) currently provide implementations of databases that are ODMG-compliant.

Table 4.2 summarizes the characteristics of data management technologies. Although object-oriented database technology is currently immature, its potential benefits seem to ensure that it will gain a growing share of the data management technology market.

TABLE 4.2 CHARACTERISTICS OF DATA MANAGEMENT TECHNOLOGIES

Technology	*Characteristics*
Flat files	Lack data independence.
	Lack data sharing.
	Lack standard language.
Relational databases	Provide data independence.
	Provide data sharing.
	Provide standard language (SQL).
Object-oriented databases	Provide data independence.
	Provide data sharing.
	Provide elaborate support for objects.
	Not yet standardized by internationally recognized standards body.

Computation Management

An information system consists of more than data: It also includes software programs that manipulate the data. An information systems architect can choose from a variety of ways to manage computation. For example, a batch-oriented COBOL system is quite different from a distributed Java system. There are four main ways of managing computation:

- A system can allocate processing to one unit or multiple units.
- A system can be written in a non-portable or portable language.
- A system can allocate processing statically or dynamically, using mobile agents.

Most systems use a single technology for management of user interface or data; however, systems commonly utilize several technologies for management of computation. Let's examine each of these three technologies.

Strictly speaking, only a standalone system allocates processing to a single unit. Even a dumb terminal contains a simple microprocessor, so a system that employs a dumb terminal will have at least two processors: one in the dumb terminal and one in the computer than controls it. However, programmers don't write code that runs on the dumb terminal's microprocessor terminal. In a typical configuration, they write code only for the mainframe computer that controls it. Because the programmer's code runs only on the mainframe, we view such a configuration as performing all its processing on a single unit.

If the dumb terminal were replaced by a PC that emulated it, nothing of significance would change. Even though the PC contains a general-purpose microprocessor, it's not being used in this configuration, which is still deemed to perform all its processing on a single unit.

However, imagine a network that links a dozen or so PCs scattered across the country, each PC containing a relational database that records inventory and sales for its region. One PC might run a program that queries the other PCs to locate an item in short supply. Processing is being performed on multiple units if the remote PCs run a program that responds to that query.

Why might this be desirable? It may be less expensive to purchase 50 ordinary computers than to purchase a single computer that has fifty times the capacity of an ordinary computer. Similarly, it may be easier to ensure that one of several computers is operational at all times than to ensure that a single computer is operational at all times. Allocating processing among several units can decrease cost and improve reliability.

Systems can also be written using a non-portable or portable language. Java, of course, is the first portable language in widespread use. By writing programs in a portable language, programmers hope to reduce or eliminate the cost of adapting programs to run on platforms other than that on which they were developed.

Many companies have suffered the misfortune of constructing large information systems that use proprietary languages or technologies, only to have the provider of the language or technology go bankrupt or charge an exorbitant price for continued support. If these companies had implemented their systems using a portable language they could have replaced the vendor without the high cost of porting the systems.

Mobile agents are software objects that can relocate themselves, or be relocated, from one processor to another. Mobile agents written in a portable language are particularly interesting and useful because they can move from a processor of one type to a processor of another type.

Mobile agents can reduce network traffic and improve the efficiency of a system. For example, suppose that an application requires two objects to exchange data in a lengthy dialog. If the objects are located on separate processors, the data must flow across the network, increasing network traffic and delaying the completion of the dialog. However, if one of the objects is a mobile agent, it can relocate itself to the processor on which the other object resides. The two objects can then complete their business using local data transfers, rather than network data transfers. This decreases network traffic and greatly increases the speed of the computation.

Now that you've been introduced to the technologies used for managing user interfaces, data, and computation, you're ready to embark on a study of specific information systems architectures. In the following sections you learn about two traditional information systems architectures. You also learn about client/server architectures and distributed architectures.

TRADITIONAL ARCHITECTURES

The two traditional information systems architectures are

- Mainframe architecture
- File-server architecture

To be honest, many experts consider the file-server architecture, which became popular in the 1980s, a modern architecture rather than a traditional architecture. However, an architecture that's been around for over a decade seems to fit the notion of *traditional* in a field where the half life of knowledge is anywhere from two to five years. Hence, the file-server architecture is included with the mainframe architecture as a traditional architecture.

Mainframe Architecture

The mainframe architecture came into widespread use during the 1960s. Featuring a "big iron" server (later versions of the mainframe architecture sometimes substituted a less expensive minicomputer for the mainframe) and dumb terminals (see Figure 4.3), the mainframe was sometimes aptly called a *smart server/dumb client* architecture. All programs were executed by the server, which was responsible for management of the user interface, data, and computation.

FIGURE 4.3

*Mainframe archi-
tecture featured a
smart server and
dumb clients.*

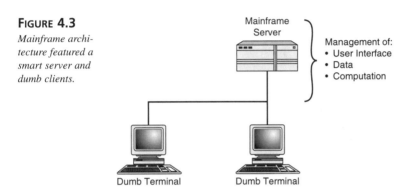

Because such systems employed dumb terminals as a user interface, they suffered from the disadvantages inherent in those primitive devices. Users found them hard to learn and companies invested significant resources in training employees to use the systems.

Although modern uses of the mainframe architecture feature relational databases, most systems built using the mainframe architecture used flat files to manage data. As a result, application programs were generally large and complex. Many of these systems continue in use today, partly because the software is so difficult to modify.

NOTE

Information systems experts expect large numbers of such systems to fail on or about the year 2000 because many antiquated systems represent years using only two digits. Such systems represent both the year 1900 and the year 2000 as 00 and therefore cannot reliably manipulate dates subsequent to December 31, 1999. This so-called Y2K problem may compel organizations to finally update these outmoded systems.

Computational technology was also primitive by modern standards. All processing was done on the mainframe server. Programs were not portable and mobile software agents were not employed. Most programs were written in COBOL, a language designed to be

4

DISTRIBUTED
ARCHITECTURES

readable by non-computer professionals rather than as a tool for efficient programming. (Of course, as it turned out, most programs were too complicated for non-programmers to understand: COBOL didn't achieve this design goal.)

However, the mainframe architecture had its bright points too. For one thing, during its day it was the only affordable architecture that allowed direct use of the computer. Computers were so expensive that organizations were fortunate to be able to afford one. More elaborate architectures featuring multiple computers were not economically feasible. An architect's choices were batch processing or the mainframe architecture.

The mainframe architecture did some things well. For example, a mainframe system could be made highly reliable. Also, data security was high because data was stored in a single location with a single point of access. Some modern architectures composing the mainframe architecture also scaled well: It was possible to build very large information systems using the mainframe architecture. Table 4.3 summarizes salient characteristics of the mainframe architecture.

TABLE 4.3 CHARACTERISTICS OF MAINFRAME ARCHITECTURE

Component	*Characteristic*
Server hardware	Mainframe computer or minicomputer
Client hardware	Dumb terminals
User interface	Keyboard input, text output
Data management	Flat files
Computation management	COBOL programs (non-portable) executed on server
Cost	Medium to high
Reliability	High
Security	High
Scalability	High
Flexibility	Low

File-Server Architecture

Decreased costs of computing hardware and advances in computing software led to a new architecture, the *file-server architecture*, which became popular during the 1980s. Many organizations had been unable to afford the high cost of the server required by the mainframe architecture. When powerful PCs first became available, these organizations sought ways to construct information systems using PCs.

Because they performed computation in the clients rather than the server, file-server systems could be built using a relatively inexpensive PC as a server. The server itself did little, functioning mainly as a repository for the common data accessed by client PCs. In contrast to the smart server/dumb client configuration of the mainframe architecture, the file-server architecture (see Figure 4.4) was *dumb server/smart client.*

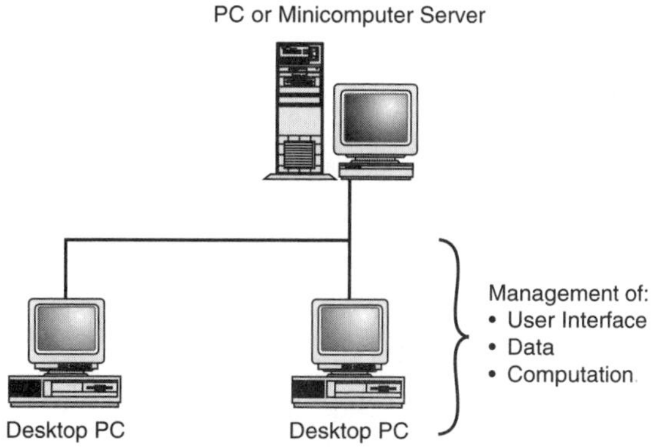

FIGURE 4.4

File-server architecture featured a dumb server and smart clients.

PC or Minicomputer Server

Management of:
• User Interface
• Data
• Computation

Desktop PC   Desktop PC

User interface management functions of file-server systems were not much more advanced than those of mainframe systems. The file-server systems usually featured color rather than monochrome displays, but both file-server and mainframe systems depended heavily on keyboard input. A user had to possess typing skills in order to use such systems.

Data management, too, was little changed: File-server systems depended on flat files just as mainframe systems did. However, the way in which file-server systems accessed their files was a little different because a program running on a client PC had to access files residing on a server PC. Typically, this was accomplished by using operating system support for file sharing that made the files appear as though they were files on the client system's local hard drive.

This approach potentially compromised both reliability and security. Because each client PC modified data on the server, a hardware or software failure in any client could corrupt the central data. Moreover, clever users could circumvent application controls by accessing the central files using, for example, a text editor, which would allow them to change or delete any data.

However, the biggest problem with the file-server approach to data management was efficiency. Suppose a user wanted to search the files for a given record. The application program would read data from the server's files, looking for the record of interest. Potentially, every record might be transmitted before the right one was found. This high

4

DISTRIBUTED
ARCHITECTURES

level of network traffic meant that the file-server architecture was suitable for use only with a high-speed local network. Large information systems extending beyond the bounds of the local network could not operate efficiently.

Computation management was similar to that of the mainframe architecture. However, languages other than COBOL (such as BASIC and dBASE) were commonly used.

Table 4.4 summarizes salient features of the file-server architecture.

TABLE 4.4   CHARACTERISTICS OF FILE-SERVER ARCHITECTURE

Component	*Characteristic*
Server hardware	PC
Client hardware	PCs
User interface	Keyboard input, text output
Data management	Flat files
Computation management	Programs written in various languages (BASIC or dBASE) executed on client
Cost	Low
Reliability	Low
Security	Low
Scalability	Low
Flexibility	Medium to high

CLIENT/SERVER ARCHITECTURE

Microsoft Windows became the predominant PC operating system during the 1990s and relational database technology matured, giving rise to the *client/server architecture* you see in Figure 4.5. In this more balanced architecture, the server and clients shared the burden of computation, making this the first *smart server/smart client* architecture.

As previously discussed, transition from a textual to a graphical user interface greatly increased ease of computer use. Many users owned PCs and required little training in order to use systems that featured GUI.

Equally important was replacement of flat files with relational databases. Early relational database management systems were notoriously inefficient. However, by the 1990s database technology had improved and hardware power had increased to the point that relational database performance was no longer a significant issue.

FIGURE 4.5

Client/server architecture featured a smart server and smart clients.

PC, Minicomputer, or Mainframe Server

Management of:
• Data
• Computation

Desktop PC   Desktop PC

Management of:
• User Interface
• Computation

SQL helped make client/server systems more scalable than file-server systems because it was no longer necessary to transmit large amounts of data across the network. Instead, the database engine could search for a desired record and return only that record. This, of course, was possible because both the server and client were fully programmable. Clients were programmed in a PC language, such as C or Visual Basic. The server commonly ran only the database engine, which executed SQL programs, but some systems featured more elaborate server programs written in C or other languages.

Because it's a relatively simple language, SQL also made client/server systems flexible. So-called *ad hoc queries*, unanticipated queries that were not pre-programmed, had been a common and significant thorn in the side of flat-file–based systems. Responding to such queries involved writing a program, a costly and time-consuming process. SQL was simple enough that programmers became much more productive; some users learned enough SQL to be able to write their own query programs.

The absence of a costly mainframe made client/server systems more cost-effective than their predecessors. The combination of cost-effectiveness and flexibility made migration to the client/server architecture a priority for many organizations. Table 4.5 summarizes salient characteristics of the client/server architecture.

4

DISTRIBUTED ARCHITECTURES

TABLE 4.5   CHARACTERISTICS OF CLIENT/SERVER ARCHITECTURE

Component	Characteristic
Server hardware	PC, minicomputer, or mainframe
Client hardware	PC
User interface	Graphical
Data management	Relational database

continues

TABLE 4.5   CONTINUED

Component	Characteristic
Computation management	Programs written in various languages executed on server or client
Cost	Low to medium
Reliability	High
Security	High
Scalability	High
Flexibility	High

By the middle of the 1990s the rush to client/server systems had become headlong. The slogan of the day was *downsizing*, which meant reducing information systems costs by replacing the big iron mainframe with a minicomputer that acted as server in a client/server configuration. Partly, downsizing was a product of cost pressures resulting from increased globalization. It was thus a logical competitive response. However, sometimes so much attention was paid to reducing costs that little attention was paid to securing the potential benefits of the client/server architecture. Consequently, not all client/server migrations were successful.

However, some understood that the proper slogan was *rightsizing*, meaning the use of appropriate and cost-effective technologies for both client and server. Those who adopted this perspective more often realized the considerable potential benefits of the client/server architecture.

Web-Server–Based Architecture

A particular form of client/server architecture has become popular since the mid 1990s—the *Web-server–based architecture* shown in Figure 4.6. This architecture features a Web server and Web browsers as clients.

Web-server–based architecture has come to play a particularly important role in organization's internal networks. There it supports functions such as project management, document tracking, and training.

Because they use a Web browser as a user interface, Web-server–based systems are easier to use than those that require complete familiarity with Microsoft Windows. Thus, they open computer use to a wider audience.

Moreover, Web-server–based architecture is not limited merely to internal use within organizations. It is the architecture of the World Wide Web itself. Using

Web-server–based architectures, many organizations have developed extensive Web sites for product information, retail sales, customer support, and other purposes. Without exaggeration, the Web-server–based architecture is *the* information systems architecture of the late 1990s.

FIGURE 4.6

Web-server–based architecture features Web server and Web browser clients.

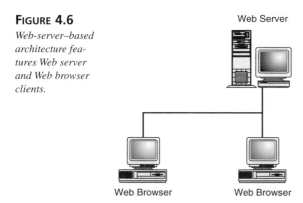

Web Server

Web Browser   Web Browser

Three-Tier Architecture

One complication affecting the client/server architecture arises in those situations in which a client accesses several different servers. If the servers use different operating systems or database engines, the client must be equipped with proper drivers for each such configuration. To complicate matters, vendors tend to update such drivers regularly. Therefore, a client must be equipped not only with drivers for the right operating system or database engine, it must be equipped with the proper versions of such drivers. When clients are numerous and geographically dispersed, this becomes a problem of system administration.

The solution (see Figure 4.7) is known as the *three-tier client/server architecture*. This architecture features a *middleware server*, which it interposes between client and server. Clients are equipped with a simple driver (a *thin driver*) that enables access to the middleware server. In turn, the middleware server provides access to servers of various types.

Middleware servers provide other useful functions, such as protocol translation. Some architects place application logic in middleware, which results in a very simple structure:

- Clients are responsible for user interface.
- Middleware servers are responsible for computation, including application logic encoding the business rules related to a system.
- The servers are responsible for data stored in a relational database.

FIGURE 4.7

Three-tier systems simplify client configuration maintenance when accessing multiple servers is a requirement.

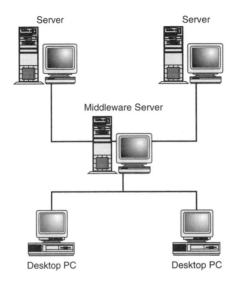

When Web browsers are used as clients, this configuration simplifies the maintenance of application programs as well as drivers. In this configuration, both the clients and the servers are general-purpose programs. All the unique parts of the information system reside in the middleware server, where they can be conveniently updated as required.

DISTRIBUTED ARCHITECTURES

A *distributed architecture* is one that includes multiple servers. If you push the point too far, many client/server systems fit this definition. For example, a three-tier client/server system usually includes multiple servers. In fact, that's the reason for having a third tier: to facilitate access to heterogeneous servers.

But clients in such systems generally connect to only a single server at a given time. To be considered truly distributed, a system should include multiple concurrent server connections. One simple distributed architecture is *peer-to-peer* networking (see Figure 4.8), in which every host potentially acts as both client and server.

Designers of distributed systems aim to place data and computation near the point of use. This reduces network traffic and improves system response time. Reliability is another potential advantage of a distributed system, which can continue working even when part of the system fails. In the past, development of distributed systems has been a difficult undertaking, owing to the novelty of the technology and the lack of adequate tools. With the advent of Java, the Web, and Common Object Request Broker Architecture (CORBA), this has finally changed. Table 4.6 summarizes salient characteristics of distributed systems.

FIGURE 4.8

A peer-to-peer network is a distributed system.

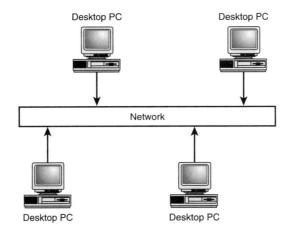

TABLE 4.6   CHARACTERISTICS OF THE DISTRIBUTED ARCHITECTURE

Components	Characteristics
Server hardware	PC, minicomputer, or mainframe
Client hardware	PC
User interface	Graphical
Data management	Relational database
Computation management	Programs written in various languages executed on server or client
Cost	Medium
Reliability	High
Security	High
Scalability	High
Flexibility	High

4

DISTRIBUTED ARCHITECTURES

Object Buses

Just as a system based on flat files can pose a maintenance problem when changes are made to data structure or format, a distributed system can pose a maintenance problem when hosts are added or deleted or when resources, such as data or programs, are relocated. A *directory service* can provide *location transparency* by enabling hosts to discover the location of resources at runtime.

When a distributed information system is object-oriented, the directory service can take the form of an object bus. An *object bus* helps objects locate remote resources, including other objects; it also enables objects to send messages to remote objects and receive responses.

The most popular object bus is that provided by CORBA, which is the subject of Chapters 21 through 33 of this book. Object bus technologies include Java's Remote Method Invocation, presented in Chapters 15 and 16, and Microsoft's DCOM, presented in Chapter 20.

Mobile Agents

Another innovation in distributed systems architecture is the *mobile agent*, an object that can move from host to host. Mobile agents allow processing to follow use dynamically; they can be used, for example, to balance the processing load of a system so as to avoid overtaxing a host that's handling many requests.

An interesting consequence of technologies like the object bus and mobile agent is that they simplify the structure of information systems. A system built using these technologies is adaptable, or even adaptive, so its structure can be tuned when necessary. Therefore, such a system better fits current organizational needs than a system built using a fixed structure.

As organizations face increased competitive pressures and environmental turbulence, the advantages offered by the distributed architecture are crucial. Data is the lifeblood of the modern organization, flowing to the remotest outpost and bringing opportunity and insight. A static information system structure is akin to hardening of the arteries, restricting the vital flow of data. Agile competitors seek information systems structures that are energetic and long-lived, such as those built using the distributed architecture.

FROM HERE

The following chapters provide additional details regarding specific state-of-the-art distributed architectures:

- Chapter 11, "Relational Databases and Structured Query Language (SQL)," more fully presents relational database technology.
- Chapter 15, "Remote Method Invocation (RMI)," describes a Java core technology that provides a simple but effective object bus for Java objects.
- Chapter 18, "Servlets and Common Gateway Interface (CGI)," describes Java servlets, a technology designed to overcome weaknesses of the Common Gateway Interface (CGI) commonly used in Web-server–based architectures.

- Chapter 21, "CORBA Overview," begins a series of chapters that describe the Common Object Request Broker Architecture, which provides an elaborate and sophisticated object bus.

- Chapter 34, "Voyager Agent Technology," introduces you to Voyager, a freely available software product that supports mobile objects and agents. In addition, Voyager is compatible with CORBA.

4

DISTRIBUTED ARCHITECTURES

DESIGN PATTERNS

IN THIS CHAPTER

Feed any programmer a thimble of gin, and chances are that he will begin complaining about unreal deadlines, being forced to release buggy software, and a general software industry that is moving too fast for its own good. Fill up his glass again, and this time he will probably start talking about something called the software crisis and how he cannot get funding to properly write software. Truth be told, the software industry is in a lot of trouble and if we don't watch out, things are going to get much worse.

The term *software crisis* is used to describe the situation brought about when software shops are forced to develop feature-packed products under unrealistic time constraints. This crisis gets exponentially worse as the number of interdependent systems grows.

A major cause of the crisis is attributed to actions taken by major companies, including Netscape and Microsoft. These companies, along with many others, operate under the bizarre new concept of Internet time. Under *Internet time*, development schedules that historically took 12 months are being shortened to 6 or 9 months. Chances are, these timetables may never turn around and only by changing the manner in which we solve problems can we overcome this crisis. In looking for solutions to the crisis, the software community looked to other engineering disciplines and studied the manner in which they solve problems.

When building a bridge, for example, civil engineers don't just start throwing wood and metal across a chasm. Instead, they study the manner that bridges were previously built, they devise a plan for a new bridge, test models, and finally, build the real bridge. Too often software projects neglect to study the successes and failures of the past, fail to plan the current project, and often fail to produce a solid piece of code. In an attempt to refocus the software industry around planning, planning, and more planning, software engineers have turned to design patterns, anti-patterns, and the Unified Modeling Language (UML).

NOTE

The UML is a collection of symbols that can be used to fully model the software cycle. For more information on this topic, see Chapter 3, "Object-Oriented Analysis and Design." *Anti-patterns*, a relatively new term describing an old concept, are the study of failed software projects. Anti-patterns are useful because they allow you to show that a piece of software has a greater chance of success if it lacks design concepts detailed by an anti-pattern.

INTRODUCING DESIGN PATTERNS

Design patterns are a tool by which the knowledge of how to build something is shared from one software engineer to another. More precisely, they allow for a logical description of a solution to a common software problem. A pattern should have applications in multiple environments, and be broad enough to allow for customization upon implementation. For example, memory management in a distributed environment is tricky. Instead of inventing a new solution for every project, many developers look to the reference counting pattern as a guide.

> **NOTE**
>
> *Reference counting* involves tracking the number of clients who have access to a unique server object. When that count reaches zero, there are no longer any clients of the object, and its allocated memory can be returned.

When working with new technologies, like distributed objects, the ability to share knowledge thorough design patterns is critical. Distributed applications introduce concerns beyond those present in standalone applications, and developers new to their use will benefit greatly from any help. These concerns, including network traffic, server scalability, and general reliability, can mean project failure if neglected. This chapter covers a history of design patterns and then covers a series of patterns that applies to distributed object development.

Like all movements in the software world, the pattern movement has a rather interesting history. Back in 1987 two engineers, Ward Cunningham and Kent Beck, were working on a project and were unsure if they would be able to finish on time. They turned to what would eventually become known as *patterns*, and were amazed at the massive assistance these patterns provided for the project. Cunningham and Beck first presented their findings at the Object-Oriented Programming Systems, Languages, and Applications (OOPSLA) conference in 1987, where they managed to generate much excitement.

> **NOTE**
>
> OOPSLA is presented every year by the Association for Computing Machinery (ACM). It is one of the premier conferences for individuals specializing in object technology.

Soon after OOPSLA, a group of four individuals—Erich Gamma, Richard Helm, John Vlissides, and Ralph Johnson—met and realized they shared a common enthusiasm for patterns. These four engineers, now known as the Gang of Four (GOF), published in the early '90s a book titled *Design Patterns: Elements of Reusable Object-Oriented Software* (Addison-Wesley, 1995). *Design Patterns*, or *the GOF book* as it is often called, has fueled the current patterns movement, which continues gaining momentum every day.

One final bit of pattern trivia is that the true father of patterns was not a software engineer at all. Christopher Alexander, an architect (not a software architect) first discussed patterns in his 1964 book, *Notes on the Synthesis of Form* (Harvard University Press, 1970). While Alexander discussed patterns as they apply to building physical structures, the issues discussed are relevant in the software community.

DEFINING PATTERN TYPES

The term *pattern* as it applies to the software process is rather broad and has numerous subcategories. Further complicating matters is the fact that patterns that apply to all parts of the software cycle are now being developed. The focus here is on patterns that specifically apply to the development of software itself. Note, however, that there are additional pattern categories that apply to analysis, organization, and risk management. Although the focus of this chapter is strictly on design patterns, it is good to have a solid understanding of other pattern categories that apply to the code writing process. These categories are described as follows:

> *Architectural patterns* describe how systems are organized as a whole. For example, an architectural pattern for an Integrated Development Environment (IDE) would discuss the manner in which the compiler, linker, text editor, and debugger all interoperate.

> *Design patterns* describe how to physically design code with respect to a single function. For example, the design of a distributed parallel processing application could take advantage of one of the many parallel processing patterns.

> *Idioms* (or *coding patterns*) describe patterns specific to a single programming language. The use of Java interfaces to describe class functionality is an example of an idiom.

The design patterns covered in this chapter are

> Factory

> Observer

> Callback

In presenting a pattern there are many criteria that should be included to provide a complete picture to the reader. The criteria should be presented in a format that is easy to read and allows readers to quickly obtain the needed pieces of information.

While a logical, easy-to-read format is required for pattern presentation, there is no standard form. The format used in this book is loosely based on what is commonly referred to as the Christopher Alexander's *Alexandrian* form. Besides not having a standard presentation format, there is no central pattern authority that guarantees a unique pattern name and function. The relatively small size of the pattern community helps eliminate redundancy, although some is bound to occur.

As stated earlier, a pattern must meet certain criteria to exist. Often people use the term pattern rather loosely and incorrectly label algorithms or data structures as "design patterns."

NOTE

The ability to determine whether something is actually a design pattern comes with time. However, algorithm and data structure confusion is common. The main difference between a design pattern and a data structure or algorithm is that a design pattern describes how a *general* problem is solved. An algorithm or data structure is a code implementation that solves a highly *specific* problem.

NOTE

All patterns in this chapter are implemented in Java. However, since many examples require explicit knowledge of a specific distributed object environment, some pseudocode is used. For example, instead of writing code that binds to a remote CORBA server, you see a line like this: "`//bind to corba server`".

The term "`bind`" refers to the process by which a client object obtains a reference to a remote object. For example, under CORBA, if you know an object's name and interface you can request that the ORB bind you to that object.

Although some variance may exist from author to author, it is generally accepted that patterns must contain all of the following criteria:

Name—Just like every other item in the world, a logical name makes identification much easier. The name should be concise, easy to remember, and logically describe the function of the pattern. An attempt should also be made to ensure that the name is not used by another pattern.

Abstract—A description of the pattern without too much regard for its implementation. This section is usually written last and is based on the problem, context, solution, and forces sections. The abstract is not necessarily a required criteria, but is an added convenience to readers.

Problem—A pattern solves a problem, and this should be clearly spelled out here. While the pattern name should hint at its function, the problem statement allows developers to clearly identify its purpose.

Context—The pattern context identifies the environment in which the pattern is applied. For example, a pattern for handling multiprocessing identifies a context for a multiprocessor machine.

Forces—The forces acting on a pattern indicate conditions that make the pattern less than optimal. Additionally, the forces section details design trade-offs that must be made to fully exploit the pattern.

Solution—Whereas the problem description states the problem solved by this pattern, the solution description states both the means to the end and the end itself. The section often includes illustrations, diagrams, and detailed text descriptions.

Examples—The examples section includes one or more code implementations of the pattern. This section is extremely important; it acts as proof that the pattern can be successfully implemented.

Resulting context—This section discusses both the desired results and side effects caused by the pattern execution.

Rationale—Discussion on why the pattern solution solves the pattern problem. Additionally present in this section are notes on why the pattern is actually needed, and the larger role that it plays in the software lifecycle.

Related patterns—If applicable, similar patterns and their relationships are mentioned here.

Known uses—In addition to meeting all criteria defined in this list, the *rule of three* is often applied to determine whether something is actually a pattern. This rule states that for a pattern to be truly proven, it must exist in at least three successful systems. The known uses section presents a discussion on known implementations of the pattern.

Now that you have a general background on design patterns, let's begin the design pattern coverage. Some of the patterns discussed in this chapter do have applications outside of distributed computing, but are not within the scope of this book.

Having covered what exactly patterns are and the problem they solve, you are ready to dive into individual discussions on a series of patterns. The rest of this chapter changes form to follow the previously discussed Alexandrian form for patterns. Each successive section introduces a new pattern in our version of the Alexandrian form.

USING THE FACTORY PATTERN

Abstract. In a distributed environment, it is not always possible to allocate memory for an object in a foreign system. The factory pattern facilitates remote instantiation of objects.

Problem. When performing distributed object-oriented programming, it is often necessary to instantiate an object on a foreign machine. While Java does provide the `new` keyword for local object instantiation, there is no explicit keyword that allows for remote object instantiation. It is not possible to directly instantiate a remote object unless the distributed environment explicitly monitors usage of the new keyword and brokers requests to a remote machine.

Context. This pattern is applicable in distributed environments where remote object instantiation is necessary.

Forces. Under the factory pattern, a single object becomes a dedicated *"factory object."* Since multiple simultaneous clients most likely use the factory object, it must be written to be totally thread-safe. If usage is going to be extremely high, or if instantiation of the target object is going to take a long while, the factory object will probably want to answer each request in a separate thread.

Solution. Under the factory pattern, client objects do not explicitly instantiate an object. Rather, they bind to a remote factory object, ask that object to perform the instantiation, and then obtain the new object from the remote factory object. This pattern mirrors many producer-to-consumer relationships in the real world. For example, if you need a shirt made, you walk down to the tailor, have your measurements taken, pick your fabrics, and then the tailor makes the shirt and gives it to you. Acting as the "factory object," the tailor accepts the burden of ensuring that the shirt meets both your requirements and the requirements of the fabric.

A *factory object* is passed data that acts as requirements for the remote object. The factory object then uses that data to instantiate the remote object and returns it to the client. Because the factory object has explicit knowledge of the remote environment, it can ensure that the instantiated object meets both the client and environmental requirements. In general, the factory object will have methods with parameter lists that mirror the constructor parameter lists. These parameters are then passed directly from the factory object method to the new object's constructor. An exception to this rule occurs when the factory needs to track data about the requestor, or when the object being instantiated needs explicit data from the factory object. Figure 5.1 shows the factory pattern in action.

Examples. Three classes are employed in the following example. A `FactoryServer` object can instantiate `ServerObject` objects. A `ClientObject` object first binds to the `FactoryServer` object and then asks for a `ServerObject` instance. `FactoryServer` is in Listing 5.1, `ServerObject` is in Listing 5.2, and `ClientObject` is in Listing 5.3.

FIGURE 5.1

Factory pattern facilitates remote object instantiation.

1. Client Requests Object From Factory

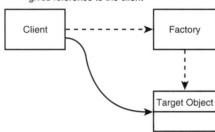

2. Factory instantiates target object, and gives reference to the client

LISTING 5.1 FactoryServer

```java
public final class FactoryServer extends Thread {
    public FactoryServer() {
        waitForConnection();
    }

    private void waitForConnection() {
        // Code to wait for an incoming connection. This code
        // specific to the distributed object technology
        // currently enabling communication.
    }

    public ServerObject createServerObject(String sName) {
        return new ServerObject(sName);
    }

    public static void main(String[] args) {
        FactoryServer server = new FactoryServer();
    }
}
```

LISTING 5.2 ServerObject

```java
public final class ServerObject {
    private final String _sName;

    public ServerObject(String sName) {
        _sName = sName;
    }
```

```
    public String getName() {
        return _sName;
    }
}
```

Listing 5.3 `ClientObject`

```
public final class ClientObject {
    public ClientObject() {
        // First bind to the remote factory object
        // object. Since the binding process is
        // specific to an actual implementation, it is
        // shown here as a comment.
        FactoryServer server = // bind to factory server

        // Request that the remote factory object instantiate
        // a ServerObject object for us.
        ServerObject serverObject = server.createServerObject("luke");
    }
}
```

Resulting Context. The factory pattern does not alter the state of the factory object, but there are memory implications that the factory server must take into account. Since many clients instantiate objects using server memory, the factory must always ensure that sufficient memory exists. In a Java environment, ensuring proper memory allocation is simply a matter of starting the Java Virtual Machine (JVM) with sufficient available memory.

Rationale. In a distributed object environment, it is usually necessary for a client to instantiate an object at the server. This pattern solves this need.

Known Uses. The factory pattern has been around in various forms for ages. It is used in non-distributed applications to centralize object instantiation and is used in countless distributed applications.

USING THE OBSERVER PATTERN

Abstract. A common requirement of distributed systems is that they possess knowledge regarding the state of a remote object. Constantly checking that remote object for changes consumes client resources, server resources, and bandwidth. The observer pattern allows for client notification upon server changes.

Problem. The function of a client object is often to either represent some state present in a corresponding server object or to take an action on a server object change. Since the client object must have instant notification of changes to the server object's state, there are two possible solutions to the notification problem. The client object could check for

5

DESIGN PATTERNS

changes every *n* units of time, or the server could notify the client only when a change occurs. Having clients constantly check for server changes is a drain on resources (both client and server) and requires that much bandwidth be dedicated to this checking. The observer pattern discusses a logical manner by which clients can receive notification of server state change.

Context. This design pattern is applicable in any environment where client objects need constant knowledge of changes to some server-side value.

Forces. Server objects conforming to the observer pattern will spend time notifying clients of changes to server state. When implementing the server object, decisions need to be made about change synchronization and the manner in which resources are allocated to telling clients about changes. In some situations the server will want to notify the client before making the actual changes to itself. In other situations, the server object will want to immediately reflect the change internally and then send off client notification in a separate (possibly low-priority) thread. Additionally, since two-way communication between client and server is required, you must ensure that external security devices allow this. If a firewall protects the client from receiving method invocations, this pattern cannot be used.

Solution: The observer pattern functions in a manner quite similar to the Java JDK1.1 delegation event model. Under the observer pattern, clients expose a method (via an interface), which is then invoked to indicate a change in the server object. The client registers with the server as an interested listener. When changes occur in the server object, the server object sends information about the change to all clients. Figure 5.2 illustrates this process.

NOTE

As with any distributed object environment, the concept of clients and servers is rather gray. Since the role of client or server may change during the application lifecycle, role should be thought of as a transient, not persistent, quality. Just because one piece of software is running on a Sun Sparc10 and the other is running on a 486 does not imply that the Sparc is the server and the 486 is the client. If the Sparc passes processing requests off to the 486, the 486 plays the role of the server.

Examples. The following examples demonstrate a simple application in which a client registers interest with a stock quote server. The client notifies the quote server of all interested ticker symbols, and the server notifies the client whenever one of those values changes. There are two classes and one interface contained in this application. The

QuoteClientI interface (see Listing 5.4) identifies the method by which the client obtains notification of a change. The QuoteClient class (see Listing 5.5) implements the QuoteClientI interface and listens for changes to a few ticker symbols. The QuoteServer class (see Listing 5.6) tracks all listeners and sends notification whenever a registered symbol has a value change.

FIGURE 5.2

The observer pattern facilitates client notification of changes in server objects.

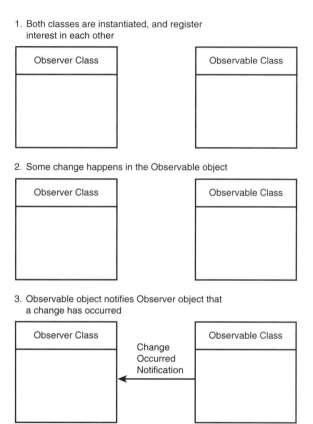

1. Both classes are instantiated, and register interest in each other

| Observer Class | Observable Class |

2. Some change happens in the Observable object

| Observer Class | Observable Class |

3. Observable object notifies Observer object that a change has occurred

| Observer Class | Change Occurred Notification | Observable Class |

LISTING 5.4   THE QuoteClientI INTERFACE

```
/**
 * Interface to be implemented by all object interested
 * in receiving quote value changed events.
 */
public interface QuoteClientI {
    public void quoteValueChanged(String sSymbol, double dNewValue);
}
```

LISTING 5.5 THE QuoteClient CLASS

```java
/**
 * The QuoteClient class registers interest with a server
 * for tracking the values of different stocks. Whenever
 * the server detects that a stock's value has changed, it
 * will notify the QuoteClient object by invoking the
 * quoteValueChanged() method.
 *
 */
import java.util.*;

public final class QuoteClient implements QuoteClientI {
    private Hashtable   _hshPortfolio;

    public QuoteClient() {
        _hshPortfolio = new Hashtable();
        regWithServer();
    }

    /**
     * Registers with the server our interest in receiving
     * notification when certian stocks change value.
     */
    private final void regWithServer() {
        QuoteServer server = // bind to quote server
        server.regListener("INKT", this);
        server.regListener("MOBI", this);
        server.regListener("NGEN", this);
        server.regListener("ERICY", this);

        _hshPortfolio.put("INKT", new Double(0));
        _hshPortfolio.put("MOBI", new Double(0));
        _hshPortfolio.put("NGEN", new Double(0));
        _hshPortfolio.put("ERICY", new Double(0));
    }

    /**
     * Invoked whenever the value associated with an interested
     * symbol changes.
     */
    public void quoteValueChanged(String sSymbol, double dNewValue) {
        // display the changes
        System.out.println("\n");
        System.out.println(sSymbol+" changed value");
        System.out.println("old value: "+_hshPortfolio.get(sSymbol));
        System.out.println("new value: "+dNewValue);

        // store the new value
        _hshPortfolio.put(sSymbol, new Double(dNewValue));
```

```
    }

    public static void main(String[] args) {
        QuoteClient client = new QuoteClient();
    }
}
```

LISTING 5.6 THE QuoteServer CLASS

```
/**
 * The QuoteServer class monitors stock feeds, and
 * notfies interested parties when a change occurs
 * to the value of a registered symbol.
 */
import java.util.*;

public final class QuoteServer {
    // listeners are stored in a hashtable or vectors. the hashtable
    // uses as a key the registered symbol, and as a value a Vector
    // object containing all listners.
    private Hashtable   _hshListeners;

    public QuoteServer() {
        _hshListeners = new Hashtable();

    }

    /**
     * Send changed values to all listeners. Since the manner
     * in which the QuoteServer object monitors the stock
     * feeds is beyond the scope of this pattern, it is
     * simply assumed that that method is invoked when needed.
     */
    private void sendChangeForSymbol(String sSymbol, double dNewValue) {
        // check if there are any listeners for this symbol
        Object o = _hshListeners.get(sSymbol);
        if(o != null) {
            Enumeration listeners = ((Vector)o).elements();
            while(listeners.hasMoreElements()) {
                ((QuoteClientI)listeners.nextElement()).
➥quoteValueChanged(sSymbol, dNewValue);
            }
        }
    }

    /**
     * Invoked by clients to register interest with the server for
     * a specific symbol.
```

continues

LISTING 5.6   CONTINUED

```
    */
    public void regListener(String sSymbol, QuoteClientI client) {
        // check if we already have a vector of listeners at this
➥ location
        Object o = _hshListeners.get(sSymbol);
        if(o != null) {
            ((Vector)o).addElement(client);
        }
        else { // create the vector
            Vector vecListeners = new Vector();
            vecListeners.addElement(client);
            hshListeners.put(sSymbol, vecListeners);
        }
    }
}
```

Resulting Context. Since the method defined by the client to indicate a server value change can be invoked at any time, clients must be developed with this in mind. Flow control cannot always be assumed, and any access to shared resources must be written in a thread-safe manner.

Rationale. The observer pattern allows for client synchronization with a server value in a manner that keeps resource use to a minimum. Since network traffic exists only when a value changes, no bandwidth is wasted. Additionally, their resources are used more efficiently because clients are not constantly pinging servers for change requests.

Known Uses. The observer pattern has obvious parallels in the world of push media. Push media involves *pushing* of content from some content source to a content listener. For example, instead of checking *The New York Times* Web site every day, push media delivers the information directly to your desktop whenever a change occurs.

USING THE CALLBACK PATTERN

Abstract. The role of a server object is often to perform some business logic that cannot be performed by a client object. Assuming that this processing takes a significant time to perform, a client may not be able to simply wait for a server request method to complete. As an alternative, the server object can immediately return void from a request method, perform the business calculations in a unique thread, and then pass the results to the client when ready.

Problem. It is common for a client object to request some data from a server object. Assuming that the processing only takes a second or two, the client need not concern itself with the processing time involved. If, however, the server processing will take 10,

15, 120, or more seconds, the client could end up waiting too long for a method return value. Having the client wait for this return value too long may cause client threads to hang and block, which is obviously not a desirable situation. Additionally, depending on the technology used to enable distributed computing, a timeout could occur if the server object takes too long before returning a value.

Context. This design pattern is applicable in any environment where server processing in response to a client request will take an extreme amount of time.

Forces. Since two-way communication between client and server is required, it must be ensured that external security devices allow this. If a firewall protects the client from receiving method invocations, this pattern cannot be used.

Solution. The callback pattern functions by allowing the client to issue a server request and then having the server immediately return without actually processing the request. The server object then processes the request and passes the results to the client. In most situations, the server performs all processing in a separate thread to allow additional incoming connections to be accepted.

This solution has obvious parallels to our earlier shirt-making example. When you visit the tailor, you give him your measurements and fabric preferences. The tailor then makes your shirt, but most likely spends at least a few weeks doing the work. Your options are to either wait for a return value (obviously not the best use of your time), or to instruct the tailor to perform a callback to you when the shirt is ready.

Examples. In this example you implement a server class that has the capability to figure out very large prime numbers. Perhaps you will have an application that requires client access to large prime numbers, but will not have client machines capable of performing the processing. Assuming this situation, the processing is offloaded to a more powerful server that performs the calculation in a unique thread and returns the value when it is found.

There are three classes that compose this example. CallbackClient (see Listing 5.7) binds to a server, requests a large prime number, and takes action upon notification that the value arrived. CallbackServer (see Listing 5.8) waits for client requests and spins each off into a separate thread using the CallbackProcessor inner-class. CallbackProcessor (see Listing 5.8) discovers the required number and returns it when found. If CallbackProcessor is unable to provide the correct value, a null value is returned.

5

DESIGN PATTERNS

LISTING 5.7   THE `CallbackClient` CLASS

```
/**
 * The CallbackClient class will bind to a server object
 * request that a large prime number be calculated, and
 * then respond to the results when delieved by the server.
 */
public final class CallbackClient {

    public CallbackClient() {
        CallbackServer server = // bind to server
        server.findLargestPrimeNumberGreaterThan(100000, this);
    }

    /**
     * Invoked by the server when the target prime number is found.
     * Accepts a Long object and not a long base-type to allow
     * for the passing of a null value if an impossible
     * request was performed.
     */
    public void primeNumberFound(Long lValue) {
        if(lValue == null) System.out.println("number not found");
        else System.out.println("number found: "+lValue);
    }
}
```

LISTING 5.8   THE `CallbackServer` CLASS

```
/**
 * The CallbackServer class finds very
 * large prime numbers. Since the calculations
 * often take much time, clients are not required to
 * wait for a return value. Instead, the CallbackServer
 * class notified the client when the value has been
 * found. All requests are performed in a
 * unique thread to allow for maximum information
 * processing.
 */
public final class CallbackServer {

    public CallbackServer() {
    }

    public void findLargestPrimeNumberGreaterThan
➥(long lBase, CallbackClient client) {
        CallbackProcessor processor = new CallbackProcessor
➥(lBase, client);
        processor.start();
        // immediately return
    }
```

```
/**
 * Inner class used to process requests in a
 * unique thread.
 */
class CallbackProcessor extends Thread {
    private long            _lBase;
    private CallbackClient  _client;

    public CallbackProcessor(long lBase, CallbackClient client) {
        _lBase = lBase;
        _client = client;
    }

    public void run() {
        long lFoundValue = //
➥ spend a lot of time figuring out the needed prime numer
        _client.primeNumberFound(new Long(lFoundValue));
    }
}
}
```

Resulting Context. Since the method defined by the client to indicate a return value from the server can be invoked at any time, clients must be developed with this in mind. Flow control cannot always be assumed, and any access to shared resources must be written in a thread-safe manner.

Rationale. Waiting for the return value of a distributed method invocation is not always possible due to a variety of constraints imposed by the system. The callback pattern offers a solution to that problem.

Known Uses. A common situation that requires the use of the callback patterns is when queries are executed against old systems that take a long time to generate a response.

I once found myself in a situation where I had to write a Java applet front end to an ancient DOS-based application. The only public interface exposed by the DOS application dictated that I write queries to an input directory and wait for a response to be written to an output directory. Through use of the callback pattern, I was able to eliminate the network overhead generated when the client would often have to wait at least a minute for a response to be generated.

USING THE SHARED INSTANCE PATTERN

Abstract. Creation of a remote object often takes a long time due to both potential database queries and object registration requirements defined by the distributed object technology. For example, in a CORBA environment a remote object must register itself with the ORB before it can be exported. Long database queries combined with potentially slow object registration can cause a rather long delay to occur between the time that a client issues a request and the time that the request is answered. CORBA, detailed in Chapters 22 through 33, is a technology that allows code written in multiple languages, running on multiple machines to communicate and share processing. CORBA technology is taking the computing world by storm, and is one of this book's major focuses.

In addition to long creation time, server objects take up memory; if the server runs out of memory, it could crash the whole system. Assuming a stateless remote object, it is possible to take this creation hit once and then allow clients to share the instance.

> **NOTE**
>
> When talking about remote objects, the terms *statefull* and *stateless* refer to the remote object's capability to be changed by a client. When a method is invoked on a statefull object, that object's member data can change. When a method is invoked on a stateless object, none of that object's member data changes.

Problem. In a distributed environment, speed is an issue that developers must constantly consider. Method invocations on a distributed object involve network traffic, and server implementations must deal with the fact that clients could create thousands of objects at the server. All of these server objects take up memory, and can take a long time to instantiate. If possible, the number of server objects created should be minimized, thus allowing for reduced resource usage and reduced response time to client queries.

Context. This pattern has applications in any distributed environment where multiple clients need access to the same server object. In general, this object must be stateless. In some situations it may be possible for clients to share a statefull object, but much care has to be taken to ensure that dirty data is never seen.

> **NOTE**
>
> *Dirty data* refers to data that has been altered by one client and that another client thinks contains historical information. For example, if two clients reference the same remote object and one alters the remote object's data, that new data is called *dirty* until everyone references the same information.

Forces. The shared instance pattern achieves its greatest success when a single server object is shared by lots of clients. If a server object is only going to be occasionally used by one or two clients, it is not worth the work required to track usage.

Solution. Serving shared instances to multiple clients places three major requirements on the server developer. First of all, the server must be able to ensure that two queries are identical. The second requirement comes into play once a query is identified as already executed. At this point, the server must be able easily locate the unique response objects. If either of these first two requirements is ignored, it is quite possible that the wrong query results will be returned to the user, which could be a major security risk. The final requirement that must be heeded by developers involves identifying when no clients have access to the shared server object. At some point, the server must be able to destroy the shared object and the only safe time to do this is when no clients are accessing the object.

The first requirement of uniquely identifying queries can easily be achieved by aggregating query parameters into a holder class and overloading that class's equals() method. If the query does not accept any parameters, you need not bother with this requirement. Listing 5.9 shows an example query holder class that might be used for searching a database of people.

LISTING 5.9   THE PersonQuery CLASS

```java
public final class PersonQuery {
    private String _sFirstName;
    private String _sMiddleName;
    private String _sLastName;

    // getter methods
    public String getFirstName() { return _sFirstName; }
    public String getMiddleName() { return _sMiddleName; }
    public String getLastName() { return _sLastName; }

    // setter methods
    public void setFirstName(String sFirstName) {
    _sFirstName = sFirstName; }
    public void setMiddleName(String sMiddleName) {
    _sMiddleName = sMiddleName; }
    public void setLastName(String sLastName) {
    _sLastName = sLastName; }

    // overload equals()
    public boolean equals(Object compare) {
        // make sure that a PersonQuery object was passed
        if(!(compare instanceof PersonQuery)) return false;

        PersonQuery personCompare = (PersonQuery)compare; //
    cast once to save time
```

continues

5

DESIGN PATTERNS

LISTING 5.9 CONTINUED

```
        // check all fields
        if(! personCompare.getFirstName().equals(getFirstName()))
→ return false;
        if(! personCompare.getMiddleName().equals(getMiddleName()))
→ return false;
        if(! personCompare.getLastName().equals(getLastName()))
→ return false;

        return true; // all good
    }
}
```

Once a query has been identified as unique, a server object must then decide if the object to be served in response already exists. To facilitate discovery of the response objects, a hashtable that uses the query as a key can be used.

All query results in Listing 5.10 are stored in a hashtable. The query object is used as the key and the query results are used as a value.

LISTING 5.10 THE SharedInstance CLASS

```
import java.util.*;

public class SharedInstance {
    private Hashtable   _hshResults;

    public SharedInstance() {
        _hshResults = new Hashtable();
    }

    public Person[] executeQuery(PersonQuery query) {
        // check if the query has already been performed
        if(_hshResults.containsKey(query)) return
→ _(Person[])hshResults.get(query);

        // query has not been performed
        Person[] returnValue = // get from database
        // register the return value with the distributed object
→ technology

        _hshResults.put(query, returnValue); // store the results

        return returnValue; // return the results
    }
}
```

It is easy for Java programmers to forget about that time long, long ago when they actually had to properly dispose of allocated memory. Java does provide a garbage collector that usually destroys any allocated unused object, but functionality is not always the same in a distributed environment. Unless the distributed object technology explicitly provides a distributed garbage collector, you as the developer are charged with this responsibility. If a remote object is given to a single client, it is easy to tie the lifecycle of the remote object to the lifecycle of the client. In situations where the remote object is shared between many clients, that number of clients must be explicitly tracked.

Listing 5.11 expands on Listing 5.10 to include support for something called reference counting. *Reference counting* involves tracking client references to a server object. When an object is served to a client, that object's reference count is incremented by 1. When the client is done with the remote object, that object's reference count is decreased by 1. When an object's reference count is 0, the server can destroy the object.

LISTING 5.11   SharedInstanceWithReferenceCounting AND PERSON CLASSES

```
import java.util.*;


public class SharedInstanceWithReferenceCounting {
    private Hashtable   _hshResults;

    public SharedInstanceWithReferenceCounting() {
        _hshResults = new Hashtable();
    }

    /**
     * Adds one to each object's reference count
     */
    private void addToReferenceCount(Person[] persons) {
        int iLength = persons.length;
        for(int i=0; i<iLength; i++) {
            persons[i].addToReferenceCount();
        }
    }

    /**
     * Adds one to each object's reference count
     */
    private void subtractfromReferenceCount(Person[] persons) {
        int iLength = persons.length;
        for(int i=0; i<iLength; i++) {
            if(persons[i].subtractfromReferenceCount())
➥ destroyObject(persons[i]);
        }
```

continues

LISTING 5.11   CONTINUED

```
    }

    /**
     * Does any needed clean-up and destroying of objects
     */
    private final void destroyObject(Person person) {
        // destroy
    }

    public Person[] executeQuery(PersonQuery query) {
        Person[] returnValue = null;

        // check if the query has already been performed
        if(_hshResults.containsKey(query)) returnValue = (Person[])
➥_hshResults.get(query);
        else returnValue = // get from database

        // register the return value with the distributed object
➥ technology

        // add to the reference count
        addToReferenceCount(returnValue);

        _hshResults.put(query, returnValue); // store the results

        return returnValue; // return the results
    }

    /**
     * Invoked by the client to indicate that he is done with all
➥ objects
     */
    public void doneWithObjects(Person[] persons) {
        subtractfromReferenceCount(persons);
    }
}


class Person {
    private int _iRefCount = 0;

    public Person() {
    }

    /**
     * Adds one to the reference count
     */
    public void addToReferenceCount() {
        _iRefCount++;
    }
```

```
/**
 * Subtracts one from the reference count.
 *
 * @return true If the refernce count is zero after subtraction
 * @return false If the reference count is non-zero after
➥ subtraction
 */
public boolean subtractfromReferenceCount() {
    _iRefCount — ;
    return (_iRefCount == 0);
}
}
```

Examples. In covering this pattern, code examples were provided in the solution section. These examples taken together provide for a working example of this pattern.

Resulting Context. Use of this pattern has obvious memory implications at the server level. Users must employ reference counting (as discussed earlier) to ensure that objects are destroyed when no longer in use.

Rationale. The shared instance pattern provides a method to speed delivery of remote objects to clients. Objects that take a long time to create can be created only once and then shared between multiple clients.

Known Uses. As with all other patterns covered in this chapter, the shared instance pattern is employed in many of the solutions that I have developed in the past few years. Most recently, I developed a piece of software to view hospital patient records. All incoming data was fed into the system via legacy system gateways, and my software provided read-only access to the data. Creating the graph of objects that compromised a single record was an involved process that took around four seconds. Through use of the shared instance pattern, I was able to reuse the same objects with multiple clients.

FROM HERE

The software industry is definitely heading toward a lot of trouble in the next few years. Unless all computers shut down in the year 2000, we will soon find ourselves forced to develop amazing feature-rich applications in hardly any time at all. Only by using patterns and other development technologies will we be able to rapidly develop the needed software.

As you continue your exploration, the following chapters aid in your understanding of the material in this chapter:

- Chapter 6, "The Airline Reservation System Model," uses the UML use-case notation to describe an airline reservation system.

5

DESIGN PATTERNS

- Chapter 15, "Remote Method Invocation (RMI)," describes a Java core technology that provides a simple but effective object bus for Java objects.
- Chapter 21, "CORBA Overview," provides a solid description of what CORBA is and how it can be used in your applications.

THE AIRLINE RESERVATION
SYSTEM MODEL

IN THIS CHAPTER

Contained within the pages of this book is detailed information on five different technologies that allow for distributed communication between applications. Even though all of these technologies enable this level of communication, each takes a radically different approach. Further complicating matters is the fact that there is no one perfect distributed object technology for all development efforts; only a careful analysis of the problem and a detailed knowledge of the technologies shows a best solution.

Given that choosing the best distributed object technology can often make or break a project, this book spends significant time teaching you how to make this decision. This knowledge is imparted in two complementary manners. First a discussion of the differences between the competing technologies is presented, and then you use each technology to implement a common piece of software.

This chapter presents a formal definition of that common piece of software, an airline reservation system. The definition is then implemented throughout the book in chapters immediately following coverage of each technology. The formal definition of the airline reservation system is presented using the Unified Modeling Language (UML), which is covered in Chapter 3, "Object-Oriented Analysis and Design." Chapter 3 provides a solid introduction to the UML. This chapter does, however, spend some time covering aspects of the UML that apply to use-cases and activity diagrams.

NOTE

The *UML* is a tool used to formally model the entire software process. By using the UML you can model a development effort from the beginning of the requirements gathering to the final implementation models. The UML is quickly becoming the de facto standard for modeling software, and proficiency in it will most likely become an essential job skill in the next five years.

DEFINING THE MODEL

As you can imagine, the software used to drive real-world airline reservations is complex. It needs to respond to thousands of simultaneous users and interact with constantly changing flight data. The airline reservation software developed for this book, however, only models a small number of transactions. The software supports multiple users, but has not been stress tested to handle thousands of users.

In adherence with the development methods defined by the UML, we first simulate a user-based requirements gathering step. We then analyze the requirements and build the necessary use-cases and activity diagrams for the system.

The Airline Reservation System Model

CHAPTER 6

119

6

THE AIRLINE
RESERVATION
SYSTEM MODEL

GATHERING REQUIREMENTS

In an actual development project, the first step is to start talking to your user base to figure out exactly what its needs are. Unfortunately, this step is often ignored and software is developed according only to how developers feel the product should work. Although projects developed without user input may be fun for developers, they often have the downside of not being used.

Although not all systems are developed in the manner they should be, we have the luxury here of pretending that we live in a perfect world. Thus, you can perform every step in the manner that it should logically happen. In addition to pretending that we live in a perfect development world, this book also gets to play both sides in a dialog with users. Of course, nothing in real life is so easy. We get to ignore the fact that users often can't find time to meet with you, or have difficulty communicating what they need.

Our airline reservation system has the following capabilities:

Search for a flight

View all open seats on a given flight

Make a flight reservation

Search for an active reservation

Of the items in the list, the two that involve searching are those that probably benefit most from user input. Only the individuals answering the phones and making reservations all day know how customers want to search for a flight.

After talking with reservation operators, the following items are ranked as the desired criteria used when searching for a flight:

Departure location

Arrival location

Departure date

Departure time

Number of required seats

The reservation operators also stated that they need the ability to specify whether queries should be strict as to departure and arrival times, or whether they should be flexible if a lower-cost flight exists. When allowing for flexibility, the operator should be able to specify a range of 1–48 hours, which defines the permitted flexibility.

The other search exposed by our system is the capability to search for an existing reservation. To perform that search, at least one of the following criteria are needed:

Reservation number

Full name

Date and approximate time of flight

Credit card number used to book flight

All searches return a collection of reservations that match the specified pattern. The burden of verifying the user, once flight data is obtained, is placed on the airline itself. In most situations, the caller is asked to verify his name and credit card number used to book the flight.

DEVELOPING THE USE-CASE

As discussed in Chapter 3, a use-case is a tool used for modeling a unique function in a system. Use-cases should be easy to read, unambiguous, and generally provide a detailed explanation of the highlighted function.

It is really important that a use-case not leave any question unanswered. Remember that the functions as they are defined in use-cases become your software. If you mean one thing, but the developers interpret your comments in a different manner, the costs can be rather large.

Another important use-case development requirement to keep in mind is that use-cases model a single function in a system. That function has a distinct starting point and a distinct end value. A common mistake made by people when developing use-cases is to model the entire system as one large use-case. Modeling a system as a single use-case leads to confusion, and should only be done if the system exposes a single function.

It should be noted that the term used to describe the entity executing a use-case is *Actor*. A use-case is performed by an Actor that may or may not be an actual person. In fact, in many situations the Actor performing a use-case is another piece of software.

A use-case is implementation-independent and, in fact, does not necessarily need to be implemented in software. One could easily write a use-case that models the process of driving a car, or even walking the dog. Although it might be rather exciting to model our entire lives via use-cases, doing so here would move this book into the self-help section, which is not a desired outcome of the "Actor writes a computer book" use-case. The use-cases developed in this chapter are implemented throughout the book in Java using each of the highlighted distributed object technologies.

Finally, use-cases apply to the general use of a system and not a specific interaction with the system. For example, a use-case titled "Actor searches for a reservation using a reservation number" is probably a valid use-case. A use-case titled "Actor searches for a reservation using reservation number #1013-42" is a use-case scenario since it represents a distinct interaction with the system. Use-case scenarios are useful for modeling how special conditions are handled.

Use-Case Notation

Just as the UML provides symbols for modeling all parts of the software process, a series of UML symbols exist that are used with use-cases. The airline-reservation system use-cases do not take advantage of every symbol (most use-cases don't), but as a reference they are all addressed here.

The first step when developing a series of use-cases is to identify the system that is being modeled. A square, with the name of the system written above it, denotes a single system. Figure 6.1 shows a model of the airline reservation system.

FIGURE 6.1

The square symbol denotes an entire system.

Airline Reservation System

After identifying the system being modeled, use-cases that identify unique functions within the system are added. A use-case is denoted using an ellipse or oval with a logical name placed below it. The names applied to both use-cases and systems should be logical, easy-to-read names, and not obscure variable-like names. For example, a use-case that models a reservation search by reservation number should be titled "Search for a Reservation by Reservation Number," not named `resSearchByNum`. Figure 6.2 shows a single use-case that becomes part of our system.

FIGURE 6.2

The ellipse or oval symbol denotes a use-case.

Actor Selects a Flight

Use-Case Relationships

Within a given system, situations may arise where two or more use-cases share some features, or where two or more use-cases use each other. For these reasons, it is possible to model three different relationships between use-cases. These relationships are defined as follows:

- Grouping—Similar to Java packages, the grouping relationship exists when multiple use-cases perform common tasks in a system.

- Uses—Similar to object composition, the uses relationship exists when multiple use-cases interact with each other.

- Extends—Similar to Java inheritance, the extends or generalization relationship allows one use-case to inherit functionality from a parent use-case.

The grouping relationship is defined using the UML package symbol. This symbol, shown in Figure 6.3, looks much like a file folder with a logical name near its top. There are zero functional implications presented by the grouping relationship. However, it does aid the logical grouping of use-cases. Systems with hundreds or thousands of use-cases employ this relationship to make their documents easier to understand.

FIGURE 6.3

The use-case grouping relationship is modeled with the package symbol.

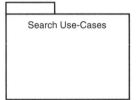

Search Use-Cases

The uses relationship is employed when one use-case takes advantage of functionality present in other use-cases. This relationship, shown in Figure 6.4, is modeled using a straight line ending in a triangle. The triangle points to the use-case being used and the line has the word *<<uses>>* written next to it.

FIGURE 6.4

The uses relationship allows one use-case to take advantage of functionality exposed by another use-case.

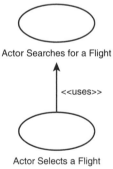

Actor Searches for a Flight

<<uses>>

Actor Selects a Flight

The extends relationship can be thought of in terms similar to Java or C++ inheritance. This relationship is used when one use-case needs to inherit functionality from a parent use-case. For example, one use-case might be used to model making a standard airline reservation. Two additional use-cases could extend this parent use-case and model the situation when reservations are made using frequent flyer miles or a *bounce pass* (a

6

ticket voucher or discount coupon given to passengers who volunteer to leave a over-booked flight). The extends relationship, shown in Figure 6.5, is shown using a line with a triangle at the end of it. The triangle points to the parent use-case and the line has the word *<<extends>>* written next to it.

FIGURE 6.5

The extends relationship allows one use-case to inherit functionality exposed by another use-case.

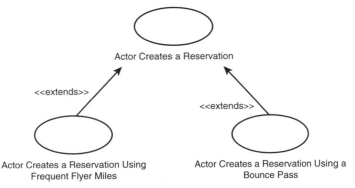

Use-Case Actors

As was earlier stated, an Actor performs a use-case. The Actor may or may not be an actual person; regardless, it is modeled using a stickman. Directly below the stickman, the Actor is labeled with a logical name. Figure 6.6 shows two potential Actors in our reservation system.

FIGURE 6.6

The stickman symbol denotes an Actor.

Reservation Client Software   Human User of Client Software

The development of a use-case is one of the most important tasks in a given software development project. Because use-cases drive the entire development process, it is critical that they unambiguously describe exactly what the software should do.

The development of a use-case is an iterative process that involves the user-base (client), project managers, and developers or development managers. Project managers through a dialog with the user base come up with initial copies of the use-cases. Often the project manager first interviews the user base to determine its needs. He then generates use-cases and presents them to the client. This presentation process often involves physically acting out the use-case with different people playing the roles represented by different systems.

Once some level of agreement has been reached between the project manager and the client, a dialog between the project manager and the development manager begins. It is the duty of the development manager to ensure that all use-cases are technologically feasible. If, for example, the project manger writes a use-case titled "Actor thinks about an item and it materializes in his hand," the development manager needs to use this opportunity to put his foot down. This example does, however, bring up another point, which is that the project manager must be either technically savvy or must work with the development manager earlier in the use-case development process. If the project manager is going to write pipe-dream use-cases, the development manger must reel him in before the client gets any far-off ideas.

MAKING ACTIVITY DIAGRAMS

In addition to the use of use-cases when modeling system functions, activity diagrams are used to model an execution path through the system. An activity diagram shows the order in which actions occur, as well as the different conditional situations that may affect the execution order. For example, one could specify that in a reservation system a flight search precedes the making of a reservation, and that a failed search leads to no reservation. It is useful to build activity diagrams after writing use-cases because the use-cases become the actions modeled by the activity diagram.

An activity diagram start point is shown as a single black dot. A line is used to show the first action or conditional to be executed after starting. The end point of an activity diagram is shown using a black dot surrounded by a black circle. Figure 6.7 shows an activity diagram start and end point.

An *action* in an activity diagram is a single function performed by the system. For example, searching in our reservation system for a flight is a distinct action. When transitioning use-cases into activity diagrams, each use-case often becomes an action. An action (shown in Figure 6.7) is modeled in an activity diagram using a rectangle with rounded corners.

A *conditional* in an activity diagram is used to alter the executing path based on some condition. For example, if no matching flights are found after a flight search is performed, another search is performed. If, however, the search did locate flights, the diagram shows a transition to a flight selection action. As shown in Figure 6.7, conditionals are represented using a diamond.

While conditionals and actions form the meat of an activity diagram, they are all tied together using *transitions*. Transitions, shown in Figure 6.7, use a solid line with an arrow pointing to the destination.

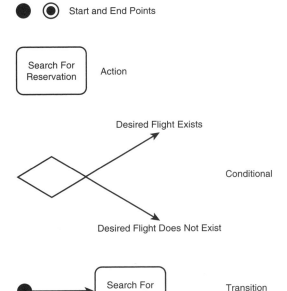

AIRLINE RESERVATION SYSTEM SERVER MODEL

Now that we have covered the technical aspects of use-case development, let's turn our user interviews into use-cases. Figure 6.8 shows the use-case diagram that depicts our system. We model the server functionality in this section. The next section models the client functionality. In developing use-cases for client/server applications, it is common to create one set of use-cases that model server functionality and another that model client functionality. As you are developing thin-client applications, all *business logic* (see following Note) is placed at the server level, and server use-cases comment on this. Client-side use-cases spend time focusing on usability issues.

The following sections contain text descriptions for each use-case. The descriptions con-form to the following outline, which allows readers to easily pick out key pieces of infor-mation. Note, however, that the outline is by no means a UML requirement. It is instead my preferred manner of developing a use-case. Also note that not all use-cases make use of every element in the outline; for example, some use-cases need no data for completion.

NOTE

The term *business logic* refers to any code that exists to represent a transaction performed in the target domain. For example, any logic in a banking environ-ment that applies interest to accounts is considered business logic. Code that obtains the name associated with an account is not considered business logic.

FIGURE **6.8**

*The airline reser-
vation server
described using
use-case notation.*

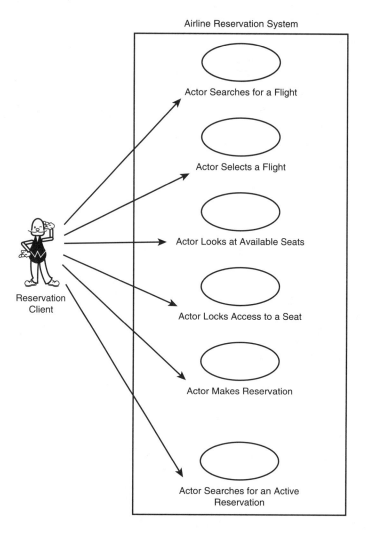

Airline Reservation System

Actor Searches for a Flight

Actor Selects a Flight

Actor Looks at Available Seats

Reservation
Client

Actor Locks Access to a Seat

Actor Makes Reservation

Actor Searches for an Active
Reservation

- Actor—Name of the Actor performing the use-case.

- Desired Outcome—Desired return value and changes to state caused by this use-case assuming an affirmative executing.

- Entered When—Discussion of pre-conditions and general entry point for the use-case.

- Finished When—Conditions that must be achieved for the use-case to complete.

- Description—Detailed description of the use-case, along with any additional information that may be needed. This section is also used to discuss general issues of how the use-case fits into the global picture of the system under development.

The Airline Reservation System Model

CHAPTER 6

127

6

THE AIRLINE
RESERVATION
SYSTEM MODEL

- Data Needed—Required information for execution to occur. This section is omitted if no data is sent to the use-case.

- Comments—Any additional information not presented under Description. This section is often used for notes on a future version of the use-case, client thoughts on the use-case, or any other additional information. This section may be omitted if not needed.

Diving into the use-case development, wherever possible we move through the system in a manner similar to that followed by an actual user. This workflow begins when an Actor searches for a flight, and ends when a reservation is booked or cancelled.

Actor Searches for a Flight

Actor. Reservation client.

Desired Outcome. Actor finds a collection of flights that meet his search criteria. Note that this collection may include zero flights if his criteria does not match any active schedules.

Entered When. Actor invokes search function in the server.

Finished When. A collection of flight entities are returned to the Actor. An empty collection is returned if no flights meet the specified criteria.

Description. The purpose of this function is to identity a single flight path from point A to point B. If the Actor desires round-trip information, multiple searches are performed. The server does support simultaneously exposing multiple flight schedules, but it is the burden of the client software to present the data in an easy-to-read fashion. In representing a single flight path, the following data elements are presented for each leg of the journey: origin airport code, origin time, origin date, arrival airport code, arrival time, and arrival date. Further information on the value expected for each element is contained in Table 6.1.

TABLE 6.1 DATA ELEMENTS USED WHEN SEARCHING FOR A FLIGHT

Name	Description
Origin airport code	Unique airport code identifying the point of origin.
Origin time	Time of day (24-hour clock) of departure.
Origin date	Date (must be year 2000-compliant) of departure.

Arrival airport code	Unique airport code identifying the arrival location.
Arrival time	Time of day (24-hour clock) of arrival.
Arrival date	Date (must be year 2000-compliant) of arrival.

Data Needed. Data is passed to this function detailing date of origin, time of origin, airport code of origin, airport of destination, number of needed seats, and a range of 0–48 hours, specifying a flexibility in schedule allowed by the Actor if a lower price exists. Again, values for these data elements are detailed in Table 6.1.

Actor Selects a Flight

Actor. Reservation client.

Desired Outcome. Actor selects a target flight from the collection of available flights presented to him.

Entered When. Flight collection is notified of choice flight.

Finished When. Both Actor and server have confirmed the choice flight, and additionally those flights that are not selected.

Description. This use-case is important because it acts as a signal to the system that the Actor has selected a single flight. Any flights that were part of the original collection of flights are no longer candidates for selection once this use-case has exited.

Data Needed. Collection of flights that meet the original search criteria. See "Actor Searches for a Flight" for additional information.

Actor Looks at Available Seats

Actor. Reservation client.

Desired Outcome. Collection of available seats is returned to the Actor.

Entered When. Actor requests seat configuration information for a unique flight.

Finished When. Seat information has been returned to the Actor.

Description. At a given point in time, any flight returned from "Actor Searches for a Flight" has at least one available seat. This function allows viewing of all unreserved and unlocked seats.

Data Needed. The seat block to be locked.

Comments. It is important to note that the system is multiuser and more than one Actor may be making reservations on the same flight at the same time. Due to this fact, a search has to be coupled with an immediate request from the Actor to lock access to the desired block of seats. See "Actor Locks Access to a Seat" for further information.

Actor Locks Access to a Seat

Actor. Reservation client.

Desired Outcome. A collection of seats is reserved in the system for a specific user.

Entered When. Actor obtains a collection of available seats on a unique flight.

Finished When. Actor identifies the desired seats as a subset of the available collection obtained from "Actor Looks at Available Seats."

Description. The multiuser nature of the reservation system requires that desired seats on a flight be locked before the actual reservation is made. This locking prevents another Actor from viewing the desired seats as available before the actual reservation is made. Since many exception situations may occur after the seats are locked and could prevent the reservation from being made, seat locks not turned into reservations become unlocked after 20 minutes.

Actor Makes Reservation

Actor. Reservation client.

Desired Outcome. A reservation is made in the system.

Entered When. Actor requests access to the parts of the system that allow for making reservations.

Finished When. A reservation that meets the Actor's requested flight criteria is made and a reservation number is returned to the Actor.

Description. Most other use-cases aid in the gathering of the data needed to make an actual reservation; in this use-case the actual reservation is made in the system. A reservation is not limited to a unique flight, but can act as an umbrella under which multiple flights are collected.

Data Needed. In order to make a reservation, the Actor must include all of the following pieces of information: flight and seat information for all flights, method of payment, and passenger demographics. Passenger demographics to be collected include name, billing address, mailing address, and frequent flyer number. Information describing the expected values of each data element is contained in Table 6.2.

TABLE 6.2   DATA ELEMENTS USED WHEN SEARCHING FOR A FLIGHT

Name	Description
Name	Both the first and last name of the passenger.
Billing address	Address to which the reservation was billed.
Mailing address	Address at which the passenger accepts mail; usually this matches the billing address.
Frequent flyer number	Alphanumeric ID of the passenger's frequent flyer account.

Comments. Since locked seats revert to the available pool if they are not turned into a reservation after 20 minutes, the reservation must occur within 20 minutes of the seat locking. As part of the reservation process, all credit card payments must be verified against available funds. If the credit card is denied, the Actor is either prompted to enter another card or to cancel the reservation. See "Actor Cancels Reservation" for information on reservation canceling.

Actor Cancels Reservation

Actor. Reservation client.

Desired Outcome. Reservation in progress, or already made, is cancelled.

Entered When. The system receives a request to cancel at least one flight owned by a reservation.

Finished When. The flight(s) is cancelled, seats are returned to the available pool, and (if applicable) a refund less cancellation fees is generated. If certain flights on a reservation are to be kept, the entire reservation is still cancelled and the flights that remain are moved to a new reservation.

Description. A user may cancel a reservation at any point after a seat lock has been obtained and before the flight takes place. The most important part of the cancellation process involves removing the lock that has been placed on reserved seats.

Data Needed. The reservation and flights to be cancelled.

Comments. To facilitate historical information gathering, nothing is ever deleted from the database itself. A cancelled flight, therefore, is simply tagged as cancelled and not deleted from the system.

Actor Searches for an Active Reservation

Actor. Reservation client.

Desired Outcome. A collection of reservations is returned to the Actor based upon search criteria. If there are no active reservations that meet the specified criteria, the returned collection is empty.

Entered When. Actor requests that a search be performed.

Finished When. The collection of available flights is returned to the Actor. If no flights meet the specified criteria, an empty collection is returned.

Description. It is a common occurrence that an Actor wants to obtain information on an active reservation after the reservation has been made. This function allows searching of the system for reservations that have either not occurred, or have occurred within the past 60 days. After 60 days, historical information is moved to a data warehouse and is obtained using another application.

Data Needed. To search for a reservation, an Actor must provide the name under which the reservation was made, in addition to any of the following data elements: credit card number used to book the reservation, date of any leg of any flight in the reservation, or time of any leg of any flight in the reservation. Due to that fact that some searches are more limiting than others, this function only returns the top 50 available reservations that match the search criteria.

Comments. This function does present security issues, since reservation information should not be given out if the requestor is not the same individual who booked the flight (or is not a trusted third party). It is up to the reservation operator to follow an authentication procedure to determine if the information requestor is approved for information dissemination.

AIRLINE RESERVATION SYSTEM CLIENT MODEL

Now that server functionality has been modeled, we can concentrate on modeling client functionality. Where the server use-cases concentrate on modeling the business logic of our system, the client use-cases can concentrate on modeling usability issues. As with the server use-cases, the client use-cases follow the outline specified earlier in this chapter.

The decision to model the client and server separately was made due to the nature of the n-tier application we are building. All business logic in an n-tier environment is placed at the server level, and a thin client attaches to the server to allow access to its functionality. The server, in turn, connects to other servers and the persistence mechanism (database, flat file, and so forth).

As an example of how the client and server differ, consider modeling the ability to search for a flight. In the real world, users rarely have a reservation consisting of a single flight but instead book at least one flight in each direction, and potentially more. At the server level, the only consideration when providing flight data is to obtain the single flight that best matches the specified criteria. At the client level, searching for a flight involves searching for multiple flights, displaying them all onscreen, and choosing certain flights to be used in a reservation. Client use-cases can also take into consideration issues regarding the User Interface (UI). The client-side use-cases are shown in Figure 6.9 and described in the following pages.

FIGURE 6.9

The reservation client use-cases.

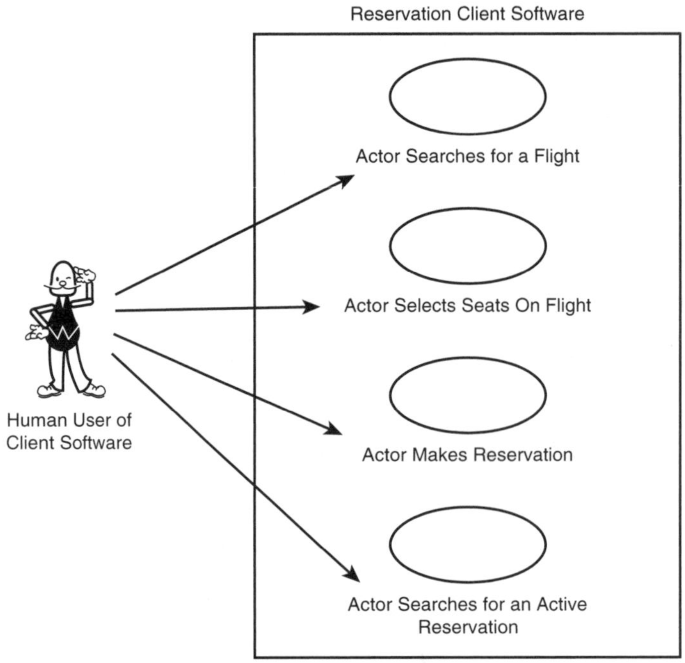

Reservation Client Software

Actor Searches for a Flight

Actor Selects Seats On Flight

Actor Makes Reservation

Actor Searches for an Active Reservation

Human User of Client Software

Actor Searches for a Flight

Actor. Human user of client software.

Desired Outcome. Collection of flights meeting search criteria is returned to the user.

Entered When. Actor clicks the UI element titled "Flight Search."

Finished When. Reservations are returned to the user and are displayed onscreen.

Description. When searching for the flights necessary to make a reservation, the Actor may want to simultaneously search for multiple fights. For example, if the flight is round-trip, the Actor wants to search for one flight from origin to destination and another

The Airline Reservation System Model

133

CHAPTER 6

6

THE AIRLINE
RESERVATION
SYSTEM MODEL

flight from destination back to origin. Additionally, Actors may want to create reservations for flights between multiple cities. For this reason, the screen that supports searching for flights should allow multiple, simultaneous search results to be displayed onscreen at the same time. Since the server only supports executing a single search, the client software has to break up all searches, execute each in a separate thread, and show all results onscreen.

Data Needed. Data is passed to this function detailing date of origin, time of origin, airport code of origin, airport of destination, number of needed seats, and a range of 0–48 hours, specifying a flexibility in schedule allowed by the Actor if a lower price exists. Further information on the expected values for these data elements is found in Table 6.1.

Actor Selects a Flight

Actor. Human user of client software.

Desired Outcome. Flights desired by the Actor are selected.

Entered When. Actor clicks a UI element adjacent to the target flight(s) and then clicks a UI element titled "Select Flights."

Finished When. Flight selection is communicated to the server and UI is updated to show available seats.

Description. After viewing the results of each search, the Actor has the option to either perform another search or to begin making flight reservations.

Data Needed. Logically, to select a flight, the Actor must have some collection of available flights from which to choose.

Actor Selects Seats on Flight

Actor. Human user of client software.

Desired Outcome. A collection of seats on the desired number of flights is reserved for the Actor.

Entered When. The UI element titled "Select Flights" mentioned in "Actor Selects a Flight" is clicked.

Finished When. The Actor clicks UI elements identifying all desired seats and clicks a UI element titled "Choose Seats."

Description. After choosing flights to place under a reservation umbrella, the next step in making a reservation is to pick seats. In this function, the UI displays seat plans for each of the planes and visually identifies each available seat.

Data Needed. To select desired seats, the Actor must be presented with a list of available seats.

Actor Makes Reservation

Actor. Human user of client software.

Desired Outcome. A reservation is made and the unique reservation number is returned.

Entered When. The UI element "Choose Seats" (mentioned in "Actor Selects Seats on Flight") is clicked.

Finished When. Actor enters demographic and payment data and clicks the UI element titled "Make Reservation"; the unique reservation is returned.

Description. The final steps in making a reservation are to enter passenger demographics, payment information, and to click the UI element titled "Make Reservation." Passenger demographics collected include billing address, mailing address, and frequent flyer number. A unique flight number is given to the Actor upon successful booking of the reservation. Further information on the expected values for these elements is found in Table 6.2.

Data Needed. Billing address, mailing address, frequent flyer number, payment information, and flight data.

Comments. In most situations this use-case terminates according to the description under "Finished When." If the server rejects payment information, the server asks the Actor to either enter new payment information or to cancel the reservation. See "Actor Cancels Reservation" for information on reservation canceling.

Actor Cancels Reservation

Actor. Human user of client software.

Desired Outcome. A reservation either in progress of being made, or already made but not taken is cancelled.

Entered When. Actor clicks any of the many "Cancel Reservation" UI elements present at various stages of the reservation process. The elements first appear once "Actor Selects a Flight" has completed execution. The element is also present when viewing the results of "Actor Searches for an Active Reservation," assuming the reservation has yet to occur.

Finished When. Reservation is cancelled and (where applicable) any of the following occur: Seats are returned to the available pool, a refund is generated, a new reservation is generated with flights not cancelled.

Description. When an Actor clicks any "Cancel Reservation" button he is presented with a list of flights present on that reservation. The Actor then clicks a UI element next to

The Airline Reservation System Model

CHAPTER 6

135

6

THE AIRLINE
RESERVATION
SYSTEM MODEL

each flight to be cancelled and then clicks a UI element titled "Process Cancellation." If less than 100% of all flights in the reservation are cancelled, a new reservation is generated and reservation number is returned to the user.

Data Needed. Reservation and flights to be cancelled.

Actor Searches for an Active Reservation

Actor. Human user of client software.

Desired Outcome. Actor obtains data on a series of reservations that match his specified search criteria.

Entered When. Actor clicks the UI element titled "Reservation Search."

Finished When. The search results are returned to the Actor.

Description. It is a common occurrence that an Actor wants to obtain information on an active reservation after the reservation was made. This function allows searching of the system for reservations that have either not occurred or have occurred within the past 60 days. After 60 days, historical information is moved to a data warehouse and is obtained by another application.

Data Needed. To search for a reservation, an Actor must provide the name under which the reservation was made as well as any of the following data elements: credit card number used to book the reservation, date of any leg of any flight in the reservation, or time of any leg of any flight in the reservation (see Table 6.3). Due to the fact that some searches are more limiting than others, this function only returns the top 50 available reservations that match the search criteria. Once the search results are obtained, the following data elements for each flight are displayed in a multi-list: departure time, departure date, arrival time, arrival date, flight duration, number of layovers. From this multi-list, the Actor may click a UI element that alters the display causing full flight details to be displayed for a unique flight.

TABLE 6.3   DATA ELEMENTS USED WHEN SEARCHING FOR A FLIGHT

Name	Description
Departure time	Time (24-hour clock) of the flight departure.
Departure date	Date (must be year 2000-compliant) of the flight departure.
Arrival time	Time (24-hour clock) of the flight arrival.
Arrival date	Date (must be year 2000-compliant) of the flight arrival.
Flight duration	Length (in hours and minutes) of the flight.
Number of layovers	Total number of layovers experienced during the flight as a whole.

Comments. This function presents security issues because reservation information should not be given out if the requestor is not the same individual who booked the flight (or is not a trusted third party). It is up to the reservation operator to follow an authentication procedure to determine if the information requestor is approved for information dissemination.

Although we now have a complete picture of the server functionality, there is one additional step that aids developers. We develop the activity diagram for the system in this last step. The diagram, shown in Figure 6.10, depicts the flow of action in the system as a whole.

FIGURE 6.10

An activity diagram for the reservation system depicts the flow of work executed within the application as a whole.

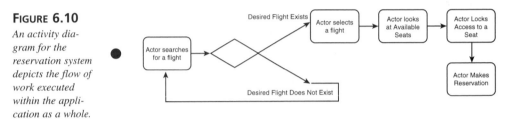

The use-cases presented in this chapter exist as a final product that has been approved by the client (user-base), product manager, and development manager. At this point it is possible to turn them over to the programming staff for modeling and code development. What is important to keep in mind is that the UML is used not only for use-case development, but also for class modeling, object and state modeling, architecture design, and all other steps in the development process. These steps are rather implementation-specific and are illustrated in the chapters of the book where the software is actually implemented.

FROM HERE

This chapter introduces the concepts behind using the UML to model a system in an implementation-independent fashion. Those concepts were then applied to model an airline reservation system. Later in this book the specifications are turned into more UML models, and then into actual software. Each of those implementations is found in one of the following chapters:

- Chapter 14, "Socket-Based Implementation of the Airline Reservation System."
- Chapter 16, "RMI-Based Implementation of the Airline Reservation System."
- Chapter 19, "Servlet-Based Implementation of the Airline Reservation System."
- Chapter 26, "CORBA-Based Implementation of the Airline Reservation System. "
- Chapter 35, "Voyager-Based Implementation of the Airline Reservation System."

JAVA

IN THIS PART

JAVA OVERVIEW

IN THIS CHAPTER

In 1891 Dutch physician Eugene Dubois discovered on the island of Java the fossil remains of a prehistoric human being, now thought to have lived 500,000 to 1.5 million years ago. *Java man* (as the species is called in utter disregard of sex) had a large face. His forehead was low and sloped, with heavy ridges above the eyes. His chinless jaw was massive and contained teeth that were huge in comparison to ours. He was short, barely over five feet tall, and his brain size was smaller than that of more modern humans.

In contrast, modern Java man and Java woman—the Java software developer—stand at the apex of human evolution. Their physical prowess is exceeded only by their intellectual acumen: Both are simply superior and entirely without peer. Does this sound like you?

If you're not a Java man or Java woman, this chapter introduces you to Java and helps you read and understand the Java sample programs used throughout this book's subsequent chapters. The chapter may not provide all that's required to transform you into Java man or Java woman, though hefting this tome will certainly help build your biceps.

Consider this chapter, if you will, "Teach Yourself Java in 24 Minutes." If you're already a Java man or Java woman, you don't need to read it. However, you might skim it as a refresher, reading only the sections on interesting or unfamiliar topics.

In this chapter you learn

- What makes Java such a unique programming language.

  Java is the first portable programming language to come into widespread use. You see here how it enables programmers to "write once and run anywhere."

- How to use the basic Java development tools included in the Java Developer's Kit (JDK).

  You don't have to purchase an expensive suite of tools in order to write Java programs. Sun Microsystems provides a free JDK that includes all the tools you need to develop Java programs.

- How to read and write programs that use Java's object-oriented and procedural constructs.

  Java includes a full range of object-oriented facilities as well as the more traditional flow-of-control facilities.

- How to read and write programs that use Java's graphical user interface (GUI) library.

  Java's Abstract Windowing Toolkit (AWT) makes it easy to write GUI programs that run on multiple platforms.

WHAT'S DIFFERENT ABOUT JAVA?

Within just a few years of its initial public release, Java has established itself as a significant programming language. At the time of this writing, pollsters estimate that there are 500,000 to 1,000,000 Java programmers. Why have so many programmers found Java a worthy object of attention? What's different about Java?

Such questions are not easily answered because Java is really quite a remarkable language. However, three characteristics stand out:

- Java programs are portable.
- Java applets automate distribution of code.
- Java is thoroughly object-oriented.

Let's take a closer look at these characteristics.

Software Portability

Most computer programs are not portable. They are written and designed to be run on a specific computing platform. Coaxing them to run on another platform is regularly more difficult and costly than writing a new program for the target platform.

To be fair, the UNIX community has long taken software portability seriously. There, the art of writing portable software has become an art. However, for the most part, the sort of portability that has been achieved is *compile-time portability*: Many UNIX programs can be successfully recompiled and run on a variety of platforms. The point is that the programs must be recompiled, which often takes minutes or even hours. Moreover, the process is not perfect: Often a programmer must tweak the code before it compiles and runs properly. This sort of portability is a genuine boon, but falls short of the incessant user demands: "faster, cheaper, better."

Java programs are portable in a different sense; they are *run-time portable*, meaning that a Java executable file can be run, without recompilation, on any platform that supports Java. The technique that makes this possible is the *bytecode*.

> **NOTE**
>
> Although Java programs are portable across platforms, you may have some trouble moving Java programs from one release of Java to another. See the upcoming section "Java Releases."

Bytecodes

Most programming languages require source programs to be compiled and linked (see Figure 7.1) before execution. Both the object code and the executable code are basically machine code for the target platform; the object code is somewhat more abstract than the machine code, but fundamentally little different. As a consequence, both the object code and the executable code are specific to the target platform. If you want to port the program to a new platform, you work with the source code; the object and executable code are of no value to you.

FIGURE 7.1

Non-Java source code must be compiled and linked.

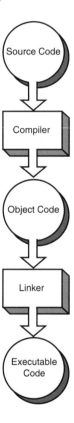

However, Java takes a different approach as you see in Figure 7.2. In a single step, the Java compiler produces *bytecodes*, a sort of machine-independent object code. The trick is that bytecodes are not directly executed by the native hardware; they are instead executed by a *Java Virtual Machine* (JVM), which functions as an interpreter. (This is generally true, but it's possible to put a JVM on a chip. In fact, several companies have done so or are doing so.)

FIGURE 7.2

Java bytecodes are portable.

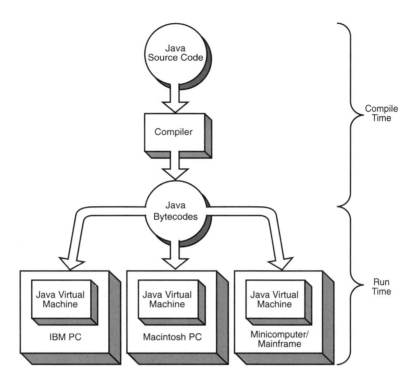

Interpretive languages are not novel: Several implementations of BASIC and Pascal featured interpreters, although they did not generally support runtime portability. Java's particular novelty lies elsewhere—in the special technologies employed to reduce the overhead inherent in interpretation. Normally, interpreted code runs about an order of magnitude more slowly than machine code. However, Java designers intended from the start for Java to rival C as a language for writing efficient application code.

Early Java compilers and virtual machines did not incorporate facilities devoted to boosting the execution speed of bytecodes, such as just-in-time compilation or hotspot optimization. At the time of this writing, these facilities are just coming into widespread use. Just-in-time compilation has significantly narrowed the speed gap between Java and C, and hotspot optimization holds the promise of effectively eliminating it. The result: a language that produces portable code and yet exacts no performance penalty. This is truly a winning combination.

Portable bytecodes, however, do not in themselves solve all the problems of making software portable. Most programs, whether written in Java, C, or another language, are not complete. They depend upon libraries of pre-written code that must be available when the program is linked (*static binding*) or executed (*dynamic binding*).

Libraries

Java provides an elaborate suite of class libraries that programmers can reference, sparing the programmer the need to write code to perform common operations. Because Java's class libraries are written in Java, they are portable. The combination of a program's bytecodes, the Java class libraries, and a Java Virtual Machine for the target platform (see Figure 7.3) are all that's needed to run a Java program.

FIGURE 7.3

Java provides an extensive portable class library.

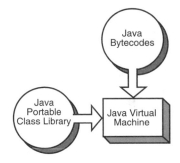

Applets

A second outstanding Java characteristic is a new kind of program called an applet. Ordinary Java programs are referred to as *applications*, to avoid confusion.

An *applet* is stored as bytecodes on a Web server, which are referenced by a Web page using a special HTML tag. When a Java-equipped browser requests the Web page that contains the applet, it discovers the applet and requests it as well. The browser then loads and executes the applet.

The applet is free to draw within a designated area of the screen. Moreover, it can interact with the user by displaying user-interface controls. The applet can even open a network connection to the Web server that stores it, enabling access to databases and other resources.

Because most computer users know how to use a Web browser, they're comfortable interacting with an applet; as long as the user's browser is Java-equipped, it doesn't matter whether the user has an IBM PC, a Macintosh PC, or some other computer. The Java applet is portable, just as other kinds of Java programs are portable.

> **NOTE**
>
> Portability is easier to achieve in principle than in practice. At the time of this writing, the JVMs in browsers are somewhat buggy and implement somewhat different Java subsets and dialects. Moreover, Sun and Microsoft are embroiled in a legal dispute over Microsoft's alleged responsibilities as a Java licensee to provide a compatible Java implementation in Internet Explorer.
>
> However, incompatibilities between browser implementations of Java may soon be alleviated. Sun's Java plug-in technology lets users run a standard Sun JVM in Microsoft Internet Explorer or Netscape Navigator. Moreover, Netscape has announced that it will incorporate a third-party JVM, possibly Sun's, in future versions of Netscape Navigator.

Applets solve one difficult application maintenance problem: software distribution. Every time the user accesses a page containing an applet, the browser downloads a fresh copy of the applet (assuming that the browser's cache doesn't intervene). If the applet has recently been changed, the user will effortlessly receive the new version of the applet. Thus, the user never runs out-of-date software.

Of course, this solution is not without complications. For one thing, some browsers may cache copies of files downloaded via the network. When this is the case, a user may unknowingly execute an out-of-date applet. Moreover, downloading itself is not without problems. The Java bytecode file is a very compact program representation; nevertheless, the overhead of downloading a large applet every time it's accessed may be objectionable. This could be avoided by means of a simple date and time stamp. Presumably, future versions of popular Web browsers will incorporate mechanisms that compare the date and time stamp of a cached applet with that of the applet residing on the server, and download the applet only if it has been updated.

Object-Oriented Programming and Program Quality

A final salient characteristic of Java is its support of object-oriented programming. Although C++ possesses object-oriented features, it's possible to write non–object-oriented software using C++. As a consequence, many C++ programmers are really C programmers in disguise, using C++ to write programs just like those they previously wrote in C. This approach to programming fails to realize the benefits inherent in object-oriented programming. Java, on the other hand, compels programmers to understand and use objects. The result is better program structure and higher program maintainability.

Bjarne Stroustrup, the designer of C++, saw backward compatibility with C as a critical language design issue. As a result, C++ is burdened with certain C facilities that have proven problematical. Although Java borrows much from C and C++, the designers of Java rejected the need for backward compatibility. The high similarity with C and C++ makes Java an easy language for C and C++ programmers to learn, and yet many troublesome C and C++ facilities, such as pointers, are not found in Java. Consequently, Java programs are potentially more reliable than comparable C or C++ programs. So far, experience with Java bears this out.

Objects and Their Properties

Because object-orientation is so fundamental to Java, it's worthwhile to spend some time reviewing its fundamentals. This will facilitate understanding the remainder of the chapter, which presents the syntax and semantics of Java.

The fundamental concept of object-oriented programming is the *object*. An object is simply a program unit, including both data and code, that is divided into two parts: *interface* and *implementation*. This separation of interface and implementation is called *encapsulation*. An object's interface is simply that portion that is publicly visible to, and therefore usable by, other objects. The implementation of an object is its hidden inner workings—those parts that are necessary to support the functions provided by the object's interface, but are not directly accessed by other objects. In addition to encapsulation, objects are also characterized by *inheritance* and *polymorphism*, topics addressed shortly.

The constituent parts of an object—the data and the code—have special object-oriented names. The data of an object describe it. Therefore, the data is called the object's *attributes*, which are stored in Java program variables called *fields*. An object's code typically consists of a set of relatively small procedures, each supporting a single *operation*, *service*, or *behavior*. (Unfortunately, object-oriented terminology remains rather inconsistent.) In Java, these procedures are called the object's *methods*, which consist of executable program statements.

For example, consider an object designed to access an email server, as is shown in Figure 7.4. Its interface might include data (such as the name of the email server and the ID of the user), code (such as a procedure to send an email message), and a procedure (to receive email messages). Its implementation might include data, such as the IP number of the email server, and code, such as a procedure to transmit the body of an email message.

FIGURE 7.4

Objects encapsulate data and code.

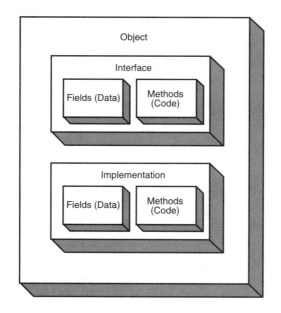

7

JAVA OVERVIEW

Object Messages

Operations in non–object-oriented programs are invoked by *calling* a function or procedure, which performs a computation and may return a result. Because a function or procedure is unique within a non–object-oriented program, it's clear which function or procedure is meant.

Object-oriented programs are somewhat more complex. Each object has its own methods (though a single, shareable copy of a method may be held in memory). Calling a method begs an important question: which method?

Instead, object-oriented programmers talk of one object *sending a message* to another as you see in Figure 7.5. The sending object sends a message to a receiving object. The receiving object handles the message by executing a method that corresponds to the message. As shown in the figure, the receiving object may return a response (called a *return value*) to the sending object.

FIGURE 7.5

Objects send and receive messages.

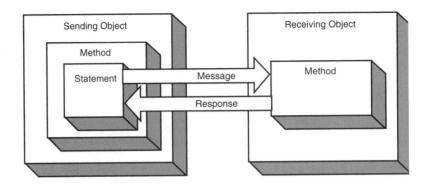

However, the difference between calling a procedure and sending a message is more than mere terminology. Even though objects may run in different processes or different computers—circumstances that preclude the simple procedure call—they can send messages to one another. The operation of sending a message outwardly resembles a procedure call but may be implemented quite differently.

Object Inheritance

In principle, objects are all that's needed for object-oriented programming. Many programs, however, work with objects that differ only in the values of their fields. The labor-saving concepts of class and inheritance were introduced to facilitate creation of such objects.

A *class* is a template that defines the common fields and methods of similar objects. In object-oriented programming, a program consists primarily of definitions of classes. Program statements can create an object that's an *instance* or *member* of a specified class.

For example, suppose you had to create objects representing purchases. Each such object may include a purchase date, a customer number, a stock number, a quantity, and a price. By creating a class named `Purchase` and specifying that instances of the class have exactly these data attributes, it becomes simple to create a new `Purchase` object.

Inheritance is a simple extension of this concept. Suppose you find that you need a set of objects that each represent a time purchase. A time purchase has all the attributes of a `Purchase`, plus two additional attributes: the interest rate and the final due date. Rather than create an entirely separate class that includes the five attributes of a `Purchase` plus the two new attributes, it's possible to extend the `Purchase` class, creating a new `TimePurchase` class that includes all the attributes of a `Purchase` (see Figure 7.6) plus the two new attributes. Conceptually, each instance of `TimePurchase` contains within it all the fields and methods of a `Purchase`. When one class extends another, the original class is called the *parent class* or *superclass* and the new class is called the *child class* or *subclass*.

Figure 7.6

Inheritance lets you extend class capabilities.

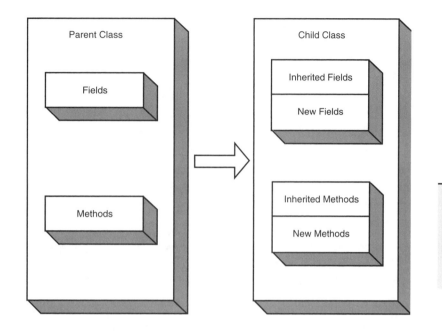

If an inherited method fails to meet a programmer's need, the programmer can redefine the method in the child class. The new definition of the method *overrides* the definition in the parent class.

Inheritance increases the productivity of programmers; with it, they can pick up where other programmers have left off. Inheritance also facilitates the creation and marketing of reusable software components. In Java, you can extend a class even if you have only its bytecodes; the source code is not necessary. This facilitates the production and sale of class libraries because vendors do not have to publicize proprietary details of the source code and yet programmers can extend the function of class library members.

Inheritance provides one payoff—the ability to extend classes—to users of object-oriented technology. Polymorphism provides another.

Object Polymorphism

Non–object-oriented code suffers from complicated flow of control, which tends to worsen as the code is revised and adapted. For example, consider a payroll system for a large company with many employee bargaining units (unions), each with different dues and policies. When the system computes an employee's pay, it must determine the bargaining unit to which the employee belongs and deduct the proper dues. Because bargaining units may negotiate various work and compensation policies, the system must also consider an employee's bargaining unit affiliation when computing overtime pay. Other computations, such as vacation time accrual, also require consideration of bargaining unit membership.

Each computation takes a form something like this:

```
if (member of unit #1)
    Compute per unit #1 policies
else if (member of unit #2)
    Compute per unit #2 policies
...
else if (member of unit #N)
    Compute per unit #N policies
```

Now consider what happens when a new bargaining unit is formed. A programmer must study each computation and revise it to include proper conditional statements to handle the new unit. If the system is sufficiently large and complex, the programmer is likely to err somewhere. Even if the programmer doesn't err, updating the payroll system is laborious and expensive.

Polymorphism provides a better way. In object-oriented programming the word *polymorphism*, which means *many forms*, refers to the capability of objects to respond distinctively to identical messages. Here's how it works:

In the object-oriented payroll system, each employee is represented by an object. Like all objects, this object belongs to a class. One simple way to solve the payroll system problem is to establish one class for each bargaining unit. Each such class is then a subclass of the `Employee` class and inherits common fields and methods. However, the computations that require consideration of bargaining unit affiliation are implemented in each subclass.

Now, when the program sends a `ComputeOvertimePay` message to an object, the object knows the pertinent bargaining unit (that is, it knows its own class identity) and its policies (that is, it implements the relevant computations in its own distinctive way). The message sender doesn't need to test what bargaining unit applies because the message receiver knows how to perform each necessary computation. Each subclass of `Employee` handles the same `ComputeOvertimePay` message polymorphically—in its own fashion.

It's much simpler to add a new bargaining unit to an object-oriented system. The programmer simply creates a class to represent the new bargaining unit. The new class handles all the necessary messages, so the programmer doesn't need to search the code and revise flow-of-control statements. As a result, the programmer is more likely to make the change quickly and properly.

Now that you know something about object-oriented programming, briefly consider the tools available to Java programmers. After doing so, you begin your survey of the Java language and libraries.

JAVA DEVELOPMENT TOOLS

Sun includes all the basic tools needed for Java programming in the free Java Developer's Kit (JDK). These free tools are not very elaborate, so many programmers prefer to purchase an Interactive Development Environment (IDE) for Java. However, even the most sophisticated IDEs provide the same three major components provided by the JDK: a compiler, an interpreter, and an appletviewer.

Java Compiler

Writing a Java program involves using an editor to prepare a source code file that has the extension .java. You must not use .JAVA as an extension. Java hails from the UNIX world, where file names are case sensitive; it hasn't lost this trait even when ported to operating systems that are not case sensitive, such as Microsoft Windows.

You use the Java compiler, known as javac, to transform your source code into byte-codes. Using the JDK, you do this at a command-line prompt:

```
javac MyJavaProgram.java
```

If the source code is error-free, the compiler produces the file MyJavaProgram.class.

If you're unaccustomed to working with a command-line prompt, you may want to get a Java IDE. However, many programmers used to IDEs find that they quickly become adept at using commands. Some actually grow to prefer using commands because of the freedom it affords.

Java Interpreter

To run a Java application—not a Java applet—you invoke the Java interpreter, known as java:

```
java MyJavaProgram
```

Notice that the program name does not specify the extension .class. Because its argument *must* be a .class file containing bytecodes, the Java interpreter doesn't require the extension. Moreover, including the extension causes an unexpected result. If you enter the following code, the Java interpreter assumes you want to run the file MyJavaProgram.class.class—probably not what you intended:

```
java MyJavaProgram.class
```

Java Appletviewer

As mentioned, Java applets can be run from Web pages loaded by Web browsers. However, this method often proves inconvenient during program development. Many browsers have a habit of caching applets. An unwary programmer may modify and recompile source code yet have the browser execute an old version of the applet. Worse yet, at the time of this writing, browser-based implementations of Java are rather buggy. Many Java programmers prefer to use the appletviewer program included in the JDK.

To execute a Java applet, you merely run appletviewer on the HTML file that contains this applet:

```
appletviewer MyWebPage.html
```

The appletviewer program brings up a window that contains only the applet: It ignores the HTML text, pictures, and styles specified in the file. Consequently, many Java programmers work with a skeleton HTML file that contains only those HTML tags necessary to run the applet. Here's an example:

```
<APPLET CODE=MyJavaApplet WIDTH=400 HEIGHT=300>
</APPLET>
```

The APPLET tag's CODE attribute names the .class file that contains the applet. The WIDTH and HEIGHT attributes specify the size of the window in which the applet runs.

JAVA RELEASES

At the time of this writing, there have been two major releases of Java and a third is imminent (see Table 7.1). Even though Java aims at making programs portable across platforms, you can encounter problems due to the evolution of Java and its libraries.

TABLE 7.1 MAJOR JAVA RELEASES

Release	Date
Java 1.0	December, 1995
Java 1.1	January, 1997
Java 1.2	December, 1998 (anticipated)

Java 1.1 introduced so many changes that Java 1.1 applets generally will not run in browsers equipped with Java 1.0, which includes the majority of browsers at the time of this writing. Programmers who want to develop applets to be hosted by public Web pages are all but compelled to use Java 1.0, even though Java 1.1 made many important improvements to the language and its libraries. Programmers writing for intranets find these incompatibilities less troublesome because they have greater control of the browser versions their users employ.

Sun has released a free product called Java Plug-in that ameliorates some of these difficulties. Java Plug-in lets Microsoft's Internet Explorer or Netscape's Navigator use Sun's Java virtual machine and library classes, rather than the Microsoft or Netscape version. Moreover, when a new version of the Java virtual machine or classes becomes available, the Plug-in automatically downloads and installs it. However, the Java virtual machine and classes are relatively large, so the download may be time consuming when a modem connection is used. Thus, Java Plug-in is of most value to intranet programmers. Those programming for public Web access are left with only the lowest-common-denominator approach: using Java 1.0.

The examples in this book are based on Java 1.1 because that's the version of Java familiar to most programmers. Don't try to run the examples using an IDE or browser that supports only Java 1.0—they simply won't work. If your IDE or browser supports Java 1.2, all should be well: Java 1.2 is backward-compatible with Java 1.1.

You're finally ready to embark on your whirlwind tour of the Java language and its libraries. The goal is to prepare you to read the Java program examples used throughout this book. If you've never written Java programs, you'll probably require further study before writing complete applications on your own.

JAVA CLASSES

A Java program, just as programs written in other object-oriented languages, consists of a collection of classes. At run-time, these classes are used to instantiate objects that perform the program's functions. Listing 7.1 shows a simple Java program. Let's dissect the program, piece by piece.

A typical Java program begins with a series of `import` statements. Strictly speaking, `import` statements are not required; they're merely a convenience to the programmer. For example, this program uses several classes, including `java.awt.Button` and `java.awt.TextField`. These names are long and rather cumbersome, so most Java programmers prefer to refer to `Button` and `TextField`. The `import` statements allow such abbreviated references. The following `import` statement tells Java that the programmer wants to abbreviate names of classes that begin with `java.awt`:

```
import java.awt.*;
```

LISTING 7.1   `JavaApplet.java`—A SIMPLE JAVA APPLET

```
import java.applet.*;
import java.awt.*;
import java.awt.event.*;
```

continues

LISTING 7.1 CONTINUED

```java
public class JavaApplet extends Applet
{
    // Fields
    private Button    theButton = new Button("Click on me.");
    private TextField theText   = new TextField(25);

    // Method
    public void init()
    {
        add(theButton);
        add(theText);
        theButton.addActionListener(new ButtonHandler());
    }

    // Inner class
    class ButtonHandler implements ActionListener
    {
        public void actionPerformed(ActionEvent evt)
        {
            theText.setText("Hello, user!");
        }
    }
}
```

Because this mechanism resembles the wildcard filename specification provided by many operating systems, some programmers attempt to go too far:

```java
import *.*.*;
```

The Java compiler will reject such an `import` statement: You can omit only the last word of a class name. The remainder of the name is called the *package*. Java uses the package name to find the class file; if the package cannot be found, Java rejects the class reference.

Class Header

The definition of a class, which begins with the *class header*, follows the `import` statements:

```java
public class JavaApplet extends Applet
```

Following the class header is the *class body*, which begins with an opening brace ({) and extends through the final closing brace (}) on the last line of the program. Let's dissect the class header before examining the contents of the class body.

The Java compiler recognizes the class header by the keyword `class`, which is followed by the name of the class, `JavaApplet`. The Java compiler requires that each source file contain only one main class and that the name of the class be the same as that of the source file, except that the source filename has the `.java` extension. The `JavaApplet` class must be contained in the `JavaApplet.java` file. This relationship between class name and source filename helps programmers trace through programs that consist of many classes, which would otherwise be a great chore.

The keyword `public` indicates that the `JavaApplet` class and its object instances are freely accessible to other classes and objects. You almost always give a program's main class public accessibility.

Finally, the keyword `extends` and the following class name indicate that the `JavaApplet` class is a subclass of `Applet`. Therefore, it inherits fields and methods from `Applet`; these give it many capabilities before you write a single line of code.

Class Body

Coming to the body of the class, you first find these lines:

```
// Fields
    private Button    theButton = new Button("Click on me.");
    private TextField theText   = new TextField(25);
```

The first line is a comment, meaning that it is ignored by the compiler. It helpfully points out that the following two lines define fields, which are program variables.

Fields

The first field, `theButton`, can refer to a `Button` object and the second, `theText`, can refer to a `TextField` object. `Button` and `TextField` are Java library classes. `Button` provides a clickable user-interface button and `TextField` provides an input block.

Each field is initialized so that it holds a reference to a valid object. Java's `new` operator constructs object instances, using arguments that specify object characteristics. Here, the argument to the `Button` constructor specifies the text that appears on the button; the argument to the `TextField` constructor specifies the number of characters that the input block accommodates. Figure 7.7 shows the applet's user interface.

Figure 7.7

Java programs look and feel like ordinary programs when executing.

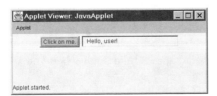

When you declare a Java field, the type you specify can name a class within Java's libraries, your program, or a so-called primitive type. *Primitive types* are simple numeric or Boolean values. Table 7.2 describes Java's primitive types. Because primitive values are not objects, you don't use the new operator to construct them. For example, you could write the following to define a field that holds the number of hairs on a human head (typically in the tens of thousands):

```
int theNumberOfHairs = 25378;
```

TABLE 7.2 JAVA'S PRIMITIVE TYPES

Type	*Description*
boolean	true/false value
byte	8-bit signed integer
char	16-bit unsigned integer
double	64-bit floating-point number
float	32-bit floating-point number
int	32-bit signed integer
long	64-bit signed integer
short	16-bit signed integer

The keyword private specifies that only the enclosing class can access the fields theButton and theText. This marks them as part of the implementation of the class, rather than the interface. You could make the fields public, in which case they would be part of the interface, accessible everywhere. Java provides a third access specifier, protected, which allows access only from within the enclosing class or one of its subclasses. If you don't specify one of the three access keywords, Java assigns package access, which allows access by classes within the same package.

In all, Java provides four levels of access:

- *package* Allows access by classes within the package.
- *private* Allows access only by the class.
- *protected* Allows access only by the class and its subclasses.
- *public* Allows unrestricted access.

You specify protected access using the keyword protected or private access using the keyword private. Java assigns package access by default when you specify neither public, protected, nor private.

You can specify the package to which your class belongs by including a `package` statement as the first statement of the class:

```
package TheGreatExperiment;
```

If you omit the `package` statement, as is the custom in small programs, Java assumes an unnamed package that consists of all the classes within the same directory as the current class.

You can also define fields with constant values. By including the keywords `static final` in the declaration of a field, you tell the Java compiler that the value of the field should not change during program execution. For example, here's a constant that represents the number of sides of a square:

```
static final int SIDES_SQUARE = 4;
```

If you erroneously write a statement that assigns a value to a `static final` field (such as `SIDES_SQUARE`), the compiler will reject your program. For example, a program containing the preceding declaration and the following statement would not compile:

```
SIDES_SQUARE = 5;
```

Methods

The second section of code within the class body defines a method, that is, a procedure that responds to a message. The message header is the line:

```
public void init()
```

This tells us the `init` method is publicly accessible and does not return a value. You specify the accessibility of a method in the same way as a field. However, fields are generally part of the implementation and have `private` access; methods are a mixed bag, some are part of the interface and some are part of the implementation.

Between a matched opening brace and closing brace are the statements that compose the method's body:

```
add(theButton);
add(theText);
theButton.addActionListener(new ButtonHandler());
```

Each of these statements sends a message. The first two statements send the `add` message and the third sends the `addActionListener` message. You can spot the name of the message by looking for the open parenthesis that immediately follows it. The third statement sends its message to the `Button` object to which the field `theButton` refers. The first two statements give no receiver; in such a case the message is sent to the current instance of the enclosing class; here, to the `JavaApplet` object.

The `add` message places a control on the screen. Thus, the effect of the first statement is to place the button on the screen and the effect of the second statement is to place the input block on the screen. The argument of the `add` message specifies the control that's to be placed on the screen. Messages can take zero, one, or more arguments.

The third statement tells the button the identity of an object that will handle user interactions with the button. The message argument specifies the object, which is constructed on-the-fly by using the `new` operator. The type of the message handler is `ButtonHandler`, a second class in the JavaApplet program, as you'll see presently.

Assignments and Operators

In addition to statements that send messages, Java also provides assignment statements. Assignments use operators to compute a value and assign it to a variable. Here's a simple assignment statement:

```
x = 2 * y + 1;
```

Java borrows many operators from C and C++. These are summarized in Table 7.3. Notice that several of the operators have different meanings, depending on the type of operand. The table gives the precedence for each operator. This determines how operators and operands are grouped. You can use parentheses to explicitly specify the grouping. For example, look at the following statements:

```
x = 2;
y = 3;
z1 = x * y + 4;
z2 = x * (y + 4);
```

The value of z1 is 10, but z2 is 14 because the addition operator in parentheses now takes precedence over the multiplication.

Java's operators are mostly left associative. The expression

```
y = x1 * x2 * x3;
```

is interpreted as

```
y = ((x1 * x2) * x3);
```

However, assignment operators are right associative, making it possible to write an expression such as the following, which assigns the value of z to y and then assigns the same value to x:

```
x = y = z;
```

Readers unfamiliar with C or C++ may at first be puzzled by several Java operators, especially the increment and decrement operators, which simply increase or decrease a value by 1. For example, the statement

```
x++;
```

increases the value of x by 1. These operators behave oddly when used within an expression. For example, consider the following snippet of code:

```
x = 1;
y = 1;
z = ++x + y++;
```

The subexpression ++x increments x and the subexpression y++ increments y; the expression assigns the value 2 to each of these variables. The value of y is trickier to determine. When the increment operator is placed before a variable, it returns the incremented value of the variable, but when it is written after a variable, it returns the unincremented value of the variable. The subexpression ++x returns the value 2 and the subexpression y++ returns the value 1. Therefore, the expression assigns the value 3 to z. The decrement operator (--) functions analogously.

Java's assignment operators are also unusual. For example, you can use the += operator to increment a variable:

```
x += 2;
```

The expression has the same meaning as this:

```
x = x + 2;
```

Java's other assignment operators function analogously (see Table 7.3).

TABLE 7.3 JAVA OPERATORS

Precedence	Operator	Operand Type	Description
1	++	numeric	increment
	--	numeric	decrement
	+, -	numeric	unary plus, unary minus
	~	integral	bitwise complement
	!	boolean	logical complement
	(*type*)	any	type cast

continues

7

JAVA OVERVIEW

TABLE 7.3   CONTINUED

Precedence	Operator	Operand Type	Description
2	*, /, %	numeric	multiplication, division, remainder
3	+, -	numeric	addition, subtraction
	+	String	concatenation
4	<<	integral	left shift
	>>	integral	right shift (signed)
	>>>	integral	right shift (unsigned)
5	<, <=	numeric	less than, less than or equal
	>, >=	numeric	greater than, greater than or equal
	instanceof	object, type	type comparison
6	==	any	equality
	!=	any	inequality
7	&	integral	bitwise AND
	&	boolean	logical AND
8	^	integral	bitwise XOR
	^	boolean	logical XOR
9	¦	integral	bitwise OR
	¦	boolean	logical OR
10	&&	boolean	conditional AND
11	¦¦	boolean	conditional OR
12	?:	boolean, any, any	conditional operator
13	=, +=, -=, =, /=, %=, <<=, >>=, >>>=, &=, ¦=, ^=	variable, any	assignment

Characters and Strings

Java provides the `String` class and character and `String` literals for representing text. Java uses the Unicode character set, a 16-bit representation that provides over 65,000 characters—enough to represent the alphabets of the world's major languages. Unicode greatly facilitates writing programs for the international market.

You write character literals as in C/C++—by surrounding a character with single quotation marks:

```
char c = 'A';
```

Alternatively, you can use the integer value of the desired Unicode character.

`String` literals are written like C/C++ strings, by surrounding text with double quotation marks:

```
String s = "Hello Mom";
```

This avoids the need to use the `new` operator to construct `String`s, an otherwise cumbersome process.

To represent common control characters, Java provides escape sequences similar to those of C/C++. For example, you can write a character literal containing a carriage return as `'\r'`. You can write a new line character as `\n` or a tab character as `\t`.

The concatenation operator (+) joins `String`s or a `String` and a `char`:

```
String s = "Hello Mo" + 'm';
```

The Java idiom for converting a numeric value to text is simple but sometimes hard to recall. You use the concatenation operator to join the numeric value to a `String`, which can be empty:

```
int n = 12;  // arbitrary value
String s = "" + n;
```

Java provides methods that extract numeric values from text. For example, the `parseInt` method of the `Integer` class extracts an `int` value from a `String`:

```
String s = "123";  // arbitrary value
int n = Integer.parseInt(s);
```

Return Values

A method can return a value of any type, either object or primitive, by executing a `return` statement that specifies the returned value. However, the type of the value returned must be compatible with the type specified in the method header. As you saw, the `init` method does not return a value and therefore its method header specifies `void` as the method's return type. Here's an example method that doubles the value of its `int` argument:

```
public int doubler(int x)
{
    return x + x;
}
```

Local Variables

Methods can define variables, known as *local variables*, that exist only during the execution of the method and cannot be accessed outside the method. Local variables are useful for storing intermediate results and clarifying code. For example, the `doubler` method could be written like this:

```
public int doubler(int x)
{
    int y;
    y = x + x;
    return y;
}
```

Inner Classes

A class can, within its body, define other classes, called *inner classes*. For example, the `JavaApplet` class defines an inner class named `ButtonHandler`, which handles messages denoting button clicks:

```
// Inner class
class ButtonHandler implements ActionListener
{
    public void actionPerformed(ActionEvent evt)
    {
        theText.setText("Hello, user!");
    }
}
```

The remarkable thing about an inner class is that it can freely access fields of the enclosing class. For example, the `ButtonHandler` class accesses the `JavaApplet` field named `theText`. Notice that the header of the `ButtonHandler` class uses an unfamiliar keyword, `implements`. The `implements` keyword is used because an `ActionListener` is not a class, but a special entity known as an *interface*.

Interfaces

An interface resembles a class; however, an interface has only constant fields and its methods include only an interface—the implementation is omitted. Java programmers use interfaces to create the "tongues and grooves" that join software units. When a programmer writes that a class implements an interface, the compiler ensures that every method named in the interface is implemented by the class; otherwise the class is considered *abstract* and cannot be instantiated. In effect, a class that implements an interface is advertising its capability to handle certain messages.

For example, the `ButtonHandler` class implements the `ActionListener` interface, a built-in interface that contains a single method, `actionPerformed`. Consistent with `ButtonHandler`'s declaration, it implements the `actionPerformed` method. You learn more about the `actionPerformed` method and its role in event handling shortly.

Constructors

When the `new` operator instantiates an object, the numeric fields of the object are set to 0 and the object fields are set to refer to a non-existent object named `null`. You'll often prefer some other initial values, which you can establish by coding a constructor. A *constructor* closely resembles a method, but its name is always the same as that of the enclosing class, and the header of a constructor never specifies a return type. After all, the purpose of a constructor is to initialize an object, not return a value.

Here's a simple example of a class that has a constructor:

```
public class Ball
{
    private float theRadius;  // radius in centimeters

    public Ball(int size_in_inches)
    {
        theRadius = 2.54 * size_in_inches;
    }
}
```

The `Ball` class contains a single field, `theRadius`, which holds the radius of a ball. The constructor accepts a single `int` argument, which it converts from inches to centimeters and stores in the field.

The `JavaApplet` class, like other applets, has no constructor. Instead, it uses an `init` method to initialize itself. A browser always calls an applet's `init` method after it constructs the applet.

Before you lose track of the JavaApplet example program, perhaps you'd like to run it. Listing 7.2 shows the HTML you need. Be sure to compile the Java source program before running the applet.

LISTING 7.2   WebPage.html—A WEB PAGE THAT HOSTS AN APPLET

```
<APPLET CODE=JavaApplet WIDTH=400 HEIGHT=100>
</APPLET>
```

FLOW OF CONTROL

Like its ancestors, C and C++, Java provides a variety of flow of control statements, including if-else, switch, for, while, and do-while.

Conditional Statements

The if statement evaluates an expression and conditionally executes a statement. When combined with an else, the if can execute one or the other of a pair of statements, based on the value of an expression. You may nest if-else statements and use braces to group multiple statements for conditional execution. Unlike C/C++, an if expression must have boolean type; it cannot be numeric. The familiar C/C++ idiom of treating 0 as false and other values as true doesn't work in Java.

For example, the following if-else statement increments top and bottom if x is 0; otherwise it decrements them:

```
if (x == 0)
{
    top++;
    bottom++;
}
else
{
    top--;
    bottom--;
}
```

Whereas the if performs a two-way conditional branch, the switch statement performs a multi-way conditional branch. The switch statement includes an integer expression and a series of case statements; it evaluates the expression and then executes the case statement that has a matching value. The switch statement may also include a default statement; if no case statement within the switch has a matching value, the switch executes the default statement. Like C/C++, once a case statement is executed, control flows to the following case or default statement. To prevent this, you can use a break statement to transfer control to the statement following the `switch`. Altogether too often, programmers neglect to include `break` statements where needed, resulting in program bugs.

Here's a typical `switch` statement, with a complement of `case` and `break` statements and a `default` statement:

```
int y = 0;
switch (num / 100)
{
    case 0:
        y = 1;
        break;
    case 1:
        y = 2;
        break;
    case 2:
        y = 8;
        break;
    default:
        y = 32;
        break;
}
```

Loop Control Statements

Like C/C++, Java provides three sorts of loops. The `for` statement is especially convenient for writing counted loops in which the number of iterations is fixed. The `for` typically includes three expressions:

- An *initilization* expression, which is executed when the loop is entered.
- A `boolean` *test* expression, which is executed before each iteration. When the test expression evaluates to `false`, iteration ceases.
- An *update* expression, which is executed at the end of each iteration.

Here's an example `for` loop that sums the numbers from 1 to n:

```
int i;
int sum = 0;
for (i = 1; i <= n; i++)
{
    sum += i;
}
```

Loop variables that exist only for the duration of the `for` can be defined inside the `for`, like this:

```
for (int i = 1; i <= n; i++)
```

The do and do-while statements are essentially simpler forms of the for statement. The do statement features a test expression. If the expression evaluates false, the do statement terminates; otherwise, the body of the do executes and the test expression is reevaluated. Iteration continues until the test expression evaluates to false. Here's a do that sums the numbers from 1 to n, just as the previous for statement did:

```
int i = 1;
int sum = 0;
while (i <= n)
{
    sum += i;
    i++;
}
```

Notice that the initialization and update expressions that were incorporated within the for are performed by auxiliary statements rather than the do. The do is most useful when the loop requires no initialization and update operations because other program statements have already established the proper initial conditions and iteration.

The do-while resembles the do, but its test expression is not evaluated until the completion of the first iteration. Therefore, a do-while always executes its body at least once. Here's a do-while loop that computes the same result as the previous loops. Notice that the computation fails if the initial value of n is less than 1:

```
int i = 0;
int sum = 0;
do
{
    i++;
    sum += i;
} while (i <= n)
```

Program Exceptions

Java provides an elegant mechanism for dealing with unexpected program conditions: the *exception*. When a Java virtual machine encounters a problem it *throws an exception*, a special object that records information about the problem. A try-catch statement can be used to trap exceptions thrown within a block of code:

```
try
{
    // statements that cause exception to be thrown
}
catch (IOException ex)
{
    // statements the deal with the exception
}
```

The catch functions somewhat like a method, including an argument (here ex) that has a type that subclasses Exception. Java's libraries define many such subclasses. It's also possible to associate multiple catch blocks with a single try; the first catch block with an argument matching the type of the actual exception executes.

If a statement that could throw a given exception is not within a try block with a catch for that exception, the Java compiler will reject the program unless special steps are taken. The header of the method enclosing the statement must be tagged with a throws clause that advertises the possibility of the uncaught exception. This allows the compiler to efficiently check that statements that invoke the method are enclosed within an appropriate try-catch or that the enclosing method also throws the exception.

Java's exception mechanism ensures that programmers deal with the most likely sources of unexpected program termination. As a result, Java programs tend to be highly reliable.

USER INTERFACE

When programming the client side of a system, the user interface is paramount. Most modern systems employ a graphical user interface, but you can write Java programs that use either a text-based or graphical style of user interface.

Text-Based User Interfaces

Java's System class mediates access to the three standard input/output streams provided by most operating systems: input, output, and error. The System.in object models the input stream; its read method lets you read a Unicode character from the input stream:

```
character data = System.in.read();
```

If the input stream is at end of file, the read method returns the value -1, which corresponds to no Unicode character.

The System.out and System.err objects model the output and error streams, respectively. Their print and println methods let you write text. Each takes a single argument, which must be a String or capable of conversion to a String. Unlike the print method, the println method adds a line termination sequence to its output and flushes the output buffer. For example, the following statement writes the familiar "Hello World!" message to the output stream:

```
System.out.println("Hello World!");
```

Abstract Window Toolkit (AWT) Interfaces

For writing GUI programs, Java provides the Abstract Window Toolkit (AWT). The AWT uses the facilities of the host platform to create and display buttons and other user-interface controls. Therefore, the AWT preserves the familiar look and feel of the host platform, making users feel thoroughly at home. However, experience shows that writing portable programs using the AWT is difficult (though by no means impossible), owing to subtle differences from platform to platform in the behavior of native controls.

The AWT classes are too extensive to be thoroughly covered in the space of a single chapter. The most important aspects of the AWT are summarized in Table 7.4, which shows key AWT classes, and Table 7.5, which shows key AWT event listeners. You should be able to understand the user-interface aspects of the example programs by reading the explanations and referring to these tables. If you're interested in a more detailed presentation of Java and the AWT, consider *Object-Oriented Programming in Java*, by Gilbert and McCarty (Waite Group Press, 1997).

TABLE 7.4   KEY AWT CLASSES

Class	*Description*
Button	Clickable button
Canvas	Surface for drawing
Checkbox	On/off button
Choice	Drop-down list
Dialog	Dialog box
FileDialog	Dialog box for opening/saving files
Frame	Top-level window
Label	Static text
List	Scrollable list
Menu	Clickable menu
MenuItem	Clickable menu item
Panel	Container for controls
Scrollbar	Standard scrollbar
ScrollPane	Container with integral scrollbars
TextArea	Multi-line text box
TextField	Single-line text box
Window	A generic window

TABLE 7.5 KEY AWT EVENT LISTENERS

Listener	Description
ActionListener	Listens for mouse click on a control
AdjustmentListener	Listens for change to scrollbar position
FocusListener	Listens for change in focus (user tabbing to next control)
ItemListener	Listens for user selection from list
KeyListener	Listens for key press
MouseListener	Listens for mouse click within a window
MouseMotionListener	Listens for mouse movement within a window
TextListener	Listens for changes to contents of a text control
WindowListener	Listens for reposition, resize, or close of window

Despite the intention to be brief, one useful but unusual AWT characteristic must be mentioned. In order to facilitate writing portable programs, the AWT lets programmers avoid hard-coding sizes and positions of controls and other user-interface objects. Most AWT programs use one or more *layout managers* to automatically position their controls. By dividing a window into regions controlled by different layout managers, programmers can create a portable screen layout that functions well over a wide range of video monitor resolutions. Table 7.6 summarizes the most popular of the AWT's layout managers.

TABLE 7.6 POPULAR AWT LAYOUT MANAGERS

Layout Manager	Description
BorderLayout	Places controls in one of five positions: north (top), south (bottom), west (left), east (right), or center.
CardLayout	Places controls on a panel within a group of panels that resembles index cards. The user can click a card for access, bringing it to the front of the group.
FlowLayout	Places controls in rows, filling each from left to right and then moving down to the next row.
GridBagLayout	Places controls according to parameters that specify size, location, and so on.
GridLayout	Places controls in a horizontal row, vertical column, or matrix of equally sized cells.

Java Foundation Classes

To overcome limitations of the AWT, Sun created the Java Foundation Classes (JFC, also known as *Swing*). Unlike the AWT, JFC does not utilize native peer components of the host platform. It is a pure-Java facility whose behavior—by design—is consistent across platforms. Because it requires architectural improvements made subsequent to Java 1.0, JFC can be used only with Java 1.1 or later.

Our example programs use the AWT rather than JFC for a number of reasons. First—and primarily—more programmers are familiar with the AWT than JFC. Second, AWT-based code tends to be simpler than JFC-based code. Devoting less space to presentation of user-interface issues is consistent with this book's emphasis on the non-client aspects of distributed systems. Third, Sun intends JFC as an alternative to, rather than a replacement of, the AWT. Finally, at the time of this writing, the current beta version of JFC is rather slow and buggy. Even though it appears that JFC represents the future of client-side Java, the AWT is chosen as the vehicle for presenting user-interface code.

FROM HERE

This chapter has taken you on a whirlwind tour of the Java language and its libraries. Obviously, there's much more to Java than could be presented in a single chapter. This chapter's goal was to jump-start your ability to read Java programs so that you'll be able to understand the many Java example programs used throughout subsequent chapters.

You need to understand a few advanced Java facilities before jumping into the examples. The following chapters provide additional details regarding the Java language and its libraries:

- Chapter 8, "Java Threads," presents threads, explaining why they're useful in building distributed systems and how to create and use them. It also discusses thread synchronization, alerting you to some subtle pitfalls that can cause your programs to fail.

- Chapter 9, "Java Serialization and Beans," presents serialization and Java Beans, both of which are especially important to building distributed systems.

JAVA THREADS

IN THIS CHAPTER

Unlike other popular programming languages, Java has threads—not clothes, of course, but lightweight processes capable of concurrent, asynchronous execution. Java's easy access to threads makes it simpler than ever to build efficient, threaded client servers. In this chapter, you'll learn:

- How concurrency can improve program performance

  Concurrent programs can do several things at once. Often, a concurrent program can outperform an equivalent nonconcurrent program.

- How to create and manage threads

  Java provides extensive capabilities for creating and controlling threads as part of its core API.

- How to avoid pitfalls of concurrency

  Concurrent programs may contain subtle bugs that cause them to hang or produce incorrect results. You'll learn how to recognize and avoid such problems.

CONCURRENCY

We're all familiar with concurrency—which is simply performing several tasks at the same time—in our daily lives. When the boss asks where the Mulligan report is, we'd better have it ready. The reply "It's not ready: I've been working on the Needham analysis" won't cut the mustard. We're expected to do several things at once and do them well.

However, until recently, computers couldn't rise to this expectation. For example, you couldn't run your word processor and spreadsheet at the same time. If the boss asked for a copy of the Mulligan report while you were working with a spreadsheet, you had to shut down the spreadsheet, launch the word processor, print the report, shut down the word processor, launch the spreadsheet, and resume work. No wonder days seemed so frantic.

Microsoft Windows changed that, giving desktop computer users the power of concurrency. Provided your computer has enough memory, you can run your word processor and spreadsheet at the same time. The programs can even cooperate, sharing data in a way that lets you insert a spreadsheet into your report so that the report stays up-to-date, even if you change the formulas in the spreadsheet. As you know from experience, concurrency provides enormous potential for improved efficiency.

THREADS

Running multiple programs—a feat called *multitasking*—is not the only form of concurrency. In fact, it's not the most powerful form, because it's hobbled by several constraints. In multitasking, each program lives in its own address space. To exchange data with other programs, a program must use a rather elaborate protocol that overcomes the lack of access to a common area of memory (for example, UNIX shared memory). You can't simply call another program's procedures. Moreover, from the perspective of an operating system, launching a program is a major event, requiring exclusive access to many shared resources. Consequently, it takes many clock ticks to launch a new program, and other programs must stand down during that interval.

You can write a concurrent system as a suite of programs, but this architecture suffers from the constraints of multitasking. Your system will probably have a fixed number of *tasks*—running copies of a program—because it's so costly to launch a new task. What's more, you'll probably spend quite a bit of time programming the system, coaxing tasks that live in private address spaces to cooperate with one another.

Now, imagine a better way. Instead of multiple programs that share no common memory, suppose you could have a single program with multiple parts that execute concurrently. The parts would cooperate without coaxing, because they're part of the same program and share common data and procedures. Also, because they're part of a single program, they could come and go without major operating system overhead. Such an architecture would make it easy to create fast, efficient servers because you could instantiate one of your hypothetical parts each time a client requests service. That way, multiple clients could be processed concurrently.

Sound too good to be true? It's not: You've just imagined Java's threads, which are quite real. Let's see how to actually create and use them.

Creating Threads

Java provides the `java.lang.Thread` class to model threads, which it supports using facilities of the host platform. This poses a few unfortunate consequences, because threads do not behave consistently across platforms. We'll take up these problems and propose some workarounds later in the chapter.

The most obvious way to create a thread is by instantiating an instance of the `Thread` class. However, the most straightforward way is to first create an instance of a class that implements the `Runnable` interface. The sample program ThreadCreation shows how to create a pair of threads. Copy it from the book's CD-ROM (you'll find both the Java and HTML source files) and run it on your own system. Its screen displays two single-digit counters—one that counts up and one that counts down (see Figure 8.1). The counters run asynchronously, because each has its own thread.

FIGURE 8.1

Threaded programs perform tasks concurrently.

Listing 8.1 shows the Java code for the ThreadCreation program, which consists of an Applet subclass, ThreadCreation, that defines two fields, a method, and an inner class. Let's look at the inner class, Digit, because it's the heart of the program.

LISTING 8.1   ThreadCreation.java—INSTANTIATING A THREAD

```java
import java.applet.*;
import java.awt.*;

public class ThreadCreation extends Applet
{
    Digit   theUpCounter   = new Digit(+1);
    Digit   theDownCounter = new Digit(-1);

    public void init()
    {
        setLayout(new GridLayout(1, 0));
        add(theUpCounter);
        add(theDownCounter);
        Thread t1 = new Thread(theUpCounter);
        Thread t2 = new Thread(theDownCounter);
        t1.start();
        t2.start();
    }

    class Digit extends TextField implements Runnable
    {
        int     theStep;
        int     theState  = 0;

        public Digit(int step)
        {
            theStep = step;
            setFont(new Font("SansSerif", Font.BOLD, 96));
            setEditable(false);
        }
```

```
public void run()
{
    while (true)
    {
        theState += theStep;
        if (theState < 0) theState = 9;
        if (theState > 9) theState = 0;
        setText("" + theState);
        try
        {
            Thread.sleep(500);
        }
        catch (Exception ex) { ; }
    }
}
}
}
```

The inner class `Digit` extends `TextField` and implements `Runnable`. You may have expected that it would extend `Thread`; it's possible to create a thread by extending `Thread`, but `Digit` demonstrates the more common approach. The `Runnable` interface requires its implementing class to define one method: `run`. As you'll see in a moment, the `run` method functions as a gateway for threads; when you want a class to be able to run as a thread, you should specify that the class implements `Runnable` and define a `run` method.

A class can implement as many interfaces as you choose, but it can only extend a single base class. By implementing `Runnable`, your class is free to extend a base class that provides fields and methods useful to your application. For example, the `Digit` class extends `TextField`, which gives it the ability to display itself on the screen as a text box. Because the Java language—not its libraries—provides thread capabilities, you don't need to extend `Thread`.

Looking more closely at the `Digit` class, you can see that it defines two fields, a constructor, and a method. One field, `theState`, holds the current value of the counter, which is initialized to zero. The other field, `theStep`, holds the increment/decrement value by which the counter is adjusted each time it steps.

The constructor accepts an argument that specifies the step value; the constructor copies the value of the argument to the field `theStep`. It then configures itself, via methods inherited from `TextField`, to use a large font and to disallow user editing of its contents.

The `run` method steps the counter. It consists of an endless loop that steps the value of `theState` and wraps the value when it falls outside single-digit range. It then updates the contents of the `TextField` to reflect the new value of `theState`. Finally, it invokes the `Thread.sleep` method from within a `try-catch` block.

The `Thread.sleep` method puts a program "on hold" for a specified interval; `Digit` uses the value 500, which means 500 milliseconds. By calling `Thread.sleep`, `Digit` courteously gives other programs and threads a chance to run; otherwise, it might monopolize the system, making the system seem sluggish to users. Because its nap might be interrupted (by an `InterruptedException`), `Digit` must call `Thread.sleep` within a `try-catch` or throw the exception to its caller. `Digit` handles the exception itself, because the exception is relatively inconsequential; the precise timing of the counting is not important. In effect, `Digit` ignores the exception, because the `catch` block contains no executable statements. Although `Digit` runs as a thread, it does not create the `Thread` in which it runs; the ThreadCreation applet performs this task in its `init` method.

Let's examine ThreadCreation. Its two fields are instances of `Digit`, one counting up by one and the other counting down by one, as specified by the argument passed to the constructor. The `init` method establishes a horizontal `GridLayout` (one row and an unspecified number of columns) as the applet's layout manager and adds each `Digit` to the applet's window.

The `init` method then creates two `Thread` objects, one for each instance of `Digit`. The `Thread` constructor imposes restrictions on the class it accepts as an argument. The class must extend `Thread` or implement `Runnable`. Because `Digit` implements `Runnable`, it's acceptable as an argument to `Thread`'s constructor. Once you create a thread, it simply sits idle until started via the `start` method; therefore, `init` is used to send a `start` message to each new `Thread`.

In response to a `start` message, a `Thread` begins executing its `run` method asynchronously: The calling program and the thread execute in parallel. (Unless your computer has multiple CPUs, it can't perform parallel computation; it merely causes the calling program and the thread to execute in turn. However, given a fast computer, this presents the illusion of parallel computation.)

You can invoke `start` several times on the same instance of `Thread`. Each thread will then share access to the fields of the shared instance. This makes it easy for threads to share information; however, as you'll soon see, it also opens the way for certain kinds of subtle program bugs that don't affect nonthreaded programs.

Thread Characteristics

`Thread` objects, like other objects, possess attributes that store their characteristics. Here are the most important characteristics of a thread:

- The *thread group* to which the thread belongs
- The *priority* of the thread

- The *name* of the thread
- The *type* of the thread
- The *status* of the thread

The ThreadChars program, shown as Listing 8.2, shows how to access these characteristics. This program follows the general pattern established by ThreadCreation. It consists of an applet that has two fields: a TextArea for displaying output and an instance of DummyThread, which is a subclass of Thread. The program's init method sets up the user interface and starts the thread. Then, it commences sending messages to the DummyThread and displaying the responses. Notice that the init method does not need to create the Thread instance. As you'll see, DummyThread extends Thread rather than implementing Runnable, so the initializer of the field theThread creates the Thread.

LISTING 8.2   ThreadChars.java—THREAD CHARACTERISTICS

```java
import java.applet.*;
import java.awt.*;

public class ThreadChars extends Applet
{
    TextArea      theOutput = new TextArea();
    DummyThread theThread = new DummyThread();

    public void init()
    {
        setLayout(new BorderLayout());
        add(theOutput);
        theOutput.setFont(new Font("Monospaced", Font.BOLD, 12));
        theOutput.setEditable(false);
        theThread.start();
        theOutput.append("\nActive Count: " + theThread.activeCount());
        theOutput.append("\n");
        theOutput.append("\nName       : " + theThread.getName());
        theOutput.append("\nPriority   : " + theThread.getPriority());
        theOutput.append("\nAlive      : " + theThread.isAlive());
        theOutput.append("\nDaemon     : " + theThread.isDaemon());
        ThreadGroup t = theThread.getThreadGroup();
        while (t != null)
        {
            theOutput.append("\n");
            theOutput.append("\nName       : " + t.getName());
            theOutput.append("\nGroup Count : " + t.activeGroupCount());
            theOutput.append("\nMax Priority: " + t.getMaxPriority());
            t = t.getParent();
        }
    }
```

continues

LISTING 8.2 CONTINUED

```java
class DummyThread extends Thread
{
    public void run()
    {
        while (true)
        {
            try
            {
                Thread.sleep(500);
            }
            catch (Exception ex) { ; }
        }
    }
}
```

The inner class `DummyThread` consists of little more than a `run` method. An instance of `DummyThread` has no function beyond mere existence: We simply want to probe it in the `init` method of ThreadChars. That's why `DummyThread` extends `Thread` rather than implementing `Runnable`; it doesn't need to inherit any capability from another base class.

Figure 8.2 shows the output of the ThreadChars program. The first paragraph displays the number of active threads in the Java virtual machine. The second paragraph displays the characteristics of the `DummyThread` instance. Each subsequent paragraph describes the characteristics of a *thread group*, from `DummyThread`'s immediate parent to the root of the thread group hierarchy.

FIGURE 8.2

Threads are members of thread groups.

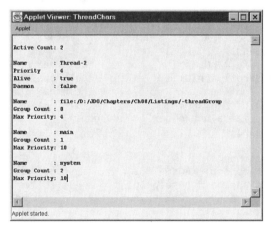

Java associates threads as thread groups for convenience. Thread groups let you send a single message to a group of threads rather than sending a message to each member of the group. A thread group can also impose restrictions on its members and their children. For example, thread groups restrict the maximum priority their members and their children can assume.

Thread priority governs access to the CPU. When a thread of higher priority is ready to run, it preempts lower priority threads. Your application may run poorly unless you assign thread priorities properly. Generally, high-priority tasks that consume little CPU time (such as user interaction) should run as high-priority threads, whereas low-priority tasks, as well as tasks that are CPU intensive, should run as low-priority threads.

In addition to group membership and priority, threads have names. However, names are mainly useful for debugging, because they don't normally appear in user-oriented output.

Threads are of two varieties: daemon and nondaemon. Daemon threads typically perform background tasks of low priority. When the last nondaemon thread terminates, Java automatically terminates any remaining daemon threads.

Using and Controlling Threads

In addition to their relatively fixed characteristics, threads have characteristics that reflect their state. A thread can be in any of several states:

- Alive or dead
- Sleeping or awake
- Suspended or nonsuspended
- Interrupted or noninterrupted

You kill a thread by sending it a `stop` message. However, this unfriendly act may not allow the thread an opportunity to put its affairs in order, leaving the program in an inconsistent state. Therefore, Sun has deprecated use of the `stop` message. You'll learn a better way to terminate a thread in the next section, "Pitfalls and Solutions." You can test whether a thread is alive by sending it the `isAlive` message. You can free the resources associated with a thread by sending it the `destroy` message.

A thread sleeps when it receives a `sleep` message. It awakens after the specified time interval expires or when it's interrupted.

You can suspend a thread—temporarily block it from execution—by sending it a `suspend` message. You can subsequently allow it to execute by sending it a `resume` message.

8

JAVA THREADS

You can interrupt a thread by sending it the `interrupt` message, which throws it an `InterruptedException`. The `isInterrupted` method lets you determine whether a thread has been interrupted.

Java provides messages that let you set the characteristics of a thread:

- `setName(String name)` lets you set the name of a thread.
- `setPriority(int priority)` lets you set the priority of a thread.
- `setDaemon(boolean daemon)` lets you change the daemon status of a thread. Sending `true` as the argument makes the thread a daemon, and sending `false` makes the thread a nondaemon.

You can send the `setMaxPriority` message to a thread group, changing the restrictions it imposes on its members and their children. Also, you can send the `setDaemon` message to a thread group, thereby changing the daemon status of every member of the group.

PITFALLS AND SOLUTIONS

Subsequent chapters present sample programs that use Java's thread capabilities, so we won't take time to present such practical examples here. (If you're eager to see a useful application of threads, see Chapter 13, "Sockets," which shows how to create a threaded Internet server.) Instead, we'll focus here on some of the pitfalls that accompany thread use, showing you both the pit and the path around it.

Stopping a Thread

Java's `Thread` class includes a `stop` method that terminates a running thread. However, Java 1.2 deprecates the method, because abruptly terminating a thread may leave program data in an inconsistent state. The ThreadStopper program, shown in Listing 8.3, demonstrates the proper technique for terminating a thread: You should allow the thread to terminate itself.

LISTING 8.3 `ThreadStopper.java`—How to Safely Stop a Thread

```
import java.applet.*;
import java.awt.*;
import java.awt.event.*;

public class ThreadStopper extends Applet
{
    TextArea     theOutput  = new TextArea();
    DummyThread theThread  = new DummyThread(theOutput);
    Button       theStop    = new Button("Stop");
    Button       theSuspend = new Button("Suspend");
```

```
Button      theResume  = new Button("Resume");

public void init()
{
    setLayout(new BorderLayout());
    add(theOutput, BorderLayout.CENTER);
    Panel p = new Panel();
    p.setLayout(new GridLayout(1, 0));
    add(p, BorderLayout.SOUTH);
    p.add(theStop);
    p.add(theSuspend);
    p.add(theResume);
    theOutput.setFont(new Font("Monospaced", Font.BOLD, 12));
    theOutput.setEditable(false);
    theStop.addActionListener   (new Stopper());
    theSuspend.addActionListener(new Suspender());
    theResume.addActionListener (new Resumer());
    theThread.start();
}

class Stopper implements ActionListener
{
    public void actionPerformed(ActionEvent evt)
    {
        theThread.stopThread();
    }
}

class Suspender implements ActionListener
{
    public void actionPerformed(ActionEvent evt)
    {
        theThread.suspend();
    }
}

class Resumer implements ActionListener
{
    public void actionPerformed(ActionEvent evt)
    {
        theThread.resume();
    }
}

class DummyThread extends Thread
{
    TextArea theOutput;
    boolean  isStopPending = false;
```

8

continues

LISTING 8.3   CONTINUED

```java
    public DummyThread(TextArea out)
    {
        theOutput = out;
    }

    public void stopThread()
    {
        isStopPending = true;
    }

    public void run()
    {
        while (! isStopPending)
        {
            theOutput.append("\nRunning...");
            try
            {
                Thread.sleep(1000);
            }
            catch (Exception ex) { ; }
        }
        theOutput.append("\nStopped.");
    }
}
}
```

Examine the DummyThread inner class and notice that it includes a boolean variable called isStopPending. This variable is initialized to false and set to true by the stopThread method. You might prefer to name such a method stop; however, the Thread.stop method is final and thus cannot be overridden.

DummyThread's run method includes a conditional while rather than the unconditional while of previous examples. When the while discovers that isStopPending is true, it exits. Therefore, you can view its output—the DummyThread appends messages to a text block set up by the applet, which passes a reference to the text block to DummyThread's constructor.

As you can see from DummyThread's user interface, DummyThread not only lets you stop a thread, it lets you suspend and resume it (see Figure 8.3). Let's see how the user interface and the suspend/resume feature work.

The user interface includes three buttons: one to stop the thread, one to suspend it, and one to resume it. Once you stop the thread, it cannot be restarted; you must exit and launch the program again.

Figure 8.3

Threads can be stopped, suspended, and resumed.

The `init` method creates a `BorderLayout` to control the placement of controls and puts the `TextArea` (a multiline text box) at the center of the applet's window so that it fills the available space. Next, the method creates a `Panel` (an invisible container) and places it along the bottom edge of the applet's windows, allowing it to expand horizontally but not vertically. A `GridLayout` governs the placement of controls within the `Panel`; the `Panel`'s constructor parameters (1,0) instruct it to place the controls in a single row. The method then adds the buttons to the `Panel`, styles the `TextArea`, sets an `ActionListener` for each button, and starts the thread.

Each `ActionListener` merely sends an appropriate message to the `Thread`:

- The Stop button's `ActionListener` sends a `stopThread` message.
- The Suspend button's `ActionListener` sends a `suspend` message.
- The Resume button's `ActionListener` sends a `resume` message.

When you use this method of stopping a thread (or more accurately, prompting a thread to stop itself), the thread can perform any desired clean up of program variables before it exits its `run` method and terminates. You should never send a thread the `stop` message.

Platform Variation

Like AWT, Java's threads use facilities of the host platform. Specifically, the host platform's scheduler determines when threads are preempted and which thread is scheduled for execution. Because hosts do not schedule threads consistently, the behavior of Java's threads varies across platforms.

Here's an example of the inconsistency that most often proves troublesome. Assume that a thread of priority 4 is running as the highest-priority thread. Then, the program creates a new thread of equal priority. When does the new thread run? On some platforms (for example, Microsoft Windows) the two equal-priority threads share access to the CPU; on others (for example, Sun Solaris) the first thread continues running until it voluntarily relinquishes the CPU. The former type of platform is said to schedule threads *preemptively*, whereas the latter schedules them *nonpreemptively*. Programmers often refer to preemptive scheduling as *round-robin* scheduling, because it allows every thread its turn.

Platforms that implement a nonpreemptive schedule can prove troublesome for threaded programs. Usually a nonpreemptive schedule works adequately because a task runs for only a short time before it requires input or writes output. Depending on how the host handles input/output buffering, these time-consuming operations may cause the task to relinquish the CPU, allowing other tasks to run. Alternatively, a courteous thread may invoke the yield method from time to time; the yield method lets other tasks of equal priority have access to the CPU.

However, in the worst case, a long-running thread may block other threads from accessing the CPU for an extended period; such threads are said to be *CPU-starved*, or simply *starved*. The consequence, from the perspective of the user, may be a sluggish and unresponsive program, particularly if the starved tasks are responsible for processing user interactions.

You can avoid thread starvation by writing software only for platforms that provide a preemptive schedule; of course, this solution is not in keeping with the Java spirit of "write once, run *anywhere*." You can also avoid thread starvation by writing your own thread scheduler that suspends and resumes Java threads in a round-robin fashion. However, that involves a great deal of work.

A more realistic way of avoiding thread starvation is to write courteous threads that invoke yield regularly. Of course, you must be careful to do this consistently; even one discourteous thread can cause program performance problems. If you're part of a large programming team, it may be worthwhile to invest resources in implementing a scheduler. Even if programmers neglect to include appropriate yield methods, program threads won't experience starvation.

Safety (Races)

Thread starvation is not the only—or greatest—risk in developing threaded programs. When a thread violates the conditions that computer scientists refer to as *safety*, serious data corruption can result. If you've worked with electronic hardware, you may know the term *race condition*, which refers to the same phenomenon.

Let's look at an example of a safety failure. Listing 8.4 shows the Unsafe class, which includes unsafe threads. The init method of Unsafe creates and starts two threads that share a single instance of EvenCounter, an inner class that's roughly similar to the DummyThread inner class of previous examples. However, EvenCounter counts in steps of two, always displaying even values. Moreover, it doesn't display its counter value; it merely displays the word *even* when the count is even or *odd* when the count is odd.

LISTING 8.4   Unsafe.java—AN UNSAFE PROGRAM

```java
import java.applet.*;
import java.awt.*;

public class Unsafe extends Applet
{
    EvenCounter  theCounter = new EvenCounter();

    public void init()
    {
        setLayout(new GridLayout(1, 0));
        add(theCounter);
        Thread t1 = new Thread(theCounter);
        Thread t2 = new Thread(theCounter);
        t1.start();
        t2.start();
    }

    class EvenCounter extends TextField implements Runnable
    {
        int theState = 0;

        public EvenCounter()
        {
            setText("Even");
            setFont(new Font("SansSerif", Font.BOLD, 32));
            setEditable(false);
        }

        public void run()
        {
            while (true)
            {
                theState += 1;
                try
                {
                    Thread.sleep(500);
                }
                catch (Exception ex) { ; }
                theState += 1;
                if (theState%2 == 1) setText("Odd");
            }
        }
    }
}
```

The applet's output indicates that the count is odd (see Figure 8.4). This may seem contradictory: If the EvenCounter, which starts at 0, counts by two, how could it ever contain an odd value? Because EvenCounter is not thread safe, its data becomes corrupted during execution. After running for a few moments, the counter value becomes odd. Let's see why that occurs.

Figure 8.4

Unsafe threads can corrupt data.

The EvenCounter class seems quite ordinary. It contains an int state variable, theState, that holds the counter. The class constructor simply sets the initial text, styles the font, and prevents the user from editing the text within the control.

As usual, the run method does the real work. It increments the counter by one, sleeps for 500 milliseconds, increments the counter by one, and updates the text. Notice that the text does not reflect the current state of the counter: Once the text is changed to *odd*, it never reverts to *even*.

This occurs because the operation of stepping the counter is *nonatomic*: It occurs as two discrete steps. Between the two steps another thread can access and update the counter, thus corrupting its data. The phenomenon is similar to the familiar database update anomaly. Admittedly, the sample program is contrived. It uses sleep so that the interval between the two nonatomic steps is quite wide. Moreover, the program could have updated the int state variable in a single step. However, Java operations on objects, as well as on some primitives (for example, long), are inherently nonatomic. What's more, the wide time interval simply causes a failure quickly and reliably; in the real world, the same result will occur every so often by chance.

If you feel you must try Unsafe before you're ready to accept our results, you can run it yourself. Because Java threads behave differently across platforms, it's possible you won't be able to duplicate our results, which were obtained using JDK 1.1.6 under Microsoft Windows 95. If you don't get an *odd* result, you should tweak the sleep interval; most platforms will exhibit a race condition for some sleep interval.

At this point you may protest that if the bug is so hard to reproduce, it can't be worth worrying about. On the contrary, users exercise a program far more heavily than an individual developer. If your program has hundreds of users who log several hours per day of execution time, once a week a user will see an occurrence that would take you about 5,000 hours of testing to reproduce. If the consequences of the data corruption are sufficiently severe, such a subtle bug may render an entire system unusable. Don't mistake *rare* for *irrelevant*.

Because thread-related bugs are so difficult to detect by using execution-based testing, many software development organizations are supplementing their execution-based testing with techniques such as software walkthroughs or inspections. A group of programmers who know what to look for (for example, nonatomic updates) can often find thread-related problems more quickly and inexpensively than a skilled testing team.

Synchronization

Now that you know how thread safety can fail, you're probably interested in how to fix an unsafe program. Just as the problem of thread safety resembles the problem of database update anomalies, the solution to thread safety problems resembles that of the database update anomaly problems: a lock. Java provides the synchronized keyword, which can be used to write a synchronized statement or method. Let's examine synchronized methods first.

Listing 8.5 shows the Safe class, a modified version of Unsafe that's not susceptible to race conditions. The statements of the run method have been moved to a new method, update, that's specified as synchronized. For each object instance, Java will allow only one thread at a time to execute a synchronized method. Of course, several threads can execute the same method of several objects without restriction, because separate objects do not share fields.

LISTING 8.5 Safe.java—A SAFE PROGRAM

```
import java.applet.*;
import java.awt.*;

public class Safe extends Applet
{
    EvenCounter  theCounter = new EvenCounter();

    public void init()
    {
        setLayout(new GridLayout(1, 0));
        add(theCounter);
        Thread t1 = new Thread(theCounter);
        Thread t2 = new Thread(theCounter);
        t1.start();
        t2.start();
    }

    class EvenCounter extends TextField implements Runnable
    {
        int theState = 0;
```

continues

*doesn't
put a
semaphore
on the
function?*

8

JAVA THREADS

LISTING 8.5   CONTINUED

```java
    public EvenCounter()
    {
        setText("Even");
        setFont(new Font("SansSerif", Font.BOLD, 32));
        setEditable(false);
    }

    public void run()
    {
        while (true)
        {
            update();
        }
    }

    private synchronized void update()
    {
        theState += 1;
        try
        {
            Thread.sleep(500);
        }
        catch (Exception ex) { ; }
        theState += 1;
        if (theState%2 == 1) setText("Odd");
    }
  }
}
```

Synchronizing the update operation makes the operation atomic, which prevents the data corruption of race conditions (see Figure 8.5). No other thread can access the state variable during the interval between the increments. If a thread attempts such access, the Java virtual machine puts the thread on a waiting list so that it can take its turn when the first thread exits the synchronized method.

FIGURE 8.5

Safe threads avoid corrupting data.

Liveness (Deadlocks)

Altogether too often, the solution to one problem leads one to the embrace of another problem. Synchronized methods are not bad, but a program that holds multiple locks (due to concurrently executing multiple synchronized methods) is subject to a phenomenon known as *deadlock*. A simple example of a non–software-related deadlock occurs when you're waiting for a friend to call you while your friend is waiting for you to call him. When a software deadlock occurs, threads cannot execute, and the program appears to hang.

Listing 8.6 shows the `Deadlock` class, which loosely illustrates Dijkstra's Dining Philosopher's problem (Dijkstra is a computer scientist famous for his work in concurrent systems and program correctness). The program uses synchronized statements merely to provide examples of their use; it could as easily have been written using synchronized methods. Either mechanism gives rise to the same problem.

LISTING 8.6   `Deadlock.java`—A PROGRAM THAT DEADLOCKS

```java
import java.applet.*;
import java.awt.*;

public class Deadlock extends Applet
{
    String thePasta = "Pasta";
    String theFork  = "Fork";
    Counter  theCounter1 = new Counter("Philosopher #1",
      thePasta, theFork);
    Counter  theCounter2 = new Counter("Philosopher #2",
      theFork, thePasta);

    public void init()
    {
        setLayout(new GridLayout(1, 0));
        add(theCounter1);
        add(theCounter2);
        Thread t1 = new Thread(theCounter1);
        Thread t2 = new Thread(theCounter2);
        t1.start();
        t2.start();
    }

    class Counter extends TextField implements Runnable
    {
        int theState = 0;
        String theName;
        String theResource1, theResource2;
```

8

continues

LISTING 8.6   CONTINUED

```java
public Counter(String name, String res1, String res2)
{
    theName = name;
    theResource1 = res1;
    theResource2 = res2;
    setFont(new Font("SansSerif", Font.BOLD, 32));
    setEditable(false);
}

public void sleep()
{
    try
    {
        Thread.sleep(2000);
    }
    catch (Exception ex) { ; }
}

public void run()
{
    while (true)
    {
        Loop1:
        while (true)
        {
            synchronized (theResource1)
            {
                System.out.println(theName +
                  " acquired " +
                  theResource1);
                sleep();
                while (true)
                {
                    synchronized (theResource2)
                    {
                        System.out.println(theName +
                          " acquired "  +
                          theResource2);
                        theState += 1;
                        break Loop1;
                    }
                }
            }
        }
        setText("" + theState);
        sleep();
    }
}
```

The synchronized statement uses a *busy flag* associated with each object. Unless a running thread can obtain exclusive access to the object named in the synchronized statement (as indicated by the object's busy flag), it skips the statement body. If it can obtain exclusive access, it sets the busy flag to exclude other threads and then executes the statement body. It tests and sets the busy flag atomically; therefore, race conditions are excluded. Because the synchronized statement skips its body when it cannot acquire exclusive access, it's usually executed within a loop that causes it to continue trying until access is acquired. Although this sample program doesn't do so, it's customary to invoke sleep at the bottom of the loop so that the loop doesn't consume too much CPU time.

The Counter inner class of the Deadlock class performs the familiar task of updating a counter. However, it updates the counter only after acquiring exclusive access to each of two objects: one representing pasta, and the other representing a fork. To understand what's going on, picture two philosophers seated opposite one another at a dining table. Each has one hand tied behind his back. On the table between them is a plate of pasta and a fork. If one grabs the fork and the other grabs the pasta, neither can eat: Deadlock has occurred. Run the program for yourself and you'll see that it hangs, usually before updating the counter a single time. (Again, our results are based on JDK 1.1.6 and Microsoft Windows 95. Your experience may vary.)

The Deadlock class instantiates two Counter objects—one that first grabs the pasta and then the fork, and another that first grabs the fork and then the pasta. The result: deadlock. Study the loops within the Counter class for a bit. They may seem complex at first, but you'll soon figure out that the outer loop acquires access to the first resource, and the inner loop acquires access to the second resource. A labeled break within the inner loop escapes both loops when access to both resources is achieved.

How can you avoid this deadlock? Easily: The NoDeadlock sample program on this book's CD-ROM shows how. You simply cause both threads to access their resources in the same order. Change the lines

```
Counter  theCounter1 = new Counter("Philosopher #1",
    thePasta, theFork);
  Counter  theCounter2 = new Counter("Philosopher #2",
    theFork, thePasta);
```

to read

```
Counter  theCounter1 = new Counter("Philosopher #1",
    theFork, thePasta);
  Counter  theCounter2 = new Counter("Philosopher #2",
    theFork, thePasta);
```

Now, both philosophers first attempt to grab the fork: One loses and one wins. The one who wins now grabs the pasta, eats his fill, and relinquishes the fork and pasta. Again,

8

JAVA THREADS

the philosophers compete to grab the fork and pasta. However, one philosopher is as likely to win the contest as the other. Therefore, over time, each eats his fill of pasta. No deadlock results as long as all threads access resources in the same order.

You should avoid nested synchronized statements, as well as nested calls to synchronized methods, when you can. However, when you must acquire multiple resources, you should acquire them in a consistent order. That way, you'll avoid deadlock.

Java provides three methods— `wait, notify,` and `notifyAll`—that provide still more control over synchronization than synchronized methods and statements, but these methods are more complicated than the techniques we've covered here. Synchronized methods and statements should prove adequate for most of your distributed computing needs. However, if you need to squeeze every ounce of performance from a program, you should consult the JDK documentation that explains these methods.

FROM HERE

This chapter was designed to expand your knowledge of *threads*, an aspect of Java that many programmers fail to understand and appreciate, and therefore fail to apply. As you've learned, Java's capabilities for creating and managing threads set it apart from other popular languages, particularly for server development. Related chapters include the following:

- Chapter 9, "Java Serialization and Beans," which presents serialization and Java Beans, additional important topics that are unfamiliar to many Java programmers.
- Chapter 13, "Sockets," which applies the principles explained in this chapter, showing how threads can be used to improve the performance of Java-based servers.

JAVA SERIALIZATION AND BEANS

IN THIS CHAPTER

People have long wondered how what they eat affects their health. One of the first modern companies to capitalize on this concern was the Kellogg Company, founded in 1900 by Dr. John Kellogg and his brother, W. K. Kellogg, who jointly developed a way to make flakes of corn, wheat, and other grains that patients at Dr. Kellogg's sanitarium enjoyed as a breakfast food. A sanitarium patient, C. W. Post, later founded a rival cereal company.

More recently, Francis Moore Lappe wrote *Diet for a Small Plant*, which presents the personal and social advantages of a diet based largely on beans and grains. According to Lappe, the world could easily sustain its present population and more if nations ceased squandering their resources on meat-based agriculture.

This chapter promotes a healthy diet for Java programmers. In homage to the Kellogg brothers, we'll take up serialization. Also, in homage to Ms. Lappe, we'll investigate the advantages of Java Beans. In this chapter you learn:

- How to use serialization to store and retrieve objects.

  Writing objects to a file presents some subtle complications. However, Java's serialization facility makes object persistence easy to achieve.

- How to use Java archive files (JARs) to store classes, objects, and data files.

  It's often more convenient and even more efficient to store classes, objects, and data in a single file. Java's jar tool lets you pack files into a JAR that can be used by appletviewer and most browsers.

- How to use Java Beans to establish runtime connections among components.

  Java Beans let your program decide at runtime what messages should go to what objects. By delaying the binding of message senders to message receivers, you increase your program's flexibility. Java Beans are an important tool for builders and users of reusable components.

SERIALIZATION

Ordinary objects lead a risky life. An object's existence can be blotted out in a twinkling of an eye by a power failure or system malfunction. Sure, when computing service is restored you can create new objects, but your newborn objects probably won't have the same state as those that existed before the failure. If they contained important data, that data has been lost.

Though they face risk of oblivion at any moment, ordinary objects lead dull and uninteresting lives: They don't get out much, spending all their time hanging with the same small clique. Ordinary objects inhabit a single Java virtual machine and cannot be transported (or transport themselves) from one system to another. They spend their existence trapped within a system, exchanging data primarily with fellow objects of their host Java virtual machine.

However, Java's serialization facility lets you create *persistent objects* that can live in a state of hibernation when computing ceases and can be awakened to thrive in any host Java virtual machine, not merely their "hometown." Serialization is so simple to use that your objects need never suffer untimely death or boredom: They can easily save their state to disk and travel the computing universe.

Persistence

Persistent objects are often described as frozen objects that can be reconstituted at the point of need. Granted, if you have no bucket, it's easier to transport an ice cube than a pint of water. What's more, *frozen* implies immobile, which correctly describes the hibernative state of a stored persistent object. However, *frozen* also carries negative connotations we'd prefer not to associate with persistent objects.

Persistent objects might be better described as *dehydrated*. An ordinary object exists, along with its class, in a Java virtual machine. In this state, the class and the object are tightly bound together. For example, when the object receives a message, it consults its class to determine the method statements it should execute. This architecture allows a single copy of the method, stored within the class, to be available to many objects, making efficient use of potentially scarce system memory.

A class, of course, is persistent. It can exist as a `.class` file that can be stored on disk (or other permanent media) and copied from one system to another. Java's serialization facility confers a similar capability on objects. Using it, you can write an object's state to a file and subsequently reconstitute the object by reading the file. Just as dehydrated foods are not palatable without water, you cannot use a stored object without its `.class` file, which must be available when the object is reconstituted.

The `Serializable` Interface

Without Java's serialization facility, you'd find it difficult to create persistent objects. Most objects contain nonprimitive fields—that is, fields that refer to other objects. Java virtual machines implement such references as *handles*, which identify objects by their location within an object table maintained by the Java virtual machine. If you naively copy the fields of an object that contains nonprimitive fields to a disk file, you accomplish little. You can't use the file to reconstitute the object in a new Java virtual machine, because the object's nonprimitive fields no longer refer to the proper locations within the object table. Instead, an object and the objects it references must be saved and reconstituted as a unit.

Java's serialization facility solves this and other problems of serialization. It includes two main components:

- The `Serializable` interface
- Special `java.io` classes that let you read and write objects

The distinguishing mark of a persistent object is that it implements the `Serializable` interface. For example, the header of the `Kellogg` class could specify that `Kellogg` objects are serializable, like this:

```
public class Kellogg implements Serializable
```

Generally, when you implement an interface, you must be concerned with implementing the methods it specifies. However, the `Serializable` interface is a null interface. It specifies no methods; therefore, an implementing class doesn't need to implement any particular methods. When you specify that a class implements `Serializable`, you're simply marking the class as eligible for processing by serialization methods. When you request that an object be written or read, the serialization facility inspects the object's class to determine whether the class implements `Serializable`. If it does, the serialization facility performs the requested operation; otherwise, it throws an exception. When you specify that a class implements `Serializable`, you give the serialization facility permission to read or write its objects.

The `java.io` package provides two classes—`ObjectInputStream` and `ObjectOutputStream`—used to read and write objects. We didn't present the `java.io` package in Chapter 7, "Java Overview," because its capabilities are extensive, requiring many pages of explanation. However, the `java.io` package provides the same basic input/output functions included in most programming languages. Assuming you've written input/output programs in some language, you'll have little trouble following a sample program. Bear in mind that the `java.io` package provides a lot of power beyond what's demonstrated here. If you're interested in more sophisticated input/output functions, you should consult the JDK documentation or a Java textbook.

The StoreObject Applet

Figure 9.1 shows the StoreObject applet, which lets you write an object to disk. You should run the applet for yourself using the files on the CD-ROM. Type a message into the text box and then click the Store button. The applet creates a disk file named temp that contains the state of the `TextField` object, including the text you typed. You can retrieve the text by running the RetrieveObject applet, which you'll meet momentarily. First, let's examine how the StoreObject applet works.

Figure 9.1

The StoreObject applet lets you store an object.

Listing 9.1 shows the source code of the StoreObject applet. As you can see, the applet includes two fields: a `TextField` that lets the user type a message and a `Button` that lets the user tell the applet to store the `TextField`. The applet's `init` method contains no surprises. It sets up a layout manager for the applet window, places the user interface components, and sets up an `ActionListener` for the `Button`.

Listing 9.1   `StoreObject.java`—Storing an Object

```java
import java.applet.*;
import java.awt.*;
import java.awt.event.*;
import java.io.*;

public class StoreObject extends Applet
{
    TextField theMessage = new TextField();
    Button    theStoreButton = new Button("Store");

    public void init()
    {
        setLayout(new BorderLayout());
        add(theMessage, BorderLayout.CENTER);
        add(theStoreButton, BorderLayout.SOUTH);
        theStoreButton.addActionListener(new StoreHandler());
    }

    class StoreHandler implements ActionListener
    {
        public void actionPerformed(ActionEvent evt)
        {
            try
            {
                FileOutputStream out = new FileOutputStream("temp");
                ObjectOutputStream sout = new ObjectOutputStream(out);
                sout.writeObject(theMessage);
                sout.close();
                System.out.println("Stored");
            }
            catch (IOException ex) { ; }
        }
    }
}
```

The interesting part of the applet is the inner class, StoreHandler, which functions as the ActionListener for the Button. Its actionPerformed method writes the TextField to disk, using an instance of ObjectOutputStream. Here are the steps it follows:

1. Create a FileOutputStream object bound to a disk file named temp. Java's FileOutputStream class represents a file open for output. The constructor lets you specify the name of the file. If the file does not exist, the FileOutputStream class creates it.

2. Create an ObjectOutputStream object bound to the FileOutputStream object. The FileOutputStream class includes no methods for writing objects. However, it's easy to create an ObjectOutputStream, which can write objects. You simply pass a reference to a FileOutputStream to the ObjectOutputStream constructor.

3. Write the TextField to the ObjectOutputStream. Writing an object to an ObjectOutputStream is child's play. Simply pass a reference to the object as an argument of the writeObject method.

   Although StoreObject writes only a single object to its ObjectOutputStream, your programs can write as many objects as you like. However, it's up to the program that reads the file to determine when to stop reading. You need to write some control information that helps the reading program determine what to do next. You'll see how to do this in a moment.

4. Close the ObjectOutputStream. When you're done writing objects to an ObjectOutputStream, you should close it. Most operating systems allow only a limited number of open files; file handles are a scarce resource that should be returned to the operating system when no longer needed. Moreover, closing a file ensures that its data is written from memory. Until a file is closed, termination of the program may leave the file in an incomplete state.

5. Display a message announcing completion of the operation. If you're using appletviewer, you'll see the message in the DOS window you used to launch appletviewer. Browsers display System.out messages in various ways. Consult your browser documentation for details.

The processing steps are enclosed within a try-catch block because input/output operations sometimes fail. For example, a disk may be full and unable to accommodate additional data. When an input/output error occurs, Java throws an IOException. The catch intercepts this exception. Of course, its response is relatively naive: It does nothing at all. This seems appropriate for a demonstration; however, it's seldom appropriate for a production program. A catch within a production program would likely include statements that report the exception or attempt to recover from it.

As mentioned, sometimes you may want to write control information to an
ObjectOutputStream along with objects. By creating your ObjectOutputStream from a
DataOutputStream, rather than a FileOutputStream, your ObjectOutputStream will
inherit useful methods:

```
FileOutputStream    out = new FileOutputStream("temp");
DataOutputStream    dout = new DataOutputStream(out);
ObjectOutputStream sout = new ObjectOutputStream(dout);
```

Table 9.1 shows some of the most useful methods of DataOutputStream. These methods
write data using a platform-independent binary format: Files written using them can be
read on any Java platform.

TABLE 9.1 KEY DataOutputStream METHODS

Method	Function
write(int b)	Writes a single byte
writeBytes(String s)	Writes a String as a series of bytes
writeChar(int c)	Writes a Unicode character
writeChars(String s)	Writes a String as a series of Unicode characters
writeDouble(double d)	Writes a double-precision floating-point number
writeFloat(float f)	Writes a single-precision floating-point number
writeInt(int n)	Writes a 32-bit integer
writeLong(long l)	Writes a 64-bit integer

The RetrieveObject Applet

Figure 9.2 shows the RetrieveObject applet, which lets you retrieve an object stored by
the StoreObject applet. The files needed to run RetrieveObject are on the CD-ROM. To
operate the applet, click Retrieve. The applet will read the stored TextField object and
add it to the applet window, where you can view it.

FIGURE 9.2

*The
RetrieveObject
applet lets you
retrieve a stored
object.*

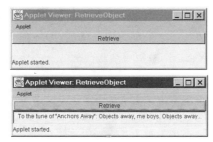

Listing 9.2 shows the source code of the RetrieveObject applet. As with the StoreObject applet, the important processing takes place in the `actionPerformed` method of the applet's inner class.

LISTING 9.2   `RetrieveObject.java`—RETRIEVING AN OBJECT

```java
import java.applet.*;
import java.awt.*;
import java.awt.event.*;
import java.io.*;

public class RetrieveObject extends Applet
{
    Button    theRetrieveButton = new Button("Retrieve");

    public void init()
    {
        setLayout(new BorderLayout());
        add(theRetrieveButton, BorderLayout.NORTH);
        theRetrieveButton.addActionListener(new RetrieveHandler());
    }

    class RetrieveHandler implements ActionListener
    {
        public void actionPerformed(ActionEvent evt)
        {
            try
            {
                FileInputStream in = new FileInputStream("temp");
                ObjectInputStream sin = new ObjectInputStream(in);
                Object c = sin.readObject();
                sin.close();
                if (c instanceof Component)
                {
                    add((Component) c, BorderLayout.CENTER);
                    invalidate();
                    validate();
                    System.out.println("Retrieved");
                }
            }
            // Possible IOException or ClassNotFoundException
            catch (Exception ex)
            {
                System.err.println(ex);
            }
        }
    }
}
```

Here are the processing steps used to restore the `TextField`:

1. Create a `FileInputStream` bound to the disk file temp.

2. Create an `ObjectInputStream` bound to the `FileInputStream`.

3. Read the object and store it in a program variable, c.

4. Close the `ObjectInputStream`. Because the `ObjectInputStream` and `FileInputStream` are bound, the `close` method also closes the `FileInputStream`.

5. Check whether the object has the expected type in order to avoid a possible `ClassCastException` in the following step. The object should be a `TextField`, but the applet expects nothing more of an object than the ability to be added to an applet window. Consequently, the applet checks for membership in the `Component` class, which is an ancestor class of `TextField`. Any `Component` can be added to an applet window.

6. If the object has the proper type, add it to the applet window and adjust the window layout. The `invalidate` and `validate` message pair causes the applet's layout manager to adjust the layout of the applet to accommodate the new `Component`.

7. Display a message announcing successful completion.

As in the StoreObject applet, the `try-catch` block guards against an `IOException`. Here, the `catch` uses a `println` to display a message when an `IOException` is thrown. Again, this response seems appropriate for a demonstration program; application programs normally require more sophisticated error handling.

You can use the `DataInputStream` class to read primitive data written to a disk file. Create the `DataInputStream` instance in much the same way as a `DataOutputStream`:

```
FileInputStream    out = new FileInputStream("temp");
DataInputStream    dout = new DataInputStream(out);
ObjectInputStream sout = new ObjectInputStream(dout);
```

You can use the methods shown in Table 9.2 to read primitive data contained in a `DataInputStream`. When you're reading multiple values from a stream, you may encounter the `EOFException`, a subclass of `IOException` that denotes reading past the end of a file.

9

TABLE 9.2   KEY `DataInputStream` METHODS

Method	Function
int readByte()	Reads a byte
char readChar()	Reads a Unicode character

continues

TABLE 9.2 CONTINUED

Method	Function
double readDouble()	Reads a double-precision floating-point number
float readFloat()	Reads a single-precision floating-point number
int readInt()	Reads a 32-bit integer
long readLong()	Reads a 64-bit integer

Recursive Serialization and transient Fields

Java's serialization facility automatically handles the complications that arise when one object refers to another. When an object refers to other objects, Java serializes them recursively so that the entire community of objects can be reconstituted. For example, if you ask Java to serialize object *x*, which refers to objects *a* and *b*, Java will serialize *x*, *a*, and *b*.

Sometimes you don't need to store every member of the community. For example, some objects may be redundant: It may be possible to recreate them by using the values of the other objects' fields. It's wasteful to write such redundant objects to the file. By specifying the keyword transient in the declaration of a field, you notify Java that it need not serialize the field. When the stored object is recreated, any transient fields receive the default initial value appropriate to their type. If you prefer some other value, you must assign it after recreating the object.

JAVA ARCHIVES (JARS)

When transferring files over a network, establishing the connection to transfer a file often requires significant time. By bundling files together, file transfer can be expedited. Java's archive files (JARs) meet this need.

The jar utility, patterned after the UNIX tar utility, creates and manipulates JARs. For example, to bundle all the class files in the current directory and the file named temp within a JAR named MyJar.jar, type this:

```
jar cf MyJar.jar *.class temp
```

Assuming you receive no error messages, you can then safely remove the archived files:

```
del *.class
del temp
```

To retrieve the files, type this:

```
jar xf MyJar.jar
```

Table 9.3 shows the parameters of the jar utility. You generally use the f parameter and either the c, t, or x parameter.

TABLE 9.3 PARAMETERS OF THE jar UTILITY

Parameter	Function
c	Creates a new JAR.
t	Lists the contents of a JAR.
x	Extracts the files within a JAR.
f	Used with the c, t, or x parameter to specify the filename. Otherwise, input is read from the standard input stream.
v	Specifies verbose output.

Java applets can be bundled with their resources (sound clips, images, data files, and so on) in a JAR file using a special HTML tag. Browsers transparently access images and sound clips from JARs. Programs that use data files contained in JARs must be specially written. Listing 9.3 shows the RetrieveJar applet, which demonstrates the technique.

LISTING 9.3 RetrieveJar.java—RETRIEVING A RESOURCE FROM A JAR FILE

```java
import java.applet.*;
import java.awt.*;
import java.awt.event.*;
import java.io.*;

public class RetrieveJar extends Applet
{
    Button      theRetrieveButton = new Button("Retrieve");

    public void init()
    {
        setLayout(new BorderLayout());
        add(theRetrieveButton, BorderLayout.NORTH);
        theRetrieveButton.addActionListener(new RetrieveHandler());
    }

    class RetrieveHandler implements ActionListener
    {
        public void actionPerformed(ActionEvent evt)
        {
            try
            {
                ObjectInputStream in = new ObjectInputStream(
```

9

continues

LISTING 9.3   CONTINUED

```
                getClass().getResourceAsStream("temp"));
            Object c = in.readObject();
            in.close();
            if (c instanceof Component)
            {
                add((Component) c, BorderLayout.CENTER);
                invalidate();
                validate();
                System.out.println("Retrieved");
            }
        }
        // Possible IOException or ClassNotFoundException
        catch (Exception ex)
        {
            System.err.println(ex);
        }
    }
  }
}
```

The program closely follows the model of the RetrieveObject applet. The important line is the one that instantiates the `ObjectInputStream`, which has been modified as follows:

```
ObjectInputStream in = new ObjectInputStream(
  getClass().getResourceAsStream("temp"));
```

Java classes are loaded by a special object known as the ClassLoader. This line uses the ClassLoader that loaded the applet to access the resource held in the file named temp, which contains the stored object. The remainder of the program works as before.

To run the RetrieveObject applet, use the HTML shown in Listing 9.4. The ARCHIVE tag tells the browser that the applet's classes and resources are located in the JAR file MyJar.jar. Applets stored in a JAR can be digitally signed by using the javakey utility. A user can grant digitally signed applets permission to perform a variety of operations that unsigned applets are not allowed to perform. Chapter 10, "Security," explains this mechanism further.

LISTING 9.4   RetrieveObject.html—RUNNING AN APPLET FROM A JAR FILE

```
<APPLET CODE=RetrieveJar ARCHIVE=MyJar.jar WIDTH=400 HEIGHT=50>
</APPLET>
```

JAVA BEANS

Software is time consuming and expensive to develop; therefore, one of the most sought-after benefits of object-oriented software development is the ability to reuse software. Software reuse aims to exploit the common functionality that typical software systems share. If this functionality can be isolated into reusable components, organizations can construct systems quickly and cheaply.

Microsoft's Visual Basic capitalized on this vision, inaugurating an extensive market for software components. Visual Basic programmers often write complete systems containing almost no code. They design a user interface, select and place ActiveX controls (components), and add a little code as glue to integrate the user interface with the controls.

If Java is to compete with Visual Basic as a vehicle for high productivity software development, it must provide an analogous software component model. Java Beans fill this role. They're reusable software components you can place in the window of a Java program, including components such as spinners, text boxes for date entry, and miniature spreadsheets. Java IDEs, such as Symantec's Visual Café for Java and Inprise's JBuilder, allow a programmer to simply drag and drop a Java Bean into a program. The programmer can customize the Bean by using a property sheet to set its properties, working in much the same way as a Visual Basic programmer. Each Bean includes meta-information that tells the IDE what properties and methods the Bean provides.

Toolsmiths, Programmers, and Users

Three people work with any Bean:

- The toolsmith, who builds the IDE or the Bean.
- The programmer, who writes a program that incorporates the Bean.
- The user, who operates the application the programmer wrote.

Each of the three has a unique perspective. The toolsmith must understand how Beans describe themselves and how they can be integrated with an IDE. The programmer must understand Bean properties and methods but can rely on the work of the toolsmith to ensure that the Bean properly installs itself within his IDE. The user doesn't even need to be aware that the Bean exists as a reusable component; all the user cares about is that the program responds properly to every keystroke or mouse gesture.

This section takes the middle road, somewhere between the concerns of the toolsmith and the programmer. You'll learn enough about Bean internals to develop a sound model of how Beans work. However, the main purpose of the section is to equip you to program using Beans. When all goes well, it's all but trivial to program using a Bean: You simply drag the Bean, drop it into a window, set its properties, and forget it. However, as you know, all does not always go well. You need to know enough about Beans to debug the code your IDE generates so that you can find and fix problems. This section will give you the necessary background knowledge.

Properties, Methods, and Events

Java's messaging infrastructure acts like a network of highways connecting your program's objects as a cooperative community. However, you may sometimes have the urge to take your Chevy Blazer four-wheeling offroad, exploring connections. As a matter of necessity, Beans are able to do exactly that.

AWT components notify other objects of user interaction by firing events. Each type of component fires events that correspond to the types of interactions it supports: A `Button` fires an `ActionEvent` when the user clicks it, and a `Scrollbar` fires an `AdjustEvent` when the user drags its thumb.

Beans must be able to inform an IDE of the properties and methods they possess as well as the data type of each property, method argument, and method return type. Beans solve this problem using the Java reflection API and a special API called `java.beans`.

Beans come in a variety of types, each type providing a distinct service. Consequently, they cannot use the ordinary AWT messaging system. Beans require a flexible messaging infrastructure, one that does not limit the communication between a Bean and its clients (that is, the objects that exchange messages with it). Beans solve this problem by using the publish/subscribe design pattern.

Let's investigate how Beans use the Java APIs and the publish/subscribe design pattern. Then we'll look at some sample programs that use Beans.

Bean Properties

Like other objects, a Bean has fields and methods. Of course, most Beans don't directly expose their fields. Instead, Beans provide *properties* that correspond to their encapsulated characteristics. Every Bean property has corresponding `get` and `set` methods. For example, suppose a Bean provides a property named `girth`. Such a Bean would have a `getGirth` method that allows you to access the value of the `girth` property and a `setGirth` method that allows you to set its value.

Java IDEs discover Bean properties in two ways. First, the Java reflection API lets an object examine another object to learn what methods it exposes. The details of the reflection API are relevant to the toolsmith, not the programmer, so we'll skip the details.

What matters is that the IDE can identify every `get` and `set` method of a Bean by simply reflecting it. The reflection API also provides the argument and return data types. Therefore, the IDE is easily able to determine the properties of a Bean.

The second way to discover Bean properties lets a toolsmith tell a programmer more than the name and data type of each Bean property. The toolsmith can design a `BeanInfo` object that describes the Bean. When an IDE examines a Bean, it looks for the Bean's `BeanInfo` object. If it finds one, it uses the information in the `BeanInfo` object to build a description of the Bean.

The Publish/Subscribe Design Pattern

Once an IDE knows the properties of a Bean, it must integrate the Bean within the user interface. The publish/subscribe design pattern provides the necessary glue. Publish/subscribe works much like the familiar AWT message paradigm. When a Bean property changes, the Bean fires an event. Of course, Beans don't fire events to every program object: In order to receive events, a client object must first subscribe.

Figure 9.3 shows the ColorSelector applet, which demonstrates Bean operation. The applet includes a text box, a scrollbar, and a color swatch. Entering a number (0–255) in the text box changes the color of the swatch. Similarly, manipulating the scrollbar changes the color of the swatch.

FIGURE 9.3

Objects of the ColorSelector program communicate via property change events.

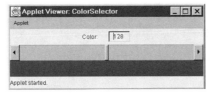

The text box and scrollbar are Beans that fire events when they're manipulated. The scrollbar listens to events fired by the text box and moves its thumb to correspond to the value in the text box. Similarly, the text box listens to the scrollbar and updates its value to correspond to the position of the scrollbar's thumb. The color swatch is an ordinary object, not a Bean. It listens to the text box and the scrollbar and updates its background color whenever either fires an event.

Listing 9.5 shows the source code of the ColorSelector applet. The applet includes fields that represent the text box, scrollbar, and color swatch. Its `init` method places them in the applet window and uses the `addPropertyChangeListener` message to subscribe each to the proper events. Inner classes do the rest.

9

LISTING 9.5 ColorSelector.java—COMMUNICATING VIA PROPERTY CHANGE EVENTS

```java
import java.applet.*;
import java.awt.*;
import java.awt.event.*;
import java.beans.*;

public class ColorSelector extends Applet
{
   TextSelector    theText   = new TextSelector();
   ScrollSelector theScroll = new ScrollSelector();
   ColorCanvas     theCanvas = new ColorCanvas();

   public void init()
   {
      setLayout(new GridLayout(0, 1));
      Panel p = new Panel();
      p.add(new Label("Color: "));
      p.add(theText);
      add(p);
      add(theScroll);
      add(theCanvas);
      theText.addPropertyChangeListener(theScroll);
      theText.addPropertyChangeListener(theCanvas);
      theScroll.addPropertyChangeListener(theText);
      theScroll.addPropertyChangeListener(theCanvas);
   }

   class TextSelector extends TextField
     implements ActionListener, PropertyChangeListener
   {
      PropertyChangeSupport theSupport = new PropertyChangeSupport(this);
      Integer theOldColor = null;

      public TextSelector()
      {
         super(3);
         addActionListener(this);
      }

      public int getColor()
      {
         return Integer.parseInt(getText());
      }

      public void setColor(int color)
      {
         setText("" + color);
         Integer newcolor = new Integer(color);
         theSupport.firePropertyChange("Color", theOldColor, newcolor);
         theOldColor = newcolor;
```

```
    }

    public void actionPerformed(ActionEvent evt)
    {
        setColor(getColor());
    }

    public void propertyChange(PropertyChangeEvent evt)
    {
        Object value = evt.getNewValue();
        if (evt.getPropertyName().equals("Color")
          && value instanceof Integer)
        {
            setText("" + ((Integer) value).intValue());
        }
    }

    public void addPropertyChangeListener(PropertyChangeListener q)
    {
        theSupport.addPropertyChangeListener(q);
    }

    public void removePropertyChangeListener(PropertyChangeListener q)
    {
        theSupport.removePropertyChangeListener(q);
    }
}

class ScrollSelector extends Scrollbar
  implements AdjustmentListener, PropertyChangeListener
{
    PropertyChangeSupport theSupport = new PropertyChangeSupport(this);
    Integer theOldColor = null;

    public ScrollSelector()
    {
        super(Scrollbar.HORIZONTAL);
        setMinimum(0);
        setMaximum(260);
        setValue(255);
        setVisibleAmount(5);
        addAdjustmentListener(this);
    }

    public int getColor()
    {
        return getValue();
    }
```

continues

LISTING 9.5   CONTINUED

```java
    public void setColor(int color)
    {
        setValue(color);
        Integer newcolor = new Integer(color);
        theSupport.firePropertyChange("Color", theOldColor, newcolor);
        theOldColor = newcolor;
    }

    public void adjustmentValueChanged(AdjustmentEvent evt)
    {
        setColor(getColor());
    }

    public void propertyChange(PropertyChangeEvent evt)
    {
        Object value = evt.getNewValue();
        if (evt.getPropertyName().equals("Color")
          && value instanceof Integer)
        {
            setValue( ((Integer) value).intValue() );
        }
    }

    public void addPropertyChangeListener(PropertyChangeListener q)
    {
        theSupport.addPropertyChangeListener(q);
    }

    public void removePropertyChangeListener(PropertyChangeListener q)
    {
        theSupport.removePropertyChangeListener(q);
    }
}

class ColorCanvas extends Canvas implements PropertyChangeListener
{
    public void propertyChange(PropertyChangeEvent evt)
    {
        Object value = evt.getNewValue();
        if (evt.getPropertyName().equals("Color")
          && value instanceof Integer)
        {
            int red = ((Integer) value).intValue();
            setBackground(new Color(red, 0, 0 ));
        }
    }
}
}
```

The `TextSelector` class models the text box. Although you may see nothing out of the ordinary, `TextSelector` is a Bean. It contains a `PropertyChangeSupport` object that helps it manage event subscriptions and get/set methods for a property named `Color`. `Color` is an `int` that represents the amount of red (0–255) in an RGB color value. The class delegates `addPropertyChangeListener` and `removePropertyChangeListener` messages to its `PropertyChangeSupport` object.

Examine the `setColor` method. You'll see that it sends the `firePropertyChange` message to the `PropertyChangeSupport` object. That's how client objects are notified of changes to the `Color` property of `TextSelector`. The message has three arguments: The first specifies the name of the property, the second specifies the old value of the property, and the third specifies the new value of the property. The second and third arguments must be objects; therefore, the `int` property value is wrapped within an `Integer`.

Recall that the `TextSelector` listens for changes in the scrollbar's properties. The `propertyChange` method executes when the scrollbar is adjusted. The method extracts the property name and the new property value from the `PropertyChangeEvent` and appropriately updates the value of the text box.

If you examine the `ScrollSelector` and `ColorCanvas` classes, you'll find they work similarly. `ScrollSelector` simply handles the `AdjustmentEvent` of `Scrollbar` rather than the `ActionEvent` of `TextField`, which is handled by `TextSelector`. `ColorCanvas` is not a Bean. Therefore, it has no properties and fires no events. However, it does receive `PropertyChangeEvents` fired by the `TextSelector` and `ScrollSelector`. In response, it updates its background color to an appropriate hue of red.

Constrained Properties

Beans can provide a more sophisticated type of property known as a *constrained property*. When a constrained property changes, any listener can veto the change by throwing an appropriate exception. Constrained properties are useful for implementing validation mechanisms. When a programmer loads your Bean into a Java IDE, the programmer can change the Bean's properties. By establishing constrained properties, you can prevent the programmer from specifying invalid values for the Bean's properties. Constrained properties can spare the programmer hours of debugging time when, for example, he tries to set your Bean's height property to a negative value.

The text box of the ColorSelector applet did not constrain its value. Of course, the only valid values for the red component of an RGB value are 0–255. Figure 9.4 shows a revised version of the ColorSelector applet, known as ChangeVetoer, that constrains the `Color` property to valid values. If you type an invalid color value—such as 900—into the text box, the applet ignores your color change request. If, on the other hand, you type a valid color value—such as 255—into the text box, the applet adjusts the position of the scrollbar and the color of the swatch to match your choice.

FIGURE 9.4

Listening objects can reject "vetoable" property change events.

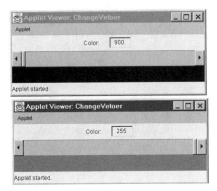

Listing 9.6 shows the source code of the ChangeVetoer applet. Because changes to the text box can be vetoed by the scrollbar, the applet subscribes the scrollbar to the text box's messages by using the addVetoableChangeListener message. You may prefer to have the color swatch veto invalid changes to the text box or have both the color swatch and the scrollbar do so. The change of the message sent to the scrollbar is the only change to the applet's init method.

LISTING 9.6 ChangeVetoer.java—VETOING PROPERTY CHANGES

```
import java.applet.*;
import java.awt.*;
import java.awt.event.*;
import java.beans.*;

public class ChangeVetoer extends Applet
{
   TextSelector    theText   = new TextSelector();
   ScrollSelector theScroll = new ScrollSelector();
   ColorCanvas    theCanvas = new ColorCanvas();

   public void init()
   {
      setLayout(new GridLayout(0, 1));
      Panel p = new Panel();
      p.add(new Label("Color: "));
      p.add(theText);
      add(p);
      add(theScroll);
      add(theCanvas);
      theText.addVetoableChangeListener(theScroll);
```

```java
      theText.addPropertyChangeListener(theCanvas);
      theScroll.addPropertyChangeListener(theText);
      theScroll.addPropertyChangeListener(theCanvas);
}

class TextSelector extends TextField
  implements ActionListener, PropertyChangeListener
{
    PropertyChangeSupport theSupport
      = new PropertyChangeSupport(this);
    VetoableChangeSupport theVetoableSupport
      = new VetoableChangeSupport(this);
    Integer theOldColor = null;

    public TextSelector()
    {
       super(3);
       addActionListener(this);
    }

    public int getColor()
    {
        try
       {
          return Integer.parseInt(getText());
       }
       catch (NumberFormatException ex)
       {
          return 0;
       }
    }

    public void setColor(int color)
    {
       Integer newcolor = new Integer(color);
       try
       {
          theVetoableSupport.fireVetoableChange(
            "Color", theOldColor, newcolor);
          theSupport.firePropertyChange("Color",
            theOldColor, newcolor);
          setText("" + color);
          theOldColor = newcolor;
       }
       catch (PropertyVetoException ex)
       {
          if(theOldColor != null)
             setColor(theOldColor.intValue());
       }
    }
```

continues

LISTING 9.6   CONTINUED

```java
public void actionPerformed(ActionEvent evt)
{
    setColor(getColor());
}

public void propertyChange(
    PropertyChangeEvent evt)
{
    Object value = evt.getNewValue();
    if (evt.getPropertyName().equals("Color")
        && value instanceof Integer)
    {
        setText("" + ((Integer) value).intValue());
    }
}

public void addPropertyChangeListener(
    PropertyChangeListener q)
{
    theSupport.addPropertyChangeListener(q);
}

public void removePropertyChangeListener(
    PropertyChangeListener q)
{
    theSupport.removePropertyChangeListener(q);
}

public void addVetoableChangeListener(
    VetoableChangeListener q)
{
    theVetoableSupport.
        addVetoableChangeListener(q);
}

public void removeVetoableChangeListener(
    VetoableChangeListener q)
{
    theVetoableSupport.
        removeVetoableChangeListener(q);
}
}

class ScrollSelector extends Scrollbar
    implements AdjustmentListener,
        VetoableChangeListener
{
    PropertyChangeSupport theSupport =
        new PropertyChangeSupport(this);
    Integer theOldColor = null;
```

```
public ScrollSelector()
{
   super(Scrollbar.HORIZONTAL);
   setMinimum(0);
   setMaximum(260);
   setValue(255);
   setVisibleAmount(5);
   addAdjustmentListener(this);
}

public int getColor()
{
   return getValue();
}

public void setColor(int color)
{
   setValue(color);
   Integer newcolor = new Integer(color);
   theSupport.firePropertyChange("Color",
     theOldColor, newcolor);
   theOldColor = newcolor;
}

public void adjustmentValueChanged(
  AdjustmentEvent evt)
{
   setColor(getColor());
}

public void vetoableChange(
  PropertyChangeEvent evt)
  throws PropertyVetoException
{
   Object value = evt.getNewValue();
   if (evt.getPropertyName().equals("Color")
     && value instanceof Integer)
   {
      int n = ((Integer) value).intValue();
      if (n < 0 || n > 255)
         throw new PropertyVetoException(
            "Color out of range", evt);
      setValue( ((Integer) value).intValue() );
   }
}

public void addPropertyChangeListener(
  PropertyChangeListener q)
{
```

9

**JAVA
SERIALIZATION
AND BEANS**

continues

LISTING 9.6   CONTINUED

```java
      theSupport.addPropertyChangeListener(q);
    }

    public void removePropertyChangeListener(
      PropertyChangeListener q)
    {
      theSupport.removePropertyChangeListener(q);
    }
  }

  class ColorCanvas extends Canvas implements
    PropertyChangeListener
  {
    public void propertyChange(
      PropertyChangeEvent evt)
    {
      Object value = evt.getNewValue();
      if (evt.getPropertyName().equals("Color")
        && value instanceof Integer)
      {
        int red = ((Integer) value).intValue();
        setBackground(new Color(red, 0, 0 ));
      }
    }
  }
}
```

The `TextSelector` class is more thoroughly revised. It now includes two support objects: one for `VetoableChangeListener` objects (such as the scrollbar) and one for `PropertyChangeListener` objects (such as the color swatch). Its `setColor` method now fires two events. The first is sent to listeners who may veto a change. The second is sent to ordinary listeners. If a listener vetoes the change, the `try-catch` handles the `PropertyVetoException`. Notice that the method does not send the `firePropertyChange` message if an exception occurs.

You can easily follow the model of these sample programs to create your own simple Beans. Moreover, you should now be able to understand the code your IDE generates when you add a Bean to your program. This will prove handy when your programs—or the Beans they contain—malfunction.

FROM HERE

This chapter concludes your study of advanced Java facilities. To see Java's serialization facility in use, see Chapter 15, "Remote Method Invocation (RMI)," which explains how serialization is important to Java distributed computing.

To study how Java Beans are being used to develop enterprise systems, see Chapter 17, "Java Help, Java Mail, and Other Java APIs," which describes key Java initiatives to facilitate development of enterprise-scale Java systems.

To see how JARs can be digitally signed, see Chapter 10, "Security," which also explains how signed applets can be granted broad privileges to access local resources.

JAVA'S NETWORKING AND ENTERPRISE APIS

IN THIS PART

SECURITY

IN THIS CHAPTER

Clifford Stoll's book *The Cuckoo's Egg* alerted the public to the danger posed by computer hackers. Unfortunately, the danger is real and grows greater by the moment: The ubiquitous Internet has greatly simplified the work of the would-be hacker, who no longer needs to discover the phone number of a dial-in modem in order to connect to a target system. If you implement systems that support remote access, you need a basic understanding of computer security and familiarity with Java's facilities for secure computing. In this chapter you'll learn:

- How Java was designed to thwart viruses, hackers, and other security threats

  From the first, Java was designed to provide a safe and reliable computing vehicle, immune to both casual and determined attacks or breaks in its security system.

- How to use Java's security tools to strike a balance between flexibility and security

  When users can access only the resources they need, security is enhanced. However, security comes at a price: A rigid security policy may hamper users' productivity, particularly if their needs change. Java lets you tailor a security policy that's neither too rigid nor too lax.

- How to write programs that work with encrypted data

  The Java Cryptography Extension (JCE) lets you write programs that encrypt and decrypt data using several popular algorithms.

- How to write programs that work with public and private encryption keys

  The `java.security` package of Java 1.2 includes classes and interfaces that let you work with public key encryption so that you can securely share data over a network.

> **NOTE**
>
> Most of the examples in this book are based on the Java 1.1 release. However, Java 1.2 significantly changes and upgrades Java's security facilities. Consequently, this chapter focuses on Java 1.2 and presents sample programs based on the Java 1.2 release. These programs were written and tested using the beta 4 release of Java 1.2. They will not operate correctly under Java 1.1.
>
> At the time of this writing, the current release of the Java Cryptography Extension (JCE) was early access release 2. The JCE API had not been frozen, so you should consult the CD-ROM and the latest information available from Sun to determine whether API changes affect the sample programs of this chapter. Also, the U.S. government has placed export restrictions on cryptographic technology that may prevent programmers outside the U.S. from obtaining the JCE. Consult the Javasoft Web site for the latest information on availability of the JCE.

SECURITY RISKS AND COUNTERMEASURES

When Sun introduced Java, the media fixated on Java applets. Netscape's early announcement of applet support within its Navigator browser excited almost everyone. Downloading cross-platform executable content was big news. Much press coverage focused on claims—some made by Sun and some made by others—that Java's security mechanisms were virtually impenetrable and that applets posed no risk to the downloader.

Soon, researchers began reporting successful breaches of Java security. Most attacks exploited obscure code or design errors that affected only a single implementation of Java, usually Netscape's Navigator or Microsoft's Internet Explorer. However, a few attacks exposed weaknesses in the security model; the new security features of Java 1.2 address some of these.

Fundamentally, attacks comprise four basic categories:

- Attacks that modify code or data
- Attacks that compromise confidentiality of information
- Attacks that acquire so many system resources that they deny legitimate users access to the resources (*denial of service* attacks)
- Attacks that annoy or antagonize users

Java's security model is designed to prevent all such attacks.

JAVA'S SECURITY MODEL

Java's security model includes three main components:

- The Byte Code Verifier, which examines the byte codes of a class before executing them
- The Class Loader, which restricts the classes that can be loaded into a Java virtual machine
- The Security Manager, which restricts access to potentially dangerous operations

By examining the byte codes of a class, the Byte Code Verifier can ensure that all byte codes represent legal Java virtual machine operations, that the class never compromises type safety of operands, that stack underflow and overflow cannot occur, and that the class methods observe all access specifiers (`public`, `private`, and `protected`). This verification rules out many types of potential attacks.

Java's Class Loader manages *name spaces* that prevent the programs running within a Java virtual machine from interfering with one another. Even if programs use identical class names, the Class Loader knows which class file each program should use. The Class Loader also ensures that users cannot load system classes. This prevents a *spoofing* attack wherein, for example, a user loads a system class that redefines the way the Java virtual machine performs file input/output.

Java's Security Manager controls access to critical system resources and operations. For example, the Security Manager prevents an applet from loading a substitute Class Loader that might inappropriately expand the applet's capabilities. Similarly, the Security Manager controls access to files. In Java 1.1, the Security Manager provided a *sandbox* in which applets ran. The sandbox restricted applets' access in many ways. For example, applets were not allowed to access files on the local system or open network connections to hosts other than the server that transmitted them. Java 1.2 provides a much more flexible Security Manager that allows you to define your own sandbox, which can be as rigid or flexible as you choose. Moreover, you can define a set of sandboxes, applying a different sandbox to each program. The next section explains how the new Security Manager works.

JAVA 1.2 SECURITY POLICIES

The Java 1.2 Security Manager lets you establish policies that govern access to system resources and operations. Under Microsoft Windows, these policies are stored in the file java.policy, which resides in the lib subdirectory of the standard JDK installation. The file contains one or more `grant` commands, which have the following syntax:

```
grant [SignedBy "signer_names"] [, CodeBase "URL"] {
  permission permission_class_name [ "target name']
    [, "action"] [, SignedBy "signer names"];
  permission ...
};
```

Each `grant` command specifies the permissions granted to a class or set of classes. The first `SignedBy` clause maps to a set of public keys that identify code signers. Java uses these keys to verify the authenticity of the classes. If you omit the `SignedBy` clause, Java does not check whether the specified class is signed or not.

You specify classes by using the `CodeBase` clause, which contains a URL. Typically, the URL specifies the `http` or `file` protocol. The `CodeBase` clause is optional: If you omit the `CodeBase` clause, the `grant` applies to every class. Rather than specify the URL of a class, you can specify the URL of a directory, in which case the `grant` applies to every class stored in the specified directory. For example, the default Microsoft Windows java.policy file contains the following entry:

```
grant codebase "file:${java.home}/lib/ext" {
  permission java.security.AllPermission;
```

This grant applies to classes that reside in the /lib/ext subdirectory of the standard JDK (represented by the Java system property `java.home`).

You specify permissions by naming the built-in Java class that enforces the policy. Table 10.1 lists some of the most important permission classes. By subclassing `Permission`, you can create your own permission classes and use them to create and enforce even more flexible security policies. Consult the JDK documentation for details.

TABLE 10.1 COMMONLY USED PERMISSION CLASSES

Class	*Function*
`java.io.FilePermission`	Controls access to files
`java.io.SocketPermission`	Controls access to sockets
`java.lang.RuntimePermission`	Controls access to threads and other system resources and operations
`java.util.PropertyPermission`	Controls access to properties

The `target` and `action` subclauses let you specify permissions more precisely. Each permission class determines the syntax and semantics of its `target` and `action` subclauses, which vary from one permission class to another. For example, the `java.io.FilePermission` class lets you specify a path in the `target` subclause and an operation ("read," "write," "execute," or "delete") in the `action` subclause. The JDK documentation for each permission class describes the class's `target` and `action` subclauses.

The second `SignedBy` clause specifies the signer of the permissions class. If Java cannot verify the signature of the permission class, the `grant` of that permission has no effect. The second `SignedBy` clause thwarts spoofing attacks; it should be used whenever the permission class does not reside within the Java runtime installation.

The following `grant` command gives local applets (and applications) all permissions, approximating their behavior under Java 1.1:

```
grant codebase "file:*" {
  permission java.security.AllPermission;
```

Of course, you may prefer a more rigid policy, particularly if others are able to load applets onto your computer. To allow local classes to access files, use this command:

```
grant codebase "file:*" {
  permission java.io.FilePermission "<<ALL FILES>>",
➥"read,write,execute,delete";
```

You can limit local classes to accessing files in a particular directory. Here's an example:

```
grant codebase "file:*" {
  permission java.io.FilePermission "c:/temp/*",
"read,write,execute,delete";
```

This command allows access only to files within the c:/temp directory. Notice that the directory is specified using a potentially platform-dependent form. As yet, Java does not support a platform-independent syntax. The preceding command does not confer ability to access files in subdirectories of c:/temp. You can allow such access by specifying this:

```
grant codebase "file:*" {
  permission java.io.FilePermission "c:/temp/-",
"read,write,execute,delete";
```

The dash allows recursive access to files and directories in and below c:/temp.

SECURITY TOOLS

Java 1.2 provides several tools that help you configure Java's security facilities. For example, the java.policy file is an ordinary text file that you can edit using a standard text editor. However, if you prefer, you can use policytool, a Java application that gives you a graphical user interface to the java.policy file.

In Java 1.1, you used javakey to write digital signatures, generate paired keys, and manage a database (the *keystore*) that associates entities with their digital keys. Java 1.2 provides a replacement tool, keytool, with enhanced functionality. You use keytool from the command line, using any of about a dozen command line options, each of which takes several options. To see these, simply type

keytool -help

at the command-line prompt. Consult the JDK documentation for up-to-date information on keytool and its options.

The jarsigner tool lets you add a digital signature to a Java archive (JAR) file. Like the policy tool, it accesses the digital signature database (keystore) maintained by keytool. You can also use the jarsigner tool to verify the signature on a JAR. Consult the JDK documentation for details on how to use this command-line tool.

THE JAVA CRYPTOGRAPHY EXTENSION (JCE)

Using the Java Cryptography Extension (JCE), you can write programs that encrypt and decrypt data and use passwords to protect against unauthorized access. To use the JCE, you need to include a line in your java.security file that names the SunJCE classes as providers of cryptographic services. Generally, your java.security file should contain only a single `policy` command. Near the middle of the file, find the following line:

```
policy.url.1=file:${java.home}/lib/security/java.policy
```

After it, add this line:

```
policy.url.2=file:${user.home}/.java.policy
```

If your java.security file contains several policy lines, you should add the new line following the last of these. Make the number following `policy.url.` the next consecutive number in the series. Your java.security file may already contain a line like the new line. If so, don't add the new line to the file.

In this section, you'll learn how to perform a variety of cryptographic tasks, including encryption and decryption of text, streams, and objects.

The Enigma Applet

Figure 10.1 shows the Enigma applet, a simple applet that demonstrates encryption and decryption. When you click the Encode button, the applet encrypts the contents of the Input text box and displays the cipher text in the Output text box. You can copy the cipher text, paste it into the Input text box, and click the Decode button. The result should be the original text.

FIGURE 10.1

The Enigma applet demonstrates encryption/decryption.

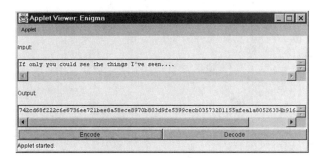

Listing 10.1 shows the source code of the Enigma applet. The applet defines two constants—`ALGORITHM` and `TRANSFORMATION`—that it uses to specify a cryptographic algorithm and related transformation. The DES algorithm, a popular cryptographic algorithm, is among several that JCE supports. The applet also defines a `SecretKey`, which it uses to hold a randomly generated key for encrypting and decrypting the data, and a `Cipher`, which performs encryption and decryption. The `try-catch` near the end of the `init` method contains statements that instantiate the `Cipher` object and generate the `SecretKey`.

LISTING 10.1   Enigma.java—ENCRYPTING AND DECRYPTING DATA

```java
import java.applet.*;
import java.awt.*;
import java.awt.event.*;
import java.security.*;
import javax.crypto.*;

public class Enigma extends Applet
{
    static final String ALGORITHM = "DES";
    static final String TRANSFORMATION = ALGORITHM + "/ECB/PKCS5Padding";

    TextArea theInputText     = new TextArea(10, 64);
    TextArea theOutputText    = new TextArea(10, 64);
    Button   theEncodeButton = new Button("Encode");
    Button   theDecodeButton = new Button("Decode");

    SecretKey theKey;
    Cipher    theCipher;

    public void init()
    {
        setLayout(new BorderLayout());
        Panel p1 = new Panel();
        Panel p2 = new Panel();
        p1.setLayout(new GridLayout(0, 1));
        p2.setLayout(new GridLayout(1, 0));
        add(p1, BorderLayout.CENTER);
        add(p2, BorderLayout.SOUTH);
        p1.add(new Label("Input:"));
        p1.add(theInputText);
        p1.add(new Label("Output:"));
        p1.add(theOutputText);
        p2.add(theEncodeButton);
        p2.add(theDecodeButton);
        Font f = new Font("Monospaced", Font.PLAIN, 12);
        theInputText.setFont(f);
        theOutputText.setFont(f);
        theOutputText.setEditable(false);
        theEncodeButton.addActionListener(new Encoder());
        theDecodeButton.addActionListener(new Decoder());

        try
        {
            theCipher     = Cipher.getInstance(TRANSFORMATION);
            KeyGenerator generator = KeyGenerator.getInstance(ALGORITHM);
            theKey        = generator.generateKey();
        }
        catch (Exception ex) { fatalError(ex); }
    }
```

```
    public void fatalError(Exception ex)
    {
        System.err.println("Fatal error:\n" + ex.toString());
        theOutputText.setText("Fatal error:\n" + ex.toString());
        ex.printStackTrace();
    }

    // inner classes omitted

}
```

Listing 10.2 shows the inner classes of the Enigma applet, which perform encryption and decryption in response to user interaction. The Cipher.init method initializes the Cipher, which operates in either ENCRYPT_MODE or DECRYPT_MODE. The doFinal method performs the cryptographic operation appropriate to the mode of Cipher. The Encode class generates a cipher text (a sequence of bytes that may include nonprintable characters). It converts the bytes to an appropriate display format by using the byteArrayToHexString method of the Hex utility class. The Decode class deals with the complementary operation—generating clear text from a sequence of bytes. It uses the hexStringToByteArray method to convert the displayed cipher text to its original binary format.

LISTING 10.2   Enigma.java—INNER CLASSES

```
class Encoder implements ActionListener
{
    public void actionPerformed(ActionEvent evt)
    {
        try
        {
            theCipher.init(Cipher.ENCRYPT_MODE, theKey);
            byte [] text = theInputText.getText().getBytes();
            byte [] codedtext = theCipher.doFinal(text);
            theOutputText.setText(Hex.byteArrayToHexString(codedtext));
        }
        catch (Exception ex) { fatalError(ex); }
    }
}

class Decoder implements ActionListener
{
    public void actionPerformed(ActionEvent evt)
    {
        try
        {
```

10

SECURITY

continues

LISTING 10.2   CONTINUED

```
            theCipher.init(Cipher.DECRYPT_MODE, theKey);
            String chars = theInputText.getText();
            byte [] text = Hex.hexStringToByteArray(chars);
            byte [] codedtext = theCipher.doFinal(text);
            theOutputText.setText(new String(codedtext));
        }
        catch (Exception ex) { fatalError(ex); }
    }
}
```

The EnigmaStream Applet

Figure 10.2 shows the EnigmaStream applet, which uses the CipherInputStream and
CipherOutputStream classes to encrypt and decrypt a data stream. When you type some
text in the Input text box and click the Encode button, the applet encodes your text and
writes it to a disk file. When you click the Decode button, the applet reads the file,
decrypts its contents, and displays them.

FIGURE 10.2

*The
EnigmaStream
applet encrypts
and decrypts a
stream.*

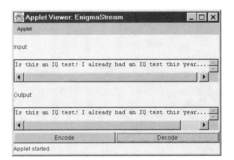

The full source code for the EnigmaStream applet resides on the CD-ROM. In the interest of conserving space, let's focus on the EnigmaStream applet's inner classes, which do
the interesting cryptographic work. These are shown in Listing 10.3.

LISTING 10.3   EnigmaStream.java—INNER CLASSES

```
class Encoder implements ActionListener
{
    public void actionPerformed(ActionEvent evt)
    {
        try
        {
            theCipher.init(Cipher.ENCRYPT_MODE, theKey);
            byte [] text = theInputText.getText().getBytes();
            CipherOutputStream out = new CipherOutputStream(
```

```
                new FileOutputStream("EnigmaStream.bin"),
                  theCipher);
                out.write(text);
                out.close();
                theOutputText.setText("");
            }
            catch (Exception ex) { fatalError(ex); }
        }
}

class Decoder implements ActionListener
{
    public void actionPerformed(ActionEvent evt)
    {
        try
        {
            theOutputText.setText("");
            theCipher.init(Cipher.DECRYPT_MODE, theKey);
            CipherInputStream in = new CipherInputStream(
              new FileInputStream("EnigmaStream.bin"),
              theCipher);
            int c;
            byte [] b = new byte [8];
            c = in.read(b);
            while (c != -1)
            {
                theOutputText.append(new String(b));
                c = in.read(b);
            }
        }
        catch (Exception ex) { fatalError(ex); }
    }
}
```

The Encoder class, like its relative in the Enigma applet, initializes a Cipher object by sending the Cipher object an init message. It places the contents of the Input text box in a byte array. It then instantiates a CipherOutputStream object, passing the constructor a FileOutputStream object and a reference to the Cipher object. Data written to the CipherOutputStream is automatically encrypted using the Cipher.

The Decoder class initializes the Cipher for decryption and instantiates a CipherInputStream. It then reads the stream, which is automatically decrypted, byte by byte. (Though reading byte by byte is simple, you may prefer to use buffered reads, which offer improved performance.)

The BlackBox Applet

Figure 10.3 shows the BlackBox applet, which shows how you can encrypt and decrypt an object, and how you can store an encrypted object in a file. When you click the Serialize button, the applet encrypts and stores the text box that appears in the upper-left part of the applet window. When you click the De-Serialize button, the applet reads the stored text box and adds it to the upper-right part of the applet window. By typing some text into the text box before you click Serialize, you can verify that the reconstituted text box faithfully preserves the state information of the original.

FIGURE 10.3

The BlackBox applet reads and writes an encrypted object.

Again, in the interest of conserving space, only the inner classes of the BlackBox applet are shown. The complete source code resides on the CD-ROM. The `Serializer` class uses the `SealedObject` class to encrypt the text box, which it writes to a disk file by using an `ObjectOutputStream`.

LISTING 10.4   `BlackBox.java`—INNER CLASSES

```java
class Serializer implements ActionListener
{
    public void actionPerformed(ActionEvent evt)
    {
        try
        {
            theCipher.init(Cipher.ENCRYPT_MODE, theKey);
            SealedObject dark = new SealedObject(theTextField, theCipher);
            ObjectOutputStream out = new ObjectOutputStream(
              new FileOutputStream("BlackBox.bin"));
            out.writeObject(dark);
            out.close();
        }
        catch (Exception ex) { fatalError(ex); }
    }
}

class DeSerializer implements ActionListener
{
    public void actionPerformed(ActionEvent evt)

        if (! isCallable) return;
```

```
    try
    {
        theCipher.init(Cipher.DECRYPT_MODE, theKey);
        ObjectInputStream in = new ObjectInputStream(
          new FileInputStream("BlackBox.bin"));
        SealedObject obj = (SealedObject) in.readObject();
        in.close();
        TextField t = (TextField) obj.getObject(theCipher);
        thePanel.add(t);
        invalidate();
        validate();
        isCallable = false;
    }
    catch (Exception ex) { fatalError(ex); }
  }
}
```

Its cousin, the DeSerializer class, reads the stored object by using an
ObjectInputStream. It casts the object returned by readObject to a SealedObject. By
sending the SealedObject the getObject message and providing the appropriate Cipher
as an argument, it decrypts the object, which it adds to the applet window. The class uses
the flag variable isCallable to prevent the user from instantiating multiple copies of the
stored object, because the user interface provides room for only the original text box and
one copy.

The Password Applet

Figure 10.4 shows the Password applet, which demonstrates how you can use a password
to authenticate access. The SecretKey used by the previous applets is a long text string
that's cumbersome—in fact, nearly impossible—for humans to recall or manipulate. By
mapping a simple password to a SecretKey, you facilitate human interaction. To operate
the applet, you enter a password and some text. When you click the Encode button, the
applet encrypts the text using a key that corresponds to the password you entered. When
you click the Decode button, the applet uses the current contents of the Password text
box to attempt to decode the cipher text. As you can see for yourself, the decryption succeeds only when you enter the same password originally used to encrypt the data.

Listing 10.5 shows the source code of the Password applet. Notice that the Password
applet imports a package, javax.crypto.spec, that the previous applets did not use. The
applet also includes two unfamiliar fields—a String that contains *salt*, and an int that
specifies an iteration count. The cryptographic algorithm uses these fields to convert the
password to a key. The salt should be a random String of eight characters that don't
need to be printable. The iteration count is usually a number in the range of 5–25; you
can use larger values, but at some cost in the amount of computation required to generate
the key.

FIGURE 10.4

The Password applet uses a password to grant access to encrypted data.

NOTE

The term *salt* refers to a random string that the cryptographic algorithm uses to convert the password to a key.

LISTING 10.5   `Password.java`—USING A PASSWORD TO GENERATE A KEY

```java
import java.applet.*;
import java.awt.*;
import java.awt.event.*;
import javax.crypto.*;
import javax.crypto.spec.*;

public class Password extends Applet
{
    static final String TRANSFORMATION = "PBEWithMD5AndDES";

    TextField thePassword      = new TextField();
    TextArea  theTextArea      = new TextArea(10, 64);
    Button    theEncodeButton  = new Button("Encode");
    Button    theDecodeButton  = new Button("Decode");

    SecretKey theKey;
    Cipher    theCipher;
    String    theSalt = "saltsalt"; // must have length of 8 characters
    int       theIterations = 17;
    byte []   theCipherText;

    PBEParameterSpec parmspec = new PBEParameterSpec(theSalt.getBytes(),
      theIterations);

    public void init()
    {
        setLayout(new BorderLayout());
        Panel p1 = new Panel();
        Panel p2 = new Panel();
        p1.setLayout(new GridLayout(0, 1));
        p2.setLayout(new GridLayout(1, 0));
```

```
        add(p1, BorderLayout.NORTH);
        add(theTextArea, BorderLayout.CENTER);
        add(p2, BorderLayout.SOUTH);
        p1.add(new Label("Password:"));
        p1.add(thePassword);
        p1.add(new Label("Text:"));
        p2.add(theEncodeButton);
        p2.add(theDecodeButton);
        Font f = new Font("Monospaced", Font.PLAIN, 12);
        thePassword.setFont(f);
        theTextArea.setFont(f);
        theEncodeButton.addActionListener(new Encoder());
        theDecodeButton.addActionListener(new Decoder());

        try
        {
            theCipher = Cipher.getInstance(TRANSFORMATION);
        }
        catch (Exception ex) { fatalError(ex); }
    }

    public void fatalError(Exception ex)
    {
        System.err.println("Fatal error:\n" + ex.toString());
        theTextArea.setText("Fatal error:\n" + ex.toString());
    }

    // inner classes omitted

}
```

Listing 10.6 shows the inner classes of the Password applet, where most of the crypto-graphic processing takes place. The PBEKeySpec object keyspec encapsulates the user-selected password. The getInstance method returns an instance of an appropriate factory for generating keys based on the transformation specified as an argument. (This, of course, is an example of the factory design pattern presented in Chapter 5, "Design Patterns.") The factory generates an appropriate key in response to the generateSecret message. Otherwise, the Encoder class functions much like the analogous inner classes of previous applets in this chapter.

LISTING 10.6   Password.java—INNER CLASSES

```
class Encoder implements ActionListener
{
    public void actionPerformed(ActionEvent evt)
    {
```

10

SECURITY

continues

LISTING 10.6 CONTINUED

```
        try
        {
            PBEKeySpec keyspec = new PBEKeySpec(
              thePassword.getText());
            SecretKeyFactory factory =
              SecretKeyFactory.getInstance(
                TRANSFORMATION);
            theKey = factory.generateSecret(keyspec);
            theCipher.init(Cipher.ENCRYPT_MODE, theKey,
              parmspec);
            byte [] text = theTextArea.getText().getBytes();
            theCipherText = theCipher.doFinal(text);
            theTextArea.setText("<Cipher text stored.>");
        }
        catch (Exception ex) { fatalError(ex); }
    }
}

class Decoder implements ActionListener
{
    public void actionPerformed(ActionEvent evt)
    {
        try
        {
            if (theCipherText == null) return;
            PBEKeySpec keyspec = new PBEKeySpec(
              thePassword.getText());
            SecretKeyFactory factory =
              SecretKeyFactory.getInstance(
                TRANSFORMATION);
            theKey = factory.generateSecret(keyspec);
            theCipher.init(Cipher.DECRYPT_MODE, theKey, parmspec);
            theCipherText = theCipher.doFinal(theCipherText);
            theTextArea.setText(new String(theCipherText));
        }
        catch (Exception ex) { fatalError(ex); }
    }
}
```

As usual, the Decoder class reverses the process. It generates a SecretKey from the password using the same process as the Encoder class. Once the key is in hand, decryption follows a pattern that should by now be familiar to you.

JAVA 1.2 SECURITY FEATURES

The previous applets of this chapter have used the JCE. However, Java 1.2 provides some useful security features of its own. In this section, you'll learn how to compute a message digest and how to use a public key to exchange secure data.

The MessageDigester Applet

A *message digest* is a hash total, or checksum, that reflects the contents of a message. Good algorithms for generating message digests yield a digest value that's sensitive to changes in the message and yet does not disclose information about the message. By comparing a transmitted message digest with a computed message digest, you can ensure that no one has tampered with the contents of the message.

Figure 10.5 shows the MessageDigester applet, which demonstrates how you can use classes of the java.security package to compute a message digest. To operate the applet, you click the Choose File button. A file dialog box pops up, letting you select a file. When you close the dialog box, the applet computes and displays a message digest for the file you selected.

FIGURE 10.5

The MessageDigester applet authenticates the contents of a message.

Listing 10.7 shows the source code for the MessageDigester class. The class includes a constant that specifies the algorithm used to compute the message digest. The SHA-1 algorithm, a popular algorithm for computing digests, is among several provided by the java.security package. Other than defining the algorithm constant, the class contains no cryptographic processing; it merely provides a user interface. The cryptographic processing is performed by the Chooser inner class.

LISTING 10.7   MessageDigester.java—COMPUTING A MESSAGE DIGEST   **10**

```
import java.applet.*;
import java.awt.*;
import java.awt.event.*;
import java.io.*;
```

continues

SECURITY

LISTING 10.7   CONTINUED

```java
import java.security.*;

public class MessageDigester extends Applet
{
    static final String ALGORITHM = "SHA-1";
    TextField theFileName = new TextField(64);
    TextField theDigest   = new TextField(64);
    Button    theChooseButton = new Button("Choose File");

    public void init()
    {
        setLayout(new GridLayout(0, 1));
        add(new Label("File Name:"));
        add(theFileName);
        add(new Label("Digest:"));
        add(theDigest);
        add(new Label(""));
        add(theChooseButton);
        Font f = new Font("Monospaced", Font.PLAIN, 12);
        theFileName.setFont(f);
        theDigest.setFont(f);
        theFileName.setEditable(false);
        theDigest.setEditable(false);
        theChooseButton.addActionListener(new Chooser());
    }

    public void fatalError(Exception ex)
    {
        ex.printStackTrace();
    }

    // inner classes omitted

}
```

Listing 10.8 shows the source code of the Chooser inner class, which provides the file dialog box for selecting a file and computes the message digest. To obtain the Frame reference that the FileDialog constructor requires, the actionPerformed method uses a little trick. It recursively examines the parent containers of the applet window, starting with the most immediate parent. When it discovers a Frame, it uses the Frame in the FileDialog constructor call. (It returns silently if no Frame is found. This is not a recommended coding technique, but it keeps the present example as simple as possible.)

LISTING 10.8   MessageDigester.java—INNER CLASS

```java
class Chooser implements ActionListener
{
    public void actionPerformed(ActionEvent evt)
    {
        Container c = getParent();
        while (c != null)
        {
            if (c instanceof Frame) break;
            c = c.getParent();
        }
        if (c == null) return;
        FileDialog fd = new FileDialog((Frame) c,
          "Choose A File", FileDialog.LOAD);
        fd.show();
        String file = fd.getFile();
        if (file != null)
        {
            try
            {
                String dir = fd.getDirectory();
                theFileName.setText(dir + file);
                MessageDigest digester =
                  MessageDigest.getInstance(ALGORITHM);
                FileInputStream in = new FileInputStream(
                  dir + file);
                int b = in.read();
                while (b != -1)
                {
                    digester.update((byte) b);
                    b = in.read();
                }
                in.close();
                byte [] digest = digester.digest();
                theDigest.setText(
                  Hex.byteArrayToHexString(digest));
            }
            catch (Exception ex) { fatalError(ex); }
        }
    }
}
```

If the user chooses a file using the file dialog box, the actionPerformed method accesses the directory and filename using getDirectory and getFile. It then instantiates a MessageDigest object for the SHA-1 algorithm. Next, it binds the specified file to a FileInputStream object and reads the contents of the file, byte by byte. The update message gives the MessageDigest object the opportunity to view each byte of the file. When the read loop reaches the end of the file, the digest message prompts the

10

SECURITY

`MessageDigest` to compute the final digest value. Like keys, the digest is a byte array that must be converted to printable form before being displayed. The `byteArrayToHexString` method performs this service.

The MessageSigner Applet

Message digests pose a problem: You must transmit both the message and the digest in a secure fashion. Otherwise, someone may modify the message and generate a new digest that reflects the surreptitious change. Public key cryptography presents one popular method of countering this threat.

In public key cryptography, keys are generated in pairs: a public key and a private key. A message sender signs a message using a private key that's known only to the sender. The result is a special type of message digest. The sender transmits the message and the digest to recipients, who already know the sender's public key. Recipients use the public key to verify that the message digest was computed using its private key counterpart. Because the private key is known only to the sender, recipients infer that the message was actually transmitted by the sender. Of course, the message can be clear text or encrypted text; its format doesn't matter to the signing and verification algorithms.

Figure 10.6 shows the MessageSigner applet, which demonstrates the signing and verification of messages by means of public key cryptography. To operate the applet, you first click the Generate Keys button to generate a public/private key pair. Then, you click the Choose File button and use a file dialog box to select a file to be used as a message. When you click the Generate Signature button, the applet generates and displays a digest that recipients can use, with the public key, to authenticate the source of the message. Finally, when you click the Verify Signature button, the applet uses the public key and digest to verify the authenticity of the message.

FIGURE 10.6

The MessageSigner applet authenticates the source and contents of a message.

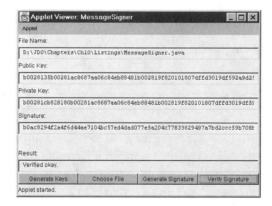

Listing 10.9 shows the source code of the MessageSigner applet. Notice that the applet imports the `java.security.spec` package, which the MessageDigest applet did not require. The MessageSigner applet uses a different algorithm than the MessageDigest applet. DSA is the popular *Digital Signature Algorithm*, which is based on the SHA-1 message digest algorithm. The `java.security` package supports several other algorithms.

LISTING 10.9   `MessageSigner.java`—SIGNING A DOCUMENT

```java
import java.applet.*;
import java.awt.*;
import java.awt.event.*;
import java.io.*;
import java.security.*;
import java.security.spec.*;

public class MessageSigner extends Applet
{
    static final String  ALGORITHM   = "DSA";
    static final int      KEY_MODULUS = 1024;
    static final byte [] SEED        =
      { (byte) 1, (byte) 2, (byte) 6, (byte) 6, (byte) 0 };

    TextField theFileName       = new TextField(64);
    TextField thePublicKey      = new TextField(64);
    TextField thePrivateKey     = new TextField(64);
    TextField theSignature      = new TextField(64);
    TextField theResult         = new TextField(64);
    Button    theGenerateButton = new Button("Generate Keys");
    Button    theChooseButton   = new Button("Choose File");
    Button    theSignButton     = new Button("Generate Signature");
    Button    theVerifyButton   = new Button("Verify Signature");

    public void init()
    {
        setLayout(new BorderLayout());
        Panel p1 = new Panel();
        Panel p2 = new Panel();
        add(p1, BorderLayout.CENTER);
        add(p2, BorderLayout.SOUTH);
        p1.setLayout(new GridLayout(0, 1));
        p1.add(new Label("File Name:"));
        p1.add(theFileName);
        p1.add(new Label("Public Key:"));
        p1.add(thePublicKey);
        p1.add(new Label("Private Key:"));
        p1.add(thePrivateKey);
```

continues

10

SECURITY

LISTING 10.9   CONTINUED

```
            p1.add(new Label("Signature:"));
            p1.add(theSignature);
            p1.add(new Label(""));
            p1.add(new Label("Result:"));
            p1.add(theResult);
            p2.setLayout(new GridLayout(1, 0));
            p2.add(theGenerateButton);
            p2.add(theChooseButton);
            p2.add(theSignButton);
            p2.add(theVerifyButton);

            Font f = new Font("Monospaced", Font.PLAIN, 12);
            theFileName.setFont(f);
            thePublicKey.setFont(f);
            thePrivateKey.setFont(f);
            theSignature.setFont(f);
            theFileName.setEditable(false);
            thePublicKey.setEditable(false);
            thePrivateKey.setEditable(false);
            theSignature.setEditable(false);
            theResult.setEditable(false);
            theGenerateButton.addActionListener(new Generator());
            theChooseButton.addActionListener(new Chooser());
            theSignButton.addActionListener(new Signer());
            theVerifyButton.addActionListener(new Verifier());
    }

    public void fatalError(Exception ex)
    {
        ex.printStackTrace();
    }

    // inner classes omitted

}
```

The applet defines a modulus value for the algorithm, which must be 512, 768, or 1024 for Sun's implementation of DSA. A larger modulus generates a more secure key, but at the cost of greater computing time. The applet also defines a random seed value. The SecureRandom class converts the specified value to a cryptographically secure random value. The main class primarily deals with the user interface. The interesting work is done by three of the four inner classes: Generator, Signer, and Verifier. The Chooser inner class merely provides the file dialog box.

Listing 10.10 shows the source code of the Generator inner class. Its actionPerformed method uses the static KeyPairGenerator.getInstance method to obtain a reference to a `KeyPairGenerator`, which it initializes and uses to generate a public/private key pair. The method then uses the `byteArrayToHexString` method to encode the keys for display. Coincidentally, the method displays a description of each key, including the format and length of the key, on `System.out`.

LISTING 10.10 `MessageSigner.java`—Generator INNER CLASS

```
class Generator implements ActionListener
{
    public void actionPerformed(ActionEvent evt)
    {
        try
        {
            KeyPairGenerator generator =
              KeyPairGenerator.getInstance(ALGORITHM);
            generator.initialize(KEY_MODULUS,
              new SecureRandom(SEED));
            KeyPair keypair = generator.generateKeyPair();
            PublicKey  pubkey  = keypair.getPublic();
            PrivateKey privkey = keypair.getPrivate();
            byte [] bytes = pubkey.getEncoded();
            thePublicKey.setText(Hex.byteArrayToHexString(bytes));
            System.out.println("Public Key Format:" +
              pubkey.getFormat() + " Length=" +
              thePublicKey.getText().length());
            bytes = privkey.getEncoded();
            thePrivateKey.setText(Hex.byteArrayToHexString(bytes));
            System.out.println("Private Key Format:" +
              privkey.getFormat() + " Length=" +
              thePrivateKey.getText().length());
        }
        catch (Exception ex) { fatalError(ex); }
    }
}
```

Listing 10.11 shows the `Signer` inner class, which computes the message signature by using the private key. The program doesn't save the value of the private key generated by the `Generate` class. Instead, the `Signer` class recovers the value of the private key from the contents of the text box that displays the value of the private key. Sun's implementation of DSA stores private keys in the PKCS#8 format; therefore, the `actionPerformed` method uses the `PKCS8EncodedKeySpec` constructor and the `KeyFactory.generatePrivate` method to instantiate a duplicate private key. The method then instantiates a `Signature` object and sends the object a sequence of `update` messages, one for each byte of the message. Finally, the method uses the `sign` message to obtain a signature from the `Signature` object.

10

SECURITY

LISTING 10.11   `MessageSigner.java`—Signer INNER CLASS

```java
class Signer implements ActionListener
{
    public void actionPerformed(ActionEvent evt)
    {
        try
        {
            String file = theFileName.getText();
            String hex = thePrivateKey.getText();
            byte [] bytes = Hex.hexStringToByteArray(hex);
            KeyFactory factory = KeyFactory.getInstance(ALGORITHM);
            KeySpec keyspec = new PKCS8EncodedKeySpec(bytes);
            PrivateKey pkey = factory.generatePrivate(keyspec);
            Signature dsa = Signature.getInstance(ALGORITHM);
            dsa.initSign(pkey);
            FileInputStream in =
              new FileInputStream(file);
            int b = in.read();
            while (b != -1)
            {
                dsa.update((byte) b);
                b = in.read();
            }
            in.close();
            byte [] signature = dsa.sign();
            theSignature.setText(
              Hex.byteArrayToHexString(signature));
        }
        catch (Exception ex) { fatalError(ex); }
    }
}
```

Listing 10.12 shows the `MessageSigner` class, which verifies a message signature. It reconstructs a public key using a technique parallel to that used in the `Generator` method. The main difference is that Sun's DSA implementation stores public keys in the X509 format, rather than the PKCS#8 format it uses for private keys. Again, this method uses the `update` message to update an instance of `Signature`, which verifies the signature upon receiving the `verify` message. The `verify` message returns `true` if the signature is authentic.

LISTING 10.12   `MessageSigner.java`—Verifier INNER CLASS

```java
class Verifier implements ActionListener
{
    public void actionPerformed(ActionEvent evt)
    {
        try
```

```
    {
        String hex = thePublicKey.getText();
        byte [] bytes = Hex.hexStringToByteArray(hex);
        KeyFactory factory = KeyFactory.getInstance(ALGORITHM);
        KeySpec keyspec = new X509EncodedKeySpec(bytes);
        PublicKey pkey = factory.generatePublic(keyspec);
        Signature dsa = Signature.getInstance(ALGORITHM);
        dsa.initVerify(pkey);
        String file = theFileName.getText();
        FileInputStream in =
          new FileInputStream(file);
        int b = in.read();
        while (b != -1)
        {
            dsa.update((byte) b);
            b = in.read();
        }
        in.close();
        hex = theSignature.getText();
        bytes = Hex.hexStringToByteArray(hex);
        if(dsa.verify(bytes))
            theResult.setText("Verified okay.");
        else
            theResult.setText("Verification failed.");
    }
    catch (Exception ex) { fatalError(ex); }
    }
}
```

FROM HERE

This chapter provided an overview of Java's security facilities and showed you how use them to implement common security functions. You learned how to encrypt and decrypt messages, how to use passwords, how to compute and verify message digests, and how to compute and verify digital signatures. The following chapters describe non-Java security facilities that are important to developers of distributed systems:

- Chapter 20, "Distributed Component Object Model (DCOM)," describes Microsoft's Component Object Model, including its security facilities.
- Chapter 33, "Other CORBA Facilities and Services," describes the security facilities of the Common Object Request Broker Architecture (CORBA).

10

SECURITY

RELATIONAL DATABASES AND STRUCTURED QUERY LANGUAGE (SQL)

IN THIS CHAPTER

If you're new to databases, you might suppose that a relational database is a database owned by someone's cousin, or that Structured Query Language is an obscure, ritualistic idiom used by tourists to request directions. However, relational databases and Structured Query Language have nothing to do with family relations or tourist information. Instead, they're the dominant vehicles for managing data in modern software systems. In this chapter you'll learn:

- Why relational databases are important to distributed systems

  Relational databases offer several advantages over flat-file data storage or object-oriented databases.

- How Structured Query Language (SQL) makes relational databases easy to use

  Because many vendors have implemented SQL databases on a variety of platforms, SQL helps you build portable applications.

- How to use SQL to define relational databases

  SQL's Data Definition Language (DDL) and Data Control Language (DCL) let you define and configure relational databases.

- How to use SQL to access and manipulate data held in a relational database

  SQL's Data Manipulation Language (DML) lets you write portable queries that extract or modify database data.

DATABASE CONCEPTS

A *database*, in the simplest sense, is merely an organized collection of data. In the early days of programming, a database consisted of a collection of files whose organization was implicit in the application programs that maintained the files. As the art of programming developed, programmers began to separate data management code from application code. By writing somewhat general data management software, they were able to use it to support multiple application systems, thus decreasing the cost of developing new applications. Eventually, data management software packages, called *database management systems* (or *DBMSs*) became commercially available. Soon thereafter, the term *database* came to refer to the DBMS as well as the data managed by the DBMS, in much the same way that we refer to a microwave oven as simply a *microwave*.

Currently, you can store application data in any of three main ways:

- In flat files (that is, ordinary sequential or random-access files)
- In a relational database
- In an object-oriented database

Each of these poses advantages or potential advantages. Let's take a minute to go over them.

Flat Files

As mentioned, the earliest way of storing application data was flat files. Because flat files are ancient (at least in the software sense of the word), you might wonder whether they have any value today. Here are some instances when you may want to use flat files to store application data:

- When the structure of the data is simple and static, the volume of data is small, and the data is accessed by one process at a time on a single, secure system

- When the cost of a database is prohibitive

- When you require extremely high performance

When the structure of the data is simple and static and the volume of data is small, flat files may be an appropriate data management vehicle. However, if you must provide remote access to the data, or if the data must be shared, you're advised to use a relational or object-oriented database. Remote access and data sharing can be difficult to implement, especially for applications programmers, who often lack training and experience in the subtleties of network and concurrent programming.

You're also advised to use a database when the structure of your data may change from time to time. When you use flat files, your application programs must organize the data. Changes to the way file data is formatted or structured often require expensive and time-consuming changes to applications programs. Occasionally, a seemingly minor change in data structure requires that an entire system be rewritten. Databases were invented to solve this very problem, so you should use one when the risk of change is substantial.

For some applications, modern databases seem prohibitively expensive. An industrial-strength database may cost thousands of dollars, putting it beyond the reach of some small organizations or nonprofit organizations. In such a case, using flat files may be the only feasible alternative. However, you should thoroughly explore the options before writing your own data management software, which you may discover costs even more to build than buy. Some shareware and freeware databases offer impressive functionality at little or no cost. By building your application around a database, you may decrease the cost of system development and ownership.

A database contains a *schema* that stores *meta information*. The meta information contained in the schema describes the location and format of every item of data stored in the database. Application programs that access the database use a special API that finds data using the schema and converts it to the requested format, regardless how the data is actually stored. This approach provides *data independence*: When the structure or format of the data within the database changes, the database can often continue to provide the data in a way acceptable to old programs, which therefore don't need to be modified to accommodate the change. The result is decreased cost of ownership—something users' managers greatly enjoy.

Modern databases are relational or object oriented. More accurately, most modern databases are somewhat relational and somewhat object oriented. To understand the difference, let's explore the notion of a relational database.

Relational Databases

Just as your kitchen blender dices carrots and celery into small, uniform pieces, a relational database dices data. By storing the structure of data in its schema and dividing data into the smallest possible atoms, relational databases achieve great flexibility. Because the unit of data is so small, it's virtually guaranteed that the schema contains everything important about the structure of the data. A complete schema lets the database API rearrange data into any requested form that's consistent with the nature of the data.

In practice, the structure of a relational database resembles that of the familiar spreadsheet, consisting of cells grouped in *rows* and *columns* (see Figure 11.1). Each row contains information about a single thing, or *entity*. Each column of the database contains cells that specify a particular entity characteristic, known as an *attribute*. For instance, an employee database might contain a row for each employee of a company. The first column might specify the employee number, the second might specify the employee name, and so on. Every row of a database has exactly the same structure: If the first column specifies employee number, the first cell in every row must contain an employee number.

FIGURE 11.1

A relational database resembles a spreadsheet with rows and columns.

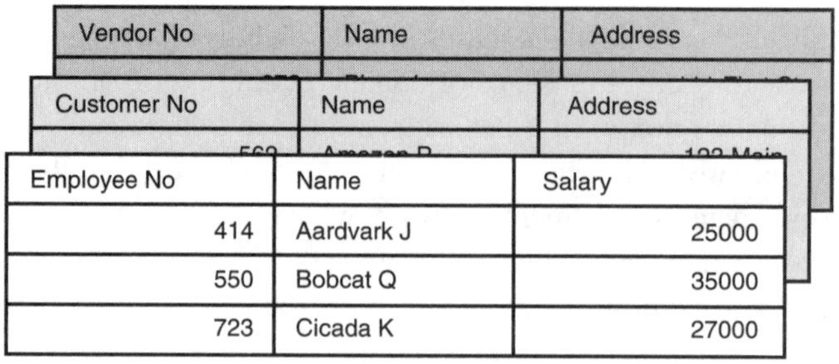

Vendor No	Name	Address

Customer No	Name	Address

Employee No	Name	Salary
414	Aardvark J	25000
550	Bobcat Q	35000
723	Cicada K	27000

Unfortunately, several terms are used to describe common database components. Rows are sometimes referred to as *records*, and columns are sometimes referred to as *fields*.

Most databases contain a variety of information. To accommodate this, databases generally include multiple *tables*, each with the familiar spreadsheet structure. For example, the database shown in Figure 11.1 includes tables describing employees, customers, and vendors.

Although a relational database is adept at storing the primitive attributes that comprise an object, it may be less capable of storing an encapsulated object that includes attributes and methods. This capability is the distinctive talent of object-oriented databases, which are becoming increasingly popular.

Object-Oriented Databases

Having an object-oriented database is like having object serialization on wheels. Rather than write objects to disk files via streams, you write them to a database that can catalog and manage them. Relational databases sometimes handle complex interobject relationships clumsily, but object-oriented databases were written with this requirement in mind. In sophisticated application domains such as CAD/CAM, object-oriented databases rule, and they're steadily making inroads into more mundane domains such as business information systems.

In response to the growing enthusiasm for object-oriented databases, most vendors of relational databases have provided some degree of object-oriented support within their databases. As a result, it's somewhat difficult to precisely characterize an object-oriented database. However, relational databases possess one important characteristic that hasn't yet been mentioned: They support Structured Query Language (SQL).

RELATIONAL DATABASE STRUCTURE

Because relational databases are vastly better standardized than object-oriented databases, the remainder of this chapter will focus on relational databases and on SQL in particular. When you're finished with the chapter, you'll know how to use SQL to perform common database tasks, such as defining tables and accessing, deleting, and updating data. Before presenting the fundamentals of SQL, let's dig a little deeper into the structure of relational databases.

Keys and Indexes

One of the basic properties of objects is identity. In an object-oriented system, you can ask whether two variables refer to the same object or different objects, and you can expect a correct, meaningful response. Relational databases store rows, which closely resemble objects. However, rows contain only data, whereas objects encapsulate data and the operations that act upon the data. If you recall that every object has a distinct identity, the similarity between rows and objects may suggest to you that each database row should have a distinct identity.

Often, one column of a database table contains values that are unique to each table row. For example, a table containing data about employees might include a column that holds an employee number that's unique to each employee. In such a case, you may designate the unique-valued column as the *primary key* of the table. Primary keys pose advantages beyond mere identification of records. Many databases provide indexes that speed retrieval of table rows. A database that indexes its employee table by employee number lets programs quickly access the row for a given employee by means of the employee number. Without a primary key, access requires a potentially time-consuming serial scan of the table rows.

When a table contains no unique-valued column, you have several alternatives. You could simply define no primary key, but the advantage of immediate access to rows is usually too great a prize to forego. Fortunately, two other alternatives present themselves: using a compound key and using an artificial key. A *compound key* is a series of columns that, taken together, are unique to every row. For example, suppose a company has two employment offices, each of which assigns serial employee numbers. Two employees could possibly have the same number. However, if the database stores a column that identifies the employment office that processed the employee, the problem of "nonuniqueness" vanishes. The combination of employment office and employee number is unique to each employee.

The other alternative is the *artificial key*, which is simply an assigned value, usually a number. In building an employee information system, you might be tempted to use the social security number column as the primary key of the employee table. However, experience shows that supposedly unique social security numbers are sometimes not unique at all. By assigning your own number, you can ensure that every employee has a unique identifier. Using the earlier example of a company with two employment offices, you might simply assign one block of numbers for use by one office and another block for use by the other. The resulting employee numbers would be unique in themselves, without recourse to a compound key that combines the employment office identifier with the employee number.

Generally, every table of a database should have a primary key. In addition, some tables may have foreign keys. A *foreign key* is simply a column that contains values that are primary key values of some database table. For example, suppose your sales database includes two tables: a customer table and a transaction table. The customer table contains the name and address of each customer, and the transaction table shows the items and quantities purchased by each customer, along with the date of purchase and the price paid.

Relational Databases and Structured Query Language (SQL)

CHAPTER 11

253

11

RELATIONAL
DATABASES AND
SQL

You could store the customer name and address in each transaction row; however, it's more efficient to store only the primary key of the customer table, which is the customer ID (as you can see in Figure 11.2). Given the customer ID, you can look up the customer's name and address, so you lose nothing by this abbreviation of content. On the contrary, you gain a great deal: Your database now stores each customer's name and address only once, rather than in each row describing a purchase by the customer. When a customer changes address, you can update a single row, rather than searching the database for all the transaction rows that pertain to the customer. This reduced redundancy improves database performance: The database occupies less storage space, and queries are processed more quickly. Those of you who have extensive database experience recognize this as *database normalization*.

FIGURE 11.2

Foreign keys help control data redundancy.

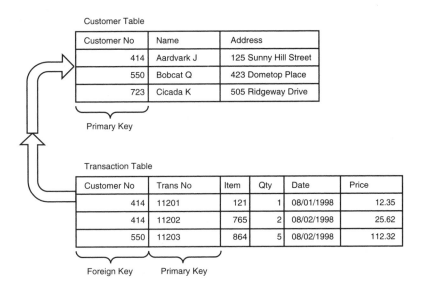

Customer Table

Customer No	Name	Address
414	Aardvark J	125 Sunny Hill Street
550	Bobcat Q	423 Dometop Place
723	Cicada K	505 Ridgeway Drive

Primary Key

Transaction Table

Customer No	Trans No	Item	Qty	Date	Price
414	11201	121	1	08/01/1998	12.35
414	11202	765	2	08/02/1998	25.62
550	11203	864	5	08/02/1998	112.32

Foreign Key   Primary Key

Constraints

Recall that a relational database schema contains a description of a database, including its contents, format, and organization. Modern relational database schemas store not only what is, but what's allowed. When you specify a database *constraint*, the database checks the result of each operation before performing the operation. If the result would violate a constraint, the database rejects the operation. This helps ensure that database data is always valid.

Databases constrain the value of database data. For instance, a database will not let you store a nonnumeric value in a numeric field. In addition to such common-sense constraints that function automatically, SQL lets you specify several additional types of constraints. One type of constraint restricts the ability to add table rows that omit specified columns. Such a constraint might prevent you from adding a row to an employee table unless the employee name column is included. Thanks to the constraint, your database won't contain any nameless employees, which might cause the payroll application to choke.

Another important type of constraint concerns the relationship between primary keys and foreign keys. Such a constraint might preclude you from adding a transaction that pertains to a nonexistent customer. The constraint is useful because the value of the foreign key customer number of the transaction table does not have a matching value in the customer table (where it's the primary key).

SQL CONCEPTS

SQL is an ANSI/ISO standardized language for defining and using relational databases. Although a few dialectical differences exist among major implementations of SQL, most relational database vendors provide a SQL interpreter that lets programmers write more-or-less portable SQL programs (or *queries*, as they're called). Incompatibilities generally arise from the use of vendor-specific SQL extensions, rather than bread-and-butter SQL syntax.

SQL includes three sublanguages:

- Data Definition Language (DDL), which lets you define and revise the structure of relational databases
- Data Control Language (DCL), which lets you specify data security and integrity mechanisms that safeguard data
- Data Manipulation Language (DML), which lets you read and write data

Most dialectical differences affect DCL, because security and integrity mechanisms vary somewhat from vendor to vendor. Consequently, vendors have sometimes elected to go their own way rather than implement orthodox DCL. In comparison, DDL and DML are relatively standard from vendor to vendor. Differences in platform characteristics, such as character collating sequence, intrude on portability more than differences in SQL syntax or semantics.

You can use SQL in a variety of ways. Most vendors provide a command-line shell that lets you type SQL queries and send them to the SQL interpreter for processing. *Interactive SQL*, as this method of use is called, is convenient for developing and debugging queries, but it provides no simple way to get query results into program variables. Consequently, most application systems use *embedded SQL*. Embedded SQL lets your

Relational Databases and Structured Query Language (SQL)

CHAPTER 11

255

11

RELATIONAL
DATABASES AND
SQL

programs send SQL queries to the SQL interpreter and receive results in program variables. Some vendors implement embedded SQL using subroutine calls, whereas others use macros that are expanded into source code by a macro preprocessor. Java's mechanism for sending and receiving SQL queries is JDBC, which is the subject of the next chapter.

Experts may disagree concerning the characteristics that an object-oriented database must possess. However, implementation of SQL is a defining characteristic of relational databases. Because almost every non-SQL database is touted as "object-oriented," it makes sense to refer to SQL databases and non-SQL databases rather than SQL databases and object-oriented databases. This is especially true because, as mentioned, SQL database vendors are including more object-oriented facilities in their databases.

However, the internal architecture of SQL-oriented databases is usually quite different from that of object-oriented databases. Even if both camps eventually provide functional support of SQL, important performance differences will probably remain. If you're interested in storing data, you should seek a suitable SQL-oriented database. If you're interested in storing objects, you should, if possible, seek an object-oriented database that provides significant SQL functionality and, where possible, use standard SQL queries rather than vendor-proprietary API calls. This approach will yield tremendous dividends if your application is ever rehosted.

Work continues on an updated SQL standard that provides object-oriented facilities. However, it seems that it will take some time to finalize the standard and an even longer period for vendors to gear up to support it. In the meantime, the choice of database vendor for distributed systems development will be somewhat problematical.

DATA DEFINITION LANGUAGE

Now that you have a solid understanding of the fundamentals of relational databases, you're ready to learn some SQL. Of course, merely reading one chapter won't make you proficient in SQL; the goals are for you to have a solid understanding of what SQL can do and to be able to read most common SQL statements. Like learning to program in Java, learning to program in SQL requires practice and therefore time. Because our goals are limited, the chapter presents some of the SQL statements in abbreviated form. You should consult your database documentation to discover what further options your database supports. Better yet, get a copy of a book on SQL that explains the SQL standard. That way, you won't be tempted to use vendor-specific statements and options that may hamper the portability of your application.

Creating a Database

Let's begin with DDL, the Data Definition Language, which you use to define the structure of a database. The most basic DDL statement is the Create Database statement, which you use to create a new database. Unfortunately, the options involved in database creation vary somewhat from vendor to vendor; consequently, the Create Database statement is one of the least standard SQL statements. You'll need to consult your database documentation or your database administrator to determine the proper syntax. You may even find that your database doesn't support the Create Database statement. To give you an idea what to expect, here's the syntax used by Microsoft SQL Server:

```
Create Database name
  [ On { default ¦ device } [ = size ] [, device [ = size ]] ... ]
  [ Log On device [ = size ] [, device [ = size ]] ... ]
  [For Load]
```

The square brackets ([ ]) indicate optional clauses. The curly braces ({}) indicate alternatives from which you must choose. Italicized tokens are names or values you must specify.

As you can see, the SQL Server form of the Create Database statement lets you name the database and create database regions on multiple devices, which are not physical devices but rather specially formatted areas controlled by SQL Server. Using the Log On clause, you can specify a set of devices to hold the database log, which records significant events. The For Load clause tells SQL Server that you plan to load a database backup image into the database; this clause lets SQL Server forego some of the work it would normally perform in preparation for use of the database.

Creating Tables

Once you've created a database, you're ready to create one or more tables. The Create Table statement has the following form:

```
Create Table name
  ( columnname datatype [ null ¦ not null ] [, ... ] )
```

Each table includes a series of columns, each having a data type. Table 11.1 summarizes some of the most useful SQL data types.

TABLE 11.1 COMMONLY USED SQL DATA TYPES

Data Type	Description
BIT(n)	A fixed-length series of exactly n Boolean (true/false) values
BIT VARYING(n)	A series of as many as n Boolean values
CHARACTER(n)	A fixed-length string of exactly n characters (abbreviated CHAR)

Data Type	Description
CHARACTER VARYING	A string of text characters
DATE	A date
DECIMAL(p,q)	A decimal number having p digits, of which q are specified as assumed decimal digits (abbreviated DEC)
FLOAT(p)	A floating-point number of precision p
INTEGER	A signed integer of implementation-defined size (abbreviated INT)
SMALLINT	A signed integer of an implementation-defined size not larger than that of INTEGER
TIME	A time of day, including hours, minutes, and seconds
TIMESTAMP	A date and time, indicating a specific time of a specific day

The NULL option specifies that the column doesn't need to be present when you add the database row; the NOT NULL option specifies that the column must be present. If you don't specify either NULL or NOT NULL, the SQL interpreter handles rows that lack data in an implementation-defined manner. That is, some database engines reject a row that contains a NULL column, whereas other database engines accept such a row. So that you can migrate your program from one database engine to another, you should always specify either NULL or NOT NULL. Doing so will cause your program to behave properly regardless of the database engine you use.

Recall that most database tables have a primary key. You can specify the primary key using the following Create Table clause:

```
Primary Key (columns)
```

Here, *columns* is a comma-separated list of columns that comprise the primary key.

Some database tables have one or more foreign keys. You can specify a foreign key using the following Create Table clause:

```
Foreign Key (columns) References table
```

As before, *columns* is a comma-separated list of columns that comprise the foreign key. Also, *table* names the table whose primary key matches the values of the foreign key of Create Table. You can include multiple Foreign Key clauses in a Create Table. If the column of the created table has a different name than the primary key of the referenced table, you can use the following form of the Foreign Key clause:

```
Foreign Key (columns) References table (columns)
```

As an example, here's a `Create Table` statement that creates a simple invoice detail file:

```
Create Table InvoiceDetail
  (InvoiceNo Char(5) Not Null,
   LineNo Char(2) Not Null,
   CustomerNo Char(5) Not Null,
   InvoiceDate Date Not Null,
   ItemNo Char(5) Not Null,
   Qty INT Not Null,
   UnitPrice DEC(10,2) Not Null)
  Primary Key (InvoiceNo, LineNo)
  Foreign Key (InvoiceNo) References Invoice
  Foreign Key (CustomerNo) References Customer
  Foreign Key (ItemNo) References Item
```

This statement creates a table named `InvoiceDetail` that includes seven columns:

- `InvoiceNo`: A five-character string
- `LineNo`: A two-character string
- `CustomerNo`: A five-character string
- `InvoiceDate`: A date
- `ItemNo`: A five-character string
- `Qty`: An integer
- `UnitPrice`: A 10-digit decimal number with two decimal digits

The primary key of the `InvoiceDetail` table is a compound key consisting of `InvoiceNo` and `LineNo`. The table has three foreign keys:

- `InvoiceNo` references a like-named column that's the primary key of the `Invoice` table.
- `CustomerNo` references a like-named column that's the primary key of the `Customer` table.
- `ItemNo` references a like-named column that's the primary key of the `Item` table.

None of the columns of the InvoiceLine table is optional; therefore, each column specification includes the `Not Null` option.

The `Alter Table` statement lets you alter the structure of an existing table. Its clauses and options are similar to those of the `Create Table` statement. The `Drop Table` statement lets you delete the table and the information it contains. Obviously, you should use the `Drop Table` statement with caution. Its form is simply this:

```
Drop table
```

DATA MANIPULATION LANGUAGE

Once you've created your database and its tables, you're ready to begin using them. The statements you use to add and maintain data derive their form from the statements you use to retrieve data. So, you'll first learn how to read database data. Later in the chapter, you'll learn how to write it.

Select

To read data, you use the Select statement. The Select statement offers a rich variety of clauses and options. To help you quickly get a grasp of SQL, this chapter focuses on the most basic forms. If you want to write efficient and sophisticated Select statements, you'll find this art a lifelong study.

The most basic Select statement has the following form:

```
Select * From table
```

This Select statement retrieves every column of every row in the specified table. You shouldn't use this simple form for three reasons:

- You probably need only a subset of the table rows and columns: This query is inefficient, wasting computer and network resources to provide and transmit unneeded data.

- You'll receive the columns in an implementation-defined sequence. Worse yet, the result of the query will change when you add or drop table columns. Such changes may cause programs that use this form of Select statement to malfunction.

- You'll often need data from several database tables, but this form of Select statement returns data from only a single table.

Here's a slightly more sophisticated form of the Select statement that avoids the cited problems:

```
Select columns From tables [Where condition]
```

Both *columns* and *tables* are comma-separated lists. For instance, here's a Select statement that returns only the ItemNo and Qty columns from the InvoiceLine table:

```
Select ItemNo, Qty From InvoiceLine
```

Here's a Select statement that should cause you to appreciate the power of relational databases and SQL:

```
Select CustomerName, InvoiceDate From InvoiceLine, Customer
  Where InvoiceLine.CustomerNo = Customer.CustomerNo
```

This statement retrieves data from two tables: InvoiceLine and Customer. The *dot notation* used in `InvoiceLine.CustomerNo` lets you refer to the CustomerNo column of the InvoiceLine table, even though the Customer table contains an identically named column. Because the two tables are related (CustomerNo is a foreign key of the InvoiceLine table, referring to the primary key of the Customer table), the SQL interpreter can *join* them. The query makes it easy to access the CustomerName column with InvoiceLine data; it's almost as though CustomerName were a column of the InvoiceLine table. Such teamwork between the relational model and SQL makes relational databases extremely useful. They let you control data redundancy—for example, by storing CustomerName only once—but let you conveniently access data spread across several tables. Of course, many such tables may contain the foreign key CustomerNo; therefore, redundancy is not eliminated but merely reduced.

Expressions

Suppose you need the dollar amount of an invoice line. The InvoiceLine table contains the quantity (Qty) and unit price (UnitPrice), but you need their product. No problem: The `Select` statement supports expressions using the familiar arithmetic operators (+, -, *, and /). To get the dollar amount of each invoice line, you can write:

```
Select Qty*UnitPrice From Invoice
```

Of course, this `Select` statement, like the previous `Select` statements you've seen, returns every row of the table. Let's see how to limit the data returned by a `Select` statement so that you don't waste computer resources.

Predicates

You've seen the `Where` clause used in a simple join that combined data from two tables. You can also use the `Where` to limit the rows returned by a query. For example, suppose you need to know the customer numbers of customers who've purchased expensive items costing over $1,000. The following statement does the trick (although it has a small flaw you'll discover momentarily):

```
Select CustomerNo From InvoiceLine Where UnitPrice >= 1000.00
```

Table 11.2 summarizes the most useful SQL comparison operators. You can also use `And`, `Or`, and `Not` to combine comparison expressions.

TABLE 11.2 COMMONLY USED SQL COMPARISON OPERATORS

Operator	Meaning
=	Equal to
>	Greater than

Operator	Meaning
<	Less than
>=	Greater than or equal to
<=	Less than or equal to
!=	Not equal to (same as <>)
<>	Not equal to (same as !=)

Sorting and Grouping

The queries that you've seen so far return their result in arbitrary order. Often, you'd prefer that results be presented in a specified order. You can achieve this by using the Order By clause. For example, to return an alphabetical list of customers, you could write:

```
Select CustomerName From Customer Order By CustomerName
```

Of course, this query won't work correctly if the CustomerName column contains values such as "John Zylingu." The SQL interpreter simply sorts the data using the specified column, putting John near the middle of the alphabet (*John*) rather than near the end (*Zylingu*). If you want to sort by customer name, the CustomerName column should contain values such as "Zylingu, John," or you should define separate columns for the customer's first and last names. If you store the names separately, you can use a query like this one to sort the names:

```
Select CustomerFirstName, CustomerLastName From Customer
  Order By CustomerLastName, CustomerFirstName
```

Recall the earlier query that returned customers who've purchased expensive items. Suppose you modified it to present the list alphabetically:

```
Select CustomerName From InvoiceLine, Customer
  Where InvoiceLine.CustomerNo = Customer.CustomerNo
    And UnitPrice >= 1000.00
  Order By CustomerName
```

The SQL interpreter presents the results alphabetically, but a customer who purchased several items appears in the list several times, once for each row of InvoiceLine. This is the flaw mentioned earlier. You can prevent this duplication by using the Group By clause:

```
Select CustomerName From InvoiceLine, Customer
  Where InvoiceLine.CustomerNo = Customer.CustomerNo
    And UnitPrice >= 1000.00
  Group By CustomerName
```

The Group By sorts the rows in the specified order, but returns only a single row for each value of CustomerName.

Aggregate Functions

If you need the total sales to customers who've purchased at least one expensive item, you need some way to total the amount of each sale. SQL provides a set of aggregate functions for such purposes. The aggregate functions are summarized in Table 11.3.

TABLE 11.3 SQL AGGREGATE FUNCTIONS

Function	*Return Value*
Avg([Distinct] *expression*)	The average of (distinct) values of the numeric expression
Count([Distinct] *expression*)	The number of (distinct) non-null values of the expression
Count(*)	The number of table rows
Max(*expression*)	The largest value of the expression
Min(*expression*)	The smallest value of the expression
Sum([Distinct] *expression*)	The total of (distinct) values of the numeric expression

For example, suppose you want the total amount of purchases by each customer who has purchased at least one expensive item. You can use the following query:

```
Select CustomerName, Sum(Qty*UnitPrice) From InvoiceLine, Customer
  Where InvoiceLine.CustomerNo = Customer.CustomerNo
    And UnitPrice >= 1000.00
  Group By CustomerName
```

You may have correctly guessed that the result of a query is itself a table. Some queries can return multiple identical rows; several aggregate functions let you ignore such duplicates by specifying the Distinct option. For example, the following query tells you how many distinct items have been sold by counting the number of distinct values of ItemNo that appear in the result:

```
Select Count(Distinct ItemNo) From InvoiceLine
```

You can use aggregate functions to report the maximum, minimum, and average unit price by using the following query:

```
Select Max(Qty * UnitPrice), Min(Qty * UnitPrice),
 Avg(Qty * UnitPrice) From InvoiceLine
```

The Where clause lets you specify which table rows are processed by a query. The similar Having clause lets you specify which groups are processed. For example, suppose you

Relational Databases and Structured Query Language (SQL)

CHAPTER 11

263

11

RELATIONAL
DATABASES AND
SQL

want a list of customers who have purchased more than $10,000 in total. The following query does just that:

```
Select CustomerName from InvoiceLine, Customer
  Where InvoiceLine.CustomerNo = Customer.CustomerNo
  Group by CustomerNo
  Having Sum(Qty * UnitPrice) > 10000.00
```

Subqueries

SQL lets you use the result of a query, called a *subquery*, as a value within another query. For example, suppose you want a list of products with higher than average price. Assuming that the Product table contains a row for each product, you could determine the average product price by using a query like this one:

```
Select Avg(UnitPrice) From Product
```

Suppose the result is $12.50. You could then get the desired list of costly products by using the following query:

```
Select ProductNo From Product Where UnitPrice > 12.50
```

A subquery lets you get this result in a single step:

```
Select ProductNo From Product
  Where UnitPrice > (Select Avg(UnitPrice) From Product)
```

The SQL interpreter processes the subquery first and then uses the result to process the main query.

SQL provides several keywords that you can use in `Where` and `Having` clause conditions that involve subqueries (see Table 11.4). As an example of using these keywords, here's a query that finds the products that have no sales:

```
Select ItemNo From Product
  Where Not Exists
    (Select ItemNo From InvoiceLine
      Where ItemNo = Product.ItemNo)
```

TABLE 11.4 COMPARISONS AND COMPARISON MODIFIERS USED WITH SUBQUERIES

Function	Comparison Evaluation
All	The condition is true only if it's true for every value returned by the subquery
Any	The condition is true if it's true for any value returned by the subquery
Exists	The condition is true if the subquery returns at least one row

continues

TABLE 11.4 CONTINUED

Function	Comparison Evaluation
In	The condition is true if the specified value is among those returned by the subquery
Not Exists	The condition is true if the subquery returns no rows
Not In	The condition is true if the specified value is not among those returned by the subquery

The subquery

```
(Select ItemNo From InvoiceLine
      Where ItemNo = Product.ItemNo)
```

is called a *correlated subquery*, because it refers to one of the columns specified in the main query, namely `Product.ItemNo`. A correlated subquery is executed multiple times, once for each row processed by the main query. This subquery returns all the invoice lines with the same item number as the current row of the main query. The `Not Exists` predicate is true exactly when no matching invoice lines are found. Therefore, only products without sales are reported.

Suppose you want to find which customers have purchased items more expensive than any purchased by customer 123. Here's a suitable query, which uses the `All` keyword:

```
Select CustomerNo From InvoiceLine
  Where UnitPrice > All
    (Select UnitPrice From InvoiceLine
      Where CustomerNo = 123)
  Group By CustomerNo
```

Here's how the query works. Notice that it consists of two parts: an outer (or *main*) query and a subquery, each with a corresponding `Select` statement. You can readily recognize the subquery because it's contained within parentheses:

```
(Select UnitPrice From InvoiceLine Where CustomerNo = 123)
```

Except for the parentheses, the subquery looks like an ordinary query. It even works in familiar fashion: The subquery simply returns the unit prices of items purchased by Customer 123.

The main query uses the results of the subquery to determine which rows it returns. To see how this works, suppose Customer 123 has purchased items with unit prices of $5, $0.02, and $215. The subquery returns exactly these values. Next, the main query compares unit prices of all purchases with these three unit prices, using the comparison operation > `All`. The comparison operation is true only for unit prices greater than all three of the values returned by the subquery. Therefore, the main query returns only unit prices of $215.01 and greater.

Perhaps you think the query should use the `Any` keyword. The peculiarities of English usage do sometimes make it difficult to choose correctly between the `All` and `Any` keywords. To see which is correct, consider this alternative query using the `Any` keyword:

```
Select CustomerNo From InvoiceLine
   Where UnitPrice > Any
      (Select UnitPrice From InvoiceLine
         Where CustomerNo = 123)
   Group By CustomerNo
```

Notice that Table 11.4 describes the `Any` modifier as returning a true value when the associated expression is true for any value returned by the subquery. Now suppose that customer 123 purchased a machine washer for $0.02 and a nuclear accelerator for $215 million. The condition `UnitPrice > Any` would be true for any `UnitPrice` above $0.02. The alternative condition—the one used in the original query—`UnitPrice > All` would be true for any `UnitPrice` above $215 million. Because the query is intended to report customers who've purchased an item more expensive than any purchased by customer 123, the condition using `All` is correct.

Often you'll find that a query expressed in English using the word *all* calls for the `Any` keyword and that a query expressed using the word *any* calls for the `All` keyword. Simply recall the definition of the `Any` and `All` modifiers and think through the query carefully. Don't blindly use the same word in the query that's used in the English explanation.

You can learn a great deal more about queries, but it's now time to move on to learn how to write data to the database. You'll find the next section easy going, because the statements that write data are patterned after the now-familiar statements that read data.

ADVANCED DATA MANIPULATION LANGUAGE

SQL allows you to perform any of three basic operations that alter the contents of a database. You can perform the following tasks:

- Insert a new row into a table
- Modify the column values of an existing table row
- Delete a table row

In this section, you'll learn how to perform each of these operations.

Inserting a Table Row

To add a table row, you use the Insert statement, which has the following form:

```
Insert Into table (columns)
  Values (values)
```

Here, *columns* is a comma-separated list of columns and *values* is a comma-separated list of values. The first column in the list takes the first value in the list as its value, and each succeeding column takes the corresponding value as its value. The number of columns and values must therefore be equal.

Here's a sample Insert statement, which adds a new row to the InvoiceLine table:

```
Insert Into InvoiceLine
  (InvoiceNo, LineNo, CustomerNo, InvoiceDate,
   ItemNo, Qty, UnitPrice)
  Values (101, 01, 203, 11/20/1998, 402, 12, 100.00)
```

Notice that the Insert statement provides a value for each column of the InvoiceLine table (look back to the InvoiceLine Create Table statement if you're unconvinced). Because the Create Table statement includes the Not Null option on several fields, the SQL Interpreter would reject the following query statement, which fails to specify values for several required columns:

```
Insert Into InvoiceLine (InvoiceNo) Values (101)
```

You can populate a database table using data from another table by writing an Insert statement that uses a Select statement to provide column values. Here's the general form of such an Insert statement:

```
Insert Into table (columns)
  Select columns From tables
  Where condition
```

Suppose, for example, your database contains a table named Backup that has the same structure as the InvoiceLine table. You can add the sales for a particular day to the Backup table, like this:

```
Insert Into Backup (InvoiceNo, LineNo, CustomerNo, InvoiceDate,
  ItemNo, Qty, UnitPrice)
  Select InvoiceNo, LineNo, CustomerNo, InvoiceDate,
   ItemNo, Qty, UnitPrice
  From InvoiceLine
  Where InvoiceDate = 11/20/1998
```

Modifying Column Values

You can modify the column values of an existing table by using the Update statement, which has the following general form:

```
Update table
  Set column = value [, column = value ] ...
  Where condition
```

For example, here's a query that raises the unit price of every product by 10 percent:

```
Update Product
  Set UnitPrice = UnitPrice * 1.1
```

Suppose you want to raise the price of only expensive products (those with a unit price in excess of $1,000). The following query does just that:

```
Update Product
  Set UnitPrice = UnitPrice * 1.1
  Where UnitPrice > 1000.00
```

You might correctly guess that it's possible to use subqueries within Update statements. Here's an Update statement that raises the prices of products with higher-than-average prices:

```
Update Product
  Set UnitPrice = UnitPrice * 1.1
  Where UnitPrice > (Select Avg(UnitPrice) From Product)
```

Deleting a Table Row

To delete a table row, you use the Delete statement, which has the following general form:

```
Delete From table
  Where condition
```

For example, to delete the inexpensive products (those priced at $1,000 or less) from the Product table, use the following query:

```
Delete From Product
  Where UnitPrice <= 1000.00
```

DATA CONTROL LANGUAGE

In addition to Data Definition Language and Data Manipulation Language, SQL provides a third sublanguage: Data Control Language (DCL). SQL's Data Control Language lets you perform the following tasks:

- Create user IDs for database users
- Specify the privileges available to each user ID (for example, the ability to access a given database table)
- Group database operations into transactions

- Configure database operating parameters
- Create and restore backups of the database or its tables

Data control operations are generally performed by a database administrator, rather than a software developer. Moreover, data control operations often involve vendor-specific extensions to the standard SQL language. Therefore, DCL is often vendor specific, rather than standardized across platforms. Consequently, this chapter doesn't attempt to survey DCL. You should consult your database documentation to determine which operations are supported as well as the syntax of the commands used to perform those operations.

FROM HERE

This chapter explained the fundamentals of relational database technology and the SQL language for accessing relational databases. You learned how to create relational databases and how to access and modify the data they hold. The following chapters provide additional information about relational databases:

- Chapter 12, "Java Database Connectivity (JDBC)," describes Java's API for access to relational databases.
- Appendix B, "Quick References," summarizes the syntax of key SQL statements for handy reference.

You'll also use your knowledge of relational databases in understanding the sample airline reservation system programs, many of which store their data in a simple relational database. Despite the growing popularity of object-oriented databases, relational databases remain the most popular means of storing information.

JAVA DATABASE CONNECTIVITY (JDBC)

IN THIS CHAPTER

You've probably seen a ship in a bottle: a fully rigged eighteenth or nineteenth century sailing vessel contained in a bottle having a mouth so small you marvel at how the builder got the components inside and assembled them. Before Sun released the Java Database Connectivity (JDBC) API, having a relational database and a Java program was a little like having a ship in a bottle: You knew where your data was but couldn't get to it. JDBC lets your Java programs perform SQL queries and process the results returned by the SQL interpreter. Using JDBC, it's a snap to access a relational database. In this chapter you learn:

- How to use JDBC to query a relational database

  JDBC makes it simple to issue a SQL query and access the results.

- How to use JDBC to determine the structure of the result set returned by a query

  JDBC makes available a host of information describing the results of a query. You can use this information to avoid hard-coding that may cause maintenance headaches.

- How to use JDBC to update the contents of a database

  JDBC lets you add, change, and delete SQL table rows. You can also group SQL statements that alter database contents into transactions, which helps avoid inconsistent database contents.

The sample programs in this chapter relate to the airline reservation system described in Chapter 6, "The Airline Reservation System Model." None of these sample programs comprises a complete airline reservation system transaction or operation; instead, they focus on data management. More complete sample programs in subsequent chapters will build on the sample programs in this chapter.

JDBC DRIVERS

To access a database via JDBC, you need a software driver. JDBC lets you work with four types of drivers:

- Type 1 drivers use a bridge to connect to the relational database. You must generally install the bridge on each client machine, making systems that use Type 1 drivers cumbersome to maintain. Sun's JDK includes the JDBC-ODBC bridge, which lets you access a relational database via ODBC, a Microsoft-designed standard way of accessing databases. Because most databases support ODBC, you can access them using the JDBC-ODBC bridge. However, ODBC drivers generally provide access to only a fraction of a database's API, are sometimes inefficient, and often are not thread-safe. Consequently, using the JDBC-ODBC bridge is a great way to learn about JDBC but not a great way to write applications.

- Type 2 drivers are native API drivers written mainly in C or C++ that use a proprietary protocol to access the database. They provide efficient access to the full database API. However, you need a different version of a Type 2 driver for every client platform. Each database vendor provides its own Type 2 drivers; therefore, you need a separate driver for each type of database engine your application accesses.

- Type 3 drivers are native API drivers that use a network protocol to communicate with a middleware server that mediates access to a database. Because Type 3 drivers are not vendor specific, you need only a single Type 3 driver no matter how many types of database engines your application accesses. However, you need a different version of the driver for every client platform.

- Type 4 drivers are pure Java drivers that communicate directly with a database. You need a different version of the driver for each database engine. However, because a Type 4 driver is pure Java, it will run on any client platform.

As you can see, you should not generally use a Type 1 driver. Nevertheless, in this chapter we'll use the JDBC-ODBC bridge. The JDBC-ODBC bridge has two advantages that are important to us: It's included in the JDK, and it can access almost any type of database. By using the JDBC-ODBC bridge, you can easily run the sample programs yourself.

Even though our examples use a Type 1 driver, you'll learn all you need to know about accessing relational databases using JDBC. If you want to experiment with more sophisticated drivers, consult Sun's Java Web site, which provides a list of JDBC-compliant drivers. You can try different drivers without changing program logic. If you like, you can even preload selected JDBC drivers each time a JVM launches. This lets you change the type of driver your application uses without modifying and recompiling the application. Consult your driver documentation to determine how to preload your driver.

READING TABLE DATA: PASSENGERLIST

Let's begin with a simple example that shows you how to read data from a relational table. The CD-ROM includes a sample Microsoft Access database named Airline.mdb. Even if you don't have Access installed on your system, you can access the database so long as you have the proper ODBC driver installed. The driver is included with Microsoft Office, Microsoft Visual C++, and other products. Therefore, if you run Microsoft Windows, it's probably already installed on your Windows 9x/NT system. If not, you may be able to download it from Microsoft's Web site.

The database contains three simple tables: Passenger, Flight, and Seat. These tables hold a subset of the data needed by the airline reservation system we use as an example throughout this book.

Copy the database from the CD-ROM to your system. In order to access the database via ODBC, you must configure a data source name (DSN). Here's how to do so:

1. Open the Windows Control Panel and double-click the ODBC applet. This launches the ODBC Data Source Administrator. Click the User DSN tab (see Figure 12.1).

Figure 12.1

The ODBC Data Source Administrator lets you create DSNs.

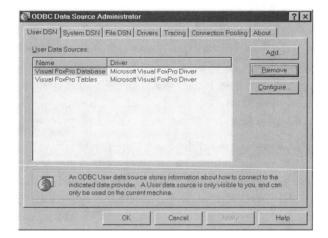

2. Click the Add button to launch the Create New Data Source dialog box shown in Figure 12.2.

Figure 12.2

The Create New Data Source dialog box lets you identify the data source of your new DSN.

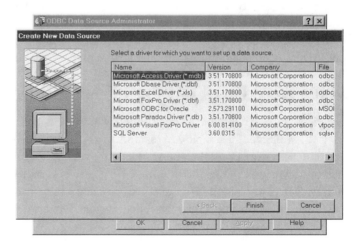

3. Select Microsoft Access Driver and click Finish. This launches the ODBC Microsoft Access 97 Setup dialog box. Type **Airline** as the data source name and then type a suitable description, as shown in Figure 12.3.

FIGURE 12.3

The ODBC Microsoft Access 97 Setup dialog box lets you associate a DSN with a database.

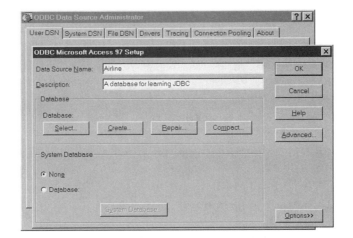

4. Click the Select button and then use the Select Database dialog box to select the file that contains your database. Click OK to return to the ODBC Microsoft Access 97 Setup dialog box. Click OK to return to the ODBC Data Source Administrator. Finally, click OK to exit. Your database is now ready for access via ODBC.

Using appletviewer, run the PassengerList applet by using the PassengerList.html file. Type a SQL query in the Query field and press Enter. The applet displays the query results in its Result field, as you can see in Figure 12.4.

FIGURE 12.4

The PassengerList applet lets you execute queries and view results.

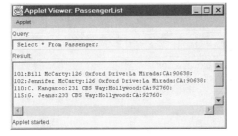

Opening a Database Connection

Let's see how the PassengerList applet works. Listing 12.1 shows its source code. Apart from the TextField and TextArea that comprise the applet's user interface, the PassengerList class defines four fields, including three constants and a field that references a Connection.

LISTING 12.1 PassengerList.java—READING A DATABASE

```
import java.applet.*;
import java.awt.*;
import java.awt.event.*;
import java.sql.*;
```

continues

LISTING 12.1   CONTINUED

```java
public class PassengerList extends Applet
{
    static final String DB = "jdbc:odbc:airline";
    static final String USER = "";
    static final String PASSWORD = "";

    TextField theQuery  = new TextField();
    TextArea  theResult = new TextArea(20, 64);

    Connection          theConnection;

    public void init()
    {
        setLayout(new BorderLayout());
        Panel p1 = new Panel();
        add(p1, BorderLayout.NORTH);
        add(theResult, BorderLayout.CENTER);
        p1.setLayout(new GridLayout(0, 1));
        p1.add(new Label("Query:"));
        p1.add(theQuery);
        p1.add(new Label("Result:"));
        theResult.setEditable(false);
        Font f = new Font("Monospaced", Font.PLAIN, 12);
        theQuery.setFont(f);
        theResult.setFont(f);
        theQuery.addActionListener(new QueryHandler());
        try
        {
            Class.forName("sun.jdbc.odbc.JdbcOdbcDriver");
            theConnection =
              DriverManager.getConnection(DB, USER, PASSWORD);
        }
        catch (ClassNotFoundException ex1) { fatalError(ex1); }
        catch (SQLException ex2) { fatalError(ex2); }
    }

    public void fatalError(Exception ex)
    {
        ex.printStackTrace();
    }

// Inner class omitted
}
```

The constants specify which database the program accesses and the user ID and password used to log on. The name of the database has the form of a special URL. The first component of the URL is the protocol name, jdbc. Every JDBC driver defines the structure of the remaining components of the URL. The JDBC-ODBC bridge uses the format jdbc:odbc:*dsn*, where *dsn* is the data source name that identifies the database.

The init method creates a Connection object and binds it to the field theConnection. As you'll see, the Connection object encapsulates the database. JDBC programs send several types of messages to the Connection object.

Let's explore the init method. It begins with the usual sort of code that establishes the applet's user interface. The last part of the method includes a try-catch that opens a connection to the database. The static method Class.forName loads the named class into the JVM (if the class has not already been loaded). The init method uses the Class.forName method to load the JDBC-ODBC driver, the full class name of which is sun.jdbc.odbc.JdbcOdbcDriver. The init method then uses the static DriverManager.getConnection method to open a connection to the database, which it stores in the field theConnection. The getConnection method checks the URL that specifies the database and selects an appropriate driver from among those loaded.

Several errors can occur while attempting to open the database. For example, the JDBC-ODBC driver may not be present or the database may be inaccessible. Two catch statements deal with these possibilities by invoking a utility method that prints a stack trace that identifies the error. Because you launch appletviewer from a command window, it displays stack traces there.

Executing a SQL Statement

The inner class QueryHandler contains the statements that create and execute the SQL query and that display the results. Its actionPerformed method creates and generates the query, which is encapsulated within a Statement object obtained by sending the createStatement message to the Connection object obtained from DriverManager.getConnection in the init method. The Statement object understands several important messages, including the executeQuery message that sends a query to the database. The query is a String argument of the executeQuery message, which returns the results encapsulated within a ResultSet object.

The actionPerformed method uses the displayResult utility method to display the contents of the ResultSet. It then closes the Statement. This action frees resources that are no longer needed. Notice that the database connection remains open: By pressing Enter in the Query field, you can repeatedly invoke the actionPerformed method. See Listing 12.2.

LISTING 12.2   PassengerList.java—INNER CLASS

```
class QueryHandler implements ActionListener
{
    public void actionPerformed(ActionEvent evt)
    {
        try
        {
            String query = theQuery.getText();
            Statement stmt = theConnection.createStatement();
            ResultSet rs  = stmt.executeQuery(query);
            displayResult(rs);
            stmt.close();
```

continues

12

JAVA DATABASE
CONNECTIVITY
(JDBC)

LISTING 12.2 CONTINUED

```
        }
        catch (SQLException ex) { fatalError(ex); }
    }

    public void displayResult(ResultSet rs)
    {
        try
        {
            ResultSetMetaData rsmd = rs.getMetaData();
            int cols = rsmd.getColumnCount();
            theResult.setText("");
             while (rs.next())
            {
                theResult.append("\n");
                for (int i = 1; i <= cols; i++)
                {
                    String text = rs.getString(i);
                    if (text == null) text = "";
                    theResult.append(text + ":");
                }
            }
            rs.close();
        }
        catch (SQLException ex) { fatalError(ex); }
    }
}
```

Displaying Query Results

The displayResult method obtains a ResultSetMetaData object by sending the getMetaData message to the ResultSet object. It uses the ResultSetMetaData object to determine the structure of the ResultSet that contains the query result. The ResultSetMetaData class supports many useful methods, which you'll explore in the next section, "Learning About Result Sets: MetaData." The displayResult method uses only one of these: getColumnCount, which returns a count of the number of columns (fields) in the ResultSet.

To access a row of the ResultSet, you send the ResultSet the next message. The ResultSet returns true if it found a row or false if you've accessed all the rows. The while loop processes each row of the ResultSet. It uses the column count to control a for loop that iterates over the columns of the ResultSet. Most ODBC database drivers require you to access columns sequentially. The for loop uses the getString message to obtain the value of each database column as a String. A family of get messages lets you get column values as other data types (see Table 12.1). However, most database data types can be conveniently converted to String, so it's often expeditious to use getString, whatever the actual data type of the column.

TABLE 12.1 DATA ACCESS METHODS OF ResultSet

Method	Meaning
getDouble(int col)	Gets the value of a column as a double
getFloat(int col)	Gets the value of a column as a float
getInt(int col)	Gets the value of a column as an int
getLong(int col)	Gets the value of a column as a long
getObject(int col)	Gets the value of a column as an Object
getShort(int col)	Gets the value of a column as a short
getString(int col)	Gets the value of a column as a String
getTime(int col)	Gets the value of a column as a Time
getTimeStamp(int col)	Gets the value of a column as a TimeStamp
getUnicodeStream(int col)	Gets the value of a column as an InputStream of Unicode characters
wasNull()	Returns true if the last column accessed had the SQL value null

The displayResult method appends the value of each column to the contents of the TextArea. After processing all the rows, it closes the ResultSet. Notice that the method uses a try-catch to handle SQLException errors, which are thrown when the SQL interpreter finds an error or another problem occurs.

LEARNING ABOUT RESULT SETS: METADATA

As previously mentioned, the ResultSet class makes a lot of useful information available via its getResultSetMetaData method, which returns a ResultSetMetaData object. Figure 12.5 shows the window of the MetaData applet. It lets you enter a query and then describes the result set the query returns. Let's analyze how the applet works.

Listing 12.3 shows the source code of the MetaData applet, which resembles the source code of the PassengerList applet. As before, the class includes fields that identify the database and the logon user ID and password. Another field holds a reference to the database Connection object. As before, the interesting part of the program is the inner class that handles ActionEvents.

FIGURE 12.5

Result set meta data describes the contents of a result set.

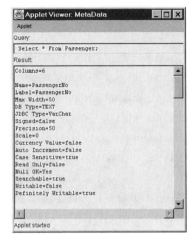

LISTING 12.3 MetaData.java—LEARNING ABOUT A ResultSet

```java
import java.applet.*;
import java.awt.*;
import java.awt.event.*;
import java.sql.*;

public class MetaData extends Applet
{
    static final String DB = "jdbc:odbc:airline";
    static final String USER = "";
    static final String PASSWORD = "";

    TextField theQuery  = new TextField();
    TextArea  theResult = new TextArea(20, 64);

    Connection         theConnection;

    public void init()
    {
        setLayout(new BorderLayout());
        Panel p1 = new Panel();
        add(p1, BorderLayout.NORTH);
        add(theResult, BorderLayout.CENTER);
        p1.setLayout(new GridLayout(0, 1));
        p1.add(new Label("Query:"));
        p1.add(theQuery);
        p1.add(new Label("Result:"));
        theResult.setEditable(false);
        Font f = new Font("Monospaced", Font.PLAIN, 12);
        theQuery.setFont(f);
```

```
        theResult.setFont(f);
        theQuery.addActionListener(new QueryHandler());
        try
        {
            Class.forName("sun.jdbc.odbc.JdbcOdbcDriver");
            theConnection =
              DriverManager.getConnection(DB, USER, PASSWORD);
        }
        catch (ClassNotFoundException ex1) { fatalError(ex1); }
        catch (SQLException ex2) { fatalError(ex2); }
    }

    public void fatalError(Exception ex)
    {
        ex.printStackTrace();
    }

    // Inner class omitted
}
```

Listing 12.4 shows the MetaData class, the inner class of the MetaData applet. The actionPerformed method closely resembles that of the PassengerList applet; however, this QueryHandler class defines the displayResult method differently.

LISTING 12.4   MetaData.java—EXECUTING A QUERY

```
class QueryHandler implements ActionListener
{
    public void actionPerformed(ActionEvent evt)
    {
        try
        {
            String query = theQuery.getText();
            Statement stmt = theConnection.createStatement();
            ResultSet rs   = stmt.executeQuery(query);
            displayResult(rs);
            stmt.close();
        }
        catch (SQLException ex) { fatalError(ex); }
    }

     public void displayResult(ResultSet rs)
    {
        try
        {
            ResultSetMetaData rsmd = rs.getMetaData();
            int cols = rsmd.getColumnCount();
            println("Columns=" + cols);
```

continues

LISTING 12.4 CONTINUED

```
println("");
for (int col = 1; col <= cols; col++)
{
    println("Name=" +
      rsmd.getColumnName(col));
    println("Label=" +
      rsmd.getColumnLabel(col));
    println("Max Width=" +
      rsmd.getColumnDisplaySize(col));
    println("DB Type=" +
      rsmd.getColumnTypeName(col));
    println("JDBC Type=" +
      getJDBCTypeName(rsmd.getColumnType(col)));
    println("Signed=" +
      rsmd.isSigned(col));
    println("Precision=" +
      rsmd.getPrecision(col));
    println("Scale=" +
      rsmd.getScale(col));
    println("Currency Value=" +
      rsmd.isCurrency(col));
    println("Auto Increment=" +
      rsmd.isAutoIncrement(col));
    println("Case Sensitive=" +
      rsmd.isCaseSensitive(col));
    println("Read Only=" +
      rsmd.isReadOnly(col));
    int nullable =
      rsmd.isNullable(col);
    switch (nullable)
    {
        case rsmd.columnNoNulls:
            println("Null OK=No");
            break;
        case rsmd.columnNullable:
            println("Null OK=Yes");
            break;
        default:
            println("Null OK=Unknown");
    }
    println("Searchable=" +
      rsmd.isSearchable(col));
    println("Writable=" +
      rsmd.isWritable(col));
    println("Definitely Writable=" +
      rsmd.isDefinitelyWritable(col));
    println("");
```

```
        }
        rs.close();
    }
    catch (SQLException ex) { fatalError(ex); }
}

// Utility methods omitted
}
```

Rather than display the contents of the result set rows, this method describes the result set table by using various `ResultSetMetaData` messages. Table 12.2 summarizes these methods and their functions. The `QueryHandler` class includes two utility methods (not shown here) in order to conserve space; they're included on the CD-ROM. The `getJDBCTypeName` method works with the `getColumnType` method, which returns an `int` corresponding to the JDBC data type of a column. The `getColumnType` method simply returns a `String` that describes the data type corresponding to its `int` argument.

The `println` is not the familiar `System.out.println`, although it does have a similar purpose. The `println` utility method appends its `String` argument to the contents of the `TextArea` called `theResult`, and then appends a line termination sequence.

TABLE 12.2 KEY ResultSetMetaData METHODS

Method	*Meaning*
`int getColumnDisplaySize(int col)`	Returns the maximum display size of the specified column
`String getColumnLabel(int col)`	Returns the suggested column heading of the specified column
`String getColumnName(int col)`	Returns the name of the specified column
`int getColumnType(int col)`	Returns the JDBC type of the specified column
`String getColumnTypeName(int col)`	Returns the vendor-specific name of the type of the specified column
`int getPrecision(int col)`	Returns the number of digits (numeric column) or characters (nonnumeric column) of the specified column
`int getScale(int col)`	Returns the implied decimal point of the specified column

continues

TABLE 12.2 CONTINUED

Method	Meaning
`boolean isAutoIncrement(int col)`	Returns `true` if the value of the specified column is generated by the database, which assigns consecutive values
`boolean isCaseSensitive(int col)`	Returns `true` if the specified column is case sensitive
`boolean isCurrency(int col)`	Returns `true` if the specified column holds a currency value
`boolean isDefinitelyWritable(int col)`	Returns `true` if the specified column is writable
`int isNullable(int col)`	Returns a value that indicates whether the specified column can contain SQL null as its value
`boolean isReadOnly(int col)`	Returns `true` if the specified column is read-only
`boolean isSearchable(int col)`	Returns `true` if the specified column can be used in a `Where` clause
`isSigned(int col)`	Returns `true` if the specified column can accommodate a signed numeric value
`isWritable(int col)`	Returns `true` if a new value can be written to the specified column

UPDATING A DATABASE: PASSENGERUPDATE

Using JDBC to update a relational database is a little more difficult than using it to read the database. Listing 12.5 shows the source code of the PassengerUpdate applet, which lets you add new passengers to the Passenger table or change the names of existing passengers. The applet does not let you delete a passenger, but you could easily add this function.

The user interface portion of the PassengerUpdate applet is somewhat different from that of the previous applets in this chapter. It provides two `TextField` objects—one for entering a passenger number and the other for entering a passenger name. When you enter a passenger number, the `FetchHandler` inner class accesses the database and displays the passenger's name. When you enter a passenger name, the `UpdateHandler` inner class tries to update the passenger's name. If this attempt fails, the `UpdateHandler` adds a new passenger with the specified number and name.

LISTING 12.5   PassengerUpdate.java—WRITING A DATABASE

```java
import java.applet.*;
import java.awt.*;
import java.awt.event.*;
import java.sql.*;

public class PassengerUpdate extends Applet
{
    static final String DB = "jdbc:odbc:airline";
    static final String USER = "";
    static final String PASSWORD = "";

    TextField thePassenger = new TextField();
    TextField theName      = new TextField();

    Connection theConnection;

    public void init()
    {
        setLayout(new GridLayout(0, 1));
        Panel p1 = new Panel();
        add(new Label("PassengerNo:"));
        add(thePassenger);
        add(new Label("Name:"));
        add(theName);
        Font f = new Font("Monospaced", Font.PLAIN, 12);
        thePassenger.setFont(f);
        theName.setFont(f);
        thePassenger.addActionListener(new FetchHandler());
        theName.addActionListener(new UpdateHandler());
        try
        {
            Class.forName("sun.jdbc.odbc.JdbcOdbcDriver");
            theConnection =
              DriverManager.getConnection(DB, USER, PASSWORD);
        }
        catch (ClassNotFoundException ex1) { fatalError(ex1); }
        catch (SQLException ex2) { fatalError(ex2); }
    }

    public void fatalError(Exception ex)
    {
        ex.printStackTrace();
    }

    // Inner classes not shown
}
```

Listing 12.6 shows the `FetchHandler` inner class of the PassengerUpdate applet. Its `actionPerformed` method is somewhat different from those you've seen previously in this chapter. It creates a SQL statement that uses a `Where` clause to access only a single row of the Passenger table. Notice how the value of the local variable `passengerno`, a `String` containing the passenger number, is joined with literals that specify the SQL keywords of the query. Notice, too, that the passenger number is enclosed in single quotes. This is not strictly necessary, because the passenger number is numeric. However, this is a common technique for dealing with text values, which may contain spaces or special characters.

LISTING 12.6   `PassengerUpdate.java`—FetchHandler INNER CLASS

```
class FetchHandler implements ActionListener
{
    public void actionPerformed(ActionEvent evt)
    {
        try
        {
            theName.setText("");
            String passengerno = thePassenger.getText();
            String query      =
              "Select Name " +
              "From Passenger " +
              "Where PassengerNo = '" +
              passengerno +
              "'";
            Statement stmt = theConnection.createStatement();
            ResultSet rs   = stmt.executeQuery(query);
            if (rs.next())
            {
                String name = rs.getString(1);
                theName.setText(name);
            }
            stmt.close();
        }
        catch (SQLException ex) { fatalError(ex); }
    }
}
```

The `UpdateHandler` inner class appears as Listing 12.7. Its `actionPerformed` method constructs a SQL `Update` statement that loads each table column with its proper value. Notice that a `Where` clause restricts the update to a single table row. The `String` containing the `Update` statement is passed as an argument of the `executeUpdate` method, which processes the query. Unlike `executeQuery`, which returns a `ResultSet`, `executeUpdate` returns an `int` that holds the number of table rows updated.

If no table rows were updated, the passenger is new. Therefore, the `actionPerformed` method constructs an appropriate SQL `Insert` statement and issues it in the same manner as the `Update` statement. As usual, the method closes the `Statement` when it's done.

LISTING 12.7   `PassengerUpdate.java`—UpdateHandler INNER CLASS

```
class UpdateHandler implements ActionListener
{
    public void actionPerformed(ActionEvent evt)
        try
        {
            String passengerno = thePassenger.getText();
            String name        = theName.getText();
            String query     =
                "Update Passenger " +
                "Set Name = '" +
                name +
                "' " +
                "Where PassengerNo = '" +
                passengerno +
                "'";
            Statement stmt = theConnection.createStatement();
            int n = stmt.executeUpdate(query);
            if (n == 0)
            {
                query = "Insert Into Passenger " +
                "(PassengerNo, Name) " +
                "Values ('" +
                passengerno +
                "', '" +
                name +
                "')";
                n = stmt.executeUpdate(query);
            }
            stmt.close();
        }
        catch (SQLException ex) { fatalError(ex); }
    }
}
```

USING DATABASE-AWARE OBJECTS: PASSENGERAPPLET

When writing distributed applications that use a relational database, you may want to encapsulate information about the database within your program objects so that they can be used more transparently. The `Passenger` class, shown in Listing 12.8, demonstrates one way to do so. The class provides accessor methods that get a passenger number (getPassengerNo) or passenger name (getName). It also provides a mutator method that changes a passenger name (setName).

LISTING 12.8   Passenger.java—A DATABASE-AWARE OBJECT

```java
import java.sql.*;

public class Passenger
{
    String thePassengerNo;
    String theName;

    public Passenger()
    {
        this("", "");
    }

    public Passenger(String passenger_no, String name)
    {
        thePassengerNo = passenger_no;
        theName = name;
    }

    public String getPassengerNo()
    {
        return thePassengerNo;
    }

    public String getName()
    {
        return theName;
    }

    public void setName(String name)
    {
        theName = name;
    }

    public static Passenger getInstance(Connection db,
      String passenger_no) throws SQLException
    {
        String query    =
          "Select Name " +
          "From Passenger " +
          "Where PassengerNo = '" +
          passenger_no +
          "'";
        Statement stmt = db.createStatement();
        ResultSet rs   = stmt.executeQuery(query);
        rs.next();
```

```
            String name = rs.getString(1);
            rs.close();
            stmt.close();
            return new Passenger(passenger_no, name);
        }

        public void dbWrite(Connection db)
          throws SQLException
        {
            String query      =
              "Update Passenger " +
              "Set Name = '" +
              theName +
              "' " +
              "Where PassengerNo = '" +
              thePassengerNo +
                "'";
            Statement stmt = db.createStatement();
            int n = stmt.executeUpdate(query);
            if (n == 0)
            {
                query = "Insert Into Passenger " +
                "(PassengerNo, Name) " +
                "Values ('" +
                thePassengerNo +
                "', '" +
                theName +
                "')";
                n = stmt.executeUpdate(query);
            }
            stmt.close();
        }
}
```

The class provides two other public methods: getInstance, which retrieves a Passenger object from the database, and dbWrite, which stores a Passenger object in the database. The getInstance method is static, so you can call it without first creating a Passenger object. It simply retrieves the name of the specified passenger from the database and then constructs and returns a Passenger object.

The code of the dbWrite method resembles that of the actionPerformed method of the PassengerUpdate applet. It first tries to update an existing row of the Passenger table; failing that, it adds a new row.

Listing 12.9 shows the PassengerApplet applet, which demonstrates how to use the Passenger class. Notice that the applet includes a Passenger field. As usual, the init method opens the database connection. The getInstance and dbWrite methods of the

Passenger class are written to accept a reference to an open database connection so that a single connection is shared among the classes and threads of the program. Because ODBC drivers are often not thread-safe, it's especially important that a single connection be shared among the classes and threads when the JDBC-ODBC bridge is used. As usual, the applet defers most processing to its inner classes.

LISTING 12.9 PassengerApplet.java—AN APPLET THAT USES THE Passenger CLASS

```java
import java.applet.*;
import java.awt.*;
import java.awt.event.*;
import java.sql.*;

public class PassengerApplet extends Applet
{
    static final String DB = "jdbc:odbc:airline";
    static final String USER = "";
    static final String PASSWORD = "";

    TextField thePassengerNo = new TextField();
    TextField theName        = new TextField();

    Passenger  thePassenger;
    Connection theConnection;

    public void init()
    {
        setLayout(new GridLayout(0, 1));
        Panel p1 = new Panel();
        add(new Label("PassengerNo:"));
        add(thePassengerNo);
        add(new Label("Name:"));
        add(theName);
        Font f = new Font("Monospaced", Font.PLAIN, 12);
        thePassengerNo.setFont(f);
        theName.setFont(f);
        thePassengerNo.addActionListener(new FetchHandler());
        theName.addActionListener(new UpdateHandler());
        try
        {
            Class.forName("sun.jdbc.odbc.JdbcOdbcDriver");
            theConnection =
                DriverManager.getConnection(DB, USER, PASSWORD);
        }
        catch (ClassNotFoundException ex1) { fatalError(ex1); }
        catch (SQLException ex2) { fatalError(ex2); }
    }
```

```
public void fatalError(Exception ex)
{
    ex.printStackTrace();
}

// Inner classes not shown
}
```

Listing 12.10 shows the inner classes of the PassengerApplet applet. The
actionPerformed method uses the getInstance method to retrieve the specified passenger from the database. If the passenger does not exist, the getInstance method throws
an SQLException. The PassengerApplet applet simply reports the exception. Instead of
reporting the exception, it might instantiate a default passenger object.

LISTING 12.10   PassengerApplet.java—INNER CLASSES

```
class FetchHandler implements ActionListener
{
    public void actionPerformed(ActionEvent evt)
    {
        try
        {
            theName.setText("");
            thePassenger = Passenger.getInstance(
              theConnection,
              thePassengerNo.getText());
            theName.setText(thePassenger.getName());
        }
        catch (SQLException ex) { fatalError(ex); }
    }
}

class UpdateHandler implements ActionListener
{
    public void actionPerformed(ActionEvent evt)
    {
        try
        {
            thePassenger.dbWrite(theConnection);
        }
        catch (SQLException ex) { fatalError(ex); }
    }
}
```

The UpdateHandler class uses the dbWrite method to update an existing table row or
add a new table row. Because the dbWrite method handles the distinction internally, it's
all the same to the UpdateHandler.

DEFINING TRANSACTIONS: PASSENGERTRANSACTION

Because the dbWrite method of the Passenger class uses a two-step process to update the database, it's vulnerable to a database anomaly similar to those that affect concurrent threads. If two users simultaneously access the same passenger record, one user may unknowingly undo a change posted by another. Recall that solving the problem affecting threads involved using synchronization to make the nonatomic operations behave atomically.

The solution to the database anomaly is similar. JDBC allows you to define a transaction that consists of a group of database operations. The transaction is not permanently posted to the database until you send the database a commit message. If a program terminates without sending a commit message, the database automatically rolls back any pending changes.

The CD-ROM contains an applet called PassengerTransaction that demonstrates the technique. Here, you'll see just those parts that differ significantly from other examples in this chapter.

Listing 12.11 shows the try-catch block of the applet's init method, where the applet opens the database connection. Notice that two new messages are sent: setTransactionIsolation and setAutoCommit. The former chooses a policy that governs transaction behavior. Although JDBC provides a number of alternative levels of transaction isolation, not all databases implement these. You'll need to consult your database documentation to determine which isolation levels are available to you.

The setAutoCommit message turns off autocommit, a JDBC facility that automatically posts database changes as they occur. Unless you turn off autocommit, your transactions will be ineffective, because they'll be posted as a single operation when the database is closed. In that case, an error relating to any transaction will cause the database to roll back every transaction.

LISTING 12.11 PassengerTransaction.java—DEFINING A DATABASE TRANSACTION

```
try
{
    Class.forName("sun.jdbc.odbc.JdbcOdbcDriver");
    theConnection =
      DriverManager.getConnection(DB, USER, PASSWORD);
    theConnection.setTransactionIsolation(
      Connection.TRANSACTION_READ_COMMITTED);
    theConnection.setAutoCommit(false);
}
catch (ClassNotFoundException ex1) { fatalError(ex1); }
catch (SQLException ex2) { fatalError(ex2); }
```

Listing 12.12 shows the `fatalError` method of the PassengerTransaction applet. Notice that it has been modified to immediately roll back any pending changes whenever an error occurs.

LISTING 12.12 `PassengerTransaction.java`—HANDLING EXCEPTIONS

```
public void fatalError(Exception ex)
{
    ex.printStackTrace();
    try
    {
        System.err.print("Attempting database rollback...");
        theConnection.rollback();
        System.err.println("Okay.");
    }
    catch (SQLException ex2)
    {
        ex2.printStackTrace();
    }
}
```

The last change necessary to establish transactions appears in Listing 12.13, which shows how to update the database when transactions are in effect. Notice that the last statement in the `try` block sends the `commit` message to the database. Because processing is complete, no further errors are likely. Committing the completed updates prevents them from being rolled back in the event of a subsequent error.

LISTING 12.13 `PassengerTransaction.java`—UPDATING THE DATABASE

```
try
{
    String passengerno = thePassenger.getText();
    String name        = theName.getText();
    String query       =   // details omitted
    Statement stmt = theConnection.createStatement();
    int n = stmt.executeUpdate(query);
    if (n == 0)
    {
        query =            // details omitted
        n = stmt.executeUpdate(query);
    }
    stmt.close();
    theConnection.commit();
}
```

FROM HERE

In this chapter, you've learned about the JDBC facility for accessing relational databases using Java. You've learned how to read and write database tables, how to determine the contents of a result set, and how to establish transactions that help prevent database anomalies.

Appendix B, "Quick References," provides additional information about relational databases and summarizes the syntax of key SQL statements for handy reference.

SOCKETS

IN THIS CHAPTER

As a child, you may have constructed a tin-can telephone system. By running a fishing line from one tree house to another, you may even have constructed a tin-can telephone network that let you contact your friends from the comfort and seclusion of your own treetop fortress. This simplest of information-exchange devices works similarly to sockets, an information exchange facility provided by TCP/IP networks. In this chapter you learn:

- How sockets let you exchange data among networked hosts

  Although sockets are low-level mechanisms for data exchange, they're simple to use and operate efficiently. When you want to exchange large volumes of data or when your data has a simple structure, the socket is an appropriate vehicle.

- How to write socket-based clients and servers

  Using the java.net library, you can easily write simple, yet powerful clients and servers that let your applications exchange data over TCP/IP networks.

- How to use threads and timeouts to construct efficient and robust clients and servers

  When servers must respond to several—perhaps many—concurrent clients, you should use a threaded server so that the clients can contact the server even when it's processing a request. Because networks are not perfectly reliable, data exchanges sometimes fail. The Java 1.1 socket timeout facility helps your applications cope with such real-world problems.

- How to use datagrams to efficiently exchange simple messages

  The datagram protocol is a lower level protocol than sockets. It performs less error checking and provides fewer features than sockets, but it provides very efficient data exchange.

SOCKETS AND THE JAVA.NET API

Sockets let you send and receive messages—called *datagrams*—over a TCP/IP network. You can use either of two types of sockets: Internet Protocol (IP) sockets or User Datagram Protocol (UDP) sockets. IP sockets send and receive IP datagrams, whereas UDP sockets send and receive UDP datagrams. IP sockets are the garden-variety socket; UDP sockets are less often used. In this chapter, you'll learn how to work with both types.

Java's java.net package supports socket input and output. Because java.net is a core Java package, it's available to every standard Java virtual machine. The classes and methods of java.net are easy to use, but powerful.

Before beginning our study of sockets, let's take time to understand their pros and cons. Even if you find that sockets don't meet your application's needs, you should spend the time to understand them thoroughly. All other TCP/IP data exchange facilities are built using sockets, which are the fundamental mechanisms of TCP/IP data transfer. You'll find a knowledge of sockets helpful in understanding how other data transfer mechanisms work.

Pros and Cons of Sockets

Sockets are the assembly language of TCP/IP data transfer, whereas other mechanisms, such as Remote Method Invocation (RMI) and Common Object Request Broker Architecture (CORBA), are the high-level languages. Just as assembly language programs—in principle—run faster and use memory more efficiently than high-level language programs, sockets offer better performance than other transfer mechanisms.

However, beware the word *offer*, because what is offered is not always achieved. Some assembly language programs are just as slow and fat as high-level language programs. Similarly, some applications that use sockets function less efficiently than some applications that use higher-level data transfer mechanisms.

If you can't be certain of the benefits of assembly language and sockets, you can be relatively certain of the cost. An assembly language program is almost always more difficult and expensive to write than an equivalent high-level language program. That's why assembly language programs have become as rare as Studebakers (a popular car during the 1940s). Similarly, if the data you want to transfer is simple—a line of ASCII text, for instance—sockets will serve you well. However, if you need to transfer an entire community of objects, you can expect to spend a great deal of time at the keyboard. Moreover, because your application will be large and complex, you can expect it to contain a relatively large number of troublesome bugs.

Sockets model network data transfers as streams of bytes. When your data is simple, sockets are an ideal choice. But when your data is complex, you should consider other options, such as RMI or CORBA. However, RMI, CORBA, and other high-level protocols do not transfer data as efficiently as sockets. When the volume of data is small, this inefficiency poses no problem. However, when an application must transfer large volumes of data, the choice of data transfer protocol is complicated. You can aim for high efficiency, trading off the increased development and maintenance effort associated with socket programming for potentially improved performance, or you can use a higher-level protocol and hope that the efficiency is acceptable.

Several factors should guide your choice. First, consider your training and skills and those of other development staff members. If you're not familiar with socket programming, for example, writing an application that uses sockets will pose special risks. Second, consider the possibility of improving system performance by means of more powerful hardware. If your application is very large, you may not have this option. Often, though, a more powerful server or a faster network can compensate for some programming shortcuts that, in the end, offer better value.

When neither of these considerations leads to a clear decision, we suggest you use a high-level protocol such as RMI or CORBA rather than sockets. By using a high-level protocol, you operate on a higher level of abstraction—one closer to the users' problems than to the technology applied to solve it. You're therefore more likely to build a correct application—one that actually solves the users' problems. Socket programming may confront you with so many technology-oriented choices that you inadvertently lose sight of the users' problems: Many projects have taken this sad path.

Once you've built a working system, you can assess its performance. You might find that it performs acceptably, in which case you've made a winning choice. Of course, you might find that performance is unacceptable. In that case, you can replace some or all of the data transfers with socket-based interaction. The work spent to implement data transfer using high-level protocols is not wasted, however. It will act as a functional specification that guides your implementation of socket-based data transfer. As a result, you're much more likely to implement a reliable data transfer than if you had originally programmed the application to use sockets.

Now that you know when to apply sockets and when to choose another data transfer mechanism, let's begin our study of sockets. We'll first examine four `java.net` classes that you'll often use in network data transfers: URL, InetAddress, Socket, and ServerSocket.

The URL Class

If your application needs to transfer data in only one direction, you may prefer to use the HTTP protocol rather than the IP or UDP protocol. The HTTP protocol, the protocol used by Web clients and servers, allows a client to download information from a Web server. The client sends the server a Uniform Resource Locator (URL) that specifies the desired document, and the server responds by transmitting the document. The URL class encapsulates a URL, letting you easily contact a server and download a document. You can create a URL by using the following constructor:

```
public URL(String url) throws MalformedURLException
```

The `String` argument specifies the document that the URL refers to. For example, the Macmillan Computer Publishing Web site is `http://www.mcp.com`. You can create a URL that refers to the Macmillan Web site by writing this:

```
URL macmillan = new URL("http://www.mcp.com");
```

The constructor throws an exception if the format of its argument does not represent a valid URL. Therefore, you must enclose the statement in a try-catch block or specify that the method that encloses the statement should throw the MalformedURLException (or one of its ancestor classes, such as Exception).

Once you've constructed a URL that points to a Web document, you can fetch the document by using the openStream method, which returns an InputStream containing the document contents. You simply read the InputStream to access the document contents. Some types of documents can be read more easily: The getContent method returns an Object that encapsulates the document contents. However, getContent succeeds only if the Java virtual machine contains an appropriate content handler for the type of document accessed.

Table 13.1 summarizes key methods and constructors of the URL class. You'll learn more about URLs in Chapter 18, "Servlets and Common Gateway Interface (CGI)," which describes the Java servlet API.

TABLE 13.1 KEY METHODS OF THE URL CLASS

Method	*Return Value*
boolean equals(Object x)	Returns true if the URL refers to the same document as the specified object, x, which should be a URL.
Object getContent()	Returns an object that encapsulates the document that the URL refers to. This method fails if the type of document content cannot be handled.
String getFile()	Returns the file portion of the URL.
String getHost()	Returns the host portion of the URL.
int getPort()	Returns the port portion of the URL.
String getProtocol()	Returns the protocol portion of the URL.
getRef()	Returns the reference portion (the HTML name tag) of the URL.
InputStream openStream()	Returns an InputStream that encapsulates the document content.

13

The InetAddress Class

The InetAddress class represents the address of an Internet host. You use InetAddress to construct Socket and DatagramPacket objects, which you'll meet in later sections of this chapter. The `InetAddress` class has no constructor; instead, it provides three static methods that each return an instance of `InetAddress`:

- `InetAddress getLocalHost()`, which returns an `InetAddress` that represents the local host (the one running the Java program).
- `InetAddress getByName(String host)`, which returns an `InetAddress` of the specified host, if the host's address can be determined. For example,

  `getByName("www.mcp.com")`

  returns the Internet address of the Macmillan Web server.
- `InetAddress [] getAllByName(String host)`, which returns an array containing all the Internet addresses of the specified host. A host has multiple addresses if it has multiple network interfaces, because each interface has a unique address.

Each of these methods throws `UnknownHostException` if it's unable to determine the Internet address of the host.

The Socket Class

An Internet host has a set of numbered ports that it can use to communicate with other hosts. The `Socket` class encapsulates a port, providing methods that let you use the port to send and receive data. You can create a `Socket` by using the constructor

`Socket(String host, int port)`

or

`Socket(InetAddress address, int port)`

For example, to open a socket that sends to port 80 of the host www.mcp.com, you write this:

```
Socket mcp = new Socket("www.mcp.com", 80;)
```

The `Socket` class also provides more specialized constructors, but you'll seldom use them. The `Socket` constructors throw exceptions if they fail; your programs need to include a `try-catch` block or a `throws` clause to handle them.

Once you've created a socket, you can use the `getInputStream` method to get an associated `InputStream` and `getOutputStream` to get an associated `OutputStream`. By using ordinary input/output methods to read and write these streams, you can perform socket input and output as simply as file input and output.

If you've worked with `InputStream` and `OutputStream`, you've probably discovered that their cousins—`BufferedInputStream` and `PrintStream`—are more convenient to use.

You could wrap the `InputStream` returned by `getInputStream` in a `BufferedInputStream` and the `OutputStream` in a `PrintStream`, but this quickly grows tiresome. An easier, more object-oriented approach is to wrap the `Socket` in a new class that provides the appropriate stream wrappers. Listing 13.1 shows the `BetterSocket` class, which does just that. The `BetterSocket` class does not extend the `Socket` class; instead, it includes a field that references a `Socket`. This makes it possible to construct a `BetterSocket` from a `Socket`. The `BetterSocket` class does not offer the full range of methods provided by the `Socket` class: You could revise `BetterSocket` to define each of them, giving each method a body that forwards the corresponding message to the `Socket` instance and returns the result. However, the `Socket` class has many methods; therefore, defining corresponding `BetterSocket` methods would be tedious. Instead, the `BetterSocket` class provides an accessor method, `getSocket`, that returns a reference to the `Socket` instance. You can accomplish any desired `Socket` operation by getting a reference to the `Socket` instance and sending the `Socket` the appropriate message.

In addition to wrapping the `Socket` streams in a `BufferedInputFile` and `PrintStream`, `BetterSocket` provides `readLine` and `println` methods that make it easy to send lines of text over the `Socket` data streams. You'll see how this works in an upcoming sample program. Notice also the `close` method that releases a `Socket` that's no longer needed.

13

LISTING 13.1   `BetterSocket.java`—AN IMPROVED SOCKET CLASS

```java
import java.net.*;
import java.io.*;

public class BetterSocket
{
    Socket         theSocket;
    BufferedReader theReader;
    PrintWriter    theWriter;

    public BetterSocket(String host, int port)
      throws UnknownHostException, IOException
    {
        this(new Socket(host, port));
    }

    public BetterSocket(Socket s)
      throws UnknownHostException, IOException
    {
        theSocket = s;
        theReader = new BufferedReader(
          new InputStreamReader(
            theSocket.getInputStream()));
```

continues

LISTING 13.1 CONTINUED

```java
        theWriter = new PrintWriter(
          theSocket.getOutputStream(), true);
    }

    public Socket getSocket()
    {
        return theSocket;
    }

    public void close()
      throws IOException
    {
        theSocket.close();
    }

    public String readLine()
      throws IOException
    {
        return theReader.readLine();
    }

    public void println(String s)
      throws IOException
    {
        theWriter.println(s);
    }
}
```

The ServerSocket Class

The last of the classes we'll study before looking at a sample program is ServerSocket. The ServerSocket class, as you may have guessed, is used by server programs. It has a method, accept, that lets a program wait for a request sent by a client and then returns a Socket that the client and server can use to exchange data. Obligingly, the Socket object on the client side automatically switches to communicate using the new Socket. Figure 13.1 illustrates the operation of a ServerSocket.

To create a ServerSocket, you use the following constructor:

```java
ServerSocket(int port)
```

This constructor throws an IOException if it fails; otherwise, your ServerSocket is ready for use. When you send the ServerSocket the accept message, it blocks until a client request arrives and then returns a Socket. For example, to create a ServerSocket that listens on port 1234 for a client request, you could write:

FIGURE 13.1

The ServerSocket *returns a* Socket *that's used to exchange data between a client and server.*

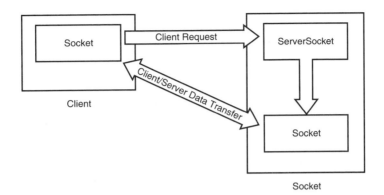

```
ServerSocket server = new ServerSocket(1234);
Socket client = server.accept();
```

You'll soon meet some additional ServerSocket methods, but let's press on to study our first sample program.

A SIMPLE SOCKET-BASED CLIENT AND SERVER

In this section, you'll see a simple socket-based client and a simple socket-based server. The client is implemented as an applet, and the server is implemented as a server. As presented, the client and server must run on the same computer, but you can easily change them to run on separate computers. You should initially run the client and server on the same computer, running the applet using appletviewer to satisfy yourself that it works. Only then should you consider running the client and server on different computers or running the client using a Web browser. You may find that you need to adjust the security configuration of your browser, particularly if you modify the applet to access a remote server.

The Socket-Based Client Applet

Figure 13.2 shows the SimpleClient applet, which connects to the SimpleServer application you'll meet in the next section. The application is a fortune cookie system (the type popular on UNIX systems) that provides a random message of the day. The client sends one of two messages—"hello" or "bye"—triggered by buttons on its window. In response, the server sends three random messages (fortune cookies). That way, you can choose the message you prefer and ignore the others, a feature not provided by run-of-the-mill fortune cookie servers.

FIGURE 13.2

The SimpleClient applet models a typical network client.

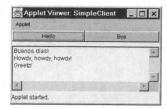

First, let's see how to run the application so you can try it for yourself; then we'll study its source code. Here are the steps you should follow. The following instructions assume you're using Windows 9x/NT (you'll need to adapt them if you're using some other operating system):

1. Copy the source files SimpleClient.java, SimpleServer.java, and SimpleClient.html from the CD-ROM to your hard drive.

2. Compile the two Java source files.

3. Start the server by typing this:

   ```
   java SimpleServer
   ```

   Soon, the server should respond with a "ready" message.

4. Open a new DOS window and start the client by typing this:

   ```
   appletviewer SimpleClient.html
   ```

5. Click the Hello button or the Bye button and observe the server response.

6. When you're done, exit the appletviewer by clicking the window's close box. Exit the server by pressing Ctrl+C.

If anything goes wrong, you'll see a Java stack trace in either the server window or client window. One possible source of problems is the port number, which is hard-coded as 1234. If this port is unavailable, the application will fail. Fixing this is simple: Choose another port number, change both the client and server source files, recompile them, and run the application.

Listing 13.2 shows the source code of the SimpleClient applet. Let's study it carefully. Notice that the port number on which the server listens is hard-coded as a constant. Notice also that the applet contains a `BetterSocket` as a field. The `init` method is straightforward, dealing exclusively with user-interface issues. The class also includes a `fatalError` method that prints a stack trace and closes the `BetterSocket`.

LISTING 13.2   `SimpleClient.java`—A SIMPLE SOCKET-BASED CLIENT

```
import java.applet.*;
import java.awt.*;
```

```java
import java.awt.event.*;
import java.net.*;
import java.io.*;

public class SimpleClient extends Applet
{
    public static final int    PORT = 1234;

    Button   theHelloButton = new Button("Hello");
    Button   theByeButton   = new Button("Bye");
    TextArea theResponse    = new TextArea(5, 64);

    BetterSocket theSocket;

    public void init()
    {
        setLayout(new BorderLayout());
        Panel p = new Panel();
        add(p, BorderLayout.NORTH);
        add(theResponse, BorderLayout.SOUTH);
        p.setLayout(new GridLayout(1, 0));
        p.add(theHelloButton);
        p.add(theByeButton);
        theResponse.setEditable(false);
        theHelloButton.addActionListener(new HelloHandler());
        theByeButton.addActionListener(new ByeHandler());
    }

    public void fatalError(Exception ex)
    {
        ex.printStackTrace();
        try
        {
            theSocket.close();
        }
        catch (Exception ex1) { ; }
    }

    class HelloHandler implements ActionListener
    {
        public void actionPerformed(ActionEvent evt)
        {
            try
            {
                theResponse.setText("");
                theSocket = new BetterSocket(
                  getCodeBase().getHost(), PORT);
                theSocket.println("Hello");
                theResponse.append(theSocket.readLine() + "\n");
```

continues

13

LISTING **13.2**   CONTINUED

```
                    theResponse.append(theSocket.readLine() + "\n");
                    theResponse.append(theSocket.readLine() + "\n");
                    theSocket.close();
                }
            catch (Exception ex) { fatalError(ex); }
        }
    }

    class ByeHandler implements ActionListener
    {
        public void actionPerformed(ActionEvent evt)
        {
            try
            {
                theResponse.setText("");
                theSocket = new BetterSocket(
                    getCodeBase().getHost(), PORT);
                theSocket.println("Bye");
                theResponse.append(theSocket.readLine() + "\n");
                theResponse.append(theSocket.readLine() + "\n");
                theResponse.append(theSocket.readLine() + "\n");
                theSocket.close();
            }
            catch (Exception ex) { fatalError(ex); }
        }
    }
}
```

The ActionListeners—HelloHandler and ByeHandler—do the interesting work. Each is similar to the other, so we'll focus on HelloHandler. Its actionPerformed method instantiates a BetterSocket, using the host address and port number. It obtains the host address by using the Applet method getCodeBase, which returns a URL that specifies the host that served the applet. The URL.getHost method returns the host portion of the URL. The actionPerformed method sends a println message to the BetterSocket, causing it to transmit the message argument—the String "Hello"—to the server. The actionPerformed method then reads the server's three-line response, displays the results, and closes the socket.

That's all there is to it: As promised, sockets are really quite simple to use. Let's move on to study the server program.

The Socket-Based Server

Listing 13.2 shows the server program that works with the client you just studied. The server's static main method instantiates a SimplerServer object and invokes its init method. The `init` method's first task is to access the server's cookies. To store the cookies, the server uses two text files—one containing "Hello" fortune cookies and one containing "Bye" fortune cookies. The `init` method reads these files and stores the cookies in two `Vector`s—one containing "Hello" messages and the other containing "Bye" messages.

LISTING 13.3 `SimpleServer.java`—A SIMPLE SOCKET-BASED SERVER

```java
import java.net.*;
import java.io.*;
import java.util.*;

public class SimpleServer
{
    public static final int    PORT = 1234;

    ServerSocket theSocket;
    BetterSocket theClient;

    Vector theHello = new Vector();
    Vector theBye   = new Vector();

    public static void main(String [] args)
    {
        new SimpleServer().init();
    }

    public void init()
    {
        try
        {
            BufferedReader in;
            String line;

            in = new BufferedReader(
              new InputStreamReader(
              new FileInputStream("hello.txt")));
            while ((line = in.readLine()) != null)
                theHello.addElement(line);
            in.close();

            in = new BufferedReader(
              new InputStreamReader(
              new FileInputStream("bye.txt")));
            while ((line = in.readLine()) != null)
                theBye.addElement(line);
            in.close();
```

continues

LISTING 13.3   CONTINUED

```java
            theSocket = new ServerSocket(PORT);
            while (true)
            {
                System.err.println("Server is ready.");
                theClient = new BetterSocket(
                  theSocket.accept());
                System.err.println("Server processing request.");
                String s = theClient.readLine();
                System.out.println("Read " + s + " from client.");
                if (s.equalsIgnoreCase("hello"))
                    sendGreeting(theHello);
                else if (s.equalsIgnoreCase("bye"))
                    sendGreeting(theBye);
                else
                    System.err.println("Invalid request: " + s);
                theClient.close();
                System.err.println("Processing complete.");
            }
        }
        catch (Exception ex)
        {
            ex.printStackTrace();
        }
    }

    public void sendGreeting(Vector v)
      throws IOException
    {
        int size = v.size();
        for (int i = 0; i < 3; i++)
        {
            int n = (int) (Math.random() * size);
            theClient.println((String) v.elementAt(n));
        }
    }
}
```

The server then creates a ServerSocket and enters an endless loop that processes client requests indefinitely. In the loop, it displays a "ready" message and then invokes the accept method. The accept method blocks execution until the ServerSocket receives a client request; then it returns a Socket. The init method wraps the Socket in a BetterSocket to simplify handling the input and output streams. Then it reads the command—"Hello" or "Bye"—sent by the client by using the readLine method. It tests the contents of the command String and passes an appropriate argument to the sendGreeting method, which sends the server's response. Finally, it closes the socket and loops, issuing another accept message that readies the server to process another client request.

The `sendGreeting` method uses the `Math.random` method to generate random numbers it uses to pick fortune cookies. It sends each fortune cookie to the client by using the `println` method. As you can see, the server is only a little more complex than the client.

Socket programming is so easy that you may wonder how it could possibly lead to the complications cited earlier in the chapter. The sample application features quite simple interaction between the client and server. The client sends one of two possible messages, and the server responds, in either case, with a three-line response. It's not socket programming as such that can become complicated, it's the client-server dialog. When clients and servers exchange dozens of message types, each requiring transmission of structured data, such as arrays or objects, programs rapidly become complicated. Therefore, the original advice stands. Use sockets only for simple data transfers; choose another technology when the data structure is more sophisticated than a simple byte stream.

THREADS AND TIMEOUTS

In order to create efficient and robust servers, you need to know about two socket programming techniques: multithreaded servers and socket timeouts. This section explains these techniques and presents examples of their use.

A Socket-Based Multithreaded Server

The server described in the previous section presents a flaw that we ignored in the interest of presenting a simple initial example. During the time the server is processing a client's request, it is unavailable to other clients. In some applications, this poses no problem. However, in others, rapid server response is critical. In this case, you need a different program structure: a multithreaded server.

Listing 13.4 shows the ThreadedServer application, a simple multithreaded server. Let's examine ThreadedServer, focusing on the points of difference between it and SimpleServer.

LISTING 13.4   `ThreadedServer.java`—A MULTITHREADED SERVER

```
import java.net.*;
import java.io.*;
import java.util.*;

public class ThreadedServer
{
    // Change the following literal if a port conflict occurs
    public static final int    PORT = 1234;
```

continues

LISTING 13.4 CONTINUED

```java
ServerSocket theSocket;

Vector theHello = new Vector();
Vector theBye   = new Vector();

public static void main(String [] args)
{
    new SimpleServer().init();
}

public void init()
{
    try
    {
        // Statements that load cookie vectors
        // omitted.

        theSocket = new ServerSocket(PORT);
        while (true)
        {
            System.err.println("Server is ready.");
            Socket s = theSocket.accept();
            Thread rp =
              new Thread(new RequestProcessor(s));
            rp.start();
        }
    }
    catch (Exception ex)
    {
        ex.printStackTrace();
    }
}
// Inner class omitted
}
```

ThreadedServer contains an inner class, RequestProcessor, that processes client
requests. You'll meet it in a moment. For now, direct your attention to the init method.
There you'll see the statement that creates the ServerSocket, followed by the "endless"
while loop. The contents of the loop are somewhat different than in SimpleServer.
ThreadedServer instantiates a Thread object based on the inner class RequestProcessor
and launches the Thread by sending it a start message. While the Thread processes the
latest client request, the init method loops back and issues a new accept message,
readying itself to handle a new client request. By handling new requests and request processing in parallel, the multithreaded server outperforms the simple server described earlier.

Listing 13.5 shows ThreadedServer's inner class, `RequestProcessor`. Its constructor saves the `Socket` reference it receives as an argument, wrapping it in a `BetterSocket` for ease of use. Its `run` method begins execution when the associated `Thread` receives a `start` message. As you can see, the `run` method contains the same statements that SimpleServer uses to handle client requests. The thread structure of the server, not its logic, is the source of its efficiency. Notice that Listing 13.5 does not show the `sendGreeting` method, which is unchanged from the version that appeared earlier in SimpleServer. The CD-ROM version of ThreadedServer contains the code for the `sendGreeting` method so that you can run ThreadedServer yourself. Just follow the same instructions given earlier, replacing references to SimpleServer with ThreadedServer.

LISTING 13.5   ThreadedServer.java—RequestProcessor INNER CLASS

```
class RequestProcessor implements Runnable
{
    BetterSocket theClient;

    public RequestProcessor(Socket s)
      throws UnknownHostException, IOException
    {
        theClient = new BetterSocket(s);
    }

    public void run()
    {
        try
        {
            System.err.println("Server processing request.");
            String s = theClient.readLine();
            System.err.println("Read " + s + " from client.");
            if (s.equalsIgnoreCase("hello"))
                sendGreeting(theHello);
            else if (s.equalsIgnoreCase("bye"))
                sendGreeting(theBye);
            else
                System.err.println("Invalid request: " + s);
            theClient.close();
            System.err.println("Processing complete.");
        }
        catch (Exception ex)
        {
            ex.printStackTrace();
        }
    }

    // sendGreeting method omitted
}
}
```

13

SOCKETS

Network Glitches

Network connections do not always function perfectly. A client might successfully contact a server, but a network outage might prevent the server from returning its response. Unless the client program anticipates this possibility, it could appear to be hung, because it's waiting indefinitely for a server response that never arrives.

Servers can suffer a similar fate if a client connects but fails to transmit the proper command. The CD-ROM includes two programs—BadServer and BadClient—that simulate network outages. BadServer contains the lines

```
System.err.println("Sleeping...");
Thread.sleep(10000);
System.err.println("Awake!");
```

right after its call to accept. The lines cause the server to become unavailable for a period of 10 seconds (10,000 milliseconds), thus mimicking a 10-second network outage. By running BadServer and SimpleClient, you can see how a network outage "hangs" SimpleClient.

The second program, BadClient, includes similar statements in its processing, just before it transmits a command. You can use it to see how network outages affect a server.

Of course, our real purpose is not merely to study the adverse consequences of a network outage. We want to prevent outages from causing programs to hang or appear to hang. The next two subsections show how to do this.

A Socket-Based Client with a Timeout Interval

To ameliorate the consequences of a network outage, you can specify a timeout interval for your sockets. When you issue a socket read or write, a clock begins counting down the interval. If the clock reaches zero before the read or write completes, the socket throws an exception that notifies your program that something has gone wrong. You specify a timeout using the message

```
setSoTimeout(int interval)
```

where *interval* specifies the timeout interval in milliseconds.

The CD-ROM includes the client applet TimeoutClient, which is based on SimpleApplet. TimeoutClient uses a timeout counter to recover from network outages. Listing 13.6 shows the pertinent source code that includes the call to setSoTimeout.

LISTING 13.6 `TimeoutClient.java` (PARTIAL LISTING)—A CLIENT WITH A TIMEOUT INTERVAL

```
class HelloHandler implements ActionListener
{
    public void actionPerformed(ActionEvent evt)
    {
        try
        {
            theResponse.setText("");
            theSocket = new BetterSocket(
              getCodeBase().getHost(), PORT);
            Socket s = theSocket.getSocket();
            s.setSoTimeout(1000);
            theSocket.println("Hello");
            theResponse.append(theSocket.readLine() + "\n");
            theResponse.append(theSocket.readLine() + "\n");
            theResponse.append(theSocket.readLine() + "\n");
            theSocket.close();
        }
        catch (Exception ex) { fatalError(ex); }
    }
}
```

You can use TimeoutClient with BadServer to see how it handles simulated network outages. TimeoutClient simply prints a stack trace when its timeout interval expires. A real application would probably take more a appropriate action that's application dependent.

A Socket-Based Server with a Timeout Interval

Listing 13.7 presents the pertinent part of a server—TimeoutServer—that uses a timeout interval to avoid tying up resources devoted to clients it can't access. The CD-ROM includes the complete source code of the server application, which you can use with BadClient to study simulated network outages.

LISTING 13.7 `TimeoutServer.java` (PARTIAL LISTING)—A SERVER WITH TIMEOUT INTERVAL

```
theSocket = new ServerSocket(PORT);
while (true)
{
    System.err.println("Server is ready.");
    Socket s = theSocket.accept();
    s.setSoTimeout(5000);
    Thread rp =
      new Thread(new RequestProcessor(s));
    rp.start();
}
```

DATAGRAMS

As mentioned near the beginning of this chapter, you can use either of two types of sockets: IP sockets or UDP sockets. Up to this point, the sample programs have used IP sockets. In this section, you'll learn how to use UDP sockets.

UDP sockets don't provide the automatic handshaking provided by the `accept` method of the `Socket` class. Moreover, TCP/IP doesn't guarantee that a host will receive UDP packets (often called *datagrams*) in the same sequence in which the originating host sent them. Therefore, UDP packets are primarily useful only for brief data transfers that involve quite simple data structures. Moreover, some organizations' network administrators configure firewalls to block UDP packets from outside their organization. If you want to use UDP packets across the Internet, you should check with your network administrator before writing code. You could save yourself a great deal of time.

A Datagram Client

Listing 13.8 shows the DatagramClient applet, a simple applet that sends and receives datagrams. As usual, the outer class sets up the user interface, which includes two buttons—one labeled "Hello" and one labeled "Bye." Clicking a button causes the applet to send a message to a server, which you'll study in a moment. The server returns a response that the applet displays.

LISTING 13.8   `DatagramClient.java`—A DATAGRAM-BASED CLIENT

```java
import java.applet.*;
import java.awt.*;
import java.awt.event.*;
import java.net.*;
import java.io.*;

public class DatagramClient extends Applet
{
    public static final int    SEND_PORT   = 1234;
    public static final int    LISTEN_PORT = 1235;

    Button    theHelloButton = new Button("Hello");
    Button    theByeButton   = new Button("Bye");
    TextArea  theResponse    = new TextArea(5, 64);

    public void init()
    {
        setLayout(new BorderLayout());
        Panel p = new Panel();
        add(p, BorderLayout.NORTH);
        add(theResponse, BorderLayout.SOUTH);
```

```
        p.setLayout(new GridLayout(1, 0));
        p.add(theHelloButton);
        p.add(theByeButton);
        theResponse.setEditable(false);
        theHelloButton.addActionListener(new HelloHandler());
        theByeButton.addActionListener(new ByeHandler());
    }

    public void fatalError(Exception ex)
    {
        ex.printStackTrace();
    }

    // Inner classes omitted
}
```

The interesting parts of the applet are the `HelloHandler` and `ByeHandler` inner classes, which are shown in Listing 13.9. Because the inner classes are similar, let's look at only the `HelloHandler` class. Its `actionPerformed` method is invoked when the user clicks the "Hello" button. By sending the `getBytes` method to a `String` constructed using a literal, the `actionPerformed` method constructs a `byte` array containing the message "Hello." The method then creates two `DatagramSockets`: the first for receiving a datagram, and the second for sending a datagram. The method creates a `DatagramPacket` using a constructor that specifies the byte array that contains the message, the length of the buffer, the Internet address of the destination host, and the port from which the datagram will be sent. Having created the datagram, the method sends it using the `send` message.

To receive the server's response, the method creates a `byte` array big enough to hold the response. It then creates a `DatagramPacket` using a simple form of the constructor that specifies only the buffer and its length. By sending the `receive` message, the method gets the server response and places it in the buffer. Finally, the method displays the response and closes the `DatagramSockets`.

LISTING 13.9   `DatagramClient.java`—INNER CLASSES

```
class HelloHandler implements ActionListener
{
    public void actionPerformed(ActionEvent evt)
    {
        try
        {
            theResponse.setText("");
            byte [] buffer = new String("Hello").getBytes();
```

continues

13

SOCKETS

LISTING 13.9   CONTINUED

```java
            DatagramSocket in  =
              new DatagramSocket(LISTEN_PORT);
            DatagramSocket out
              = new DatagramSocket();
            DatagramPacket dg;
            dg = new DatagramPacket(
              buffer, buffer.length,
              InetAddress.getByName(null), SEND_PORT);
            System.err.print("Sending datagram....");
            out.send(dg);
            System.err.println("sent.");
            buffer = new byte[255];
            dg = new DatagramPacket(
              buffer, buffer.length);
            in.receive(dg);
            theResponse.setText(new String(buffer));
            in.close();
            out.close();
        }
        catch (Exception ex) { fatalError(ex); }
    }
}

class ByeHandler implements ActionListener
{
    public void actionPerformed(ActionEvent evt)
    {
        try
        {
            theResponse.setText("");
            byte [] buffer = new String("Bye").getBytes();
            DatagramSocket in  =
              new DatagramSocket(LISTEN_PORT);
            DatagramSocket out
              = new DatagramSocket();
            DatagramPacket dg;
            dg = new DatagramPacket(
              buffer, buffer.length,
              InetAddress.getByName(null), SEND_PORT);
            out.send(dg);
            buffer = new byte[255];
            dg = new DatagramPacket(
              buffer, buffer.length);
            in.receive(dg);
            theResponse.setText(new String(buffer));
            in.close();
            out.close();
        }
        catch (Exception ex) { fatalError(ex); }
```

```
        }
    }
}
```

As you can see, the datagram client turns out to be a simple program. Let's examine the datagram server, which you'll discover is equally simple.

A Datagram Server

Listing 13.10 shows the DataServer application, a UDP-based server. Notice that the application defines two ports: one on which to receive and another on which to transmit. The complementary client applet, which you'll meet momentarily, uses these same two ports but in a mirrored fashion—the client listens on the port to which the server transmits and transmits on the port to which the server listens.

LISTING 13.10 DatagramServer.java—A DATAGRAM-BASED SERVER

```java
import java.net.*;
import java.io.*;
import java.util.*;

public class DatagramServer
{
    public static final int    LISTEN_PORT = 1234;
    public static final int    SEND_PORT   = 1235;

    Vector theHello = new Vector();
    Vector theBye   = new Vector();

    public static void main(String [] args)
    {
        new DatagramServer().init();
    }

    public void init()
    {
        try
        {
            BufferedReader in;
            String line;

            in = new BufferedReader(
              new InputStreamReader(
              new FileInputStream("hello.txt")));
            while ((line = in.readLine()) != null)
                theHello.addElement(line);
            in.close();
```

continues

LISTING 13.10 CONTINUED

```java
        in = new BufferedReader(
          new InputStreamReader(
          new FileInputStream("bye.txt")));
        while ((line = in.readLine()) != null)
            theBye.addElement(line);
        in.close();

        DatagramSocket socket =
          new DatagramSocket(LISTEN_PORT);
        byte [] buffer = new byte[255];
        DatagramPacket dg =
          new DatagramPacket(buffer, buffer.length);
        while (true)
        {
            System.err.println("Server is ready.");
            socket.receive(dg);
            System.err.println("Server processing request.");
            String s = new String(buffer);
            System.err.println("Read " + s + " \nfrom client " +
              dg.getAddress() + ".");
            if (s.startsWith("Hello"))
                sendGreeting(theHello);
            else if (s.startsWith("Bye"))
                sendGreeting(theBye);
            else
                System.err.println("Invalid request: " + s);
            System.err.println("Processing complete.");
        }
    }
    catch (Exception ex)
    {
        ex.printStackTrace();
    }
}

public void sendGreeting(Vector v)
  throws IOException
{
    String s = "";
    int size = v.size();
    for (int i = 0; i < 3; i++)
    {
        int n = (int) (Math.random() * size);
        s += v.elementAt(n) + "\n";
    }
    DatagramSocket out =
      new DatagramSocket();
    DatagramPacket dg =
      new DatagramPacket(s.getBytes(), s.length(),
```

```
                 InetAddress.getByName(null), SEND_PORT);
           out.send(dg);
           out.close();
     }
}
```

Before sending or receiving a UDP packet, your program must construct a
`DatagramPacket` object. The `init` method constructs such an object, using a byte array
capable of holding 255 bytes. The longest message that the program can handle is determined by the size of this `DatagramPacket` buffer. To listen, the server sends the `receive`
message to its `DatagramSocket`. It extracts the transmitted `String` from the byte array
buffer and handles processing in much the same fashion as its IP-packet cousin servers.

In its `sendGreeting` method, the server constructs a `DatagramSocket` for transmitting the
response to the client and a `DatagramPacket` to hold the response. It uses the
`InetAddress.getByName` method with a `null` argument to get the host address of the
client, which in this demonstration must be the same as that of the server. In a real server, you could use the `DatagramPacket` methods `getAddress` and `getPort` to obtain the
host address and port number from which the received packet originated. Sending the
assembled datagram is easily accomplished by using the `send` method.

As you can see, using UDP sockets is only a bit more complicated than using IP sockets.
Where the client/server interaction is quite simple, the lower overhead of UDP sockets
may pay performance dividends.

FROM HERE

In this chapter, you've learned about sockets—the most fundamental facility for exchanging data among networked hosts. You learned how to write socket-based clients and
servers and how to use threads and timeouts to construct efficient, robust systems. You
also learned how to use low-overhead datagrams to increase the efficiency of simple,
connectionless data exchanges. The following chapters provide additional information
about sockets:

- Chapter 14, "Socket-Based Implementation of the Airline Reservation System,"
  shows how the airline reservation system example can be implemented using sockets.

- Chapter 15, "Remote Method Invocation (RMI)," describes a Java core package
  that implements a socket-based protocol that simplifies exchanging data among
  networked hosts.

- Chapter 18, "Servlets and Common Gateway Interface (CGI)," describes the Java
  servlet API. URLs play an important role in the servlet API.

13

SOCKETS

SOCKET-BASED IMPLEMENTATION OF THE AIRLINE RESERVATION SYSTEM

IN THIS CHAPTER

In the previous chapter, you learned about Java's network API and socket programming. In this chapter, you'll see an example of a larger socket-based program—the Airline Reservation System of Chapter 6, "The Airline Reservation System Model." You'll find the source code for the program on the CD-ROM. By studying the program, you'll learn more about using sockets to exchange data across networks.

To refresh your recall of the Airline Reservation System, you should turn back to Chapter 6 and skim it quickly, focusing on the functional requirements of the system. In this section, we'll focus on the differences between the requirements presented in Chapter 6 and the program described in this chapter.

> **NOTE**
>
> Even though it includes over 1,100 lines of source code, the sample program presented in this chapter doesn't fully satisfy all the requirements described in Chapter 6.

The sample program implements only the following three transactions, which are based on those given in Chapter 6:

- Search Flights, which returns each flight stored in the database.
- Search Seats, which returns the reservation information for a specified passenger identified by passenger number.
- Book Seat, which enters a reservation for a specified passenger and flight. The transaction makes several simplifying assumptions. The passenger and flight must already exist as entities; the transaction does not create new passengers or flights. The reservation number must be unique; attempting to add a reservation with the same number as an existing reservation updates the existing reservation.

The sample program does not implement the visual interface for seat selection described in Chapter 6. Nor does it implement the reservation pool locking mechanism.

Fully implementing the requirements given in Chapter 6 is possible, but it would increase the size of the program by a factor of 2 or 3. A good way to learn more about socket programming is to extend the program to include the unimplemented transactions and features described in Chapter 6.

Let's begin our tour of the program by looking at the application classes. Later, we'll look at the client and server classes that provide the user interface and network connectivity.

APPLICATION CLASSES

The sample program includes three application classes:

- `Flight`, which models a flight
- `Passenger`, which models a passenger
- `Reservation`, which models a reservation

Let's examine each of these in turn.

The `Flight` Class

Because top-level Java classes are always stored in a file that has the same name as the class, you can correctly infer that the `Flight` class is stored in the file Flight.java. You'll find that file on the CD-ROM in the directory for this chapter.

NOTE

All the code from here until the next section, "The Passenger Class," is found in the file Flight.java in the chapter14/listings directory of the CD-ROM.

The `Flight` class defines these fields:

```
String    theFlightNo;
String    theOrigin;
String    theDestination;
String    theDeparture;
String    theArrival;
int       theSeats;
int       theReservations;
```

The `FlightNo` field uniquely identifies a flight. All the fields except two are `String` objects. The integer field `theSeats` contains the seating capacity of the flight; the integer field `theReservations` contains the number of seats currently booked.

The class has two constructors—one that lets you create a `Flight` by specifying only the flight number and another that lets you specify values for each field:

```
public Flight(String flight_no)
{
    this(flight_no, "", "", "", "", 0, 0);
}

public Flight(String flight_no, String origin,
  String destination, String departure,
```

14

SOCKET-BASED
IMPLEMENTATION

```
    String arrival, int seats, int reservations)
{
    theFlightNo = flight_no;
    theOrigin = origin;
    theDestination = destination;
    theDeparture = departure;
    theArrival = arrival;
    theSeats = seats;
    theReservations = reservations;
}
```

The Flight class has four main types of methods:

- Accessor and mutator methods

- Static methods that return one or more instances of Flight

- A method, dbWrite, that writes a Flight instance to the database

- Methods that convert a Flight instance to or from a String representation

The accessor and mutator methods present nothing remarkable; they simply provide access to the state data stored in a Flight object. Therefore, let's move on to the static methods of the Flight class—getInstance and getFlights. These methods are static, so they can be used even if you have no reference to a Flight instance. They provide the usual way of obtaining flight data from the database. The getInstance method returns the Flight object having a specified flight number:

```
public static Flight getInstance(Connection db,
  String flight_no) throws SQLException
{
    String query      =
        "Select Origin, Destination, Departure, " +
        "Arrival, Seats, Reservations " +
        "From Flight " +
        "Where FlightNo = '" +
        flight_no +
        "'";
    Statement stmt = db.createStatement();
    ResultSet rs   = stmt.executeQuery(query);
    rs.next();
    String origin       = rs.getString(1);
    String destination  = rs.getString(2);
    String departure    = rs.getString(3);
    String arrival      = rs.getString(4);
    int    seats        = rs.getInt(5);
    int    reservations = rs.getInt(6);
    rs.close();
    stmt.close();
    return new Flight(flight_no, origin,
        destination, departure, arrival, seats,
```

```
        reservations);
}
```

The similar `getFlights` method returns an array that contains every flight:

```java
public static Flight [] getFlights(Connection db)
  throws SQLException
{
    Vector f = new Vector();
    String query      =
       "Select FlightNo, Origin, Destination, " +
       "Departure, Arrival, Seats, Reservations " +
       "From Flight ";
    Statement stmt = db.createStatement();
    ResultSet rs   = stmt.executeQuery(query);
    while (rs.next())
    {
        String flight_no   = rs.getString(1);
        String origin       = rs.getString(2);
        String destination = rs.getString(3);
        String departure    = rs.getString(4);
        String arrival      = rs.getString(5);
        int    seats        = rs.getInt(6);
        int    reservations = rs.getInt(7);
        Flight flight = new Flight(flight_no, origin,
           destination, departure, arrival, seats,
           reservations);
        f.addElement(flight);
    }
    rs.close();
    stmt.close();
    int n = f.size();
    Flight [] flights = new Flight[n];
    for (int i = 0; i < n; i++)
    {
        flights[i] = (Flight) f.elementAt(i);
    }
    return flights;
}
```

Notice how `getFlights` uses a `Vector` to collect the flights and then creates an array with exactly the proper size, copying the elements of the `Vector` into the array. Notice also the use of the `getInt` method to obtain values of the proper type for the numeric fields `theSeats` and `theReservations`.

The `dbWrite` method writes a `Flight` instance into a SQL database. It first attempts to update an existing table row; failing that, it creates a new table row:

```java
public void dbWrite(Connection db)
  throws SQLException
```

14

SOCKET-BASED
IMPLEMENTATION

```java
{
    String query     =
        "Update Flight " +
        "Set Origin = '" +
        theOrigin +
        "', " +
        "Destination = '" +
        theDestination +
        "', " +
        "Departure = '" +
        theDeparture +
        "', " +
        "Arrival = '" +
        theArrival +
        "', " +
        "Seats = '" +
        theSeats +
        "', " +
        "Reservations = '" +
        theReservations +
        "' " +
        "Where FlightNo = '" +
        theFlightNo +
        "'";
    Statement stmt = db.createStatement();
    int n = stmt.executeUpdate(query);
    if (n == 0)
    {
        query = "Insert Into Flight " +
        "(FlightNo, Origin, Destination, Departure, " +
        "Arrival, Seats, Reservations) " +
        "Values ('" +
        theFlightNo +
        "', '" +
        theOrigin +
        "', '" +
        theDestination +
        "', '" +
        theDeparture +
        "', '" +
        theArrival +
        "', '" +
        theSeats +
        "', '" +
        theReservations +
        "')";
        n = stmt.executeUpdate(query);
    }
    stmt.close();
}
```

Finally, the `Flight` class provides a method, `packAsString`, that packs the field values of a `Flight` instance into a `String` and a static method, `unpackFromString`, that in turn returns a `Flight` instance it creates by parsing field values from a `String`:

```java
public String packAsString()
{
    String s = theFlightNo;
    s += "," + theOrigin;
    s += "," + theDestination;
    s += "," + theDeparture;
    s += "," + theArrival;
    s += "," + theSeats;
    s += "," + theReservations;
    return s;
}

public static Flight unpackFromString(String s)
{
    StringTokenizer st = new StringTokenizer(s, ",");
    Flight f = new Flight(st.nextToken());
    f.setOrigin(st.nextToken());
    f.setDestination(st.nextToken());
    f.setDeparture(st.nextToken());
    f.setArrival(st.nextToken());
    f.setSeats(Integer.parseInt(st.nextToken()));
    f.setReservations(Integer.parseInt(st.nextToken()));
    return f;
}
```

The `Passenger` Class

> **NOTE**
>
> All the code from here until the next section, "The `Reservation` Class," is found in the file Passenger.java in the chapter14/listings directory of the CD-ROM.

The design of the `Passenger` class resembles that of the `Flight` class, so we'll present only the most salient parts. The `Passenger` class defines the following fields:

```java
String thePassengerNo;
String theName;
String theAddress;
String theCity;
String theState;
String theZip;
String theCreditCard;
```

Like the `Flight` class, the `Passenger` class defines two constructors. One requires only a passenger number; the other requires values for each field. The `Passenger` class also provides an accessor and mutator method for each of its fields.

The `Passenger` class provides two database methods: a static method, `getInstance`, that returns the instance of `Passenger` having a specified passenger number and a method, `dbWrite`, that writes a `Passenger` instance to the database. Here's the `getInstance` method, which resembles the similarly named method of the `Flight` class:

```
public static Passenger getInstance(Connection db,
  String passenger_no) throws SQLException
{
    String query      =
      "Select Name, Address, City, State, Zip, " +
      "CreditCard " +
      "From Passenger " +
      "Where PassengerNo = '" +
      passenger_no +
      "'";
    Statement stmt = db.createStatement();
    ResultSet rs   = stmt.executeQuery(query);
    rs.next();
    String name        = rs.getString(1);
    String address     = rs.getString(2);
    String city        = rs.getString(3);
    String state       = rs.getString(4);
    String zip         = rs.getString(5);
    String credit_card = rs.getString(6);
    rs.close();
    stmt.close();
    return new Passenger(passenger_no, name, address,
      city, state, zip, credit_card);
}
```

Here's the `dbWrite` method, which resembles the similarly named method of the `Flight` class:

```
public void dbWrite(Connection db)
  throws SQLException
{
    String query      =
      "Update Passenger " +
      "Set Name = '" +
      theName +
      "', Address = '" +
      theAddress +
      "', City = '" +
      theCity +
      "', State = '" +
      theState +
      "', Zip = '" +
```

```
            theZip +
            "', CreditCard = '" +
            theCreditCard +
            "' " +
            "Where PassengerNo = '" +
            thePassengerNo +
            "'";
        Statement stmt = db.createStatement();
        int n = stmt.executeUpdate(query);
        if (n == 0)
        {
            query = "Insert Into Passenger " +
            "(PassengerNo, Name, Address, " +
            "City, State, Zip, CreditCard) " +
            "Values ('" +
            thePassengerNo +
            "', '" +
            theName +
            "', '" +
            theAddress +
            "', '" +
            theCity +
            "', '" +
            theState +
            "', '" +
            theZip +
            "', '" +
            theCreditCard +
            "')";
            n = stmt.executeUpdate(query);
        }
        stmt.close();
    }
```

The `Passenger` class also defines `packAsString` and `unpackFromString` methods. These are not shown because they closely resemble the similarly named methods of the `Flight` class, which we covered in the preceding section.

The `Reservation` Class

14

SOCKET-BASED IMPLEMENTATION

> **NOTE**
>
> All the code from here until the next section, "The `SuperSocket` Class," is found in the file Reservation.java in the chapter14/listings directory of the CD-ROM.

The third and final application class of the sample program is the Reservation class. This class defines three fields:

```
String    theReservationNo;
String    theFlightNo;
String    thePassengerNo;
```

The Reservation class defines three constructors. Two resemble those of the Flight and Passenger classes: One of these requires only a reservation number, and the other requires values for each of the three fields of the Reservation class. The additional method takes a Connection instance as an argument and uses the Connection to check whether the specified flight has an available seat. If no seat is available, the method throws a FlightBookedException; otherwise, it reduces the count of available seats:

```
public Reservation(Connection db,
  String reservation_no, String flight_no,
  String passenger_no)
  throws FlightBookedException, SQLException
{
    Flight flight = Flight.getInstance(db, flight_no);
    int seats = flight.getSeats();
    int reservations = flight.getReservations();
    if (reservations >= seats)
      throw new FlightBookedException();
    flight.setReservations(reservations + 1);
    flight.dbWrite(db);
    theReservationNo = reservation_no;
    theFlightNo = flight_no;
    thePassengerNo = passenger_no;
}
```

The BookedFlightException class is a simple methodless class that extends the Exception class.

Of course, the method the Reservation class uses to manage available sets is not an entirely adequate approach. Unless a constructed Reservation instance is subsequently booked, the corresponding seat is forever lost. Passengers might appreciate the extra leg room, but the airline's shareholders would not. The pool mechanism described in Chapter 6 is a simple solution to this problem.

Like the previous classes, the Reservation class defines accessor and mutator methods for its fields. It also defines three static methods: one that returns a specified Reservation instance, one that returns all Reservation instances associated with a specified flight, and one that returns all Reservation instances associated with a specified passenger. These follow the design of similar methods of the Flight and Passenger classes and are therefore not shown here. Similarly, the dbWrite, packAsString, and unpackFromString methods of the Reservation class are not shown. See the file Reservation.java in the chapter14/listings directory of CD-ROM for their contents.

THE SuperSocket CLASS

To transfer data across the network, the program uses the SuperSocket class, which performs a function similar to that of the BetterSocket class of Chapter 13, "Sockets." SuperSocket uses an ObjectInputStream and an ObjectOutputStream to serialize an object, transmit it over the network, and deserialize it. Rather than associate ObjectStream objects directly with the socket, the program associates them with byte arrays, using the ByteArrayInputStream and ByteArrayOutputStream classes. This is necessary because in JDK 1.1.6, associating an ObjectStream with a socket causes the socket to hang.

The SuperSocket class always transfers a Vector whose elements must be serializable objects. The readVector and writeVector methods do the real work:

> **NOTE**
>
> The code for this section is found in the file SuperSocket.java in the chapter14/listings directory of the CD-ROM.

```
public Vector readVector()
  throws IOException, ClassNotFoundException
{
    int n = theInput.readInt();
    byte [] buffer = new byte[n];
    theInput.read(buffer);
    ByteArrayInputStream bytes =
      new ByteArrayInputStream(buffer);
    ObjectInputStream in =
      new ObjectInputStream(bytes);
    Object x = in.readObject();
    in.close();
    return (Vector) x;
}

public void writeVector(Vector x)
  throws IOException
{
    ByteArrayOutputStream bytes =
      new ByteArrayOutputStream();
    ObjectOutputStream out =
      new ObjectOutputStream(bytes);
    out.writeObject(x);
    byte [] buffer = bytes.toByteArray();
    out.close();
    theOutput.writeInt(buffer.length);
    theOutput.write(buffer);
}
```

To see how to use SuperSocket, we first need to move on and consider the Server class.

THE Server CLASS

The Server class provides a simple, single-threaded server that provides remote clients access to the data contained in the application's SQL database. The main method of the Server class instantiates an instance of Server. The constructor opens a database connection and initiates listening for client requests:

> **NOTE**
>
> All the code from here until the next section, "The RemoteClient Class," is found in the file Server.java in the chapter14/listings directory of the CD-ROM.

```java
public Server()
{
    try
    {
        Class.forName("sun.jdbc.odbc.JdbcOdbcDriver");
        theConnection =
          DriverManager.getConnection(DB, USER, PASSWORD);

        theSocket = new ServerSocket(PORT);
        while (true)
        {
            System.err.println("Server is ready.");
            Socket s = theSocket.accept();
            theClient = new SuperSocket(s);
            processRequest();
        }
    }
    catch (Exception ex)
    {
        ex.printStackTrace();
    }
}
```

When the program receives a client request, the processRequest method uses SuperSocket.readObject to obtain the Vector that specifies the requested transaction:

```java
Vector v = theClient.readVector();
String opcode = (String) v.elementAt(0);
System.out.println(opcode);
```

It then tests the contents of the `String` object `opcode` and invokes a method to process the requested transaction. Here's the method that processes requests to search for a flight:

```java
public Vector searchFlights()
{
    Vector out = new Vector();
    try
    {
        Flight [] flights =
          Flight.getFlights(theConnection);
        for (int i = 0; i < flights.length; i++)
        {
            String s = flights[i].packAsString();
            out.addElement(s);
        }
    }
    catch (SQLException ex)
    {
        out.addElement("***Error***");
    }
    return out;
}
```

Each request-processing method returns a `Vector` that's transmitted as a response to the client by the `processRequest` method, which invokes `SuperSocket.writeVector`. The response contains packed `String` objects that encode `Flight` instances.

Here's the method that handles a request to search by passenger number for a specified reservation:

```java
public Vector searchSeats(Vector v)
{
    Vector out = new Vector();
    try
    {
        String passenger = (String) v.elementAt(1);
        Reservation [] res =
          Reservation.getPassenger(
          theConnection, passenger);
        if (res == null || res.length == 0)
            out.addElement("***No such record***");
        else
        {
            for (int i = 0; i < res.length; i++)
            {
                String s = res[i].packAsString();
                out.addElement(s);
            }
        }
```

```
    }
    catch (SQLException ex)
    {
        System.out.println(ex);
        out.addElement("***Error***");
    }
    return out;
}
```

Here's the final request-processing method, the one that handles a request to book a seat:

```
public Vector bookSeat(Vector v)
{
    Vector out = new Vector();
    try
    {
        String flight_no =
          (String) v.elementAt(1);
        String passenger_no =
          (String) v.elementAt(2);
        String res_no =
          (String) v.elementAt(3);
        Reservation res = new Reservation(
          theConnection, res_no, flight_no,
          passenger_no);
        res.dbWrite(theConnection);
        out.addElement("***Added ok***");
    }
    catch (Exception ex)
    {
        ex.printStackTrace();
        out.addElement("***Error***");
    }
    return out;
}
```

THE RemoteClient CLASS

The RemoteClient class provides a crude user interface, shown in Figure 14.1, for accessing the remote server. It presents the same controls for each of the three supported transactions. Actually, you don't need to enter data for the Search Flights transaction; you only need to enter the passenger number for the Search Seats transaction. The Book Seat transaction requires a reservation number, flight number, and passenger number. The program performs no input validation.

FIGURE 14.1

The RemoteClient application interface lets you access the application database over a TCP/IP network.

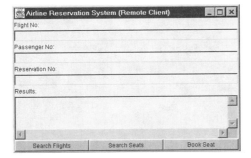

In the interest of brevity, we'll omit discussion of the user interface methods, which merely invoke the processing methods when the user interacts with the application. See the RemoteClient.java file in the chapter14/listings directory of the CD-ROM for the contents of the user interface methods. The RMI-based example program we present in Chapter 16, "RMI-Based Implementation of the Airline Reservation System," has a similar user interface to the one featured in the RemoteClient class; that chapter contains a detailed explanation of the user interface. Three processing methods each handle one of the three supported transactions. The searchFlights method handles the Search Flights transaction:

> **NOTE**
>
> All the code from this section is found in the file RemoteClient.java in the chapter14/listings directory of the CD-ROM.

```java
public void searchFlights()
{
    try
    {
        theResults.setText("");
        theSocket = new SuperSocket(
          HOST, PORT);
        theSocket.getSocket().setSoTimeout(TIMEOUT);
        Vector v = new Vector();
        v.addElement("Search Flights");
        theSocket.writeVector(v);
        v = theSocket.readVector();
        theSocket.close();
        for (int i = 0; i < v.size(); i++)
        {
            String s = (String) v.elementAt(i);
```

14

SOCKET-BASED IMPLEMENTATION

```
            theResults.append(s + "\n");
        }
    }
    catch (Exception ex) { fatalError(ex); }
}
```

The `searchSeats` method handles the Search Seats transaction:

```
public void searchSeats()
{
    try
    {
        theResults.setText("");
        theSocket = new SuperSocket(
          HOST, PORT);
        theSocket.getSocket().setSoTimeout(TIMEOUT);
        Vector v = new Vector();
        v.addElement("Search Seats");
        v.addElement(thePassengerNo.getText());
        theSocket.writeVector(v);
        v = theSocket.readVector();
        theSocket.close();
        for (int i = 0; i < v.size(); i++)
        {
            String s = (String) v.elementAt(i);
            theResults.append(s + "\n");
        }
    }
    catch (Exception ex) { fatalError(ex); }
}
```

Finally, the `bookSeat` method handles the Book Seat transaction:

```
public void bookSeat()
{
    try
    {
        theResults.setText("");
        theSocket = new SuperSocket(
          HOST, PORT);
        theSocket.getSocket().setSoTimeout(TIMEOUT);
        Vector v = new Vector();
        v.addElement("Book Seat");
        v.addElement(theFlightNo.getText());
        v.addElement(thePassengerNo.getText());
        v.addElement(theReservationNo.getText());
        theSocket.writeVector(v);
        v = theSocket.readVector();
        theSocket.close();
        for (int i = 0; i < v.size(); i++)
```

```
        {
            String s = (String) v.elementAt(i);
            theResults.append(s + "\n");
        }
    }
    catch (Exception ex) { fatalError(ex); }
}
```

To run the sample program for yourself, you must use Windows 9*x* or NT, because UNIX does not provide support for the Microsoft Access database Airline.mdb. First copy the files from the chapter14/listings directory of the CD-ROM to your local hard drive. If you prefer, you can copy only the source files and compile them yourself. Use the Control Panel ODBC Administrator tool to create a DSN named "airline," referring to the Airline.mdb file in this chapter. Be sure not to use the similarly named file for Chapter 12, "Java Database Connectivity (JDBC)." Then, start the server in one DOS window by typing

java Server

Finally, start the client in another DOS window by typing

java RemoteClient

If you get an error message indicating that the client or server was unable to open its socket, you should suspect a port conflict. Change the value of the PORT field in both the Server.java and RemoteClient.java files from 1234 to a port that your system does not use.

FROM HERE

In this chapter, you've seen a complete application of modest size that uses sockets to link a client program with a remote server. In the next chapter, you'll learn how Java's Remote Method Invocation (RMI) API makes it easier to create such applications.

14

**SOCKET-BASED
IMPLEMENTATION**

REMOTE METHOD INVOCATION (RMI)

IN THIS CHAPTER

According to German folklore, everyone has a doppelgänger, a spirit double that resembles its original in every detail. One's doppelgänger, however, is normally invisible. Remote Method Invocation (RMI) allows objects in different Java virtual machines of different hosts to send and receive messages. To perform this feat, RMI employs doppelgängers that appear as local objects even though they reside on remote hosts. In this chapter you'll learn:

- How RMI makes it easy to implement distributed applications

  Implementing a distributed application using sockets can be a chore. RMI makes it almost as easy to implement a distributed application as a nondistributed application.

- How RMI makes it possible for local objects and remote objects to interact

  A remote object can be accessed outside its host Java virtual machine. You'll see how Java's serialization facility allows remote objects to accept method calls and return method results.

- How to create remote objects

  A remote object requires only a few more lines of code than an ordinary object. You can easily create remote objects that act as servers, processing requests sent by clients on other hosts. You'll also see how such remote objects can call back their clients to inform them of state changes.

REMOTE PROCEDURE CALLS

Transferring data is a basic computational operation. Java's message-method paradigm transfers data from a calling object to a called object within a single Java virtual machine. In Chapter 13, "Sockets," you learned how to cross virtual machine boundaries using sockets to transfer data from one host to another. Consider that both paradigms—method calls and sockets—achieve the same goal: the transfer of data. Now consider which is easier to use. Most certainly you'll agree that it's easier to invoke a method than to send a message over a socket. Wouldn't you like to send data to a remote host as easily as you invoke a method? RMI provides that convenience.

One of the cornerstones of early evolutionary biology was Haeckel's theory that *ontogeny*—the development of an embryo—recapitulates *phylogeny*—the evolutionary development of the embryo's species. Adherents of the theory pointed to apparent parallels between the development of human embryos and those of animal species, such as the "fish stage" of human embryo development, in which the embryo develops "gill slits." Subsequent research determined that the alleged recapitulation of "gill slits" was merely superficial: At no point does a human embryo develop gills, a fish tail, or fins. Consequently, very few modern embryologists subscribe to Haeckel's view.

However, ontogeny often recapitulates phylogeny in the software world. Often, study of a technology's ancestors can reveal much about the technology. The immediate technological forerunner of RMI is *Remote Procedure Call (RPC)*. Although RPC is a non–object-oriented technology, understanding how it works will help you understand how RMI works and why RMI is an improvement over other technologies.

Like RMI, RPC aims to make transferring data to a remote host simple. RPC presents remote data transfers as procedure calls, the basic data transfer mechanism of non–object-oriented programs. Procedure calls differ from method calls in that the arguments and return values of a procedure always have primitive type, never object type. As you'll soon see, RMI simply extends the basic RPC model by allowing arguments and return values to have object type.

To see how RPC works, consider a simple procedure call such as the following:

```
float side = fsqrt(area);
```

This procedure call invokes the sqrt procedure, sending the value of area as an argument and storing sqrt's return value in side. Consider how you might perform this operation if the code for the sqrt procedure resides on a remote host. Assume that the remote host is already equipped with a suitable socket-based server that processes client requests. You could follow this procedure:

1. Get the Internet address of the remote host.
2. Open a socket connection to the server.
3. Convert the value whose square root you require into ASCII and send the message SQRT *number*, where *number* is the value. (Of course, you could send the value in binary, but that makes it more difficult to troubleshoot the transfer process.)
4. Read the server response and convert the value it contains from ASCII to floating point.

The inconvenient part of the procedure is converting the argument value from floating point to ASCII (known as *marshaling* the argument) and converting the return value from ASCII to floating point (known as *unmarshaling* the return value). The server must perform complementary operations—unpacking the argument value, computing its square root, and marshaling the return value. RPC takes on these tasks, making it easier to transfer data from one host to another. In Figure 15.1, the local object is termed the *client*, and the remote object is termed the *server*, because remote objects generally act as servers. However, later in this chapter, you'll see how remote objects can initiate interactions via the callback mechanism.

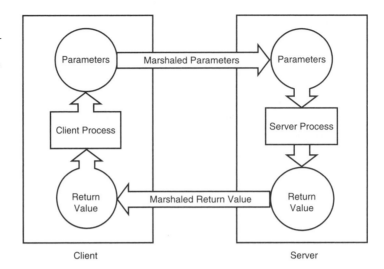

REMOTE METHOD INVOCATION

RMI goes RPC one better by automatically marshaling and unmarshaling objects as well as primitive values. To do this, it uses Java's serialization facility—simply serializing argument and return values, transmitting them over the network, and deserializing them for use. Therefore, any object that implements the `Serializable` interface can be sent by RMI as a method argument or return value.

RMI also provides a registry service that runs on the server. The registry service maintains a database of named remote objects. When a client wants to use a remote object, it asks by name for a reference to the remote object. The registry scans its database and returns a reference to the requested object. Figure 15.2 shows how RMI's registry works.

To get a reference to a remote object via the registry, you use the static `lookup` method of the `Naming` class:

```
Server server = (Server) Naming.lookup(URL);
```

The method returns a reference to the remote object as an `Object`, which you then cast to the appropriate type (`Server` in this example). The URL is a `String` that specifies the name of the host on which the registry and remote object run and the symbolic name of the remote object. The URL must specify "rmi" as its protocol field. For example, to look up a reference to a remote object known as `fred` on a host known as `bedrock`, you'd use this:

```
Server server = (Server) Naming.lookup("rmi://bedrock/fred");
```

FIGURE 15.2

The RMI registry supplies references to remote objects.

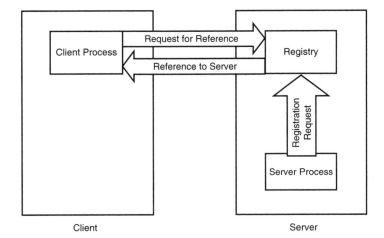

You can specify the host using a host name or IP address. For testing, you may want to use the host name localhost or the IP address 127.0.0.1, both of which refer to the local host (the one on which your program is running).

With RMI, once you have a reference to a remote object, you can use it just as you would a local object. For example, suppose you create a Calculator class that includes a sqrt method that uses a special, high-speed algorithm for computing square roots. If a client has a reference—call it theCalculator—to a remote Calculator object, it could calculate a square root like this:

```
float root = theCalculator.sqrt(number);
```

One small difference distinguishes Calculator's sqrt method from that of a local object: Calculator.sqrt may throw a RemoteException. Contact with remote objects is subject to network outages and other complications that don't affect local objects. Java can't handle this contingency; the proper response is application dependent. Therefore, Java throws an exception, which your program can catch and handle.

Stubs and Skeletons

As mentioned in the chapter introduction, RMI works its magic by means of doppelgängers. Actually, every remote object uses a pair of doppelgängers (local objects that stand in for the remote object) known as a *stub* and *skeleton*, as shown in Figure 15.3.

The stub and local object reside on the local host, whereas the skeleton and remote object reside on the remote host. The local object can easily communicate with the stub because they're in the same Java virtual machine. Likewise, the remote object can easily communicate with the skeleton because they're in the same Java virtual machine. The stub acts as a surrogate for the server so that the client can access the server transparently. When the stub receives a message from the client, it forwards it across the network to the server, obtains the server's response, and returns it to the client. The skeleton performs a similar function on behalf of the server.

FIGURE 15.3

Local and remote objects communicate via stubs and skeletons.

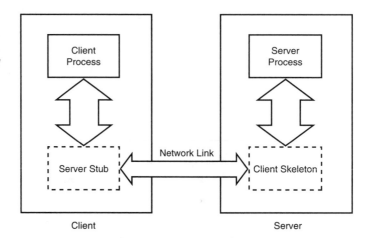

It's easy to program RMI clients and servers because their doppelgängers handle most of the complications of remote access. You need to bear in mind only these few considerations:

- A remote method call can throw a RemoteException, which your program must handle.

- All objects sent via RMI as arguments or return values must implement the Serializable interface. If an argument or return value cannot be serialized, the remote method call fails.

- Objects are not automatically remote: You must make them so. You'll learn how to do so presently. If your program sends a nonremote object as argument or receives one as a return value, the program actually receives a copy of the object. Remote object references can be transferred from host to host, but nonremote object references cannot.

The Stub and Skeleton Compiler Tool: rmic

If you've ever been had by a smooth-talking salesman, you may be apprehensive concerning the stub and skeleton. Shifting the programming burden from client and server to stub and skeleton would accomplish little if the stub and skeleton were difficult to program. Fortunately, they're not: Java provides a tool, `rmic`, that automatically generates stubs and skeletons from a compiled .class file.

Let's say you've written and compiled a class for remote use—call it the `FrisbeeServer` class. Before using the class, you run the `rmic` tool, like this:

```
rmic FrisbeeServer
```

The `rmic` tool scans the FrisbeeServer.class file and creates two new .class files: FrisbeeServer_Stub.class and FrisbeeServer_Skel.class. Any client that remotely accesses a `FrisbeeServer` object requires access to the `FrisbeeServer_Stub` class, which you should distribute along with the other classes that comprise the client. If you recompile the `FrisbeeServer` class, you should rerun `rmic` to generate a revised stub and skeleton. Strictly speaking, this isn't always necessary; however, it's difficult to predict what changes to the server necessitate a change to the stub or skeleton. It's better to be safe than sorry.

Pros and Cons of RMI

Before looking at some sample RMI programs, let's consider the pros and cons of RMI. As you'll soon see, relative to sockets, RMI applications are easier to develop and maintain. Moreover, RMI may help overcome firewall limitations that make it difficult for socket-based programs to communicate outside a protected domain. If RMI cannot connect to a remote object using its ordinary protocol, it automatically attempts to connect using an HTTP-based protocol. If a local proxy server lets Web clients access Web servers outside the firewall, RMI can contact the remote object using HTTP. The HTTP protocol is as much as an order of magnitude slower than RMI's ordinary protocol, but slow communication is often better than no communication.

At the time of this writing, Sun and IBM had recently announced that they will cooperate to develop a way for RMI to communicate across a network using the same Internet-ORB protocol (IIOP) supported by CORBA. A limited release of code for the new interface was planned for release by press time. Support for IIOP may makes it possible for RMI-based objects and CORBA-based objects to interoperate. Should this occur, RMI's ease of use could make it the development path of choice even for CORBA systems.

RMI also makes it simple to move behavior from one host to another—a difficult feat to accomplish using sockets. Software agents that migrate from host to host can choose to execute on the host that offers the best mix of local resources, thus minimizing the amount of data that must be transported across the network and thereby improving throughput and response time.

15

RMI does pose some possible cons. Some have found Java's serialization facility ineffi-cient, requiring large amounts of memory and CPU cycles to serialize and deserialize large objects. Of course, this is not a limitation of RMI in principle, merely a potential performance bottleneck of RMI's current implementation. If you plan to transfer large objects across the network, you're advised to do some simple benchmarking before choosing RMI as your application architecture.

RMI is also a proprietary technology, solely directed by Sun. Those who prefer open standards may shy away from RMI on this account, just as they avoid other proprietary technologies such as Microsoft's Distributed Component Object Model (DCOM). Microsoft, a Java licensee, has announced that it will not support RMI—those who work with Microsoft software may have reason to avoid RMI owing to Microsoft's cold shoulder. Some feel that Sun's own attitude toward RMI is lukewarm; that Sun is more committed to its IDL implementation of CORBA. As evidence, they point out that Sun originally promised IIOP support for RMI in June of 1997. Sun has yet (at the time of this writing) to fulfill this promise. Of course, Sun's real strategy at any moment is any-one's guess and likely, in any case, to change over time.

A commonly cited disadvantage of RMI is that it's a Java-only architecture. In fairness to RMI, Java provides the Java Native Interface (JNI) facility that allows C and C++ pro-grams to invoke methods on Java objects. Because you can use JNI to build a Java inter-face to a non-Java legacy system, it's possible to overcome the Java-only limitation.

A SIMPLE RMI PROGRAM

Now that you've absorbed the necessary background information, let's study an RMI program and learn how to implement and run remote objects. Our example is a simple program designed to assist the customers of Bennie the Bookie's Wagering Service. The program, shown in Figure 15.4, displays a list of ongoing sports games and lets the user obtain the current score directly from Bennie's server. Don't try to run the program just yet: Some special instructions are required to make it operate.

Figure 15.4

RMIClient dis-plays game scores obtained from a remote server.

The program consists of six source files, each of which is located in the chapter15/list-ings directory of the CD-ROM:

- Score.java, which contains the Score class that encapsulates a game score
- Scores.java, which contains the Scores class that encapsulates a collection of game scores
- ScoresServerInterface.java, which contains the ScoresServerInterface interface that defines the methods exported by the remote object
- RMIClient.java, which contains the main code for the client applet
- RMIServer.java, which contains the main code for the remote object
- RMIClient.html, which contains the HTML code used to run the client applet

Listing 15.1 shows the Score class, which presents little that is remarkable. Notice that the class is marked as implementing the Serializable interface, which permits it to be processed by RMI.

LISTING 15.1   Score.java—A CLASS THAT ENCAPSULATES A GAME SCORE

```
import java.io.Serializable;

class Score implements Serializable
{
    String theHomeCity;
    String theHomeTeam;
    String theVisitorTeam;
    int    theHomeScore;
    int    theVisitorScore;
    int    theQuarter;

    public Score(String homecity, String hometeam,
      String visitorteam, int homescore, int visitorscore,
      int quarter)
    {
        theHomeCity     = homecity;
        theHomeTeam     = hometeam;
        theVisitorTeam  = visitorteam;
        theHomeScore    = homescore;
        theVisitorScore = visitorscore;
        theQuarter      = quarter;
    }

    public String getKey()
    {
        return theHomeCity + " vs " + theVisitorTeam;
    }

    public String toString()
    {
```

continues

15

REMOTE METHOD
INVOCATION
(RMI)

LISTING 15.1 CONTINUED

```
        String s = theHomeTeam;
        s += " vs " + theVisitorTeam;
        s += " at " + theHomeCity;
        s += ": "   + theHomeScore;
        s += "-"    + theVisitorScore;
        s += " ("   + theQuarter + "Q)";
        return s;
    }
}
```

Listing 15.2 shows the `Scores` class, which also implements `Serializable`. The class encapsulates a `Hashtable` that provides keyed access to stored game scores. The key, provided by the `getKey` method of the `Score` class, consists of the names of the competing teams. The class provides a method (`getGames`) to obtain an array containing the keys of all games in progress and methods to access and update the game scores (`getScore` and `putScore`).

LISTING 15.2 `Scores.java`—A CLASS THAT ENCAPSULATES A COLLECTION OF GAME SCORES

```java
import java.io.Serializable;
import java.util.*;

public class Scores implements Serializable
{
    Hashtable theScores = new Hashtable();

    public String [] getGames()
    {
        int elemcount = theScores.size();
        String [] games = new String [elemcount];
        Enumeration elements = theScores.elements();
        for (int i = 0; i < elemcount; i++)
        {
            Score score = (Score) elements.nextElement();
            games [i] = score.getKey();
        }
        return games;
    }

    public void putScore(Score score)
    {
        String key = score.getKey();
        theScores.remove(key);
        theScores.put(key, score);
    }
```

```
    public Score getScore(String key)
    {
        return (Score) theScores.get(key);
    }
}
```

The Server Interface

Listing 15.3 shows `ScoresServerInterface`, an interface that specifies the methods exported by the remote object. The `fetchGames` method returns an array containing the keys of the games in progress, and the `getScore` method returns the current score of a specified game. Notice that the interface extends the `Remote` interface. Every remote object must define a similar interface extending `Remote` that identifies its exported methods.

LISTING 15.3   `ScoresServerInterface.java`—AN INTERFACE TO A REMOTE OBJECT

```
import java.rmi.*;

public interface ScoresServerInterface extends Remote
{
    public String [] fetchGames() throws RemoteException;
    public Score fetchScore(String game) throws RemoteException;
}
```

The Client

Listing 15.4 shows the `RMIClient` class. Notice that the class defines a `String` field named `URL`, which refers to the host on which the remote object resides. It also "scores" the symbolic name by which the remote object is known. As you'll see later, the server registers itself using this symbolic name. The remainder of the `RMIClient` class simply establishes the user interface. Its inner classes, as usual, handle the processing.

LISTING 15.4   `RMIClient.java`—A SIMPLE RMI-BASED CLIENT APPLET

```
import java.applet.*;
import java.awt.*;
import java.awt.event.*;
import java.rmi.*;
import java.rmi.server.*;

public class RMIClient extends Applet
{
    static final String URL = "rmi://localhost/scores";
```

continues

LISTING 15.4   CONTINUED

```
Button    theFetchGames    = new Button("Fetch Games");
Button    theFetchScore    = new Button("Fetch Score");
Choice    theGames         = new Choice();
TextArea theScore          = new TextArea(20, 64);

FetchScoreHandler theFetchScoreHandler =
  new FetchScoreHandler();

public void init()
{
    setLayout(new BorderLayout());
    Panel p = new Panel();
    add(theGames, BorderLayout.NORTH);
    add(theScore, BorderLayout.CENTER);
    add(p, BorderLayout.SOUTH);
    p.setLayout(new GridLayout(1, 0));
    p.add(theFetchGames);
    p.add(theFetchScore);
    theScore.setEditable(false);
    theScore.setFont(new Font(
      "Monospaced", Font.BOLD, 12));
    theGames.addItemListener(
      new GameHandler());
    theFetchGames.addActionListener(
      new FetchGamesHandler());
    theFetchScore.addActionListener(
      theFetchScoreHandler);
}

public void fatalError(Exception ex)
{
    ex.printStackTrace();
}

// Inner classes omitted
}
```

Listing 15.5 shows the inner classes of the RMIClient class: GameHandler, FetchGamesHandler, and FetchScoresHandler. Both FetchGamesHandler and FetchScoreHandler invoke methods remotely. Because the two methods are similar, let's examine only FetchScoreHandler.

LISTING 15.5   RMIClient.java—INNER CLASSES

```
class GameHandler implements ItemListener
    {
        public void itemStateChanged(ItemEvent evt)
```

```
        {
            String choice = theGames.getSelectedItem();
            theFetchScoreHandler.fetchScore(choice);
        }
    }

    class FetchGamesHandler implements ActionListener
    {
        public void actionPerformed(ActionEvent evt)
        {
            try
            {
                theGames.removeAll();
                ScoresServerInterface server =
                  (ScoresServerInterface) Naming.lookup(URL);
                String [] games = server.fetchGames();
                for (int i = 0; i < games.length; i++)
                {
                    theGames.addItem(games[i]);
                }
            }
            catch (Exception ex) { fatalError(ex); }
        }
    }

    class FetchScoreHandler implements ActionListener
    {
        public void actionPerformed(ActionEvent evt)
        {
            fetchScore(theGames.getSelectedItem());
        }

        public void fetchScore(String game)
        {
            try
            {
                ScoresServerInterface server =
                  (ScoresServerInterface) Naming.lookup(URL);
                Score score = server.fetchScore(game);
                theScore.setText(score.toString());
            }
            catch (Exception ex) { fatalError(ex); }
        }
    }
}
```

15

FetchScoreHandler's actionPerformed method is invoked when the user clicks the Fetch Score button, requesting an updated score for the currently selected game. The actionPerformed method in turn invokes the fetchScore method (which is organized as a method separate from `actionPerformed` so that it can be called by the `actionPerformed` method of the `GameHandler` class). To access the remote method, `fetchScore` obtains a reference to the remote object by using the `Naming.lookup` method. It casts the returned instance of `Object` to a `ScoresServerInterface` and invokes the `fetchScore` method of the remote object. It uses the `Score` object returned by the remote object to update the output `TextArea`. Of course, these statements are enclosed in a `try-catch` block that handles a possible `RemoteException`.

Notice that only a few statements accomplish all the work needed to access the remote object. As promised, programming an RMI client is easy. Let's move on to see an RMI server. Then we'll show you how to run the program.

The Server

Listing 15.6 shows the RMI-based server. Notice that the server extends the base class `UnicastRemoteObject`, which implements appropriate remote semantics for `Object` methods such as `hashCode`, `equals`, and `toString`. If the operation of these methods is not important to your class, it's not necessary that the class extend `UnicastRemoteObject`. The server defines a field that contains its symbolic name "scores," the name the client uses to access the server.

LISTING 15.6   `RMIServer.java`—A SIMPLE RMI-BASED SERVER

```
import java.rmi.*;
import java.rmi.server.*;

public class RMIServer extends UnicastRemoteObject
  implements ScoresServerInterface
{
    static final String SERVERNAME = "scores";

    Scores theScores = new Scores();

    public static void main(String [] args)
    {
        System.setSecurityManager(new RMISecurityManager());
        try
        {
            RMIServer server = new RMIServer();
            Naming.rebind(SERVERNAME, server);
            System.out.println("Server ready.");
        }
        catch (Exception ex)
        {
            ex.printStackTrace();
        }
```

```
    }

    public RMIServer() throws RemoteException
    {
        theScores.putScore(new Score("Denver", "Broncos",
          "Dolphins", 6, 0, 1));
        theScores.putScore(new Score("Dallas", "Cowboys",
          "Packers", 6, 6, 2));
    }

    public String [] fetchGames() throws RemoteException
    {
        return theScores.getGames();
    }

    public Score fetchScore(String game) throws RemoteException
    {
        return theScores.getScore(game);
    }
}
}
```

Before creating an instance of the RMIServer class, the main method installs a security manager. The security manager prevents client objects from misusing their access to the server. Its default policies are adequate for most applications. Next, the main method creates the server instance and enters it in the registry, which binds the symbolic name to the server.

The constructor adds two sample records to the database maintained by the Scores object. Notice that the constructor may throw a RemoteException, as indicated by its throws clause.

Following the constructor are the implementations of the two methods exported by the remote object in its interface. Notice that the only thing that distinguishes these methods from methods of a nonremote object is the throws clause in the method header. The server-side skeleton, as always, performs the hard parts.

Running the RMI-Based Program

Running the RMI-based program is somewhat more complicated than running an ordinary program. Recall that the program is configured to run both the server and the client on a single host. If you want to run them on separate hosts, you must revise the host name in both source files and recompile them. Here are the steps you should follow to run the program on your own Windows 9x/NT system:

1. Compile all the .java files. You can do this in a single step:

   `javac *.java`

2. Process the RMIServer.class file through the `rmic` tool:

   `rmic RMIServer`

3. Start the registry:

   `start rmiregistry`

4. Start the server:

   `java RMIServer`

5. Open a second DOS window and start the client:

   `appletviewer RMIClient.html`

You should be able to use the Fetch Games button and the Fetch Score button to query the scores database.

> **NOTE**
>
> The current release of the JDK includes a known bug that causes some systems to incorrectly report an access error when the server starts. If you encounter this bug, check the Javasoft Web site (`http://www.javasoft.com`) or the JDK release notes for a workaround. Besides the solutions suggested there, you may find that dialing up your ISP resolves the problem.

CALLBACKS

A problem with the current version of the sample application is that the user must click Fetch Score to obtain an updated game score. Of course, the user doesn't know when a new score is available and therefore has little recourse other than to periodically click Fetch Score, hoping to see a new result. Given a little more elaborate programming, an RMI remote object can invoke a method on its client. Let's look at an improved version of the sample application that uses this technique to automatically update scores as soon as they're received. Figure 15.5 shows the new version of the program in operation. Notice that it lacks the buttons of the previous version, because its automatic operation renders them pointless.

Listing 15.7 shows the `AutoScoresServerInterface`, which specifies the sole method exported by the revised server. The `addScoresClient` method allows a client to subscribe to the regularly updated scores provided by the server. A subscriber must implement the `AutoScoresClientInterface`, which appears as shown in Listing 15.8. The server sends clients an `updateScores` message whenever an updated score is available. In the interest of brevity, the server takes the expedient route of sending the entire updated scores database. A somewhat more sophisticated server might transmit only the updated score.

FIGURE 15.5

The AutoScoresClient automatically receives and displays updated scores.

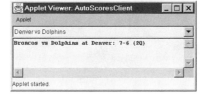

LISTING 15.7 AutoScoresServerInterface.java—THE SERVER INTERFACE

```
import java.rmi.*;

public interface AutoScoresServerInterface extends Remote
{
    public void addScoresClient(AutoScoresClientInterface client)
      throws RemoteException;
}
```

LISTING 15.8 AutoScoresClientInterface.java—THE CLIENT INTERFACE

```
import java.rmi.*;

public interface AutoScoresClientInterface extends Remote
{
    public void updateScores(Scores scores)
      throws RemoteException;
}
```

Listing 15.9 shows the revised client. Notice the symbolic name of the revised server, "autoscores." Notice also that the client is considerably simpler than before. By eliminating much of the user interface, we've streamlined the entire application. In order to receive callbacks from the server, the client must export itself as a remote object. Because the client class extends Applet rather than UnicastRemoteObject, it uses the static UnicastRemoteObject.export method to export itself. If the operation of the hashCode, equals, or toString methods were important, the client should provide overriding implementations of these methods. None of these methods is important to this application; therefore, the AutoScoresClient relies on the semantics inherited from Object, even though these are inadequate for remote objects.

LISTING 15.9   AutoScoresClient.java—THE CLIENT APPLET

```java
import java.applet.*;
import java.awt.*;
import java.awt.event.*;
import java.rmi.*;
import java.rmi.server.*;

public class AutoScoresClient extends Applet
  implements AutoScoresClientInterface
{
    static final String URL = "rmi://localhost/autoscores";

    Choice    theGames       = new Choice();
    TextArea  theScore       = new TextArea(20, 64);

    Scores theScores;

    public void init()
    {
       setLayout(new BorderLayout());
       add(theGames, BorderLayout.NORTH);
       add(theScore, BorderLayout.CENTER);
       theScore.setEditable(false);
       theScore.setFont(new Font(
         "Monospaced", Font.BOLD, 12));
       theGames.addItemListener(
         new GameHandler());
       try
       {
          UnicastRemoteObject.exportObject(this);
          AutoScoresServerInterface server =
            (AutoScoresServerInterface) Naming.lookup(URL);
          server.addScoresClient(this);
       }
       catch (Exception ex) { fatalError(ex); }
    }

    public void fatalError(Exception ex)
    {
       ex.printStackTrace();
    }

    public void updateScores(Scores scores)
    {
       theScores = scores;
       String [] games = theScores.getGames();
       String selected = theGames.getSelectedItem();
       theGames.removeAll();
       for (int i = 0; i < games.length; i++)
       {
```

```
            theGames.addItem(games[i]);
      }
      if (selected != null)
      {
         theGames.select(selected);
         showScore();
      }
   }

   public void showScore()
   {
      String selected = theGames.getSelectedItem();
      Score score = theScores.getScore(selected);
      theScore.setText(score.toString());
   }

   class GameHandler implements ItemListener
   {
      public void itemStateChanged(ItemEvent evt)
      {
         showScore();
      }
   }
}
```

Once the client has obtained a reference to the remote server, it sends the server an `addScoresClient` message, requesting that it be added to the server's list of clients that are notified of updated scores. The client also implements the `updateScores` method, which the server invokes to communicate the updated scores.

Listing 15.10 shows the `AutoScoresServer`, the remote object that provides the updated scores. Most of the complexity of the server results not from RMI, but from the requirement that it provide updated scores. Otherwise, it would closely resemble the `RMIServer` class presented earlier.

LISTING 15.10 `AutoScoresServer.java`—THE SERVER

```
import java.rmi.*;
import java.rmi.server.*;
import java.util.*;

public class AutoScoresServer extends UnicastRemoteObject
   implements AutoScoresServerInterface, Runnable
{
      static final String SERVERNAME = "autoscores";
```

continues

15

REMOTE METHOD
INVOCATION
(RMI)

Listing 15.10 CONTINUED

```java
Scores theScores  = new Scores();
Vector theClients = new Vector();

public static void main(String [] args)
{
    System.setSecurityManager(new RMISecurityManager());
    try
    {
        AutoScoresServer server = new AutoScoresServer();
        Naming.rebind(SERVERNAME, server);
        System.out.println("Server ready.");
        new Thread(server).start();
    }
    catch (Exception ex)
    {
        ex.printStackTrace();
    }
}

public AutoScoresServer() throws RemoteException
{
    theScores.putScore(new Score("Denver", "Broncos",
        "Dolphins", 6, 0, 1));
    theScores.putScore(new Score("Dallas", "Cowboys",
        "Packers", 6, 6, 2));
}

public void run()
{
    try
    {
        System.out.println("Counting down to update...");
        Thread.sleep(60000);
        theScores.putScore(new Score("Denver", "Broncos",
            "Dolphins", 7, 6, 2));
        System.out.println("Updating.");
        updateScores();
        System.out.println("Updated.");
    }
    catch (Exception ex) { ; }
}

public void updateScores()
  throws RemoteException
{
    Enumeration clients = theClients.elements();
    while (clients.hasMoreElements())
    {
        AutoScoresClientInterface client =
```

```
               (AutoScoresClientInterface) clients.nextElement();
           client.updateScores(theScores);
       }
   }

   public void addScoresClient(
     AutoScoresClientInterface client)
     throws RemoteException
   {
       theClients.addElement(client);
       client.updateScores(theScores);
   }
}
```

The `addScores` method processes requests to join the list of clients notified of updates. The method simply adds a remote reference to a requesting client to a `Vector`. It then sends the client an `updateScores` message that provides the client the current scores. Notice again that the remote reference is handled the same way as a local reference; only the `throws` clause in the method header distinguishes `addScoresClient` and `updateScores` from methods that deal solely with local references.

To provide the updated score, the server's `main` method spawns a new thread. The `run` method executed by the thread pauses for one minute (60,000 milliseconds) and then posts a revised score to the scores database and transmits the change to all registered clients. To help you observe this behavior, the `run` method includes several `System.out.println` calls.

As you can see, RMI is as simple as it is powerful. With just a few lines of extra code, you can create distributed objects that invoke remote methods and perform callbacks. The next section reveals that even more is in store.

RMI-BASED SOFTWARE AGENTS

The CD-ROM contains a sample program that shows how to use RMI to implement software agents that can migrate from host to host. Figure 15.6 shows the program's output. We won't take up the topic of agents at this point—they're covered in Chapter 34, "Agents." However, you might enjoy studying the program now, thereby gaining a preview of what's to come in Chapter 34. Like other RMI programs, the implementation is simple and straightforward. Here are the instructions for running the program:

1. Compile all the .java files from the chapter15/listings directory of the CD-ROM. You can do this in a single step:

   ```
   javac *.java
   ```

15

REMOTE METHOD
INVOCATION
(RMI)

FIGURE 15.6

A software agent can migrate from host to host.

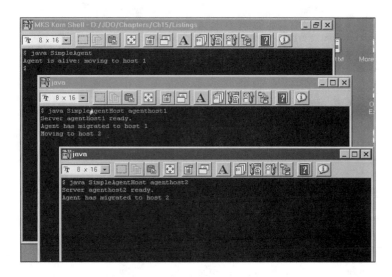

2. Process the SimpleAgent.class file through the `rmic` tool:

   `rmic SimpleAgentHost`

3. Start the registry:

   `start rmiregistry`

4. Start the first instance of the server:

   `java SimpleAgentHost agenthost1`

5. Open a second DOS window and start the second instance of the server:

   `java SimpleAgentHost agenthost2`

6. Open a third DOS window and start the client:

   `java SimpleAgent`

The agent should quickly move from the client process to the first server and then the second server.

FROM HERE

In this chapter, you've learned how RMI works and the advantages it offers. You've learned how to create RMI-based servers that process client requests and issue callbacks to keep clients informed of state changes. The following chapters provide additional information about RMI and other distributed computing technologies:

- Chapter 16, "RMI-Based Implementation of the Airline Reservation System," shows how the Airline Reservation System example can be implemented using RMI.

- Chapter 18, "Servlets and Common Gateway Interface (CGI)," describes the Java Servlet API. Using servlets is another simple way of implementing a distributed system.

- Chapter 20, "Distributed Component Object Model (DCOM)," describes Microsoft's proprietary distributed computing model.

- Chapter 21, "CORBA Overview," provides an introduction to the Common Object Request Broker Architecture, an alternative technology for distributed computing. The remaining chapters of Part V, "The CORBA Approach to Distributed Computing," present CORBA in depth.

- Chapter 34, "Voyager Agent Technology," describes agent technology and ObjectSpace Voyager, a freeware package for developing Java-based agents.

RMI-BASED IMPLEMENTATION OF THE AIRLINE RESERVATION SYSTEM

IN THIS CHAPTER

In the previous chapter, you learned about Java's Remote Method Invocation (RMI) API. In this chapter you'll see an example of a larger RMI-based program: the Airline Reservation System of Chapter 6, "The Airline Reservation System Model." You'll find the source code for the program on the CD-ROM. By studying the program, you'll learn more about using sockets to exchange data across networks.

To refresh your recall of the Airline Reservation System, you should turn back to Chapter 6 and skim it quickly, focusing on the functional requirements of the system. You should also refresh your recollection of the socket-based implementation of the Airline Reservation System presented in Chapter 14, "Socket-Based Implementation of the Airline Reservation System," because the RMI-based program described in this chapter is functionally equivalent to the socket-based program described in Chapter 14.

One of the advantages of using RMI over sockets is that RMI lets you work at a higher level of abstraction. For example, you don't have to code serialization routines or command dispatchers. As a result, your code is more compact. The RMI-based program described in this chapter consists of a little over 800 lines, whereas the socket-based program has over 1,100 lines. Research has demonstrated that the time required to write a line of code is approximately the same, regardless which programming language or API is used. This implies that the smaller size of RMI programs translates into increased programmer productivity: A programmer using RMI should be almost 1.5 times as productive as one using sockets.

Here are the three transactions implemented by the sample program:

- Search Flights, which returns each flight stored in the database.
- Search Seats, which returns the reservation information for a specified passenger identified by passenger number.
- Book Seat, which enters a reservation for a specified passenger and flight. The transaction makes several simplifying assumptions. The passenger and flight must already exist as entities; the transaction does not create new passengers or flights. The reservation number must be unique; attempting to add a reservation with the same number as an existing reservation updates the existing reservation.

Like the sample program of Chapter 14, the sample program of this chapter does not implement the visual interface for seat selection described in Chapter 6. Also, it doesn't implement the reservation pool locking mechanism. However, near the end of this chapter, we'll show you how to implement such a mechanism.

As before, let's begin our tour of the program by looking at the application classes. Later, we'll look at the client and server classes that provide the user interface and network connectivity.

APPLICATION CLASSES

The application classes are not much different from those presented in Chapter 14. The biggest difference is that we've omitted the methods to pack and unpack field values as Strings. Because RMI handles serialization automatically, we don't need to provide these methods.

> **NOTE**
>
> Because the classes are changed very little, they're not shown here. You can examine them by copying them from the CD-ROM to your system's hard drive.

Recall that every RMI server must define an interface that specifies the methods that the server makes available to its clients. Therefore, every RMI server has two source files: one defining the class, and one defining its interface. Let's examine the interface first.

The Server Interface

The server supports three transactions and provides a method for each transaction:

> **NOTE**
>
> The following code is found in the file ServerInterface.java in the chapter16/ listings directory of the CD-ROM.

```
public interface ServerInterface extends Remote
{
    public Flight [] searchFlights()
      throws RemoteException, SQLException ;
    public Reservation [] searchSeats(
      String passenger_no)
      throws RemoteException, SQLException ;
    public void bookSeat(String flight_no,
      String passenger_no, String res_no)
      throws RemoteException, SQLException,
      FlightBookedException ;
}
```

These three methods are all that the application requires, because the server can invoke methods on the application objects to perform most of its processing. Notice that the interface extends Remote and that each method may throw the RemoteException, in addition to any exceptions thrown by application processing, such as SQLException and FlightBookedException. Notice also that two of the methods return arrays. Because a

Java array is an object, an array is serializable and can be passed as a remote method argument or return value, as long as the elements of the array are primitive or serializable.

Notice also that none of the application classes has been revised to extend the `UnicastRemoteObject` class. Therefore, RMI will pass instances of the application classes by value, rather than by reference. If several clients request access to the same `Flight` instance, for example, each receives its own instance rather than a reference to a single instance. This behavior is appropriate for the Airline Reservation System, which uses a SQL database to centrally store its persistent state.

However, some applications require that there be only one object instance associated with each real-world entity. To accommodate this requirement, simply define any such objects as extending `UnicastRemoteObject`. Alternatively, you can invoke the static `exportObject` method of the `UnicastRemoteObject` class, passing a reference to the object instance that you want passed by reference, not value. Doing so registers the instance reference as a remote reference. Of course, in either case, you must use the `rmic` utility to generate the skeleton class required by the RMI runtime system.

The Server Class

> **NOTE**
>
> All the code from here until the next section, "The Client Class," is found in the file Server.java in the chapter16/listings directory of the CD-ROM.

In addition to the three methods specified in its interface, the server class defines several fields, a `main` method, and a constructor. The class header specifies that the class extends the `UnicastRemoteObject` class and that it implements the `ServerInterface`:

```
public class Server extends UnicastRemoteObject
  implements ServerInterface
```

The class defines four constant fields:

```
static final String SERVERNAME = "ARServer";
static final String DB = "jdbc:odbc:airline";
static final String USER = "";
static final String PASSWORD = "";
```

The `SERVERNAME` field specifies the name under which the server registers itself in the RMI registry. The `DB` field specifies the JDBC URL of the database, including the DSN "airline." Because the DSN was created without user ID and password, these are specified as null Strings. Defining these four values as constants makes it easier to revise them.

The only nonstatic field of the server class is the field used to hold the database connection once the database is opened:

```
Connection theConnection;
```

The main method performs these functions:

- It installs a security manager that prevents clients from misusing server resources.
- It registers the server instance in the RMI registry.
- It displays a console message announcing that the server is ready.

Here's the source code for the main method:

```
public static void main(String [] args)
{
    System.setSecurityManager(new RMISecurityManager());
    try
    {
        Server server = new Server();
        Naming.rebind(SERVERNAME, server);
        System.out.println("Server ready.");
    }
    catch (Exception ex)
    {
        ex.printStackTrace();
    }
}
```

The constructor is responsible for opening a connection to the database:

```
public Server() throws Exception
{
    Class.forName("sun.jdbc.odbc.JdbcOdbcDriver");
    theConnection =
      DriverManager.getConnection(DB, USER, PASSWORD);
}
```

The forName call can throw a NoClassDefFoundException, and the getConnection call can throw a SQLException; therefore, the constructor specifies that it can throw an Exception, a common superclass of NoClassDefFoundException and SQLException.

The searchFlights method is one of the three methods exported by the server, as specified in its interface. This method simply invokes the getFlights method of the Flight class, which returns an array containing an instance of Flight for each row of the Flight database table:

```
public Flight [] searchFlights()
  throws RemoteException, SQLException
{
    Flight [] flights =
      Flight.getFlights(theConnection);
    return flights;
}
```

The searchSeats method works similarly. It simply invokes the getPassenger method of the Reservation class, which returns an array containing an instance of Reservation for each row of the Reservation database table:

```
public Reservation [] searchSeats(
  String passenger_no)
  throws RemoteException, SQLException
{
    Reservation [] res =
      Reservation.getPassenger(
      theConnection, passenger_no);
    return res;
}
```

The final exported method, bookSeat, invokes the Reservation constructor to create a new instance of Reservation that has the appropriate values for reservation number, flight number, and passenger number. It then uses the dbWrite method of the Reservation class to create a table row that contains the specified values:

```
public void bookSeat(String flight_no,
  String passenger_no, String res_no)
  throws RemoteException, SQLException,
  FlightBookedException
{
    Reservation res = new Reservation(
      theConnection, res_no, flight_no,
      passenger_no);
    res.dbWrite(theConnection);
}
```

The Client Class

Just as the RMI-based server class is much simpler than the socket-based server class, the RMI-based client class is much simpler than the socket-based client class. The client is implemented as an application, rather than an applet; therefore, its class header specifies that the class extends the Frame class:

```
public class RemoteClient extends Frame
```

The class defines two fields involved with accessing the RMI server and several user interface fields. A constant field specifies the URL of the server:

NOTE

All the code from here until the section on "The Locking Mechanism" is found in the file RemoteClient.java in the chapter16/listings directory of the CD-ROM.

```
public static final String URL = "rmi://127.0.0.1/ARServer";
```

The protocol, of course, is RMI. Notice that the server host is specified using an IP number rather than a host name. However, either can be used. The final component of the URL is the symbolic name of the server object, `ARServer`. Recall that the server registered itself using that name.

Another field holds the remote reference to the server object:

```
ServerInterface theServer;
```

This field is initialized in the default constructor.

Here are the user interface–related fields of the class:

```
Button theSearchFlights = new Button("Search Flights");
Button theSearchSeats   = new Button("Search Seats");
Button theBookSeat      = new Button("Book Seat");

TextField theFlightNo       = new TextField();
TextField thePassengerNo    = new TextField();
TextField theReservationNo  = new TextField();

TextArea  theResults        = new TextArea();
```

The socket-based sample program of Chapter 14 is relatively complicated; therefore, we can't offer significant explanation of its user interface. Because the RMI-based program is simpler, let's look more thoroughly at its user interface, which is quite similar to that used by the socket-based sample program. Figure 16.1 shows the application window, which holds three `TextField` objects, a `TextArea` object, and three `Button` objects.

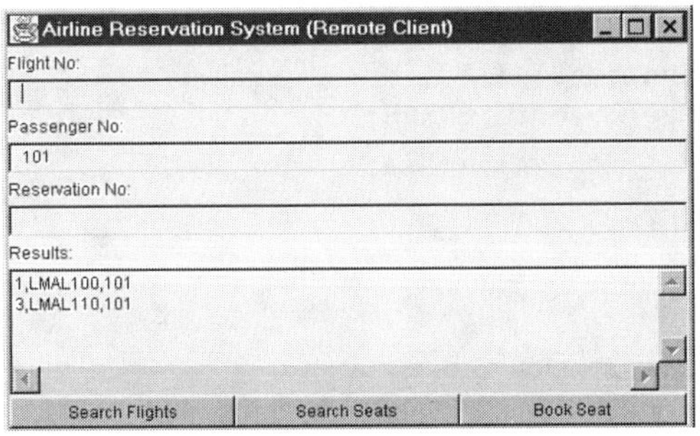

FIGURE 16.1

The RMI-based client and server are simpler than their socket-based counterparts.

The TextField objects allow the user to enter a flight number, passenger number, and reservation number. Not every transaction uses every value. Table 16.1 summarizes the values used by each transaction. If you fail to provide a required input value, the program generally throws an exception. You'll discern this by the stack trace the program displays on the console. If you provide unneeded input values, the program ignores them.

TABLE 16.1   INPUT VALUES USED BY AIRLINE RESERVATION SYSTEM TRANSACTIONS

Transaction	Input Value(s)
Book Seat	Flight number, passenger number, reservation number
Search Flights	Passenger number
Search Seats	(None)

Before examining the default constructor, which lays out the application window, take a quick look at the main method, which is quite short:

```
public static void main(String [] args)
{
    new RemoteClient();
}
```

The main method simply instantiates a RemoteClient object. The object's default constructor does the rest. Now, take a look at the constructor (you'll see the rest shortly):

```
public RemoteClient()
{
    super("Airline Reservation System (Remote Client)");
    setLayout(new BorderLayout());
    Panel p;
    p = new Panel(new GridLayout(0, 1));
    add(p, BorderLayout.NORTH);
    p.add(new Label("Flight No:"));
    p.add(theFlightNo);
    p.add(new Label("Passenger No:"));
    p.add(thePassengerNo);
    p.add(new Label("Reservation No:"));
    p.add(theReservationNo);
    p.add(new Label("Results:"));
    add(theResults, BorderLayout.CENTER);
    p = new Panel(new GridLayout(1, 0));
    add(p, BorderLayout.SOUTH);
    p.add(theSearchFlights);
    p.add(theSearchSeats);
    p.add(theBookSeat);
    theResults.setEditable(false);
    theSearchFlights.addActionListener(
      new ButtonHandler());
```

```
theSearchSeats.addActionListener(
  new ButtonHandler());
theBookSeat.addActionListener(
  new ButtonHandler());
addWindowListener(new WindowHandler());
setSize(600, 400);
setVisible(true);
```

The default constructor uses the super constructor to pass an argument to the constructor of its superclass, Frame, which uses the argument to set the window title. Then, the constructor establishes a BorderLayout layout manager that divides the screen into three areas: north (the top of the window), center, and south (the bottom of the window). The program does not use the east and west areas. The constructor then creates a Panel that establishes a multirow GridLayout layout manager for the north area and places the three TextField objects in the Panel, with three Label objects that describe the TextField objects and a fourth Label that describes the TextArea that appears in the center area of the window, immediately below the north area.

Next, the constructor adds the TextArea, referenced by the field theResults, to the center area of the window. In the south area of the window, the constructor places a Panel controlled by a second GridLayout—this one specifying a multicolumn layout. The constructor places the three Button objects in this Panel, causing them to appear in the south area of the screen.

To prevent user editing of the contents of the TextArea, the constructor invokes the setEditable message. The constructor then establishes an ActionListener for each of the three Button objects, using instances of the ButtonHandler inner class. Finally, the constructor invokes setSize to set the size of the application window to a value appropriate to a standard VGA monitor; it then makes the application window visible by invoking setVisible.

The constructor also obtains a reference to its remote server:

```
try
{
    theServer =
      (ServerInterface) Naming.lookup(URL);
}
catch (Exception ex) { fatalError(ex); }
```

The static lookup method of the Naming class returns a reference to an object that implements the Remote interface. Because the object must be a reference to a Server instance that implements the ServerInterface, the constructor casts the returned value to a ServerInterface. This operation fails with a ClassCastException if returned objects fail to implement the ServerInterface. This might occur, for instance, if you use an incorrect URL, causing the RMI runtime to connect to the wrong server. If some other RMI-related error occurs, the call can throw a `RemoteException`. If you want to handle the two types of exceptions differently, you can associate distinct `catch` statements with the `try`.

The three transaction-handling methods are simple, just as they are in the server. Here's the `searchFlights` method:

```
public void searchFlights()
  throws Exception
{
    theResults.setText("");
    Flight [] flights =
      theServer.searchFlights();
    for (int i = 0; i < flights.length; i++)
    {
        theResults.append(flights[i] + "\n");
    }
}
```

Notice that the `searchFlights` method simply invokes the corresponding `searchFlights` method on the server object and processes the result the server returns.

The `searchSeats` and `bookSeat` methods work similarly:

```
public void searchSeats()
  throws Exception
{
    theResults.setText("");
    Reservation [] seats =
      theServer.searchSeats(thePassengerNo.getText());
    for (int i = 0; i < seats.length; i++)
    {
        theResults.append(seats[i] + "\n");
    }
}

public void bookSeat()
  throws Exception
{
    theResults.setText("");
    theServer.bookSeat(theFlightNo.getText(),
      thePassengerNo.getText(),
      theReservationNo.getText());
}
```

The `ButtonHandler` inner class dispatches button-related events by invoking the appropriate transaction-handling method:

```
    class ButtonHandler implements ActionListener
{
    public void actionPerformed(ActionEvent evt)
    {
        try
        {
            String cmd = evt.getActionCommand();
            if (cmd.equals("Search Flights"))
                searchFlights();
            else if (cmd.equals("Search Seats"))
                searchSeats();
            else if (cmd.equals("Book Seat"))
                bookSeat();
        }
        catch (Exception ex) { fatalError(ex); }
    }
}
```

It uses the getActionCommand method to obtain the default action String associated with the Component—in this case a Button—that generated the ActionEvent. By default, this method returns the label that appears on the face of the Button. The method uses the equals method to test for a match between a String literal and the action String.

NOTE

Many programmers—and several Java authors—mistakenly use the equals operator (==) to perform such comparisons. When the operands of the equals operator are object references, the operator tests whether the references refer to the same object. Two String objects can be different objects, even though they contain precisely the same characters. Therefore, as in the code example, you should use the equals method rather than the equals operator when comparing the contents of String objects.

A second inner class, WindowHandler, lets the user close the application by clicking the application window's close box:

```
class WindowHandler extends WindowAdapter
{
    public void windowClosing(WindowEvent evt)
    {
        setVisible(false);
        System.exit(0);
    }
}
```

Finally, the class defines a simple error-handling routine, `fatalError`, called by several of the methods in the class. The `WindowHandler` method attempts no recovery, but neither does it shut down the application. It simply displays a message on the console and returns:

```
public void fatalError(Exception ex)
{
    ex.printStackTrace();
}
```

RUNNING THE SAMPLE PROGRAM

To run the sample program, copy the source files from the chapter16/listings directory on the CD-ROM to your local hard drive. Because the application classes of the sample program use an Access database, you must run the program using Windows 9x or Windows NT. It won't operate under UNIX, for example.

Enter the following commands at a DOS prompt:

```
javac *.java
rmic Server
start rmiregistry
java Server
```

Once the server displays a message indicating that it's ready, start the client by entering the following command in a second DOS window:

```
java RemoteClient
```

If the RMI facility throws unexpected exceptions, look back to Chapter 15, "Remote Method Invocation (RMI)" for troubleshooting hints. Also examine the release notes that accompany the JDK or Java Interactive Development Environment you're using. If you have a network, you can run the client and server on separate hosts. After you've successfully launched and operated the client and server on a single host, change the host name in the client's source file, recompile the client, and run the client and server on separate hosts.

THE LOCKING MECHANISM

To facilitate comparison with the socket-based sample program of Chapter 14, the sample program we've presented here doesn't implement the locking protocol described in Chapter 6, which specifies the application's requirements. However, it's instructive to see how to perform such an operation, because many applications require a similar facility.

One simple way to implement the required locking protocol is to create within the Airline database a new database table called LockedSeat, which stores information on seats held pending completion of a reservation. Here's a simple `lockSeat` method that places a hold on a seat by inserting a record into the LockedSeat database table. The method also increments the reservation count maintained in the Flight table of the Airline database, which is described in Chapter 12, "Java Database Connectivity (JDBC)," and used in subsequent chapters:

```
public lockSeat(Connection db)
  throws FlightBookedException, SQLException
{
    Flight flight = Flight.getInstance(db, flight_no);
    int seats = flight.getSeats();
    int reservations = flight.getReservations();
    if (reservations >= seats)
      throw new FlightBookedException();
    flight.setReservations(reservations + 1);
    flight.dbWrite(db);

    Statement stmt = db.createStatement();
    query = "Insert Into LockedSeat " +
      "(ReservationNo, FlightNo, " +
      "PassengerNo, TimeStamp) " +
      "Values ('" +
      theReservationNo +
      "', '" +
      theFlightNo +
      "', '" +
      thePassengerNo +
      "', '" +
      new Timestamp(new Date()) +
      "')";
    stmt.executeUpdate(query);
    stmt.close();

    db.commit();
}
```

Notice that the method throws a `BookedFlightException` if no seats are available. Moreover, various SQL errors can throw a `SQLException`. Notice that the LockedSeat table includes a column that holds a timestamp value. In a moment, you'll see why this column is needed. As its last operation, the method invokes the `commit` method to close the current database transaction. The `commit` method causes the operations of incrementing the reservation count and inserting the new row in the LockedSeat table to function atomically, thereby avoiding database anomalies. For the call to `commit` to work properly, you must turn off autocommit after opening the database connection. You must also add a similar call to `commit` after each database update in every method of the `Reservation`, `Flight`, and `Passenger` classes.

The lockSeat method does not create a Reservation table row; that's the function of the bookSeat method:

```java
public void bookSeat(Connection db)
  throws SQLException, NoLockException
{
    Statement stmt = db.createStatement();
    String query;
    int n;

    query = "Delete From LockedSeat" +
      " Where ReservationNo ='" +
      theReservationNo +
      "'";
    n = stmt.executeUpdate(query);
    if (n == 0) throw new NoLockException();

    query = "Insert Into Reservation " +
      "(ReservationNo, FlightNo, PassengerNo) " +
      "Values ('" +
      theReservationNo +
      "', '" +
      theFlightNo +
      "', '" +
      thePassengerNo +
      "')";
    n = stmt.executeUpdate(query);

    stmt.close();

    db.commit();
}
```

The bookSeat method deletes the lock record from the LockedSeat table. If no such record exists, the method throws an application exception, NoLockException. Otherwise, the reservation count in the Flight table would be incorrect. The method then inserts a new row into the Reservation table and commits its database changes.

The timestamp column in the LockedSeat table is necessary to cope with locked seats that are somehow never booked. A simple way to avoid falsely seeming to run out of seats is to periodically delete any stale locks. The following reaper method does just that:

```java
public void reaper(Connection db)
{
    Statement stmt = db.createStatement();
    while (true)
    {
        try
        {
```

```
        Thread.sleep(NAPLENGTH);
        Timestamp cutoff =
          new Timestamp(new Date() - 30 * 60 * 1000);
        query = "Select ReservationNo, " +
          "FlightNo, TimeStamp " +
          "From LockedSeat";
        ResultSet rs = stmt.executeQuery(query);
        while (rs.next())
        {
            String res_no = rs.getString(1);
            String flight_no = rs.getString(2);
            Timestamp ts  = rs.getTimestamp(3);
            if (ts.before(cutoff))
            {
                query = "Delete From LockedSeat" +
                  " Where ReservationNo ='" +
                  res_no +
                  "'";
                n = stmt.executeUpdate(query);

                Flight flight = Flight.getInstance(db, flight_no);
                int reservations = flight.getReservations();
                flight.setReservations(reservations - 1);
                flight.dbWrite(db);
                db.commit();
            }
        }
        rs.close();
    }
    catch (Exception ex) { ex.printStackTrace(); }
  }
}
```

The reaper method is designed to run as a thread. It awakens every thirty minutes and deletes any locks held thirty minutes or longer, resetting the available seat counter within the Flight table as appropriate. You can use this technique to implement numerous useful routines for periodically pruning your SQL databases.

FROM HERE

In this chapter, you've seen a complete application of modest size that uses RMI to link a client program with a remote server. RMI is one of the easiest distributed computing technologies to use. The following chapters provide information about *servlets*, another distributed computing technology:

- Chapter 18, "Servlets and Common Gateway Interface (CGI)," shows how to write distributed systems using Java's servlet facility.

- Chapter 19, "Servlet-Based Implementation of the Airline Reservation System," presents a sample program that's functionally equivalent to the one presented in this chapter, but it uses servlets rather than RMI.

JAVA HELP, JAVA MAIL, AND OTHER JAVA APIS

IN THIS CHAPTER

Before distributed systems, users' lives were simple, as were programmers' lives. When Marge, the accounts payable clerk, clicked the wrong button on the posting screen, she picked up the phone and called Fred, the applications programmer responsible for the accounts payable system. Or, if she was sufficiently anxious to justify a high-calorie snack, she'd stop by Fred's office, which was near the lunchroom that contained the vending machines. Fred knew from experience how to handle Marge when she was stressed out. He'd ask her about her grandchildren and chat about other trivialities, inquiring what had prompted her call or visit only after her stress index was well below redline.

Such friendships between users and programmers were once common. However, the symbiotic relationship between users and programmers was disrupted when distributed systems geographically separated users from programmers. A distributed system that fails to address the social implications of dispersed staff may fail, even though it's technically perfect.

This chapter presents two Java APIs that, at the time of this writing, are in early release status: Java Help and Java Mail. The Help and Mail APIs can help you build distributed systems that partially compensate for the absence of Fred, the friendly programmer. Also, a section at the end of this chapter highlights some other Java APIs that haven't yet been fully released. In this chapter you learn

- How to use Java Help to build application help files

  Java Help lets you build a pure Java help facility that includes features such as nested folders, hyperlinks, indexes, full-text searches, and context-sensitive help.

- How to use Java Mail to send Internet mail messages

  Java Mail lets your applications send and receive mail by interfacing with standard Internet mail servers. Using the Java Mail API, you can build applications that notify you when, or even before, something goes wrong, helping you respond rapidly to problems so that they don't escalate into catastrophes.

- What other Java APIs are under development

  Sun has many other Java APIs under development. You'll learn what they are and how they can help you build better distributed applications.

JAVA HELP

The Java Help API lets you include stylish, modern help facilities in your applications. It supports nested folders of help information, hyperlinks that let the user jump from topic to topic, indexes, full-text searches, and context-sensitive help. The Java Help API is in early release, meaning that the API is subject to change. Therefore, this section emphasizes the architecture and operation of Java Help, rather than the API. You'll learn how to build basic help facilities for Java applications and applets. The more exotic help capabilities, however, are discussed, not demonstrated.

Java Help uses the Java Foundation Classes (also known as *JFC* or *Swing*) rather than the Abstract Window Toolkit (AWT) classes. Therefore, to explore Java Help, you'll need JDK 1.1 and the Swing packages or JDK 1.2, which includes Swing as an integral component. If you want to use Java Help with applets, check your Web browser vendor's Web site and the Sun Web site for information on downloading and installing browser support for JDK 1.1 and Swing or JDK 1.2. You may want to use Sun's Java Activator, which provides such support for Netscape Navigator and Microsoft Internet Explorer.

Sun implemented Java Help as a Java extension, meaning that Java Help is distributed as a JAR file containing packages with names that begin with javax. Doing so avoids a restriction imposed by Web browsers: Most Web browsers treat packages with names that begin with java as core packages and prevent you from accessing such packages lest you thereby commit a security breach. Because they're named differently than Java core packages, you can access Java extension packages freely and therefore use Java Help with both applications and applets. Check the Java Mail release notes for information on installing Java Mail for access by Web browsers.

Java Help provides an attractive user interface that resembles Microsoft's Windows Explorer (see Figure 17.1). The left panel, called the *navigator*, lets the user access a hierarchy of folders containing help topics.

FIGURE 17.1

The Java Help facility provides an Explorer-style user interface.

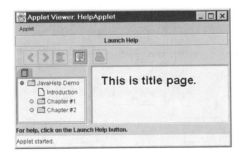

The right panel shows the contents of the currently selected folder. Icons let the user move forward and backward through the topics, access a history of viewed topics, hide or show the left panel, or print a topic. (JDK 1.1 does not support printing of topics.) Tabs in the left panel let the user choose from among multiple views (the help file in the figure has only a single tab and provides only a single view). For example, you can provide one view organized as a table of contents, another organized as an index, and another that performs a full-text search. Let's see how you build a Java Help facility.

A basic Java Help facility, called a *help set*, includes the following elements, as shown in Figure 17.2:

- The HelpSet file, which identifies the opening topic, the map file, and the views provided by the help set.
- A Java program (application or applet) that launches a help viewer.
- Topic pages, which contain the information the user will access. Each topic page resides in an HTML file.
- The map file, which provides pseudonyms for each HTML file.
- View files, which describe a view—a way of accessing the help topics. A help set can have multiple views, each described by a distinctively formatted view file. For example, the view file for a table of contents view specifies the hierarchical structure of topics, whereas the view file for an index view specifies the index entries and the related topics.

For convenience, the various files are normally stored within a JAR file. Let's begin our study of Help facility implementation by examining a topic page.

FIGURE 17.2

A Help facility includes a structured set of files.

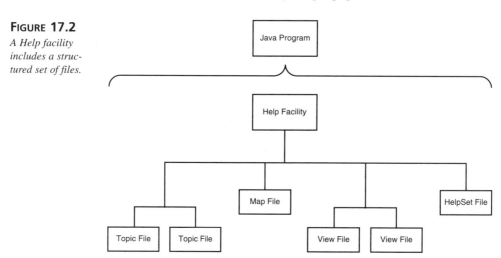

Help Topic Pages

Java Help uses HTML to specify the contents of a help topic page. For example, Listing 17.1 shows the HTML file that generated the topic page shown in Figure 17.1. This is a particularly simple topic page. More sophisticated pages can include colors, hyperlinks, images, and other familiar HTML devices. (Hyperlinks within topics should normally use relative, rather than absolute, addresses to facilitate installation of the help facility.)

Because the topic page is known by a URL, its content can even be dynamically generated by a server. For the ultimate in sophistication, you can embed Java applets in topics, giving your help topic multimedia or interactive capabilities not possible using ordinary HTML.

LISTING 17.1   Title.html—TOPIC FILE

```
<HTML>
<HEAD>
<TITLE>This is the title page.</TITLE>
</HEAD>
<BODY>
<H1>This is title page.</H1>
</BODY>
</HTML>
```

Map File

The map file establishes pseudonyms, called *topic IDs*, for the URLs that identify the HTML files containing topic information. Topic IDs afford compact references to the HTML files and facilitate renaming files or reorganizing directories. Topic IDs are particularly helpful when your program provides context-sensitive help, because your program can reference topics indirectly. This often lets you update or change help content without recompiling and redistributing your program. Listing 17.2 shows the map file used by the help demonstration on the CD-ROM. Each entry has the simple form *ID=URL*. Notice that all the URLs in the example are relative URLs.

LISTING 17.2   Map.jhm—THE MAP FILE

```
toplevelfolder=images/toplevel.gif

top=Title.html
intro=Intro.html
section0101=Section0101.html
section0102=Section0102.html
section0201=Section0201.html
section0202=Section0202.html
```

Java 1.2 supports a new URL protocol, jar:, that lets you access files within a JAR file. This protocol is handy for use within a map file when you choose to place your topic files within a JAR.

Here's a typical jar: URL:

```
jar:file:/c:/helpstuff/helpfile.jar!topic1.html
```

This URL references a JAR file named `c:/helpstuff/helpfile.jar` on the local hard drive by using the `file:` protocol. When this URL is used, Java will open the JAR file and extract the file `topic1.htm`.

View Files

Each view file describes a different structure or organization of the help topics. You write view files using XML, which you can consider to be a superset of HTML. The main difference between HTML and XML is that HTML's tags and attributes are standard, whereas XML's tags and attributes are application dependent.

Listing 17.3 shows the view file used by the help program example. Notice that the file uses two types of tags:

- The `toc` tag encloses every line but the first. It specifies that this file describes the help set's table of contents. A single help set can have more than one table of contents, each described in its own file. A help set can also have one or more index views. Files describing index views use the `index` and `indexitem` tags.

- The `tocitem` describes an item within the table of contents. Items can be nested. For example, in Listing 17.3, the `top` item is the parent of every other item. Notice that some items have associated IDs and some don't. The items with IDs are defined in the map file, which relates each such item to an HTML document that describes its content and appearance.

LISTING 17.3 HelpDemoTOC.xml—THE TABLE OF CONTENTS FILE

```
<?xml version='1.0' encoding='ISO-8859-1' standalone='yes' ?>
<toc>
<tocitem id=top>JavaHelp Demo

    <tocitem id=intro>Introduction</tocitem>

    <tocitem>Chapter #1
        <tocitem id=section0101>Section #1</tocitem>
        <tocitem id=section0102>Section #2</tocitem>
    </tocitem>

    <tocitem>Chapter #2
        <tocitem id=section0201>Section #1</tocitem>
        <tocitem id=section0202>Section #2</tocitem>
    </tocitem>

</tocitem>
</toc>
```

HelpSet File

The most important file used by Java Help is the HelpSet file, which describes the overall structure of the help set. Like the view files, the HelpSet file is written using XML. Listing 17.4 shows the HelpSet file used by the help program example.

LISTING 17.4 HelpDemo.hs—THE HELPSET FILE

```xml
<?xml version='1.0' encoding='ISO-8859-1' standalone='yes' ?>
<helpset>
  <title>JavaHelp Demo</title>
  <homeID>top</homeID>
  <map>
     <data>Map.jhm</data>
  </map>
  <view>
    <name>TOC</name>
    <label>Table Of Contents</label>
    <type>javax.javahelp.JHelpTOCNavigator</type>
    <data>HelpDemoTOC.xml</data>
  </view>
</helpset>
```

This HelpSet file uses the following XML tags:

- `helpset`, which defines the file as one describing a help set.
- `title`, which specifies a title by which this help set is known.
- `homeID`, which specifies the topic that's initially present. Here, the topic named `top` is identified as the initial topic. The map file identifies the HTML file corresponding to this ID.
- `map`, which specifies the name of the map file associated with the help set. The `map` tag encloses a `data` tag that specifies the URL of the map file.
- `data`, which specifies a URL. The `data` tag is used with the `map` and `view` tags.
- `view`, which describes a view. If a help set contains multiple views, its HelpSet file contains multiple `view` tags.
- `name`, which names the view.
- `label`, which specifies a label that appears on the tab in the navigator.
- `type`, which specifies the name of the Java Help class that handles the view.

The Java Help API provides three classes commonly used to process views:

- `javax.javahelp.JHelpTOCNavigator`, which handles table of contents views
- `javax.javahelp.JHelpIndexNavigator`, which handles index views

- `javax.javahelp.JHelpSearchNavigator`, which handles full-text search views

We don't present the latter two classes here. Consult the documentation that accompanies the Java Help distribution for information about them.

A Helpful Applet

Listing 17.5 shows a simple applet, HelpApplet, that launches a help viewer on command. Figure 17.1 showed the appearance of this applet. Let's examine its source code and see how it works.

LISTING 17.5   `HelpApplet.java`—AN APPLET WITH HELP

```
import java.applet.*;
import java.awt.*;
import java.awt.event.*;
import java.net.*;
import javax.javahelp.*;
import com.sun.java.swing.*;

public class HelpApplet extends JApplet
{
    JButton theLauncher = new JButton("Launch Help");

    public void init()
    {
        getContentPane().setLayout(new BorderLayout());
        getContentPane().add(theLauncher,
          BorderLayout.NORTH);
        JLabel lbl = new JLabel(
          "For help, click on the Launch Help button.");
        Font f = new Font("Helvetica", Font.BOLD, 12);
        lbl.setFont(f);
        getContentPane().add(lbl, BorderLayout.SOUTH);
        theLauncher.addActionListener(new Launcher());
    }

    public void fatalError(Exception ex)
    {
        ex.printStackTrace();
    }

    class Launcher implements ActionListener
    {
        public void actionPerformed(ActionEvent evt)
        {
            try
            {
                URL url = new URL(getCodeBase(),
```

```
          "HelpDemo/HelpDemo.hs");
        HelpSet hs = new HelpSet(
          getClass().getClassLoader(), url);
        JHelp jh = new JHelp(hs);
        jh.setVisible(true);
        getContentPane().add(jh, BorderLayout.CENTER);
        invalidate();
        validate();
      }
      catch (Exception ex) { fatalError(ex); }
    }
  }
}
```

You may notice some unfamiliar features as you study the HelpApplet class. As we mentioned, the Java Help API uses the Swing user-interface classes. Therefore, it seemed appropriate to use these rather than the usual AWT classes in the applet itself. It's possible to mix Swing components and AWT components. However, in beta releases of Swing and JDK 1.2, this was a frequent source of bugs. Therefore, whether by habit or cautiousness, we continue to use one or the other rather than both.

In comparing a Swing-based program to a non–Swing-based program, two differences stand out:

- Swing includes many components that extend the capabilities of similar AWT components. These are named with a *J* prefix. For example, Swing includes JApplet, JLabel, JButton, and JTextField components rather than Applet, Label, Button, and TextField components.

- You generally don't directly add components to a Swing container; instead, you add components to the container's content pane, which you access by using the getContentPane method.

Apart from these differences, a Swing-based program looks much the same as an AWT-based program. Of course, further differences arise if you choose to take advantage of Swing capabilities that have no AWT counterpart. If you're interested in learning about these, you might enjoy *Java 1.2 Interactive Course* (Waite Group Press, 1999), which was co-authored by one of the authors of this book.

The heart of the applet, contained within the actionPerformed method of its inner class, can be found in the following lines:

```
URL url = new URL(getCodeBase(),
  "HelpDemo/HelpDemo.hs");
HelpSet hs = new HelpSet(
  getClass().getClassLoader(), url);
JHelp jh = new JHelp(hs);
jh.setVisible(true);
```

The first statement constructs a URL that refers to the HelpSet file. Although it's usual to enclose help files within a JAR, the help example doesn't do so, because that makes them more cumbersome to examine. The URL references a subdirectory, HelpDemo, that contains the HelpSet file, HelpDemo.hs. You can copy the files from the CD-ROM to try the applet yourself. Be sure to recursively copy the subdirectory and its contents along with the .class and .html files for the applet.

The second statement, which appears on the third and fourth lines, constructs a HelpSet object. Doing so requires a reference to a ClassLoader instance that can load the proper view classes and the URL of the HelpSet file. Getting the ClassLoader is actually easier than it seems. The value null tells the HelpSet constructor to use the default ClassLoader. Here, we've gone to some extra trouble to write code that will work even in odd circumstances where nondefault ClassLoaders are at work. Under normal circumstances, the value returned by getClass().getClassLoader() will be null. However, if a special ClassLoader is in use, the expression returns a reference to that ClassLoader.

The third and fourth statements, which appear on the last two lines, construct a JHelp object from the HelpSet object and make the JHelp visible. Because the view is a table of contents view, the created JHelp object is an instance of javax.javahelp.TOCNavigator, the appropriate help viewer for a table of contents. The remaining statements of the actionPerformed method add the JHelp to the applet window and reformat the applet window as needed to accommodate the JHelp.

That's all there is to it. Simply clicking the Launch Help button loads and displays the help viewer. Of course, in a real application you might want to consider some issues we've swept under the carpet in the interests of brevity and simplicity:

- In this applet, nothing prevents the user from clicking the Launch Help button multiple times, creating a new JHelp instance each time. If a JHelp is active, you should reuse it rather than create a new instance.

- Creating the JHelp requires parsing the help files, which is a time-consuming process. You may prefer to create the JHelp during program initialization and simply display it when the user requests help.

- You may prefer to display help in a separate window rather than in the applet window. To do this, you can create a JFrame and place the JHelp within it. The next example, an application that offers help, demonstrates this technique.

A Helpful Application

Applications and applets are rather dissimilar. Swing exaggerates the differences somewhat, so an example of a help-equipped application is in order. Figure 17.3 shows how the sample application looks, and Listing 17.6 contains its source code.

FIGURE 17.3

Java Help supports applications and applets.

LISTING 17.6 `HelpApplication.java`—AN APPLICATION WITH HELP

```java
import java.awt.*;
import java.awt.event.*;
import java.net.*;
import javax.javahelp.*;
import com.sun.java.swing.*;

public class HelpApplication extends JFrame
{
    JButton theLauncher = new JButton("Launch Help");

    public static void main(String [] args)
    {
        new HelpApplication().init();
    }

    public HelpApplication()
    {
        super("HelpApplication");
    }

    public void init()
    {
        getContentPane().setLayout(new BorderLayout());
        getContentPane().add(theLauncher, BorderLayout.NORTH);
        getContentPane().add(
          new Label("Click on the button for help."),
          BorderLayout.CENTER);
        theLauncher.addActionListener(new Launcher());
        addWindowListener(new WindowHandler());
```

continues

LISTING 17.6   CONTINUED

```
        pack();
        setVisible(true);
    }

    public void fatalError(Exception ex)
    {
        System.err.println(ex);
    }
    // Inner classes omitted
}
```

As usual, we've deferred the inner classes to a subsequent listing, which we'll explain momentarily. As you can see, the logic of the HelpApplication class is typical for an application, although some Swing-related differences are evident. For example, the class extends JFrame and adds components to its main container by using the getContentPane method you saw in the HelpApplet class.

Listing 17.7 shows the inner classes of HelpApplication. The first inner class, WindowHandler, handles the event generated when the user clicks the close box of the main application window.

LISTING 17.7   HelpApplication.java—INNER CLASSES

```
class WindowHandler extends WindowAdapter
{
    public void windowClosing(WindowEvent evt)
    {
        setVisible(false);
        System.exit(0);
    }
}

class Launcher implements ActionListener
{
    public void actionPerformed(ActionEvent evt)
    {
        try
        {
            URL url = new URL("file", "", "HelpDemo/HelpDemo.hs");
            HelpSet hs = new HelpSet(
              getClass().getClassLoader(), url);
            JHelp jh = new JHelp(hs);
            JFrame frame = new JFrame("Help Window");
            frame.getContentPane().add(jh);
            frame.pack();
            frame.setDefaultCloseOperation(
```

```
                WindowConstants.DISPOSE_ON_CLOSE);
            frame.setVisible(true);
        }
        catch (Exception ex) { fatalError(ex); }
    }
}
```

The second inner class, `Launcher`, responds to a click on the Launch Help button by popping up a help viewer. The initial statements of its `actionPerformed` method resemble those of the similar method of the HelpApplet. However, HelpApplication creates a `JFrame` that presents its help viewer in a window separate from its main window. It uses the `pack` method to size the pop-up window and the `setDefaultCloseOperation` to specify that the help window closes automatically when the user clicks its close box. You can use this same technique to launch a separate help window for use with an applet.

That completes our tour of the Java Help facility. You should now be able to create your own help sets and launch appropriate help viewers from Java applets or applications. Bear in mind that the Java Help API has not yet been finalized. You should consult the Javasoft Web site for the latest available information about Java Help.

In the next section, you'll learn how to send Internet mail messages from your application.

JAVA MAIL

At the time of this writing, the Java Mail API is in early release and can be downloaded from the Javasoft Web site. Java Mail requires the Java Activation Framework (JAF), so be sure to download and install both products. Without JAF, many Java Mail operations fail silently, issuing `NullPointerException` errors.

The sample program, called TinyMail, sends a mail message via an SMTP mail server. Three main classes of the Java Mail API do the real work:

- `Session`, which represents properties that define the interface between the mail client and the network. The `Session` class also acts as a factory for creating `Transport` objects.
- `Message`, which represents a mail message.
- `Transport`, which represents the transport agent that sends a message. The primary method of the `Transport` class is send, which transmits a message.

Tables 17.1 and 17.2 summarize the methods of the `Session` class and the `Message` class, respectively, used in the example program, along with several other important methods. These classes as well as other classes of the Java Mail API provide many additional methods. Consult the Java Mail API documentation for the latest information.

TABLE 17.1 KEY METHODS OF THE Session CLASS

Method	Function
static Session getDefaultInstance(s)	Returns a Session instance Properties *p*, Authenticator created using the specified properties and authentication.
Properties getProperties()	Returns the properties associated with the Session.
Transport getTransport()	Returns a Transport object that implements the protocol associated with the Session.
setDebug(boolean *debug*)	Sets or resets the debug flag, as specified.

TABLE 17.2 KEY METHODS OF THE Message CLASS

Method	Function
void setFrom(Address *from*)	Sets the sender (from) address of the message.
void setRecipients(MessageRecipientType *type*, Address *recipient*)	Adds a recipient address to the message.
void setSentDate(Date *date*)	Sets the sent data of the message.
void setSubject(String *subj*)	Sets the subject of the message.

Listing 17.8 shows the source code of the TinyMail class. The class provides a non-GUI interface that lets the user type the name of the SMTP (mail) host, the from address, the to address (receipt), the subject, and the message. Because most users have a mail client on their PC, you'll probably never implement a program with a user interface like TinyMail's. Instead, you're more likely to write a program that obtains the host name and other information programmatically. Such a program may be used, for instance, to alert a system administrator of a system problem.

LISTING 17.8 TinyMail.java—AN SMTP MAIL CLIENT

```java
import java.io.*;
import javax.mail.*;
import javax.mail.internet.*;
import java.net.*;
import java.util.*;

public class TinyMail {
    static final String MAILER = "TinyMail";
```

```
public static void main(String[] args)
{
    new TinyMail();
}

public TinyMail()
{
    String   theSMTPHost;
    String   theSender;
    String   theRecipient;
    String   theSubject;

    BufferedReader in =
            new BufferedReader(new InputStreamReader(System.in));

    try {
        System.out.print("SMTP Host: ");
        System.out.flush();
        theSMTPHost = in.readLine();

        System.out.print("From: ");
        System.out.flush();
        theSender = in.readLine();

        System.out.print("To: ");
        System.out.flush();
        theRecipient = in.readLine();

        System.out.print("Subject: ");
        System.out.flush();
        theSubject = in.readLine();

        Properties props = new Properties();
        props.put("mail.smtp.host", theSMTPHost);
        Session session =
          Session.getDefaultInstance(props, null);

        Message msg = new MimeMessage(session);
        msg.setFrom(new InternetAddress(theSender));
        msg.setRecipients(Message.RecipientType.TO,
          InternetAddress.parse(theRecipient, false));
        msg.setSubject(theSubject);

        getMessageText(in, msg);

        msg.setHeader("X-Mailer", MAILER);
        msg.setSentDate(new Date());

        Transport.send(msg);
```

17

JAVA HELP, JAVA
MAIL, AND OTHER
JAVA APIS

continues

LISTING 17.8 CONTINUED

```
            System.out.println("\nMailed okay.");
        }
        catch (Exception e)
        {
            e.printStackTrace();
        }
    }

    public void getMessageText(BufferedReader in, Message msg)
      throws MessagingException, IOException
    {
        String line;
        StringBuffer buffer = new StringBuffer();
        System.out.println("Enter message (Ctl-Z ends)");
        while ((line = in.readLine()) != null)
        {
            buffer.append(line);
            buffer.append("\n");
        }
        msg.setText(buffer.toString());
    }
}
```

The program is quite simple. It establishes a `BufferedReader` associated with `System.in`, the default program input stream. It prompts the user for necessary data, reads the user's responses, and stores the responses in program variables.

When all the necessary information has been read, the program creates a `Session` object, using the SMTP host name as the only explicit property. Then, the program creates a `MimeMessage` object. `MimeMessage` is a subclass of message that provides several additional methods, including `setHeader`, which allows specification of a mail message header, and `setText`, which allows specification of the mail message body. Finally, the program uses the `send` method to transmit the message.

The Java Mail API also has the capability to manipulate folders and messages stored by an Internet Mail Application Protocol (IMAP) server. Because the Java Mail API is in early release at the time of this writing, you should consult the Javasoft Web site for the latest information on this and other capabilities.

FORTHCOMING JAVA APIS

Apart from Java Help and Java Mail, Sun has several other Java APIs of interest to developers of distributed systems. These APIs are at varying stages of development:

- Enterprise JavaBeans (EJB), a component architecture for building reusable server-side software components. The EJB architecture is CORBA compliant. It provides a mapping between CORBA protocols and EJB protocols so you can access CORBA APIs from Java. EJB also supports Java's Remote Method Invocation (RMI). An early access release of EJB is available.

- Java Naming and Directory Interface (JNDI), which provides a single point of access to the potentially many naming and directory services used within an organization. JNDI lets you access directory services such as the Lightweight Directory Services Protocol (LDAP), Novell's NetWare Directory Services (NDS), and Sun's Network Information Service (NIS) in a common, Java-oriented way. JNDI can provide access to security certificates, e-mail addresses, databases, network file systems, and other resources and services. At the time of this writing, version 1.1 of the JNDI specification and code were available.

- Java Media APIs, including Java Media Framework (JMF), Java Sound API, Java Speech API, and Java Telephony API. JMF supports streaming of audio and video media over networks and control and synchronization of playback. At the time of this writing, the Java Sound API provides 32-channel high-quality audio output and can operate under Musical Instrument Digital Interface (MIDI) control. The Java Speech API provides text-to-speech and speech recognition capabilities. The Java Telephony API is a programming interface for computer-telephony applications. These APIs are in various stages of development.

- Java Transaction API (JTA), which defines a high-level transaction management interface and manager for distributed transaction systems. The JTA API specification is available for review.

- Java Transaction Service (JTS), which defines a low-level transaction management specification intended for use by vendors who provide transaction management systems. The revised JTS specification includes a standard Java mapping of the CORBA Object Transaction Service. The specification and Java mappings are available for download.

Consult the Javasoft Web site for the latest information on these APIs.

FROM HERE

You learned how to use the Java Help API and the Java Mail API to add help and mail facilities to your applications. This chapter is the final chapter of Part III, "Java's Networking and Enterprise APIs," which describes Java and Java facilities for distributed computing. Part IV, "Non-CORBA Approaches to Distributed Computing," describes two non-Java approaches to distributed computing: the Common Gateway Interface (CGI) and Microsoft's Distributed Component Object Model (DCOM). If you're a Java fan, don't skip Part IV, thinking that it contains no Java. Chapters 18, "Servlets and Common Gateway Interface (CGI)," and 19, "Servlet-Based Implementation of the Airline Reservation System," describe and demonstrate Java servlets, which support CGI and offer advantages over more common CGI technologies.

NON-CORBA APPROACHES TO DISTRIBUTED COMPUTING

PART IV

IN THIS PART

SERVLETS AND COMMON GATEWAY INTERFACE (CGI)

IN THIS CHAPTER

Two of the greatest tennis stars of all time were Australians Rod Laver and Ken Rosewall. During the 1970s, they played opposite one another in tournament after tournament. You never knew who'd win Wimbledon, for instance, but most years you could be sure it would be either Laver or Rosewall. Though they were fellow countrymen, the two were otherwise quite unalike. Laver was tall with a devastatingly powerful first serve. Rosewall, at only 5 feet and 6 inches, seemed barely tall enough to peer over the net; yet he moved with such agility that no passing shot seemed beyond his reach. Nevertheless, in tennis just as in basketball, height has its advantages: In comparison to Laver's serve, Rosewall's was merely a "servlet."

In this chapter, you'll learn about servlets of a different variety: small Java programs that run on a server, providing HTML documents to remote clients. Some, particularly Microsoft, have impugned the potential of client-side Java (not that we agree with them, mind you). However, even detractors acknowledge that server-side Java is a technology to reckon with. In this chapter you learn:

- How to use the URLConnection class to obtain data from a Web server

  The URLConnection class makes it a snap to download information from a server, whether the server is an ordinary Web server, a CGI-based Web server, or a Java servlet-based Web server.

- How to use HTML forms to transfer data to a server using the Common Gateway Interface (CGI)

  HTML pages called *forms* can contain user interface controls such as pushbuttons and check boxes. You can define a button that triggers the transmission of the values of a page's controls to a server, which can process the data and return a response for display by the Web client. Because Web clients are ubiquitous, HTML forms let a user access a server, no matter what hardware platform or operating system the user runs.

- How to write a servlet that processes a Web client's GET request

  To access a Web page, a Web client sends a GET request via the HTTP protocol to a Web server. You'll learn how to use a servlet to receive and process a Web client's GET request.

- How to write a servlet that processes a Web client's POST request

  To send the contents of a Web form to a Web server, a Web client uses the POST request. You'll learn how to use a servlet to receive and process POST requests.

USING THE URLCONNECTION CLASS

Recall that the URL class, which you met in Chapter 13, "Sockets," lets you download the document identified by a URL. Its cousin class URLConnection provides access to many attributes that describe the document and the server response that provided it. You don't use a constructor to obtain an instance of URLConnection; instead, you use the openConnection method of the URL class. Once you have a URLConnection instance, you can invoke any of the methods summarized in Table 18.1. The getHeaderField method returns the value of a specified field of the server's response header. Table 18.2 describes the most commonly used fields.

TABLE 18.1   KEY METHODS OF THE URLConnection CLASS

Method	*Function*
Object getContent()	Returns an object that represents the contents of the document associated with the URLConnection, if an appropriate content handler is available.
String getContentEncoding()	Returns a String that describes the type of encoding used by the document associated with the URLConnection.
int getContentLength()	Returns the length (in bytes) of the document associated with the URLConnection.
String getContentType()	Returns a String that describes the type of encoding used by the document associated with the URLConnection.
long getDate()	Returns a long that holds the creation date and time of the server's response.
long getExpiration()	Returns a long that holds the expiration date and time of the server's response.
String getHeaderField(String *name*)	Returns a String that holds the value of the specified field of the response header returned by the server. (See Table 18.2 for the names of the response header fields.)
String getHeaderField(int *n*)	Returns a String that holds the value of the specified field of the response header returned by the server. Response header fields are numbered beginning with 0.

continues

18

TABLE 18.1 CONTINUED

Method	Function
`long getIfModifiedSince()`	Returns a `long` that holds the modification date and time that force refetching of the document associated with the `URLConnection`.
`InputStream getInputStream()`	Returns an `InputStream` that contains the bytes of the document associated with the `URLConnection`.
`long getLastModified()`	Returns a `long` that holds the date and time at which the document associated with the `URLConnection` was last modified.

TABLE 18.2 KEY SERVER RESPONSE HEADER FIELDS

Field	Meaning
Allowed	The request methods (for example, GET, PUT, and POST) that the user can issue for this URL
Content-Encoding	The type of encoding of the response message (for example, x-zip-compressed)
Content-Language	The language of the response message
Content-Length	The length (in bytes) of the response message
Content-Transfer-Encoding	The type of encoding used for MIME messages
Content-Type	The MIME type and subtype of the content of this message (for example, text/plain)
Cost	The cost of retrieving the document
Date	The creation time (GMT) of the document
Derived-From	The version of the document from which this document derives
Expires	The time (GMT) at which the document expires and should be refetched
Last-Modified	The time (GMT) at which the document was last modified
Message-ID	A unique identifier for this message
Public	The request methods anyone can issue for this URL
Title	The title of this document
URI	The URI (Universal Resource Identifier; for practical purposes, the term is synonymous with *URL*) or URL of the document
Version	The version of the document
WWW-Authenticate	The authorization method used by the server
WWW-Link	The HTML link reference of the document

Figure 18.1 shows the output of WebClient, a simple applet that uses the URL and URLConnection classes to download a Web page and its description. The applet doesn't render the HTML contents of the document, it merely displays them. To operate the applet, you merely type a URL in the text box and press Enter. Let's see how the applet works.

FIGURE 18.1

The WebClient applet displays the attributes and content of a Web document.

Listing 18.1 shows the source code of the WebClient applet, except for the inner class URLHandler, which provides an actionPerformed method that handles ActionEvents associated with the TextField used to input a URL. The main point of interest is the array theHeaders, which contains the names of the response field headers the applet retrieves. Otherwise, most of the code is user interface oriented.

LISTING 18.1 WebClient.java—AN APPLET THAT DISPLAYS WEB DOCUMENT CONTENTS AND CHARACTERISTICS

```java
import java.applet.*;
import java.awt.*;
import java.awt.event.*;
import java.io.*;
import java.net.*;
import java.util.Date;

public class WebClient extends Applet
{
```

continues

Listing 18.1 CONTINUED

```java
TextField theURL     = new TextField(32);
TextArea  theData    = new TextArea(6, 64);
TextArea  theContent = new TextArea(10, 64);

String [] theHeaders = {
    "Allowed",
    "Content-Encoding",
    "Content-Language",
    "Content-Length",
    "Content-Transfer-Encoding",
    "Content-Type",
    "Cost",
    "Date",
    "Derived-From",
    "Expires",
    "Last-Modified",
    "Message-ID",
    "Public",
    "Title",
    "URI",
    "Version",
    "WWW-Authenticate",
    "WWW-Link",
};

public void init()
{
    Font f = new Font("Monospaced", Font.PLAIN, 12);
    setFont(f);
    Panel p1 = new Panel();
    Panel p2 = new Panel();
    setLayout(new BorderLayout());
    add(p1, BorderLayout.NORTH);
    add(p2, BorderLayout.CENTER);

    p1.setLayout(new GridLayout(0, 1));
    p1.add(new Label("URL:"));
    p1.add(theURL);

    p2.setLayout(new GridLayout(0, 1));
    Panel p3 = new Panel();
    Panel p4 = new Panel();
    p2.add(p3);
    p2.add(p4);

    p3.setLayout(new BorderLayout());
    p3.add(new Label("URL Data:"),
      BorderLayout.NORTH);
    p3.add(theData, BorderLayout.CENTER);
```

```
        p4.setLayout(new BorderLayout());
        p4.add(new Label("URL Content:"),
          BorderLayout.NORTH);
        p4.add(theContent, BorderLayout.CENTER);

        theURL.addActionListener(new URLHandler());
        theData.setEditable(false);
        theContent.setEditable(false);
    }

    public void println(String s)
    {
        theData.append(s + "\n");
    }

    public void fatalError(Exception ex)
    {
        ex.printStackTrace();
    }
    // Inner class omitted
}
```

Listing 18.2 shows the `URLHandler` inner class of the `WebClient` class. The `actionPerformed` method retrieves and displays the document contents and characteristics. To do so, it constructs a `URL` using the text input by the user. It invokes the `openConnection` method to obtain a `URLConnection` and calls several `URLConnection` methods that provide document characteristics. It uses a simple `for` loop to obtain and display the response header fields. It displays the document characteristics in the upper `TextArea`, `theData`, by using the `println` method of its enclosing class.

LISTING 18.2   `WebClient.java`—`URLHandler` INNER CLASS

```
class URLHandler implements ActionListener
{
    public void actionPerformed(ActionEvent evt)
    {
        try
        {
            theData.setText("");
            theContent.setText("");
            URL url = new URL(theURL.getText());
            URLConnection connect =
              url.openConnection();
            println("Content Encoding: " +
              connect.getContentEncoding());
            println("Length: " +
```

continues

LISTING 18.2   CONTINUED

```
            connect.getContentLength());
        println("Type: " +
          connect.getContentType());
        println("Date: " +
          new Date(connect.getDate()));
        println("Expiration: " +
          new Date(connect.getExpiration()));
        println("Last Modified: " +
          new Date(connect.getLastModified()));
         for (int i = 0; i < theHeaders.length; i++)
        {
            String header =
              connect.getHeaderField(theHeaders[i]);
            println(theHeaders[i] + ": " +
              header);
        }
         BufferedReader in =
          new BufferedReader(
          new InputStreamReader(
          url.openStream()));
        String line;
        while ((line = in.readLine()) != null)
        {
            theContent.append(line + "\n");
        }
        in.close();
    }
    catch (Exception ex) { fatalError(ex); }
  }
}
```

To obtain the document contents, the actionPerformed method uses the
URL.openStream method. It wraps the returned InputStream reader within a
BufferedReader, which provides the convenient readLine method for reading the stream
one line at a time. The method simply appends each line of input to the lower TextArea,
theContent.

Generally, your programs will need to access only a few (if any) document characteristics. Therefore, your programs using URLConnection and URL to access a document won't
usually be this long. Notice that you can download the contents of a URL with less than a
dozen lines of code. URL is simple to use, but powerful.

COMMON GATEWAY INTERFACE (CGI)

The WebClient program from Listing 18.2 demonstrates one of the two fundamental
capabilities of a Web client: the ability to download information from a Web server by

issuing an HTTP GET request. Modern Web clients also have the capability to upload data to a Web server, using techniques referred to as the *Common Gateway Interface* (or *CGI*). CGI defines two methods for uploading data: GET and POST. The POST method is more powerful and secure than the GET method, which is not implemented by Java servlets. Therefore, we'll omit discussion of using the GET method to upload data.

To use the POST method, you define an HTML page that includes tags that specify user interface controls. Your page can include pushbuttons, input boxes, radio buttons, and so on. When the user clicks a designated submit button, the Web client uploads the values of the controls to the Web server. The Web server processes the incoming data and generally returns a response in the form of an HTML page that the Web client displays. Let's discuss how to build such a form.

The source code of a typical HTML page includes several structural tags in the following form:

```
<HTML>
<HEAD>
<TITLE>This is the title</TITLE>
</HEAD>
<BODY>
    ... the body of the page is defined here ...
</BODY>
</HTML>
```

To create an HTML form, you follow this same pattern. Within the body of the HTML document, you define a form using a pair of tags like these:

```
<FORM METHOD=POST ACTION="url">
    ... the body of the form goes here ...
</FORM>
```

url specifies the protocol (HTTP), the host name, and possibly the port of the Web server in the same fashion as a URL used to access a document. However, the path and document part of *url* do not refer to a document to be fetched; instead, they refer to a program the Web server runs (possibly a Java servlet) to process the form's input. The path and name don't need to be the actual path and name of the file containing the program. Most Web servers provide a table that translates between a "document" path and name specified by the user and the actual path and name of the program that should be run.

Within the body of the form, you use HTML tags to define the controls you want. You can also include ordinary HTML text, images, and so on. Table 18.3 summarizes HTML tags you can use to include various input elements within a form. Most of the tags support attributes that modify their appearance or function. The purpose in presenting this information is to help you read HTML forms prepared by others. If you want to create your own HTML forms, you might consult a book on basic HTML. An easier approach

18

SERVLETS AND
CGI

is to use an HTML editor that lets you build forms using a point-and-click, WYSIWYG interface, such as Adobe's PageMill or Microsoft's FrontPage.

TABLE 18.3   SUMMARY OF FORM INPUT ELEMENTS

Tag and Attribute	Input Element
`<INPUT TYPE=TEXT …>`	Defines a text box.
`<INPUT TYPE=CHECKBOX …>`	Defines an on/off check box.
`<INPUT TYPE=RADIOBUTTON …>`	Defines a radio button. All controls that have the same name are considered part of a single set of radio buttons, only one of which can be in the "on" state at any time.
`<INPUT TYPE=SUBMIT …>`	Defines a submit button.
`<INPUT TYPE=RESET …>`	Defines a reset button.
`<INPUT TYPE=HIDDEN …>`	Defines a hidden field, the value of which is transmitted to the Web server. It cannot be manipulated by the user.
`<TEXTAREA COLS=cols ROWS=rows …>`	Defines a multiline text box.
`<SELECT SIZE=n …>`	Defines a drop-down list box. Used with `CHOICE`.
`<OPTION …>`	Specifies an item within the drop-down list box created by `SELECT`. Must be nested between the `<SELECT>` and `</SELECT>` tags that define the list box.

Form input elements include a `NAME` attribute, which specifies a name for the control, and a `VALUE` attribute, which specifies a default initial value of an input field or the text that appears on a button. Every form must include a submit button that initiates the data upload. You should usually also include a reset button that restores the values of all controls to their initial values.

Listing 18.3 shows the simple HTML form you'll use later in this chapter to run a Java servlet that processes form input. Study the tags and attributes used in the form and try to determine how it should operate. Figure 18.2 shows how the form looks.

Use a Web browser (not the appletviewer, which cannot display HTML text) to verify your conclusions. Then, experiment by replacing the tags and attributes to see what sorts of forms you can create. Use a WYSIWYG HTML editor such as PageMill or FrontPage if you have one. Of course, your forms won't operate until you build an appropriate Java servlet, which you'll learn how to do later in this chapter.

LISTING 18.3   TestPoster.java—A SIMPLE HTML FORM

```
<HTML>
<HEAD>
<TITLE>Poster Test Page</TITLE>
</HEAD>
<BODY>
<FORM ACTION="http://127.0.0.1:8080/servlet/poster" METHOD=POST>
<H1>Poster Test Page</H1>
<P>Name:
<INPUT TYPE=TEXT NAME=name>
<P>Type:
<P> <INPUT TYPE=RADIO NAME=type VALUE=Human> Human
<P> <INPUT TYPE=RADIO NAME=type VALUE=Clone> Clone
<P> <INPUT TYPE=RADIO NAME=type VALUE=Replicant> Replicant
<P>Status:
<P> <INPUT TYPE=CHECKBOX NAME=status VALUE=Off-world> Off-world
<P> <INPUT TYPE=SUBMIT>
<INPUT TYPE=RESET>
</FORM>
</BODY>
</HTML>
```

FIGURE 18.2

A simple input form, such as the Poster Test Page example, can upload data to a Web server.

18

SERVLETS AND
CGI

SERVLETS: SERVER-SIDE JAVA

Now that you've learned a bit about the client side of Web data exchange, let's shift focus to the server side. In this section you'll learn how to write servlets. First you'll learn how to write a servlet that handles a GET request; later in this chapter, you'll learn how to write a servlet that handles a POST request. Along the way, you'll learn how to access initialization arguments, request context data, and examine the servlet context.

Most servlets are instances of the `HttpServlet` class, which extends the `GenericServlet` class. These classes provide much of the functionality of a servlet: All you must do is provide the application-dependent functions. Table 18.4 summarizes key `GenericServlet` methods, and Table 18.5 summarizes key `HttpServlet` methods.

The most important servlet methods are the `doGet` and `doPost` methods. To create a servlet, you provide overriding implementations of these methods. When your `doGet` or `doPost` method gets control, it receives two arguments: one, an `HttpServletRequest`, encapsulates the HTTP request, and the other, an `HttpServletResponse`, encapsulates the server response. By invoking methods on these objects, your program can inspect the request and construct and send an appropriate response.

TABLE 18.4 SUMMARY OF KEY `GenericServlet` METHODS

Method	*Function*
`void destroy()`	The network service automatically calls this method whenever it removes the servlet.
`String getInitParameter(String name)`	Returns the value of the specified initialization parameter from the servlet's properties file.
`Enumeration getInitParameterNames()`	Returns the names of the servlet's initialization parameters.
`ServletContext getServletContext()`	Returns a `ServletContext` object describing the servlet's context.
`String getServletInfo()`	Returns a description of the servlet.
`void init(ServletConfig config)`	Initializes the servlet. Servlet classes that override `init` should call `super.init` so that the servlet can be properly initialized.
`void log(String msg)`	Writes a message to the servlet log.

TABLE 18.5 SUMMARY OF KEY HttpServlet METHODS

Method	*Function*
void doGet(HttpServletRequest *request*, HttpServletResponse *response*)	Processes an HTTP GET request.
void doPost(HttpServletRequest *request*, HttpServletResponse *response*)	Processes an HTTP POST request.

The HttpServletRequest class extends the ServletRequest class, which provides many useful methods. Table 18.6 summarizes these. The HttpServletRequest provides several additional methods that may be of value, including methods that handle Web browser cookies. Consult the Servlet Development Kit documentation or the Java 1.2 JDK documentation for further information.

TABLE 18.6 SUMMARY OF KEY ServletRequest METHODS

Method	*Function*
Object getAttribute(String *name*)	Returns the value of the specified request attribute.
String getCharacterEncoding()	Returns the name of the character set used to encode the request.
int getContentLength()	Returns the length of the request.
String getContentType()	Returns the media type of the request.
ServletInputStream getInputStream()	Returns a ServletInputStream associated with the request.
String getParameter(String *name*)	Returns the value of the specified request parameter.
Enumeration getParameterNames()	Returns an Enumeration containing the names of the request parameters.
String [] getParameterValues(String *name*)	Returns the values of the specified request parameter.
String getProtocol()	Returns a description of the request protocol.
BufferedReader getReader()	Returns a BufferedReader associated with the request.
String getRemoteAddr()	Returns the Internet address of the client.
String getRemoteHost()	Returns the host name of the client.
String getServerName()	Returns the host name of the server.
int getServerPort()	Returns the port number of the server.

18

SERVLETS AND
CGI

The `HttpServletReponse` class and its parent class, `ServletResponse`, provide many useful methods. The most important of these are shown in Table 18.7.

TABLE 18.7   KEY `HttpServletResponse` AND `ServletResponse` METHODS

Method	Function
`PrintWriter getWriter()`	Returns a `PrintWriter` for writing text responses.
`ServletOutputStream getOutputStream()`	Returns a `ServletOutputStream` for writing binary responses.
`void setContentType(String type)`	Sets the content type of the response.

IMPLEMENTING A SERVLET

Now that you're acquainted with the main method used to implement servlets, let's examine a sample servlet. Figure 18.3 shows the output of a servlet known as SimpleServlet, as rendered by a Web browser. Don't try to run the servlet just yet. It requires the servletrunner utility (or a compatible Web server) as a host; the servletrunner utility is the topic of the next section. Listing 18.4 shows the source code of the servlet.

> **NOTE**
>
> Listing 18.4 was compiled with JDK 1.1.6 with the Servlet Development Kit 2.0. The Servlet Development Kit is not presently bundled with JDK 1.1 (now at release 7) or JDK 1.2 (now at beta 4), so it's necessary to separately download and install it. No special measures are necessary to work with the Servlet Development Kit: Simply follow the installation instructions provided with the download.

FIGURE 18.3
The SimpleServlet transmits a static HTML page.

LISTING 18.4 SimpleServlet.java—A SERVLET THAT HANDLES AN HTTP GET REQUEST

```java
import javax.servlet.*;
import javax.servlet.http.*;
import java.io.*;

public class SimpleServlet extends HttpServlet
{
    public void doGet(HttpServletRequest request,
      HttpServletResponse response)
      throws ServletException, IOException
    {
        response.setContentType("text/html");
        PrintWriter out = response.getWriter();
        out.println("<HEAD>\n");
        out.println(
          "<TITLE>A SimpleServer Page</TITLE>\n");
        out.println("</HEAD>\n");
        out.println("<BODY>\n");
        out.println(
          "<H1>SimpleServlet was here.</H1>\n");
        out.println("</BODY>\n");
        out.close();
    }

    public String getServletInfo()
    {
        return (
          "I'm a little servlet, 29 lines long.");
    }
}
```

18

SERVLETS AND CGI

The servlet extends the HttpServlet class, overriding the doGet method to provide its application-specific processing, which merely transmits a static HTML page. Notice that the method can potentially throw a ServletException; many servlet-related methods throw this exception, which requires you to program a try-catch block or a throws clause.

The first task performed by this servlet, and most other servlets, is to set the content type of its output. Most servlets return HTML text to the requesting client; therefore, "text/html" is the most commonly used argument value. Next, the servlet uses the getWriter method to obtain a reference to a PrintWriter that encapsulates the response that will be transmitted to the client. Using the PrintWriter.println method, it writes a series of HTML tags that comprise the static output shown in Figure 18.3. Finally, the servlet closes the PrintWriter and exits its doGet method.

The servlet also implements the getServletInfo method, which returns a String that describes the servlet. All servlets should implement this method.

To run the servlet, you need the servletrunner utility or a compatible Web server. So that you can run the servlet, let's examine the servletrunner utility that's included in the Servlet Development Kit.

THE servletrunner UTILITY

The servletrunner utility, like most JDK utilities, is a command-line program that accepts several command arguments. To see these, type servletrunner -h, which causes servletrunner to display the following menu of options:

```
D:\JDO\Chapters\Ch18\Listings>servletrunner -h
Usage: servletrunner [options]
Options:
  -p port     the port number to listen on
  -b backlog  the listen backlog
  -m max      maximum number of connection handlers
  -t timeout  connection timeout in milliseconds
  -d dir      servlet directory
  -s filename servlet property file name
  -r dir      document root directory
java.exe: No error
```

Most of these options have default values. For example, the port defaults to 8080, and the servlet property filename defaults to servlet.properties. Unless you place your servlet .class files and HTML documents in the JDK directory tree, you'll need to specify the servlet and document root directories. The easiest way to use servletrunner is to navigate to the directory that contains your servlet's .class file and launch servletrunner from its own DOS window, giving explicit values to the -d and -r options:

```
servletrunner -d c:\servlets -r c:\servlets
```

Once servletrunner has initialized itself, you can use a Web browser to access your servlet by using the following URL:

```
http://localhost:8080/servlet/SimpleServlet
```

If you find that *SimpleServer* is too laborious to type, you can use the servlet.properties file to establish a pseudonym for your servlet. Simply include a line like the following:

```
servlet.simple.code=SimpleServlet
```

This entry establishes *simple* as a pseudonym for *SimpleServer*, allowing you to use the URL http://localhost:8080/servlet/simple to access the SimpleServlet servlet. Try it for yourself before reading on.

A PARAMETERIZED SERVLET

The servlet.properties file also lets you establish parameter name-value pairs that can help you initialize a servlet. They let you change a servlet's initial state without recompiling it. The multiline entry used for this purpose will look like this:

```
servlet.pseudonum.initArgs=\
  name=value, \
  name=value, \
    ...
  name=value
```

Here, *pseudonym* is the pseudonym of the servlet, and each line after the first associates a value with the specified name. Notice the backward slash (\) that ends each line (other than the last). As an example, the following entry for the servlet named coins gives values for some common U.S. coins:

```
servlet.coins.initArgs=\
  penny=1, \
  nickel=5, \
  dime=10, \
  quarter=25
```

To see how to access these initialization parameters within a servlet, see Listing 18.5. The servlet uses the `getInitParameterNames` method to obtain an `Enumeration` containing the names of its initialization parameters. Then it uses the `getInitParameter` method to obtain the value of each, including the value in the HTML page it returns to the client. The servlet.properties file on the CD-ROM contains entries for the ParameterizedServlet servlet. If you run the servlet, you should see output like that shown in Figure 18.4.

LISTING 18.5 ParameterizedServlet.java—A SERVLET THAT ACCESSES INITIALIZATION PARAMETERS

```java
import javax.servlet.*;
import javax.servlet.http.*;
import java.io.*;
import java.util.Enumeration;

public class ParameterizedServlet extends HttpServlet
{
    public void doGet(HttpServletRequest request,
      HttpServletResponse response)
      throws ServletException, IOException
    {
        response.setContentType("text/html");
        PrintWriter out = response.getWriter();
```

continues

18

SERVLETS AND
CGI

LISTING 18.5   CONTINUED

```
            out.println("<HEAD>\n");
            out.println(
              "<TITLE>A SimpleServer Page</TITLE>\n");
            out.println("</HEAD>\n");
            out.println("<BODY>\n");
            out.println(
              "<H1>Parameters:</H1>");
            out.println("<DL>\n");
            Enumeration parms = getInitParameterNames();
            while (parms.hasMoreElements())
            {
                String pname = (String) parms.nextElement();
                String pval  = getInitParameter(pname);
                out.println("<DT><B>" + pname + ":</B>");
                out.println("<DD><I>" + pval + "</I><P>");
            }
            out.println("</DL>\n");
            out.println("</BODY>");
            out.close();
        }

    public String getServletInfo()
    {
        return (getClass().getName());
    }
}
```

FIGURE 18.4

*The
ParameterizedSer
vlet accesses ini-
tialization para-
meters.*

A SERVLET THAT HANDLES POST REQUESTS

The PostServlet program example handles an HTTP POST request. PostServlet logs its input to a disk file and returns a reply to the client. You can use PostServlet as a model for more complex servlets that handle HTML form-based input, storing results in a file or database. Listing 18.6 shows the source code for PostServlet.

Following in the footsteps of SimpleServlet, the first task of PostServlet is to set the content type of its response, which again is "text/html." PostServlet then accesses an initialization parameter that identifies the directory that contains its data file. It uses the Java system property `file.separator` (which usually specifies a slash or backward slash) to join the directory name and the filename. The servlet then calls `getParameterNames` to obtain an `Enumeration` over the names of parameters included in its request data. Each parameter holds the value of an HTML form control. By using the `getParameterValues` method, the servlet obtains the data associated with each control. It writes the data to its disk file and returns a grateful response to the client.

LISTING 18.6   `PostServlet.java`—A SERVLET THAT HANDLES POST REQUESTS

```java
import javax.servlet.*;
import javax.servlet.http.*;
import java.io.*;
import java.util.Enumeration;

public class PostServlet extends HttpServlet
{
    public void doPost(HttpServletRequest request,
      HttpServletResponse response)
      throws ServletException, IOException
    {
        response.setContentType("text/html");
        PrintWriter out = response.getWriter();

        String dir = getInitParameter("dir");
        String sep = System.getProperties().
          getProperty("file.separator");

        PrintWriter fout =
          new PrintWriter(
          new FileWriter(dir + sep + "data.txt", true));
        Enumeration parms =
          request.getParameterNames();
        while (parms.hasMoreElements())
        {
            String pname = (String) parms.nextElement();
```

18

SERVLETS AND CGI

continues

LISTING 18.6 CONTINUED

```java
                fout.print(pname + "=");
                String [] pval  =
                  request.getParameterValues(pname);
                for (int i = 0; i < pval.length; i++)
                {
                    if (i > 0) fout.print(",");
                    fout.print(pval[i]);
                }
                fout.println();
            }
            fout.close();

            out.println("<HEAD>\n");
            out.println(
              "<TITLE>A PostServer Page</TITLE>\n");
            out.println("</HEAD>\n");
            out.println("<BODY>\n");
            out.println(
              "<H2>Thanks for the yummy data!</H2>");
            out.println("</BODY>");
            out.close();
        }

        public String getServletInfo()
        {
            return (getClass().getName());
        }
    }
}
```

The HTML file shown earlier in Listing 18.3 provides an HTML form suitable for use by PostServlet so that you can try it yourself. Figure 18.5 shows the output PostServlet returns to its clients.

FIGURE 18.5

The PostServlet servlet thanks the user for the data received.

CLIENT REQUEST AND SERVLET CONTEXT INFORMATION

The CD-ROM contains the sample program RequestInfo, which transmits a formatted page that describes the client's request. Figure 18.6 shows the output of the RequestInfo servlet. You may find RequestInfo useful in debugging HTML forms, because it displays the name and value of each control on the form.

FIGURE **18.6**

The RequestInfo servlet dumps the client request.

The CD-ROM also contains the sample program ContextDumper, which transmits a formatted page that describes the servlet context, including a list of active servlets. The list of active servlets is obtained using this code:

```
ServletContext context =
  getServletContext();
Enumeration servlets =
  context.getServletNames();
while (servlets.hasMoreElements())
{
    String name =
      (String) servlets.nextElement();
    out.println(name + "<BR>");
}
```

Sun advises that the getServletNames method may leave the servletrunner or Web server in an inconsistent state. Therefore, you should not run the ContextDumper servlet in a production environment. Most Web servers that support servlets provide a built-in facility that performs an operation similar to that of ContextDumper.

Figure 18.7 shows the output of the ContextDumper servlet.

FIGURE 18.7

The ContextDumper servlet dumps the current servlet context.

SERVLET CONSIDERATIONS

Java servlets are becoming increasingly popular, but their use is not yet widespread. Consequently, it's too early to make a thorough and accurate assessment of servlet technology. However, here are some issues to consider:

- Virtually any Web browser can access a servlet. Consequently, applications using a servlet-based architecture support essentially every common computing platform and architecture.

- The HTML form-based user interface, although widely available, is a "least common denominator" user interface, offering relatively few features. Of course, it's possible to use Java servlets with other sorts of front ends. HTML form-based user interfaces are simply easier to construct and more popular than alternative types of user interfaces.

- Servlets appear to be more secure and perform more efficiently that CGI programs written in C, C++, or Perl.

- Because they're written in Java, servlets are relatively simple to create and are portable across server platforms.

FROM HERE

You learned how to use the URLConnection class to download data from a Web server. You've learned how to construct and use HTML forms that transmit their contents to a Web server. What's more, you've learned how to write Java servlets that handle GET and POST requests.

Chapter 19, "Servlet-Based Implementation of the Airline Reservation System," provides additional information about servlets. It shows how servlets might be used to implement this book's running sample application system.

SERVLET-BASED IMPLEMENTATION OF THE AIRLINE RESERVATION SYSTEM

IN THIS CHAPTER

In the previous chapter, you learned about Java's servlet facility. In this chapter, you'll see an example of a larger servlet-based program—one that implements the Airline Reservation System of Chapter 6, "The Airline Reservation System Model." The program is similar in function to the RMI-based program presented in Chapter 16, "RMI-Based Implementation of the Airline Reservation System." You'll find the source code for this chapter's program in the chapter19/listings directory of the CD-ROM. By studying the program, you'll learn more about using servlets to provide data and transactions to remote users.

To refresh your recall of the Airline Reservation System, you should turn back to Chapter 6 and skim it quickly, focusing on the functional requirements of the system. You should also refresh your recollection of the socket-based implementation of the Airline Reservation System presented in Chapter 14, "Socket-Based Implementation of the Airline Reservation System," because the servlet-based program described in this chapter is functionally equivalent to the socket-based program described in Chapter 14. As you'll see, it's much easier to write applications using servlets than either sockets or RMI.

Here are the three transactions implemented by the sample program in this chapter:

- Search Flights, which returns each flight stored in the database.
- Search Seats, which returns the reservation information for a specified passenger identified by passenger number.
- Book Seat, which enters a reservation for a specified passenger and flight. The transaction makes several simplifying assumptions. The passenger and flight must already exist as entities; the transaction does not create new passengers or flights. The reservation number must be unique; attempting to add a reservation with the same number as an existing reservation updates the existing reservation.

Like the sample program of Chapter 16, the sample program of this chapter does not implement the visual interface for seat selection described in Chapter 6. Nor does it implement the reservation pool locking mechanism. You could implement such a mechanism by elaborating on the solution sketched near the end of Chapter 16.

We won't need to study the application classes, because they're unchanged from the versions presented with the RMI version of the program in Chapter 16. You can examine them by copying them from the CD-ROM to your system's hard drive. So, let's dive in and study the servlet classes themselves. The program design assigns each of the three supported transactions to a distinct servlet; each of the next three sections presents one of these servlets.

THE SEARCHFLIGHTS SERVLET

The SearchFlights servlet displays a list of flights contained in the SQL database. You can see the servlet's output in Figure 19.1. The SearchFlights transaction requires no input data; therefore, the SearchFlights servlet implements the `doGet` method, which handles the clients' HTTP `GET` requests. To access the servlet, first compile the source file (SearchFlights.java) and then launch the servletrunner utility (or your servlet-capable Web server). You can access the servlet by pointing your Web browser to the following URL:

```
http://localhost:8080/servlet/SearchFlights
```

(If you're using a Web server, you may need to use a different URL: See your Web server's documentation.) The output of the SearchFlights servlet is formatted as a data dump. However, if your HTML skills are up to the task, you can easily revise the servlet to generate output that includes tags that format the data into an HTML table, making the data easier to read.

FIGURE 19.1

The SearchFlights servlet displays a complete list of flights.

> **NOTE**
>
> All the code from here until the next section, "The SearchSeats Servlet," is found in the file SearchFlights.java in the chapter19/listings directory of the CD-ROM.

Let's walk through the source code of the SearchFlights servlet. Like most Java programs, it begins with a set of imports. Because SearchFlights is a servlet, it imports two servlet packages:

```
import javax.servlet.*;
import javax.servlet.http.*;
import java.io.*;
import java.sql.*;
```

The class header specifies that SearchFlights extends the HttpServlet class:

```
public class SearchFlights extends HttpServlet
```

The class defines only three fields—the familiar fields used to establish a database connection using the JDBC-ODBC bridge (for a refresher on JDBC, see Chapter 12, "Java Database Connectivity (JDBC)"):

```
static final String DB = "jdbc:odbc:airline";
static final String USER = "";
static final String PASSWORD = "";
```

The class defines only two methods: getServletInfo and doGet. The getServletInfo method returns a String describing the servlet:

```
public String getServletInfo()
{
    return (getClass().getName());
}
```

Like the doGet methods of other servlets, the doGet method of SearchFlights may throw a ServletException or IOException:

```
public void doGet(HttpServletRequest request,
  HttpServletResponse response)
  throws ServletException, IOException
```

The first tasks of the doGet method are to specify that its response stream will contain HTML and to open the response stream:

```
response.setContentType("text/html");
PrintWriter out = response.getWriter();
```

Because the first part of the output HTML page will be the same whether the transaction succeeds or fails, doGet next sends the first part of the page:

```
out.println("<HTML>");
out.println("<HEAD>");
out.println(
"<TITLE>Search Flights Results Page</TITLE>");
out.println("</HEAD>");
out.println("<BODY>");
```

Most of the remaining processing of the doGet method occurs inside a try statement. Let's first look at the associated catch statement, which completes the output HTML page by sending an error message:

```
catch (Exception ex)
{
    out.println("<H2>Error:</H2>");
    out.println(ex);
}
```

```
out.println("</BODY>");
out.println("</HTML>");
out.close();
```

The three statements following the `catch` statement are executed even if the `try` statement succeeds. They finish the output page and close the response stream.

The statements within the body of the `try` statement open a connection to the database and execute the `Flight.getFlights` method, passing a reference to the open database. After closing the database connection, the program formats the output lines that comprise the body of the HTML page:

```
Class.forName("sun.jdbc.odbc.JdbcOdbcDriver");
Connection db =
DriverManager.getConnection(DB, USER, PASSWORD);

Flight [] flights =
  Flight.getFlights(db);

db.close();

out.println("<H2>Flight Information:</H2>");

for (int i=0; i < flights.length; i++)
    out.println(flights[i] + "<BR>");
```

A more sophisticated version of the servlet might open the database connection only once rather than every time it processes a transaction. You could accomplish this by defining the database connection reference as a static field and opening the database connection only if the field has a `null` value. If you're using the JDBC-ODBC bridge and you make this change, you must also specify that the servlet implements `SingleThreadModel`, a marker interface that requires no methods. A servlet that implements `SingleThreadModel` will run as a single thread; this avoids problems that might otherwise arise because many ODBC drivers are not thread safe.

As you can see, servlets are easy to write, and they're very flexible. However, bear in mind that the client performs only user interface processing: The servlet does all the real work. Nevertheless, you can create fully distributed applications using servlets, because servlets can easily communicate with one another using a fully object-oriented protocol such as RMI or CORBA's IIOP. One simple architecture associates a "gateway" server with each client. The gateway server provides a set of servlets that act on behalf of the client, contacting remote servers as needed to satisfy requests. Figure 19.2 depicts this configuration.

FIGURE 19.2
*Servlets can coop-
erate to provide a
fully distributed
architecture.*

THE SEARCHSEATS SERVLET

The SearchSeats servlet lists all seat reservations associated with a specified passenger. Figure 19.3 shows the input HTML page associated with the SearchSeats servlet, and Figure 19.4 shows a sample output HTML page.

FIGURE 19.3
*The SearchSeats
servlet processes a
request sent by an
HTML form.*

Here's the HTML source code used to create the test page that exercises the SearchSeats servlet:

FIGURE 19.4

The SearchSeats servlet returns an HTML page that lists the seats reserved by a specified passenger.

> **NOTE**
>
> The following code is found in the file SearchSeats.html in the chapter19/listings directory of the CD-ROM.

```html
<HTML>
<HEAD>
<TITLE>Search Seats Test Page</TITLE>
</HEAD>
<BODY>
<FORM ACTION="http://127.0.0.1:8080/servlet/SearchSeats"
 METHOD=POST>
<H1>Search Seats Test Page</H1>
<P>Passenger No:
<INPUT TYPE=TEXT NAME=passenger_no>
<P>
<INPUT TYPE=SUBMIT>
<INPUT TYPE=RESET>
</FORM>
</BODY>
</HTML>
```

> **NOTE**
>
> All the code from here until the next section, "The BookSeat Servlet," is found in the file SearchSeats.java in the chapter19/listings directory of the CD-ROM.

Let's study the source code of the servlet itself. The servlet imports the same packages and defines the same fields as the SearchFlights servlet. However, because the SearchSeats servlet requires a passenger number as input, it implements the doPost method rather than the doGet method implemented by the SearchFlights servlet:

```
public void doPost(HttpServletRequest request,
HttpServletResponse response)
throws ServletException, IOException
```

Like the SearchFlights servlet, SearchSeats first specifies its response type, opens its response stream, and transmits the first page of the output HTML page:

```
response.setContentType("text/html");
PrintWriter out = response.getWriter();

out.println("<HTML>");
out.println("<HEAD>");
out.println(
  "<TITLE>Search Seats Results Page</TITLE>");
out.println("</HEAD>");
out.println("<BODY>");
```

Next, SearchSeats obtains the value of the passenger number input by the user:

```
String passenger_no =
request.getParameter("passenger_no");
```

Notice that the HTML source code for the input form specifies passenger_no as the name of the input text field (refer to Figure 19.3).

The main processing of SearchSeats closely resembles that of SearchFlights; however, it invokes Reservation.getPassenger rather than Flight.getFlights:

```
try
{
    Class.forName("sun.jdbc.odbc.JdbcOdbcDriver");
    Connection db =
      DriverManager.getConnection(DB, USER, PASSWORD);

    Reservation [] seats =
      Reservation.getPassenger(
      db, passenger_no);

    db.close();

    out.println("<H2>Seat Information:</H2>");
    for (int i=0; i < seats.length; i++)
        out.println(seats[i] + "<BR>");
}
catch (Exception ex)
{
    System.err.println(ex);
    out.println("<H2>Error:</H2>");
    out.println(ex);
}

out.println("</BODY>");
```

```
out.println("</HTML>");
out.close();
```

THE BOOKSEAT SERVLET

The BookSeat servlet creates and makes a database record of a fight reservation. Figure 19.5 shows the HTML input form, and Figure 19.6 shows sample output. The following input form provides the flight number, passenger number, and reservation number that specify the flight reservation:

> **NOTE**
>
> The following code is found in the file BookSeat.html in the chapter19/listings directory of the CD-ROM.

```html
<HTML>
<HEAD>
<TITLE>Book Seat Test Page</TITLE>
</HEAD>
<BODY>
<FORM ACTION="http://127.0.0.1:8080/servlet/BookSeat"
 METHOD=POST>
<H1>Book Seat Test Page</H1>
<P>
Flight No:
<INPUT TYPE=TEXT NAME=flight_no>
<P>
Passenger No:
<INPUT TYPE=TEXT NAME=passenger_no>
<P>
Reservation No:
<INPUT TYPE=TEXT NAME=reservation_no>
<P>
<INPUT TYPE=SUBMIT>
<INPUT TYPE=RESET>
</FORM>
</BODY>
</HTML>
```

> **NOTE**
>
> All the code from here until the end of the chapter is found in the file BookSeat.java in the chapter19/listings directory of the CD-ROM.

FIGURE 19.5

The BookSeat servlet requires the user to enter flight number, passenger number, and reservation number information.

FIGURE 19.6

The BookSeat servlet records a flight reservation.

The BookSeat servlet closely resembles the SearchSeats servlet. Both implement the doPost method and receive parameter values from an HTML input form. The BookSeat servlet receives three such parameters:

```
String flight_no =
  request.getParameter("flight_no");
String passenger_no =
  request.getParameter("passenger_no");
String reservation_no =
  request.getParameter("reservation_no");
```

The main processing of the BookSeat servlet, which is enclosed within the usual try-catch block, instantiates a Reservation object, invokes its dbWrite method, and outputs a confirmation message:

```
Reservation res = new Reservation(
  db, reservation_no, flight_no, passenger_no);
res.dbWrite(db);
db.close();

out.println("Seat Booked.");
```

FROM HERE

In this chapter, you've seen a complete application of modest size that uses servlets to display and update database data. As you can see, using servlets is very easy. Yet, servlets are enormously powerful and flexible. Moreover, because they're written in Java, they're also portable. Here's a preview of what's coming up:

- Chapter 20, "Distributed Component Object Model (DCOM)," describes Microsoft's proprietary distributed computing model.
- Chapter 21, "CORBA Overview," begins the first of two parts of this book that present the Common Object Request Broker Architecture (CORBA).

19

SERVLET-BASED
IMPLEMENTATION

DISTRIBUTED COMPONENT OBJECT MODEL (DCOM)

IN THIS CHAPTER

Developing distributed components with Java and DCOM simplifies developing distributed applications. If you're already familiar with COM, CORBA, or RMI, it won't take you long to understand DCOM. Even if you don't have a good background with the Component Object Model (COM), the Microsoft Java virtual machine (JVM), the run-time environment for Java, makes it painless to develop both COM and DCOM components.

> **NOTE**
>
> Chapters 15, "Remote Method Invocation (RMI)," and 16, "RMI-Based Implementation of the Airline Reservation System," cover Remote Method Invocation (RMI). Part V of this book, "The CORBA Approach to Distributed Computing," provides a detailed discussion of the Common Object Request Broker Architecture (CORBA).

This chapter covers the following:

- An overview of DCOM
- A brief architecture review
- A comparison of DCOM to other technologies
- Code examples

The exercises are provided to help you become comfortable with the technology and to drive home the concepts in the architecture section. After completing the code examples, we'll compare DCOM to other technologies such as CORBA and RMI. After you complete this chapter and the exercises, you should have a solid understanding of DCOM and be able to develop DCOM clients and servers in Java. In addition, you can use most of the techniques and design patterns from the other chapters of this book with DCOM.

No matter what your background, you'll probably at some point have to deal with COM/DCOM. Understanding DCOM may be a great skill to master as you conquer your next distributed applications. This is especially true if you have to interface with commercial off-the-shelf components and applications or existing in-house applications that use DCOM.

Windows NT is prevalent in the client/server market, and DCOM is heavily integrated with the NT operating system. Therefore, DCOM is important to understand because of the proliferation of Windows NT and the size of the COM component market.

OVERVIEW OF COM AND DCOM

The Component Object Model (COM) provides a means to create extensible services called components. As components mature (evolve) and add new features and functions, the services they provide remain backward compatible with older incarnations of the components they replace. This enables older applications (COM clients) to treat new components like older components. Therefore, when you upgrade the component, older client applications should continue working.

NOTE

Even within Windows NT and Windows 95, there's a trend to provide more operating system services in the form of COM services because of their flexible nature. If you've ever installed software that uses new DLLs that make older applications stop working, you'll realize the importance of this trend.

COM uses object-oriented techniques, namely *polymorphism*, to accomplish the extensible component architecture. COM compares to a local procedure call (LPC) roughly the way C++ compares to C—one being procedural and one being object oriented. Therefore, a remote procedure call (RPC) is to DCOM as C is to C++. DCOM groups data and methods into objects, which you can use through various interfaces.

DCOM may be viewed as COM with a longer wire. Therefore, the terms *DCOM* and *COM* are often used interchangeably throughout the text. Even though the first few iterations of COM did not have distributed support, the design for distributed objects was included. COM was designed from the ground up to support distributed computing. Therefore, you can use a legacy COM client with a DCOM server just by changing a few Windows NT Registry settings.

The major difference between DCOM and COM is that DCOM uses RPC as shown in Figures 20.1 and 20.2. Therefore, the use of DCOM can be transparent to the COM client; DCOM servers can work with an older COM client. For that matter, you can use

20

DISTRIBUTED
COMPONENT
OBJECT MODEL

most existing COM servers that predate the release of DCOM as DCOM servers, again, just by changing a few Registry settings.

FIGURE 20.1

The regular Component Object Model (COM).

FIGURE 20.2

COM with a long wire (DCOM).

In addition to this transparent mode of operation for interfacing with older COM services, DCOM adds the ability for the client to ask to connect to a specific server. Also, DCOM adds security features, which are important for secure distributed computing. Again, LPC is based on RPC, so architecturally, the usage model and techniques for using DCOM are similar in nature to COM.

Only the core operating system runs in kernel mode while most of the operating system runs in separate processes in the user mode. Applications that want to use those operating system processes have to go through the LPC manager, which resides in the kernel. The LPC manager marshals the request from the application to the OS process. Therefore,

Windows NT is designed from the ground up using the client/server architecture, which is also referred to as the *services architecture*. COM is an object-oriented extension to LPC. Therefore, LPC in not an afterthought; it's a core part of Windows/NT.

COM/DCOM TOOL SUPPORT

Many development tools support COM. Microsoft's Visual Basic, which is heavily centered on COM, commands a hefty portion of the programming language market. Other prominent tools that support COM are Visual C++, C++ Builder, Delphi, and others. Most of these tools support both the creation of COM components and the hosting of COM objects. Development tool support is a major strength of DCOM.

In addition to these tools, Microsoft has made sure that Java integrates well with DCOM. For instance, Java classes can be treated like COM objects. Visual J++ 6.0 is a rapid application development (RAD) tool, and it integrates with COM seamlessly. Also, Sun provides an ActiveX bridge to expose JavaBeans as ActiveX controls (an *ActiveX control* is a type of COM component).

You can use the Java classes you create as scriptable components, which can be scripted using Visual Basic, VBScript, JScript, Perl, Python, and other tools. Therefore, you can use the classes you build, for example, inside of a Web browser, an Excel spreadsheet, or as part of an Active Server Page. Essentially, you can use your Java classes anywhere you can use Automation. *Automation* enables users to take control of components and applications through easy-to-use scripting languages such as Visual Basic. We'll discuss Automation later in the chapter.

You may wonder why all this matters to Java. It's simple really. There are a lot of COM components out there and chances are you'll need to integrate them in one of your projects. For that matter, there are a lot of COM component developers in the market, and you may need to integrate their skills in your next project.

> **NOTE**
>
> Many of the Java application server providers, such as WebLogic's Tengah and Bluestone's Sapphire, provide DCOM support.

DCOM ARCHITECTURE

All distributed object architecture must provide the following basic features:

- Interface definition
- Directory services

20

DISTRIBUTED COMPONENT OBJECT MODEL

- Marshaling
- Object persistence
- Security

Interface negotiation is important to distributed systems. It allows distributed objects the opportunity to communicate and evolve separately without breaking the existing contract. *Directory services* provide a means of finding, activating, and connecting to remote objects. *Marshaling* is a means to make the object appear to be in a local process, yet communicate the invocation of methods along with their parameters over process and machine boundaries. Marshaling allows access to interfaces from remote sites and moves data to and from the client process and the server process. Marshaling is just a means of formatting data between clients and components so they can communicate clearly at the bit and byte level.

Object persistence is saving an object state to a persistent storage, such as a flat file or database. It's also how to connect to a unique instance of an object; for example, when the object is already running in another process. Finally, *security* is needed to protect access to components at various levels. The rest of this section briefly discusses these architectural issues in order to help you understand the DCOM architecture well enough to write Java/DCOM programs effectively.

Interfaces

Defining an interface between a client and a component is like defining a contract between two people. The interface exposes a collection of methods that state what behavior and functionality the component will provide.

In DCOM, you don't deal with objects directly. Instead, you deal with interfaces to objects. A DCOM *interface* is a collection of methods that define a service contract. Actually, what you get is an interface pointer that points to a vtable (a vtable is a collection of pointers to methods). Java does not support interface pointers or any pointers for that matter (see the following note). However, Microsoft allows Java developers to access COM objects in a natural way. The interface defines the behavior of an object independently of any one implementation of an object. DCOM is a binary interoperability agreement for how clients interact with interfaces via pointers and local and remote proxies. Proxies act as surrogate objects that are involved in marshaling the parameters to and from the components.

> **NOTE**
>
> Microsoft JVM is a precursor to COM+. The way DCOM is handled in Java is like a precursor to the way DCOM will be handled in other languages with the introduction of COM+. COM+ will make DCOM programming a lot easier. For example, let's compare getting a pointer to an interface in Java to doing the same thing in C++:
>
> ```
> IHelloDCOM pHelloDCOM;
> CoCreateInstance (CLSID_HelloDCOM, NULL,
> CLSCTX_INPROC_SERVER,
> IID_HelloDCOM,
> (void **) &pHelloDCOM);
> ```
>
> Here's the equivalent Java code:
>
> ```
> IHelloDCOM helloDCOM = (IHelloDCOM) new HelloDCOM();
> ```
>
> As you know, there are no pointers in Java. Therefore, instead of dealing with pointers, the Microsoft JVM handles all the low-level complexity. The Microsoft JVM also allows you to cast an interface to an object instead of using the IUnknown interface negotiation, which makes programming COM in Java much easier than doing it in C++ in many cases. Actually, Java's multiple interfaces inheritance model maps nicely to working with IUnknown.

DCOM provides standard interfaces for dealing with objects. One such interface is IUnknown. Every DCOM object must support IUnknown. Also, Java classes, via the Microsoft JVM, support a lot of other standard interfaces. So what's a COM object? A *COM object* is a component that supports one or more interfaces; a *COM interface* refers to a collection of related methods. There are standard interfaces and there are user-defined interfaces. COM objects are accessed only through interfaces. A COM class implements one or more interfaces, and COM objects are runtime instantiations of COM classes.

IDispatch is a standard interface, which all COM objects that support late binding (Automation) must have. Java classes in the Microsoft JVM, by default, support Automation via the IDispatch interface.

COM works with many computer programming languages. However, there's a special language for describing interfaces called the *Interface Definition Language (IDL)*.

20

DISTRIBUTED
COMPONENT
OBJECT MODEL

> **NOTE**
>
> Java classes also support the following interfaces:
>
> `IConnectionPointContainer, IDispatchEx, IExternalConnection, IMarshal,`
> `IProvideClassInfo, IProvideClassInfo2, ISupportErrorInfo` and, of course,
> `IUnknown.`

Interface Definition Language (IDL)

IDLs are high-level, English-like languages for describing which interfaces an object supports. You can define an interface via IDL independent of any programming language. DCOM, like CORBA, has an IDL, which unlike CORBA's IDL, is based on the existing DCE standard IDL for RPC. Before Windows NT 4.0, Microsoft had two types of IDL. One was called *IDL*, and one was called *ODL*. ODL works with Automation, which was known as OLE Automation and for a brief while as ActiveX Automation. Since Windows NT 4.0 was released, there's only one type of IDL. Therefore, ODL has been merged into IDL.

IDL is a special C-like language for specifying DCOM interfaces. You compile it with Microsoft's IDL compiler (MIDL) to create a type library. You then use another tool to create Java or C++ stubs and proxies, which act as surrogate objects involved in marshaling the parameters between the COM client and the COM components.

> **NOTE**
>
> A DCOM *stub* equates to a CORBA or RMI *skeleton*. A DCOM *proxy* equates to an RMI or CORBA *stub*. Therefore, *stub* in CORBA speak is the *client*, whereas *stub* in DCOM speak is the *server*.

DCOM's IDL, unlike CORBA IDL, does not support inheritance, which is a key ingredient to object-oriented design. Instead, DCOM supports containment, delegation, and aggregation. It also uses interface negotiation (`IUnknown`), which provides the key feature of inheritance (that is, *polymorphism*). Therefore, DCOM can support many interfaces.

The good news is you don't have to know IDL to do DCOM programming. Microsoft and others have a lot of development tools that can create type libraries and COM objects; most of the tools approach the power of using IDL without the hassle. Visual Basic, Visual C++, Visual J++, and Inprise's Delphi all have the ability to create type libraries, so you never have to use IDL. Also, with the release of COM+, there will be even less reason to use IDL.

One of the keys to COM's success is ease of use. DCOM is not tied to IDL the way CORBA is. In fact, there's nothing special about IDL. It's just a C-like language for creating proxies and stubs. Again, you don't have to use IDL to do DCOM programming. For Java programming, you never have to touch IDL. Even if you use the Microsoft Java SDK and JVM and no fancy integrated development environment (IDE), you don't have to write any IDL. Toward the end of the chapter we'll go through the process of creating COM and DCOM objects without using IDL.

Check out Part V of this book for a detailed look at CORBA IDL. CORBA syntax and structure is different than DCOM, but the intent is similar. COM IDL, like Latin, may be a dead language in a few years.

Invocation

Invocation is the means to invoke a method on an object. *Dynamic invocation* is the ability to call an object from a late bound language, such as a scripting language. A scripting language typically is not compiled. Rather, scripting languages are associated with interpreted languages. Conversely, compiled languages, such as C++, use static invocation. Java is an interpreted language with statically compiled language features; it's a hybrid, so to speak. Therefore, Java can work with both `vtable` and `Dispinterface` interfaces (`IDispatch`-based interfaces) in Microsoft's JVM.

DCOM, like CORBA, provides both static and dynamic invocation of objects. The type library provides the meta data to do the dynamic invocation and introspection similar to CORBA's interface repository or Java's introspection mechanism. (For more on CORBA dynamic invocation, introspection, and reflection, see Chapter 32, "Interface Repository, Dynamic Invocation, Introspection, and Reflection.") The type libraries are analogous, in many respects, to CORBA's interface repository, and dynamic invocation is needed for languages that require late binding.

NOTE

Meta data is a term used to describe data that, instead of representing some entity, serves to describe other data.

Directory Services and Activation

As mentioned earlier, object location provides a means of finding, activating, and connecting to remote objects. Once a COM client knows a component's name, it can use the COM library to look up the component's class that corresponds to a unique identifier. It can then determine whether the COM object should be run locally or remotely (if remotely, it can work with the remote machine to activate the component).

COM uses the Registry and the COM library to perform object lookup. When a COM client tries to create a COM object, the COM libraries look up the associated COM class implementation in the Registry. (This is somewhat analogous to the way RMI uses the `RMIRegistry` or CORBA uses `COSNaming`.) The COM class implementation is executable code called by the server. The executable code that the COM class is associated with could be a dynamic link library, executable file, or a Java class. (See the section on COM servers for more details.) The COM libraries load the COM server and work with the server to create the object (the instance of the COM class) and then return an interface pointer to the COM client. With DCOM, the COM libraries are updated to create COM objects on remote machines.

In order to create remote objects, the COM libraries read the network name of the remote server machine from the Registry to create remote COM objects. Alternatively, the name can be passed to the COM libraries' `CoCreateInstanceEx` function call. We'll cover a code example that uses `CoCreateInstanceEx` with the name of the server passed as a parameter.

For remote components (that is, DCOM components), the COM libraries use the *service control manager* (SCM, pronounced "scum"), to perform object activation. In this scenario, when a COM client attempts to create a COM component, the COM library looks up the COM object in the Windows NT Registry as usual. What it finds in the Registry is information on how to instantiate the COM object just as before. However, if the COM class configuration in the Registry specifies a remote server, the COM library will collaborate with SCM. SCM's job is to contact the SCM on the remote server. The remote SCM then works with the COM library on the remote machine to instantiate the object and return an instance to the client application.

> **NOTE**
>
> `CoCreateInstanceEx` is an extended version of `CoCreateInstance` of the original COM library. `CoCreateInstance` is the standard way to look up COM objects in the Registry. `CoCreateInstanceEx` adds parameters for security and remote machine specification.

Identifiers for Locating Objects

You can find an interface by looking it up in the Windows Registry by its name or its globally unique identifier (GUID). GUIDs are guaranteed to be unique. The GUIDs for interfaces are called interface identifiers (IIDs). The GUIDs for COM classes are called class identifiers (CLSIDs). All calls to `CoCreateInstance` need the CLSID to uniquely identify the class the COM client is requesting. CLSID are listed in the Registry with a list of the IIDs they support.

DCOM uses the remote server name and CLSID to interact with the COM client's SCM. As shown in Figure 20.3, the SCM uses this identifier when it connects to the remote SCM on the server machine and requests creation of the COM object on the client's behalf.

FIGURE 20.3
DCOM activation.

NOTE

Unlike CORBA, DCOM has no `objectId`. Instead, if you want to connect to the same unique instance of an object, you use a moniker.

DCOM has two other types of identifiers called the application identifier (AppID) and the program identifier (ProgID). The AppID was added to COM as part of its security support. The AppID essentially represents a COM server process namespace that's shared by multiple CLSIDs. All COM objects in this server process namespace have the same security settings. The AppID concept is like a container for CLSID associated with a process to avoid a lot of excessive Registry keys that all contain the same server name. We'll work with these different identifiers in the code samples.

ProgID is a user friendly name of the component that's associated with the CLSID. Therefore, in Visual Basic, for example, you can pass the name of the ProgID to `CreateObject`, and `CreateObject` will look up the ProgID in the Registry and get the corresponding CLSID.

20

**DISTRIBUTED
COMPONENT
OBJECT MODEL**

With the release of Windows NT 5.0, COM adds a central store for COM classes. All activation-related information about a component can be stored in the Active Directory of the domain controller. The COM libraries will get activation information, such as the remote server name, transparently from the Active Directory. Reconfiguring the component will be a simple matter of changing the setting for the component in the Active Directory. Then, Active Directory proliferates these changes to all the clients connected to the portion of the Active Directory that contains the component's information. This further closes the gaps between CORBA's activation model and DCOM's. This is really a leapfrog contest between CORBA, RMI, and DCOM.

Object Persistence and Unique Instances of Objects

As mentioned earlier, CORBA provides an `objectId` to connect to specific instances of an object. This object reference is used by various CORBA services. The object reference can be used to reload the state of an object. Essentially, you can covert the object reference to a string and copy it to a file or some other type of persistent storage. Then, a year later you can use that object reference to instantiate that object to the state you left it a year ago, assuming of course, that some other client did not change the state of that object in the last year. CORBA clients use the object reference to connect to a particular instance of an object. Conversely, COM objects, by default, are stateless objects. COM objects do not have object identifiers. Instead, they use monikers to connect to a particular instance.

COM's instance-naming mechanism is extremely flexible but at the price of complexity. An `IMoniker` specifies an instance for COM. Monikers, also referred to as instance names, for COM objects are themselves COM objects. This explains their flexibility and, for that matter, their complexity (compared to the CORBA approach). The standard COM interface for these naming objects is `IMoniker`.

If the COM object that the moniker is referring to is not already running in a server process, `IMoniker` can create and initialize a COM object instance to the state it had before. If, on the other hand, the COM object that `IMoniker` is referring to is running in an existing COM server process, `IMoniker` can connect to the running instance of the COM object via the COM server.

The COM library maintains a list of currently running, explicitly named COM object instances called the running object table (ROT), which `IMoniker` uses to find the running COM object instances. Essentially, if the COM object instance is not in the ROT, `IMoniker` initializes a new one usually from some type of persistent storage. (With acronyms such as SCM and ROT, it makes you wonder who comes up with this stuff and what their fixation is with nasty sounding acronyms!) There are a few monikers built in to COM, such as the File moniker, the URL moniker, and the Class moniker.

DCOM Servers

Once you create a COM object, you need a server to serve the objects up to the world. A *COM server* is container that holds COM objects. In essence, a COM server is either a class, a dynamic link library, or an executable file that contains COM classes, which in the case of Java, relates to Java classes. The COM server has the ability to turn classes into objects. The server implements the `IClassFactory` interface, which provides a standard way to request having a COM class instantiated into a COM object.

You won't need to create servers because MIDL (a fancy IDE) generates them for you. In addition, COM clients won't need to deal with `IClassFactory` directly, because the COM library handles this when you call `CoCreateInstance` or the extended version, `CoCreateInstanceEx`.

The COM client asks the COM library for a given class via a CLSID. The CLSID can be looked up in the Registry. The COM library goes to the Registry and looks up the CLSID. The COM library then instantiates a server, which must provide an `IClassFactory` interface so that the COM server can create the object on behalf of the COM library. In order for the COM client to ask the COM library for a class, the COM client has to find the CLSID in the Registry. Therefore, the server must register a CLSID for every COM object it's able to create.

Here are the three types of COM servers:

- *In-process servers*. In the same process (DLL, OCX, INPROC)
- *Local servers*. Local, separate process (EXE)
- *Remote servers*. Separate process on a remote machine

In-process servers execute in the same process context as the client. Fundamentally, an in-process server is a DLL, which means, among other things, that if there's a bug in the in-process server, it could bring down the client process. For example, OCXs always run in the context of the client. (ActiveX controls are sometimes referred to as *OLE controls*. An OLE control is an ActiveX control, but an ActiveX control is not necessarily an OCX.) An OCX is a DLL with a different extension that supports Automation and events. (*Automation* is dynamic invocation support for late-bound languages.) Local Java classes that are exported as COM objects run in this mode, unless they're using a surrogate process.

Local servers run in a separate process from their clients but still on the same machine. Basically, local servers run over LPC. An example of a local server is Excel (and just about every other Office Suite application for the Windows market). Most Office Suite applications support Automation and OLE.

Remote servers execute in a separate process on another machine. The clients use RPC to talk to the remote server. However, a client does not have to know that the server is remote. This may be completely transparent to the client. Java classes that have been exported as COM objects can be run in this mode only if they use a surrogate process, which can be the default surrogate process provided by the COM library. This process is covered in the code examples.

The COM library supplies three ways for COM clients to attach to a remote server and request a COM object:

- The server name is associated with the `ProgID` of the object in the Windows Registry.
- An explicit parameter is passed to `CoCreateInstanceEx`, `CoGetInstanceFromFile`, `CoGetInstanceFromStorage`, or `CoGetClassObject` specifying the server name.
- Monikers are used.

As mentioned earlier, COM clients are backward compatible with DCOM servers; therefore, all a COM client has to know is the CLSID of the component it wants to use. The COM client calls `CoCreateInstance`, and the COM libraries create the component on the remote server as configured in the Registry. Therefore, older COM clients, which predate the release of DCOM, can transparently use remote COM objects. However, newer clients have the flexibility to specify the server they want to connect to, which is essential with some applications. The newer servers can specify the server name as a parameter to `CoCreateInstanceEx`. Table 20.1 shows a list of calls used when creating objects from persistent storage.

TABLE 20.1 DCOM COMPONENTS USED TO REQUEST COM OBJECTS

DCOM API Calls	*Description*
`CoCreateInstance`	Creates an interface pointer to a stateless COM object.
`CoCreateInstanceEx`	Creates an interface pointer to a stateless COM object.
`CoGetInstanceFromFile`	Creates a new instance from a file. The COM object is initialized from the file.
`CoGetInstanceFromStorage`	Creates a new instance from storage. The COM object is initialized from the storage.

Marshaling

A key concept to local/remote transparency is *marshaling*, which means to take an interface pointer to a COM object in one process and allow a client in another process to call member functions through that interface pointer. RMI, CORBA, and DCOM do some form of marshaling. There are two ways to achieve marshaling in COM: COM standard marshaling and COM custom marshaling.

COM marshaling allows a client in one process to make interface method calls on COM objects in another process. The COM objects in the other process can be down the hall or on the other side of the globe. The COM clients are not aware of the differences between local and remote calls. Marshaling involves taking an interface pointer in a server's process and making that interface pointer available to the client process. Therefore, marshaling involves setting up interprocess communication (either RPC or LPC). Next, marshaling must take the arguments to an interface method call, as passed from the client, and serialize those arguments to the remote object's process.

Different argument types are marshaled differently. A simple value such as an `int` is marshaled by copying the value. However, a more complex object, such as `java.lang.String`, is marshaled by copying the data pointed to it. The arguments to method calls must be moved to the server's address space, which again, may be across the hall or around the world. In order to use nonstandard, user-defined COM interfaces, you must define your own marshaling. Microsoft defines custom marshaling for its Java implementation.

Custom marshaling is fundamental for certain applications. However, Microsoft recognized that most applications do not need or desire to optimize their marshaling mechanism. Therefore, COM offers standard marshaling for the built-in standard COM interfaces. With standard marshaling, COM furnishes a generic proxy and a generic stub that communicate through standard RPC for each standard COM interface.

On the other hand, each custom interface must implement an interface marshaler that knows how to marshal all the arguments of those functions of the interface properly. The interface marshaler actually performs the transportation, serialization, and deserialization of the argument structures among the processes. COM's architecture allows developers to plug in their own marshalers for their own custom interfaces. Therefore, COM objects can use these interfaces' custom marshalers to transparently handle marshaling as if the interface was supplied with COM. If a COM object supports `IMarshal`, it supports custom marshaling. The Microsoft JVM supports `IMarshal`, so it does some level of custom marshaling for Java.

An example of custom marshaling is the Microsoft Active Data Connector (ADC), which uses optimized marshaling to move an entire row set of OLE data, thus reducing network traffic for accessing rows in a database.

> **NOTE**
>
> You probably won't ever need to write your own custom marshaler because DCOM/Java integration centers around IDispatch. IDispatch is a built-in interface. Therefore, COM provides a marshaler for it. In addition, Microsoft provides a special optimized marshaler for Java COM objects.

Standard Interfaces

IUnknown is the ubiquitous interface. IUnknown is used for interface negotiations, life cycle management, and containment and delegation. All COM objects must implement IUnkown's QueryInterface(), AddRef(), and Release() methods.

Interface negotiation is the ability to ask a COM object at runtime which other interfaces it supports. Because all COM objects must implement the IUnknown interface, all COM objects support interface negotiation. Therefore, COM clients can access any COM object and use QueryInterface to determine which interfaces the COM object supports. The ability to query the interface supported allows COM clients to decide, at runtime, which interface to use.

QueryInterface allows the COM object to pass an interface pointer to other COM objects, which don't even have to be on the same machine. COM uses QueryInterface to aggregate many COM objects. It allows components to evolve overtime and yet still be backward compatible with older clients, while new clients are allowed to access new features through new interfaces.

This interface negotiation feature gives COM architectural appeal. COM objects describe their features at a high level of abstraction. This permits COM clients the ability to query the COM object to see whether it supports a particular interface (a *feature-set*). Compare this to a CORBA object's single interface model. The ability of a COM client to request the feature-set of a COM object allows for flexibility that you would expect for a component object model. In other words, COM objects should be allowed to mature and develop new features without breaking old clients.

Life cycle management is the ability to create and destroy components. IUnknown supports two methods for performing life cycle management: AddRef() and Release(). COM uses reference counting to control a COM object's lifetime. The COM system is not responsible for the life cycle of the object. Rather, the individual object is responsible for its own life cycle. Therefore, reference counting works a lot like memory management (that is, objects are destroyed when they're no longer being used).

When clients first get an interface pointer to an object, they must call AddRef(). When the clients are done with the interface pointer, they must call Release(). Therefore, when the client is finished with the COM object, it calls Release(), and if the object determines that there are no other clients, it will destroy itself. This puts a lot of responsibility on the client—especially considering that in a distributed environment the client machine may crash, be rebooted, turned off abruptly, or otherwise disconnected before the COM client is able to call Release(). COM components can be connected to many clients, in different processes on different machines, and the COM object has to wait for all clients to release their reference before the COM object can be freed. Once all the COM objects associated with a COM server are freed, the COM server can exit.

DCOM has many features for optimizing and enhancing the life cycle management of remote COM objects. As mentioned earlier, clients might disconnect prematurely; therefore, remote operations need a way to tell whether the client is still alive. Pinging is one way to detect whether clients are still around. On the server machine, each remote object being hosted has a ping period. If the ping period ends without receiving a ping from the client, that remote COM object can be terminated. The ping period is approximately six minutes in length. DCOM does not ping per COM object. Rather, it uses sets of pings grouped by certain criteria for optimization.

No chapter about Java DCOM would be complete without a section on Dispinterface and IDispatch. COM objects can support a Dispinterface, which is a dispatch interface. Dispinterface works differently from a vtable interface. vtable interfaces, or regular COM interfaces, have some limitations. COM clients of such interfaces have to bind to the interface methods based on absolute locations of the methods in the vtable. This scheme works for compiled code such as C++, but it does not work for interpreted languages such as VBScript, Python, JScript, and Perl.

Of course, vtable access is much faster; the only downside is that creating your own custom vtable-based interface requires you to write your own custom marshaler, which is less than straightforward with Java. On the other hand, if you use IDispatch and a Dispinterface, you don't have to worry about custom marshaling. IDispatch is a standard built-in interface; therefore, Microsoft provides the marshaling.

The speed issues are really just noise if you're doing remote servers. If you're doing remote servers, most of your speed issues are due to network latency. CORBA, DCOM using IDispatch, and RMI execute at similar speeds. Here's an example of what a Dispinterface might look like:

```
dispinterface HelloCOM
    {
      properties:
        [id(0)] long count;
```

```
methods:
    [id(1)] BSTR getHelloMessage(void);
};
```

The count property is assigned a dispID of zero, and the getHelloMessage method is assigned a dispID of one. A COM client, called an *Automation controller*, can use dispIDs to get/set properties and to invoke the method call. In the code examples, we're going to write a Java program that uses IDispatch to do just this. In the sample program, instead of accessing a COM object directly through a wrapper class, we control a COM object by passing dispID to IDispatch. IDispatch has the methods for invoking methods and properties given a dispID using IDispatch::Invoke.

As referenced in Table 20.2, a *variant* is a class that can contain any kind of data. Invoke uses variants to pass arguments to methods, to return properties and for method returns. We'll cover variants further in the code examples.

TABLE 20.2 IDispatch METHODS FOR ACCESSING A Dispinterface

Member Method	Description
Invoke	Gets or sets a property or invokes a method given a dispID. You can pass an array of variants for arguments. Invoke returns a variant.
GetIDsOfNames	Given a string representing the name of a property, method, or method argument, it returns the corresponding dispID.
GetTypeInfoCount	Determines whether Type info is available.
GetTypeInfo	Retrieves Type information.

If all this talk about IDispatch and Dispinterface has you worried, relax. As this chapter has mentioned many times before (and will mention again), if you use the Microsoft JVM and Java SDK, you don't have to write any IDL. The Microsoft JVM makes all Java classes look like COM objects and all COM objects look like Java classes. We'll explore how the Microsoft JVM does this magic in the next section.

Java and DCOM

Java programmers do not need to create interface definition files (IDL/ODL) to create COM objects. Also, special tools such as IDL compilers are not necessary.

Microsoft's JVM allows you to create two types of COM objects with Java:

- COM objects that implement only IDispatch and do not contain any type information

- COM objects that implement any COM interface (that is, custom, dual, or `Dispinterface`)

The first type that uses `IDispatch`, as mentioned before, is great for scripting languages such as Perl, Python, VBScript, JScript, and so on. The Microsoft JVM implements `IDispatch` automatically for all Java objects. Microsoft refers to this feature as `AutoIDispatch`. Before `AutoIDispatch`, Java programmers had to write their own IDL files. Now all we have to do is create a Java class. Any public methods or member variables are automatically exposed via Automation. Anything that makes my job easier, I like.

The second type of COM object is for use with strongly typed languages such as C++ and Java.

To implement a COM object in Java using `AutoIDispatch`, follow these steps:

1. Write a Java class and compile it. The class must have public members and methods.

2. Register the class using `JavaReg`.

There may be times when you don't want a class to be scriptable—perhaps to hide certain properties to the outside world—yet still make them accessible from other Java classes internal to the package. The Microsoft JVM allows you to turn off the `AutoIDispatch` on a class-by-class basis. The class that doesn't want scripting just has to implement the `com.ms.com.NoAutoScripting` interface. This interface, like `java.io.Serializable`, doesn't contain any methods. Like `Serializable`, it tells the VM that this object can be serialized. `NoAutoScripting` just tells the VM not to expose `IDispatch` for this class.

> **NOTE**
>
> Visual J++ 6.0 automates COM creation. If you create a COM DLL in Visual J++ 6.0, the `inproc` server name is not `msjava.dll`. Instead, the name of the DLL is `NameOfClass.dll`. There's an example on how to use Visual J++ to create COM objects in the coding exercises.

This completes our survey of COM/DCOM architecture. We now take a look at some of the differences between COM/DCOM and other distributed object technologies, such as RMI and CORBA. We then move on to the coding examples.

20

DISTRIBUTED COMPONENT OBJECT MODEL

COMPARING DCOM TO RMI AND CORBA

I don't think it's fair to advocate any one distributed object framework (DCOM, RMI, or CORBA) over another, because each object framework has advantages that give it an edge for certain types of applications. Also, using one distributed object framework does not preclude using another.

> **NOTE**
>
> Different CORBA ORB vendors implement different CORBA services, and not all CORBA service implementations are equal. This comparison does not point out specific differences between vendors. Therefore, as we cover CORBA services, features, and architecture advantages, make sure the ORB you're considering supports the particular services, features, and implementations you need—don't base buying a particular CORBA ORB on this discussion alone.

Ease of Development and IDL

Java's transparent DCOM support clearly gives it an architectural advantage—namely, you don't have to learn another language to create DCOM/Java components. Conversely, when you develop a CORBA component, you typically start by creating an IDL file. Then you have to derive your client and server from another class. However, it should be noted that there are tools, such as Inprise's Caffeine, that allow you to reduce some CORBA complexity by allowing you to define your interfaces in Java.

As mentioned earlier, you don't need IDL to create Java DCOM components. However, there are times when you do need to create IDL files (for example, when you want to provide custom marshaling, or you want to create `vtable` components). Concerning comparisons of the IDL languages (Microsoft's IDL to CORBA's IDL), it has been stated that CORBA's IDL seems more thought out and easier to use. CORBA (possibly) has a cleaner IDL syntax because it doesn't extend an existing IDL like Microsoft extends RPC IDL for DCOM.

Java's RMI has no IDL; it does not need one because it provides only Java-to-Java communication. You define your remote interfaces in Java. You then create an implementation class in Java that implements the remote interface you defined. Although it doesn't have an IDL to deal with like CORBA does, the inheritance model of defining a remote object is a bit more complicated than the DCOM approach. RMI is bit less complicated than the CORBA approach (unless you use something like Inprise's Caffeine). Again, I have seen demonstrations of IDEs that make RMI development fairly trivial. (I've always used Notepad, Javac, and RMIC to do RMI development.)

There seems to be a lot of work by various companies to make CORBA and RMI development easier. Therefore, any advantage DCOM has in development ease of use may be short lived.

Directory Services

RMI is currently lacking a solid default directory service. However, there are third-party tools that implement Java naming and directory interface, which give RMI a robust directory service. CORBA has an advanced directory service called COSNaming, which provides transparent location of objects, depending on your CORBA vendor COSNaming implementation. DCOM's current directory service lacks a truly distributed transparent nature like CORBA's COSNaming. This lack of support appears to be more of different approaches to solve a similar problem than a missing feature or an architecture advantage.

However, in Windows NT 5.0, DCOM can be used in connection with Active Directory. Activation-related information about a component will be stored in the Active Directory of the domain controller. The COM libraries will get activation information, such as the remote server name, transparently from the Active Directory. Active Directory will proliferate configuration changes to all the clients that are registered to receive a component's information.

Marshaling

RMI has good support for marshaling—both in ease of use and overall feature-set. With RMI, if an object defines a remote interface, it's passed by reference. *Passed by reference* means that when the client calls a method of a remote interface, the call is marshaled over the wire. However, RMI can pass objects by value.

Imagine defining a remote hashtable type of class that contains results to a query. Every time your client accesses the remote hashtable object, the call goes over the wire, which can really slow things down because of the latency of the network. RMI gives you another option. If you pass a parameter to a remote method and that parameter does not implement a remote interface, and that parameter is an instantiation of a class that implements Serializable, then the parameter will be marshaled over the network. If the code for the parameter is not available on the client machine, RMI will load the class from the remote machine. Therefore, not only are the values moved across the network, but the code that accesses those values is moved across the network as well. In essence, you've moved code and data such that the object has been relocated to the client's process.

Therefore, RMI has an architectural advantage at doing marshaling. Neither CORBA nor DCOM approaches this technique of moving the code from one JVM to another, but both allow you to pass by value. By default, DCOM, like CORBA, uses "pass by reference," whereas RMI allows both "pass by reference" and "pass by value." In addition, RMI allows to you to pass code.

Future versions of CORBA will have support for pass by value. It's possible to create your own pass by value support with DCOM, but it isn't as straightforward as the RMI approach. To perform pass by value in DCOM, you need to define your own custom vtable interface, and you need to write you own custom marshaler for the custom vtable, which involves using C programming and Raw Native Interface (RNI). There are ways around the DCOM marshaling issue. For example, you could pack all class data in a string and then write your own unpacker, but this is not an elegant solution.

Security and Administration

As far as security goes, DCOM has some clear architecture advantage with its tight integration with the NT security model. This gives DCOM an edge in administration and ease of development. Therefore, the same or similar tools that are included with the OS can manage DCOM security. In other words, if you know how to administer Windows NT, you can learn to administer DCOM easily.

Interoperability and Bridging

It seems RMI is moving closer to interoperating with CORBA, which is a big plus for RMI and CORBA. Of course, RMI interoperating with CORBA will degrade some of its functionality (you would have to give up its most innovative feature, which is its ability to transfer code and data in a pass by value call).

Already there's a lot of bridging technologies from one distributed object architecture to another. For example, IONA has a CORBA/COM bridge that takes a CORBA object and makes it appear as an ActiveX control, which can then be embedded easily in a Visual Basic program (or a Visual J++ or Delphi program, for that matter). Here's another example: The forthcoming CORBBeans implementation will allow CORBA distributed objects to look like JavaBeans on the client. This, in effect, gives CORBA a local component model and will make CORBA "toolable" on the client. Making CORBA toolable makes it easier to use CORBA in applications such as Visual Basic by using the ActiveX bridge to bridge the CORBA bean to look like an ActiveX control.

Persistence

CORBA seems to have a fairly straightforward persistence mechanism for reconnecting to unique instances of an object. Java and DCOM don't seem to provide a straightforward approach to handling persistence. DCOM does provide a flexible way to manage persistence, yet it's not as implicit as the CORBA technique. Therefore, at this point in time, it's more complex to implement.

The Component Revolution

Declaring one technology the winner, and any of the other technologies the loser, is impossible. There's something else of greater importance that all these technologies supply—the plumbing for the *component revolution*.

All these technologies enable the component revolution, which allows companies to assemble frameworks of components into working solutions. Most information technology (IT) shops have the option to buy commercial off-the-shelf components on the basis of what functionality they provide, not on the basis of what distributed object technology they were built with. The IT shops have this option because there are enough bridging tools to bridge between any two technologies at least half a dozen ways.

The component revolution is based on the following precepts:

- Whenever possible and feasible, buy before you build.
- Do not reinvent the wheel. Be distributed object/component architecture agnostic and buy the components that best fit your organization's objectives.

Following these precepts accomplishes the following:

- It allows IT shops to embrace and extend frameworks. Instead of focusing on the mundane, they can focus on the IT tools that will give the organization the competitive edge.
- It saves support and development costs.
- It invests money in the component industry, which will grow and prosper, thus pushing more applications features into the mundane space and allowing more innovation and creation of cutting-edge IT tools.

Using a Model That Works

Splitting hairs over architecture issues may be the wrong way to pick a distributed object framework. Rather, which component model you use may depend heavily on the talent pool at your company. If you have a department full of Visual Basic programmers, you should consider using DCOM mostly, and RMI and CORBA when you have to connect to third-party components and frameworks. Conversely, if you use Java a lot on both the middle-tier and the client, you might consider using RMI and only use COM when you want to capitalize on a huge install base of applications that have ActiveX Automation support. If you need to connect to a lot of legacy applications that support CORBA, CORBA is the obvious choice.

DCOM is an excellent tool to have in your arsenal of tools for creating distributed applications, as well as for enabling the next revolution in history: the component revolution. Using the Microsoft Java SDK, you can easily write both DCOM clients and DCOM servers, and you can integrate with existing applications and in-house components developed by Visual Basic, Delphi, and Visual C++ developers. You can still use CORBA, DCOM, and RMI from the Microsoft JVM, so you don't have to select just one distributed object technology.

COM AND DCOM CODING EXERCISES

The strategy of the code examples is to keep them simple. The intent is to show how to expose and use COM objects from Java. We'll explore how what's covered in the architecture section applies to the code example. If you do the code examples, you'll understand the architecture better.

Without further ado, let's create our first COM program.

Creating a Java COM Object

This code example assumes you have Microsoft's Java SDK 3.1 or higher. The Microsoft Java SDK is freely downloadable from its Web site. If you don't have the Microsoft Java SDK, go to www.microsoft.com/java and get it. Once you've downloaded it, follow the install instruction closely.

For the first code example, we're going to just create a simple COM server; then we're going to register that COM server in the system Registry so other programs can find it.

In your favorite editor, enter the code in Listing 20.1.

LISTING 20.1   CREATING THE HelloCOM COM PROGRAM

```
class HelloCOM
{
  public int count = 0;

  public String getHello()
  {
    count ++;
    return "Hello from COM " + count;
  }
```

Save this in a file as HelloCOM.java.

Now you need to compile it. Use the Microsoft compiler; from the command line, type this:

```
C:\jsdk>jvc HelloCOM.java
```

Next, you need to register it with `JavaReg` by typing the command exactly as shown in the following command line. If successful, you should get a dialog box, as shown in Figure 20.4.

```
C:\jsdk>javareg /register /class:HelloCOM /progid:Acme.HelloCOM
```

FIGURE 20.4
OLE/COM Object Viewer HelloCOM *Registration dialog box.*

JavaREG is tool for registering Java classes as COM components in the system Registry. This tool also enables you to configure the COM classes you create to execute remotely.

You now need to copy the HelloCOM.class file to \java\lib in the Windows directory. You'll need to substitute drives and directories as needed:

```
C:\jsdk>copy HelloCOM.class d:\winnt\java\lib\HelloCOM.class
```

That's it! You just created your first COM object. Remember, the only difference between COM and DCOM, from the programmer's perspective, is a few Registry settings and the length of the wire. Let's do some poking around and see this first hand.

Exploring COM with OLEVIEW

OLEVIEW is the OLE/COM object viewer; it is a development, administration, and testing tool. You'll use this tool extensively to browse the COM classes you create. Reading the Registry with RegEdit is no fun, and it's quite time consuming. OLEVIEW allows you to easily see the Registry entries for the COM objects you create. It also allows you to configure the COM classes you're going to create. This includes distributed COM activation and security settings.

> **NOTE**
>
> OLEVIEW comes with Visual J++, Visual C++, and the DCOM SDK. You likely have OLEVIEW somewhere on your machine. If you can't find it, you can download it at www.microsoft.com/oledev/olecom/oleview.htm.

Another great feature of OLEVIEW is that it allows you to instantiate a COM class into a COM object. This allows you to test the COM classes you create simply by double-clicking their names in the OLEVIEW program. The list of interfaces of the classes you create is displayed in OLEVIEW, and you can activate COM classes locally or remotely. Here's the bottom line: OLEVIEW is a real nice tool to know if you're doing DCOM development.

With the above in mind let's work with OLEVIEW to get a feel for how HelloCOM is configured in the registry.

1. If OLEVIEW is on your path, type **OLEVIEW** at the DOS prompt. Otherwise, find it and execute it.
2. Select View, ExpertMode.
3. Select Object, CoCreateInstanceFlags, CLSCTX_INPROC_SERVER.
4. Expand the node labeled Grouped by Component.
5. Expand the Java Classes mode under Grouped by Component.
6. Find the class you created in the previous exercise (HelloCOM).
7. Click this node once.

> **NOTE**
>
> The CLSCTX_INPROC_SERVER component will not run as a remote server. Local and remote servers run in separate processes. Inproc is associated with a DLL, so when the class is registered, it's associated with the DLL that runs Java classes (namely, msjava.dll).

Notice that under the Registry tab on the right side, the CLSID and AppID are listed. When we executed JavaREG earlier, we used the following for the class and ProgID arguments:

```
/class:HelloCOM /progid:Acme.HelloCOM
```

Notice how the names map to this ProgID.

Now let's look at the information we can glean from the Registry tab:

- The inproc server is listed as msjava.dll.
- The threading model is specified as Both.
- The Java class associated with this COM object is HelloCOM.
- The ProgID is Acme.HelloCOM.

Think about all the ways you can use this information if something goes wrong. OLEVIEW is a great tool for debugging configuration problems.

Now let's test this COM object. When you double-click the HelloCOM node, OLEVIEW will try to instantiate the COM class associated with the CLSID listed. The following events will happen when you double-click this node:

- OLEVIEW takes the ProgID and finds the CLSID (remember, the CLSID is a 128-bit GUID that identifies our COM class) for this COM class.
- OLEVIEW calls CoCreateInstance, passing it the CLSID and the CLSCTX_INPROC_SERVER.
- The COM library loads msjava.dll and negotiates with its IFactory to get a COM object representing our Java class.

The bottom line is that OLEVIEW is actually loading a live version of our class. This is a powerful tool for testing classes.

Next, notice that the node has been expanded to show all the interfaces that this COM class supports. Notice also that it supports the following interfaces:

- IUnknown. Interface negotiation and life cycle management
- IDispatch. Dynamic invocation for scripting languages
- IMarshal. Custom marshaling

You should be familiar with these interfaces from the earlier discussion of the architecture. From there, we can ascertain that Microsoft has defined some kind of custom marshaler to marshal parameters to methods and return types between processes and machines.

Now, double-click IDispatch. A dialog box should pop up. Press the View Type Info button. An ITypeInfo viewer should pop up. The type information is missing, as you can see in Figure 20.5, because we didn't create a type library.

20

DISTRIBUTED COMPONENT OBJECT MODEL

FIGURE 20.5

The OLEVIEW dialog box's view type information.

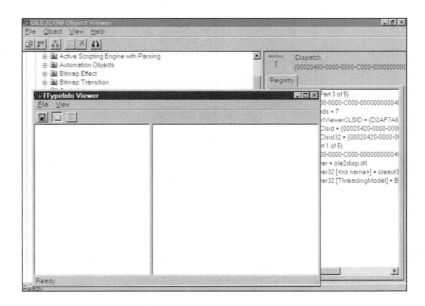

FIGURE 20.5

The OLEVIEW dialog box's view type information.

Type libraries are good to have around. Visual Basic has a tool called *Object Browser* in its IDE that uses type libraries to gather meta data on components. This tool is so useful that if a component provides these type libraries, developers will use them extensively. Visual Basic even has a feature that as you type an object's variable name in the editor, the editor gives you a list of methods that the object supports. This feature is called *intellisense*, and it makes development easier. Therefore, we definitely want to include type libraries. But how? Keep reading.

Scripting the `HelloCOM` Object

We're going to use the COM server you just created with Visual Basic.

This code example assumes you have some form of scripting language that works as an Automation controller. If you don't have such a language, don't worry about it. The next example shows you how to create an Automation controller in Java.

I chose Visual Basic for this example because many people know how to use it, and it's widely available. LotusScript is similar in syntax to Visual Basic. If you can't find a scripting language that suits your fancy, don't sweat it. Just skip the scripting section of this example.

> **NOTE**
>
> Any Automation-capable scripting language will do. You can use Lotus Script, which comes with Notes and Lotus 1-2-3, VBScript, and Visual Basic for Applications (VBA), which comes with Word and Excel. Two of my favorite Automation-capable scripting languages are Perl and Python. Both Perl and Python provide examples for doing Automation. They're freely available at www.perl.org and www.python.org, respectively.

From your favorite Automation controller scripting language, add a button to a form called Command1. Then add the code from Listing 20.2.

LISTING 20.2 SCRIPTING THE HelloCOM OBJECT WITH VISUAL BASIC

```
Private Sub Command1_Click()
    Dim helloCOM As Object
    Dim count As Integer

    Set helloCOM = CreateObject("Acme.HelloCOM")
    MsgBox helloCOM.getHello
    count = helloCOM.count
End Sub
```

Now run the program and press the Command1 button. Your output should look like what is shown in Figure 20.6.

FIGURE 20.6

Output of HelloCOM *using Visual Basic scripting.*

Notice that we use Visual Basic's CreateObject to instantiate the COM class into an object. Also notice that we pass CreateObject the ProgID of the COM class. You can probably guess what Visual Basic is doing underneath, but let's recap to make sure:

- CreateObject takes the ProgID and finds the CLSID for this COM class in the system Registry.
- CreateObject then calls CoCreateInstance, passing it the CLSID and the CLSC-TX_INPROC_SERVER, which tells CoCreateInstance to create this object as an in-process COM server.

20

- The COM library loads msjava.dll and negotiates with IUnknown to get an IFactory interface.

- The COM library then uses the IFactory to get a COM object representing the Java class. (Actually, at this point, IFactory returns an IDispatch that represents the interface to the COM object.)

See Figure 20.7 for a diagram of this sequence.

FIGURE 20.7

Visual Basic sequence diagrams.

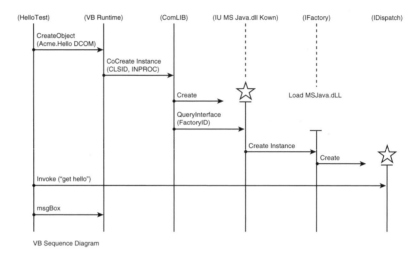

VB Sequence Diagram

Now let's consider what happens when the code example makes the following call:

```
MsgBox helloCOM.getHello
```

Here we're taking what helloCOM.getHello returns to use as a parameter to MsgBox. MsgBox is just a Visual Basic method that pops up a message box with a string that you give it. Underneath, Visual Basic is calling the IDispatch.Invoke method with the name of the method we defined in the Java class getHello. IDispatch.Invoke passes back a return type of Variant. A variant, as you'll remember from the architecture section, can hold any type of value. Visual Basic then works with the variant to see what it contains (in this case, it contains a string).

You may wonder why you're being prepped with all this background information. AutoIDispatch does not provide a type library. If it did, you could use JActiveX (a tool from the Microsoft Java SDK that wraps COM objects into Java classes) to create wrapper functions around the COM class you created (which we cover in the code examples). Without JActiveX, creating wrapper classes can be a little tough.

Using Java and "Raw" Dispatch Calls

Actually, using Visual Basic to do Automation is kind of like cheating, considering this is a book on Java. However, this demonstrates how easy it is to control Java from scripting languages.

You could do the preceding example in Java; however, we did not create a type library. (We'll go into the various ways of creating type libraries in other exercises.) For now the question is this: How are you supposed to use this class if you can't have JActiveX generate a wrapper class via a type library?

The obvious recommendation is just to use this as a regular Java class (use it like any other java class and import HelloCOM). Although efficient, this technique does not teach you how to work with Automation objects that do not have a type library. Also, this technique does not work when you do remote objects, which is covered in the next example.

> **NOTE**
>
> In order to do this exercise, you need the files from the examples that ship with Microsoft Java SDK 3.1.

So let's go through the "Raw" Dispatch Example step by step.

1. Copy the HelloCOMController.java file from the CD-ROM to a new directory.
2. Go to RegEdit and copy the CLSID for this class. You can do this by searching for "HelloCOM" with the RegEdit utility. Use Find from RegEdits menu bar. When you find "HelloCOM," select Edit and copy the CLSID to the clipboard.
3. Put the CLSID in the source file like so (note that your CLSID will be different):

```
private final String app_id = "{68068FA0-5FF5-11D2-A9AF}";
```

Now find the Java SDK examples. These are in the Microsoft Java SDK 3.1 directory:

`\Samples\DCOM\Dispatch\Sample\util`

The two files you want are DCOMLib.class and DCOMParam.class. Copy all the Java *.class files from this directory to your Windows directory in the following path:

`\Java\Lib\sample\util`

This puts the files you need in the class path.

Listing 20.3 is on the CD-ROM. Copy this file into the class files directory.

LISTING 20.3 THE HelloCOMController CLASS

```java
import com.ms.com.Variant;
import com.ms.com.Dispatch;
import java.util.Vector;
import sample.util.DCOMLib;
import sample.util.DCOMParam;

public class HelloCOMController
{
                //CLSID shorten for appearance
    private final String app_id = "{68068FA0-5FF5-11D2-111-111111}";
    private final String serverName = "localhost";

    public static void main(String[] args)
    {
        HelloCOMController helloController =
new HelloCOMController();
    }

    public HelloCOMController()
    {
        Object helloCOM = null;
        String strHello;
        int getHelloID;
        Variant [] arguments;

        DCOMParam appId = new DCOMParam(app_id);

        appId.setServerName(serverName);

        try{
            helloCOM = DCOMLib.CoCreateInstanceEx(appId);
        }catch(Exception e){
            System.out.println("HelloClient: Exception "+ e);
        }finally{
        }

        arguments = new Variant[0];
        getHelloID = Dispatch.getIDOfName(helloCOM,"getHello");

        Variant retVal = Dispatch.invokev(helloCOM,
                        getHelloID,
                        Dispatch.Method,
                        arguments,
                        null);

        strHello = (String)retVal.toString();

System.out.println("The hello COM servers says: " +
strHello);
```

```
    }

}
```

Now you need to compile the code. From the command prompt enter

jvc HelloCOMController.java

Finally, run it by typing

jview HelloCOMController

You should get a message in the console that says

```
The hello COM server says: Hello from COM 1
```

Let's do an analysis on the following snippet from the earlier code:

```
import com.ms.com.Variant;
import com.ms.com.Dispatch;
```

First, we're importing two Microsoft classes that are used a lot with COM: `Variant` and `Dispatch`.

`Variant` is used to map the Automation Variant type to Java. `Variant` can hold any value, `int`, `string`, `float`, `double`, `DATE`, or even an `IDispatch`. You need the `Variant` class to work with COM components that do not supply type libraries. `Variant` is used exclusively by `Dispatch.Invoke` to pass both return values and arguments. `Variant` allows you to change what types a variant has. Most `Variant` methods fall into two types: coercion (`toTypeXXX`) and access (`getTypeXXX` and `putTypeXXX`).

The `Dispatch` class, a class with only static members, allows COM clients written in Java to invoke methods and get/set properties of Automation objects. Automation objects are COM components that support the `IDispatch` interface, as discussed in the architecture section. `IDispatch` includes a lot of methods, but all of them boil down to two capabilities:

- `getIDsOfNames`, which maps methods or property names to `dispids`
- `invokev`, which invokes methods and get/set properties

We'll use forms of both of these methods in this example. The `IDispatch` class has many forms of these two methods. This helps developers with default types, as well as doing a subset or a frequently used superset of this functionality.

The two other classes used are `DCOMLib` and `DCOMParam`:

```
import sample.util.DCOMLib;
import sample.util.DCOMParam;
```

20

DISTRIBUTED COMPONENT OBJECT MODEL

These classes are included with the examples that ship with the Microsoft Java SDK 3.1. Microsoft used its J/Direct tool to create the `DCOMLib` classes that allow you to access the COM library directly. These are not supported classes; however, if enough people use them, they will probably either be supported or their functionality will be included in the core Microsoft API. (This happened in the past with MFC for VC++. So many people used the sample classes that they became part of MFC in future releases.)

`DCOMLib` contains methods for helping create DCOM objects more easily. It uses J/Direct for importing the required COM functions and for mapping C structures needed to create COM objects. It has one static function that we'll cover:

```
public static IUnknown CoCreateInstanceEx(DCOMParam param)
```

`DCOMParam` simplifies the parameters used to create a DCOM object with `DCOMLib.CoCreateInstanceEx`. It fills in common default value parameters that you would pass to `DCOMLib.CoCreateInstanceEx`. Here's an abbreviated list of some of the methods `DCOMParam` defines:

```
public void setServerName(String server)
public String getServerName()
public void setUser(String user)
public String getUser()
public void setDomain(String domain)
public String getDomain()
public void setPassword(String password)
public String getPassword()
public int getHRESULT()
```

All these features will be useful when we create remote objects. As you can see by this list of methods, you can manipulate the user name and password you use to connect. You can also specify to which server on which domain you should connect. This is a nice class to have around.

Let's look more closely at `HelloCOMController`. This constructor has five local variables:

- `helloCOM` holds the `Dispatch` pointer to an instance of the `HelloCOM` COM class we created in the first code example.

- `strHello` contains the hello string that we're going to retrieve using the `getHelloString` method from the `HelloCOM` COM class we created previously.

- `getHelloID` holds the dispatch identifier of the method we want to call (`getHello`).

- `Variant[]` arguments holds the list of arguments to our method (which in this case is none).

- The `DCOMParam` appID holds the parameters for the call to `CoCreateInstanceEx`.

Before we create the COM object, we must set the DCOMParam class used for the call to CoCreateInstanceEx. HelloCOMController initializes the class DCOMParam with the app_id we took from the Registry in step 1. Next, we'll set the server to the local server string constant. Here's a snippet of what the code for this looks like:

NOTE

HelloCOMController uses two similar, but separate, variables: appID and app_ID. app_ID is a String constant and appID is an instance of DCOMPARAM class.

```
        // Create the DCOMParam and initialize it to
        // the app_id we got out of the registry in step one
        //
    DCOMParam appId = new DCOMParam(app_id);

        // Set the server to the server name
        // server name equals localhost
        //
    appId.setServerName(serverName);

        // Create the helloCOM COM Object
        // Pass the appId to CoCreateInstanceEx
        //
     helloCOM = DCOMLib.CoCreateInstanceEx(appId);
```

Now that HelloCOMController has an IUnknown representing the HelloCOM COM object class, it's time to invoke its getHello method. First, we initialize arguments to a zero-length Variant array, because the getHello method has no arguments. Next, we get the Dispinterface ID of the getHello method. Then we use this ID to invoke the method using Dispatch.invokev:

```
        // We don't need any arguments for "getHello".
        //
    arguments = new Variant[0];

        // Get the dispinterface identifier for "getHello"
        //
    getHelloID = Dispatch.getIDOfName(helloCOM,"getHello");

        // Invoke the dispinterface method
        // The return type is returned as a Variant
        //
    Variant retVal = Dispatch.invokev(helloCOM,
                    getHelloID,
                    Dispatch.Method,
                    arguments,
                    null);
```

20

DISTRIBUTED COMPONENT OBJECT MODEL

```
                    // Convert the Variant to a string
                    //
           strHello = (String)retVal.toString();

      //Write the hello message out to the console.
      //
System.out.println("The hello COM servers says: " +
strHello);
```

Creating a Java DCOM Object

In this exercise, we're going to create a remote COM object. This exercise is a duplicate of the first. We're going to use a different class name than the HelloCOM Java class. The class name will be HelloDCOM. This is so you can compare the Registry settings of HelloDCOM to HelloCOM in the next exercise.

As you did in the first example, using your favorite editor, enter the code in Listing 20.4.

LISTING 20.4 CREATING THE HelloDCOM DCOM OBJECT

```
class HelloDCOM
{
  public int count = 0;

  public String getHello()
  {
    count ++;
    return "Hello from COM" + count;
  }
}
```

Also, as before, you need to compile. Use the Microsoft compiler, like so:

C:\jsdk>jvc HelloDCOM.java

Next, you need to register it with JavaReg:

C:\jsdk>javareg /register /class:HelloDCOM /progid:My.HelloDCOM /surrogate

The only real difference in this step to what you did in the first exercise is the addition of the /surrogate parameter, which is essential for doing remote objects. The JavaReg /surrogate parameter allows the system-provided surrogate process to wrap the msjava.dll file in a process. This is needed because otherwise the DLL would have to run inproc, which can't be used with remote objects.

Again, as before, you need to copy this HelloDCOM.class file to the Windows directory:

C:\jsdk>copy HelloDCOM.class d:\winnt\java\lib\HelloDCOM.class

To test this setup, let's run the OLEVIEW program from the second exercise. Go to the HelloDCOM class and try to instantiate. This will test to see if everything is working okay.

From OLEVIEW, select `View.ExpertMode` and also set the `Object.CoCreateInstance` flags to `CLSCTX_LOCAL_SERVER` and `CLSCTX_REMOTE_SERVER`.

NOTE

It's essential that `CLSCTX_INPROC_SERVER` is not selected.

Now expand the Java Classes node. Then expand the Class HelloDCOM node. If the node opens, then the COM class you created was instantiated to a COM object. Now compare all the parameters and settings in the Registry with the settings to HelloCOM. Go through the steps from the second exercise with HelloDCOM.

To actually use the COM object remotely, you're going to need to get familiar with another tool. The name of this tool is DCOM Configuration (DCOMCNFG). DCOMCN-FG is included with DCOM for Windows 95 and Windows NT with Service Pack 2 (SP2) or Service Pack 3. You can use DCOMCNFG to set application properties, such as security and location. On the computer running the client application, you must also specify the location of the server application that will be accessed or started. For the server application, you'll specify the user account that has permission to access and start the application to the client computer.

Configuring the Server

Here are the steps needed to configure the server:

1. At the DOS prompt, type **DCOMCNFG** (or launch it any way you prefer; it's in the Windows \System32 directory).
2. Select Java Class: HelloDCOM in the Applications tab's Application list box.
3. Double-click Java Class: HelloDCOM or press the Properties button.
4. Another dialog box pops up called Java Class: HelloDCOM. Ensure that the words "DLL Surrogate" appear next to the application type in the General tab. This is required for remote operation of Java classes.
5. Go to the Security tab.
6. Select the Use Custom Access permission.
7. Press the Edit button to edit the access permissions.
8. Add the user name with the Add button. (Press Show Users in the Add Users and Groups dialog box.)

9. Set their permissions to Allow Access in the type of permission.

10. Select the Use Custom Launch permission.

11. Press the Edit button to edit the access permissions.

12. Add the user name with the Add button. (Press Show Users in the Add Users and Groups dialog box.)

13. Set their permissions to Allow Access in the type of permission.

Configuring the Client

Here are the steps needed to configure the client:

1. Run the JavaReg tool on the client machine. The following line is entered as a continuous line at the DOS prompt without a line break:

```
C:\jsdk>javareg /register /class:HelloDCOM /progid:My.HelloDCOM
/clsid:{CLSID}  /remote:servername
```

2. Plug in the value of the *CLSID* to the 128-bit CLSID associated with this class. You can get this value by looking it up in OLEVIEW.

3. Set *servername* to the name of your remote machine.

   Here's an example of what it might look like:

```
javareg /register /class:HelloDCOM /progid:My.HelloDCOM
/clsid:{064BEED0-62FC-11D2-A9AF-00A0C9564732} /remote:azdeals08
```

4. Next, you can use OLEVIEW on the client to ensure that you can connect to the remote server. This step should be familiar to you by now. This is the third time we've used OLEVIEW. Go through the steps from the second exercise with OLE-VIEW and note the differences between HelloDCOM on the client and HelloDCOM on the server.

Testing the Configuration with OLEVIEW

To test this setup, let's run the OLEVIEW program (again) from the second example. You're going to go to the HelloCOM COM class and try to instantiate it into an object just like you did before. This will test to see if everything is working okay:

1. Run OLEVIEW on the client machine.

2. Select View.ExpertMode and also set Object.CoCreateInstance flags to CLSCTX_REMOTE_SERVER.

3. Expand the Java Classes node. Then expand the Class: HelloDCOM node. If the node opens, then the COM class you created was instantiated to a COM object. This essentially tests that you have everything running okay.

Let's recap what this actually does from the architecture standpoint:

1. OLEVIEW takes the `ProgID` and finds the CLSID for this COM class.

2. OLEVIEW calls `CoCreateInstanceEx`, passing in the CLSID and the `CLSCTX_REMOTE_SERVER`.

3. Based on the `CLSCTX_REMOTE_SERVER`, the COM library knows that this object is on a remote machine, so it looks up the name of the machine in the Registry.

4. At this point, the COM library starts interacting with the client SCM to load the COM server.

5. The client SCM interacts with the server SCM.

6. The server SCM loads up the default DLL surrogate, which in turn loads msjava.dll, which then loads the classes' *IFactory* COM class.

7. The COM library on the server negotiates with `IUnknown` from the COM server to get an `IFactory` interface.

8. The COM library will then use the `IFactory` to get a COM object representing the Java class. (Actually, at this point, it returns an `IDispatch` that represents the interface to the COM object.)

Demonstrating Access

From your favorite Automation controller scripting language, add a button to a form called Command1 and then add the code shown in Listing 20.5.

LISTING 20.5 DEMONSTRATING HelloDCOM CLASS ACCESS

```
Private Sub Command1_Click()
    Dim helloDCOM As Object
    Dim count As Integer

    Set helloDCOM = CreateObject("My.HelloDCOM")
    MsgBox helloDCOM.getHello
    count = helloDCOM.count

    MsgBox helloDCOM.getHello
    count = helloDCOM.count
End Sub
```

At this point, we pass the name of the COM class's `ProgID` to `CreateObject`. The Visual Basic runtime library initiates a similar process, as described in previous exercises.

Notice that we use Visual Basic's `CreateObject` to instantiate the DCOM class into an object. Also notice that again we pass `CreateObject` the `ProgID` of the COM class. By this point you should be able to guess what Visual Basic might be doing underneath, but let's recap one more time:

20

DISTRIBUTED
COMPONENT
OBJECT MODEL

- CreateObject takes the ProgID and finds the CLSID for this COM class in the system Registry. The Visual Basic runtime notices that the object being requested is a remote object.
- CreateObject then calls CoCreateInstance, passing it the CLSID which tells CoCreateInstance to create this object as an remote process COM server.
- The local machine's SCM contacts the remote machine's SCM.
- The remote machine's SCM uses the COM library to load msjava.dll in a surrogate process and then negotiates with IUnknown to get an IFactory interface.
- The COM library then uses the IFactory to get a COM object representing the Java class. (Actually, at this point, IFactory returns an IDispatch that represents the interface to the COM object.)
- The IDispatch reference gets marshaled back to the local machine so that the VB application (the COM client) can begin making calls.

Now use the example you created in the previous exercise as the client and do the following:

1. Go to RegEdit and copy the class ID for this class. The way to do this is to search for HelloDCOM with RegEdit using Edit, Find.
2. Put the value of the CLSID in the file, like so:

   ```
   private final String app_id = "{68068FA0-5FF5-11D2-A9AF}";
   ```

   Where *CLSID* is the class ID you copied from RegEdit.
3. Change the name of the server:

   ```
   private final String serverName = NAME_OF_REMOTE_HOST;
   ```

   Here, *NAME_OF_REMOTE_HOST* is the name of the machine with your COM class on it.
4. Compile and run it on the client machine.
5. Finally, move it to a different client machine and run DCOMCNFG if you have to set up security settings for the new client machine.

Before moving on, let's summarize what we've covered to this point in the coding exercises.

You know how to create a local COM server and a remote COM server. You know how to test both a local and a remote COM server with OLEVIEW. You know how to configure a COM server to be a remote server with JavaReg and DCOMCNFG. In addition to this, you know how to access COM objects that do not supply type libraries.

The next thing we're going to cover is how to create type libraries and how to use those type libraries to generate wrapper classes with JActiveX.

You can use JActiveX to generate wrapper classes from any COM class that supplies type libraries and supports IDispatch. In other words, you can use JActiveX to access Visual Basic programs that support Automation and OCXs that you build with Visual Basic. For instance, you can use JActiveX to create class wrappers with any tool that's able to create COM objects and type libraries, such as Delphi, Visual C++, C++ Builder, and others. You can even use it to wrap Excel Automation services. There's an excellent example of using Java to control Excel in the Samples directory of the Java SDK 3.1. (I've personally used JActiveX to generate class wrappers for Outlook, so my application was an Automation controller for Outlook.)

Creating a Type Library with Visual J++

In this section, you're going to create a class using Visual J++ 6.0. If you do not have Visual J++, don't worry. We'll cover how to create type libraries with Microsoft's Java SDK.

Start up Visual J++ 6.0. If the New Project dialog box does not come up, do the following:

1. Go to File, New Project.
2. From the New tab's tree, select node Visual J++ Projects, Components.
3. Select the COM DLL icon.
4. Name the project "Hello."
5. Press the Open button.

Once the new project is opened, do the following:

1. Double-click Class1 in the Project Explorer view.
2. Rename the class to HelloVJpp. You have to do this in the edit window and the Project Explorer view.
3. Add a public member called count, like so:

   ```
   public int count = 0;
   ```
4. Add the following method (you can right-click HelloVJpp in the class outline, which pops up an Add Method dialog box):

   ```
   public String getHello()
   {
   return "Hello First VJ ++ program";
   }
   ```

Now, to compile it, go to Build, Build, and you're done. You've created your first Java component with a type library.

To show you that this does indeed have a type library, let's fire up OLEVIEW and see it:

1. Start OLEVIEW.
2. Select `Hello.HelloVJpp`. Make sure `CLSCTX_INPROC_SERVER` is selected in the Object menu. Notice that the project name became part of the `ProgID`.
3. Expand the node. This tests whether it was registered correctly.
4. Select `Hello.HelloVJpp` again.
5. Look at the Registry tag and notice that this has a `TypeLib` GUID.
6. If you know how to use Visual Basic (4.0 or higher), start it up and use the Object Browser to view the COM class you created.

It does not get much easier than this to create a type library for a Java class.

For the next exercise, let's use JActiveX to build wrapper classes around this COM class you created with Visual J++. Note that you can use Visual J++ to do this. Select Project, Add COM Wrapper to automatically wrap a COM object. (For those who do not have Visual J++, we'll do it the JActiveX way.)

Creating a COM Wrapper with JActiveX

Among other things, the JActiveX tool can generate class wrappers for COM objects from type libraries. JActiveX generates *.java files for the COM classes and interfaces that are in a type library. When you compile the Java classes into *.class files, the classes allow a program to access COM objects. You deal with Java classes and interfaces instead of `IDispatch`, which makes life a lot easier. You just import and use the classes as you would any other Java class. You can specify a type library (*.tlb) or a dynamic link library (*.dll) that contains the type library as a resource.

> **NOTE**
>
> If you specify an .ocx file and leave out the `/javatlb` switch, the JActiveX tool will create a JavaBean wrapper for the ActiveX control.

JActiveX generates Java source files that use `com` directives. These directives appear inside comments. The jvc compiler knows how to take these `com` directives and create a class that will call the COM class (from information JActiveX receives out the type library). Here is an example of a COM directive:

```
/** @com.method(vtoffset=3, dispid=3, type=METHOD, name="getHelloString")
    @com.parameters() */
```

> **NOTE**
>
> Only the newer compilers that ship with the Java SDK accept com directives
> (1.023.3920 or later). Earlier versions of jvc won't work.

Let's use the JActiveX tool to create a wrapper around the last class that you created. Go to the directory that contains the DLL you created in the last exercise.

Now run the JActiveX tool against it. The format for JActiveX is as follows:

```
jactivex /d output_path   file_name_of_type_lib
```

Here, `file_name_of_type_lib` can be *.tlb, *.olb, *.ocx, *.dll, or *.exe, and the /d option specifies the output directory path. Here's an example of what this might look like on your machine:

```
C:\jsdk>jactivex /d c:\jsdk\Exercise8 Hello.dll
```

This action should have created two files in your output directory:

```
HelloVJpp.java
```

```
HelloVJpp_Dispatch.java
```

These classes have a lot of warnings in them. Here's an example:

```
// notifyAll UNMAPPABLE: Name is a keyword or conflicts
//                       with another member.
//   /** @com.method()
//       @hidden */
//   public native void notifyAll();
```

You can ignore these warnings. Because the COM classes were created with Java classes, a bunch of name conflicts exist. However, because we're more interested in the custom methods, we don't really care.

Listings 20.6 and 20.7 are the listings for the classes. These listings are shortened for display. The full listings can be found on the CD-ROM.

LISTING 20.6   CLASSES FOR HelloVJpp

```
package hello;

import com.ms.com.*;
```

continues

LISTING 20.6 CONTINUED

```
import com.ms.com.IUnknown;
import com.ms.com.Variant;

/** @com.class(classid=D130B670-63C5-11D2-A9B0-00A0C9564732,
      DynamicCasts) */
public class HelloVJpp implements
      IUnknown,com.ms.com.NoAutoScripting,hello.HelloVJpp_Dispatch
{

  /** @com.method()
      @hidden */
  public native String getHello();

  public static final com.ms.com._Guid clsid = new com.ms.com._Guid(...);
}
```

LISTING 20.7 CLASSES FOR HelloVJpp_Dispatch

```
package hello;

import com.ms.com.*;
import com.ms.com.IUnknown;
import com.ms.com.Variant;

// Dispatch-only interface HelloVJpp_Dispatch
/** @com.interface(iid=13076493-63C6-11D2-A9B0-00A0C9564732,
      thread=AUTO, type=DISPATCH) */

public interface HelloVJpp_Dispatch extends IUnknown
{
/** @com.method(dispid=100, type=METHOD, name="getHello", returntype=VOID)
      @com.parameters([type=STRING] return) */
  public String getHello();


  public static final com.ms.com._Guid iid = new com.ms.com._Guid(...);
}
```

Notice that there are com directives in the comments. Some of these directives specify the IID; some are being used to demarcate methods. When the jvc compiler sees these com directives, it knows how to generate the corresponding hooks into COM. Now all you have to do is compile these classes. Then, with a few Registry settings, you can use the COM object you created as a remote COM object (that is, DCOM).

The next step is to compile the generated files with jvc. Then you'll test this as a local COM object. You must create a small program that exercises the classes you just created with JActiveX:

```
class HelloTest
{
    public static void main(String [] args)
    {
        hello.HelloVJpp_Dispatch helloVJpp = new hello.HelloVJpp();
        System.out.println(helloVJpp.getHello());
    }
}
```

Next, you need to compile this code example and run it (for now, run it all on the same machine). As always, ensure that all the classes you create are in your class path. Then, move the compiled files to client machine.

Now do the following:

1. Open up OLEVIEW and select `Hello.HelloVJpp` from the treeview.

2. Go to the Implementation tab.

3. Select Use Surrogate Process. (Typically, you do this with JavaReg; however, because you're working with a DLL instead of a Java class, you do it differently for the server.)

4. Use DCOMCNFG to configure `Hello.HelloVJpp` the same way you did before. Essentially, what you want to do is give the user name you're going to use on the client machine and the privileges to launch and run this DCOM server. Refer to the previous exercise if you don't remember how to do this.

5. Next, copy the Hello.dll file over to the client. You need it for the type library information it contains.

6. Run regsvr32 to register Hello.dll. This sets up the pointer to the type library information. The wrapper classes needs this type library information to function properly.

7. Finally, you need to register the `Hello.HelloVJpp` on the client using JavaReg:

```
C:\jsdk>javareg /register /class:HelloVJpp /progid:Hello.HelloVJpp
                /clsid:{CLSID} /remote:servername
```

As you did before, set the CLSID to the 128-bit CLSID associated with this class. You can get this value by looking it up in OLEVIEW. (Right-click the class in the treeview and then select Copy to Clipboard.)

Set the server name to the name of your remote machine.

Note that regsvr32 registers DLLs in the Registry. Now, you may be thinking that because the DLL is the code that contains the class, if the DLL is registered on the client, the client will use the DLL locally. Yes, this is true. However, when you use JavaReg, you register Hello.HelloVJpp to access the remote server. You need these two steps because the DLL contains the TLB (type library) within itself as a Windows resource. You need the TLB information; otherwise, the wrapper classes you generated with JActiveX will not work. If you skip using regsvr32 to register the type library, you can still call this remote COM object using IDispatch. You could also use this remote COM object with Visual Basic using the CreateObject feature instead of using New.

Next, you need to use OLEVIEW on the client to test whether it's connecting to the DCOM server (HelloVJpp); then run the HelloTest sample program against it (use Jview).

> **NOTE**
>
> You can also create type libraries using JavaReg. In this case, the first exercise JavaReg command-line arguments would look like this:
>
> ```
> C:\test>javareg /register /class:HiCOM /clsid:{guid} /typelib:HiCOM.tlb
> ```
>
> This creates the type library and puts it in the Registry for you. You may want to try the last exercise using nothing but the Java SDK.

Other COM bridges are available besides Microsoft's. Sun provides a unidirectional bridge from JavaBeans to ActiveX controls. ActiveX controls are COM objects that support events and are displayable in a container. Also, Halcyon and other vendors provide bi-directional COM/DCOM interaction with Java from non-Microsoft JVMs.

Registering Callbacks

This exercise will show you how to create a callback in DCOM. Essentially, you pass a callback object to a COM server object. The COM server object uses this COM callback object to make a call on the client. Therefore, the server can initiate communication with the client. (Actually, in this scenario, both the server and the client act as server and client to each other; however, I'll refer to the COM object that's actually registered in the Registry as the server for simplicity of explanation.)

Listing 20.8 shows what the code should look like in concept.

LISTING 20.8 THE callMeAnyTime CALLBACK OBJECT USING DCOM

```
class Callback
{
    public void callMeAnyTime (Hashtable hashtable)
    {
        //use hashtable, in our case just display it
    }
    . . .
    . . .
}

class ComServerObject
{
  Callback callback;
  public void registerCallback(Callback callback)
  {
    this.callback = callback;
    //return right away
  }
  public void queryState()
  {
    //fire off thread to do a query
    //on the state of something and then return
  }
 public void gotQueryBack()
 {
   Hashtable queryResults;
     //populate hashtable with query results
   callback.callMeAnyTime(queryResults);
 }
}
class ComClient
{
    void getStatus()
    {
        Callback callback = new Callback();
        IComServerObject server = new ComServerObject();
        server.registerCallback(callback);
        server.queryState();
    }
}
```

The callback class will be passed to the ComServer from the ComClient via a call to ComServer.registerCallback. Once the ComServer has the Callback that the ComClient creates, it can use the ComClient's IDispatch interface to make calls in the ComClient's address space.

Essentially, you want the ComServerObject class to be a COM object. Also, the Callback object needs to be accessible from DCOM.

I recommend you use the following technique to implement this callback example: First, you do this as an all-Java solution. You test and develop the code with Java, not DCOM. Next, you try exposing ComServerObject to COM via Visual J++ 6.0 and then use the Visual J++ Create COM Wrapper feature to generate classes for dealing with the COM server object. You then write and test an all-local COM object solution. Finally, you try setting up ComServerObject as a DCOM component. You then test this as a remote solution.

The all-Java approach is shown in Listing 20.9 (the complete listing can be found on the CD-ROM).

LISTING 20.9   THE Callback CLASS USING JAVA

```
class Callback
{
   public void callMeAnyTime (Hashtable hashtable)
   {
               //use hashtable, in our case just display each element
      for (Enumeration e = hashtable.elements();
                              e.hasMoreElements();)
      {
         Object object = e.nextElement();
          System.out.println("default " + object);
      }//end of for

   }//end of method

}//end of Callback class
```

You can see by the class definition that the Callback class only contains one method: callMeAnyTime. This method just goes through a hashtable and prints out each element in the hashtable (using the toString of each object, which is implicitly called when using the addition operator with any object and a string).

Listing 20.10 shows the ComClient class.

LISTING 20.10   THE ComClient CLASS

```
class ComClient
{
    class MyCallback extends Callback
    {
       public void callMeAnyTime (Hashtable hashtable)
       {
           System.out.println("Received callback    ");
           System.out.println("      " + hashtable);
        }//end of callMeAnyTime method
```

```
    }//end of inner class MyCallBack

    void getStatus()
    {
        Callback callback = new MyCallback();
        ComServerObject server = new ComServerObject();
        server.registerCallback(callback);
        server.queryState();
    }//end of getStatus

    public static void main(String [] args)
    {
        ComClient cc = new ComClient();
        cc.getStatus();
    }//end of main

}//end of class
```

MyCallback extends the Callback object and defines a method that overrides the callMeAnyTime method. The getStatus method creates an instance of MyCallback and registers the Callback instance with an instance of the ComServerObject. The main method creates an instance of the ComClient and calls the getStatus method. The main method essentially just bootstraps and tests the ComClient.

Finally, Listing 20.11 shows the ComServerObectClass class.

LISTING 20.11 THE ComServerObjectClass CLASS

```
class ComServerObject
{
    Callback callback;

    public void registerCallback(Callback callback)
    {
      this.callback = callback;
      //return right away
    }

    public void queryState()
    {
      SimulateQuery sq = new SimulateQuery();
      sq.start();
    }

    public void gotQueryBack()
    {
      Hashtable queryResults = new Hashtable();
```

continues

20

DISTRIBUTED
COMPONENT
OBJECT MODEL

LISTING 20.11   CONTINUED

```
        //populate hashtable
    ...
    ...

    callback.callMeAnyTime(queryResults);
  }

  class SimulateQuery extends Thread
  {

    public void run()
    {

      for (int index = 0; index < 10; index++)
      {
        try {sleep(2000);} catch (Exception e) {}
        ComServerObject.this.gotQueryBack();
      }
    }//end of run

  }//end of simulate query

}
```

Here, you define a SimulateQuery class, which is essentially a class to simulate getting a query result from some type of database. SimulateQuery just pretends that it got some results every two seconds.

Here's the sequence:

1. You start the ComClient with Jview.
2. The ComClient creates an instance of MyCallback class and the ComServerObject.
3. The ComClient registers the MyCallback instance with the ComServerObject.
4. ComServerObject starts up an instance of the SimulateQuery class.
5. SimulateQuery fires ten query results set to the callback object via the callMeAnyTime method.

Now, you need to test this program as a local class. Then, you want to start up Visual J++ and create a project for the Callback class:

1. Create a COM DLL project.
2. Rename Class1 to Callback.
3. Cut and paste the callMeAnyTime method from Callback.java. Compile this project into a COM DLL.

These steps expose `Callback` as a COM object. Repeat this for the `ComServerObject`.

Next, you want to start up Visual J++ and create a project for the `ComServerObject` class and add it to the same solution as the previous one:

1. Create another COM DLL project in the same solution as before.
2. Rename `Class1` to `ComServerObject`.
3. Cut and paste all the methods and the inner class from `ComServerObject.java`.
4. Select the project that contains the `ComServerObject` class.
5. Select Project, Add COM Wrapper.
6. Select `Callback` from the list of COM objects available.
7. Add the `import` statement to the top of the `ComServerObject.java` file:

   ```
   import callback.Callback
   ```
8. Compile this project into a COM DLL.

This changes the code to access the `Callback` object as a COM object instead of as a COM class.

In order to put `ComClient` in the solution, you want to start up Visual J++ and create a project for the `Callback` class:

1. Create an empty project and add the `ComClient.java` file to it.
2. Change the first line from

   ```
   import Callback;
   ```

   to

   ```
   import callback.*;
   ```

   This specifies that you want to use the `Callback` class as a COM object.
3. Select the project that contains the `ComClient` class.
4. Select Project, Add COM Wrapper.

Select `ComServerObject` from the list of COM objects available.

This creates the following two COM wrapper files in a package called `comserverobject`:

- `ComServerObject.java`—This is the COM wrapper.
- `ComServerObject_Dispatch.java`—This is the Dispatch interface.

Now we need to change the class `MyCallback` to implement the `callback.Callback_Dispatch` interface.

Listing 20.12 defines the `ComServerObjectClass` class, which is what the `ComClient` class looks like, and which is now DCOM enabled.

20

DISTRIBUTED COMPONENT OBJECT MODEL

LISTING 20.12 THE `ComServerObjectClass` CLASS DCOM ENABLED

```
import comserver.*;   //import the comserver wrapper classes
import callback.*;    //import the callback wrapper classes
import java.util.*;
import com.ms.com.*;  //for using Variant

class ComClient
{

        // Note this class implements callback.Callback_Dispatch
        // Instantiating this interface identifies this class as
        // COM object
        //////////////////////////////////////////////////////////
    class MyCallback implements callback.Callback_Dispatch
    {
      ...
      ...
        //Call back method that the server uses to call the client
      public void callMeAnyTime (Object object)
      {
        System.out.println("Recieved callback   ");
        System.out.println("     " + object);
      }

    }//inner MyCallback class ////////////////////////////////////

    void getStatus()
    {
      MyCallback callback = new MyCallback();
      ComServerObject server = new ComServerObject();
      server.registerCallback(callback);
      server.queryState();
    }

    public static void main(String [] args)
    {
        ComClient cc = new ComClient();
        cc.getStatus();
    }
}
```

COMClient has an inner class called MyCallBack that defines an inner class that extends callback.Callback_Dispatch. By extending callback.Callback_Dispatch we have identified this class as a type of Callback_Dispatch so when we pass this object to the server it can call us back. Thus, when we pass an instantiation of the call back to the ComServerObject, it now knows how to talk to the server via DCOM. The getStatus method creates an instance of MyCallback and registers the Callback instance with an instance of the `ComServerObject`. The main method creates an instance of the `ComClient` and calls the `getStatus` method. The main method just bootstraps and tests the `ComClient`.

Next, you want to make sure that the all of the classes are on the class path. Then refer to the earlier example using Visual J++ and make the server remote. Make sure that the COM wrapper files and the two dlls are on both the client and the server.

You do not have to use Visual J++ to create the COM dll. You can use the Microsoft Java SDK. Instead of creating COM dll, you just create regular Java classes and compile them normally with the Java SDK. Then you use JavaReg with the /tlb option to create type libraries. After you compile, you use JActiveX to run against the type library you created to give you the Java COM wrapper files. You have to do this for each of the COM objects.

We now turn our attention to COM IDL. We're not going to cover DCOM IDL for several reasons. To do a decent job of covering DCOM IDL, we would need to dedicate a whole chapter. Conversely, all that using DCOM IDL would buy us over `AutoIDispatch` would be the ability to do custom marshaling. However, we won't cover it because it involves Raw Native Interface (RNI), which is beyond the scope of this chapter. Granted, there are valid reasons for using IDL. However, if you examine the reasons, most of the time you'll find that you simply don't need to use IDL. All the reasoning and warnings behind, it's at least a good idea to know how the Java types map to the Microsoft IDL types. Microsoft IDL is the common language to the COM, so we discuss it here briefly.

Creating a COM Object with IDL

There's another way to create COM objects. This way uses JActiveX again, but you need to write some IDL and use MIDL (Microsoft's IDL compiler). Essentially, what you do is create an IDL file. Compile the IDL file into a type library. Run the type library through the JActiveX, which will generate some Java source code. You then extend the `*Impl` class that JActiveX creates for you. You either extend the class that JActiveX generates directly (by editing the source) or you subclass the class that JActiveX generates. The second technique is recommended.

For this exercise we are going to use a new (IDL) version of our Hello class. We will add several do-nothing methods to show how to specify Java types in IDL.

Here is what our class looks like:

LISTING 20.13   THE HelloIDL CLASS DCOM ENABLED

```java
public class HelloIDL
{

        public HelloIDL()
        {
        }

        public String sayHello(String name)
        {
                return "Hello " + name;
        }

        public int giveInt(int number)
        {
                return number;
        }

        public Integer giveInteger(Integer number)
        {
                return number;
        }


        public float giveFloat(float number)
        {
                return number;
        }

        public byte giveByte(byte number)
        {
                return number;
        }

        public char giveChar(char number)
        {
                return number;
        }

}
```

Listing 20.14 shows what the IDL for this class would look like.

LISTING 20.14   THE HelloIDLLib IDL FILE

```
[
    uuid(c250ad52-69ce-11d2-99d6-00a0c9569583),
    helpstring("HelloIDLLib Type Library"),
```

```
    version(1.0)
]
library HelloIDLLib
{
   importlib("stdole32.tlb");
   [
     object,
     uuid(c250ad51-69ce-11d2-99d6-00a0c9569583),
     dual,
     pointer_default(unique),
     helpstring("IHelloIDL Interface")
   ]
  interface IHelloIDL : IDispatch
  {
   [ helpstring("giveChar Method") ]
   HRESULT giveChar([in] char p1, [out, retval] char * rtn);

   [ helpstring("giveInt Method") ]
   HRESULT giveInt([in] long p1, [out, retval] long * rtn);

   [ helpstring("giveFloat Method") ]
   HRESULT giveFloat([in] float p1, [out, retval] float * rtn);

   [ helpstring("giveByte Method") ]
   HRESULT giveByte([in] unsigned char p1, [out, retval] unsigned char*
rtn);

   [ helpstring("sayHello Method") ]
   HRESULT sayHello([in] BSTR p1, [out, retval] BSTR * rtn);
  }//end of interface

   [
      uuid(c250ad50-69ce-11d2-99d6-00a0c9569583),
      helpstring("CHelloIDL Object")
   ]
   coclass CHelloIDL
   {
      interface IHelloIDL;
   };//end of co class
};//end of library


[
    uuid(c250ad52-69ce-11d2-99d6-00a0c9569583),
    helpstring("HelloIDLLib Type Library"),
    version(1.0)
]
```

The preceding are settings for the attributes of the COM library that we are creating. It is here that we specify version information and `helpstrings` to identify this component.

The IDL also specifies the Universal Unique identifier (UUID) to identify our library: in this case, `c250ad51-69ce-11d2-99d6-00a0c9569583`. The UUID is the same as the GUID that we talked about earlier.

```
interface IHelloIDL : IDispatch
  { ...
```

defines the VTABLE interface definition for our class. As you can see, our interface supports `IDispatch`, which is the ability to do late bound calls. This interface supports the dual interface, which means that it supports both `dispinterface` and VTABLE interfaces as defined by the dual keyword in the `HelloIDLLib` declaration.

```
coclass CHelloIDL
    {
        interface IHelloIDL;
...
```

The above snippet defines our `dispinterface` for this component.

So let's see how the Java methods map to this IDL file.

`giveChar in Java snippet`

```
        public char giveChar(char number)
        {
                return number;
        }
```

`giveChar in IDL snippet`

```
    [ helpstring("giveChar Method") ]
    HRESULT giveChar([in] char p1, [out, retval] char * rtn);
```

Here we see that `char` in Java corresponds to `char` in IDL.

We also see that return types for `char` in Java are `char` pointers in IDL.

`giveInt in Java snippet`

```
        public int giveInt(int number)
        {
                return number;
        }
```

`giveInt in IDL snippet`

```
[ helpstring("giveInt Method") ]
HRESULT giveInt([in] long p1, [out, retval] long * rtn);
```

Similarly, we see that int in Java corresponds to long in IDL. And return types for int in Java are pointer to longs in IDL.

We summarize these data type mappings in Table 20.3.

TABLE 20.3 DATA TYPE MAPPING FROM JAVA TO COM IDL

Java Data Type	*COM IDL Data Type*
Void	void
Char	char
Double	double
Int	long
Float	float
String	BSTR
Pointer to interface	IDispatch
Short	short
Byte	unsigned char
Boolean	boolean

In order to use this IDL we first create a type library out of it. Then we use the type library in conjunction with JActiveX to create an IHelloIDL interface for the class that we want to extend. If you have done CORBA development, these steps are similar to what you would do with CORBA. We then run the IDL through the MIDL compiler, which then gives us a type library file.

To run it we enter MIDL HelloIDLlib.IDL at the DOS prompt. Then we run the Type library file through JActiveX.

To Run JActiveX, enter the following at the DOS prompt:

JActiveX /D . HelloIDLLib.TLB

JActiveX would generate two Java class files.

- CHelloIDL.java is the file we need to use the COM object from the client perspective.
- IHelloIDL.java is the file we need to extend in our component class to expose it as a COM object.

20

DISTRIBUTED
COMPONENT
OBJECT MODEL

Listing 20.15 shows the CHelloIDL class generated.

LISTING 20.15   THE CHelloIDL CLASS

```
package helloidllib;

import com.ms.com.*;
import com.ms.com.IUnknown;
import com.ms.com.Variant;

/** @com.class(classid=C250AD50-69CE-11D2-99D6-00A0C9569583,DynamicCasts)
*/
public class CHelloIDL implements
IUnknown,com.ms.com.NoAutoScripting,helloidllib.IHelloIDL
{
  /** @com.method() */
  public native char giveChar(char p1);

  /** @com.method() */
  public native int giveInt(int p1);

  /** @com.method() */
  public native float giveFloat(int p1);

  /** @com.method() */
  public native byte giveByte(byte p1);

  /** @com.method() */
  public native String sayHello(String p1);

  public static final com.ms.com._Guid clsid = new com.ms.com.
      Guid((int)0xc250ad50, (short)0x69ce, (short)0x11d2, (byte)0x99,
      (byte)0xd6, (byte)0x0, (byte)0xa0, (byte)0xc9, (byte)0x56,
      (byte)0x95, (byte)0x83);
}
```

Notice that this class gives us the same methods as our original class. It also has COM directives that specify that the methods are really COM methods for a COM object. When jvc runs across these COM directives it puts hooks in the bytecode so that when JView or IE runs across these hooks, they know how to dispatch a method call to the COM object.

Listing 20.16 shows the IHelloIDL class generated by JActiveX.

LISTING 20.16 THE IHelloIDL CLASS

```
IHelloIDL.java Listing

package helloidllib;

import com.ms.com.*;
import com.ms.com.IUnknown;
import com.ms.com.Variant;

// Dual interface IHelloIDL
/** @com.interface(iid=C250AD51-69CE-11D2-99D6-00A0C9569583,
     thread=AUTO, type=DUAL) */
public interface IHelloIDL extends IUnknown
{
  /** @com.method(vtoffset=4, dispid=1610743808, type=METHOD,
      name="giveChar", addFlagsVtable=4)
      @com.parameters([in,type=I1] p1, [type=I1] return) */
  public char giveChar(char p1);

  /** @com.method(vtoffset=5, dispid=1610743809, type=METHOD,
      name="giveInt", addFlagsVtable=4)
      @com.parameters([in,type=I4] p1, [type=I4] return) */
  public int giveInt(int p1);

  /** @com.method(vtoffset=6, dispid=1610743810, type=METHOD,
      name="giveFloat", addFlagsVtable=4)
      @com.parameters([in,type=I4] p1, [type=R4] return) */
  public float giveFloat(int p1);

  /** @com.method(vtoffset=7, dispid=1610743811, type=METHOD,
      name="giveByte", addFlagsVtable=4)
      @com.parameters([in,type=U1] p1, [type=U1] return) */
  public byte giveByte(byte p1);

  /** @com.method(vtoffset=8, dispid=1610743812, type=METHOD,
      name="sayHello", addFlagsVtable=4)
      @com.parameters([in,type=STRING] p1, [type=STRING] return) */
  public String sayHello(String p1);


  public static final com.ms.com._Guid iid = new com.ms.com._
      Guid((int)0xc250ad51, (short)0x69ce, (short)0x11d2, (byte)0x99,
      (byte)0xd6, (byte)0x0, (byte)0xa0, (byte)0xc9, (byte)0x56,
      (byte)0x95, (byte)0x83);
}
```

CHelloIDL.java is the file we use as a client and IHelloIDL.java is the file we need to extend in our component class.

Compile the preceding two classes and make sure they are in the class path. Change the `HelloIDL` to implement `IHelloIDL` and add the UUID to the class file as follows:

From

```
public class HelloIDL
{

        public HelloIDL()
        {
        }
...
...
```

To

```
public class HelloIDL implements helloidllib.IHelloIDL
{
        private static final String CLSID =
                "c250ad50-69ce-11d2-99d6-00a0c9569583";


        public HelloIDL()
        {
        }
...
...
```

Compile `HelloIDL` and make sure it is in the classpath.

Register the class in the register like so:

```
C:\msjsdk >javareg /register /class:HelloIDL /progid:DEAL.HelloIDL /
clsid:{c250ad50-69ce-11d2-99d6-00a0c9569583}
```

Now we need to write a simple test program to test this class. The test program uses the class as a COM object, not a Java object. We use the `CHelloIDL` class. (We could now use this COM object from any language, such as Visual Basic.) Here is the `TestHelloIDL.java` class file.

```
import helloidllib.*;

class TestHelloIDL
{
 public static void main(String [] args){
    helloidllib.IHelloIDL hello = new helloidllib.CHelloIDL();
    System.out.println("Say Hello: " + hello.sayHello("Hello"));
    System.out.println("Say 5: " + hello.giveInt(5));
    System.out.println("Say 5.0: " + hello.giveFloat(5));
  }//end of main
}//end of class TestHelloIDL
```

As you can see in the main method, we assign an IHelloIDL reference and a new instance, CHelloIDL class. We can then make calls on this COM object.

You should try to activate this object through the OLEVIEW program before you start trying to test it with this local program. This will let you know if you have copied all the classes to the classpath and registered the COM class correctly.

Now compile TestHelloIDL and run it.

To make this class remote you use JActiveX or DCOMCNFG like we did earlier. The main difference between this class and the other classes we created is that this class works with both a dispinterface or vtable interface. So you get a performance advantage if you're using a statically compiled language as opposed to a late bound language that needs dispinterface. Of course, you only see this advantage if you used all the classes locally.

FROM HERE

This chapter covered a brief overview of COM/DCOM and distributed object architecture. After discussing some of the advantages and disadvantages of COM/DCOM technologies, we ran through some basic exercises for developing COM/DCOM objects.

This chapter completes Part IV, "Non-CORBA Approaches to Distributed Computing." Part V, "The CORBA Approach to Distributed Computing," which includes Chapters 21 through 27, delves into the CORBA approach to distributed computing.

THE CORBA APPROACH TO DISTRBUTED COMPUTING

IN THIS PART

CORBA OVERVIEW

IN THIS CHAPTER

Computer technology has evolved in a rather interesting fashion. As development moved from the military into the private sector, two camps of developers formed. One camp was comprised of individuals working in academia, producing—in an *ad hoc* manner—software that ran on various UNIX platforms. The other camp was comprised of individuals working for software corporations, attempting to develop software for home and business markets. With all this development occurring, one might think that all forces would join together and produce complementary software. Unfortunately, this did not occur, and virtually everyone out there decided on their own proprietary manner to solve a problem.

All this development gave us more operating systems than we can shake a stick at, more network transport protocols than anyone knows what to do with, and way too many opinions on what solution is the best. The truth of the matter is that most solutions are pretty similar in that they all solve a common problem and take about the same time to function.

This chapter takes a look at a technology called CORBA, which is an attempt to link together all the disparate development projects that occur around the world. In covering this material, the following topics are addressed:

- What CORBA really is, and what components make up the CORBA universe
- How an entity (specification) enters the CORBA universe
- Details on each of the various entities in the CORBA universe
- How the OMG came into existence, and the problems it solves

THE PUSH TOWARD OPEN COMPUTING

As with many things in this world, software quality does not matter as much as software marketing. Those companies with the best marketing departments found their software in use by more and more people. As a prime example of this, many people argue that until Windows 95 came out, the Macintosh Operating System ran circles around Windows 3.1. Microsoft marketing did not let this hold it back, and it worked hard to make sure that regardless of quality, Windows was the dominant operating system.

Although marketing departments did push forward many proprietary platforms, and—in some cases—achieve a large market presence, there has been a shift in the past few years from the proprietary computer world to one that is more open.

Under an open computing model, companies agree to develop software that adheres to a standard; therefore, companies can develop similar pieces of software based on the same standard. To keep from favoring a single vendor, the standard is often maintained by an independent third party. As you consider the implications of this, think about what would happen if the same thing happened with natural languages.

There are thousands and thousands of natural languages currently in use right now all over the world. Of those languages, most business transactions are conducted in English, Spanish, French, German, Russian, Chinese, and Japanese. Companies wishing to do business in multiple countries are forced to spend millions on translation services. If everyone were to learn a common language, this problem would go away, and business would no longer be conducted in some proprietary language but rather in one common open language.

> **NOTE**
>
> Many attempts at getting the world to speak a common second language have been launched but none have achieved too much success. A language called Esperanto did achieve some success, but its popularity is fading.

As part of the push toward open standards for computing, a specification called Common Object Request Broker Architecture (CORBA) has been developed and is supported by an incredibly large developer population. CORBA is a standard maintained by the largest software consortium in the world—the Object Management Group (OMG). With over 800 members, the OMG's membership list is a who's who of the software industry, even boasting the membership of Microsoft, who pushes a competitive standard called DCOM.

> **NOTE**
>
> Not content to use CORBA at Microsoft, it decided to develop its own technology called *Distributed Component Object Model* (or *DCOM*). DCOM is a technology that allows for distributed object communication between multiple Win32 systems. Support for various flavors of UNIX along with the Macintosh Operating System has been announced but not fully released. DCOM is covered in Chapter 20, "Distributed Component Object Model (DCOM)."

CORBA is rather amazing in that it allows for easy communication between objects written in multiple languages, all running on different machines. For example, one could write a Java application that runs on a Macintosh and talks to a collection of COBOL objects running on a VMS machine.

CORBA FOR UPPER MANAGEMENT

When jumping into a new technology, I always find it useful to read a high level description of that technology. I like to call this description the *upper management perspective*, because it describes the technology without getting too specific. For those readers lucky enough to have worked only for companies with highly intelligent upper management, you'll have to pretend for a moment. If you find yourself asking upper management to move to a CORBA development model in the future, this section should provide a good starting point for your discussions.

CORBA is a specification for a technology that allows objects on one machine to communicate with objects running on any number of different machines. The objects can be written in virtually any language (including non–object-oriented languages such as COBOL and C) and can run on virtually any machine in existence. CORBA is currently the only technology that supports such a broad range of languages and hardware environments.

> **NOTE**
>
> To state that CORBA objects can be implemented in a non–object-oriented language may generate some level of confusion. As you'll learn in upcoming chapters, CORBA allows non–object-oriented legacy code to parade as a CORBA object.

CORBA, as in independent entity, only specifies how individual objects communicate with each other. No inherent support exists for locating objects, services, or functions such as security. Complementing CORBA, and forming the Object Management Architecture (OMA), are three other entities charged with adding functionality. These entities—CORBAservices, CORBAdomains, and CORBAfacilities—are specifications for specific pieces of functionality that can aid the CORBA developer.

With all this excitement surrounding CORBA and open computing in general, the question that begs asking is "Why"? If we never looked to open computing before, why do so now? Why not let companies such as Microsoft, Novell, and Sun duke it out with competing proprietary standards? A detailed answer to this question could fill a book on its own, but the main reason is that only through open standards will the needed level of software reuse ever be obtained. *Software reuse* doesn't mean that code is copied and pasted from one application into another, but rather that compiled code is easily reused between multiple applications.

21

Software development efforts being undertaken today place more and more requirements on the developer and throw in shorter deadlines for good measure. The software community is also forced to face a growing developer shortage that shows no signs of slowing. To meet these new deadlines, developers must be able to leverage both existing in-house code and code developed by third-party vendors.

Application-level reuse has existed for a long while now (for example, you don't write a new database server for each new application), but this reuse must move to all levels of a development effort. By writing code that adheres to an open model, developers produce code that is both reusable in-house and by other companies. If a component-centric development model continues to gain popularity, chances are that application development will take on a very new face. Developers and programmers will actually write components, analysts will identify business needs, and power users will string together components to form entire applications.

As you begin to learn about CORBA, it's important to stress that the OMG produces absolutely no software—its purpose is to produce *specifications*. Once the OMG has certified a specification, various third-party vendors produce the software that conforms to the specification. As we begin our exploration into the world of CORBA, we'll first look at the manner in which an idea becomes an OMG specification.

OMG SPECIFICATION PROCESS

As was earlier stated, the purpose of the OMG is to produce specifications for the technologies that make up the Object Management Architecture. Through its members, along with the developer community as a whole, specifications are developed, voted upon, and implemented in a fully functional form. The process by which an idea moves into an accepted specification is well defined and allows for a logical progression.

The first step in developing a specification is for a *request for proposal* (or *RFP*) to be issued. The RFP details the problem that needs to be solved and any additional information that members might need in order to produce a solution. The RFP is first issued by an OMG task force electronically, and then it's formally presented at a task force technical meeting. Electronic distribution of the RFP occurs at least three weeks before the physical meeting where it's presented. This lag time allows members to fully study the RFP before having to discuss it in person.

After an RFP has been formally presented, all parties intending to respond have at least 60 days to issue a *letter of intent* (or *LOI*). This 60-day waiting period is not etched in stone as an OMG requirement, but it has become the *de facto* standard. Once the LOI deadline has passed, an initial submission deadline is set. This time period (at least 12 weeks after the LOI deadline) gives submitters time to both prepare a specification and an implementation. Although the OMG only produces specifications, no proposals are accepted if they're not paired with a fully functional implementation. By forcing the development of an implementation along with the specification, the OMG is assured that an impossible-to-implement specification is not submitted. All submissions are formally presented to the voting body.

If there's a single submission, chances are that it will become an official OMG standard. Assuming that conflicting submissions exist, one will either be chosen or some submitters may choose to merge the solutions themselves. In any situation, the OMG member body must vote upon a specification before it becomes a standard. A single submission is not a guarantee of standardization, because it may fail to fully solve the problem.

As you begin to work more and more with CORBA, you may decide that you want to take an active role in determining its future. The OMG membership is always open and demands only a modest fee. If, however, you're not ready to commit to being a member, you can still be a part of the specification process. The OMG Web site contains all current RFPs, and any person in the world is welcome to submit a proposal.

> **NOTE**
>
> All OMG specifications can be tracked online at
> `http://www.omg.org/schedule/`.

With an understanding of how the OMG functions, you're now ready to dive under the covers and learn about what really makes the CORBA universe tick.

OBJECT MANAGEMENT ARCHITECTURE

The CORBA universe, as defined by the OMG, is comprised of four different entities. These entities include a specification for distributed object communication as well as many specifications for add-on functionality. The following list describes all entities in detail:

- ORB: The *Object Request Broker* (or *ORB*) is the piping that connects all developments within the CORBA universe. It specifies how all objects written in any language running on any machine can communicate with each other.

- CORBAservice: A *CORBAservice* is a specification for some added CORBA functionality with implications in a horizontal arena. A CORBAservice will usually define some object-level functionality that you need to add to an application but do not want to produce in-house. Because all vendors producing a given

CORBAservice conform to the specifications produced by the OMG, you can easily swap one vendor's solution for another vendor's solution. An example of a CORBAservice is the event service that allows events to be delivered from one source object to a collection of listener objects.

- CORBAfacility: Like a CORBAservice, a *CORBAfacility* is also a specification for some added CORBA functionality. However, the implications can be either horizontal or vertical. A CORBAfacility differs in that it specifies functionality at a higher level than a CORBAservice. For example, CORBAfacilities define functionality for transactions such as email and printing.

- CORBAdomain: A *CORBAdomain* is a specification for some level of CORBA added functionality with applications in a unique industry or domain. A CORBAfacility used in finance might calculate derivative prices, and a CORBAfacility used in healthcare might match up patient records contained in heterogeneous systems.

All the technologies in the previous list are housed under the umbrella term *Object Management Architecture (OMA)*. The OMA is rather amazing in that it's fully backed by over 800 independent (and often competing) technology vendors. In the next few sections, we'll take a look at each of the currently available CORBAservices, CORBAfacilities, and CORBAdomains.

CORBAservices

CORBAservices add functionality to a CORBA application at the server level. They provide services to objects that are necessary for various tasks, including event management, object lifecycle, and object persistence. New CORBAservices are constantly being produced, but at the time of this writing, only the following 15 services are in existence (a full list of available CORBAservices can be found on the OMG Web site at `http://www.omg.org`):

- Collection Service: This service provides access to a variety of data structures.

- Concurrency Control Service: This service enables multiple clients to coordinate access to shared resources. For example, if two clients are attempting to withdraw funds from the same back account, this service could be used to ensure that the two transactions do not happen at the same time.

- Event Service: This service enables events to be delivered from multiple event sources to multiple event listeners.

- Externalization Service: This service enables an object (or objects) or a graph to be written out as a stream of bytes. This is similar to *object serialization* in JDK1.1.

- Licensing Service: This service enables control over intellectual property. It allows content authors to ensure that their efforts are not being used by others for profit.

- Life Cycle Service: This service defines conventions for creating, deleting, copying, and moving objects.

- Naming Service: This service allows objects to be tagged with a unique logical name. The service can be told of the existence of objects and can also be queried for registered objects.

- Persistent Object Service: This service enables objects to be stored in some medium. This medium will usually be a relational or object database, but it could be virtually anything.

- Property Service: This service enables name/value pairs to be associated with an object. For example, some image file could be tagged with name/value pairs describing its content.

- Query Service: This service enables queries to be performed against collections of objects.

- Relationship Service: This service enables the relationship between entities to be logically represented.

- Security Service: This service enables access to objects to be restricted by user or by role.

- Time Service: This service is used to obtain the current time along with the margin of error associated with that time. In general, it's not possible to get the exact time from a service due to various factors, including the time delta that occurs when messages are sent between server and client.

- Trader Object Service: This service allows objects to locate certain services by functionality. The object will first discuss with the trader service whether a particular service is available; then it negotiates access to those resources.

- Transaction Service: This service manages multiple, simultaneous transactions across a variety of environments.

CORBAservices are always being developed by the OMG; chances are that by the time you read this list, there will be a few more services. Already steps are being taken to finalize firewall and fault tolerance services. For additional information on CORBAservices, take a look at Chapter 30, "The Naming Service," Chapter 31, "The Event Service," and Chapter 33, "Other CORBA Facilities and Services."

CORBAfacilities

As stated earlier, CORBAfacilities add additional functionality to an application at a level closer to the user. Facilities are similar to services in that they both aid a CORBA application; however, CORBAfacilities need not be simply targeted at a broad audience. CORBAfacilities are categorized into horizontal and vertical services.

Vertical CORBAfacilities

A vertical CORBAfacility has specific applications in a unique industry or domain. Obvious parallels exist between a vertical CORBAfacility and a CORBAdomain; however, CORBAdomains usually have much broader applications within the domain. The following list describes the eight existing vertical CORBAfacilities:

- Accounting: This facility enables commercial object transactions.
- Application Development: This facility enables communication between application development objects.
- Distributed Simulation: This facility enables communication between objects used to create simulations.
- Imagery: This facility enables interoperability between imaging devices, images, and image data.
- Information Superhighways: This facility enables multiuser application communication across wide area networks.
- Manufacturing: This facility enables interoperability between objects used in a manufacturing environment.
- Mapping: This facility enables communication between objects used for mapping.
- Oil and Gas Industry Exploitation and Production: This facility enables communication between objects used in the petroleum market.

Horizontal CORBAfacilities

Horizontal CORBAfacilities are broad in their function and should be of use to virtually any application. Due to their broad scope, there are four categories of horizontal CORBAfacilities. This list of categories is not at all static and can be added to at some point in the future:

- User Interface: All facilities in this category apply to the user interface of an application.
- Information Management: All facilities in this category deal with the modeling, definition, storage, retrieval, and interchange of information.

- System Management: All facilities in this category deal with management of information systems. Facilities should be neutral in vendor support, because any system should be supported.

- Task Management: All facilities in this category deal with automation of various user- or system-level tasks.

The User Interface common facilities apply to an application's interface at many levels. As shown in the following list, this includes everything from physically rendering object to the aggregation of objects into compound documents:

- Rendering Management: This facility enables the physical display of graphical objects on any medium (screen, printer, plotter, and so forth).

- Compound Presentation Management: This facility enables the aggregation of multiple objects into a single compound document.

- User Support: This facility enables online help presentation (both general and context sensitive) and data validation.

- Desktop Management: This facility supports the variety of functions needed by the user at the desktop.

- Scripting: This facility exists to support user automation scripts.

The Information Management common facilities enable the myriad functions required in a data ownership situation. These facilities, defined in the following list, range in function from information management to information storage:

- Information Modeling: This facility supports the physical modeling of data storage systems.

- Information Storage and Retrieval: This facility enables the storage and retrieval of information.

- Compound Interchange: This facility enables the interchange of data contained in compound documents.

- Data Interchange: This facility enables the interchange of physical data.

- Information Exchange: This facility enables the interchange of information as an entire logical unit.

- Data Encoding and Representation: This facility enables document encoding discovery and translation.

- Time Operations: This facility supports manipulation and understanding of time operations.

The System Management common facilities aid in the difficult task of managing a heterogeneous collection of information systems. These facilities, defined in the following list, range in function from managing resources to actually controlling their actions:

- Management Tools: This facility enables the interoperation of management tools and collection management tools.
- Collection Management: This facility enables control over a collection of systems.
- Control: This facility enables actual control over system resources.

The Task Management common facilities assist with the automation of user- and system-level tasks:

- Workflow: This facility enables tasks that are directly part of a work process.
- Agent: This facility supports manipulation and creation of software agents.
- Rule Management: This facility enables objects to both acquire knowledge and to also take action based on that knowledge.
- Automation: This facility allows one object to access the key functionality of another object.

Like CORBAservices, CORBAfacilities are constantly growing, and they're definitely an important piece of the OMA. Full details on all facilities are always available on the OMG Web site at `http://www.omg.org`, as are details on new and upcoming facilities.

CORBAdomains

CORBAdomains are solutions that target an individual industry. They differ from vertical CORBAfacilities in that they often fully model some specific business process. Most CORBAdomains are developed and maintained by different task forces within the OMG itself. For example, the CORBAmed task force oversees all developments targeted at the healthcare industry. Covering all CORBAdomains in this section would be rather tedious (most readers will likely only have interest in less than 10 percent of what is covered). What you should know, however, is that virtually every industry is represented by a collection of CORBAdomain solutions. Some of the represented domains are healthcare, finance, manufacturing, and telecomm.

OMG HISTORY AND BACKGROUND

In the computer world, it's often hard to get even a handful of developers to work together in a productive manner. There are often squabbles and people who refuse to accept that another idea may work better. This inability to function as a large group extends to all reaches of the software community, and it's almost commonplace to hear two people from the same company represent conflicting viewpoints on a major technological issue. Assuming that the situation does not get out of hand, conflicting viewpoints can create important new developments. If everyone agreed on things, we might have all agreed that the abacus was the pinnacle of computing.

Given that developers often cannot agree on many points, it's really amazing that the OMG has managed to collect well over 800 members so far. This strong membership does owe a tip of the hat to the history leading up to the OMG's inception and the manner in which it was formed.

The OMG was formed in 1989 by representatives from 3Com Corporation, American Airlines, Canon Inc., Data General, Hewlett-Packard, Philips Telecommunications N.V., Sun Microsystems, and Unisys Corporation with the express goal of furthering global component-based development. The founding companies and most of the software community knew that components were the key to the future, but without a standard, one vendor's components would not work with another vendor's components.

When the founding companies decided that a standard for distributed computing was necessary, they also decided that this standard must be open and therefore not controlled by a single company. When a single company attempts to further a standard, that standard is often directed to further the direct needs of the company and not the industry as a whole. Microsoft's DCOM is an example of a distributed object technology benefiting mostly one vendor. DCOM runs wonderfully on Win32 platforms but will not run on Macintosh or UNIX machines at all.

NOTE

Microsoft has announced intentions to port DCOM to both Macintosh and UNIX platforms, but a version that is as fully functional as the Win32 port has yet to be seen.

The formation of the OMG in 1989 as a not-for-profit organization started the movement for an open model for distributed computing. Soon after its inception, the OMG released the first draft of the Object Management Architecture in the fall of 1990. That's when the CORBA movement started to make itself really known. As the CORBA 1.1 specification became known and realized in commercial implementations, the OMG members were hard at work on the CORBA 2.0 specification.

> **NOTE**
>
> The first functional version of CORBA was 1.1; the 1.0 specification was basically a working draft.

One of the main weaknesses of the CORBA 1.1 specification was that it produced applications that could not interoperate across ORBs from different vendors. An application was written to support one and only one ORB, and code written to one ORB could not easily communicate with another ORB. For developers working only with in-house development, this did not prove to be too much of a problem. However, if a development shop was using ORB A and wanted to access objects written by a third-party vendor, which was using ORB B, chances were the code would not interoperate. In an attempt to solve this problem, CORBA 2.0 added an important new feature to the CORBA universe: the Internet Inter-ORB Protocol (IIOP). IIOP is a protocol that allows ORB-to-ORB communications to occur over the Internet's TCP/IP backbone. In time, this could very well lead to an Internet that's fully populated by available CORBA objects. Full details on IIOP are covered in Chapter 29, "Internet Inter-ORB Protocol (IIOP)."

> **NOTE**
>
> This book generally refers to the CORBA 2.0 specification, because it is widely implemented. The most recent version from the OMG is CORBA 2.3.

MOVING FORWARD

Having read this chapter, you should have a very solid understanding of what CORBA is all about. Moving into a new technology can be a challenge; fortunately, CORBA adds few technical hurdles to be crossed. Moving to a CORBA world means learning a few new technologies, but most importantly, it means learning about working in a distributed universe. CORBA applications execute on machines scattered all over the world and add concerns not present with applications that execute on a single machine. All of a sudden, you're forced to consider network usage, enterprisewide fault tolerance, and a host of other concerns that do not exist when an application exists on one machine.

What you should know going into all of this is that distributed objects are the future of computing. As more and more computers attach themselves to the Internet, more and more computers become candidates for CORBA applications. Chances are that in the very near future, you'll be running all forms of consumer applications—from home banking to recipe management—as CORBA applications executing on your home computer and all kinds of servers scattered around the world. Only by mastering distributed object skills now will you prepare yourself for the job market of the future.

FROM HERE

As you continue on your exploration of CORBA, the following chapters will prove interesting:

- Chapter 22, "CORBA Architecture"
- Chapter 28, "The Portable Object Adapter (POA)"
- Chapter 29, "Internet Inter-ORB Protocol (IIOP)"

CORBA ARCHITECTURE

IN THIS CHAPTER

Approximately 100 years ago, L. L. Zamenhof invented a natural language called *Esperanto*. Esperanto was developed not to replace the native tongue of any speaker but to be a common tongue shared between all speakers. Zamenhof realized that it was not possible for everyone to agree on a common native language, and also that asking most of the world to learn French, English, or Spanish as a second language would create barriers. Asking someone to learn a second language that's already the native tongue of an existing group of people puts one group at a disadvantage. Native speakers always have an edge over those who learn the language as a second language due to the many idiosyncrasies present in any language. In developing a common, easy-to-learn second language, Zamenhof saw a world where everyone continued to use their native tongues but used Esperanto for all multinational dealings.

Even though Esperanto was developed as a solution to a natural language crisis, it has many parallels in the software movements of today. There's not currently one perfect programming language for all problems but rather a collection of languages that all serve a unique purpose. Some of Java's biggest proponents argue that it's the best language for all development efforts, but as anyone who has developed advanced software—for example, medical imaging software—will tell you, Java is not a silver bullet. C, C++, Lisp, COBOL, Fortran, and many other languages all play important roles in modern computing and will not be replaced any time soon.

Because different programming languages all solve different problems, developers should be encouraged to take their pick of languages when solving a given problem. A single application will most likely need to solve many business problems, and chances are that the application will be best written in more than one language. For example, an application might need to search the Internet for weather data, store the data in a COBOL-based legacy system, and build some complex graphical representations of the data. The Internet surfing component could be easily implemented in Java, the legacy storage would have to be written in COBOL, and the graphical processing would likely be best written in C. These languages have few, if any, inherent constructs for interlanguage communication and would be best served by a new language that all could use as a common second language.

CORBA, as you learned in Chapter 21, "CORBA Overview," is a tool for enabling multi-language, multiplatform communication. Two important technologies, Interface Definition Language (IDL) and the Object Request Broker (ORB), facilitate this broad level of communication. The first technology, IDL, is the Esperanto of software. It's a language that allows for the description of a block of code without regard to its implementation language. The second technology, the ORB, acts as a highway over which all communication occurs. For example, a Java application to support fingering could expose a single method called `finger()` that accepts a username as a parameter. The function would be described in IDL, and any application wishing to finger a user would attach to the Java finger application, invoke its method, and obtain a return value. All this communication would occur across the ORB, which transparently manages most details associated with remote object communication.

> **NOTE**
>
> finger is a UNIX application that allows users to find information about other users.

In Chapter 21, we looked at CORBA from the perspective of a high-level manager who has probably not seen a line of code since COBOL was trendy. This high-level introduction is useful in that it provides a solid introduction to the technology, but it probably left you looking for a lot more. In this chapter, we'll dive under the hood and figure out exactly what makes the whole CORBA universe tick.

> **NOTE**
>
> The term *CORBA universe* is often used to encompass all entities that are used in CORBA development. This includes the ORB, BOA, and any other software developed for the OMA.

In digging around the CORBA universe, you'll learn the following topics:

- The technologies that form the CORBA universe
- How to describe an object in a language-independent fashion
- How to work around the shortcomings of IDL

As was stated earlier, CORBA exists due to two important technologies: IDL and the ORB. In this first section, we'll look at exactly how these two technologies allow CORBA development to occur as well as at some secondary technologies that aid in the process.

CORBA TECHNOLOGIES

At first glance, IDL looks somewhat like C++ or Java. This commonality is rooted in a desire to make learning the syntax rather easy, but you should note that IDL is *not* a programming language at all. There are constructs for describing method signatures, but absolutely no constructs for describing things such as flow control. IDL exists for one and only one purpose: to describe class functionality. As an example, let's return back to the earlier example of a finger application. Listing 22.1 contains the CORBA IDL used to describe that method. Note that nowhere in the code is any actual functionality present; rather, we only specify method parameters and return values.

LISTING 22.1   CORBA IDL DEFINING AN INTERFACE IMPLEMENTED BY AN OBJECT THAT SUPPORTS FINGERING

```
interface FingerServer {
    string finger(in string userName);
};
```

After documenting the functionality in IDL, we must write Java code to implement the functionality, and the two are to be distributed as a remote server. Before getting into the inner details of IDL and the ORB, we'll take a look at what's needed to turn the IDL in Listing 22.1 into a full application. If you don't understand everything at first, don't worry—by the time you finish this chapter, everything will make complete sense.

The IDL Compiler: Stubs and Skeletons

An important tool in the arsenal of any CORBA developer is an IDL compiler. The IDL compiler, as shown in Figure 22.1, accepts an IDL file as input and then writes out two important files: the stub and the skeleton. The stub file is given to the client as a tool to describe server functionality, and the skeleton file is implemented at the server. The two files are written using the programming languages in place at the client and the server. For example if the server is developed using Java, we need a Java skeleton; if the client is developed using C++, we need a C++ stub. There are mappings available from IDL to virtually every language out there, and the CORBA environment allows for clients and servers to be written in any combination of supported languages. What should be noted is that an ORB vendor does not need to support all available languages on all platforms. If you want to mix and match languages and platforms, you must find a vendor with a product that supports your project. Chapter 23, "Survey of CORBA ORBs," covers the languages and platforms supported by a number of different ORBs.

FIGURE 22.1

The IDL compiler turns IDL into stubs and skeletons.

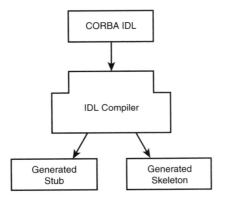

> **NOTE**
>
> A compiler is often thought of as the tool that turns a language such as C++ into a native executable; however, the term *compiler* actually applies to any translator. In this case, the IDL compiler acts as a software translator.

The stub and skeleton files, although special in terms of CORBA development, are perfectly standard files in terms of their target language. Each file exposes the same methods specified in the IDL; invoking a method on the stub file causes the method to be executed in the skeleton file. The fact that the stub file appears as a normal file in the client allows the client to manipulate the remote object with the same ease with which a local object is manipulated. In fact, until you begin to optimize remote object access to minimize network traffic, there's no need to even regard the remote object as anything special.

> **NOTE**
>
> Even though CORBA allows remote objects to masquerade as local objects, projects often end with a stage in which code is reworked to minimize the times that a remote object is accessed. Each time a remote object is accessed, network traffic is generated, and too many accesses can cause an application to become slow. Chapter 24, "A CORBA Server," and Chapter 25, "A CORBA Client," examine optimization to minimize network traffic.

Now that you fully understand what the output of the IDL compiler is, we'll generate
Java stubs and skeletons for the IDL in Listing 22.1. As with most development efforts in
this book, the code is generated using the Inprise Visibroker suite of CORBA tools. This
suite includes an ORB, an IDL compiler, and some advanced tools that will be covered
later in this chapter. The Inprise (formally Borland) suite of tools was chosen due to the
fact that, especially in the Java space, it's a market leader. Netscape has integrated the
client libraries into its browser, and many other major companies have announced support as well. The Inprise tool set came about as a result of Inprise's purchase of
Visigenic, a pioneer in the field of Java and CORBA development. If you haven't done
so already, take the time to install the Inprise software contained on the accompanying
CD-ROM.

The IDL compiler is invoked from the command line using the command `idl2java`
`fileName.idl`. Listing 22.2 contains the client stub, and Listing 22.3 contains the server
skeleton produced by running the code in Listing 22.1 through the IDL-to-Java compiler.
In this first example, the code is provided as a reference, but you'll usually not need to
pay too much attention to it. The skeleton file is usually extended and directly implemented, whereas the stub file is simply compiled with the client.

LISTING 22.2   THE STUB CLASS IS AUTOMATICALLY GENERATED BY THE IDL COMPILER

```
public class _st_FingerServer extends
           org.omg.CORBA.portable.ObjectImpl implements FingerServer {
    public java.lang.String[] _ids() {
       return __ids;
    }

    private static java.lang.String[] __ids = { "IDL:FingerServer:1.0" };

    public java.lang.String finger( java.lang.String userName) {
        try {   org.omg.CORBA.portable.OutputStream _output =
                    this._request("finger", true);
                _output.write_string(userName);
                org.omg.CORBA.portable.InputStream _input =
                    this._invoke(_output, null);
                java.lang.String _result;
                _result = _input.read_string();
                return _result;
        }
        catch( org.omg.CORBA.TRANSIENT _exception) {
            return finger(userName);
        }
    }
}
```

Listing 22.3 The Skeleton Class Is Automatically Generated by the IDL Compiler

```
abstract public class
_FingerServerImplBase extends org.omg.CORBA.portable.Skeleton
                    implements FingerServer {
    protected _FingerServerImplBase(java.lang.String name) {
        super(name);
    }

    protected _FingerServerImplBase() {
    }

    public java.lang.String[] _ids() {
        return __ids;
    }

    private static java.lang.String[] __ids = { "IDL:FingerServer:1.0"};

    public org.omg.CORBA.portable.MethodPointer[] _methods() {
        org.omg.CORBA.portable.MethodPointer[] methods =
            { new org.omg.CORBA.portable.MethodPointer("finger", 0, 0),};
        return methods;
    }

    public boolean_execute(org.omg.CORBA.portable.MethodPointer method,
                        org.omg.CORBA.portable.InputStream input,
                        org.omg.CORBA.portable.OutputStream output) {
        switch(method.interface_id) {
            case 0: {
            return _FingerServerImplBase._execute(this, method.method_id,
                                            input, output);
            }
        }
        throw new org.omg.CORBA.MARSHAL();
    }


public static boolean execute(FingerServer self, int_method_id,
                        org.omg.CORBA.portable.InputStream_input,
                        org.omg.CORBA.portable.OutputStream_output) {
        switch(_method_id) {
            case 0: {
            java.lang.String userName;
            userName = _input.read_string();
            java.lang.String _result = _self.finger(userName);
            _output.write_string(_result);
            return false;
            }
        }
        throw new org.omg.CORBA.MARSHAL();
    }
}
```

The next step after generating the stub and skeleton files is to actually implement server functionality by extending the skeleton. Listing 22.4 contains the code for the `FingerServerImplementation` class. Once you've looked it over, we'll step through it and figure out exactly what's happening.

LISTING 22.4 THE `FingerServerImplementation` CLASS

```
import java.io.*;
import org.omg.CORBA.*;

public class FingerServerImplementation extends _FingerServerImplBase {

    public FingerServerImplementation(String name) {
        super(name);
    }

    /**
     * Invoked by the client when a finger request
     * is issued.
     *
     * @param userName The user to be fingered
     * @return Any available data on the fingered user. If
     * an exception is raised during the finger process,
     * the phrase "exception occurred". If anything else
     * happens that keeps the application from functioning,
     * a "command not processed" message is returned.
     */
    public String finger(String userName) {
        // attempt to execute a finger command
        try{    Process returnValue =
                        Runtime.getRuntime().exec("finger "+userName);
                InputStream in = returnValue.getInputStream();
                StringBuffer sbReturnValue;
                int iValue = -1;
                while( (iValue = in.read()) != -1) {
                    System.out.print((char)iValue);
                }
                System.out.println(returnValue.exitValue());
        }
        catch(  Exception e ) { return "exception occurred"; }

        return "command not processed";
    }

    public static void main(String[] args) {
        // obtain references to the ORB and the BOA
        ORB orb = ORB.init();
        BOA boa = orb.BOA_init();
```

```
        // create a new FingerServerImplementation object
        FingerServerImplementation fingerServer =
                    new FingerServerImplementation("Finger Server");

        // notify the ORB that the
        // FingerServerImplementation object is ready
        boa.obj_is_ready(fingerServer);

        // wait for an incoming connection
        boa.impl_is_ready();
    }
}
```

22

CORBA
ARCHITECTURE

The first section of the FingerServerImplementation class that you want to pay attention to is the class signature. FingerServerImplementation is declared to extend FingerServerImplBase, which you'll remember from Listing 22.3 as the server skeleton. By extending the skeleton class, you provide an implementation for all public methods, but you also allow certain CORBA-specific tasks to be managed in the skeleton parent class itself.

Another important piece of the FingerServerImplementation class is the implementation of the finger() method. What's interesting about this method is that, even though it accepts a parameter from a remote object and also sends a return value back to that remote object, no CORBA-specific code is contained in it.

The final section of the FingerServerImplementation class that needs attention is the main() method. This method does contain CORBA-specific code and, later on in this chapter when we cover the ORB in detail, we'll address all CORBA-specific development. What you should note now about the main() method is that it first obtains a reference to the ORB and then creates a new FingerServerImplementation object and registers that object with the ORB. Finally, the application enters a wait state, where it simply waits for a client to invoke a method. This wait state is entered when the boa.impl_is_ready() method is executed and is only necessary in servers without a GUI. If the server has a GUI, the GUI keeps the server active until a request is issued.

To complete the exploration of this application, take a look at the client software contained in Listing 22.5. Stop for a minute, study the code, and pay specific attention to the manner in which remote objects are manipulated. Once we've interacted with the ORB to obtain a reference to the remote object, that object is manipulated in the same manner as a local object. If the application were written in a manner such that the client altered the state of the server object, that state would remain constant across all method invocations.

LISTING 22.5 A `FingerClient` OBJECT ISSUES `finger` REQUESTS AGAINST A REMOTE `FingerServer` OBJECT

```
import org.omg.CORBA.*;

/**
 * The FingerClient class binds to a FingerServer object
 * and attempts to finger a user.
 */
public class FingerClient {

    public static void main(String[] args) {
        // connect to the ORB
        ORB orb = ORB.init();
        // obtain a reference to a FingerServer object
        FingerServer fingerServer =
            FingerServerHelper.bind(orb, "Finger Server");
        // finger a user
        String sResult = fingerServer.finger("lukecd");
        // print out the results of the finger command
        System.out.println(sResult);
    }
}
```

To run these two applications, first install the Inprise Visibroker ORB software and launch the application called *OSAgent*. Depending on your hardware and the manner in which you performed the Visibroker install, this application may be set up as an NT Service or something that's launched from the command line. If the OSAgent is running an NT Service, it's likely already running. If you're running it from the command line, make sure it's in your system's PATH environment variable and then type

osagent

The OSAgent application is basically the ORB itself and must be running for the applications to function.

With the OSAgent active, first run the server by typing

java FingerServerImplementation

Now, open an alternate command window and type

java FingerClient

This launches the client software. The client software should bind to the server, finger the user "lukecd," and print out the results. If you're running the server on a machine that does not have finger installed, you should get back some error message. Assuming the command is successful, you'll obtain finger data on the user "lukecd." Note that the client will immediately exit after invoking operations on the server, but the server will remain running. When a CORBA server enters a wait loop by invoking `boa.impl_is_ready()`, that server stays active until it is quit.

For all the trepidation that you may have had entering into a CORBA development effort, you must admit that it's really not all that complicated. A lot of hype surrounds CORBA, but this does not mean things must get complicated. In just a few pages of code, you can develop a simple application!

Now that we've developed a simple application, we'll continue our exploration of CORBA technologies with a look at the ORB and the BOA.

The Object Request Broker (ORB) and the Basic Object Adapter (BOA)

As was stated earlier, the ORB is the highway over which all CORBA communication occurs. In the previous example, every time the `FingerClient` application invokes the `finger()` method on the remote `FingerServer` object, the ORB gets involved. All issues regarding interacting between the local and remote objects are managed completely by the ORB; this includes marshaling of method parameters and return values, along with object location management and any other nitty-gritty details.

22

CORBA
ARCHITECTURE

> **NOTE**
>
> The term *marshal* refers to the process when data formatted to be readable by one language or architecture is translated so that it's readable by a different one. This could be as simple as translating a C-style string into a Java-style string or as complicated as byte-order reversing.

Data marshaling is a process that happens automatically via the ORB, and other than knowing that it happens, you don't need to spend too much time thinking about it. The server also takes care of the issue of *object location management*, which is a great benefit to the developer. Object location management deals with locating remote objects when the client asks for them. In the client code in Listing 22.5, a reference to the remote object is obtained with the following line of code:

```
FingerServer fingerServer =
            FingerServerHelper.bind(orb, "Finger Server");
```

What's interesting about this method is that we don't ask for an object on a specific machine or IP address, but rather we ask the ORB for an object that implements the `FingerServer` interface and has the logical name "Finger Server." As you'll remember, when the server is started, the constructor passes the logical name "Finger Server" to its parent, thus telling the ORB that the server is named "Finger Server." The ORB matches up the request for an object with its internal registry of existing objects.

The fact that the ORB makes object location something that developers need not worry about means that the finger application previously developed could be run on more than one machine in the same fashion as it's run on one. Figure 22.2 depicts a common server architecture in a CORBA environment. The ORB is running on its own machine, the server is on another, and two instances of the client application are running on the other two machines.

FIGURE 22.2

A common architecture for a CORBA environment.

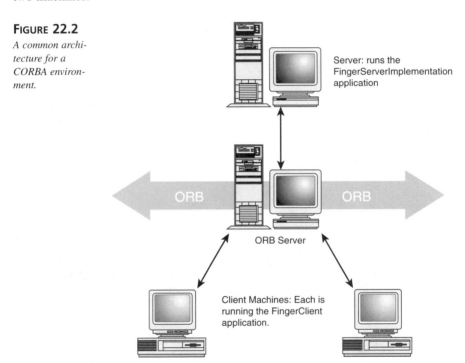

Server: runs the FingerServerImplementation application

ORB   ORB

ORB Server

Client Machines: Each is running the FingerClient application.

In addition to dealing with the ORB during your development efforts, you'll also deal with an entity called the *Basic Object Adapter* (or *BOA*). An Object Adapter, in general, defines how an object is activated into the CORBA universe. An Object Adapter is a required feature in a CORBA application because it manages communication with the ORB for many objects. Although any Object Adapter could be used, the CORBA specification defines the Basic Object Adapter, which must be provided by all vendors. The BOA is fully featured, and according to the Object Management Group (OMG), it "can be used for most ORB objects with conventional implementations." In Listing 22.4, the line of code `boa.obj_is_ready()` is invoked with a `FingerServer` object as a parameter, which asks the BOA to tell the ORB that the `FingerServer` object is ready to accept remote method invocations.

> **NOTE**
>
> Although the BOA is currently the desired Object Adapter, the CORBA 3.0 specification deprecated it in favor of the new *Portable Object Adapter* (or *POA*). The POA is covered in detail in Chapter 28, "The Portable Object Adapter (POA)."

Interacting with the ORB and BOA

To provide developer access to both the ORB and BOA, two important Java classes are presented. The first such class, `org.omg.CORBA.ORB`, represents the ORB singleton. Second, the class `org.omg.CORBA.BOA` is provided, which represents the BOA.

> **NOTE**
>
> The term *object singleton* refers to any object that has one and only one instance in a given environment. At any one point in time, regardless of the number of active clients and servers, there's only one ORB object.

The following lines of code highlight two important methods in the ORB class. The first method, `init()`, is a static method that obtains a reference to the ORB singleton. This method is overloaded to function in different environments, including those that require special parameters as well as situations in which the client is a Java applet. Due to certain security restrictions placed on the applet developer by the strict browser security model (often called the *security sandbox*), it's not always possible for the applet to connect to an ORB on any machine. In Chapter 25, we fully examine how the Inprise ORB allows applet clients to connect to the server.

The second method, highlighted at the bottom of this code, shows the two overloaded versions of the `BOA_init()` method. This method, invoked on the ORB, obtains a reference to the BOA. The following are the overloaded versions of the ORB class's `init()` method:

```
public static org.omg.CORBA.ORB init();
```

```
public static org.omg.CORBA.ORB init(java.lang.String[],
java.util.Properties);

public static org.omg.CORBA.ORB init(java.applet.Applet);

public static org.omg.CORBA.ORB init(java.applet.Applet,
java.util.Properties);

public org.omg.CORBA.BOA BOA_init();

public org.omg.CORBA.BOA BOA_init(java.lang.String, java.util.Properties);
```

Once a reference to the BOA has been obtained, it's used to facilitate communication with the ORB. These lines highlight four important BOA methods. The two versions of the obj_is_ready() method tell the ORB that the object parameter is ready to interact with remote clients. Before an object can be exported, this method must be called; otherwise, an error will occur.

The third method highlighted by this code is one that Java developers might not expect to see. deactivate_obj() accepts as a parameter an activated object and tells the ORB that the object parameter can no longer be used by remote clients. As Java developers, we're accustomed to not having to manage an object's life cycle, but once we enter into a distributed environment, it does become an issue. If you fail to deactivate all activated objects, the server will eventually enter an out-of-memory state. Chapters 24 and 25 spend significant time discussing how to best implement distributed memory management.

The fourth important method, impl_is_ready(), tells the ORB that the server is ready to accept client requests. In Listing 22.4, the FingerServer application invokes this method once it is fully ready to accept requests. The following is a list of important methods in the BOA class:

```
public abstract void obj_is_ready(org.omg.CORBA.Object);

public abstract void obj_is_ready(org.omg.CORBA.Object, java.lang.String,
byte[]);

public abstract void deactivate_obj(org.omg.CORBA.Object);

public abstract void impl_is_ready();
```

Although the ORB and BOA are, by far, not the only objects that you'll need to exist in the CORBA universe, they are the major ones. As you learn more about CORBA in these next few chapters, you'll learn about other objects that are supplied to aid CORBA development.

CORBA IDL AND THE CORBA OBJECT MODEL

In the previous section, we looked briefly at CORBA IDL, the language used to describe objects for remote access. In this next section, we examine IDL in detail—first by looking at each supported construct and its Java equivalent and then by looking at the shortcomings of the language.

IDL Constructs

As has been stated over and over, IDL allows developers to describe code such that virtually any programming language can understand it. The example of COBOL code invoking methods on a Java object is often used, but this example also implies that the COBOL application fully understands the methods exposed by the Java application. If the Java application has a method that returns a `java.awt.Image` object, the COBOL application must be able to fully understand that object. Unfortunately, it's not possible to wave a magic wand and magically have all legacy applications understand modern programming constructs. Many of those legacy applications were written before computers could even display any form of image. To allow all languages to intercommunicate, IDL allows lowest-common-denominator communication, which basically means that all methods must accept as parameters, and return as a return value, either a byte, some form of number, or a string. This, of course, does present some challenges to the developer, but there are possible workarounds. As a conclusion to this section, we'll look at an application that allows image data to be passed from client to server.

IDL Data Types

All communication with CORBA objects is performed using any of the data types supported by IDL. If some entity does not have a CORBA equivalent, it must be abstracted using one of the supported data types. Table 22.1 contains all data types, along with their Java equivalent. The only type that may not be familiar to you is the any data type. An any, as its name implies, is a holder class that can reference any entity in the CORBA universe.

TABLE 22.1 IDL-TO-JAVA MAPPING

IDL	Java
char	char
octet	byte
boolean	boolean
TRUE	true
FALSE	false
string	java.lang.String
short	short
long	int
float	float
double	double
any	CORBA.Any

module

Starting at the highest level, the first IDL construct that we examine is the module. The module, like its Java equivalent the package, allows for the logical grouping of entities. Listing 22.6 contains an IDL snippet that makes use of the module construct. Note that the construct starts with the keyword module and is immediately followed by the logical name associated with it. The entire module is delimited by curly braces, and a semicolon immediately follows the closing brace.

LISTING 22.6 THE IDL module CONSTRUCT MAPS TO THE JAVA PACKAGE CONSTRUCT

```
module userData {
        interface Person {
                string getName();
        };
};
```

If your application design calls for subpackages, the module should be placed inside of another module. Listing 22.7 contains an example that would map into the Java package org.luke.userData.

LISTING 22.6   USING SUBMODULES TO CREATE A MULTILEVEL PACKAGE STRUCTURE

```
module org {
        module luke {
                module userData {
                        interface Person {
                                string getName();
                        };
                };
        };
};
```

interface

As you may have guessed from the development we've done in this chapter, the `inter face` keyword maps to a Java `interface`. This should not be confused with mapping directly to a Java class, because it's quite possible that many Java classes might implement the interface defined by a single IDL interface or one Java class might implement many IDL interfaces. When the idl2java compiler compiles an IDL interface, the Java interface is named `interfaceNameOperations`. In most situations, you'll not deal directly with this interface. You simply extend the skeleton class, which in turn implements the `interfaceNameOperations` interface.

Interface inheritance is supported and, like much of IDL, uses syntax borrowed from C++. Listing 22.7 contains two interfaces, `ParentInterface` and `ChildInterface`, where `ChildInterface` inherits `ParentInterface`.

LISTING 22.7   INHERITANCE IN IDL USES A SYNTAX SIMILAR TO C++

```
interface ParentInterface {
        string parentMethod();
};
interface ChildInterface : ParentInterface {
        string childMethod();
};
```

Operations

An `interface` as a whole is comprised of a collection of operations. An *operation* maps directly into a Java *method*; however, an IDL operation signature is slightly more complicated. All parameters passed into an operation must be specified as either "in," "inout," or "out" parameters. This specification tells the ORB exactly how it needs to manage data as it travels from client to server, and potentially back again. Table 22.2 discusses how each of the modifiers function, and Listing 22.8 contains some IDL that uses each modifier.

22

CORBA ARCHITECTURE

In keeping with the goal of supporting the lowest-common-denominator programming language, there's no support for method overloading in IDL.

TABLE 22.2   IDL OPERATION MODIFIERS

Parameter Modifier	Function
in	Specifies a parameter that passes data into a method but is not changed by the method invocation
inout	Specifies a parameter that passes data into a method and is potentially changed during the method invocation
out	Specifies a parameter that does not pass data into the method but is potentially modified by the method execution

LISTING 22.8   PARAMETER MODIFIERS IN CORBA IDL

```
interface ParameterModifierExample {
        string getDataForIn(in string name);
        void getDataForInout(in string name, inout results);
        void getDataForOut(in string name, out results);
};
```

attribute

In addition to associating methods with an interface, it's also possible to specify an attribute exposed by the interface. An attribute maps to a private member variable, which is obtained using *getter* and *setter* methods. Listing 22.9 contains some IDL that makes use of the attribute keyword. The mapping of this IDL to Java is shown in Listing 22.10.

LISTING 22.9   ATTRIBUTES IN IDL ARE USED TO MODEL THE NONBEHAVIORAL ASPECTS OF AN OBJECT

```
interface AttributeDemo {
    attribute string attribute1;
    attribute long attribute2;
};
```

LISTING 22.10   IDL ATTRIBUTES MAP TO PRIVATE INSTANCE VARIABLES WITH PUBLIC
GETTER AND SETTER METHODS

```
public class AttributeDemoImplementation
        extends AttributeDemoImplBase {
    private String attribute1;
    private int attribute2;

    public String attribute1() {
        return attribute1;
    }

    public void attribute1(String attribute1) {
        this.attribute1 = attribute1;
    }

    public int attribute2() {
        return attribute2;
    }
    public void attribute2(int attribute2) {
        this.attribute2 = attribute2;
    }
}
```

struct

In addition to specifying CORBA entities using the `interface` keyword, it's also possible to specify an entity using the `struct` keyword. Although a `struct` may have little meaning to the Java developer, those of us with experience in C/C++ have an intimate understanding of its use. A `struct` is basically a collection of data that includes no behavior at all. A `struct` maps directly into a Java class with public member variables matching all `struct` attributes. Listing 22.11 contains a simple `struct` defined using IDL. Listing 22.12 contains the mapping of that `struct` into Java.

LISTING 22.11   THE struct CONSTRUCT IS USED TO CREATE ENTITY OBJECTS

```
struct StructDemo {
        string attribute1;
        string attribute2;
        long attribute3;
};
```

LISTING 22.12 AN IDL struct MAPS TO A CLASS WITH PUBLIC MEMBER VARIABLES

```
public class StructDemo {
        public String attribute1;
        public String attribute2;
        public int attribute3;
}
```

enum

The enum construct allows for the creation of enumerated data types. For example, if you have an `interface` called "rainbow," you might want to model each of its colors using a data type that can only take on a value of red, orange, yellow, green, blue, indigo, or violet. A CORBA enum maps to a Java class with `public final static int` member variables matching each element in the enumerated data type. Listing 22.13 contains the IDL for the rainbow example, and Listing 22.14 contains the Java code that maps to the color enum.

LISTING 22.13 ENUMERATED DATA TYPES ARE CREATED IN CORBA USING THE enum CONSTRUCT

```
enum Color {red, orange, yellow, green, blue, indigo, violet};
interface Rainbow {
    attribute Color color1;
    attribute Color color2;
    attribute Color color3;
    attribute Color color4;
    attribute Color color5;
};
```

LISTING 22.14 THE MAPPING OF AN IDL enum TO A JAVA CLASS

```
final public class Color {
    final public static int _red = 0;
    final public static int _orange = 1;
    final public static int _yellow = 2;
    final public static int _green = 3;
    final public static int _blue = 4;
    final public static int _indigo = 5;
    final public static int _violet = 6;
    final public static Color red = new Color(_red);
    final public static Color orange = new Color(_orange);
    final public static Color yellow = new Color(_yellow);
    final public static Color green = new Color(_green);
    final public static Color blue = new Color(_blue);
    final public static Color indigo = new Color(_indigo);
    final public static Color violet = new Color(_violet);
    private int __value;
```

```
    private Color(int value) {
        this.value = value;
    }

    public int value() {
        return __value;
    }

    public static Color from_int(int $value) {
        switch($value) {
        case _red : return red;
        case _orange : return orange;
        case _yellow : return yellow;
        case _green : return green;
        case _blue : return blue;
        case _indigo : return indigo;
        case _violet : return violet;
        default : throw new org.omg.CORBA.BAD_PARAM
                    ("Enum out of range: [0.." + (7 - 1) + "]: " + $value);
        }
    }

    public java.lang.String toString() {
        org.omg.CORBA.Any any = org.omg.CORBA.ORB.init().create_any();
        ColorHelper.insert(any, this);
        return any.toString();
    }
}
```

union

The IDL union construct allows for a single entity to store any one of many different data types. When the union is declared, all possible data types are listed, and during usage, it may take on one and only one at a single point in time. During its life cycle, the active data type may change. An IDL union maps into a Java class with getter and setter methods corresponding to each available data type. Listing 22.15 contains the IDL declaration for a simple union, and Listing 22.16 contains the generated Java code.

LISTING 22.15 A SIMPLE UNION IN IDL

```
enum Color {red, orange, yellow, green, blue, indigo, violet};

union ColorUnion switch (Color) {
    case red:long rgbValue;
    case orange:long rgbValue;
    case yellow:long rgbValue;
    case green:long rgbValue;
    default:boolean bNoColor;
};
```

LISTING 22.16 THE GENERATED JAVA CODE ASSOCIATED WITH THE IDL IN LISTING 22.15

```
final public class ColorUnion {

private .Object _object;
    private Color _disc;

    public ColorUnion() {
    }

    public Color discriminator() {
        return _disc;
    }

    public int rgbValue() {
        if(_disc != (Color) Color.red &&
           _disc != (Color) Color.orange &&
           _disc != (Color) Color.yellow &&
           _disc != (Color) Color.green &&
           true) {
            throw new org.omg.CORBA.BAD_OPERATION("rgbValue");
        }
        return ((.Integer) _object).intValue();
    }

    public boolean bNoColor() {
        if(_disc == (Color) Color.red ¦¦
           _disc == (Color) Color.orange ¦¦
           _disc == (Color) Color.yellow ¦¦
           _disc == (Color) Color.green ¦¦
           false) {
            throw new org.omg.CORBA.BAD_OPERATION("bNoColor");
        }
        return ((.Boolean) _object).booleanValue();
    }

    public void rgbValue(int value) {
        _disc = (Color) Color.red;
        _object = new .Integer(value);
    }

    public void rgbValue(Color disc, int value) {
        _disc = disc;
        _object = new .Integer(value);
    }

    public void bNoColor(Color disc, boolean value) {
        _disc = disc;
        _object = new .Boolean(value);
    }
```

```
    public .String toString() {
        org.omg.CORBA.Any any = org.omg.CORBA.ORB.init().create_any();
        ColorUnionHelper.insert(any, this);
        return any.toString();
    }
}
```

sequence and array

The IDL sequence and array data types are used to specify collections of elements. Both data types map to Java arrays. When declaring either a sequence or an array, you first declare it using the typedef keyword and then use it in context. Listing 22.17 demonstrates how each is used. Note that because the sequence and array data types map directly into Java arrays, no Java class is generated by the idl2java compiler for them.

LISTING 22.17   CREATING SEQUENTIAL COLLECTIONS OF INFORMATION USING THE sequence CONSTRUCT

```
typedef sequence<string> StringSequence;
typedef string StringArray[1013];

interface LotsOfStrings {
    attribute StringSequence StringCollection1;
    attribute StringArray StringCollection2;
};
```

exception

As Java developers, we're accustomed to programming in an environment that allows for the use of exceptions. Just as in Java, an IDL exception is raised when some exceptional situation occurs during the invocation of a method. For example, a server might expose a login() method that returns a reference to a now-logged-in user. If that login were to fail, the method could raise an exception that indicates the failed login. An IDL exception maps to a Java exception and is declared using the raises clause after the target method. Listing 22.18 contains the IDL for the login example.

LISTING 22.18   MODELING EXCEPTIONAL SITUATIONS USING THE exception CONSTRUCT

```
exception InvalidLoginException {
    string reason;
};

interface User {
    attribute string name;
```

continues

LISTING 22.18   CONTINUED

```
    attribute string password;
};

interface LoginServer {
    User loginUser(in string name, in string password)
        raises (InvalidLoginException);
}
```

HACKING IDL

When we began our exploration into the depths of IDL, we started with the disclaimer that it's geared to the lowest-common-denominator programming language. Stripping the advanced features present in many languages does allow wonderful things such as multi-language communication, but it also causes problems when developers want to work with features common in modern languages. Earlier in the chapter, we used the example of the two Java applications communicating using CORBA with the need of passing image data back and forth. Because it's not possible to declare a method using IDL that accepts a `java.awt.Image` object as a parameter, we must perform some tricky work to get everything to function properly. In this final section, we look at solving both the problem of passing `java.awt.Image` objects around the CORBA universe and the broader problem of IDL's shortcomings.

Working with Image Objects in the CORBA Universe

In looking at the problem of passing an `Image` object around the CORBA universe, one must break down the object into some smaller pieces that can be described in IDL. Looking at the properties that form an image, we arrive at an ordered collection of pixels, a height, and a width. With these three properties in mind, the IDL in Listing 22.19 can be used to describe an image.

LISTING 22.19   MODELING THE IMPORTANT ATTRIBUTES OF AN IMAGE IN IDL

```
typedef sequence<long> LongSequence;

interface IDLImageI {
    long getHeight();
    long getWidth();
    LongSequence getImageData();
};
```

Building on the IDL description of an image object, we design a CORBA application that can both create and display IDLImage objects. As with most CORBA applications, the effort is divided into two separate applications. A client application reads in a local image file, binds to a server application, and passes over the image data. The server application accepts the data, reads it in, and finally displays the image onscreen. This application is a great building block if you ever need to write CORBA applications that are charged with managing images. Building on the IDL in Listing 22.19, Listing 22.20 contains the full IDL for the application.

LISTING 22.20   THE FULL IDL FOR THE IMAGE SHARING APPLICATION

```
module imageConverter {
    typedef sequence<long> LongSequence;

    interface IDLImageI {
        long getHeight();
        long getWidth();
        LongSequence getImageData();
    };

    interface ImageServerI {
        void displayImage(in IDLImageI image);
    };

};
```

The Server Application

As is common in many client/server applications, we start development with the server. The server is composed of three classes that listen for incoming display requests and then parse and display the IDLImage objects. Listing 22.21 contains the code for the ImageServer class. This class is the implementation of the ImageServerI interface. It performs ORB registration and listens for client invocations of the displayImage() method.

LISTING 22.21   IMPLEMENTATION OF THE ImageServerI INTERFACE

```
import org.omg.CORBA.*;
import imageConverter.*;

/**
 * The ImageServer class is the server implementation
 * of the ImageServerI interface.
 */
public class ImageServer extends _ImageServerIImplBase {
```

continues

LISTING 22.21   CONTINUED

```
    private ImageServerGUI gui = null;

    public ImageServer() {
        super("Image Server");

        gui = new ImageServerGUI();
        gui.pack();
        gui.setVisible(true);
    }

    /**
     * Invoked when a client wishes to display
     * an image at the server
     */
    public void displayImage(IDLImageI idlImage) {
        gui.displayImage(idlImage);
    }

    public static void main(String[] args) {
        // obtain reference to ORB
        ORB orb = ORB.init();
        // obtain reference to BOA
        BOA boa = orb.BOA_init();
        // create a new ImageServer object
        ImageServer server = new ImageServer();
        // register the ImageServer object with the ORB
        boa.obj_is_ready(server);
        // wait for connections
        boa.impl_is_ready();

    }

}
```

The other two classes that form the server are charged with server GUI maintenance and image display. Listing 22.22 contains the code for the ImageServerGUI class, which is the GUI screen for the server. It has no widgets to accept user input, but it does display status messages indicating whether the server is waiting for or processing a request.

LISTING 22.22   THE UI FOR IMAGE SERVER

```
import java.awt.*;
import java.awt.image.*;
import imageConverter.*;

/**
```

```
 * The ImageServerGUI class is the GUI associated with
 * the ImageServer.
 */
public final class ImageServerGUI extends Frame {
    private Label    _lblStatus;

    public ImageServerGUI() {
        super("Image Server");
        setLayout(new FlowLayout());
        _lblStatus = new Label();
        setWait();
        add(_lblStatus);
    }

    private void setWait() {
        _lblStatus.setText("Waiting For An Image");
    }

    private void setProcessing() {
        _lblStatus.setText("Processing Image");
    }

    /**
     * Invoked when an image should be displayed
     */
    public void displayImage(IDLImageI idlImage) {
        setProcessing();
        // create an Image object using the parameters supplied
        // in the IDLImage object
        Image image =
            createImage(new MemoryImageSource(idlImage.getWidth(),
                                              idlImage.getHeight(),
                                              idlImage.getImageData(),
                                              0, idlImage.getWidth()));
        // display the image in its own frame
        Frame f = new Frame();
        f.setLayout(new FlowLayout());
        f.add(new ImagePanel(image));
        f.pack();
        f.setVisible(true);
        setWait();
    }
}
```

An additional class, ImagePanel, simply extends java.awt.Panel and facilitates the display of java.awt.Image objects. The ImagePanel class is contained in Listing 22.23.

LISTING 22.23 THE ImagePanel CLASS

```java
import java.awt.*;

/**
 * The ImagePanel class facilitates the display of
 * java.awt.Image objects.
 */
public class ImagePanel extends Panel {
    private Image image;

    public ImagePanel(Image image) {
        this.image = image;
    }

    public final void paint(Graphics g) {
        g.drawImage(image, 0, 0, this);
    }

    public final Dimension getMinimumSize() {
        return new Dimension
                (image.getWidth(this), image.getHeight(this));
    }

    public final Dimension getPreferredSize() {
        return new Dimension
                (image.getWidth(this), image.getHeight(this));
    }
}
```

The Client Application

Having built a server application that understands and displays images, we now build a client application. The client allows the user to select an image file from his hard drive and then request that the server display the image. Upon loading, the client binds to an `ImageServerI` object and then waits for user input.

In addition to the implementation of a client UI for the client application, there's also the `IDLImage` class, an implementation of the `IDLImageI` interface. This class holds a reference to a `java.awt.Image` object and makes available pixel, height, and width information. Listing 22.24 contains the code for the `IDLImage` class, and Listing 22.25 contains the `ImageClient` class, which is the client UI.

LISTING 22.24 THE CLASS USED TO MODEL A `java.awt.Image` OBJECT SO THAT IT CAN BE MANIPULATED BY REMOTE OBJECTS

```java
import java.awt.*;
import java.awt.image.*;
import imageConverter.*;

/**
 * Implementation of the IDLImageI interface
 */
public final class IDLImage extends _IDLImageIImplBase {
    private Image      _image;
    private int[]      _iImageData;
    private Component  _observer;
    private int        _iHeight;
    private int        _iWidth;

    public IDLImage(Image image, Component observer) {
        _image = image;
        _observer = observer;
        obtainImageData();
    }

    /*          methods defined in the IDL          */
    public int[] getImageData() {
        return _iImageData;
    }

    public int getHeight() {
        return _iHeight;
    }

    public int getWidth() {
        return _iWidth;
    }

    /**
     * Obtains all needed data on the Image object
     */
    private void obtainImageData() {
        try{    MediaTracker track = new MediaTracker(_observer);
                track.addImage(_image, 0);
                track.waitForAll();
        }
        catch(  Exception e ) { System.out.println("error at load: "+e); }

        _iHeight = _image.getHeight(_observer);
        _iWidth = _image.getWidth(_observer);

        _iImageData = new int[_iWidth * _iHeight];
        PixelGrabber grabber = new PixelGrabber
```

continues

LISTING 22.24   CONTINUED

```
                                  (_image, 0, 0, _iWidth,
                                  _iHeight, _iImageData, 0, _iWidth);
        try {   grabber.grabPixels();   }
        catch (InterruptedException e) {
            System.err.println("interrupted waiting for pixels!");
            return;
        }
        if ((grabber.getStatus() & ImageObserver.ABORT) != 0) {
            System.err.println("image fetch aborted or errored");
            return;
        }
    }
}
```

LISTING 22.25   AN ImageClient OBJECT READS IN GIF OR JPEG FILES AND REQUESTS THAT A REMOTE SERVER DISPLAY THEM

```
import java.awt.*;
import java.awt.event.*;
import org.omg.CORBA.*;
import imageConverter.*;


public final class ImageClient extends Frame
                               implements ActionListener {
    private Image           _imageActive = null;
    private ImageServerI    _imageServer = null;
    private BOA             _boa = null;
    private Button          _buttonLoad = null;
    private Button          _buttonSendToServer = null;
    private Label           _lblImageActive;

    public ImageClient() {
        doBind();
        buildScreen();
    }

    /**
     * Binds to the ORB, and obtains references to the
     * BOA and ImageServer objects.
     */
    private void doBind() {
        ORB orb = ORB.init();
        _boa = orb.BOA_init();
        _imageServer = ImageServerIHelper.bind(orb, "Image Server");
    }

    /**
```

```
 * Builds the GUI
 */
private void buildScreen() {
    setLayout(new GridLayout(2,2,10,10));
    add(new Label("Active Image"));
    add(_lblImageActive = new Label("None Selected"));
    add(_buttonLoad = new Button("Load Image"));
    add(_buttonSendToServer = new Button("Send Image To Server"));

    _buttonLoad.addActionListener(this);
    _buttonSendToServer.addActionListener(this);
}

/**
 * Invoked when a Button object is clicked
 */
public void actionPerformed(ActionEvent ae) {
    java.lang.Object target = ae.getSource();
    if(target == _buttonLoad) doLoad();
    else sendImageToServer();
}

/**
 * Prompts the user to load an image, and if a proper file
 * is selected, reads in that image
 */
private final void doLoad() {
    FileDialog dlgOpen =
            new FileDialog(this, "Choose An Image", FileDialog.LOAD);
    dlgOpen.setVisible(true);

    if(dlgOpen.getFile() == null) return;
    StringBuffer bufFile = new StringBuffer();
    bufFile.append(dlgOpen.getDirectory());
    bufFile.append(dlgOpen.getFile());

    String sFile = dlgOpen.getFile();
    if(isValid(sFile)) {
        Image image = null;
        try{    String sFileName =
                        sFile.substring(0, sFile.indexOf('.'));
                image = getToolkit().getImage(bufFile.toString());
                _lblImageActive.setText(sFile);
        }
        catch(  Exception e ) { System.out.println; };
        _imageActive = image;
    }
}

/**
 * Determines if the user has selects a valid image
 *
```

continues

22

CORBA
ARCHITECTURE

LISTING 22.25 CONTINUED

```
 * @return true If the file name ends with gif, jpg, or jpeg
 * @return false If the true condition is not satisfied
 */
private boolean isValid(String name) {
    String extension =
        name.substring(name.indexOf('.')+1, name.length());
    if(extension.equalsIgnoreCase("gif")) return true;
    if(extension.equalsIgnoreCase("jpg")) return true;
    if(extension.equalsIgnoreCase("jpeg")) return true;
    return false;
}

/**
 * Creates an IDLImage object and asks that
 * the server display it
 */
private void sendImageToServer() {
    if(_imageServer == null) return;
    IDLImageI idlImage = new IDLImage(_imageActive, this);
    _boa.obj_is_ready(idlImage);
    _imageServer.displayImage(idlImage);
}

public static void main(String[] args) {
    ImageClient client = new ImageClient();
    client.pack();
    client.setVisible(true);
}
}
```

PUTTING IT ALL TOGETHER

Now that you've gone over the code, you need to enter it all in, compile the IDL, and then compile the application. To run the application, first start the OSAgent (Inprise Visibroker ORB), then launch the server and finally the client. You should be able to load in images at the client and force the server to display them. If you have access to a LAN, try running the client and server on different machines.

As was shown in the simple image manipulation example, the shortcomings of IDL can be worked around. Moving a complex object to IDL means breaking it down into smaller pieces and then shipping those pieces through the ORB. As long as both the client and server know how to break apart and reassemble the object, you'll have no problems.

FROM HERE

In this chapter, you learned a lot about what makes CORBA tick. We looked under the hood at the ORB, the BOA, and at IDL. As we further explore CORBA in the next few chapters, your understanding will move from knowledge of syntax and basic workings to an evolved understanding of how to build CORBA applications.

The following chapters complement the material covered in this chapter:

- Chapter 24, "A CORBA Server"
- Chapter 25, "A CORBA Client"
- Chapter 26, "CORBA-Based Implementation of the Airline Reservation System"

22

CORBA ARCHITECTURE

SURVEY OF CORBA ORBS

IN THIS CHAPTER

When shopping for clothing, two individuals will rarely find that an identical item fits one as well as it fits another. What's more, there may be abstract features of a clothing item that appeals to one of shoppers, but if it does not fit the needs defined by his or her body shape, chances are it will sit in the back of the closet forever. Even though it's not as much fun as shopping for clothing, shopping for an ORB does involve similar concerns. No two ORB vendors provide the same solution, and no one implementation is best for all environments. Even though all ORBs conform to a common standard, different vendors have decided to tailor their Object Request Broker (ORB) such that its market is well defined. When making a purchase, one must take the time to identify the optimal vendor.

CORBA coverage to this point in the book has made use of the Inprise Visibroker ORB. The Visibroker ORB, originally developed by Visigenic (Visigenic was acquired by Borland, which then changed its name to Inprise), is in use by millions of customers all over the world, including Oracle and Netscape. The ORB was chosen for inclusion in this book due to the fact that it has solid support for Java on the NT and Solaris platforms, as well as wide industry acceptance. If the focus of this book were developing COBOL-based CORBA solutions on VMS, another ORB would have been selected. This chapter looks at the concerns facing CORBA developers, not when producing a CORBA solution, but when deciding which ORB to use. In addition, this chapter looks at two development tools that make developing CORBA applications much easier.

Specifically, the following points are addressed in this chapter:

- Why ORBs differ
- What to look for in an ORB
- How Rational Rose helps with application design
- How the SNiFF+ development environment makes development easier

WHY ORBS DIFFER

Given the fact that all ORBs implement a common specification, it's easy to think there's no difference between ORBs from competing vendors. Unfortunately, due to both the evolving nature of the CORBA specification (see Chapter 21, "CORBA Overview") and its shear breadth, vendors often have very different products.

The first issue of the evolving CORBA specification is one that has the potential to cause great confusion. The CORBA specification currently stands at version 2.3 and is considered to be rather rich in features. This level of richness has not always been present, and without certain pieces of the specification complete, vendors have been in a bit of a quandary. If, for example, a certain feature has yet to be added to the CORBA specification but a vendor is facing client demand, the vendor is likely to implement the feature in a proprietary fashion in order to please the client. As is to be expected, vendors often make decisions based on where the money is, which leads to vendors implementing proprietary solutions. Vendors taking this level of initiative is good because it tends to feed the development of an Object Management Group (OMG) specification, but it also presents problems if their versions differ from the eventual OMG specification. This was seen early on when vendors wanted to release an ORB that supported Java before the OMG was finished with the Java-to-Interface Definition Language (IDL) mapping. What ended up happening was that vendors created their own mappings, submitted them to the OMG to be the Java-to-IDL specification, and sold the ORB software that supported their mapping. Up until the point of the OMG releasing the final specification, there were two different mappings in use by a variety of vendors. After the OMG released the specification, all vendors had to modify their products to support the new mapping. This also had the unfortunate downside of causing all developers to modify their applications accordingly.

CHOOSING AN ORB

When deciding on an ORB, there are a lot of concerns you'll want to keep in mind. Each and every application you develop has certain needs, and the correct ORB should meet each and every one of those needs. The following list takes a look at some topics you want to consider when choosing an ORB:

- Platform choice
- Language bindings
- Available CORBAservices
- Available CORBAfacilities
- Available CORBAdomains
- Core competency within an organization
- Features beyond those contained in the CORBA specification
- Availability of third-party components
- Cost

Starting at the top of the list, the two features that will likely narrow down the number of available choices with greatest ease are *platform choice* and *language bindings*. The other items can often be worked around if missing, but support for your implementation language(s) and platform(s) is crucial. If your developers are all seasoned Java developers and your IS department only supports Solaris servers, you must choose an ORB with Java and Solaris support.

Moving further down the list, CORBAservices, CORBAfacilities, and CORBAdomains are items that can significantly reduce your development time. As Chapter 21 discusses, CORBAservices, CORBAfacilities, and CORBAdomains are plugged into your application to provide some level of functionality that you would otherwise have to write yourself. As you design an application, check to see if any of its features overlap with features implemented by a CORBAservice, CORBAfacility, or CORBAdomain. If there's an overlap, you'll want to look for an implementation of that entity that fits in with the ORB you're looking at.

Core competency within an organization looks not at a feature of the product but rather at the level of skill your developers have with the target ORB. Although similar, all ORBs have idiosyncrasies that can be exploited to achieve superior performance. If your staff really understands the ORB from a certain vendor, the cost of training them for an alternate ORB should be a consideration.

Features beyond those contained in the CORBA specification should also be considered. In addition to looking at the development time saved by available CORBAservices, CORBAfacilities, and CORBAdomains, you should also look at the potential time-savings with other additions to the CORBA environment. If a vendor has extended the features of the target ORB to perform some task that, although beyond the CORBA specification, is of need to you, this product should be considered. For example, many vendors offer support for tunneling through a firewall. If your application involves a client applet outside of a firewall and a server application behind the firewall, this tunneling feature will save you a lot of development time. Development time can be further saved if a third-party vendor releases an application that works with a target ORB to add needed functionality. In general, all five of the add-on functionality considerations are something that will potentially increase your time to market. Each represents code that will not have to be written by your staff but instead will be purchased and integrated into your product.

One thing to note when integrating third-party components, such as CORBAservices, CORBAfacilities, or CORBAdomains, is that the component really is a good fit. If you have to do more work integrating the component than you save by not writing the purchased code, you're better off to simply write the code yourself.

A final consideration that helps when deciding on an ORB is, unfortunately, cost. Regardless of the number of problems the ORB solves, if you cannot get approval to purchase it, it cannot be considered. Fortunately, if an ORB is significantly more expensive, this is often due to a large number of features. If you can prove to management that purchasing the features is actually less expensive than paying salaries to develop them in-house, your chances of getting the expensive ORB purchased are increased. What should be noted when talking about cost is that some free ORBs are available. Usually these ORBs are not as fast or as rich in features as the ones that cost money, but they might help you to sneak CORBA into an organization.

COMPARING ORB PRODUCTS

As a tool to help in choosing an ORB, Table 23.1 presents a comparison of a variety of ORBs. Note that one obvious omission is ORB price. In general, ORBs do not have a basic price and availability at Egghead software. The ORB pricing structure is usually something that is haggled out between vendor and client, and it depends on topics such as reselling, number of users, and number of servers.

TABLE 23.1 AN ORB COMPARISON CHART

Vendor	Product	Platforms	Languages	CORBAservices	Notes
Inprise (INPR) http://www.inprise.com	Visibroker	Windows Solaris IRIX AIX HP-UX Digital UNIX	Java C++	Event Naming	Client code is freely distributed with the Netscape Navigator browser.
Iona http://www.iona.com	Orbix	Solaris HP/UX IRIX AIX Digital Alpha/Open MVS Sequent DYNIX/ptx Windows MVS VXWorks		Naming Trader Event Security	Includes COM/ Also includes software used when integrating with object databases.
Expersoft http://www.expersoft.com/	CORBAplus	Windows HP-UX Solaris AIX DEC UNIX	Java C++	Transaction	Also includes a CORBA/ COM bridge.
Peerlogic http://www.peerlogic.com	DAIS	Windows Solaris Open VMS HP/UX	C C++ Java Eiffel	Security Event Transaction	Also includes support for COM.
Gerald Brose http://www.inf.fu-berlin.de/~brose/jacorb/	JacORB	Any with a 1.1 version of the JDK	Java	Naming Event	Written in Java, and is freely available.

CORBA DEVELOPMENT TOOLS

This chapter started out with an exploration of competing ORBs, which will help you when making a decision about the ORB that will be deployed in your enterprise. In this section, we look at two development tools that will aid in the application development process.

These products are complementary and help the application design process all the way from the initial design stages up to the final debugging process:

- Rational Rose (http://www.Rational.com)
- SNiFF+ (http://www.TakeFive.com)

Rational Rose

The first product we examine is Rational Rose from Rational software. Rational Rose is a visual modeling tool that uses a variety of modeling languages to model applications from initial requirements right down to the final deliverable. This broad scope of functionality is actually rather impressive, and although all features do not apply specifically to CORBA, each of these features does aid the application development process. As we examine Rose, we first take a high-level look at each of its features and then dive into the CORBA-specific aspects of the tool.

As was earlier stated, Rose is used to fully model the lifecycle of an application. The tool allows models to be built using the UML, Booch notation, or ,OMT.

> **Note**
>
> The UML, OMT, and Booch notation are all languages that allow for modeling all aspects of the application development process. Because it's becoming the de facto industry standard, the UML is used throughout this book. For more information, flip back to Chapter 3, "Object-Oriented Analysis and Design," and Chapter 6, "The Airline Reservation System Model."

Once launched, Rose presents a screen similar to what's shown in Figure 23.1. A workspace is shown on the right side of the screen, and a component browser is shown along the left side.

Figure 23.1

*The Rational Rose
default window,
Use-Case view.*

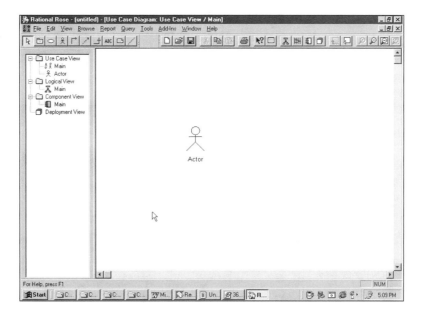

Looking at the component browser, you'll note that there are four views into an application that are developed during the modeling process. The first view (and the one active in Figure 23.1) is the *Use-Case view*. In this view, you add the actors, use-cases, packages, and associated relationships that model what the system is supposed to do. In addition to containing actors and individual use-cases, the Use-Case view also contains any number of individual diagrams. If your application is modeled using a lot of use-cases, you may want to call out various relationships for inclusion in their own diagram.

Moving further down the component browser window, the next section you encounter is the *Logical view*. Inside of the Logical view, you actually model the individual classes that are to form the system. Figure 23.2 shows a class created with Rose that models a stock.

FIGURE **23.2**

*The Rational Rose
default window's
Logical view.*

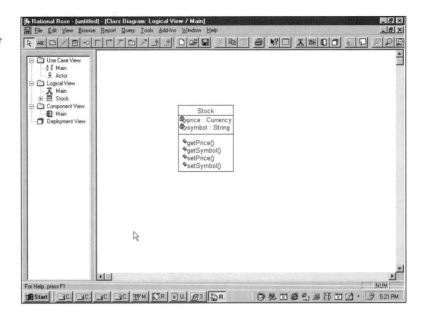

According to the diagram, the Stock class contains two private attributes (price and symbol) and publishes four public *getter* and *setter* methods. In addition to modeling classes in the Logical view, you may also model class relationships, package structure, and descriptive notes. Like the Use-Case view, the Logical view may also contain any number of diagrams. A good rule of thumb to follow when building diagrams is that if you need to scroll your screen to understand what's being depicted, the diagram is a candidate for being broken down into smaller pieces. Computer-based modeling tools are meant to replace paper, and if you need to print out your diagram, tape together a collection of pages, and hang them on the wall, you are taking one large step backwards.

Moving beyond the Logical view, the next level of modeling performed is the *Component view*. This level acts to aggregate the different classes that form your system into logical components. For example, you might move all classes charged with database access into a data access component and then move all classes charged with object-to-relational mapping in a translation component. In general, a component is a tool that facilitates logical grouping of entities in an application.

The final level of modeling provided by Rose is the *Deployment view*. In this view, you physically model the hardware architecture upon which the application runs. This level of modeling is especially important in *n*-tier applications, because the fact that certain pieces may need a dedicated machine needs to be documented. As an example, consider an application server. Under such an application, processor- or memory-insensitive pieces such as object caches or object-to-relational translators will likely need a dedicated machine. On the other hand, pieces such as an asynchronous audit trail service could easily share access to a machine.

With this overview of how Rose aids the application development process, let's return to the manner in which it specifically aids CORBA applications. As you may imagine, one of the least enjoyable aspects of developing a CORBA application is synchronizing the IDL files with their implementation files. Although well-designed systems generally produce a design that leads to classes that require few changes to the public methods, experience shows that change is inevitable. As you work with the classes that form your application, oversights in the initial design become apparent. Unfortunately, no matter how much you may examine the different classes and their relationships, snafus always manage to rear their ugly heads.

To help keep your IDL files synchronized with their implementation classes, and consequently the UML model itself, Rose can automatically generate both the Java skeleton and CORBA IDL file for every class in the logical model. Because you'll be actually working with the Java files produced, Rose fully supports round-trip engineering, thus ensuring the safety of your code. Unfortunately, the current version of Rose does have some shortcomings when it comes to the automatic generation of IDL and Java files due to the manner in which data types are handled. When you create a class in Rose, the data type of all method parameters, return values, and attributes must be specified. Because the UML has no native data types, you must enter in language-specific data types as the model is built. Chances are you can probably guess where this issue is headed. Because the IDL and Java have different names for basic data types (string vs. String, for example), the same model cannot be easily used to produce both IDL and Java files. The addition of an automatic data type translation function to Rose would be a boon to development, but for now there are alternatives.

NOTE

Round-trip engineering is a term used to describe the process of creating a visual model, generating code from it, making changes to the code, and finally having those changes reflected in the visual model. Support for round-trip engineering in a tool is a big plus because it eases the process of synchronizing the model with the code.

I recently used Rose to model a piece of software used in healthcare that contained well over 200 classes. We decided that Rose would be used to contain the model and that we would use IDL data types when modeling a class that was to be exposed in the CORBA environment. We then used the Inprise idl2java compiler to produce the Java skeleton files. Classes that were internal to the application did not utilize IDL data types but instead used Java data types, thus allowing for Java skeletons to be generated directly from the model. Only generating IDL from certain files is actually a relatively easy process due to the fact that Rose permits certain classes to have their IDL generation globally suppressed. Once we had ironed out the kinks, the code generation worked out well.

SNiFF+

SNiFF+ from TakeFive Software is a development environment for projects developed using C, C++, Fortran, Java, and CORBA IDL. In this study, we examine the Java and IDL features, but if you're developing cross-language applications, note that support is provided. In addition to support for a variety of languages, SNiFF+ is available for virtually every operating system. At present, the list of supported operating systems includes Windows, Solaris, SunOS, HP/UX, AIX, Digital UNIX, Irix, SCO UNIX, SNI Sinix, and Linux.

Before we dive into specifics on the SNiFF+ feature-set, it should be noted that simply calling SNiFF+ a "development environment" understates it capabilities. SNiFF+ is over-flowing with all kinds of features that make the process of developing enterprise servers much easier.

In the general Java/CORBA development tool market, many vendors attempt to differentiate their offerings with features such as GUI builders and other such items that benefit the client developer. Although these features may make someone's job easier, they are of little concern to the server developer. At the server, we face issues including thread management, sharing code between large groups of developers, application design management, and versioning. This is especially true in thin-client environments where the client is simply a thin access layer into a complex server that maintains all business logic. In fact, in many such environments, the client may be designed by a collection of UI designers but is likely coded by only one or two. In comparison, 5 to 50 (or more) developers may develop the server. Situations like these call for a tool set that allows server engineers to not only easily understand their own work but to also easily understand the work performed by other members in the team. If you're changing the signature of a public method, it's critical that you instantly know every other line of code that invokes the public method. In applications with only a handful of classes, it's easy to simply build the application and see where it fails. If that build is going to take over five minutes, you need a much faster route to the answer.

SNiFF+ targets the server developer with a collection of features that can save many hours during the initial development process as well as help prevent bugs sneaking into the code, thus shortening the alpha-to-release cycle. Specifically, the following features are made available to the developer:

- Code analysis
- Code editing
- Build execution
- Debugging
- Version management

When you initially load SNiFF+, the first task performed is to create a new project. The project consists of a collection of source files, along with various other files generated automatically by SNiFF+. A given project can contain files implemented in different languages (for example, Java and IDL), and the project browser actively supports simultaneous projects. Figure 23.3 shows a SNiFF+ project window that contains the server code you'll develop in Chapter 24, "A CORBA Server."

FIGURE 23.3

The SNiFF+ project manager.

Once you've created a new project in SNiFF+, you have a variety of different steps you can take. Assuming you're beginning a new project, you may add new source files and take them through the full edit/compile/debug cycle. Let's step through the manner in which these features are implemented. We'll begin with an existing project and look at the manner in which SNiFF+ exploits its feature-set.

Starting with the code analysis functions, SNiFF+ provides a variety of functions that allow for code visualization. In general, code visualization is a pretty broad topic that could potentially include any number of features. Within the SNiFF+ environment, this feature-set has been defined to include the following features:

- Symbol locating
- Hierarchy browsing
- Difference checking

Symbol locating involves locating all lines of code in a project where a given symbol (method, variable, and so on) is referenced. This function is most useful when you need to calculate the impact on a project of a change to a public method. Whenever a public method encounters a signature change, all locations in the application that invoke the method must be updated. In large group projects, the public methods exposed by a class you develop might very well be utilized by any number of classes you did not develop. Figure 23.4 shows SNiFF+ displaying what's called a method *refers-to relationship*. A refers-to relationship displays all the locations in the active project where a given method is invoked. Automatically calculating this relationship is very important because it allows developers to see the impact of a method change on the project as a whole. In addition to calculating this relationship for methods, SNiFF+ has the ability to calculate the relationship for classes, interfaces, and variables.

FIGURE 23.4

Checking refers-to relationships with SNiFF+.

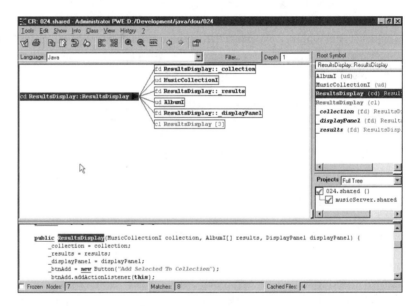

Hierarchy browsing provides a visual representation of the class hierarchy present in a given project. All classes and interfaces are shown, with lines connecting child classes to their parents. As shown in Figure 23.5, SNiFF+ enhances this view by using different symbols to represent different types of classes and interfaces. Classes are shown as rectangles, interfaces as rectangles with rounded corners (such as `MusicCollectionI` and `MusicServerI`), abstract classes as blue rectangles, and so on.

FIGURE 23.5

Visualizing class hierarchy with SNiFF+.

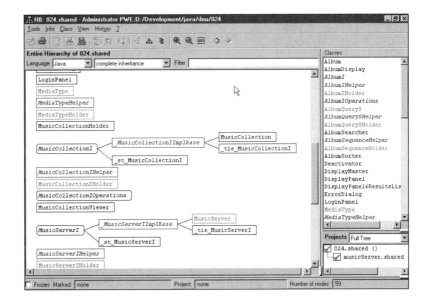

Now, let's move on to *difference checking*. SNiFF+ has the ability to take two versions of the same file or two different files and locate all points where they are different. This is a very useful feature due to the fact that with large applications, it's often hard to remember the exact locations where changes were made. When checking a source file back into a version control system, it's customary to add comments describing the changes you made. Through the use of the difference-checking tool, you can rapidly locate the changes you made. In addition, the tool is useful when more than one person is working on a single file. If, for example, the IDL files for a single project are maintained by more than one person, it's very useful to be able to rapidly locate positions in those files altered by other developers.

Next, let's move from code analysis to *code editing*. SNiFF+ provides a fully featured source code editor. The editor, shown in Figure 23.6, displays the active source file along the left and center of the screen, with a listing of all methods along the right side of the screen. At any point in time, a method name can be clicked to jump immediately to its location in the source code. Although the editor does alter the text color of keywords and comments, it does not perform this change in real time. Both the updates to the text display color and the list of active methods is updated when the file is saved. One especially nice feature of the editor—sadly missing in many competing editors—is the ability to double-click a curly brace and have the code between the target brace and its pair highlighted.

23

SURVEY OF CORBA ORBs

FIGURE 23.6

*The SNiFF+
source code editor.*

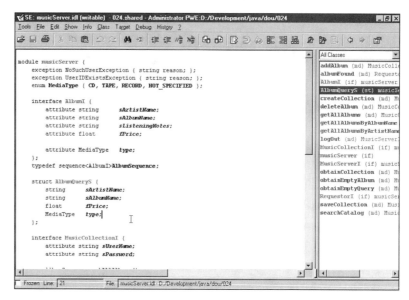

In addition, the code editor provides the ability to—with just one click—comment or uncomment a series of lines, adjust the tabs applied against a series of lines, and interact with the other tools exposed by SNiFF+. For example, you can highlight a method name, right-click it, and instantly see all the other files that invoke the method. Due to the manner in which IDL files map to Java files, this allows you to browse your IDL file and determine all Java files that invoke a given operation.

A project is generally of minimal use if it cannot be compiled; for this reason, SNiFF+ contains full support for the execution of builds. Builds executed in SNiFF+ are performed with the aid of a make file, and either individual files or whole projects can be compiled at the touch of a button. For those of you who (like myself) have not touched a make file since those days in college when professors refused to admit that any development tool other than vi, cc, and make exist, don't fear. SNiFF+ does automatically generate the make file for you (note that this file may be manually edited if needed). In the time I have used the tool, I have never once had to modify the make file at all. There's a project settings GUI through which you set attributes such as your class path and output directory, and SNiFF+ takes care of folding these values into the make file. Of course, if you feel like diving in yourself, the make file is yours to edit.

The next SNiFF+ feature we explore is the *debugger*, used during the phase enjoyed by only the most hardcore developers. Like most modern debugging applications, the SNiFF+ debugger is operated from a GUI and contains the ability to set breakpoints, watch variables, track changes, and to examine the status of multiple concurrent threads.

The ability to track threads is one of the more powerful features that server developers will likely need to take advantage of. If, for example, you allocate a new thread to each incoming connection and those threads access common data, you'll want to track that they do not corrupt any other views into the same information.

Finally, we arrive at the *version management* features present in SNiFF+. SNiFF+ is fully integrated with the ClearCase, PVCS, and RCS version control applications. From within the editor, you have the ability to perform the check in, check out, and rollback functions exposed by the underlying version control system. An individual project is tied to no more than one version control system, and this setting may be changed at any point in time.

Having used a wide variety of Java and CORBA development environments over the past few years, I'm rather happy to note that SNiFF+ is one of the best systems I have ever encountered. It's obviously not for the client developer, but as a server developer, it's great to find a tool that appeals directly to my needs. The ability to deal with multiple languages is also a boon, because with CORBA applications, one always deals with Java and IDL, and any legacy integration will likely need C or C++. Not having to switch between Visual C++ and Symantec Café helps to speed up development cycles.

As a side note, if for any reason you prefer some aspect of another tool to SNiFF+ (perhaps you want to use vi for an editor), SNiFF+ is completely configurable. You can easily integrate your preferred tool.

FROM HERE

In this chapter, we looked at a collection of different ORBs on the market, as well as two development tools that you'll want to consider taking advantage of in your development efforts. Rational Rose presents an industry-standard manner to take applications through their life cycles, and it helps to cut down on the code you have to write via its code generation tools. SNiFF+ helps you out once you start writing code with advanced visualization tools as well as great debugging and editing utilities.

This chapter is slightly different from the other CORBA chapters, because it focuses on the tool rather than the technology side of the development process. Although tools are important, they are useless if you do not understand the technology they benefit. As you spend time with the rest of this book, the following chapters will expand on your knowledge of the technology that makes CORBA work:

- Chapter 22, "CORBA Architecture"
- Chapter 24, "A CORBA Server"
- Chapter 25, "A CORBA Client"

23

SURVEY OF
CORBA ORBs

A CORBA SERVER

IN THIS CHAPTER

The term *client/server* is applied to applications that exist as at least two components. A server application is often more powerful and is charged with tasks such as execution of business rules and database access. The client application often interacts with human users and presents an interface through which the server is accessed. CORBA applications are client/server in the true sense of the term; however, an application's role as client or server often changes during that application's lifecycle. CORBA applications are made up of distributed objects, all of which can communicate during an application's existence.

This chapter looks at CORBA's role as a client/server–enabling technology and implements a fully featured server application. This application differs from the other sample servers developed in this book, because it does not demonstrate a single technology but rather demonstrates how to build a production-grade server. The application is fully multiuser, includes support for garbage collection, and, as an added bonus, demonstrates the callback design pattern from Chapter 5, "Design Patterns." A client for this application is developed in Chapter 25, "A CORBA Client."

APPLICATION DESIGN

The application developed in this chapter allows for the management of a collection of music CDs, records, and cassettes. The client developed in the following chapter is an applet and uses the server to store all information pertaining to an individual's collection. The IDL exposed by the server is contained in Listing 24.1.

LISTING 24.1 THE IDL FOR THE MUSIC SERVER APPLICATION

```
module musicServer {
    exception NoSuchUserException { string reason; };
    exception UserIDExistsException { string reason; };
    enum MediaType { CD, TAPE, RECORD, NOT_SPECIFIED };

    interface AlbumI {
        attribute string      sArtistName;
        attribute string      sAlbumName;
        attribute string      sListeningNotes;
        attribute float       fPrice;

        attribute MediaType   type;
    };
    typedef sequence<AlbumI>AlbumSequence;

    struct AlbumQueryS {
        string      sArtistName;
        string      sAlbumName;
        float       fPrice;
```

```
            MediaType    type;
        };

        interface MusicCollectionI {
            attribute string sUserName;
            attribute string sPassword;

            AlbumSequence getAllAlbums();
            AlbumSequence getAllAlbumsByArtistName();
            AlbumSequence getAllAlbumsByAlbumName();
            void addAlbum(in AlbumI album);
            void deleteAlbum(in AlbumI album);

            AlbumI obtainEmptyAlbum();
        };

        interface RequestorI {
            void albumFound(in AlbumSequence album);
        };

        interface MusicServerI {
            MusicCollectionI obtainCollection(in string sUserName,
                                              in string sPassword)
            raises(NoSuchUserException);

            MusicCollectionI createCollection(in string sUserName,
                                              in string sPassword)
            raises(UserIDExistsException);
            void logOut(in MusicCollectionI collection);

            void saveCollection();

            AlbumQueryS obtainEmptyQuery();
            void searchCatalog(in AlbumQueryS query, in RequestorI requestor);
        };
};
```

Starting with the main entity, focus your attention on the MusicServerI interface. This interface exposes operations that manage client lifecycle. This lifecycle starts when a user logs into the server using the obtainCollection() operation or creates a new account using the createCollection() operation, and it ends when the logOut() operation is invoked. The interface also exposes an operation called saveCollection(), which saves information on all users to a file. Saving user information to a file allows information to be preserved after a server restart. The last operation of the MusicServerI interface, searchCatalog(), performs an exhaustive search of a collection of music catalogs. The obtainEmptyQuery() operation is a utility operation that returns an AlbumQueryS object with default values.

Moving from the `MusicServerI` interface, focus your attention on the `MusicCollectionI` and `AlbumI` interfaces. The `AlbumI` interface models a unique album, and the `MusicCollectionI` interface represents a unique collection of `AlbumI` objects. Contained in the `MusicCollectionI` interface are operations to add and remove objects as well as attributes that indicate the user name and password needed to obtain a reference to the collection.

The only other entity that deserves significant attention is the `RequestorI` interface. This interface is actually implemented by the applet client and allows for delayed delivery of the results of an album search. Due to the fact that an album search may take significant time to perform, it could be a rather large waste of resources to have the `searchCatalog()` operation return the results of a search itself. Instead, the operation accepts a parameter indicating the entity performing the request and notifies that entity when the search is complete.

IMPLEMENTATION

Moving from the design of the application to its implementation, the next sections address the manner in which the interfaces in Listing 24.1 are actually implemented.

The `MusicServer` Class

Starting with the `MusicServerI` interface, the `MusicServer` implementation class is contained in Listing 24.2.

LISTING 24.2 THE `MusicServer` CLASS IMPLEMENTS THE `MusicServerI` INTERFACE

```java
import musicServer.*;
import org.omg.CORBA.*;

/**
 * Main server class
 */
public final class MusicServer extends _MusicServerIImplBase {
    private static BOA          _boa;
    private MusicCollectionHolder   _musicCollectionHolder;

    public MusicServer() {
        super("MusicServer");
        _musicCollectionHolder = new MusicCollectionHolder(_boa);
    }

    /**
     * Invoked by the client when he wants to attempt a login
     */
```

```java
public MusicCollectionI obtainCollection(String sUserName,
                                         String sPassword)
                     throws NoSuchUserException {
    MusicCollectionI collection = _
        musicCollectionHolder.obtainCollection(sUserName, sPassword);
    if(collection == null) {
        throw new NoSuchUserException("Invalid Login Information");
    }

    _boa.obj_is_ready(collection);
    return collection;
}

/**
 * Invoked by the client when he wants to create a new
 * MusicCollectionI object.
 */
public MusicCollectionI createCollection(String sUserName,
                                         String sPassword)
                     throws UserIDExistsException {
    if(_musicCollectionHolder.doesUserNameExist(sUserName)) {
        throw new UserIDExistsException(sUserName+
                                        " is already in use");
    }

    MusicCollectionI collection =
        new MusicCollection(sUserName, sPassword, _boa);
    _boa.obj_is_ready(collection);
    _musicCollectionHolder.addMusicCollection(collection);

    return collection;
}

/**
 * Helper method that obtains an AlbumQueryS
 * object populated with dummy data.
 */
public AlbumQueryS obtainEmptyQuery() {
    return new AlbumQueryS("", "", 0f, MediaType.NOT_SPECIFIED);
}

/**
 * Performs an exhaustive search of all available
 * catalogs. Demonstrates the callback design pattern.
 */
public void searchCatalog(AlbumQueryS query, RequestorI requestor) {
    AlbumSearcher searcher =
        new AlbumSearcher(query, requestor, _boa);
    searcher.start();
}
```

24

A CORBA
SERVER

continues

LISTING 24.2 CONTINUED

```
/**
 * Invoked by the client when he wants to logout, deactivates
 * all activated objects.
 */
public void logOut(MusicCollectionI collection) {
    Deactivator deactivator = new Deactivator(collection, _boa);
    deactivator.start();
}

public void saveCollection() {
    _musicCollectionHolder.saveCollection();
}

public static void main(String[] args) {
    ORB orb = ORB.init();
    _boa = orb.BOA_init();

    MusicServer server = new MusicServer();

    _boa.obj_is_ready(server);
    _boa.impl_is_ready();
}
}
```

Looking at the code in Listing 24.2, you'll not notice anything too unusual. This class is rather similar to others developed so far in this book. Two methods, however, do perform operations that are rather interesting. Looking at the searchCatalog() method, you'll notice that even though it performs a search, the results of that search are not immediately returned. Because the search could take a long time to perform, the method returns immediately and spawns off a new thread to perform the search and then notify the client when the results are ready. To facilitate notification, the searchCatalog() method accepts a reference to the client in the form of a RequestorI object. This method demonstrates the callback pattern from Chapter 5.

The other method of interest is the logOut() method. This method also spawns off a new thread. However, this thread is charged with deactivating all objects activated by the client during this session. As stated earlier in the book, every call to BOA.obj_is_ready() needs to be paired with a call to BOA.deactivate_obj(). Not deactivating objects will lead to the server running out of memory after being used for awhile. The manner in which activated objects are tracked is covered later in the section on the MusicCollectionI implementation.

The `AlbumSearcher` Class

As stated earlier, the `searchCatalog()` method in the `MusicServer` class spawns off a unique thread in which the actual catalog search is performed. The class that performs this search, `AlbumSearcher`, is contained in Listing 24.3. Note, however, that due to the space constraints of this book, an actual music catalog is not implemented. The class simply invents a new album based on the search parameters supplied by the client.

LISTING 24.3 THE `AlbumSearcher` CLASS PERFORMS AN ALBUM SEARCH IN A UNIQUE THREAD AND NOTIFIES THE REQUESTOR WHEN COMPLETE

```
import musicServer.*;
import org.omg.CORBA.*;

/**
 * The AlbumSearcher  class Performs an exhaustive search of all
 * available sources looking for the specified AlbumI object.
 * When the search is finished, the requestor is notified of the results.
 *
 * This class is an example of the Callback Pattern covered
 * in chapter 5.
 */
public class AlbumSearcher extends Thread {
    private AlbumQueryS      _query;
    private RequestorI       _requestor;
    private BOA              _boa;

    public AlbumSearcher(AlbumQueryS query,
                         RequestorI requestor, BOA boa) {
        _query = query;
        _requestor = requestor;
        _boa = boa;
    }

    /**
     * Search for the album in a unique thread. In this example,
     * the search is not actually performed, and the end result
     * is simply invented.
     */
    public void run() {
        AlbumI album = new Album();
        album.sArtistName(_query.sArtistName);
        album.sAlbumName(_query.sAlbumName);
        album.fPrice(_query.fPrice);
        album.type(_query.type);

        _boa.obj_is_ready(album);
```

continues

24

A CORBA SERVER

LISTING 24.3   CONTINUED

```
        AlbumI[] returnValue = {album};
        _requestor.albumFound(returnValue);
    }

}
```

The Deactivator Class

The other processing class utilized by the MusicServer class performs object deactivation upon logout. This class, contained in Listing 24.4, is actually rather simple. It first asks the target MusicCollection object to deactivate all activated AlbumI objects and then deactivates the MusicCollection object itself.

LISTING 24.4   THE Deactivator OBJECT IS CHARGED WITH DEACTIVATING ALL ACTIVATED OBJECTS

```
import org.omg.CORBA.*;
import musicServer.*;

public class Deactivator extends Thread {
    private MusicCollectionI    _musicCollection;
    private BOA                 _boa;

    public Deactivator(MusicCollectionI musicCollection, BOA boa) {
        _musicCollection = musicCollection;
        _boa = boa;
    }

    public void run() {
        ((MusicCollection)_musicCollection).deactivateObjects();
        _boa.deactivate_obj(_musicCollection);
    }
}
```

The Album and MusicCollection Classes

So far, we've concentrated on the classes that allow the music collection to exist but have not actually looked at the classes that model the collection itself. Listing 24.5 contains the implementation of the AlbumI interface, and Listing 24.6 contains the implementation of the MusicCollectionI interface.

The AlbumI implementation is rather basic—it does little more than expose a few variables with getter and setter methods. Looking forward to the MusicCollectionI implementation, you'll notice a lot of new concepts being introduced.

LISTING 24.5 THE Album CLASS IMPLEMENTS THE AlbumI INTERFACE

```java
import java.io.*;
import musicServer.*;

/**
 * Models a unique album, with all of its properties
 */
public class Album extends _AlbumIImplBase implements Serializable {
    private String      _sArtistName;
    private String      _sAlbumName;
    private String      _sListeningNotes;
    private float       _fPrice;

    private MediaType   _type;

    public Album() {
        this("", "", "", 0f, MediaType.NOT_SPECIFIED);
    }

    public Album(String sArtistName,
                 String sAlbumName,
                 String sListeningNotes,
                 float fPrice,
                 MediaType type) {
        _sArtistName = sArtistName;
        _sAlbumName = sAlbumName;
        _sListeningNotes = sListeningNotes;
        _fPrice = fPrice;
        _type = type;
    }

    public String sArtistName() {
        return _sArtistName;
    }

    public void sArtistName(String sArtistName) {
        _sArtistName = sArtistName;
    }

    public String sAlbumName() {
        return _sAlbumName;
    }

    public void sAlbumName(String sAlbumName) {
        _sAlbumName = sAlbumName;
    }

    public String sListeningNotes() {
```

24

A CORBA SERVER

continues

LISTING 24.5   CONTINUED

```
        return _sListeningNotes;
    }

    public void sListeningNotes(String sListeningNotes) {
        _sListeningNotes = sListeningNotes;
    }

    public float fPrice() {
        return _fPrice;
    }

    public void fPrice(float fPrice) {
        _fPrice = fPrice;
    }

    public MediaType type() {
        return _type;
    }

    public void type(MediaType type) {
        _type = type;
    }
}
```

LISTING 24.6   THE MusicCollection CLASS IMPLEMENTS THE MusicCollectionI
INTERFACE

```
import musicServer.*;
import java.util.*;
import java.io.*;
import org.omg.CORBA.*;

/**
 * Models a collection of albums.
 */
public class MusicCollection extends
            _MusicCollectionIImplBase implements Serializable {
    private Vector          _vecAlbums;
    private String          _sUserName;
    private String          _sPassword;

    private transient BOA   _boa;
    private Vector          _vecActivatedObjects;

    private boolean         _bObjectsDeactivated = false;

    public MusicCollection(String sUserName, String sPassword, BOA boa) {
        super();
```

```
        _sUserName = sUserName;
        _sPassword = sPassword;
        _vecAlbums = new Vector();
        _boa = boa;
        _vecActivatedObjects = new Vector();
    }

    /**
     * Invoked after being de-serialized with a new reference to the BOA
     */
    public void updateTransientData(BOA boa) {
        _boa = boa;
    }

    /**
     * Obtains all AlbumI objects ordered by artist name
     */
    public AlbumI[] getAllAlbumsByArtistName() {
        AlbumI[] albums = getAllAlbums();
        AlbumSorter.sortByArtistName(albums);
        return albums;
    }

    /**
     * Obtains all AlbumI objects ordered by album name
     */
    public AlbumI[] getAllAlbumsByAlbumName() {
        AlbumI[] albums = getAllAlbums();
        AlbumSorter.sortByAlbumName(albums);
        return albums;
    }

    /**
     * Obtains all AlbumI objects in default order
     */
    public AlbumI[] getAllAlbums() {
        if(_bObjectsDeactivated) {
            _bObjectsDeactivated = false;
            Enumeration e = _vecAlbums.elements();
            while(e.hasMoreElements()) {
                _boa.obj_is_ready((org.omg.CORBA.Object)e.nextElement());
            }
        }

        AlbumI[] returnValue = new AlbumI[_vecAlbums.size()];
        _vecAlbums.copyInto(returnValue);
        return returnValue;
    }
```

continues

24

A CORBA
SERVER

LISTING 24.6   CONTINUED

```java
/**
 * Adds an AlbumI object to the collection
 */
public void addAlbum(AlbumI album) {
    _vecAlbums.addElement(album);
}

/**
 * Removes an AlbumI object from the collection
 */
public void deleteAlbum(AlbumI album) {
    _vecAlbums.removeElement(album);
}

/**
 * Obtains an empty AlbumI object
 */
public AlbumI obtainEmptyAlbum() {
    AlbumI returnValue = new Album();
    _boa.obj_is_ready(returnValue);
    _vecActivatedObjects.addElement(returnValue);
    return returnValue;
}

public void sUserName(String sUserName) { _sUserName = sUserName; }
public String sUserName() { return _sUserName; }

public void sPassword(String sPassword) { _sPassword = sPassword; }
public String sPassword() { return _sPassword; }

/**
 * Deactivates all activated objects
 */
public void deactivateObjects() {
    _bObjectsDeactivated = true;
    Enumeration e = _vecAlbums.elements();
    while(e.hasMoreElements()) {
        _boa.deactivate_obj((org.omg.CORBA.Object)e.nextElement());
    }
}

}
```

Looking at the MusicCollection class, first focus your attention on the steps taken to support serialization. Because MusicCollection objects are going to be serialized when the server saves all objects, this class needs to implement the java.io.Serializable interface. In addition to implementing the serialization tagging interface, the class also marks its BOA reference as transient. A *transient object* is one that is not serialized when the rest of the object is. The fact that the variable exists is saved; however, the information pointed to by that variable is lost.

When you're serializing objects that reference any sort of remote object, all remote references must be tagged as transient. This step is required due to the fact that a remote object reference is only a pointer to an implementation object, not the implementation object itself. If the reference is serialized, there's no guarantee that the item it points to will still be there after deserialization. Because the BOA reference is needed, a method called updateTransientData() is provided, with the understanding that it will be passed a new BOA reference immediately following deserialization.

The next aspect of the MusicCollection class that you'll want to concentrate on is the manner in which activated objects are tracked and then deactivated. If you look at the obtainEmptyAlbum() method, you'll notice that it pairs every call to obj_is_ready() with a line that places the newly activated object inside the Vector object pointed to by the _vecActivatedObjects variable. The obtainEmptyAlbum() method is invoked by the client when it wants to obtain an empty AlbumI object that will be added to its collection.

Also contained in the class, and presented here, is the deactivateObjects() method. This method iterates through the collection of activated objects and individually deactivates each one. The class also sets a boolean member variable called _bObjectsDeactivated to true, indicating that the objects have, in fact, been deactivated. This boolean is referenced in the getAllAlbums() method to determine whether the AlbumI objects need to be activated before being returned. Because the AlbumI objects are deactivated during logout, they must be reactivated before being served again. An alternative to activating the objects in the getAllAlbums() method would be to activate them immediately following login.

```
public void deactivateObjects() {
      _bObjectsDeactivated = true;
      Enumeration e = _vecAlbums.elements();
      while(e.hasMoreElements()) {
          _boa.deactivate_obj((org.omg.CORBA.Object)e.nextElement());
      }
  }
```

The decision to place the activation code in this method was made so as to not slow down the login process. Users often expect certain operations to take longer than others, and applications should be designed around these expectations. Although no overall speed is gained by placing the activation code in the getAllAlbums() method, a perceived gain exists. Because users often expect searches to take longer than the login process, taking the time to activate objects during the search is something the user expects. If, however, we were to activate the objects during the login, the user might be surprised how long it takes for a login to occur.

The final area you'll want to note is the two methods that obtain AlbumI objects in a sorted fashion. These objects invoke a static utility method in the AlbumSorter class, which performs the sort itself.

The AlbumSorter Class

Listing 24.7 contains the AlbumSorter class, which uses a bubble sort to sort the array of AlbumI objects by either album or artist name. This sorting algorithm functions by continuously iterating through the array of elements, swapping those that are out of place. The algorithm exits when a pass is made through the array that does not require sorting. In general, the bubble sort is rather slow, especially if the items are in reverse order. This algorithm was simply used because it's rather easy to understand and is taught in most CS101 classes. Figure 24.1 demonstrates how the algorithm would function for an array containing the values a, z, d, c, a.

FIGURE 24.1

Sorting with the bubble sort algorithm.

Pass	Values				
1	A	Z	D	C	A
2	A	D	C	A	Z
3	A	D	A	C	Z
4	A	A	D	C	Z
5	A	A	C	D	Z

LISTING 24.7   THE AlbumSorter CLASS USES A BUBBLE SORT TO SORT A COLLECTION OF AlbumI OBJECTS

```
import musicServer.*;

public class AlbumSorter {

    /**
     * Sorts, using the bubble sort, all AlbumI objects
     * by artist name.
     */
    public static void sortByArtistName(AlbumI[] albums) {
        int iLength = albums.length;
        iLength — ;
        boolean bSwapHappened = true;
```

```
        while(bSwapHappened) {
            bSwapHappened = false;
            for(int i=0; i<iLength; i++) {
                if(albums[i].sArtistName().charAt(0) >
                   albums[i+1].sArtistName().charAt(0)) {
                    bSwapHappened = true;
                    AlbumI temp = albums[i];
                    albums[i] = albums[i+1];
                    albums[i+1] = temp;
                }
            }
        }
    }

    /**
     * Sorts, using the bubble sort, all AlbumI objects
     * by album name.
     */
    public static void sortByAlbumName(AlbumI[] albums) {
        int iLength = albums.length;
        iLength—;
        boolean bSwapHappened = true;
        while(bSwapHappened) {
            bSwapHappened = false;
            for(int i=0; i<iLength; i++) {
                if(albums[i].sAlbumName().charAt(0) >
                   albums[i+1].sAlbumName().charAt(0)) {
                    bSwapHappened = true;
                    AlbumI temp = albums[i];
                    albums[i] = albums[i+1];
                    albums[i+1] = temp;
                }
            }
        }
    }
}
```

The `MusicCollectionHolder` Class

Well, stop for a moment and pat yourself on the back. We're definitely in the home stretch as far as developing the server goes. Just two more classes need coverage; then we can move on to the client.

As you may have noticed when looking at the `MusicServer` class, method invocations that involve managing `MusicCollection` objects are performed with the aid of a `MusicCollectionHolder` object. This class, contained in Listing 24.8, is charged with maintaining a collection of `MusicCollectionI` objects.

24

A CORBA SERVER

LISTING 24.8   THE MusicCollectionHolder OBJECT IS CHARGED WITH MAINTAINING A
COLLECTION OF MusicCollectionI OBJECTS

```java
import musicServer.*;
import java.util.*;
import java.io.*;
import org.omg.CORBA.*;


/**
 * Utility class that holds references to MusicCollectionI
 * objects, and facilitates the login process.
 */
public class MusicCollectionHolder {
    private Hashtable    _hshUsers;
    private BOA          _boa;

    public MusicCollectionHolder(BOA boa) {
        _hshUsers = readInHash();
        _boa = boa;
    }


    /**
     * Reads in the contents of the _hshUsers object
     */
    private Hashtable readInHash() {
        try{    File file = new File("users.ser");
                if(! file.exists()) return new Hashtable();

                Hashtable hshUsers = null;
                FileInputStream fIn = new FileInputStream(file);
                ObjectInputStream oIn = new ObjectInputStream(fIn);
                hshUsers = (Hashtable)oIn.readObject();
                oIn.close();
                fIn.close();
                updateTransientData();
                return hshUsers;
        }
        catch( Exception ioe ) {
                return new Hashtable();
        }
    }


    /**
     * Updates the BOA reference in all MusicCollectionI objects
     */
    private void updateTransientData() {
        Enumeration e = _hshUsers.elements();
        while(e.hasMoreElements()) {
            ((MusicCollection)e.nextElement()).updateTransientData(_boa);
        }
```

```
    }

    /**
     * Obtains the MusicCollectionI object associated with the
     * specified name and password.
     */
    public MusicCollectionI obtainCollection(String sUserName,
                                             String sPassword) {
        MusicCollectionI collection =
            (MusicCollectionI)_hshUsers.get(sUserName);
        if(collection == null) return null;

        if(collection.sPassword().equals(sPassword)) return collection;

        return null;
    }

    /**
     * Adds a MusicCollectionI object to the collection of
     * objects monitored by this object.
     */
    public void addMusicCollection(MusicCollectionI collection) {
        _hshUsers.put(collection.sUserName(), collection);
    }

    /**
     * Checks if the specified user name is already in use
     */
    public boolean doesUserNameExist(String sUserName) {
        return _hshUsers.containsKey(sUserName);
    }

    /**
     * Saves the contents of the hashtable to a file.
     */
    public void saveCollection() {
        // lock access to the hashtable. this prevents
        // a user from being added or removed while we
        // are saving.
        synchronized(_hshUsers) {
            try{    FileOutputStream fOut =
                        new FileOutputStream("users.ser");
                    ObjectOutputStream oOut =
                        new ObjectOutputStream(fOut);
                    oOut.writeObject(_hshUsers);
                    oOut.flush();
                    oOut.close();
                    fOut.close();
            }
```

24

*A CORBA
SERVER*

continues

LISTING 24.8 CONTINUED

```
            catch(  IOException ioe ) {}
        }
    }

}
```

In managing the collection of MusicCollection objects, the MusicCollectionHolder object gets to perform a lot of interesting operations. Looking first at the Hashtable object in which MusicCollection objects are stored, note the readInHash() and saveCollection() methods.

The saveCollection() method is invoked to trigger the serialization of all MusicCollection objects. The method creates a FileOutputStream object pointing at a file titled users.ser and then creates an ObjectOutputStream object on top of the FileOutputStream object. Once the ObjectOutputStream object is created, its writeObject() method is invoked with the target Hashtable object as a parameter.

What should also be noted about this method is that during the time that the Hashtable object is being serialized, we lock access to it using the synchronized keyword. In a multithreaded environment, it's very possible that more than one thread might attempt to access the same physical variable at the same time. Regarding this situation, that could mean a new MusicCollection object might be added to the Hashtable object at the same time a save is occurring. This situation is not one we would want to happen because it could invalidate the integrity of the Hashtable's collection.

Once the contents of the Hashtable have been saved by the saveCollection() method, it becomes possible to read them back in. The readInHash() method is invoked from the constructor and attempts to perform the deserialization. First off, the method creates a new File object that points to the users.ser file on the hard drive. The method then checks to see whether this file actually exists and simply returns a new Hashtable object if the file does not exist. If the file does exist, the method creates a new FileInputStream object on top of the File object and an ObjectInputStream object on top of the FileInputStream object. The readObject() method in the ObjectInputStream object is now invoked, and its return value is cast as a Hashtable object. Finally, we invoke the updateTransientData() method, which updates the BOA reference in each MusicCollection object.

Although the object serialization is the most complicated task performed by the MusicCollectionHolder object, it's not the only task that deserves attention. You'll want to take note of the obtainCollection(), addMusicCollection() and doesUserNameExist() methods. Respectively, they allow searching for

MusicCollection objects by user name and password, the addition of a new MusicCollection object, and checking whether a user name is already in existence.

The UserSaver Class

The last class we'll cover is a standalone utility class called UserSaver (see Listing 24.9). This class simply binds to the MusicServerI instance and asks it to save its collection of users. This class is provided to allow for server management to occur without having to add a GUI to the server itself. Because server applications usually run minimized or in the background, the addition of a GUI is simply not needed and would only add to screen clutter.

LISTING 24.9   THE UserSaver OBJECT PROMPTS THE SERVER TO SAVE ITS COLLECTION OF USERS

```
import musicServer.*;
import org.omg.CORBA.*;

public class UserSaver {

    public static void main(String[] args) {
        ORB orb = ORB.init();
        MusicServerI musicServer = MusicServerIHelper.bind(orb);
        musicServer.saveCollection();
    }
}
```

FROM HERE

At this point, you should have a solid understanding of what it takes to actually develop a production CORBA server application. We tackled some pretty tricky issues, including memory management, object persistence, and general design with respect to efficiency. As you go out into the world and begin designing and coding your own servers, keep in mind the decisions that were made in this chapter.

As you read about the development of the client software in Chapter 25, "A CORBA Client," the discussion of this application will continue to some extent. We'll cover how to run the server (although by now, you should be able to figure that out yourself) and talk further about the design decisions we made.

A CORBA CLIENT

IN THIS CHAPTER

In Chapter 24, "A CORBA Server," you spent some time developing a server application that has features that allow for creating, viewing, and modifying a collection of music albums. In this chapter, you again look at the problem of developing an application that facilitates the maintenance of a music collection; however, this time the focus is on client development. If you skipped over Chapter 24, you really should go back and read it; this chapter builds on the material covered in Chapter 24.

As was discussed in Chapter 24, client/server applications are those applications that divide their functionality into at least two separate pieces. The client side is usually charged with interacting with the human user, gathering input, and passing off data to the server for processing. The server, in turn, is charged with executing business logic, interacting with persistence mechanisms (such as databases, flat files, and so forth), and any processing that is too time-consuming to be performed by the client.

In building the client application, the following topics are covered:

- Designing a thin-client applet
- Implementing callbacks in an applet
- Using the gatekeeper application to tunnel IIOP over HTTP

APPLICATION DESIGN

As with all applications, the first step in the development process is to take a look at your requirements and to design the application. Often, engineers want to dive right into the code-writing process and neglect the ever-important first step of design. Unfortunately, as discussed in Chapters 5, "Design Patterns," and 6, "The Airline Reservation System Model," these design-free software projects usually fail to work (or even fail to reach completion). Designing the client component of a client/server application is often easier than the server component, due to the fact that the client can leverage the server design. The client exists to exploit functionality in the server and therefore has its functionality specified by the server.

CORBA IDL serves as a contract between two distributed objects (in our case, this means between all client and server components), making the IDL an important piece of the design process. In general, the server exposes some functionality, which is then exploited by the client. Therefore, in developing the client in this chapter, we can base its design on the IDL developed for the server in Chapter 24.

Listing 25.1 contains a reprint of the server IDL developed and implemented in Chapter 24. Read over the listing to refresh your memory. If you have any questions, flip back a few pages and reread the chapter.

LISTING 25.1 THE IDL FOR THE MUSIC SERVER APPLICATION

```
module musicServer {
    exception NoSuchUserException { string reason; };
    exception UserIDExistsException { string reason; };
    enum MediaType { CD, TAPE, RECORD, NOT_SPECIFIED };

    interface AlbumI {
        attribute string      sArtistName;
        attribute string      sAlbumName;
        attribute string      sListeningNotes;
        attribute float       fPrice;

        attribute MediaType   type;
    };
    typedef sequence<AlbumI>AlbumSequence;

    struct AlbumQueryS {
        string      sArtistName;
        string      sAlbumName;
        float       fPrice;
        MediaType   type;
    };

    interface MusicCollectionI {
        attribute string sUserName;
        attribute string sPassword;

        AlbumSequence getAllAlbums();
        AlbumSequence getAllAlbumsByArtistName();
        AlbumSequence getAllAlbumsByAlbumName();
        void addAlbum(in AlbumI album);
        void deleteAlbum(in AlbumI album);

        AlbumI obtainEmptyAlbum();
    };

    interface RequestorI {
        void albumFound(in AlbumSequence album);
    };

    interface MusicServerI {
        MusicCollectionI obtainCollection(in string sUserName,
                                          in string sPassword)
                    raises(NoSuchUserException);

        MusicCollectionI createCollection(in string sUserName,
                                          in string sPassword)
                    raises(UserIDExistsException);

        void logOut(in MusicCollectionI collection);
```

continues

LISTING 25.1 CONTINUED

```
        void saveCollection();

        AlbumQueryS obtainEmptyQuery();
        void searchCatalog(in AlbumQueryS query, in RequestorI requestor);
    };
};
```

Moving beyond the details of the server, take a look at Table 25.1. This table discusses each of the client-side classes implemented to bring about communication between the human user and the data-processing server. These classes present a user interface (UI) and make use of the Abstract Windowing Toolkit (AWT) to build their screens.

TABLE 25.1 CLIENT-SIDE CLASSES

Class	Function
MusicCollectionViewer	The class that extends java.applet.Applet, binds to remote services, and builds the initial user interface.
AlbumDisplay	Displays a unique AlbumI object and allows for modification of its values. It also prompts for user input before executing a catalog search.
DisplayPanel	Displays all available AlbumI objects, allows for the creation of new objects, and deletes objects from the collection.
ResultsDisplay	Displays the results after a catalog search and prompts the user to add any albums in the result set to his collection.
DisplayMaster	Aids in the display of multiple AlbumI objects.
ErrorDialog	Used to display error messages.
LoginPanel	Allows a user to either log in or create a new account.

THE MUSICCOLLECTIONVIEWER CLASS

To begin your exploration of the client development process, take a look at the MusicCollectionViewer class contained in Listing 25.2. This class extends the Applet class and is charged with setting up the default look of our client.

LISTING 25.2   THE MusicCollectionViewer CLASS

```java
import java.awt.*;
import java.awt.event.*;
import java.applet.*;
import org.omg.CORBA.*;
import musicServer.*;

/**
 * Main Applet class.
 */
public class MusicCollectionViewer extends
            Applet implements ActionListener {
    private MusicServerI       _musicServer;
    private MusicCollectionI   _collection;
    private Button             _btnLogout;
    private BOA                _boa;

    public void init() {
        establishServiceReferences();
        setLayout(new BorderLayout(1,1));
        Panel pnlButtons = new Panel();
        pnlButtons.setLayout(new FlowLayout(FlowLayout.RIGHT));
        pnlButtons.add(_btnLogout = new Button("Logout"));
        add(pnlButtons, BorderLayout.NORTH);
        add(new LoginPanel(this), BorderLayout.CENTER);

        _btnLogout.addActionListener(this);
        _btnLogout.setEnabled(false);
    }

    /**
     * Invoked when the logout button is pressed
     */
    public void actionPerformed(ActionEvent ae) {
        // notify the server that we are done
        _musicServer.logOut(_collection);
        _collection = null;

        // place the GUI in login mode
        _btnLogout.setEnabled(false);
        removeAll();
        Panel pnlButtons = new Panel();
        pnlButtons.setLayout(new FlowLayout(FlowLayout.RIGHT));
        pnlButtons.add(_btnLogout);
        add(pnlButtons, BorderLayout.NORTH);
        add(new LoginPanel(this), BorderLayout.CENTER);
        doLayout();
        validate();
    }
```

continues

LISTING 25.2 CONTINUED

```
/**
 * Establishes references to the ORB, BOA and
 * MusicServerI object.
 */
private void establishServiceReferences() {
    ORB orb = ORB.init(this);
    _boa = orb.BOA_init();
    _musicServer = MusicServerIHelper.bind(orb);
}

/**
 * Invoked after a successful login or create new
 * account transaction. Changes the active display
 * to show the collection of AlbumI objects.
 */
private void displayCollection() {
    removeAll();
    Panel pnlButtons = new Panel();
    pnlButtons.setLayout(new FlowLayout(FlowLayout.RIGHT));
    pnlButtons.add(_btnLogout);
    add(pnlButtons, BorderLayout.NORTH);
    add(new DisplayPanel(_collection,
                         _musicServer,
                         _boa), BorderLayout.CENTER);
    doLayout();
    validate();
}

/**
 * Invoked by the LoginPanel class when the user
 * wants to login.
 */
public void attemptLogin(String sUserName, String sPassword) {
    try{   _collection = _musicServer.obtainCollection(sUserName,
                                                       sPassword);
           displayCollection();
           _btnLogout.setEnabled(true);
    }
    catch(  NoSuchUserException nsue ) {
           ErrorDialog dialog =
               new ErrorDialog(getFrame(this),
                               "Invalid Login, Try Again");
               dialog.setLocation(getLocationOnScreen().x+100,
                               getLocationOnScreen().y+100);
           dialog.pack();
           dialog.show();
    }
}
```

```
/**
 * Invoked by the LoginPanel class when the user
 * wants to create a new account.
 */
public void createNewAccount(String sUserName, String sPassword) {
    try{    _collection = _musicServer.createCollection(sUserName,
                                                        sPassword);
            displayCollection();
            _btnLogout.setEnabled(true);
    }
    catch(  UserIDExistsException uidee ) {
            ErrorDialog dialog =
                new ErrorDialog(getFrame(this),
                                "User ID In Use, Choose Another");
                dialog.setLocation(getLocationOnScreen().x+100,
                            getLocationOnScreen().y+100);
            dialog.pack();
            dialog.show();
    }
}

/**
 * Helper method used to obtain the parent
 * Frame object. Used when spawning a Dialog
 * object.
 */
public static Frame getFrame(Component component) {
    if(component instanceof Frame) return (Frame)component;

    while((component = component.getParent()) != null) {
        if(component instanceof Frame)
            return (Frame)component;
    }
    return null;
}
}
```

In general, as you look over the class, you should find that most of the code is easy to understand. With the exception of the establishServiceReferences() method, all code simply performs the manipulation of the UI. In the establishServiceReferences() method, we obtain references to the MusicServerI object developed in Chapter 24 along with the ORB and BOA. The ORB object is simply used to bind to the MusicServerI object and therefore is only needed in the scope of the method itself. The BOA object, however, is needed later when registering to receive callbacks.

As you know from the development of the MusicServer class in Chapter 24, the searchCatalog() method accepts a RequestorI instance and notifies this object when the catalog search is complete. Because the RequestorI object reference is passed through the ORB, it's necessary to use the BOA at the client-side to register the RequestorI object with the ORB. This is further covered in this chapter when we implement the DisplayPanel and ResultsDisplay classes.

In addition to taking note of the manner in which remote object references are managed, note the general workflow present in the application. Upon loading, the Applet displays a LoginPanel object on the screen. This class—detailed later in this chapter—prompts the user to either log in or create a new account. After receiving a command from the LoginPanel object, the applet either displays the user's music collection or an error message, indicating an incorrect login or in-use login ID (when creating new accounts). All changes to the active display are not made directly through the MusicCollectionViewer object, but rather are made by requesting a change from the DisplayMaster object.

THE ALBUMDISPLAY CLASS

As we move around the client, the next class discussed is the AlbumDisplay class. This class serves to either display information on an album, to collect album-related information for a search, or to collect album-related information used when creating a new album.

Take a look at the code for the AlbumDisplay class in Listing 25.3 (try not to get too overwhelmed). The class uses the GridBagLayout layout manager to design the screen. This layout manager allows for advanced UI design but has the unfortunate downside of leading to a lot of code. If you don't immediately understand exactly how the UI is coming together, don't worry. When you actually run the application on your machine, the UI will make perfect sense. What you should concentrate on in your examination is the manner in which the class serves each of its purposes.

LISTING 25.3   THE AlbumDisplay CLASS

```java
import java.awt.*;
import java.awt.event.*;
import musicServer.*;

/**
 * The AlbumDisplay class displays the contents
 * of an AlbumI object, and—optionally—allow for
 * the values to be updated. This class is also used
 * to collect information allowing for the creation of
 * a new AlbumI object.
 */
public class AlbumDisplay extends Panel implements ActionListener {
    public static int        VIEW_ONLY = 10;
    public static int        VIEW_AND_MODIFY = 13;
```

```java
public static int          CREATE_NEW = 1013;
public static int          SEARCH = 42;

private int                _iMode;

private AlbumI             _album;
private MusicCollectionI   _collection;

private TextField          _txtArtistName = null;
private TextField          _txtAlbumName = null;
private TextField          _txtPrice = null;
private Choice             _chcMediaType = null;
private TextArea           _txtListeningNotes = null;

private Button             _btnAction;
private DisplayPanel       _displayPanel;

/**
 * Constructor used when we are in CREATE_NEW or SEARCH mode
 */
public AlbumDisplay(MusicCollectionI collection,
                    int iMode,
                    DisplayPanel displayPanel) {
    this(null, iMode, collection);
    _displayPanel = displayPanel;
}

/**
 * Constructor used when we are in either VIEW_ONLY
 * or VIEW_AND_MODIFY mode.
 */
public AlbumDisplay(AlbumI album,
                    int iMode,
                    MusicCollectionI collection) {
    // assign local variables
    _album = album;
    _iMode = iMode;
    _collection = collection;

    // build the GUI
    GridBagLayout gbl = new GridBagLayout();
    GridBagConstraints gbc = new GridBagConstraints();
    setLayout(gbl);

    Label lblArtistName = new Label("Artist Name");
    gbc.gridx = 0;
    gbc.gridy = 0;
    gbc.gridwidth = 1;
    gbc.gridheight = 1;
    gbc.anchor = GridBagConstraints.NORTH;
```

continues

LISTING 25.3   CONTINUED

```java
gbc.fill = GridBagConstraints.NONE;
gbc.insets = new Insets(2,2,2,2);
gbl.setConstraints(lblArtistName, gbc);
add(lblArtistName);

gbc = new GridBagConstraints();
Label lblAlbumName = new Label("Album Name");
gbc.gridx = 0;
gbc.gridy = 1;
gbc.gridwidth = 1;
gbc.gridheight = 1;
gbc.anchor = GridBagConstraints.NORTH;
gbc.fill = GridBagConstraints.NONE;
gbc.insets = new Insets(2,2,2,2);
gbl.setConstraints(lblAlbumName, gbc);
add(lblAlbumName);

    gbc = new GridBagConstraints();
Label lblPrice = new Label("Price");
gbc.gridx = 0;
gbc.gridy = 2;
gbc.gridwidth = 1;
gbc.gridheight = 1;
gbc.anchor = GridBagConstraints.NORTH;
gbc.fill = GridBagConstraints.NONE;
gbc.insets = new Insets(2,2,2,2);
gbl.setConstraints(lblPrice, gbc);
add(lblPrice);

gbc = new GridBagConstraints();
Label lblMediaType = new Label("Media Type");
gbc.gridx = 0;
gbc.gridy = 3;
gbc.gridwidth = 1;
gbc.gridheight = 1;
gbc.anchor = GridBagConstraints.NORTH;
gbc.fill = GridBagConstraints.NONE;
gbc.insets = new Insets(2,2,2,2);
gbl.setConstraints(lblMediaType, gbc);
add(lblMediaType);

gbc = new GridBagConstraints();
Label lblListeningNotes = new Label("Listening Notes");
gbc.gridx = 0;
gbc.gridy = 4;
gbc.gridwidth = 1;
gbc.gridheight = 1;
gbc.anchor = GridBagConstraints.NORTH;
gbc.fill = GridBagConstraints.NONE;
```

```
gbc.insets = new Insets(2,2,2,2);
gbl.setConstraints(lblListeningNotes, gbc);
add(lblListeningNotes);

gbc = new GridBagConstraints();
_txtArtistName = new TextField((album == null) ?
    "" : album.sArtistName(), 30);
gbc.gridx = 1;
gbc.gridy = 0;
gbc.gridwidth = 1;
gbc.gridheight = 1;
gbc.anchor = GridBagConstraints.NORTH;
gbc.fill = GridBagConstraints.NONE;
gbc.insets = new Insets(2,2,2,2);
gbl.setConstraints(_txtArtistName, gbc);
add(_txtArtistName);

gbc = new GridBagConstraints();
_txtAlbumName = new TextField((album == null) ?
    "" : album.sAlbumName(), 30);
gbc.gridx = 1;
gbc.gridy = 1;
gbc.gridwidth = 1;
gbc.gridheight = 1;
gbc.anchor = GridBagConstraints.NORTH;
gbc.fill = GridBagConstraints.NONE;
gbc.insets = new Insets(2,2,2,2);
gbl.setConstraints(_txtAlbumName, gbc);
add(_txtAlbumName);

gbc = new GridBagConstraints();
_txtPrice = new TextField((album == null) ?
    "" : Float.toString(album.fPrice()), 30);
gbc.gridx = 1;
gbc.gridy = 2;
gbc.gridwidth = 1;
gbc.gridheight = 1;
gbc.anchor = GridBagConstraints.NORTH;
gbc.fill = GridBagConstraints.NONE;
gbc.insets = new Insets(2,2,2,2);
gbl.setConstraints(_txtPrice, gbc);
add(_txtPrice);

_chcMediaType = new Choice();
_chcMediaType.add("CD");
_chcMediaType.add("Tape");
_chcMediaType.add("Record");
_chcMediaType.add("Not Specified");
    int iTypeValue = (album == null)
    ? MediaType._NOT_SPECIFIED : album.type().value();
```

continues

25

A CORBA CLIENT

LISTING 25.3 CONTINUED

```java
if(iTypeValue == MediaType._CD) {
    _chcMediaType.select("CD");
}
else if(iTypeValue == MediaType._TAPE) {
    _chcMediaType.select("Tape");
}
else if(iTypeValue == MediaType._RECORD) {
    _chcMediaType.select("Record");
}
else if(iTypeValue == MediaType._NOT_SPECIFIED) {
    _chcMediaType.select("Not Specified");
}
gbc = new GridBagConstraints();
gbc.gridx = 1;
gbc.gridy = 3;
gbc.gridwidth = 1;
gbc.gridheight = 1;
gbc.anchor = GridBagConstraints.NORTH;
gbc.fill = GridBagConstraints.HORIZONTAL;
gbc.insets = new Insets(2,2,2,2);
gbl.setConstraints(_chcMediaType, gbc);
add(_chcMediaType);

gbc = new GridBagConstraints();
_txtListeningNotes = new TextArea((album == null)
    ? "" : album.sListeningNotes(), 5, 30);
gbc.gridx = 1;
gbc.gridy = 4;
gbc.gridwidth = 1;
gbc.gridheight = 5;
gbc.anchor = GridBagConstraints.NORTH;
gbc.fill = GridBagConstraints.NONE;
gbc.insets = new Insets(2,2,2,2);
gbl.setConstraints(_txtListeningNotes, gbc);
add(_txtListeningNotes);

if(iMode == VIEW_ONLY) {
    // if we are in view-only mode, disable
    // entry on all text fields
    _txtArtistName.setEnabled(false);
    _txtAlbumName.setEnabled(false);
    _txtPrice.setEnabled(false);
    _chcMediaType.setEnabled(false);
    _txtListeningNotes.setEnabled(false);
}
else {
    // only add the action button if we
    // are in a mode that allows for updating
    // or for searching. depending on the mode
```

```
                    // setting, set the button text.
                    if(iMode == SEARCH) {
                        _btnAction = new Button("Search");
                        // disable listening notes for search mode
                        _txtListeningNotes.setEnabled(false);
                    }
                    else _btnAction = new Button("Save Album");
                    _btnAction.addActionListener(this);

                    gbc = new GridBagConstraints();
                        gbc.gridx = 1;
                        gbc.gridy = 10;
                        gbc.gridwidth = 1;
                        gbc.gridheight = 5;
                        gbc.anchor = GridBagConstraints.SOUTHEAST;
                        gbc.fill = GridBagConstraints.NONE;
                        gbc.insets = new Insets(5,2,2,2);
                        gbl.setConstraints(_btnAction, gbc);
                        add(_btnAction);
        }
    }

    /**
     * Invoked when the current data should be converted
     * into a new AlbumI object, and saved at the server.
     */
    private void doSaveNew() {
        AlbumI album = _collection.obtainEmptyAlbum();
        album.sArtistName(_txtArtistName.getText());
        album.sAlbumName(_txtAlbumName.getText());
        try{    album.fPrice(
                new Float(_txtPrice.getText()).floatValue()); }
        catch(  NumberFormatException nfe) {
                album.fPrice(0f);
        }
        album.type(getMediaType());
        album.sListeningNotes(_txtListeningNotes.getText());
        _collection.addAlbum(album);
        _displayPanel.newAlbum(album);
    }

    /**
     * Helper method used to obtain a MediaType
     * object reflecting the currently selected
     * value present in the _chcMediaType Choice.
     */
    private MediaType getMediaType() {
        String sMediaType = _chcMediaType.getSelectedItem().trim();
        if(sMediaType.equals("CD")) return MediaType.CD;
        if(sMediaType.equals("Tape")) return MediaType.TAPE;
```

continues

LISTING 25.3 CONTINUED

```
        if(sMediaType.equals("Record")) return MediaType.RECORD;
        return MediaType.NOT_SPECIFIED;
    }

    /**
     * Invoked when the current data should be placed
     * inside of the current AlbumI object.
     */
    private void doSaveChanges() {
        _album.sArtistName(_txtArtistName.getText());
        _album.sAlbumName(_txtAlbumName.getText());
        try{    _album.fPrice(
                    new Float(_txtPrice.getText()).floatValue()); }
        catch(  NumberFormatException nfe) {
                    _album.fPrice(0f);
        }
        _album.type(getMediaType());
        _album.sListeningNotes(_txtListeningNotes.getText());
    }

    /**
     * Triggers a search
     */
    private void doSearch() {
        float fPrice = 0f;
        try{    fPrice = new Float(_txtPrice.getText()).floatValue(); }
        catch(  NumberFormatException nfe) { }
        _displayPanel.doSearch(_txtAlbumName.getText(),
                                _txtArtistName.getText(),
                                fPrice,
                                getMediaType());
    }

    /**
     * Invoked the save Button object is pressed
     */
    public void actionPerformed(ActionEvent ae) {
        if(_iMode == CREATE_NEW) doSaveNew();
        else if(_iMode == SEARCH) doSearch();
        else doSaveChanges();
    }

}
```

As was earlier stated, the AlbumDisplay class serves a series of different purposes; however, each object may serve only one purpose. The unique purpose of a single
AlbumDisplay object is defined by passing any one of four constants into the object's
constructor during the instantiation process. These constants, shown next, allow for the

object to display an AlbumI object as VIEW_ONLY or VIEW_AND_MODIFY. In addition, the constants allow for the collection of album-related information that's used either in a catalog search or during the creation of a new AlbumI object, which is then added to the user's collection.

```
public static int          VIEW_ONLY = 10;

public static int          VIEW_AND_MODIFY = 13;

public static int          CREATE_NEW = 1013;

public static int          SEARCH = 42;
```

Because the value of the mode variable has an effect on the UI itself, some runtime UI decisions are made. These decisions—all made at the end of the constructor code—affect items such as the addition of a Save or Search button and the disabling of certain input fields (if text entry is not allowed for that mode). As is logical, VIEW_ONLY mode allows no entry at all in any field; however, also note that SEARCH mode disallows entry in the listening notes field. Because the catalog search is executed against a collection of albums not owned by the user himself, listening notes are not present.

During the designing of the UI, two directions could have been taken when dealing with the listening notes entry field for search mode. One direction would have been to simply remove the field from the screen altogether; however, this could lead to user confusion. When looking at a UI, users like consistency because it helps them to recognize the purpose of a widget without having to read its accompanying label. Through location recognition, users are able to use applications much faster than if they have to constantly figure out where a desired widget is. By keeping the listening notes field on the screen and simply disabling it (the second direction), we maintain the same look whenever album information is collected or displayed.

Moving down toward the bottom of the code listing, take note of the actionPerformed() method. This method, reprinted here, is invoked when either the Save or Search button is pressed:

```
public void actionPerformed(ActionEvent ae) {
    if(_iMode == CREATE_NEW) doSaveNew();
    else if(_iMode == SEARCH) doSearch();
    else doSaveChanges();
}
```

What's interesting about the code in the actionPerformed() method is the fact that it must take into account the active mode to determine a course of action. If the object is in CREATE_NEW mode, the button press is a request from the user to collect information in the UI, package it as an AlbumI object, and add it to the active collection. If the object is in SEARCH mode, the button press is a request from the user to perform a catalog search.

If, however, the user is in VIEW_AND_MODIFY mode, the button press is a request from the user to save changes to the AlbumI object currently being modified.

With this understanding of how each button press causes a mode-specific method to be invoked, the next few pages discuss each of those methods. First up is the doSaveNew() method, which is invoked in CREATE_NEW mode.

This method, highlighted earlier, first obtains a reference to a remote AlbumI object from the active collection. As discussed when covering the server in Chapter 24, obtaining a new AlbumI object involves a call to BOA.obj_is_ready(), which means that at some point a call to BOA.deactivate_obj() is needed. When implementing the server, we placed the code to track obj_is_ready() calls there, which means we're freed from having to do it at the client. After a reference to the new AlbumI object is obtained, its attributes are set using the data entered into the UI, and finally the AlbumI object is added to the user's collection. The last line of code in the method does not interact with any remote objects but rather notifies the UI that a new AlbumI object has been added and that the display should update itself.

```
private void doSaveNew() {
    AlbumI album = _collection.obtainEmptyAlbum();
    album.sArtistName(_txtArtistName.getText());
    album.sAlbumName(_txtAlbumName.getText());
    try{    album.fPrice(new Float(_txtPrice.getText()).floatValue()); }
    catch(  NumberFormatException nfe) {
            album.fPrice(0f);
    }
    album.type(getMediaType());
    album.sListeningNotes(_txtListeningNotes.getText());
    _collection.addAlbum(album);
    _displayPanel.newAlbum(album);
}
```

The next method that might get called when a button is pressed is the doSearch() method, which is called when a search action is to begin. This method, highlighted next, collects all information entered into the UI and asks the DisplayPanel instance to perform a search. The DisplayPanel class is covered in the next section.

```
private void doSearch() {
    float fPrice = 0f;
    try{    fPrice = new Float(_txtPrice.getText()).floatValue(); }
    catch(  NumberFormatException nfe) { }
    _displayPanel.doSearch(_txtAlbumName.getText(), _
            txtArtistName.getText(), fPrice, getMediaType());
}
```

The final method that might be called in response to a button press is the doSaveChanges() method, which is called when an AlbumI object has been modified at the UI and needs its server values updated. This method, highlighted next, is interesting in that it only interacts with the active `AlbumI` object itself. Because that `AlbumI` object is only a reference to an implementation object sitting at the server, invoking any of its setter methods immediately reflects the change at the client and at the server.

```
private void doSaveChanges() {
    _album.sArtistName(_txtArtistName.getText());
    _album.sAlbumName(_txtAlbumName.getText());
    try{    _album.fPrice(new Float(_txtPrice.getText()).floatValue()); }
    catch(  NumberFormatException nfe) {
            _album.fPrice(0f);
    }
    _album.type(getMediaType());
    _album.sListeningNotes(_txtListeningNotes.getText());
}
```

At this point, the only method not yet covered is the `getMediaType()` helper method. When invoked, this method looks at the active media type selection and creates a `MediaType` object representing its value. A `MediaType` object, as covered in Chapter 24, is defined in the server IDL and represents the media upon which the active album is recorded.

THE DISPLAYPANEL CLASS

The next class you come into contact with is the `DisplayPanel` class, which creates the main UI used when interacting with the application (see Listing 25.4). Take a brief look over the UI code, but, again, do not spend too much time with it. The code uses the `GridBagLayout` layout manager to place a `List` object displaying the collection of albums along the left, and it places any one of many `AlbumDisplay` objects along the right side of the screen. Additional elements allow for changing how the list is sorted, deleting albums, and loading the screens that allow for entering new albums or searching the album catalog.

LISTING 25.4   THE `DisplayPanel` CLASS

```
import java.awt.event.*;
import java.awt.*;
import musicServer.*;
import java.util.*;
import org.omg.CORBA.*;

/**
 * Main UI screen
 */
public class DisplayPanel extends Panel
```

continues

LISTING 25.4   CONTINUED

```
                              implements ActionListener, ItemListener {
// mark as protected to allow for access in
// inner class by Netscape VM.
protected DisplayMaster      _displayMaster;

private Checkbox             _chkByArtist;
private Checkbox             _chkByAlbum;
private List                 _lstAlbums;
private Hashtable            _hshAlbums;
private MusicCollectionI     _collection;
private MusicServerI         _musicServer;
private BOA                  _boa;

private Button               _btnNew;
private Button               _btnDeleteSelcted;
private Button               _btnSearch;

public DisplayPanel(MusicCollectionI collection,
                    MusicServerI musicServer,
                    BOA boa) {
    _collection = collection;
    _musicServer = musicServer;
    _boa = boa;

    // create instance variables
    CheckboxGroup grp = new CheckboxGroup();
    _chkByArtist = new Checkbox("Artist", true, grp);
    _chkByAlbum = new Checkbox("Album", false, grp);
    _lstAlbums = new List(15);
    showAlbumsByArtist();
    _displayMaster = new DisplayMaster(_collection, this);
    _btnNew = new Button("New Album");
    _btnDeleteSelcted = new Button("Delete Selected");
    _btnSearch = new Button("Search Screen");

    // establish event listeners
    _btnNew.addActionListener(this);
    _btnDeleteSelcted.addActionListener(this);
    _lstAlbums.addActionListener(this);
    _btnSearch.addActionListener(this);
    _chkByArtist.addItemListener(this);
    _chkByAlbum.addItemListener(this);

    // build the GUI
    GridBagLayout gbl = new GridBagLayout();
    GridBagConstraints gbc = new GridBagConstraints();
    setLayout(gbl);

    // left half
```

```
Label lblOrder = new Label("Order By");
      gbc.gridx = 0;
 gbc.gridy = 0;
 gbc.gridwidth = 1;
 gbc.gridheight = 1;
 gbc.anchor = GridBagConstraints.WEST;
 gbc.fill = GridBagConstraints.NONE;
 gbc.insets = new Insets(2,2,2,2);
 gbl.setConstraints(lblOrder, gbc);
 add(lblOrder);

 gbc = new GridBagConstraints();
 gbc.gridx = 0;
 gbc.gridy = 1;
 gbc.gridwidth = 1;
 gbc.gridheight = 1;
 gbc.anchor = GridBagConstraints.WEST;
 gbc.fill = GridBagConstraints.NONE;
 gbc.insets = new Insets(2,2,2,2);
 gbl.setConstraints(_chkByArtist, gbc);
 add(_chkByArtist);

 gbc = new GridBagConstraints();
 gbc.gridx = 0;
 gbc.gridy = 2;
 gbc.gridwidth = 1;
 gbc.gridheight = 1;
 gbc.anchor = GridBagConstraints.WEST;
 gbc.fill = GridBagConstraints.NONE;
 gbc.insets = new Insets(2,2,2,2);
 gbl.setConstraints(_chkByAlbum, gbc);
 add(_chkByAlbum);

 gbc = new GridBagConstraints();
 gbc.gridx = 0;
 gbc.gridy = 3;
 gbc.gridwidth = 1;
 gbc.gridheight = 5;
 gbc.anchor = GridBagConstraints.NORTH;
 gbc.fill = GridBagConstraints.BOTH;
 gbc.insets = new Insets(2,2,2,2);
 gbl.setConstraints(_lstAlbums, gbc);
 add(_lstAlbums);

 // right half
 gbc.gridx = 4;
 gbc.gridy = 1;
 gbc.gridwidth = 1;
 gbc.gridheight = 1;
 gbc.anchor = GridBagConstraints.EAST;
```

continues

LISTING 25.4   CONTINUED

```
        gbc.fill = GridBagConstraints.NONE;
        gbc.insets = new Insets(2,2,2,2);
        gbl.setConstraints(_btnNew, gbc);
        add(_btnNew);

        gbc = new GridBagConstraints();
        gbc.gridx = 3;
        gbc.gridy = 1;
        gbc.gridwidth = 1;
        gbc.gridheight = 1;
        gbc.anchor = GridBagConstraints.EAST;
        gbc.fill = GridBagConstraints.NONE;
        gbc.insets = new Insets(2,2,2,2);
        gbl.setConstraints(_btnDeleteSelcted, gbc);
        add(_btnDeleteSelcted);

        gbc = new GridBagConstraints();
        gbc.gridx = 2;
        gbc.gridy = 1;
        gbc.gridwidth = 1;
        gbc.gridheight = 1;
        gbc.anchor = GridBagConstraints.WEST;
        gbc.fill = GridBagConstraints.NONE;
        gbc.insets = new Insets(2,2,2,2);
        gbl.setConstraints(_btnSearch, gbc);
        add(_btnSearch);

        gbc = new GridBagConstraints();
        gbc.gridx = 1;
        gbc.gridy = 3;
        gbc.gridwidth = 5;
        gbc.gridheight = 5;
        gbc.anchor = GridBagConstraints.NORTH;
        gbc.fill = GridBagConstraints.BOTH;
        gbc.insets = new Insets(2,2,2,2);
        gbl.setConstraints(_displayMaster, gbc);
        add(_displayMaster);
    }

    /**
     * Invoked when the album display should be sorted
     * by album
     */
    private void showAlbumsByAlbum() {
        AlbumI[] albums = _collection.getAllAlbumsByArtistName();
        int iLength = albums.length;
        _hshAlbums = new Hashtable();
        _lstAlbums.removeAll();
        for(int i=0; i<iLength; i++) {
```

```
            String sAlbumName = albums[i].sAlbumName();
            _lstAlbums.addItem(sAlbumName);
            _hshAlbums.put(sAlbumName, albums[i]);
        }
    }

    /**
     * Invoked when the album display should be sorted
     * by artist
     */
    private void showAlbumsByArtist() {
        AlbumI[] albums = _collection.getAllAlbumsByArtistName();
        int iLength = albums.length;
        _hshAlbums = new Hashtable();
        _lstAlbums.removeAll();
        for(int i=0; i<iLength; i++) {
            String sArtistName = albums[i].sArtistName();
            _lstAlbums.addItem(sArtistName);
            _hshAlbums.put(sArtistName, albums[i]);
        }
    }

    /**
     * Invoked when a new Album is added to the collection,
     * allows for the local display to be updated without
     * a network interaction.
     */
    public void newAlbum(AlbumI album) {
        String sAlbumName = album.sAlbumName();
        _hshAlbums.put(sAlbumName, album);
        _lstAlbums.addItem(sAlbumName);
    }

    /**
     * Triggers the display of a screen that will collect
     * new album information and prompt for a save
     */
    private void doNew() {
        _displayMaster.showEmpty();
    }

    /**
     * Deletes the currently selected album from
     * the collection.
     */
    private void doDeleteSelected(String sName) {
        AlbumI album = (AlbumI)_hshAlbums.get(sName);
        _collection.deleteAlbum(album);
        _lstAlbums.remove(sName);
    }
```

continues

25

A CORBA Client

LISTING 25.4 CONTINUED

```java
/**
 * Updates the detail display to show the currently
 * selected album
 */
private void displaySelected(String sName) {
    _displayMaster.updateActiveAlbum((AlbumI)_hshAlbums.get(sName));
}

/**
 * Triggers a display of the search screen
 */
private void showSearchScreen() {
    _displayMaster.showSearch();
}

/**
 * Invoked when either of the Checkbox objects changes
 * state. Causes a re-display of the albums.
 */
public void itemStateChanged(ItemEvent ie) {
    if(_chkByArtist.getState()) showAlbumsByArtist();
    else showAlbumsByAlbum();
}

/**
 * Invoked when a search is requested.
 */
public void doSearch(String sAlbumName,
                     String sArtistName,
                     float fPrice,
                     MediaType type) {
    // create the query object
    AlbumQueryS query = new AlbumQueryS(sAlbumName,
                                        sArtistName,
                                        fPrice,
                                        type);
    // create the callback listener
    ResultsListener listener = new ResultsListener();
    // register the callback listener with the ORB
    _boa.obj_is_ready(listener);
    // perform the search
    _musicServer.searchCatalog(query, listener);
}

/**
 * Inner class used to listen for the results of
 * a catalog search.
 */
class ResultsListener extends _RequestorIImplBase {
```

```
        public ResultsListener() {
            super();
        }

        /**
         * Invoked when the search results are
         * ready.
         */
        public void albumFound(AlbumI[] albums) {
            _displayMaster.showSearchResults(albums);
        }
    }

    /**
     * Invoked when any of the Button objects, or the List
     * object is clicked.
     */
    public void actionPerformed(ActionEvent ae) {
        java.lang.Object source = ae.getSource();

        if(source == _btnNew) {
            doNew();
        }
        else if(source == _lstAlbums) {
            displaySelected(ae.getActionCommand());
        }
        else if(source == _btnSearch) {
            showSearchScreen();
        }
        else {
            doDeleteSelected(ae.getActionCommand());
        }
    }
}
```

As you examine the DisplayPanel class, note the fact that two categories of actions can take place in response to user interaction. First off, the user can request that the active display show details on a single item, show the new album screen, or show the search screen. The other category of actions involves interacting with a server object to update the album list, delete an album, or perform a search.

The first category of actions (those that involve updating the display) are rather simple due to the fact that a DisplayMaster object performs UI changes. Each of the methods in the DisplayPanel class that perform a UI update actually delegates the call to a DisplayMaster object. The DisplayMaster class is covered later in this chapter.

The second category of actions (those that involve server interaction) are a touch more complicated. This is especially true when performing the search, due to the fact that call-backs must be implemented.

The first piece of server interaction code involves obtaining the sorted list of AlbumI objects and then displaying them onscreen. The UI allows the user to sort albums by artist as well as by album, but it uses the server to perform the physical sorting. Highlighted next is the showAlbumsByArtist() method, which first obtains the sorted list of AlbumI objects from the server, sticks them in a Hashtable object, and then adds them to the List object for onscreen display. A Hashtable object is used for storage because it allows for easy reference of a single AlbumI object when the user clicks one in the List object.

If the user desires the albums to be sorted by album name, the showAlbumsByAlbum() method is invoked. Although not highlighted here, the method is identical to the showAlbumsByArtist() method, save for the fact that it asks the server for the AlbumI objects sorted by album.

```
private void showAlbumsByArtist() {
    AlbumI[] albums = _collection.getAllAlbumsByArtistName();
    int iLength = albums.length;
    _hshAlbums = new Hashtable();
    _lstAlbums.removeAll();
    for(int i=0; i<iLength; i++) {
        String sArtistName = albums[i].sArtistName();
        _lstAlbums.addItem(sArtistName);
        _hshAlbums.put(sArtistName, albums[i]);
    }
}
```

The second server interaction to focus on is the doDeleteSelected() method, which is invoked when the user clicks an item in the List object and then clicks the Delete Selected button. This method, highlighted next, is passed a String object that's both the logical name displayed in the List object and the Hashtable key for the target AlbumI object. The method then uses the String object to obtain a reference to the target AlbumI object, removes it from the server collection, and then removes it from the onscreen display.

```
private void doDeleteSelected(String sName) {
    AlbumI album = (AlbumI)_hshAlbums.get(sName);
    _collection.deleteAlbum(album);
    _lstAlbums.remove(sName);
}
```

The code highlighted next contains the doSearch() method and the ResultsListener inner class. These two entities form the final server interactions performed by this class, and they're also the most complicated. As discussed earlier, this class implements the callback design pattern. Under the callback pattern, a client issues a query against a remote object but is not returned the results of that query. Instead, the client passes a reference to another object that is then notified by the server when the results of the query are ready. In the following example, the doSearch() method is invoked when the user desires a search to be performed. The inner class ResultsListener represents the listener class in this situation. The doSearch() method is passed parameters that represent the user's search criteria. The method next packages up the search parameters in an AlbumQueryS object, creates a new ResultsListener object, registers that object with the ORB, and finally invokes the searchCatalog() method on the server.

Once the searchCatalog() method is invoked, the code returns and simply waits for the server to finish searching for the albums. When the server is finished searching, it invokes the albumFound() method in the ResultsListener object and passes an object reference containing the results of the search. With the search complete, the albumFound() method requests that the DisplayMaster object display the result set.

```
public void doSearch(String sAlbumName,
                     String sArtistName,
                     float fPrice,
                     MediaType type) {
    AlbumQueryS query =
    new AlbumQueryS(sAlbumName, sArtistName, fPrice, type);
    ResultsListener listener = new ResultsListener();
      _boa.obj_is_ready(listener);
      _musicServer.searchCatalog(query, listener);
}
class ResultsListener extends _RequestorIImplBase {
    public ResultsListener() {
        super();
    }

        public void albumFound(AlbumI[] albums) {
        _displayMaster.showSearchResults(albums);
    }
}
}
```

THE RESULTSDISPLAY CLASS

Continuing on in our exploration of the search mechanism, Listing 25.5 contains the ResultsDisplay class. This class is instantiated and displayed by a DisplayMaster object once a catalog search is complete. The class displays a list of all albums in the found set and gives the user the option to add any of those albums to his collection. In general, this class is much simpler when compared to earlier classes, but it does demonstrate the manner in which albums are added to a collection.

LISTING 25.5 THE ResultsDisplay CLASS

```java
import java.awt.*;
import java.awt.event.*;
import musicServer.*;

/**
 * Displays the results after a catalog search.
 */
public class ResultsDisplay extends Panel implements ActionListener {
    private MusicCollectionI    _collection;
    private AlbumI[]            _results;
    private List               _lstResults;
    private Button             _btnAdd;
    private DisplayPanel       _displayPanel;

    public ResultsDisplay(MusicCollectionI collection,
                          AlbumI[] results,
                          DisplayPanel displayPanel) {
        _collection = collection;
        _results = results;
        _displayPanel = displayPanel;
        _btnAdd = new Button("Add Selected To Collection");
        _btnAdd.addActionListener(this);
        _lstResults = new List(10);

        // build the GUI
        int iLength = _results.length;
        StringBuffer sbBuilder;
        for(int i=0; i<iLength; i++) {
            sbBuilder = new StringBuffer();
            sbBuilder.append(results[i].sAlbumName());
            sbBuilder.append(" — ");
            sbBuilder.append(results[i].sArtistName());
            _lstResults.add(sbBuilder.toString());
        }

        setLayout(new BorderLayout());
        add(_lstResults, BorderLayout.CENTER);

        Panel pnlButtons = new Panel();
        pnlButtons.setLayout(new FlowLayout(FlowLayout.RIGHT));
        pnlButtons.add(_btnAdd);
        add(pnlButtons, BorderLayout.SOUTH);
    }

    /**
     * Invoked when the Add button is pressed
     */
    public void actionPerformed(ActionEvent ae) {
        int iSelectedIndex = _lstResults.getSelectedIndex();
```

```
            // add to the collection
            _collection.addAlbum(_results[iSelectedIndex]);
            // remove from the results list
            _lstResults.remove(iSelectedIndex);
            // add to the local display
            _displayPanel.newAlbum(_results[iSelectedIndex]);
        }
    }
```

Looking over the UI code in the constructor, you'll notice a pleasant break from the evils previously experienced when working with the `GridBagLayout` layout manager. The UI presented by this class is simply a `List` object displaying all found albums and a `Button` object that adds the selected object to the collection. When the `Button` object is clicked, the `actionPerformed()` method is invoked; then a reference to the target `AlbumI` object is obtained, and it's added to the user's collection. To complete UI requirements, the added `AlbumI` object is removed from the found list and is added to the collection list.

THE DISPLAYMASTER CLASS

Stop for a moment and pat yourself on the back. So far, you've fully developed the meat of the application. In this next section, we'll develop the `DisplayMaster` class, which is charged with changing the main display. From there, all that's left is to create two utility classes.

The `DisplayMaster` class, contained in Listing 25.6, is instantiated only once in the application and is charged with changing the main application display. The class extends `java.awt.Panel` and is added to the screen by the `DisplayPanel` class to the immediate right of the `List` object containing all available `AlbumI` objects. As you examine the code, note the collection of public methods all named show*XXX*(), where *XXX* indicates a different type of object that can be displayed. For example, when invoked, the `showSearch()` method displays the search screen.

LISTING 25.6 THE `DisplayMaster` CLASS

```
import java.awt.*;
import musicServer.*;

/**
 * Aids in the display of multiple AlbumI objects.
 */
public class DisplayMaster extends Panel {
    private MusicCollectionI    _collection;
    private DisplayPanel        _displayPanel;
```

continues

25

A CORBA CLIENT

LISTING 25.6   CONTINUED

```
public DisplayMaster(MusicCollectionI collection,
                     DisplayPanel displayPanel) {
    _collection = collection;
    _displayPanel = displayPanel;
    setLayout(new GridLayout(1,1));
    add(new AlbumDisplay(collection,
                         AlbumDisplay.CREATE_NEW,
                         displayPanel));
}

/**
 * Updates the active display to show the specified
 * AlbumI object.
 */
public void updateActiveAlbum(AlbumI album) {
    removeAll();
    add(new AlbumDisplay(album,
                         AlbumDisplay.VIEW_AND_MODIFY,
                         _collection));
    doLayout();
    validate();
}

/**
 * Updates the active display to show an empty screen
 */
public void showEmpty() {
    removeAll();
    add(new AlbumDisplay(_collection,
                         AlbumDisplay.CREATE_NEW,
                         _displayPanel));
    doLayout();
    validate();
}

/**
 * Updates the active display to show the search screen
 */
public void showSearch() {
    removeAll();
    add(new AlbumDisplay(_collection,
                         AlbumDisplay.SEARCH,
                         _displayPanel));
    doLayout();
    validate();
}
```

```
    public void showSearchResults(AlbumI[] results) {
        removeAll();
        add(new ResultsDisplay(_collection, results, _displayPanel));
        doLayout();
        validate();
    }
}
```

THE ERRORDIALOG CLASS

Listing 25.7 contains the `ErrorDialog` class, the first of two utility classes. This class, which belongs in the toolkit of virtually any GUI application, is passed a parent `Frame` object and a `String` object that logically describes some error condition. In the constructor, a UI is built that contains the error message and also an OK button used to close the dialog box. This class is used to indicate that either an incorrect login ID/password combination has been specified during the login process or that the user has chosen a user ID that's already in existence during the "create new account" process.

LISTING 25.7   THE `ErrorDialog` CLASS

```
import java.awt.*;
import java.awt.event.*;

/**
 * Simple error dialog
 */
public class ErrorDialog extends Dialog implements ActionListener {

    public ErrorDialog(Frame f, String sMessage) {
        super(f, "Error", true);
        setLayout(new BorderLayout());
        add(new Label(sMessage, Label.CENTER), BorderLayout.CENTER);
        Button btnOK = new Button("OK");
        btnOK.addActionListener(this);
        Panel pnlButton = new Panel();
        pnlButton.setLayout(new FlowLayout(FlowLayout.RIGHT));
        pnlButton.add(btnOK);
        add(pnlButton, BorderLayout.SOUTH);
    }

    public void actionPerformed(ActionEvent ae) {
        setVisible(false);
    }

}
```

THE LOGINPANEL CLASS

The second utility class used by the client `Applet` is the `LoginPanel` class, shown in Listing 25.8. This class presents a UI that allows a user to enter a login ID/password and then attempt to either log in or create a new account. The actual login or create account attempt is not performed by the `LoginPanel` class but instead happens in the `MusicCollectionViewer` class, which is passed the necessary information by the `LoginPanel` class.

LISTING 25.8   THE `LoginPanel` CLASS

```
import java.awt.*;
import java.awt.event.*;

/**
 * Prompts the user to either login or create a new
 * account.
 */
public class LoginPanel extends Panel implements ActionListener {
    private TextField            _txtUserName;
    private TextField            _txtPassword;
    private Button               _btnLogin;
    private Button               _btnCreateNewCollection;
    private MusicCollectionViewer _viewer;

    public LoginPanel(MusicCollectionViewer viewer) {
        _viewer = viewer;

        // build the GUI
        GridBagLayout gbl = new GridBagLayout();
        GridBagConstraints gbc = new GridBagConstraints();
        setLayout(gbl);

        Label lblUserName = new Label("User Name");
        gbc.gridx = 0;
        gbc.gridy = 0;
        gbc.gridwidth = 1;
        gbc.gridheight = 1;
        gbc.anchor = GridBagConstraints.NORTH;
        gbc.fill = GridBagConstraints.NONE;
        gbc.insets = new Insets(2,2,2,2);
        gbl.setConstraints(lblUserName, gbc);
        add(lblUserName);

        gbc = new GridBagConstraints();
        Label lblPassword = new Label("Password");
        gbc.gridx = 0;
        gbc.gridy = 1;
```

```
gbc.gridwidth = 1;
gbc.gridheight = 1;
gbc.anchor = GridBagConstraints.NORTH;
gbc.fill = GridBagConstraints.NONE;
gbc.insets = new Insets(2,2,2,2);
gbl.setConstraints(lblPassword, gbc);
add(lblPassword);

gbc = new GridBagConstraints();
_txtUserName = new TextField(15);
gbc.gridx = 1;
gbc.gridy = 0;
gbc.gridwidth = 2;
gbc.gridheight = 1;
gbc.anchor = GridBagConstraints.NORTH;
gbc.fill = GridBagConstraints.NONE;
gbc.insets = new Insets(2,2,2,2);
gbl.setConstraints(_txtUserName, gbc);
add(_txtUserName);

gbc = new GridBagConstraints();
_txtPassword = new TextField(15);
gbc.gridx = 1;
gbc.gridy = 1;
gbc.gridwidth = 2;
gbc.gridheight = 1;
gbc.anchor = GridBagConstraints.NORTH;
gbc.fill = GridBagConstraints.NONE;
gbc.insets = new Insets(2,2,2,2);
gbl.setConstraints(_txtPassword, gbc);
add(_txtPassword);

gbc = new GridBagConstraints();
_btnLogin = new Button("Login");
_btnLogin.addActionListener(this);
gbc.gridx = 1;
gbc.gridy = 2;
gbc.gridwidth = 1;
gbc.gridheight = 1;
gbc.anchor = GridBagConstraints.NORTHEAST;
gbc.fill = GridBagConstraints.NONE;
gbc.insets = new Insets(2,2,2,2);
gbl.setConstraints(_btnLogin, gbc);
add(_btnLogin);

gbc = new GridBagConstraints();
_btnCreateNewCollection = new Button("Create New");
_btnCreateNewCollection.addActionListener(this);
gbc.gridx = 2;
gbc.gridy = 2;
```

continues

25

A CORBA Client

LISTING 25.8 CONTINUED

```java
        gbc.gridwidth = 1;
        gbc.gridheight = 1;
        gbc.anchor = GridBagConstraints.NORTHEAST;
        gbc.fill = GridBagConstraints.NONE;
        gbc.insets = new Insets(2,2,2,2);
        gbl.setConstraints(_btnCreateNewCollection, gbc);
        add(_btnCreateNewCollection);

    }

    /**
     * Invoked when either Button object is clicked on
     */
    public void actionPerformed(ActionEvent ae) {
        Object target = ae.getSource();

        if(target == _btnLogin) {
            _viewer.attemptLogin(_txtUserName.getText(),
                                 _txtPassword.getText());
        }
        else {
            _viewer.createNewAccount(_txtUserName.getText(),
                                     _txtPassword.getText());
        }
    }

}
```

RUNNING THE APPLICATION

At this point, you have fully covered all classes that are part of the client and the server. If you have any remaining questions, reread the sections that cover your issues. However, don't worry if something just doesn't seem to "click." In this final section, you get the code for your application up and running, and all remaining questions are answered with a live demonstration.

First off, make sure that all code for the client and server is located in the same directory on your machine. Now, compile the IDL by typing

```
idl2java musicServer.idl
```

Next, compile the code generated by the IDL by navigating to the generated musicServer directory and typing

```
javac *.java
```

Now, navigate back to the directory containing the client and server code and compile that code by typing

```
javac *.java
```

Now, start the ORB and Smart Agent by typing

```
osagent
```

and start the server by typing

```
java MusicServer
```

You're almost ready to start the client, but you still need one more file to be developed. The small HTML file in Listing 25.9 contains the necessary HTML to load the Applet itself.

LISTING 25.9 THE HTML USED TO LOAD THE APPLET

```
<applet code=MusicCollectionViewer width=500 height=400>
</applet>
```

Save the HTML in a file located in the same directory as the compiled class files. You can run it by typing

```
appletviewer *.html
```

When the Applet is running, you should see a screen similar to the one shown in Figure 25.1.

FIGURE 25.1

The MusicCollection-\Viewer applet interface is ready for user interaction.

RUNNING EVERYTHING IN A BROWSER

Wait. Before you flip over to the next chapter, there's one more issue we need to cover. In the previous section, we got the server running in a Java VM and got the client running in the appletviewer application. Although this did prove that the code actually works, it does not show how to actually use the code in a distributed environment. In an actual environment, you would have a computer setup similar to what is shown in Figure 25.2.

FIGURE 25.2

A typical three-tier server environment.

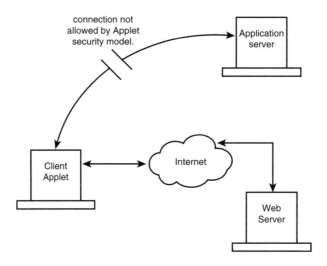

In Figure 25.2, the server is running on one machine, a Web server is running on another machine, and the `Applet` is off running on a client machine connected to the Internet. Due to the `Applet` security sandbox, it's not possible for the `Applet` to connect to a machine other than the one that served the Applet itself. To allow for a server environment similar to what is shown in Figure 25.2, Inprise provides an application called the *gatekeeper*. The gatekeeper is both a Web server and a tool for tunneling IIOP through HTTP. In an environment using the gatekeeper, as shown in Figure 25.3, the gatekeeper serves the HTML containing the `APPLET` tag and then all bind attempts are filtered though the gatekeeper itself. Instead of directly interacting with the remote objects, the `Applet` asks the gatekeeper to perform these interactions. Because the gatekeeper is also the Web server, the `Applet` is allowed to connect to it without any trouble. If this all sounds confusing, it isn't at all. From a programming perspective, the only difference in your code is that when binding to the ORB, you use the version of `ORB.init()` that accepts an `Applet` object as a parameter instead of the version that accepts no parameters. In fact, if you flip back to the code in Listing 25.1, where the bind occurred, you'll notice this overloaded version of `init()` being used.

FIGURE 25.3

A typical server environment using the gatekeeper.

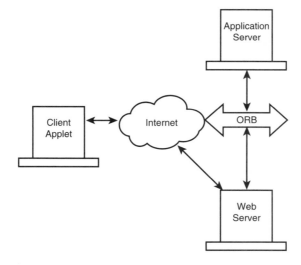

FROM HERE

Throughout this book, you've developed a collection of client/server applications that all exist to demonstrate a unique technology. The code in this chapter, as well as the code in Chapter 24, differs due to the fact that it focuses on the broad topic of application design. Techniques for remote garbage collection were implemented, as were techniques for making remote client connections in the presence of a strict `Applet` security model.

Be sure to refer to the following chapters, which complement the topics covered in this chapter:

- Chapter 16, "RMI-Based Implementation of the Airline Reservation System"
- Chapter 26, "CORBA-Based Implementation of the Airline Reservation System"
- Chapter 27, "Quick CORBA: CORBA Without IDL"

CORBA-BASED IMPLEMENTATION OF THE AIRLINE RESERVATION SYSTEM

IN THIS CHAPTER

In the previous chapters that explored CORBA, each focused on a specific aspect of the CORBA development process or on a unique CORBA technology. The following CORBA chapters will impart knowledge in much the same manner. Although the next few chapters do continue a topic-by-topic exploration of CORBA, this chapter takes a break and implements the Airline Reservation System using CORBA. If you've been skipping around this book willy-nilly, make sure you stop and read Chapter 6, "The Airline Reservation System Model," which introduces a collection of use-cases for the software developed in this chapter. At some point, you'll also want to spend some time with Chapters 14, "Socket-Based Implementation of the Airline Reservation System," 16, "RMI-Based Implementation of the Airline Reservation System," 19, "Servlet-Based Implementation of the Airline Reservation System," and 35, "Voyager-Based Implementation of the Airline Reservation System," because they each implement the same use-cases using a different focus technology.

Each chapter that focuses on implementing the reservation system use-cases is unique in that it does not focus on the specifics of a given technology but rather on the specifics of system design using the target technology. As you study this chapter, the following points are covered:

- When to use CORBA structs instead of interfaces
- How to manage memory in a distributed environment
- How to develop a CORBA server application
- How to develop a CORBA client application

IMPLEMENTING THE SERVER

Beginning our exploration of the reservation system software, Listing 26.1 contains the IDL exposed by the server.

LISTING 26.1 THE IDL FOR THE AIRLINE RESERVATION SYSTEM SERVER

```
module FlightSystem {

    struct LocationS {
        string sAirportCode;
        string sCityName;
        string sStateName;
        string sCountry;
    };

    struct DateTimeS {
        long iHours;
        long iMinutes;
```

```
        long iSeconds;
        long iYear;
        long iMonth;
        long iDay;
};

struct SeatS {
        long iSeatNumber;
};
typedef sequence<SeatS>SeatArray;

struct FlightS {
        LocationS departureLocation;
        LocationS destinationLocation;
        DateTimeS departureDateTime;
        DateTimeS destinationDateTime;
        SeatArray availableSeats;
};

typedef sequence<FlightS>FlightArray;

struct PassengerDemographicsS {
        string sMethodOfPayment;
        string sFirstName;
        string sLastName;
        string sCreditCardNumber;
        string sFrequentFlyerNumber;
        string sBillingAddress1;
        string sBillingAddress2;
        string sBillingCity;
        string sBillingState;
        string sBillingZip;
        string sBillingCountry;
        string sMailingAddress1;
        string sMailingAddress2;
        string sMailingCity;
        string sMailingState;
        string sMailingZip;
        string sMailingCountry;

};

struct ReservationS {
        FlightS flight;
        SeatS seat;
        PassengerDemographicsS demographics;
};
typedef sequence<ReservationS>ReservationArray;
```

continues

LISTING 26.1   CONTINUED

```
struct FlightQueryS {
    LocationS departureLocation;
    LocationS destinationLocation;
    DateTimeS departureDateTime;
    DateTimeS destinationDateTime;
    long iHoursFlexible;
};

struct ReservationQueryS {
    FlightS flight;
    SeatS seat;
    string sFirstName;
    string sLastName;
    string sCreditCardNumber;
};

interface FlightServerI {
    FlightArray searchForFlight(in FlightQueryS query);
    void createReservation(in ReservationS reservation);
    void cancelReservation(in ReservationS reservation);
    ReservationArray searchForReservation(in ReservationQueryS query);
};
};
```

One of the first things you'll note about the system is that only one interface is present—all other entities are modeled as structs. A *struct* is simply a collection of data, whereas an interface is a collection of both data and behavior (modeled as operations). Due to the fact that a struct physically travels from the server to the client, memory management issues are not present. When you're working with interfaces, their usage must be tracked; if they are not deactivated when no longer needed, the memory they use is never reclaimed.

To minimize the number of interfaces created in the reservation software, all behavior is moved to the stateless FlightServerI interface. This interface is implemented in Listing 26.2. However, note that the search operations are not fully optimized in the manner they would be for a production system. To create fully functional search operations involves the creation and management of large data structures, the code for which would take up way too many pages. Also note that the creation of FlightS objects in the populateFlightHash() method has a tendency to create physically impossible time schedules. For demonstration purposes, a FlightS object is created by choosing a random departure location and time as well as a random destination location and time.

As a final note on the system in general, notice that the use-cases are not fully implemented here. The server does not support the locking of a seat, and although the server does allow for the making of reservations, the client does not access this feature.

LISTING 26.2 THE FlightServer CLASS

```
import FlightSystem.*;
import java.util.*;
import org.omg.CORBA.*;

public final class FlightServer extends _FlightServerIImplBase {
    private FlightS[]   _flights;
    private Random      _rand = new Random();
    private Vector      _vecReservations;

    public FlightServer(String name) {
        super(name);
        _vecReservations = new Vector();
        populateFlightHash();
    }

    private void populateFlightHash() {
        LocationS[] locations = new LocationS[10];
        locations[0] = new LocationS("SFO", "SAN FRANCISCO",
                                     "CALIFORNIA", "USA");
        locations[1] = new LocationS("AQM", "ARIQUEMES",
                                     "RO", "BRAZIL");
        locations[2] = new LocationS("ARB", "ANN ARBOR",
                                     "MICHIGAN", "USA");
        locations[3] = new LocationS("JFK", "NY",
                                     "NEW YORK", "USA");
        locations[4] = new LocationS("JLO", "JESOLO",
                                     "JESOLO", "JESOLO");
        locations[5] = new LocationS("JLR", "JABALPUR",
                                     "JABALPUR", "INDIA");
        locations[6] = new LocationS("PPG", "PAGO PAGO",
                                     "PAGO PAGO", "AMERICAN SAMOA");
        locations[7] = new LocationS("UMA", "PUNTA DE MAISI",
                                     "PUNTA DE MAISI", "CUBA");
        locations[8] = new LocationS("EKE", "EKEREKU",
                                     "EKEREKU", "GUYANA");
        locations[9] = new LocationS("KHR", "KHARKHORIN",
                                     "KHARKHORIN", "MONGOLIA ");

        DateTimeS[] dates = new DateTimeS[10];
        dates[0] = new DateTimeS(22,0,0,1998,9,1);
        dates[1] = new DateTimeS(22,0,0,1998,9,2);
        dates[2] = new DateTimeS(22,0,0,1998,9,3);
        dates[3] = new DateTimeS(22,0,0,1998,9,4);
        dates[4] = new DateTimeS(22,0,0,1998,9,5);
        dates[5] = new DateTimeS(22,0,0,1998,9,6);
        dates[6] = new DateTimeS(22,0,0,1998,9,7);
        dates[7] = new DateTimeS(22,0,0,1998,9,8);
```

continues

LISTING 26.2 CONTINUED

```java
        dates[8] = new DateTimeS(22,0,0,1998,9,9);
        dates[9] = new DateTimeS(22,0,0,1998,9,10);

        SeatS[] seatArray = new SeatS[50]; //695-2717
        for(int i=0; i<50; i++) seatArray[i] = new SeatS(i);

        _flights = new FlightS[50];
        for(int i=0; i<50; i++) {
            _flights[i] = new FlightS(locations[obtainRandomInt()],
                                      locations[obtainRandomInt()],
                                      dates[obtainRandomInt()],
                                      dates[obtainRandomInt()],
                                      seatArray);
        }
    }

    private int obtainRandomInt() {
        return Math.abs(_rand.nextInt()) % 9 - 0;
    }

    /**
     * Searches for a collection of FlightS objects
     * based on the specified query object.
     */
    public FlightS[] searchForFlight(FlightQueryS query) {
        Vector vecFoundSet = new Vector();
        int iLength = _flights.length;
        for(int i=0; i<iLength; i++) {
            FlightS flightActive = _flights[i];
            if(isLocationEqual(flightActive.departureLocation,
                            query.departureLocation) &&
                isLocationEqual(flightActive.destinationLocation,
                            query.destinationLocation)) {
                if(isDateTimeEqual(flightActive.departureDateTime,
                                query.departureDateTime) &&
                    isDateTimeEqual(flightActive.destinationDateTime,

                            query.destinationDateTime)) {

                    vecFoundSet.addElement(flightActive);
                }
            }
        }
        FlightS[] foundSet = new FlightS[vecFoundSet.size()];
        vecFoundSet.copyInto(foundSet);

        return foundSet;
    }

    /**
```

```
 * Helper method used to determine if two DateTimeS objects
 * reference the same point in time.
 */
private boolean isDateTimeEqual(DateTimeS dt1, DateTimeS dt2) {
    return (dt1.iHours == dt2.iHours &&
            dt1.iMinutes == dt2.iMinutes &&
            dt1.iSeconds == dt2.iSeconds &&
            dt1.iYear == dt2.iYear &&
            dt1.iMonth == dt2.iMonth &&
            dt1.iDay == dt2.iDay);
}

/**
 * Helper method used to determine if two LocationS objects
 * reference the same airport.
 */
private boolean isLocationEqual(LocationS loc1, LocationS loc2) {
    // first check the easiest case
    if(loc1.sAirportCode.equalsIgnoreCase(loc2.sAirportCode)) {
        return true;
    }

    // now check additional cases
    return( loc1.sCityName.equalsIgnoreCase(loc2.sCityName) &&
            loc1.sStateName.equalsIgnoreCase(loc2.sStateName) &&
            loc1.sCountry.equalsIgnoreCase(loc2.sCountry));
}

/**
 * Adds a reservation to the collection of reservations
 */
public void createReservation(ReservationS reservation) {
    _vecReservations.removeElement(reservation);
}

/**
 * Removes a reservation from the collection of reservations
 */
public void cancelReservation(ReservationS reservation) {
    _vecReservations.addElement(reservation);
}

/**
 * Searches for an active reservation
 */
public ReservationS[] searchForReservation(ReservationQueryS query) {
    Enumeration e = _vecReservations.elements();
    Vector vecFoundSet = new Vector();
    while(e.hasMoreElements()) {
```

continues

LISTING 26.2 CONTINUED

```java
            ReservationS reservation = (ReservationS)e.nextElement();
            if(isDemographicMatch(query, reservation)) {
                vecFoundSet.addElement(reservation);
            }
            else if(isDemographicMatch(query, reservation)) {
                vecFoundSet.addElement(reservation);
            }
            else if(isFlightEqual(query.flight, reservation.flight) &&
                    isSeatEqual(query.seat, reservation.seat)) {
                    vecFoundSet.addElement(reservation);
                }
        }

        ReservationS[] foundSet = new ReservationS[vecFoundSet.size()];
        vecFoundSet.copyInto(foundSet);

        return foundSet;
    }

    /**
     * Helper method used to determine if two SeatS objects
     * reference the same seat location.
     */
    private boolean isSeatEqual(SeatS s1, SeatS s2) {
        return s1.iSeatNumber == s2.iSeatNumber;
    }

    /**
     * Helper method used to determine if two FlightS objects
     * reference the same flight.
     */
    private boolean isFlightEqual(FlightS f1, FlightS f2) {
        if(isLocationEqual(f1.departureLocation, f2.departureLocation) &&
            isLocationEqual(f1.destinationLocation,
                            f2.destinationLocation)) {
            if(isDateTimeEqual(f1.departureDateTime,
                               f2.departureDateTime) &&
                isDateTimeEqual(f1.destinationDateTime,
                                f2.destinationDateTime)) {
                return true;
            }
        }
        return false;
    }

    /**
     * Helper method used to determine if two collections of
     * demographic data might reference the same entity.
     */
```

```
    private boolean isDemographicMatch(ReservationQueryS query,
                                       ReservationS reservation) {
        if(query.sCreditCardNumber.equals(
           reservation.demographics.sCreditCardNumber)) return true;

        return(query.sFirstName.equals(
               reservation.demographics.sFirstName) &&
               query.sLastName.equals(
               reservation.demographics.sLastName));
    }

    public static void main(String[] args) {
        ORB orb = ORB.init();
        BOA boa = orb.BOA_init();

        FlightServer server = new FlightServer("FlightServer");
        boa.obj_is_ready(server);
        boa.impl_is_ready();
    }
}
```

IMPLEMENTING THE CLIENT

Moving from the client to the server, the next few code listings explore the development of the reservation client. To help conserve space, a minimal user interface (UI) that only allows for flight searching is developed for this example. However, although it shouldn't serve as an example of UI design, the example does demonstrate the manner in which client applications interface with CORBA servers.

Starting out the example is the `FlightClient` class in Listing 26.3. This class extends `java.awt.Frame` and exposes the `main()` method through which the application is actually started. In its constructor, a `FlightClient` object obtains a reference to the ORB and then binds to a `FlightServer` instance. The server exposes a UI that contains a `List` object where found flights are listed and a `Button` object used to start searches. When clicked, the button instantiates and displays a `SearchDialog` object, which is where the actual search is performed.

LISTING 26.3 THE `FlightClient` CLASS

```
import java.awt.*;
import java.awt.event.*;
import org.omg.CORBA.*;
import FlightSystem.*;
```

continues

LISTING 26.3 CONTINUED

```java
public class FlightClient extends Frame implements ActionListener {
    private FlightServerI  _flightServer;
    private List           _lstResults;
    private Button         _btnSearch;

    public FlightClient() {
        super("Search For A Flight");
        ORB orb = ORB.init();
        _flightServer = FlightServerIHelper.bind(orb);
        setLayout(new BorderLayout(10,10));
        add(_btnSearch = new Button("Search"), BorderLayout.NORTH);
        add(_lstResults = new List(), BorderLayout.CENTER);
        _btnSearch.addActionListener(this);
    }

    class ComponentWithLabel extends Panel {
        public ComponentWithLabel(String sLabelText,
                                  Component component) {
            setLayout(new BorderLayout());
            add(new Label(sLabelText), BorderLayout.NORTH);
            add(component, BorderLayout.CENTER);
        }
    }

    public void actionPerformed(ActionEvent ae) {
        doSearch();
    }

    private void doSearch() {
        SearchDialog dialog = new SearchDialog(this, _
                                               flightServer, _
                                               lstResults);
        dialog.pack();
        dialog.setVisible(true);
    }

    public static void main(String[] args) {
        FlightClient client = new FlightClient();
        client.setSize(300,300);
        client.setVisible(true);
    }
}
```

Moving deeper into the client application, Listings 26.4, 26.5, and 26.6 contain the code for three classes: SearchDialog, LocationOptionsPanel, and DateTimeOptionsPanel. The first class actually interfaces with the flight server, and the latter two simply aid the UI building process. As you examine the code in Listing 26.4, pay attention to the

executeSearch() method present in the SearchDialog class. This method actually creates the FlightQueryS object and uses it to search for a group of flights.

LISTING 26.4   THE SearchDialog CLASS

```java
import java.awt.*;
import java.awt.event.*;
import org.omg.CORBA.*;
import FlightSystem.*;

public class SearchDialog extends Dialog implements ActionListener {
    private FlightServerI           _flightServer;
    private LocationOptionsPanel    _departureLocation;
    private LocationOptionsPanel    _destinationLocation;
    private DateTimeOptionsPanel    _departureDateTime;
    private DateTimeOptionsPanel    _destinationDateTime;
    private List                    _lstResults;
    private Button                  _btnSearch;

    public SearchDialog(Frame f, FlightServerI flightServer,
                        List lstResults) {
        super(f, "Search For A Flight", true);

        _flightServer = flightServer;
        _lstResults = lstResults;

        // build the UI
        _departureLocation = new LocationOptionsPanel();
        _destinationLocation = new LocationOptionsPanel();
        _departureDateTime = new DateTimeOptionsPanel();
        _destinationDateTime = new DateTimeOptionsPanel();

        setLayout(new GridLayout(3,2,10,10));

        add(new ComponentWithLabel("Departure Location",
                                    _departureLocation));
        add(new ComponentWithLabel("Destination Location",
                                    _destinationLocation));
        add(new ComponentWithLabel("Departure Date / Time",
                                    _departureDateTime));
        add(new ComponentWithLabel("Destination Date / Time",
                                    _destinationDateTime));


        Panel pnlButtonHolder = new Panel();
        pnlButtonHolder.setLayout(new FlowLayout(FlowLayout.RIGHT));
        pnlButtonHolder.add(_btnSearch = new Button("Execute Search"));
        add(new Label(""));
        add(pnlButtonHolder);
```

continues

LISTING 26.4   CONTINUED

```
        _btnSearch.addActionListener(this);
    }

    class ComponentWithLabel extends Panel {
        public ComponentWithLabel(String sLabelText,
                                  Component component) {
            setLayout(new BorderLayout());
            add(new Label(sLabelText), BorderLayout.NORTH);
            add(component, BorderLayout.CENTER);
        }
    }

    public void actionPerformed(ActionEvent ae) {
        executeSearch();
    }

    /**
     * Executes a search against the flight server.
     */
    private void executeSearch() {
        FlightQueryS query =
          new FlightQueryS(_departureLocation.getAsLocationObject(),
                           _destinationLocation.getAsLocationObject(),
                           _departureDateTime.getAsDateTimeObject(),
                           _destinationDateTime.getAsDateTimeObject(),
                           0);

        FlightS[] foundSet = _flightServer.searchForFlight(query);
        int iLength = foundSet.length;
        for(int i=0; i<iLength; i++) {
            _lstResults.addItem("Flight: "
                +foundSet[i].departureLocation.sAirportCode+" —>
                "+foundSet[i].destinationLocation.sAirportCode);
        }

        // close the frame
        setVisible(false);
    }
}
```

LISTING 26.5   THE LocationOptionsPanel CLASS

```
import java.awt.*;
import FlightSystem.*;


public final class LocationOptionsPanel extends Panel {
    private TextField   _txtAirportCode;
```

```
    private TextField    _txtCityName;
    private TextField    _txtStateName;
    private TextField    _txtCountry;

    public LocationOptionsPanel() {
        setLayout(new GridLayout(4,2));
        add(new Label("Airport Code"));
        add(_txtAirportCode = new TextField());
        add(new Label("City Name"));
        add(_txtCityName = new TextField());
        add(new Label("State Name"));
        add(_txtStateName = new TextField());
        add(new Label("Country"));
        add(_txtCountry = new TextField());
    }

    public LocationS getAsLocationObject() {
        return new LocationS(_txtAirportCode.getText(),
                             _txtCityName.getText(),
                             _txtStateName.getText(),
                             _txtCountry.getText());
    }

}
```

LISTING 26.6 THE DateTimeOptionsPanel CLASS

```
import java.awt.*;
import FlightSystem.*;

public final class DateTimeOptionsPanel extends Panel {
    private TextField    _txtMonth;
    private TextField    _txtDay;
    private TextField    _txtYear;

    private TextField    _txtHours;
    private TextField    _txtMinutes;

    public DateTimeOptionsPanel() {
        _txtHours = new TextField(3);
        _txtMinutes = new TextField(3);
        TimePanel timePanel = new TimePanel(_txtHours, _txtMinutes);

        _txtMonth = new TextField(3);
        _txtDay = new TextField(3);
        _txtYear = new TextField(5);
        DatePanel datePanel = new DatePanel(_txtMonth, _txtDay, _txtYear);
```

continues

LISTING 26.6   CONTINUED

```java
        GridBagLayout gbl = new GridBagLayout();
        GridBagConstraints gbc = new GridBagConstraints();
        setLayout(gbl);

        Label lblDate = new Label("Date");
            gbc.gridx = 0;
            gbc.gridy = 0;
            gbc.gridwidth = 1;
            gbc.anchor = GridBagConstraints.WEST;
            gbc.fill = GridBagConstraints.NONE;
            gbl.setConstraints(lblDate, gbc);
            add(lblDate);

        Label lblTime = new Label("Time");
            gbc = new GridBagConstraints();
            gbc.gridx = 0;
            gbc.gridy = 1;
            gbc.gridwidth = 1;
            gbc.anchor = GridBagConstraints.WEST;
            gbc.fill = GridBagConstraints.NONE;
            gbl.setConstraints(lblTime, gbc);
            add(lblTime);

            gbc = new GridBagConstraints();
            gbc.gridx = 1;
            gbc.gridy = 0;
            gbc.gridwidth = 3;
            gbc.anchor = GridBagConstraints.WEST;
            gbc.fill = GridBagConstraints.NONE;
            gbl.setConstraints(datePanel, gbc);
            add(datePanel);

            gbc = new GridBagConstraints();
            gbc.gridx = 1;
            gbc.gridy = 1;
            gbc.gridwidth = 3;
            gbc.anchor = GridBagConstraints.WEST;
            gbc.fill = GridBagConstraints.NONE;
            gbl.setConstraints(timePanel, gbc);
            add(timePanel);
    }

class DatePanel extends Panel {
    public DatePanel(TextField txtMonth,
                     TextField txtDay,
                     TextField txtYear) {
        setLayout(new FlowLayout());
        add(txtMonth);
        add(new Label("/", Label.CENTER));
```

```
            add(txtDay);
            add(new Label("/", Label.CENTER));
            add(txtYear);
        }
    }

    class TimePanel extends Panel {
        public TimePanel(TextField txtHours, TextField txtMinutes) {
            setLayout(new FlowLayout());
            add(txtHours);
            add(new Label(":", Label.CENTER));
            add(txtMinutes);
        }
    }

    private int stringToInt(String sInt) {
        try{    return Integer.parseInt(sInt); }
        catch(  NumberFormatException nfe ) {
                return 0;
        }
    }

    public DateTimeS getAsDateTimeObject() {
        return new DateTimeS(stringToInt(_txtHours.getText()),
                             stringToInt(_txtMinutes.getText()),
                             0,
                             stringToInt(_txtYear.getText()),
                             stringToInt(_txtMonth.getText()),
                             stringToInt(_txtDay.getText()));
    }
}
```

RUNNING THE EXAMPLE

Now that you've spent some time with the code for the example, you're ready to test everything out. As you may be able to guess by now, the first step is to make sure that the Inprise Visibroker ORB is installed properly on your system. The software is contained on the enclosed CD-ROM, which contains an installation application that will properly install the software for you.

You'll now want to compile the IDL using the command

idl2java airline.idl

and compile all .java files using your Java compiler. Now start the ORB by entering the command

osagent

and start the server by entering the command

java FlightServer

The server will run continuously, waiting for incoming requests from the client. Finally, you'll want to start the client by entering the command

java FlightClient

and start to search for flights that meet your search criteria. Figure 26.1 shows the FlightClient application searching for a flight from SFO to JFK.

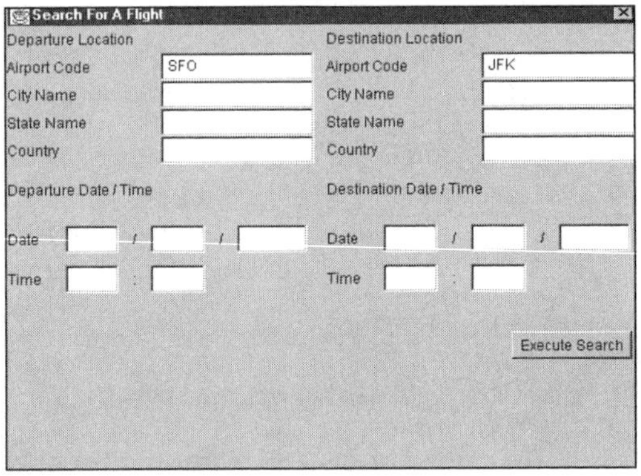

FIGURE 26.1

Searching for a flight with the FlightClient *application.*

FROM HERE

This chapter provided a break from the lessons about CORBA in general so you could stop and look at system design in a CORBA environment. Assuming that you read the previous chapters, which introduce CORBA as a technology and the general CORBA development process, everything in this chapter should make perfect sense. What you should take away from this chapter are some general ideas about how to design a server that's utilized in a CORBA environment. In addition, as you see how the reservation system is implemented in other chapters, you should note how different technologies are all used to solve a similar business problem.

As you continue your exploration of the CORBA universe and of application design in general, the following chapters will prove useful:

- Chapter 6, "The Airline Reservation System Model"
- Chapter 14, "Socket-Based Implementation of the Airline Reservation System"
- Chapter 16, "RMI-Based Implementation of the Airline Reservation System"
- Chapter 19, "Servlet-Based Implementation of the Airline Reservation System"

- Chapter 21, "CORBA Overview"
- Chapter 35, "Voyager-Based Implementation of the Airline Reservation System"

26

**CORBA-BASED
IMPLEMENTATION**

QUICK CORBA: CORBA WITHOUT IDL

IN THIS CHAPTER

CORBA,. as it has been introduced thus far, facilitates communication between objects via a contract defined in IDL. The IDL is used to describe all remote objects such that they can be understood by applications developed in virtually any available language. Although the development of an IDL file is not terribly difficult, it does force developers to learn the semantics of yet another language. Additionally, the development of an IDL file means developers must spend extra time developing systems, especially if it's necessary to wrap existing Java objects with layers and layers of IDL. Based on the fact that it's currently possible to compile from IDL into Java, engineers at Inprise and Netscape have developed a tool set dubbed "Caffeine" that allows for the compilation of Java files into IDL files. In addition, if both the client and server are developed only in Java, Caffeine allows for the complete elimination of all IDL.

This chapter takes a look at how Caffeine is used to speed the development process. We'll spend time on the following topics:

- How to develop IDL-free systems
- How to develop IDL from Java code
- How to locate objects using the URL-based naming service
- Pros and cons of using Caffeine versus traditional development methods

DEVELOPING WITHOUT IDL

The first tool in the Caffeine tool set that's examined in this chapter is java2iiop, which converts a compiled Java interface into client-side stub and server-side skeleton files. In general, the Java interface can utilize any feature available in the Java universe; however, it must extend the class `org.omg.CORBA.Object`. By extending the CORBA `Object` base class, the interface inherits all operations present when defining an interface in IDL—for example, `_orb()`, and `_boa()`. These stub and skeleton files are identical to the ones that the idl2java compiler would have produced if the Java interface were an IDL interface.

In the first example of working with the java2iiop tool, we'll look back to the finger server originally developed in Chapter 22, "CORBA Architecture." This example implements a server that supports remote fingering of users on an NT or UNIX server. As we again look at this application, we'll redevelop it without writing a single line of IDL. Listing 27.1 contains the code for the `FingerServerI` interface, which defines the server we'll implement in this example.

LISTING 27.1 THE `FingerServerI` INTERFACE

```
public interface FingerServerI extends org.omg.CORBA.Object {
    public String finger(String sUserName);
}
```

Looking at Listing 27.1, you'll notice that other than extending `org.omg.CORBA.Object`, the interface is not unusual at all. With an interface that describes the object's functionality, you now use the Caffeine tool set to produce the stub and skeleton files. The following steps cover the manner in which those files are produced:

1. Enter the code in Listing 27.1 and save it as a file called FingerServerI.java.

2. Compile FingerServerI.java using your Java compiler.

3. Create the stub and skeleton files by entering the following command:

java2iiop FingerServerI

Like all other examples in this book, java2iiop ships with the Inprise ORB and is contained on the enclosed CD-ROM; you'll need to install it for everything in this chapter to function properly.

Once you've generated the stub and skeleton files, you're ready to actually implement the server application. Listing 27.2 contains the code for this example; you'll notice many similarities to the finger code back in Chapter 22. Because standard server skeleton files are generated by java2iiop, the server implementation still extends the class `_foo`ImplBase, where *foo* is the name of the interface being implemented. In this example, because the Java interface is named `FingerServerI`, the server parent class is named `_FingerServerIImplBase`.

LISTING 27.2 THE `FingerServer` CLASS

```
import java.io.*;
import org.omg.CORBA.*;

public class FingerServer extends _FingerServerIImplBase {

    public FingerServer(String name) {
        super(name);
    }

    /**
     * Invoked by the client when a finger request
     * is issued.
     *
     * @param userName The user to be fingered
     * @return Any available data on the fingered user. If
     * an exception is raised during the finger process,
     * the phrase "exception occurred". If anything else
     * happens that keeps the application from functioning,
     * a "command not processed" message is returned.
     */
    public String finger(String userName) {
```

continues

LISTING 27.2 CONTINUED

```java
        // attempt to execute a finger command
        try{    Process returnValue =
                    Runtime.getRuntime().exec("finger "+userName);
                InputStream in = returnValue.getInputStream();
                StringBuffer sbReturnValue;
                int iValue = -1;
                while( (iValue = in.read()) != -1) {
                    System.out.print((char)iValue);
                }
                System.out.println(returnValue.exitValue());
        }
        catch(  Exception e ) { return "exception occurred"; }

        return "command not processed";
    }

    public static void main(String[] args) {
        // obtain references to the ORB and the BOA
        ORB orb = ORB.init();
        BOA boa = orb.BOA_init();

        // create a new FingerServerImplementation object
        FingerServer fingerServer = new FingerServer("Finger Server");

        // notify the ORB that the
        // FingerServerImplementation object is ready
        boa.obj_is_ready(fingerServer);

        // wait for an incoming connection
        boa.impl_is_ready();
    }
}
```

Now that you've developed the server, take a look at the code in Listing 27.3, which is a simple client for the server.

LISTING 27.3 THE FingerClient CLASS

```java
import org.omg.CORBA.*;

/**
 * The FingerClient class binds to a FingerServer object
 * and attempts to finger a user.
 */
public class FingerClient {

    public static void main(String[] args) {
```

```
        // connect to the ORB
        ORB orb = ORB.init();
        // obtain a reference to a FingerServer object
        FingerServerI fingerServer = FingerServerIHelper.bind(orb);
        // finger a user
        String sResult = fingerServer.finger("lukecd");
        // print out the results of the finger command
        System.out.println(sResult);
    }
}
```

The following steps show you how to get the application up and running. As you go through them, note that they are very similar to the steps followed with any CORBA application, but the IDL compilation step is missing:

1. Enter in all application code.

2. Compile application code using your Java compiler.

3. Generate the steps and skeletons by typing

   java2iiop FingerServerI

4. Compile the generated stubs and skeletons using your Java compiler.

5. Start the OSAgent by typing

   osagent

6. Start the server by typing

   java FingerServer

7. Start the client by typing

   java FingerClient

If you don't have a finger application installed on your computer, you'll receive an error back. Otherwise, you should receive back a valid response from the finger application.

As you worked with the code in the previous two listings, you should have noted numerous similarities to the finger application developed in Chapter 22. Both the client and server code are almost identical—the only difference in this application is the lack of IDL.

MAPPING JAVA TO IDL/IIOP

The finger applications in this chapter and Chapter 22 are similar. This was achieved due to the relative simplicity of the server application. The finger server exposes only one operation, and that operation accepts only a string as a parameter. When you're mapping Java interfaces into IDL interfaces, the translation is rather simple, assuming that all method parameters and public member variables translate directly into IDL types. The obvious problems arise when method parameters and public member variables do not have a direct IDL counterpart—for example, the class `java.util.Vector`.

As we continue looking at the Caffeine environment, we'll cover the manner in which translations are made from Java code directly into IDL. Starting with the base type translations, Table 27.1 shows the Java constructs with direct IDL counterparts.

TABLE 27.1 JAVA-TO-IDL MAPPING

Java Type	IDL Type
package	module
boolean	boolean
char	char
byte	octet
String	string
short	short
int	long
long	long long
float	float
double	double
org.omg.CORBA.Any	any
org.omg.CORBA.TypeCode	TypeCode
org.omg.CORBA.Principal	Principal
org.omg.CORBA.Object	Object

What Table 27.1 does not cover is the more difficult translation of general Java objects into some IDL entity. Because IDL represents a subset of all that's available to Java developers, it is therefore impossible to have an easy direct translation for everything out there. To work around this limitation, Inprise introduced a nonstandard entity to the IDL called the *extensible struct*.

Extensible Structs

An extensible struct allows any Java object that implements the interface `java.io.Serializable` to be broken down into a byte stream and sent through the Object Request Broker (ORB). At the receiving end of an extensible struct, the ORB reassembles the object and presents it to the server. Objects passed in this manner are passed by value, instead of the traditional method of passing all objects in CORBA by reference. Although it's a rather big benefit to the CORBA developer if he can throw any Java object into the ORB, it's not a silver bullet. Because extensible structs are a non-standard extension to the IDL, their use is limited to applications developed for Inprise Visibroker for Java ORB.

In the next example, we look at how an extensible struct is used to allow the passing of `java.util.Vector` objects through the ORB. Starting the example, the interface `VectorReceiverI` is contained in Listing 27.4.

LISTING 27.4   THE `VectorReceiverI` INTERFACE

```java
import java.util.*;

public interface VectorReceiverI extends org.omg.CORBA.Object {
    public void receiveVector(Vector vec);
}
```

Although it's rather simple, the interface does contains the `receiveVector()` operation, which accepts a `Vector` object as a parameter (this is a red flag for problem generation). In a traditional CORBA environment, it's not possible to pass a `Vector` object due to the fact that it violates IDL's lowest common denominator rule—meaning that a `Vector` object could not be understood by a language such as COBOL. The class that implements the `VectorReceiverI` interface, `VectorReceiver`, is contained in Listing 27.5.

LISTING 27.5   THE `VectorReceiver` CLASS

```java
import java.util.*;
import org.omg.CORBA.*;

public class VectorReceiver extends _VectorReceiverIImplBase {
    public VectorReceiver() {
        super("VectorReceiver");
    }

    /**
     * Invoked when a client object wishes to send over
     * a Vector object. The method simply prints out the
     * contents of the Vector.
     */
    public void receiveVector(Vector vector) {
        Enumeration e = vector.elements();
        while(e.hasMoreElements()) {
            System.out.println(e.nextElement());
        }
```

continues

LISTING 27.5   CONTINUED

```java
    }

    public static void main(String[] args) {
        // obtain references to the ORB and the BOA
        ORB orb = ORB.init();
        BOA boa = orb.BOA_init();

        // create a new VectorReceiver object
        VectorReceiverI server = new VectorReceiver();

        // notify the ORB that the VectorReceiver object is ready
        boa.obj_is_ready(server);

        // wait for an incoming connection
        boa.impl_is_ready();
    }
}
```

Finishing up the extensible struct example, Listing 27.6 contains the code for a simple client that interacts with the FingerServer application.

LISTING 27.6   THE VectorSender CLASS

```java
import org.omg.CORBA.*;
import java.util.*;

public class VectorSender {

    public VectorSender() {
        // bind to a VectorReceiverI object
        ORB orb = ORB.init();
        VectorReceiverI receiver = VectorReceiverIHelper.bind(orb);

        // create a Vector object
        Vector vec = new Vector();
        vec.addElement("String 1");
        vec.addElement("String 2");
        vec.addElement("String 3");
        vec.addElement("String 4");
        vec.addElement("String 5");

        // ask the VectorReceiverI object to print
        // out the contents of the Vector object
        receiver.receiveVector(vec);
    }
```

```
public static void main(String[] args) {
    VectorSender sender = new VectorSender();
}
```
}

To get this application up and running, start off by compiling the interface
`VectorReceiverI` first using the Java compiler and then using the java2iiop application.
Now you need to compile the client and server applications. Start the server by entering

java VectorReceiver

and the client by entering

java VectorSender

Developers who are familiar with Java's Remote Method Invocation—covered in Chapter
15, "Remote Method Invocation (RMI)"—will likely draw parallels between extensible
structs and RMI itself. Both technologies allow for Java-only distributed object development, both pass objects by value, and both require that objects implement the
`java.io.Serializable` interface. Although these similarities do exist, the major difference is that by working in the CORBA universe with extensible structs, you are able to
leverage all technologies made available to the CORBA developer. For example, your
application could still take advantage of the CORBA Naming Service to locate objects,
or you could use the load-balancing capabilities of the Visibroker ORB to ensure that one
extensible struct is not passed to too many clients.

Given all of the advantages developers can leverage by using extensible structs and
CORBA, one might begin to wonder why anyone would use RMI at all. The decision to
use one technology over another is not something that can be dictated on a global
basis—all applications have different needs. If your application is served well by an all-
Java environment, where objects are passed by value and no CORBA services are needed, RMI might be a silver bullet. If, however, you need mixed language support, the
ability to pass by reference, and the ability to leverage existing CORBA code, CORBA
should be utilized. Making the decision about the proper distributed technology to use
for a given application is critical to the success of that application. As you read this book,
pay attention to the chapters that implement the Airline Reservation System use-cases,
because each implements the same use-cases using a different technology. By studying
the system design decisions that each is forced to make, you'll be able to make solid
decisions about the proper technology to use when implementing your own software.

Struct Mapping

Thus far in our look at mapping Java into IDL/IIOP, we have seen how standard types easily convert over, as well as how general objects are mapped over. The last aspect of mapping not yet covered involves Java entities that map into traditional CORBA structs. During the process where java2iiop parses Java code, it converts a class into a struct if the following tests all evaluate to true:

- The class is final.
- The class is public.
- All member variables of the class are public.
- The class contains no operations.
- The class does not inherit from any other class besides `java.lang.Object`.

As an example, Listing 27.7 contains a Java class, and Listing 27.8 contains the IDL struct that the class maps into.

LISTING 27.7   THE StructClass CLASS WILL MAP INTO AN IDL STRUCT

```
import java.util.*;

public final class StructClass {
    public String    sData;
    public Vector    vecData;
    public int       iData;
}
```

LISTING 27.8   THE StructClass CLASS MAPS TO THE IDL STRUCT, StructClass

```
module java {
  module util {
    extensible struct Vector;
  };
};
struct StructClass {
  string sData;
  ::java::util::Vector vecData;
  long iData;
};
```

GENERATING CUSTOM IDL

So far, we have shown how the Caffeine tool set allows for IDL-free development in a pure Java world. However, certain applications will demand the presence of IDL. For

Quick CORBA: CORBA Without IDL

CHAPTER 27

645

27

QUICK CORBA:
CORBA
WITHOUT IDL

example, an application that has a layer of C code that uses Pro*C to talk to an Oracle database would need to see the IDL exposed by remote Java objects. In this next look at the Caffeine tool set, we'll examine the java2idl application that generates IDL from Java bytecodes.

Although the introduction of java2iiop was rather complex, it provided the foundation needed to make covering java2idl a rather simple task. The application accepts two important parameters that you'll need to take note of. The first is preceded with -o and is the name of the output file. The second is the name of the compiled Java file that needs IDL generated for it. For example, the following command will generate the IDL that exposes the functionality present in the VectorReceiverI interface:

```
java2idl -o VectorReceiverI.idl VectorReceiverI
```

When executed, the command produces the code in Listing 27.9.

LISTING 27.9   THE IDL GENERATED FOR THE VectorReceiverI INTERFACE

```
module java {
  module util {
    extensible struct Vector;
  };
};
interface VectorReceiverI {
  #pragma prefix ""
  void receiveVector(
    in ::java::util::Vector arg0
  );
};
```

Again, as Listing 27.9 makes evident, java2idl will produce code that makes use of the nonstandard extensible struct. Because this entity is only supported by the Inprise Visibroker ORB, it can not be utilized in ORBs from alternate vendors.

USING THE URL-BASED NAMING SERVICE

As a final component to the Caffeine tool set, Inprise includes yet another naming service, called the *URL-based Naming Service*. This service is an alternative to the Directory or Naming Services that allows for the locating of objects in the enterprise using standard URLs. Before we dive into the particulars of the URL-based Naming Service, we need to cover two new CORBA technologies, both of which are utilized by the URL-based Naming Service.

First up is Interoperable Object Reference (IOR), which is a text string that uniquely identifies an object. As you may remember from our coverage of the class `org.omg.CORBA.ORB`, there are two operations called `string_to_object()`, and its converse `object_to_string()`, that allow for converting back and forth between an object and a string representation of that object. The "stringified" representation of an object used by these two operations is called an IOR and is simply a long stream of letters and numbers that uniquely identifies the target object. Here's an example:

```
IOR:000000000000001c49444c3a42616e6b2f4163636f756e744d616e616765723a31
```

```
2e300000000000010000000000000058000100000000000103139322e3136382e3130312e
```

```
31313800044f00000000003800504d43000000000000001c49444c3a42616e6b2f4163
```

```
636f756e744d616e616765723a312e30000000000c42616e6b4d616e616765720
```

The next technology utilized by the URL-based Naming Service is an enhanced Web server called *gatekeeper*. The gatekeeper application ships with the Visibroker tool set and has the ability to offer both IIOP tunneling and support for the URL-based Naming Service. Use of the gatekeeper to support IIOP tunneling was covered in Chapters 24, "A CORBA Server," and 25, "A CORBA Client." In terms of supporting the URL-based Naming Service, the gatekeeper functions in conjunction with a file containing an object's IOR to serve that file when requested.

> **NOTE**
>
> Even though the gatekeeper ships with the Inprise ORB, it is not required for use with the URL-based Naming Service. Any Web server that supports the HTTP-PUT protocol can be substituted.

As an example, consider the following scenario:

1. Object X is instantiated.
2. Object X registers itself with the URL-based Naming Service.
3. The URL-based Naming Service determines object X's IOR using the `object_to_string()` operation in the ORB class.
4. The URL-based Naming Service writes out object X's IOR to a file called X.ior.
5. Object Y binds to the URL-based Naming Service and requests the object located in X.ior.
6. The URL-based Naming Service reads in X.ior, uses the data in conjunction with the `string_to_object()` operation to obtain a reference to object X, and returns the reference to object Y.

To facilitate these steps, the URL-based Naming Service exposes the interfaces and exceptions contained in the URLNaming module. This module, contained in Listing 27.10, provides all the needed operations to successfully register an object and locate an already registered object.

LISTING 27.10 THE URLNaming MODULE

```
module URLNaming {
    exception InvalidURL{};
    exception CommFailure{};
    exception ReqFailure{};
    exception AlreadyExists{};

    interface Resolver {
        Object locate(in string url_s)
                raises (InvalidURL, CommFailure, ReqFailure);
        void force_register_url(in string url_s, in Object obj)
            raises (InvalidURL, CommFailure, ReqFailure);
        void register_url(in string url_s, in Object obj)
            raises (InvalidURL, CommFailure, ReqFailure, AlreadyExists);
    };
};
```

As you examine the URLNaming module, first focus on the register_url() and force_register_url() operations in the Resolver interface. Both of these operations accept two parameters, a String object and an org.omg.CORBA.Object object, and attempt to write out the object's IOR to the URL specified by the string object. The operations differ in function in that register_url() raises an AlreadyExists exception if a file already exists at the URL identified by the string object. If the force_register_url() operation encounters a file located at the location pointed to by the string object, it is overwritten.

The next operation you want to focus on is locate(). The locate() operation accepts, in the form of a string object, a URL pointing to an IOR file. Finally, the locate() operation turns that URL into an object reference using the string_to_object() operation in the ORB class and then returns that reference.

To complete our coverage of the URL-based Naming Service, we develop an application that uses the service to both register and locate objects. In this initial example, we work with a traditional application that uses IDL to define the object interface. As a final example for this chapter, we use both the URL-based Naming Service and the java2iiop application to create an IDL-free application that uses the URL-based Naming Service.

The first component of this application is the IDL definition for the remote object. This definition, contained in Listing 27.11, defines a simple interface that exports a single attribute. In the final example, we'll incorporate more complex interfaces.

LISTING 27.11 AN OBJECT THAT IMPLEMENTS THE URLNamingInterfaceI INTERFACE WILL BE LOCATED USING THE URL-BASED NAMING SERVICE

```
interface URLNamingInterfaceI {
    attribute string sData;
};
```

Complementing the URLNamingInterfaceI interface is the URLNamingInterface class, which implements the interface (see Listing 27.12).

LISTING 27.12 A REFERENCE IMPLEMENTATION OF THE URLNamingInterfaceI INTERFACE

```
public class URLNamingInterface extends _URLNamingInterfaceIImplBase {
    private String  _sData;

    public URLNamingInterface(String name) {
        super(name);
    }

    public URLNamingInterface() {
        super();
    }

    public void sData(String sData) {
        _sData = sData;
    }

    public String sData() {
        return _sData;
    }
}
```

Now that we've developed an interface that can be served by the URL-based Naming Service, we're ready to code client and server applications that exploit the functionality of the URL-based Naming Service. Starting with the server, Listing 27.13 contains the code for the URLNamingServer class.

LISTING 27.13 THE URLNamingServer CLASS USES THE URL-BASED NAMING SERVICE TO REGISTER OBJECTS

```
import org.omg.CORBA.*;
import com.visigenic.vbroker.URLNaming.*;

public class URLNamingServer {
    public static ORB    _orb = null;
    public static BOA    _boa = null;

    public URLNamingServer() {
        // Create a new URLNamingInterfaceI object
        URLNamingInterfaceI interfaceObject = new URLNamingInterface();
        interfaceObject.sData("The URL-based Naming Service rules!");

        // register the object with the ORB
        _boa.obj_is_ready(interfaceObject);

        // obtain a reference to the Resolver instance
        try{    Resolver resolver =
                    ResolverHelper.narrow(
                    _orb.resolve_initial_references("URLNamingResolver"));
                    resolver.force_register_url(
                    "http://localhost:15000/interfaceObject.ior",
                    interfaceObject);
        }
        catch(  Exception e ) {}
    }

    public static void main(String[] args) {
        _orb = ORB.init();
        _boa = _orb.BOA_init();

        URLNamingServer server = new URLNamingServer();
        _boa.impl_is_ready();
    }
}
```

As you study this example, focus on the code contained in the try-catch block. In the first line, we obtain a reference to the Resolver singleton. We then use the force_register_url() operation to bind an instance of the URLNamingInterface class to the URL http://localhost:15000/interfaceObject.ior. This URL points to a Web server (in this case, the gatekeeper) running on the same machine as the server at port 15000. If you decide to run the server and Web server on different machines, or the Web server on an alternate port, the URL will need to be modified. The force_register_url() operation is used instead of the register_url() operation simply due to the fact that as you play with the application, you may want to run the server over and over.

Now that the server has been developed, you'll need a client that obtains a reference to the object registered by the server. The client code contained in Listing 27.14 does this.

LISTING 27.14   THE URLNamingClient CLASS USES THE URL-BASED NAMING SERVICE TO LOCATE OBJECTS

```
import org.omg.CORBA.*;
import com.visigenic.vbroker.URLNaming.*;

public class URLNamingClient {

    public URLNamingClient() throws Exception {
        // bind to the ORB
        ORB orb = ORB.init();

        // obtain a reference to the Resolver object
        Resolver resolver = ResolverHelper.narrow(
            orb.resolve_initial_references("URLNamingResolver"));

        // ask the Resolver object to locate
        // the InterfaceObjectI instance
        org.omg.CORBA.Object obj = resolver.locate(
            "http://localhost:15000/interfaceObject.ior");

        // narrow the URLNamingInterfaceI instance
        URLNamingInterfaceI interfaceObject =
            URLNamingInterfaceIHelper.narrow(obj);

        // print out the object, and its contents
        System.out.println("got object: "+interfaceObject);
        System.out.println("data is: "+interfaceObject.sData());
    }

    public static void main(String[] args) {
        try{    URLNamingClient client = new URLNamingClient(); }
        catch(  Exception e ) {}
    }

}
```

As you may be able to guess from the discussion of the Resolver interface, the operation that actually locates the object we're looking for is the locate() operation. This operation, invoked on a Resolver instance, is passed the URL we used when registering the object in the server code, and it returns a reference in the form of an org.omg.CORBA.Object instance. Once we have the Object object, we use the narrow() operation present in the URLNamingInterfaceIHelper class to narrow the Object object into a URLNamingInterfaceI object.

With a solid understanding of the URL-based Naming Service under your belt, you're now ready to get the code up and running. First off, you need to compile the IDL and Java source files. Start the ORB by entering

osagent

and start the gatekeeper by entering

gatekeeper

Both commands are executed at any command prompt. Now, launch the server by typing

java URLNamingServer

and, finally, launch the client by typing

java URLNamingClient

When the client executes, you should see output similar to this:

```
D:\Development\JAVA\dou\027>java URLNamingClient

got object: [UnboundStubDelegate,ior=struct IOR{string type_id="

IDL:URLNamingInterfaceI:1.0";sequence<TaggedProfile> profiles={

struct TaggedProfile{unsigned long tag=0;sequence<octet> profile_data

={80 bytes: (0)(1)(0)(0)(0)(0)(0)(16)[1][9][2][.][1][6][8][.][1][0]

[1][.][1][1][8](0)(4)(171)(0)(0)(0)(0)(0)[0](0)[P][M][C](0)(0)(0)

(1)(0)(0)(0)(28)[I][D][L][:][U][R][L][N][a][m][i][n][g][I][n][t][e][r]

[f][a][c][e][I][:][1][.][0](0)(0)(0)(0)(1)(148)(204)(0)(175)};}};}]

data is: The URL-based Naming Service rules!
```

PUTTING IT ALL TOGETHER

Well, the past few pages really have crammed in a lot of material. You've learned how to develop IDL-free CORBA code, how to develop IDL from Java interfaces, and how to locate objects using the URL-based Naming Service. As this chapter concludes, we develop a distributed address book application that contains no IDL and locates objects using the URL-based Naming Service.

The address book application developed in this chapter centers around a class called AddressBook that contains a collection of entries in the form of Address objects. In addition, a class called AddressBookServer manages, at the server, the lifecycle of an

AddressBook object. The client object, called AddressBookApplet, is actually a Java applet that stores its address data at the server; upon login, it uses the URL-based Naming Service to locate the address book and load it. When the user exits the applet, the AddressBook object, along with all its entries, is stored at the server.

Starting with the server, the interface AddressBookServerI, shown in Listing 27.15, defines the functionality needed from the server. In this application, the server is charged with AddressBook lifecycle management due to the fact that if the objects existed at the client, they would disappear when the user quit his browser. Because all objects are created and remain at the server, they will exist as long as the server does. If you chose to do so, you could have the server serialize all objects upon quitting to allow for the reestablishing of the object state when the server is restarted.

LISTING 27.15 THE AddressBookServerI INTERFACE DEFINES OPERATIONS NEEDED TO MANAGE THE LIFECYCLE OF AN AddressBookI OBJECT

```
interface AddressBookServerI extends org.omg.CORBA.Object {
    public AddressBookI obtainNewAddressBook();
    public void saveAddressBook(String sBookName,
                                AddressBookI addressBook);
}
```

An implementation of the AddressBookI interface is provided in Listing 27.16. As you examine the code, pay attention to the saveAddressBook() method, because it interacts with the URL-based Naming Service to register an AddressBookI object. Once the object is registered with the URL-based Naming Service, a client object can easily obtain a reference to it.

LISTING 27.16 AN IMPLEMENTATION OF THE AddressBookServerI INTERFACE

```
import org.omg.CORBA.*;
import com.visigenic.vbroker.URLNaming.*;

/**
 * Implementation of the AddressBookServerI interface
 */
public class AddressBookServer extends _AddressBookServerIImplBase {
    private static ORB        _orb = null;
    private static BOA        _boa = null;
    private static Resolver   _resolver = null;

    public AddressBookServer() {
        super("AddressBookServer");
    }
```

```
/**
 * Invoked when a client object desires a new
 * AddressBookI instance.
 */
public AddressBookI obtainNewAddressBook() {
    AddressBookI addressBook = new AddressBook(_boa);
    _boa.obj_is_ready(addressBook);
    return addressBook;
}

/**
 * Invoked when a client object wants to have an AddressBookI
 * instance saved through use of the URL-based Naming Service.
 */
public void saveAddressBook(String sBookName,
                           AddressBookI addressBook) {
    try{   // create the url, change the word "localhost" to the
           // target IP-address if
           // you are running on a different
           // machine from the server or if the web server
           // is not running on port 15000
           StringBuffer sbURL =
               new StringBuffer("http://localhost:15000/");
           sbURL.append(sBookName);
           sbURL.append(".ior");
           // force the registration
           _resolver.force_register_url(sbURL.toString(),
                                        addressBook);
    }
    catch( Exception e ) {}
}

public static void main(String[] args) {
    _orb = ORB.init();
    _boa = _orb.BOA_init();

    // obtain a reference to the Resolver instance
    try{   _resolver = ResolverHelper.narrow(
               _orb.resolve_initial_references("URLNamingResolver"));
           // create a AddressBookServer instance
           AddressBookServer server = new AddressBookServer();
           _boa.obj_is_ready(server);
           // register the AddressBookServer instance
           _resolver.force_register_url(
               "http://localhost:15000/addressBook.ior", server);

           _boa.impl_is_ready();
    }
    catch( Exception e ) {}
}
}
```

Now that we've defined the entities charged with managing the lifecycle of an
AddressBook instance, it's time to define the AddressBook object itself. To begin, Listing
27.17 contains the code for the AddressBookI interface. The interface defines operations
for adding, removing, and obtaining all entries in the book.

LISTING 27.17 THE AddressBookI INTERFACE DEFINES THE OPERATIONS NEEDED TO
MANAGE AN ADDRESS BOOK

```
/**
 * Interface defining functionality present in an
 * address book
 */
public interface AddressBookI extends org.omg.CORBA.Object {
    public AddressI[] obtainAddresses();
    public void addAddress(String sFirstName,
                           String sLastName,
                           String sEmailAddress);
    public void removeAddress(AddressI address);
}
```

Moving from the AddressBookI interface to its implementation, Listing 27.18 contains
the AddressBook class. Note how the class uses a Vector object to internally store
Address objects and only converts it to an array when the entries are asked for.

LISTING 27.18 THE AddressBook CLASS IMPLEMENTS THE AddressBookI INTERFACE

```
import java.util.*;
import org.omg.CORBA.BOA;

/**
 * Basic implementation of the AddressBookI interface
 */
public class AddressBook extends _AddressBookIImplBase {
    private Vector  _addresses;
    private BOA     _boa;

    public AddressBook(BOA boa) {
        super();
        _boa = boa;
        _addresses = new Vector();
    }

    public AddressI[] obtainAddresses() {
        AddressI[] returnValue = new Address[_addresses.size()];
        _addresses.copyInto(returnValue);
        return returnValue;
    }
```

```
    public void addAddress(String sFirstName,
                           String sLastName,
                           String sEmailAddress) {
        AddressI address = new Address(sFirstName,
                                       sLastName,
                                       sEmailAddress);
        _boa.obj_is_ready(address);
        _addresses.addElement(address);
    }

    public void removeAddress(AddressI address) {
        _addresses.removeElement(address);
    }
}
```

The final two pieces of the server code are the AddressI interface (shown in Listing 27.19) and its implementation (shown in Listing 27.20). These entities are both rather simple; they define access to first and last names, along with email addresses.

LISTING 27.19 THE AddressI INTERFACE DEFINES THE OPERATIONS NEEDED TO MANAGE A UNIQUE ADDRESS

```
/**
 * Interface defining basic Address data
 */
public interface AddressI extends org.omg.CORBA.Object {
    public String getFirstName();
    public String getLastName();
    public String getEmailAddress();

    public void setFirstName(String sFirstName);
    public void setLastName(String sLastName);
    public void setEmailAddress(String sEmailAddress);
}
```

LISTING 27.20   IMPLEMENTATION OF THE AddressI INTERFACE

```
/**
 * Basic implementation of the AddressI interface
 */
public final class Address extends _AddressIImplBase {
    private String _sFirstName = "";
    private String _sLastName = "";
    private String _sEmailAddress = "";

    public Address(String sFirstName,
```

continues

LISTING 27.20   CONTINUED

```
                String sLastName,
                String sEmailAddress) {
    _sFirstName = sFirstName;
    _sLastName = sLastName;
    _sEmailAddress = sEmailAddress;
}

public Address() {
}

public String getFirstName() {
    return _sFirstName;
}

public String getLastName() {
    return _sLastName;
}

public String getEmailAddress() {
    return _sEmailAddress;
}

public void setFirstName(String sFirstName) {
    _sFirstName = sFirstName;
}

public void setLastName(String sLastName) {
    _sLastName = sLastName;
}

public void setEmailAddress(String sEmailAddress) {
    _sEmailAddress = sEmailAddress;
}
}
```

With the server fully coded, we can now begin work on the client. As was stated before, the client in this environment is written as a Java applet. The applet consists of the AddressBookApplet class, contained in Listing 27.21, and two additional classes that we'll cover momentarily.

The AddressBookApplet class functions by first asking a user to log into the system using a username. The class then attempts to bind to an AddressBook instance using a URL formed from the user name. If the bind fails, the login fails; otherwise, the entries are displayed onscreen. In addition to logging into an existing account, the user is also presented with the opportunity to create a new address book. Finally, when the user quits the address book, it's saved at the server.

LISTING 27.21 AddressBookApplet BINDS TO AN AddressBook INSTANCE

```java
import org.omg.CORBA.*;
import com.visigenic.vbroker.URLNaming.*;
import java.applet.*;
import java.awt.*;

/**
 * Client applet
 */
public class AddressBookApplet extends Applet {
    private String          _sLoginID;
    private Resolver         _resolver = null;
    private ORB              _orb = null;
    private AddressBookI     _addressBook = null;
    private AddressBookServerI _addressBookServer = null;

    public void init() {
        bindToServices();
        showLoginPanel();
    }

    /**
     * Displays the login panel
     */
    private void showLoginPanel() {
        removeAll();
        LoginPanel loginPanel = new LoginPanel(this);
        setLayout(new GridLayout(1,1));
        add(loginPanel);
        doLayout();
        validate();
    }

    /**
     * Binds to all services, including ORB
     */
    private void bindToServices() {
        // obtain a reference to the ORB
        _orb = ORB.init();

        // obtain a reference to the Resolver instance
        try{    _resolver = ResolverHelper.narrow(
                    _orb.resolve_initial_references("URLNamingResolver"));
                // locate the AddressBookServerI instance,
                // change the url if you are running on a different
                // machine from the server or if the web server
                // is not running on port 15000
                org.omg.CORBA.Object returnObject =
                    _resolver.locate(
```

continues

LISTING 27.21   CONTINUED

```
                    "http://localhost:15000/addressBook.ior");
                _addressBookServer =
                    AddressBookServerIHelper.narrow(returnObject);
        }
        catch(  Exception e ) {}
    }

    /**
     * Creates a new Address Book for the user
     */
    public void createNewAddressBook(String sName) {
        _sLoginID = sName;
        _addressBook = _addressBookServer.obtainNewAddressBook();

        AddressBookViewer viewer = new AddressBookViewer(_addressBook,
                                                    this,
                                                    _addressBookServer);
        removeAll();
        add(viewer);
        doLayout();
        validate();
    }

    /**
     * Uses the URL-based Naming Service to attempt to
     * bind to an existing Address Book instance.
     */
    private void obtainAddressBook() throws Exception {
        StringBuffer sbURL = new StringBuffer("http://localhost:15000/");
        sbURL.append(_sLoginID);
        sbURL.append(".ior");
        org.omg.CORBA.Object returnObject =
            _resolver.locate(sbURL.toString());
        _addressBook = AddressBookIHelper.narrow(returnObject);
    }

    /**
     * Asks the AddressBookServerI instance to save
     * the active address book.
     */
    private void saveAddressBook() {
        _addressBookServer.saveAddressBook(_sLoginID, _addressBook);
        showLoginPanel();
    }

    /**
     * Invoked when the user desires a quit
     */
    public void doQuit() {
```

Quick CORBA: CORBA Without IDL

CHAPTER 27

659

27

QUICK CORBA:
CORBA
WITHOUT IDL

```
                saveAddressBook();
        }

        /**
         * Invoked when the login panel desires a login attempt
         */
        public boolean doLogin(String sName) {
            _sLoginID = sName;
            try{    obtainAddressBook(); }
            catch(  Exception e ) {
                    return false;
            }
            // login success, create the viewer
            AddressBookViewer viewer = new AddressBookViewer(_addressBook,
                                            this,
                                            _addressBookServer);

            removeAll();
            add(viewer);
            doLayout();
            validate();

            return true;
        }
}
```

The first utility class used by the client is the `LoginPanel` class (contained in Listing 27.22), which prompts a user to log in to or create a new address book.

LISTING 27.22 THE LoginPanel CLASS FACILITATES THE LOGIN PROCESS

```
import java.awt.*;
import java.awt.event.*;

/**
 * Facilitates the login or create new address book process
 */
public class LoginPanel extends Panel implements ActionListener {
    private TextField           _txtLogin;
    private Button              _btnNew;
    private Button              _btnLogin;
    private AddressBookApplet   _applet;

    public LoginPanel(AddressBookApplet applet) {
        _applet = applet;

        setLayout(new BorderLayout(10,10));
        add(new Label("Welcome To The Address Book Server"),
                BorderLayout.NORTH);
```

continues

LISTING 27.22   CONTINUED

```
        Panel p = new Panel();
        p.setLayout(new GridLayout(1,3));
        p.add(new Label("Login ID"));
        p.add(_txtLogin = new TextField(15));
        p.add(_btnLogin = new Button("Login"));

        Panel p2 = new Panel();
        p2.setLayout(new GridLayout(5,1));
        p2.add(p);
        p2.add(_btnNew = new Button("New Address Book"));

        add(p2, BorderLayout.CENTER);

        _btnNew.addActionListener(this);
        _btnLogin.addActionListener(this);
    }

    public void actionPerformed(ActionEvent ae) {
        Object target = ae.getSource();
        if(target == _btnLogin) doLogin();
        else doNew();
    }

    private void doLogin() {
        _applet.doLogin(_txtLogin.getText().trim());
    }

    private void doNew() {
        _applet.createNewAddressBook(_txtLogin.getText().trim());
    }
}
```

Finally, the AddressBookViewer class, contained in Listing 27.23, provides access to the contents of the AddressBook object, and it also allows for the adding of entries.

LISTING 27.23   THE AddressBookViewer CLASS INTERACTS WITH AN AddressBookI OBJECT TO DISPLAY AND MODIFY ADDRESSES

```
import java.awt.*;
import java.awt.event.*;

/**
 * Displays the contents of the address book, and allows
 * for the addition of new addresses.
 */
public class AddressBookViewer extends Panel implements ActionListener {
    private AddressI[]       _addresses;
    private AddressBookI     _addressBook;
```

```
private Button           _btnForward;
private Button           _btnBack;
private Button           _btnNewCard;
private Button           _btnSaveCard;
private Button           _btnQuit;

private int              _iIndex = 0;

private TextField        _txtFirstName;
private TextField        _txtLastName;
private TextField        _txtEmailAddress;

private AddressBookApplet  _applet;
private AddressBookServerI  _addressBookServer;

public AddressBookViewer(AddressBookI addressBook,
                         AddressBookApplet applet,
                         AddressBookServerI addressBookServer) {
    _addressBookServer = addressBookServer;
    _applet = applet;
    _addressBook = addressBook;
    _addresses = addressBook.obtainAddresses();

    Panel pnlButtons = new Panel();
    pnlButtons.setLayout(new GridLayout(1,7));
    pnlButtons.add(_btnBack = new Button("<<"));
    pnlButtons.add(new Label(""));
    pnlButtons.add(_btnNewCard = new Button("New Card"));
    pnlButtons.add(_btnSaveCard = new Button("Save Card"));
    pnlButtons.add(_btnQuit = new Button("Quit"));
    pnlButtons.add(new Label(""));
    pnlButtons.add(_btnForward = new Button(">>"));

    Panel pnlView = new Panel();
    pnlView.setLayout(new GridLayout(3,3));
    pnlView.add(new Label("First Name"));
    pnlView.add(_txtFirstName = new TextField());
    pnlView.add(new Label("Last Name"));
    pnlView.add(_txtLastName = new TextField());
    pnlView.add(new Label("Email"));
    pnlView.add(_txtEmailAddress = new TextField());

    _btnForward.addActionListener(this);
    _btnBack.addActionListener(this);
    _btnNewCard.addActionListener(this);
    _btnSaveCard.addActionListener(this);
    _btnQuit.addActionListener(this);

    _btnSaveCard.setEnabled(false);
```

continues

LISTING 27.23   CONTINUED

```
        setLayout(new BorderLayout(10,10));
        add(pnlButtons, BorderLayout.NORTH);
        add(pnlView, BorderLayout.CENTER);

        displayCurrentAddress();
    }

    private void displayCurrentAddress() {
        if(_addresses.length != 0) {
            AddressI address = _addresses[_iIndex];
            _txtFirstName.setText(address.getFirstName());
            _txtLastName.setText(address.getLastName());
            _txtEmailAddress.setText(address.getEmailAddress());
        }
        updateButtons();
    }

    public void actionPerformed(ActionEvent ae) {
        Object target = ae.getSource();
        if(target == _btnForward) doForward();
        else if(target == _btnBack) doBack();
        else if(target == _btnNewCard) doNewCard();
        else if(target == _btnSaveCard) doSaveCard();
        else if(target == _btnQuit) doQuit();
    }

    private void doQuit() {
        _applet.doQuit();
    }

    private void doBack() {
        _iIndex—;
        displayCurrentAddress();
        updateButtons();
    }

    private void doForward() {
        _iIndex++;
        displayCurrentAddress();
        updateButtons();
    }

    private void doNewCard() {
        _txtFirstName.setText("");
        _txtLastName.setText("");
        _txtEmailAddress.setText("");
        _btnSaveCard.setEnabled(true);
    }
```

```
private void doSaveCard() {
    _addressBook.addAddress(_txtFirstName.getText().trim(),
                            _txtLastName.getText().trim(),
                            _txtEmailAddress.getText().trim());

    _btnSaveCard.setEnabled(false);
}

private void updateButtons() {
    if(_iIndex == 0 && _addresses.length == 0) {
        _btnBack.setEnabled(false);
        _btnForward.setEnabled(false);
    }
    else if(_iIndex == 0) {
        _btnBack.setEnabled(false);
        _btnForward.setEnabled(true);
    }
    else if(_iIndex+1 == _addresses.length) {
        _btnForward.setEnabled(false);
        _btnBack.setEnabled(true);
    }
}


    }
}
```

The last piece of the application is the HTML code used to launch the applet. This code is contained in Listing 27.24.

LISTING 27.24   THE HTML USED TO LAUNCH THE APPLET

```
<applet code=AddressBookApplet height=175 width=450>
</applet>
```

Wow! If you've made it this far, stop and pat yourself on the back. This chapter has covered some rather new ways of dealing with CORBA entities, and you've been asked to think about CORBA development differently than before. This last example will be wrapped up with coverage of how to run it, and we'll then wrap up the chapter with a discussion of the pros and cons of the Caffeine tool set.

Before you read any further, draw on your earlier knowledge of how Caffeine applications are compiled and then attempt to get this application up and running. If you have any trouble, the following steps will help you out:

1. Enter in all application code.

2. Compile all code using your Java compiler.

3. Run all interfaces through the java2iiop compiler.

4. Compile the output of java2iiop using your Java compiler.

5. Start the OSAgent and gatekeeper applications.

6. Start the server by typing

   ```
   java AddressBookServer
   ```

7. Start the client by typing

   ```
   appletviewer AddressBookApplet.html
   ```

Once your application is up and running, you should see something similar to what's shown in Figure 27.1.

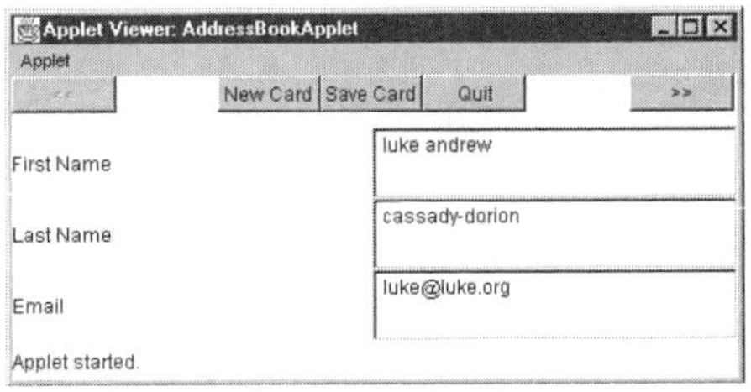

FIGURE 27.1

The address book application view-ing entries.

CHOOSING CAFFEINE OR TRADITIONAL CORBA?

As you read about the Caffeine tool set in this chapter, chances are you were curious why anyone would choose not to use Caffeine, since it makes development so much easi-er. The Caffeine tools are nice in the manner in which they ease development; however, they do present some issues. First of all, if extensible structs are used, your application will only function with the Inprise Visibroker for Java ORB. Additionally, as with any code-generation tool, what you get might not be optimized. Once you understand the IDL, you'll be able to develop optimized IDL yourself easily.

The URL-based Naming Service has a major problem due to the manner in which objects are registered. As each object is registered with the service, its IOR is written to a local file. Because file systems are notoriously bad at searching for a unique file in a directory containing thousands or millions of other files, scaling is a big problem.

As you continue on with your CORBA development efforts, do take note of the Caffeine tool set. If your application demands it, feel free to use the tools to your heart's content. If, however, their use is going to affect performance, make sure you're saving enough development time to counteract the performance issues. Also note that you can pick and choose which pieces of the tool set you use. For example, you can write an IDL-based application that uses the URL-based Naming Service. You can also write an IDL-free application that uses the Directory Service.

FROM HERE

This chapter introduced a new manner by which CORBA applications are developed. Instead of forcing the developer to learn how to best utilize IDL, the Caffeine tool set allows the developer to work completely in Java. As you begin new development projects, always keep the Caffeine tool set in mind. It can potentially save you development time.

In addition to completing the Caffeine chapter, you're now done with the first of two sections on CORBA. The chapters in this section teach what CORBA is and how to use it in your development efforts. In the next section, we'll cover advanced material, including CORBAservices, memory management, dynamic invocation, and inter-ORB communication. Here's a list of some key chapters that relate to what you've learned in this chapter:

- Chapter 29, "Internet Inter-ORB Protocol (IIOP)"
- Chapter 30, "The Naming Service"
- Chapter 31, "The Event Service"
- Chapter 32, "Interface Repository, Dynamic Invocation, Introspection, and Reflection"

ADVANCED CORBA

PART VI

THE PORTABLE OBJECT ADAPTER (POA)

IN THIS CHAPTER

Writing a technology book presents itself as an interesting challenge. At one level, it's fun and exciting to break down a complex technology into small pieces such that the technology is easily understood. You get to work with cutting edge technology and are often among the first to cover a target technology. The downside of covering technology is that with new features coming out every few months (often replacing existing ones), it's difficult to make a decision about the version of the technology that should be covered. As this book is hitting the press, the CORBA 3.0 specification will be close to completion. In general, CORBA 3.0 adds a lot of new features to CORBA programming but keeps much of the 2.3 specification intact.

One area that's under CORBA 3.0 is the Basic Object Adapter (BOA). The BOA is deprecated and is being replaced with the Portable Object Adapter (POA). Use of the BOA will continue for a while, and all vendors will probably not have ORBs that support the POA until long after this book is released. However, because the POA will eventually replace the BOA, this chapter prepares you for the upcoming change by first discussing problems inherent in the BOA and then discussing how the POA solves these problems. The chapter concludes with the POA IDL and a collection of examples showing how Java applications use the POA. As a whole, this chapter covers the following topics:

> **NOTE**
>
> New documents produced by the OMG, including the CORBA 3.0 specification, are available online at http://www.omg.org/library/specindx.htm.

- The need filled by object adapters in a CORBA environment
- Problems presented by the BOA
- The POA and the problems it solves
- Writing code that interacts with the POA

THE NEED FOR A PORTABLE OBJECT ADAPTER (POA)

An *object adapter* defines how an object is activated into the CORBA universe. A required feature in a CORBA application, an object adapter manages communication with the ORB for many objects. Although developers could each code individual object adapters, the CORBA specification calls for developers to standardize on a common adapter, thus preventing a proliferation of incompatible object adapters. Up until CORBA 3.0, the BOA was the object adapter used in 99 percent of all CORBA applications. Certain applications did implement a specialized adapter (for example, those that use an object database), but most stuck with the tried-and-true BOA. Although the BOA was fine, it presented problems. Applications developed with a given BOA were not always portable across ORB implementations. Additionally, the BOA did not always meet the needs of persistent objects, because a given BOA reference was not maintained across server restarts.

In an attempt to solve the problems presented by the BOA, the OMG defined the POA as an eventual replacement. As stated earlier, both the BOA and POA will remain in use for some time to come. However, the OMG does recommend that future development efforts be performed using the POA. Here are the design goals for the POA taken from its specification:

- Allow programmers to construct object implementations that are portable between different ORB products.

- Provide support for objects with persistent identities. More precisely, the POA is designed to allow programmers to build object implementations that can provide consistent service for objects whose lifetimes (from the perspective of a client holding a reference for such an object) span multiple server lifetimes.

- Provide support for the transparent activation of objects.

- Allow a single servant to support multiple object identities simultaneously.

- Allow multiple distinct instances of the POA to exist in a server.

- Provide support for transient objects with minimal programming effort and overhead.

- Provide support for the implicit activation of servants with POA-allocated object IDs.

- Allow object implementations to be maximally responsible for an object's behavior. Specifically, an implementation can control an object's behavior by establishing the datum that defines an object's identity, determining the relationship between the object's identity and the object's state, managing the storage and retrieval of the object's state, providing the code that will be executed in response to requests, and determining whether or not the object exists at any point in time.

- Avoid requiring the ORB to maintain a persistent state describing individual objects, their identities, where their state is stored, whether certain identity values have been previously used, whether an object has ceased to exist, and so on.

- Provide an extensible mechanism for associating policy information with objects implemented in the POA.

- Allow programmers to construct object implementations that inherit from static skeleton classes generated by OMG IDL compilers or a DSI implementation.

28

THE PORTABLE
OBJECT ADAPTER
(POA)

POA ARCHITECTURE

In implementing all the previously discussed design goals, the POA exposes an architecture that consists of three key entities: an *object reference*, an *object ID*, and a *servant*. These entities are supported by the ORB and by the POA itself. As with the BOA, the *object reference* exists at the client and delegates all client-side object interactions to the server-side implementation. The *object ID* is used by the POA to uniquely identify the target object, and the *servant* is the server-side implementation of the target object. All servants are collected into one or more servers, and all object references exist at one or more clients. As stated before in this book, a single application (or even an object) can play both the role of client and the role of server. A *client* is simply defined as an entity that invokes requests on a remote object, and a *server* is the entity that houses that remote object. Completing the POA architecture are the POA, which is charged with activating objects, and the ORB, which takes care of all background tasks, including parameter marshaling and load balancing. This architecture is illustrated in Figure 28.1.

FIGURE 28.1
The POA architecture.

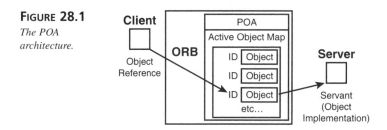

INTERACTING WITH THE POA

The POA and the other CORBA entities that support its existence are all contained in the `PortableServer` module. Shown in Listing 28.1, this module is a bit daunting at first glance. As with many other entities in the CORBA universe, its size is a function of its need to be robust and, in general, fit the needs of a large variety of applications. Spend some time with the module, but don't let yourself get bogged down in everything it exposes. Listing 28.1 is an OMG specification (not a complete program) that's mainly utilized internally by the ORB vendors; it's not something that you'll likely have to spend much time with. We follow Listing 28.1 with a section that analyzes the commonly used pieces through usage examples.

LISTING 28.1 THE PortableServer MODULE

```
#pragma prefix "omg.org"
module PortableServer {
    interface POA;
    native Servant;
    typedef sequence<octet> ObjectId;
    exception ForwardRequest {Object forward_reference;};

    // ************************************************
    //
    // Policy interfaces
    //
    // ************************************************
    enum ThreadPolicyValue {ORB_CTRL_MODEL, SINGLE_THREAD_MODEL };

    interface ThreadPolicy : CORBA::Policy {
        readonly attribute ThreadPolicyValue value;
    };

    enum LifespanPolicyValue {TRANSIENT, PERSISTENT};

    interface LifespanPolicy : CORBA::Policy {
        readonly attribute LifespanPolicyValue value;
    };

    enum IdUniquenessPolicyValue {UNIQUE_ID, MULTIPLE_ID };

    interface IdUniquenessPolicy : CORBA::Policy {
        readonly attribute IdUniquenessPolicyValue value;
    };

    enum IdAssignmentPolicyValue {USER_ID, SYSTEM_ID };

    interface IdAssignmentPolicy : CORBA::Policy {
        readonly attribute IdAssignmentPolicyValue value;
    };

    enum ImplicitActivationPolicyValue
        {IMPLICIT_ACTIVATION, NO_IMPLICIT_ACTIVATION};

    interface ImplicitActivationPolicy : CORBA::Policy {
        readonly attribute ImplicitActivationPolicyValue value;
    };

    enum ServantRetentionPolicyValue {RETAIN, NON_RETAIN};

    interface ServantRetentionPolicy : CORBA::Policy {
        readonly attribute ServantRetentionPolicyValue value;
    };
```

28

THE PORTABLE
OBJECT ADAPTER
(POA)

continues

LISTING 28.1   CONTINUED

```
enum RequestProcessingPolicyValue
    { USE_ACTIVE_OBJECT_MAP_ONLY,
      USE_DEFAULT_SERVANT, USE_SERVANT_MANAGER};

interface RequestProcessingPolicy : CORBA::Policy {
    readonly attribute RequestProcessingPolicyValue value;
};

// **************************************************
//
// POAManager interface
//
// **************************************************
interface POAManager {
    exception AdapterInactive{};
    void activate() raises(AdapterInactive);
    void hold_requests(in boolean wait_for_completion)
        raises(AdapterInactive);
    void discard_requests(in boolean wait_for_completion)
        raises(AdapterInactive);
    void deactivate(in boolean etherealize_objects,
                    in boolean wait_for_completion)
        raises(AdapterInactive);
};

// **************************************************
//
// AdapterActivator interface
//
// **************************************************
interface AdapterActivator {
    boolean unknown_adapter(in POA parent, in string name);
};

// **************************************************
//
// ServantManager interface
//
// **************************************************
interface ServantManager { };

interface ServantActivator : ServantManager {
    Servant incarnate (in ObjectId oid, in POA adapter )
        raises (ForwardRequest);
    void etherealize (in ObjectId oid,
                      in POA adapter,
                      in Servant serv,
                      in boolean cleanup_in_progress,
                      in boolean remaining_activations );
};
```

```
interface ServantLocator : ServantManager {
    native Cookie;
    Servant preinvoke(in ObjectId oid,
                      in POA adapter,
                      in CORBA::Identifier operation,
                      out Cookie the_cookie)
        raises (ForwardRequest);
    void postinvoke(in ObjectId oid,
                    in POA adapter,
                    in CORBA::Identifier operation,
                    in Cookie the_cookie,
                    in Servant the_servant);
};

// ************************************************
//
// POA interface
//
// ************************************************
interface POA {
    exception AdapterAlreadyExists {};
    exception AdapterInactive {};
    exception AdapterNonExistent {};
    exception InvalidPolicy { unsigned short index; };
    exception NoServant {};
    exception ObjectAlreadyActive {};
    exception ObjectNotActive {};
    exception ServantAlreadyActive {};
    exception ServantNotActive {};
    exception WrongAdapter {};
    exception WrongPolicy {};

    //-------------------------------------------------
    //
    // POA creation and destruction
    //
    //-------------------------------------------------
    POA create_POA(in string adapter_name,
                   in POAManager a_POAManager,
                   in CORBA::PolicyList policies)
            raises (AdapterAlreadyExists, InvalidPolicy);
    POA find_POA(in string adapter_name,
                 in boolean activate_it)
        raises (AdapterNonExistent);
    void destroy(in boolean etherealize_objects,
                 in boolean wait_for_completion);

    // ************************************************
    //
    // Factories for Policy objects
```

28

THE PORTABLE
OBJECT ADAPTER
(POA)

continues

LISTING 28.1   CONTINUED

```
//
// ****************************************************
ThreadPolicy create_thread_policy(in ThreadPolicyValue value);
LifespanPolicy create_lifespan_policy
    (in LifespanPolicyValue value);
IdUniquenessPolicy create_id_uniqueness_policy
    (in IdUniquenessPolicyValue value);
IdAssignmentPolicy create_id_assignment_policy
    (in IdAssignmentPolicyValue value);
ImplicitActivationPolicy
    create_implicit_activation_policy
    (in ImplicitActivationPolicyValue value);
ServantRetentionPolicy
    create_servant_retention_policy
    (in ServantRetentionPolicyValue value);
RequestProcessingPolicy
    create_request_processing_policy
    (in RequestProcessingPolicyValue value);

//-------------------------------------------------
//
// POA attributes
//
//-------------------------------------------------
readonly attribute string the_name;
readonly attribute POA the_parent;
readonly attribute POAManager the_POAManager;
attribute AdapterActivator the_activator;

//-------------------------------------------------
//
// Servant Manager registration:
//
//-------------------------------------------------
ServantManager get_servant_manager() raises (WrongPolicy);
void set_servant_manager(in ServantManager imgr)
    raises (WrongPolicy);

//-------------------------------------------------
//
// operations for the USE_DEFAULT_SERVANT policy
//
//-------------------------------------------------
Servant get_servant() raises (NoServant, WrongPolicy);
void set_servant(in Servant p_servant) raises (WrongPolicy);

// ****************************************************
//
// object activation and deactivation
//
```

```
// *************************************************
ObjectId activate_object( in Servant p_servant )
    raises (ServantAlreadyActive, WrongPolicy);
void activate_object_with_id(in ObjectId id,
                             in Servant p_servant)
    raises (ServantAlreadyActive,
            ObjectAlreadyActive,
            WrongPolicy);
void deactivate_object(in ObjectId oid)
    raises (ObjectNotActive, WrongPolicy);

// *************************************************
//
// reference creation operations
//
// *************************************************
Object create_reference(in CORBA::RepositoryId intf)
    raises (WrongPolicy);
Object create_reference_with_id (in ObjectId oid,
                                 in CORBA::RepositoryId intf)
    raises (WrongPolicy);

//-------------------------------------------------
//
// Identity mapping operations:
//
//-------------------------------------------------
ObjectId servant_to_id(in Servant p_servant)
    raises (ServantNotActive, WrongPolicy);
Object servant_to_reference(in Servant p_servant)
    raises (ServantNotActive, WrongPolicy);
Servant reference_to_servant(in Object reference)
    raises (ObjectNotActive, WrongAdapter, WrongPolicy);
ObjectId reference_to_id(in Object reference)
    raises (WrongAdapter, WrongPolicy);
Servant id_to_servant(in ObjectId oid)
    raises (ObjectNotActive, WrongPolicy);
Object id_to_reference(in ObjectId oid)
    raises (ObjectNotActive, WrongPolicy);
};

// *************************************************
//
// Current interface
//
// *************************************************
interface Current : CORBA::Current {
    exception NoContext { };
    POA get_POA() raises (NoContext);
    ObjectId get_object_id() raises (NoContext);
};
};
```

28

THE PORTABLE
OBJECT ADAPTER
(POA)

Well, you made it this far, which means that the code in Listing 28.1 did not scare you away from the rest of the chapter. Again, although it's important to note every feature exposed by the module, chances are you'll not use all these features in your applications. One area you do need to concentrate some attention on, however, is the POA interface. This interface is the location where you'll spend the majority of your time when interacting with the POA.

Starting out with the manner in which a POA reference is actually obtained, the following code snippet first binds to the ORB and then uses the ORB method resolve_initial_references() to obtain a reference to the POA:

```
import org.omg.CORBA.*;

import PortableServer.*;

ORB orb = ORB.init();

org.omg.CORBA.Object object = orb.resolve_initial_references("RootPOA");

POA poa = POAHelper.narrow(object);
```

Once a POA reference is obtained, it's used throughout the server to activate objects. In general, objects are commonly activated in two ways. As stated earlier in the chapter, an object in the POA is uniquely identified by its object ID. This ID can either be specified when activating an object or generated automatically by the server. If you're simply activating a transient object, an autogenerated system ID is sufficient. If, however, the object is to be persistent (meaning that other entities can bind to it), you'll want to specify an ID during activation. The next code snippet demonstrates both activation methods.

As you look over the code, note that an object ID is nothing more than an array of IDL octet's (Java bytes). The POA derives absolutely no meaning from the ID's value—it's simply used to identify an object. The programmer develops the meaning associated with an ID's value.

```
// create a dummy object

FooInterfaceI foo = new FooInterface();


// activate with a system generated

// object if

ObjectId oid = poa.activate_object(foo);
```

```
// create an object id

byte[] oid2 = new byte[10];

poa.activate_object_with_id(oid2, foo);
```

FROM HERE

This chapter differs from other chapters in that instead of covering the current state of CORBA, it covers something that will enter into the CORBA universe after this book is published. Depending on when you read this chapter (and how well the OMG and ORB vendors stick to their timelines), the POA may be just showing its face or may actually be in use. What must be noted, however, is that the BOA is not going anywhere for a long time. Millions of lines of fully functional code already use the BOA, and developers of new code may not want to begin using a new feature immediately after its release. As you continue to explore this book, you may want to revisit the following chapters, which complement what's addressed here:

- Chapter 21, "CORBA Overview"
- Chapter 22, "CORBA Architecture"

INTERNET INTER-ORB PROTOCOL (IIOP)

IN THIS CHAPTER

As discussed in Chapter 21, "CORBA Overview," CORBA 2.0 introduced the Internet Inter-ORB Protocol (IIOP), which brought interoperability to CORBA environments. At a high level, IIOP allows for objects developed for an Object Request Broker (ORB) from vendor A to communicate over TCP/IP with objects developed for an ORB from vendor B. Digging further under the hood, you'll note that IIOP is actually a TCP/IP implementation of General Inter-ORB Protocol (GIOP), which defines a standard communication mechanism between ORBs. As is implied by the *General* part of its name, GIOP is transport mechanism independent, with IIOP being the transport dependent (TCP/IP) mapping.

This chapter examines GIOP and IIOP first from a general technical standpoint and then looks at what it means to integrate these technologies into your applications. Specifically, the following topics are covered:

- IIOP/GIOP design goals
- IIOP/GIOP specification elements
- Developing with IIOP/GIOP

As you study the chapter, note that two types of information are presented. The first section presents a general overview of IIOP/GIOP and then digs under the hood to present some of the nitty-gritty details. The second section actually develops a multi-ORB application. In general, this first section is interesting but is presented for reference purposes only. It's important to know why IIOP/GIOP came into existence as well as how exactly they work, but this knowledge is not necessary to work with IIOP. The second section actually develops an application that uses IIOP to enable inter-ORB communication and therefore is of greater use to developers.

DESIGN GOALS

In the initial request for proposal (RFP) that led to GIOP, the OMG outlined a series of design requirements for submissions to adhere to. These requirements generally called for a highly scalable, easy-to-understand addition to the Object Management Architecture (OMA) that allowed for inter-ORB communication. As these goals led to the eventual GIOP and IIOP specifications, the following bulleted points (taken from the CORBA 2.3 specification) were defined to describe the final IIOP/GIOP specification:

NOTE

The OMG RFP process (fully described in Chapter 21) is a standard mechanism used to gather third-party input on potential specifications.

- *Widest possible availability.* The GIOP and IIOP are based on the most widely used and flexible communications transport mechanism available (TCP/IP) and define the minimum additional protocol layers necessary to transfer CORBA requests between ORBs.

- *Simplicity.* The GIOP is intended to be as simple as possible while meeting other design goals. Simplicity is deemed the best approach to ensure a variety of independent, compatible implementations.

- *Scalability.* The IIOP/GIOP protocol should support ORBs, and networks of bridged ORBs, up to the size of today's Internet, and beyond.

- *Low cost.* Adding support for IIOP/GIOP to an existing or new ORB design should require small engineering investment. Moreover, the runtime costs required to support IIOP in deployed ORBs should be minimal.

- *Generality.* Whereas the IIOP is initially defined for TCP/IP, GIOP message formats are designed to be used with any transport layer that meets a minimal set of assumptions; specifically, the GIOP is designed to be implemented on other connection-oriented transport protocols.

- *Architectural neutrality.* The GIOP specification makes minimal assumptions about the architecture of agents that will support it. The GIOP specification treats ORBs as opaque entities with unknown architectures.

As you examine this set of requirements, it quickly becomes apparent that any piece of software actually able to achieve all goals is an impressive offering. Not only does GIOP need to enable communication between different ORBs, but it must also be scalable, have a low cost, function between any compliant ORBs, and allow for implementation using any transport protocol. Because TCP/IP is the transport protocol with the widest use, a logical next step after developing GIOP was to implement it using TCP/IP. (As stated earlier, the TCP/IP implementation of GIOP is called *IIOP.*)

UNDER THE HOOD

With knowledge of the problem solved by IIOP/GIOP, we now move into coverage of how exactly the technologies are implemented. Because the focus is specifically on IIOP, and not on GIOP and IIOP as independent entities, the remaining sections cover the two in conjunction.

The GIOP specification consists of four distinct elements; these elements work in conjunction to facilitate the inter-ORB communication. After looking over the elements, we'll dive into a discussion of each:

- The Common Data Representation (CDR) definition
- GIOP message formats

- GIOP transport assumptions
- Internet IOP message transport

The first element in the list—Common Data Representation (CDR)—exists to facilitate representation of IDL data types in a low-level format suitable for transfer between entities. This format breaks down IDL data types into the physical bytes they consist of, and it can be passed to entities in either forward or reverse order. When one ORB attempts to communicate with another over GIOP, they exchange information on their preferred byte order, and that information is taken into account when placing the IDL data elements into the CDR.

The second element in the list—GIOP message formats—is a collection of seven different formats that messages can use when traveling between ORBs. These formats fully support all aspects of CORBA communication, including dynamic object location and remote operation invocation.

The third element in the list—GIOP transport assumptions—is a collection of assumptions that are made about the target implementation technology. The final element in the list—Internet IOP message transport—continues the discussion of transport mechanisms to detail how TCP/IP connections are utilized; this section is specific to the IIOP specification.

To finish up the exploration of GIOP and IIOP implementation and specification details, take a look at the IDL in Listing 29.1. This listing contains two modules, GIOP and IIOP, that each expose functionality used when two ORBs communicate with each other.

LISTING 29.1   IDL FOR THE GIOP AND IIOP MODULES

```
module GIOP {
    struct Version {
        octet major;
        octet minor;
    };

    enum MsgType_1_0{
        Request, Reply, CancelRequest,
        LocateRequest, LocateReply,
        CloseConnection, MessageError
    };


    enum MsgType_1_1{
        Request, Reply, CancelRequest,
        LocateRequest, LocateReply,
```

```
        CloseConnection, MessageError,
        Fragment
    };

    struct MessageHeader_1_0 {
        char magic [4];
        Version GIOP_version;
        boolean byte_order;
        octet message_type;
        unsigned long message_size;
    };

    struct MessageHeader_1_1 {
        char magic [4];
        Version GIOP_version;
        octet flags; // GIOP 1.1 change
        octet message_type;
        unsigned long message_size;
        };

struct RequestHeader_1_0 {
        IOP::ServiceContextList service_context;
        unsigned long request_id;
        boolean response_expected;
        sequence <octet> object_key;
        string operation;
        Principal requesting_principal;
    };

    struct RequestHeader_1_1 {
        IOP::ServiceContextList service_context;
        unsigned long request_id;
        boolean response_expected;
        octet reserved[3]; // Added in GIOP 1.1
        sequence <octet> object_key;
        string operation;
        Principal requesting_principal;
    };

    enum ReplyStatusType {
        NO_EXCEPTION,
        USER_EXCEPTION,
        SYSTEM_EXCEPTION,
        LOCATION_FORWARD
    };

    struct ReplyHeader {
        IOP::ServiceContextList service_context;
        unsigned long request_id;
```

continues

LISTING 29.1 CONTINUED

```
        ReplyStatusType reply_status;
    };

    struct CancelRequestHeader {
        unsigned long request_id;
    };

    struct LocateRequestHeader {
        unsigned long request_id;
        sequence <octet> object_key;
    };

    enum LocateStatusType {
        UNKNOWN_OBJECT,
        OBJECT_HERE,
        OBJECT_FORWARD
    };

    struct LocateReplyHeader {
        unsigned long request_id;
        LocateStatusType locate_status;
    };
};


module IIOP {
    struct Version {
        octet major;
        octet minor;
    };

    struct ProfileBody_1_0 {
        Version iiop_version;
        string host;
        unsigned short port;
        sequence <octet> object_key;
    };

    struct ProfileBody_1_1 {
        Version iiop_version;
        string host;
        unsigned short port;
        sequence <octet> object_key;
        sequence <IOP::TaggedComponent> components;
    };
};
```

WORKING WITH IIOP

Continuing our exploration of IIOP, we'll now develop an application that uses IIOP to enable communication between a server object using one ORB and a client object using an alternate ORB.

The application uses the Inprise Visibroker ORB that has been used throughout the book, as well as a free ORB called JacORB. JacORB is contained on the CD-ROM and is also available on the Web at `http://www.inf.fu-berlin.de/~brose/jacorb`. Both ORBs support IIOP; however, JacORB is especially interesting due to the fact that it's freely available and is written in pure Java. If you're producing a Java/CORBA solution on a platform that no other ORB supports or if you're working on a shoestring budget, you should look at JacORB as a primary development platform. For more information on different ORBs, see Chapter 23 "Survey of CORBA ORBs."

An important feature of a distributed environment is that of locating distributed objects in the enterprise. A client object decides which server objects it will need to take advantage of and uses some mechanism to locate those objects. In earlier chapters where the Inprise Visibroker ORB is used exclusively, object location is performed using the Directory Service. Due to the fact that the Directory Service is Visibroker specific, an alternate mechanism for locating objects needs to be utilized in this example.

In addition to the Inprise-specific Directory Service, objects can also be located using the Naming Service and the Interoperable Object Reference (IOR). The Naming Service, which is covered in Chapter 30, "The Naming Service," is an OMG specification for locating and categorizing objects. The IOR is a string that uniquely identifies a given object. The IOR is obtained using the `ORB.object_to_string()` operation and resolved using the `ORB.string_to_object()` operation. Here's an example:

```
IOR:000000000000001c49444c3a42616e6b2f4163636f756e744d616e616765723a312e
```

```
300000000001000000000000000580001000000000103139322e3136382e3130312e313
```

```
0000000013800044f003800504d43000000000000000001c49444c3a42616e6b2f4163636f75
```

```
6e744d616e616765723a312e30000000000c42616e6b4d616e616765720000
```

Due to the fact that the Naming Service is rather complex and is not fully addressed until the following chapter, this next sample application uses the IOR for object location purposes.

The server component of the application brings an object into existence using the JacORB and writes the IOR to a file. The client component is then brought into existence using the Inprise Visibroker ORB; the IOR file is read into memory and used to locate the remote object. Starting out this application is the simple IDL file contained in Listing 29.2.

LISTING 29.2   THE `IIOPTestCaseI` INTERFACE

```
interface IIOPTestCaseI {
    void displayMessage(in string message);
    long addTheseNumbers(in long firstNumber, in long secondNumber);
};
```

The `IIOPTestCaseI` interface exposes two methods: one that simply prints its parameters to the standard output and one that adds its parameters and returns the result. An implementation of this interface is contained in Listing 29.3.

LISTING 29.3   THE `IIOPTestCase` CLASS

```
public class IIOPTestCase extends _IIOPTestCaseIImplBase {

    public IIOPTestCase(String name) {
        super(name);
    }

    public IIOPTestCase() {
        super();
    }

    public void displayMessage(String message) {
        System.out.println(message);
    }

    public int addTheseNumbers(int firstNumber, int secondNumber) {
        return firstNumber + secondNumber;
    }
}
```

Moving toward the development of the server itself, Listing 29.4 contains the code for the `IIOPServer` class, which creates a new `IIOPTestCase` object, obtains the IOR, and then writes the IOR to a file.

LISTING 29.4   THE `IIOPServer` CLASS

```
import jacorb.Orb.*;
import jacorb.Naming.NameServer;
import java.io.*;

public class IIOPServer {
```

```java
    public IIOPServer() {
        // bind to the ORB
        org.omg.CORBA.ORB orb = org.omg.CORBA.ORB.init();
        org.omg.CORBA.BOA boa = orb.BOA_init();

        // create the object
        org.omg.CORBA.Object iiopTestCase =
        boa.create(new IIOPTestCase(),"IDL:IIOPTestCaseI:1.0");

        // activate the object
        boa.obj_is_ready(iiopTestCase);

        // obtain and write out the IOR
        String sIOR = orb.object_to_string(iiopTestCase);
        try{    writeIOR(sIOR, " c:\\IIOPTestCase.ior"); }
        catch(  Exception e ) { System.out.println(e); }

        // wait
        boa.impl_is_ready();
    }

    /**
     * Prints the specified string to the specified file.
     *
     * @param sIOR The string to output
     * @param sFileName The file to house the string.
     */
    private void writeIOR(String sIOR,
                          String sFileName) throws Exception {
        FileWriter fw = new FileWriter(sFileName);
        PrintWriter pw = new PrintWriter(fw);
        pw.println(sIOR);

        pw.flush();
        pw.close();
        fw.close();
    }

        public static void main( String[] args ) {
            new IIOPServer();
        }
}
```

As you examine the IIOPServer class shown in Listing 29.4, keep in mind that it uses the JacORB ORB, not the Inprise version. Because the ORB and BOA interfaces are standardized, interactions with those objects are similar to what you have come to expect from previous chapters.

Upon instantiation, a `IIOPServer` object creates a new `IIOPTestCase` object, obtains the IOR using the `object_to_string()` operation, and then writes the IOR to a file named IIOPTestCase.ior. Once the server is up and running, the Inprise client object can bind to the JacORB server object. Listing 29.5 contains the `IIOPClient` class, which performs this task.

LISTING 29.5 THE `IIOPClient` CLASS

```
import org.omg.CORBA.*;
import java.io.*;

public class IIOPClient {

    public IIOPClient() {
        // bind to the ORB
        ORB orb = ORB.init();

        // read in the IOR
        String sIOR = "";
        try{    sIOR = readIOR("c:\\IIOPTestCase.ior"); }
        catch(  Exception e ) {}

        // resolve the object
        org.omg.CORBA.Object object = orb.string_to_object(sIOR);

        // narrow the object
        IIOPTestCaseI iiopTestCase = IIOPTestCaseIHelper.narrow(object);

        // print out the object
        System.out.println(iiopTestCase);

        // invoke methods on the object
        iiopTestCase.displayMessage("IIOP Rules!");
        System.out.println(iiopTestCase.addTheseNumbers(555, 458));
    }

    /**
     * Reads in the IOR located at the specified location.
     *
     * @param sFileName The location of the IOR.
     */
    private String readIOR(String sFileName) throws Exception {
        FileReader fr = new FileReader(sFileName);

        StringBuffer sbBuilder = new StringBuffer();
        int iChar = -1;
        while( (iChar = fr.read()) != -1) {
            sbBuilder.append((char)iChar);
        }
```

```
        fr.close();

        return sbBuilder.toString();
    }

    public static void main(String[] args) {
    }

}
```

The `IIOPClient` class, when instantiated, reads in the contents of the IIOPTestCase.ior file and uses the `string_to_object()` operation to resolve the IOR. The `IIOPTestCase` object then has its methods invoked.

To run the application, first install (from the CD-ROM) both the JacORB ORB and the Inprise Visibroker ORB on your computer. Next, enter all the code. Then place the IDL and server code in one directory and the IDL and client code in another. Now use the JacORB IDL compiler to compile the IDL in the server directory by entering the following command:

idl2j IIOPTestCaseI.idl

Next, change to the client directory and use the Inprise IDL compiler to compile the IDL by entering this command:

idl2java IIOPTestCaseI.idl

Now compile all generated client and server code.

At this point, you're ready to begin using the application. First, start the JacORB ORB by typing

jacorbd

and then start the server by typing

java IIOPServer

Once the IOR file has been written to a file, start the Inprise Visibroker ORB by typing

osagent

and then run the client by typing

java IIOPClient

FROM HERE

This chapter covered IIOP—an important technology developers will want to take advantage of when moving into the multi-ORB world. Here are some additional chapters that complement the knowledge imparted in this chapter:

- Chapter 21, "CORBA Overview"
- Chapter 22, "CORBA Architecture"
- Chapter 28, "The Portable Object Adapter (POA)"

THE NAMING SERVICE

IN THIS CHAPTER

In a distributed environment, one of the more complicated tasks one must deal with is locating objects needed at a given point in time. Large distributed environments may exist such that hundreds or thousands of different objects all publish some level of functionality that other objects will want to take advantage of. Of course, it's possible to give each object a different logical name, but this isn't as easy as it may sound.

Consider the real-world problem of applying a unique identifier to a human. Most individuals have some spoken logical name that can be used to identify them; however, this name is only useful in a specific context. Assuming the name is not replicated within a certain context, few problems will exist. If, for example, I have both a friend named John and a coworker named John, the context in which I reference "John" will identify that person. If, however, there are two Johns at my office, an additional layer will need to be added—one John might become "John in sales," and the other might become "John in engineering." Adding contextual layers could obviously occur infinitely until no possible naming conflicts remain.

Just as it's difficult to name humans in an easy to understand manner, it is also difficult to name distributed objects in an easy to understand manner. In an attempt to ease the object naming problem, the OMG has released a specification for a context-sensitive naming scheme called the *Naming Service*. The Naming Service allows for context-sensitive names to be associated with objects, and for those objects to be referenced using their names. This chapter examines the Naming Service, including the following important points:

- The information required when creating a context-sensitive name
- The manner in which multiple Naming Services interact
- How to use the Naming Service in your applications
- Inprise alternatives to the Naming Service

WHAT'S IN A NAME?

As stated earlier, the Naming Service allows for context-sensitive names to be associated with objects. As shown in Figure 30.1, using wine as an example, a context-sensitive name is one that not only identifies the object itself but also categorizes that object. Placing a named object in a series of categories not only aids in searching for it but also eliminates potential confusion that might occur when two different objects have the same name.

FIGURE 30.1

A context-sensitive naming scheme for wine.

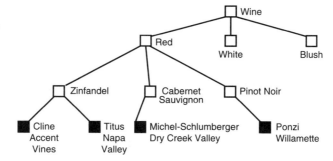

In addition to demonstrating how wines might be categorized using the Naming Service, Figure 30.1 also demonstrates the fact that name contexts are represented using a *naming graph*. The path formed from the graph entry point to an actual object is referred to as the object's *compound name*. For example, the compound name associated with the Cline Ancient Vines wine would be this:

Wine->Red->Zinfandel->Cline Ancient Vines

FEDERATED NAMING SERVICES

Distributed systems have always been developed with attention paid to their potential grand scale. Of course, some distributed applications may only exist on a handful of computers, but more and more systems exist across the entire Internet. With a general desire to support incredible size, the Naming Service allows multiple Naming Services (or *namespaces*) to be tied together, forming a larger, federated Naming Service.

Joining multiple namespaces together is performed as a simple extension of the existing name graph. When multiple namespaces are joined, a node from one namespace is assigned as the parent node relative to the root node of another namespace. Figure 30.2 expands on the earlier wine example by moving each type of wine (red, white, blush) into a unique namespace.

FIGURE 30.2

*Creating a feder-
ated namespace.*

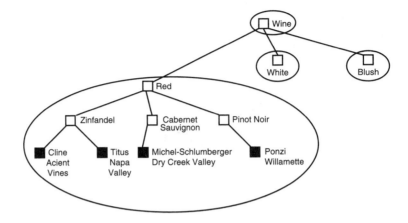

USING THE NAMING SERVICE IDL

Thus far, we've explored the Naming Service on the surface but have yet to actually dig
under the hood to see how to make everything function. This next section further examines the implementation details of the Naming Service, builds a small simple application,
and then builds a wine cellar management application.

As with all CORBAservice specifications, the principle deliverable for the Naming
Service is a collection of interfaces described using CORBA IDL. The Naming Service
IDL, contained in Listing 30.1, has two important interfaces: `NamingContext` and
`BindingIterator`. Let's stop for a moment and examine the interfaces. They are relative-
ly self-explanatory and should be easy to understand. Once you have a feeling for the
interfaces, we'll discuss them in detail.

LISTING 30.1   THE CosNaming MODULE CONTAINS ALL CODE FOR THE CORBA
NAMING SERVICE

```
module CosNaming {
    typedef string Istring;

    struct NameComponent {
        Istring id;
        Istring kind;
    };

    typedef sequence <NameComponent> Name;

    enum BindingType {nobject, ncontext};

    struct Binding {
```

```
    Name binding_name;
    BindingType binding_type;
};

typedef sequence <Binding> BindingList;

interface BindingIterator;

interface NamingContext {
    enum NotFoundReason { missing_node, not_context, not_object};

    exception NotFound {
        NotFoundReason why;
        Name rest_of_name;
    };

    exception CannotProceed {
        NamingContext cxt;
        Name rest_of_name;
    };

    exception InvalidName{};

    exception AlreadyBound {};

    exception NotEmpty{};

    void bind(in Name n, in Object obj)
        raises(NotFound, CannotProceed, InvalidName, AlreadyBound);
    void rebind(in Name n, in Object obj)
        raises(NotFound, CannotProceed, InvalidName);
    void bind_context(in Name n, in NamingContext nc)
        raises(NotFound, CannotProceed, InvalidName, AlreadyBound);
    void rebind_context(in Name n, in NamingContext nc)
        raises(NotFound, CannotProceed, InvalidName);
    Object resolve (in Name n)
            raises(NotFound, CannotProceed, InvalidName);
    void unbind(in Name n) raises(NotFound,
                                    CannotProceed,
                                    InvalidName);
    NamingContext new_context();
    NamingContext bind_new_context(in Name n)
                raises(NotFound, AlreadyBound,
                        CannotProceed, InvalidName);
    void destroy() raises(NotEmpty);
    void list(in unsigned long how_many,
            out BindingList bl,
            out BindingIterator bi);
};
```

continues

30

THE NAMING
SERVICE

LISTING 30.1 CONTINUED

```
interface BindingIterator {
    boolean next_one(out Binding b);
    boolean next_n(in unsigned long how_many,out BindingList bl);
    void destroy();
};
};
```

Before diving into the interfaces themselves, we need to cover two important terms. The purpose of the Naming Service is to allow objects to be associated with a name and for those objects to be discovered using their name. The task of associating a name graph with an object is called *binding*. The task of discovering an object by using the name graphs is called *resolving*.

As you may have guessed when examining the interfaces, most of the functionality of the Naming Service is present in the NamingContext interface. This interface exposes methods for binding and resolving objects, along with other housekeeping methods. The following list provides an explanation of these interfaces, starting with the bind() and resolve() methods and then moving on to everything else:

- bind() The bind() operation, which is probably the first operation you'll invoke, is obviously used to bind an object to a name graph. It accepts as a parameter both a name graph and the object that's to be bound to that graph. The name graph is formed by creating an array of NameComponent objects, where the first object in the array is the highest level descriptor, and the last object is the most specific. A NameComponent object is formed using two strings: a logical name and a description of the data.

- rebind() The rebind() operation creates a binding of a name graph and an object in the naming context, even if the name is already bound in the context.

- resolve() Once an object is bound to a name graph, it is discovered using the resolve() operation. This operation accepts a name graph as a parameter and searches for an object associated with the same graph. If no object can be found, an exception is raised.

- bind_context() and rebind_context() The bind_context() and rebind_context() operations allow for the binding of an object that's actually a name graph itself. This context can then be discovered using the traditional resolve() operation and allows for the creation of interconnected namespaces.

- new_context() and bind_new_context() A unique context is used to represent an independent namespace. To create a new context object, the new_context() operation is used. If, when you're creating a new context, it's best served by associating it with an existing context. The `bind_new_context()` operation accepts a name graph as a parameter and returns a new context bound to the specified graph.

- `unbind()` The `unbind()` operation accepts a name graph as a parameter and removes it from the context.

- `destroy()` If a naming context is no longer needed, it can be removed from existence by invoking its `destroy()` operation.

- `list()` In addition to querying the naming context for specific objects, you can also simply browse all name graphs. Applications in which human users are required to choose some object, can graphically render the name graphs using the list() operation and then resolve the actual object once a unique graph is chosen. The `list()` operation allows access to all graphs. Unlike other operations, which simply return the requested data, the `list()` operation accepts two *out* parameters that are populated using the data contained in the name graphs and an *in* parameter indicating the amount of data to be returned. The first out parameter is a `BindingList` object that references an array of name graphs. The number of graphs referenced by the `BindingList` object is specified by the in parameter. If there are additional name graphs not referenced by the `BindingList` object, they are accessed through the second out parameter, a `BindingIterator` object.

- `BindingIterator` Because naming contexts may reference large numbers of name graphs, the `BindingIterator` object is used to obtain these graphs in smaller chunks. It exposes a `next_one()` method that populates an out parameter with the next available name graph. In addition, a `next_n()` method populates an out parameter with the number of name graphs specified by the in parameter.

DEVELOPING WITH THE NAMING SERVICE

At this point in our discussion of the Naming Service, you should have a solid understanding of its purpose and feature set. Additionally, the prior examination of the IDL should give you a basic understanding of how to interact with the service. In this section, we first develop a small application that performs name binding and resolution. After this initial development effort, we look at how the Naming Service can be used in the real world by writing a wine cellar management application.

Because binding and name resolution are probably the most common tasks performed using the Naming Service, we'll begin our development effort there. Listing 30.2 contains the code for a class called `NameServiceDemo`. The class binds to the Naming Service, creates a name graph, binds an object to that graph, and then resolves the object using the initial name graph. Let's stop for a minute and study the code. We'll then go through each step in the process.

LISTING 30.2   PERFORMING BIND AND NAME RESOLUTION OPERATIONS USING THE NAMING SERVICE

```java
import org.omg.CORBA.*;
import org.omg.CosNaming.*;
import com.visigenic.vbroker.services.CosNaming.*;

public class NameServiceDemo {
    private NameComponent[] _nameGraph = null;
    private NamingContext   _root = null;
    private BOA             _boa = null;

    public NameServiceDemo() {
        ORB orb = ORB.init();
        _boa = orb.BOA_init();
        try{    _root = NamingContextHelper.bind(orb); }
        catch(  Exception e ) { }

        createNameGraph();
        bindObject();
        resolveObject();
    }

    /**
     * The createNameGraph() method creates a new
     * name graph that is then used in binding
     * and resolution.
     */
    private final void createNameGraph() {
        _nameGraph = new NameComponent[3];
        _nameGraph[0]
            = new NameComponent("great-grandparent category", "string");
        _nameGraph[1]
            = new NameComponent("grandparent category", "string");
        _nameGraph[2]
            = new NameComponent("parent category", "string");
    }


    /**
     * The bindObject() method creates a new
     * NameServiceObject object and binds it
     * to the name graph created by the createNameGraph()
     * method.
     */
    private final void bindObject() {
        NamingContext root = _root;

        NameServiceObjectI object = new NameServiceObject();
        object.sData("some information");
```

```
        _boa.obj_is_ready(object);
        int iLength = _nameGraph.length-1;
        // iterate through the name graph, binding
        // each context on its own
        NameComponent[] componentHolder = new NameComponent[1];
        for(int i=0; i<iLength; i++) {
            componentHolder[0] = _nameGraph[i];
            try{    root = root.bind_new_context(componentHolder); }
            catch( Exception e ) { }
        } // for

        // bind the target object to the last
        // item in the name graph
        componentHolder[0] = _nameGraph[iLength];
        try{    root.bind(componentHolder, object); }
        catch( Exception e ) {
                System.out.println("exception at object bind: "+e);
        }
        System.out.println("bound object, data is: "+object.sData());
    }

/**
 * The resolveObject() method using the name
 * graph created by the createNameGraph() method
 * to discover the bound NameServiceObject object.
 */
private final void resolveObject() {
    try{    // resolve using the last entry in the name graph
            NameComponent[] componentHolder = new NameComponent[1];
            componentHolder[0] = _nameGraph[2];
            org.omg.CORBA.Object resolvedObject =
                _root.resolve(_nameGraph);
            // narrow the result into a NameServiceObject object
            NameServiceObjectI object =
                NameServiceObjectIHelper.narrow(resolvedObject);
            System.out.println("resolved object, data is: "+
                            object.sData());
    }
    catch( Exception e ) {
            System.out.println("exception at object resolve: "+e);
    }
}

public static void main(String[] args) {
    NameServiceDemo demo = new NameServiceDemo();
}

}
```

The first task undertaken by the `NameServiceDemo` class is the creation of the name graph itself. This step, represented in the `createNameGraph()` method, simply creates an array of `NameComponent` objects. The first item in the array is the top-most parent, and the last item in the array is the bottommost parent.

After the creation of the name graph itself, the next task undertaken is to bind an object to the graph previously created. In this example, the bound object is an instance of the `NameServiceObjectI` class. This class, described using IDL in Listing 30.3, is a simple class that has a single string attribute.

LISTING 30.3   THE `NameServiceObjectI` INTERFACE

```
interface NameServiceObjectI {
    attribute string sData;
};
```

The process of binding the object to the name graph takes place in the `bindObject()` method and is accomplished in two steps. First, we iterate through the name graph, calling the `bind_new_context()` method to individually bind each `NameComponent` object to a new context. We then call the `bind()` method to bind the last `NameComponent` object to the `NameServiceObjectI` object itself.

Once we've bound the target object to the name graph, that same name graph can be used to resolve the object. The last method invoked in this example, `resolveObject()`, uses the `resolve()` method to resolve the previously bound object.

Now that you fully understand the introduction to the Naming Service, you're ready to run the sample application. If you've not already installed the Inprise ORB and Naming Service component (an option during the install), do so now. This software is included on the enclosed CD-ROM. With the proper software installed, first compile the IDL by entering

idl2java NameServiceObjectI.idl

and then compile the Java code using your Java compiler. Now start the ORB using the following command:

osagent

Start the Naming Service using this command:

vbj -DORBservices=CosNaming
            com.visigenic.vbroker.services.CosNaming.ExtFactory
            ExampleServiceName example_log

The command to start the Naming Service takes two parameters. The first, `ExampleServiceName`, indicates the unique name associated with this Naming Service instance; the second, `example_log`, indicates the name of the file to be used as a log.

In this example, the same class performs all binding and resolving in sequence right after each other, but this does not have to be the case. The `bindObject()` and `resolveObject()` methods could be pulled out of the `NameServiceDemo` class and placed individually in their own classes. To fully test your understanding of the name service, you might want to actually separate the methods yourself and then run them on different machines.

ADVANCED USES FOR THE NAMING SERVICE

In the previous example, we looked at the two most basic uses for the Naming Service: binding and resolution. Although these two functions are often the most used, they are by no means the only functions published by the Naming Service. In the next example, we build a distributed wine cellar management application. The server component stores a collection of wines, and the client application can browse the server's wines as well as add to the collection. Once the client finds a wine in the server's collection that it owns, that wine can be added to a client-side collection.

Starting with the server component, Listing 30.4 contains the IDL for the server, and Listing 30.5 contains the implementation of the `WineServer` class. The `WineServer` class simply exposes one method, `addWine()`, that accepts a wine to be categorized and the collection of categories used to classify the wine.

LISTING 30.4   THE IDL FOR THE WINE SERVER

```
interface WineI {
    attribute string sVineyardName;
    attribute string sType;
    attribute string sAdditionalNotes;
    attribute long   vintage;
    attribute long   points;
    attribute string sPointSource;
};

typedef sequence<string> stringSequence;

interface WineServerI {
    void addWine(in stringSequence categories, in WineI wine);
};
```

LISTING 30.5 THE WineServer CLASS

```
import org.omg.CORBA.*;
import org.omg.CosNaming.*;
import com.visigenic.vbroker.services.CosNaming.*;

/**
 * The WineServer class uses the CORBA Naming Service
 * to maintain a collection of wines as categorized
 * by the user.
 */
public class WineServer extends _WineServerIImplBase {
    private NamingContext  _root;
    private static ORB     _orb;
    private static BOA     _boa;

    public WineServer() {
        super("Wine Server");
        // obtain the root context
        _root = NamingContextHelper.bind(_orb, "NameService/1");
    }

    /**
     * The addWine() method is invoked by the client
     * when he wishes to add a new wine to the collection
     * maintained by the Naming Service.
     *
     * @param categories Collection of categories used to
     *                    classify the wine
     * @param winw The wine to be added
     */
    public void addWine(String categories[], WineI wine) {
        NamingContext root = _root;

        int iLength = categories.length;
        iLength—;

        NameComponent[] componentHolder = new NameComponent[1];
        for(int i=0; i<iLength; i++) {
            componentHolder[0] = new NameComponent(categories[i], "");
            // see if the context is already bound
            try{    root =
                        NamingContextHelper.narrow(
                        root.resolve(componentHolder)); }
            catch(  Exception e ) {
                    // bind the new context
                    try{    root =
                                root.bind_new_context(componentHolder); }
                    catch(  Exception innerE ) {
                            System.out.println("inner: "+innerE);
                    }
```

```
            } // catch
        } // for

        // create a copy of the original WineI object
        WineI newWine = new Wine();
        newWine.sVineyardName(wine.sVineyardName());
        newWine.sType(wine.sType());
        newWine.sAdditionalNotes(wine.sAdditionalNotes());
        newWine.vintage(wine.vintage());
        newWine.points(wine.points());
        newWine.sPointSource(wine.sPointSource());

        // activate the new object
        _boa.obj_is_ready(newWine);

        componentHolder[0] = new NameComponent(categories[iLength], "");
        // bind the object
        try{    root.bind(componentHolder, newWine); }
        catch(  Exception e ) { System.out.println("e: "+e); }
    }

    public static void main(String[] args) {
        _orb = ORB.init();
        _boa = _orb.BOA_init();
        // create the WineServer application
        WineServer server = new WineServer();
        // tell the BOA about the WineServer application
        _boa.obj_is_ready(server);
        // notify the BOA that we are ready to wait for incoming
connections
        _boa.impl_is_ready();
    }
}
```

Looking at the code in Listing 30.5, you'll see some obvious parallels to the code in the initial example. However, in this situation, the object-binding process is expanded to be more robust. In the initial example, all binds were performed under the assumption that the NameComponent object being bound was not already in use. The bindObject() method simply iterated through the new NameComponent objects and called the bind_new_context() method to add them to the name graph. In this example, every call to bind_new_context() is preceded with an invocation of the resolve() method. If the resolve() method does not throw an exception, we know that the NameComponent object is already part of the name graph. If an exception is thrown, we know that the NameComponent object is not present in the name graph and can proceed to add it. Due to the fact that we may be adding many unique wines that all have the same parent categories, this more robust version of the bindObject() method is very much needed.

Moving from the server to the client itself, we perform a two-step exploration of the code. First, we look at the code that interacts with the Naming Service. Second, we explore the code that builds the User Interface (UI). After all code has been examined, we fire up the application and give the Naming Service a run for its money.

Listing 30.6 contains the code for the class `WineClient`. This class contains methods used to traverse the name graph, bind to the Naming Service, and ask the `WineServer` to add wines to the collection. Some additional code is used to launch the GUI. As you examine the class, pay specific attention to the code that interacts with the Naming Service (all GUI specific code will be covered later).

LISTING 30.6 THE `WineClient` CLASS INTERACTS WITH `WineServer` AND THE NAMING SERVICE

```
import java.awt.*;
import java.util.*;
import org.omg.CORBA.*;
import org.omg.CosNaming.*;
import com.visigenic.vbroker.services.CosNaming.*;


public class WineClient {
    private BOA            _boa;
    private NamingContext  _root;
    private WineServerI    _wineServer;

    public WineClient() {
        ORB orb = ORB.init();
        _boa = orb.BOA_init();
        _root = NamingContextHelper.bind(orb, "NameService/1");
        _wineServer = WineServerIHelper.bind(orb);

        WineClientGUI gui = new WineClientGUI(this, _wineServer, _boa);
        gui.setSize(350,350);
        gui.setVisible(true);
    }

    public void addWine(String[] sCategories, WineI wine) {
        _boa.obj_is_ready(wine);
        _wineServer.addWine(sCategories, wine);
    }

    public List obtainNameGraph() throws Exception {
        return obtainNameGraph(_root, new List(), 0);
    }

    /**
     * Obtains a List object displaying a hierarchical
```

```
    * view of all wines represented by the specified
    * name graph.
    *
    * @param root       The name graph to traverse
    * @param lstWines   The list being build
    * @param iLevel     Indicator of the current indent
    */
    public List obtainNameGraph(NamingContext root,
                                List lstWines,
                                int iLevel) throws Exception {
        // create the holder objects used for out parameters
        BindingIterator iterator = null;
        BindingIteratorHolder iteratorHolder
            = new BindingIteratorHolder(iterator);
        BindingListHolder listHolder
            = new BindingListHolder(new Binding[0]);

        // obtain the first 100 bindings
        root.list(100, listHolder, iteratorHolder);

        // place the graph items into the string array;
        Binding[] bindingList = listHolder.value;
        int iLength = bindingList.length;
        for(int i=0; i<iLength; i++) {
            Vector vecNext = new Vector();
            NameComponent[] name = bindingList[i].binding_name;
            int iNameLength = name.length;
            for(int j=0; j<iNameLength; j++) {
                StringBuffer sbCurrentItem = new StringBuffer();
                for(int k=0; k<iLevel; k++) {
                    sbCurrentItem.append("   "); // 3 spaces per indent
                }
                sbCurrentItem.append(name[j].id);
                lstWines.addItem(sbCurrentItem.toString());;
            }
            // recurse with new context
            if(bindingList[i].binding_type == BindingType.ncontext) {
                obtainNameGraph(NamingContextHelper.narrow
                    (root.resolve(name)), lstWines, iLevel+1);
            }
            else { // references a WineI object
                StringBuffer sbCurrentItem = new StringBuffer();
                for(int k=0; k<iLevel+1; k++) {
                    sbCurrentItem.append("   "); // 3 spaces per indent
                }
sbCurrentItem.append(WineIHelper.narrow(root.resolve(name))
                                .sVineyardName());
                lstWines.addItem(sbCurrentItem.toString());
            }
```

continues

LISTING 30.6   CONTINUED

```
        }
        return lstWines;
    }

    public static void main(String[] args) {
        WineClient client = new WineClient();
    }
}
```

In the WineClient class, the most interesting code is executed during the obtainNameGraph() method. In this method, the NamingContext.list() method is executed recursively, giving a picture of all NamingContext and WineI objects represented by the root node. In addition to traversing the name graph, the obtainNameGraph() method places all found information in a hierarchically formatted List object.

Moving beyond the WineClient class, two additional classes help form the client application. The class WineClientGUI (contained in Listing 30.7) is the base GUI for the whole system. It displays the collection of available wines, the collection of owned wines, and prompts the user to add wines to the local collection or to the server collection. When a user asks to add a wine to the server collection (contained in Listing 30.8), the WineInfo dialog is spawned. It collects the appropriate information and asks the server to add the wine to the collection. When a user asks that a server wine be added to the local collection, the doBuyWine() method in the WineClientGUI takes care of the transfer.

LISTING 30.7   THE WineClientGUI CLASS IS THE BASE GUI FOR THE ENTIRE CLIENT
APPLICATION

```
import java.awt.*;
import java.awt.event.*;
import java.util.*;
import org.omg.CORBA.*;
import org.omg.CosNaming.*;

public class WineClientGUI extends Frame implements ActionListener {
    private WineClient    _wineClient;
    private List          _listWinesOwned;
    private Vector        _vecWinesOwned;
    private List          _listWinesAvailable;
    private Button        _btnBuySelected;
    private Button        _btnAddWine;

    private WineServerI   _wineServer;
    private BOA           _boa;
```

```
public WineClientGUI(WineClient wineClient,
                     WineServerI wineServer, BOA boa) {
    _wineClient = wineClient;
    _wineServer = wineServer;
    _boa = boa;

    _listWinesOwned = new List();
    _vecWinesOwned = new Vector();
    buildScreen();
}

/**
 * Builds or rebuilds the screen
 */
public void buildScreen() {
    removeAll();
    try{    _listWinesAvailable = _wineClient.obtainNameGraph(); }
    catch(  Exception e) {}

    Panel pnlWines = new Panel();
    pnlWines.setLayout(new GridLayout(1,2,10,10));
    pnlWines.add(new ListPanel("Wines Available",
                               _listWinesAvailable));
    pnlWines.add(new ListPanel("Wines Owned", _listWinesOwned));

    Panel pnlButtons = new Panel();
    pnlButtons.setLayout(new GridLayout(1,2,10,10));
    pnlButtons.add(_btnBuySelected =
        new Button("Buy Selected Wine"));
    pnlButtons.add(_btnAddWine = new Button("Add Wine To Server"));
    _btnBuySelected.addActionListener(this);
    _btnAddWine.addActionListener(this);

    setLayout(new BorderLayout(10,10));
    add(pnlWines, "Center");
    add(pnlButtons, "North");
    doLayout();
}

/**
 * Invoked when the human user clicks on a Button object
 */
public void actionPerformed(ActionEvent ae) {
    if(ae.getSource() == _btnAddWine) doAddWine();
    else doBuyWine();
}

/**
 * Adds a wine to the collection represented
 * by the name graph.
```

continues

30

THE NAMING SERVICE

LISTING 30.7   CONTINUED

```java
     */
    private void doAddWine() {
        WineInfo info = new WineInfo(this, _wineServer, _boa);
        info.pack();
        info.setVisible(true);
    }

    /**
     * Adds the selected wine to our personal
     * collection.
     */
    private void doBuyWine() {
        // add vineyard name to list
        _listWinesOwned.addItem(_listWinesAvailable.getSelectedItem());
    }

    /**
     * Utility class used to facilitate GUI building
     */
    class ListPanel extends Panel {
        public ListPanel(String sLabel, List lst) {
            setLayout(new BorderLayout(10,10));
            add(new Label(sLabel), "North");
            add(lst, "Center");
        }
    }
}
```

LISTING 30.8   THE `WineInfo` DIALOG PROMPTS THE USER TO ADD A NEW WINE TO THE SERVER COLLECTION

```java
import java.awt.*;

import java.awt.event.*;

import org.omg.CORBA.*;


/**
 * Prompts the user to add a new wine, and adds it to the name graph
 */
public final class WineInfo extends Dialog implements ActionListener {
    private Choice      _chcVarietal;
    private Choice      _chcGrape;
    private TextField   _txtVineyardName;
    private TextField   _txtNotes;
    private TextField   _txtVintage;
```

```
private TextField    _txtPoints;
private TextField    _txtPointSource;
private Button       _btnAdd;
private Button       _btnCancel;

private WineServerI    _wineServer;
private BOA            _boa;
private WineClientGUI  _gui;

public WineInfo(WineClientGUI gui, WineServerI wineServer, BOA boa) {
    super(gui, "Add Wine", true);
    _wineServer = wineServer;
    _boa = boa;
    _gui = gui;

    _chcVarietal = new Choice();
    _chcVarietal.addItem("Red");
    _chcVarietal.addItem("White");
    _chcVarietal.addItem("Blush");

    _chcGrape = new Choice();
    _chcGrape.addItem("Zinfandel");
    _chcGrape.addItem("Cabernet Sauvignon");
    _chcGrape.addItem("Chardonnay");
    _chcGrape.addItem("Merlot");
    _chcGrape.addItem("Pinot Noir");
    _chcGrape.addItem("Shiraz");

    setLayout(new GridLayout(8,2,10,10));
    add(new Label("Varietal"));
    add(_chcVarietal);
    add(new Label("Grape"));
    add(_chcGrape);
    add(new Label("Vineyard name"));
    add(_txtVineyardName = new TextField(20));
    add(new Label("Notes"));
    add(_txtNotes = new TextField(20));
    add(new Label("Vintage"));
    add(_txtVintage = new TextField(20));
    add(new Label("Points"));
    add(_txtPoints = new TextField(20));
    add(new Label("Point Source"));
    add(_txtPointSource = new TextField(20));
    add(_btnCancel = new Button("Cancel"));
    add(_btnAdd = new Button("Add"));

    _btnCancel.addActionListener(this);
    _btnAdd.addActionListener(this);
}
```

30

THE NAMING
SERVICE

continues

LISTING 30.8   CONTINUED

```java
/**
 * Invoked when the user clicks on a Button
 */
public void actionPerformed(ActionEvent ae) {
    if(ae.getSource() == _btnAdd) doAdd();
    setVisible(false);
}

/**
 * Adds a wine to the server
 */
private void doAdd() {
    WineI wine = getDataAsWineObject();
    _boa.obj_is_ready(wine);
    String[] sCat = new String[2];
    sCat[0] = wine.sType();
    sCat[1] = _chcGrape.getSelectedItem();
    _wineServer.addWine(sCat, wine);
    _gui.buildScreen();
}

/**
 * Creates a WineI object using the data in
 * the UI widgets
 */
private WineI getDataAsWineObject() {
    WineI wine = new Wine();
    wine.sVineyardName(_txtVineyardName.getText());
    wine.sType(_chcVarietal.getSelectedItem());
    wine.sAdditionalNotes(_txtNotes.getText());
    try{   wine.vintage(Integer.parseInt(_txtVintage.getText())); }
    catch(  NumberFormatException nfe ) {}
    try{   wine.points(Integer.parseInt(_txtPoints.getText())); }
    catch(  NumberFormatException nfe ) {}
    wine.sPointSource(_txtPointSource.getText());

    return wine;
}

}
```

Once you've spent some time with the code in the previous listings, you should finalize your understanding by actually running the application. You should already have the Inprise ORB and Naming Service installed from running the first application. If not, do so now. After the ORB software is up and running, compile all IDL and Java code for the wine application and then launch the Naming Service by entering

```
java -DORBservices=CosNaming
     com.visigenic.vbroker.services.CosNaming.ExtFactory
     NameService wine_log
```

Next, launch the server by entering

java WineServer

and the client by entering

java WineClient

When the application is up and running, you should see something similar what's shown in Figure 30.3.

FIGURE 30.3

The wine application in action.

INPRISE ALTERNATIVES TO THE NAMING SERVICE

This chapter has focused on finding objects in the enterprise using the Naming Service itself. What you are probably wondering is how code examples in the previous chapters performed the same task without using the Naming Service. Throughout this book, there are many, many examples of CORBA applications, few of which make use of the Naming Service when locating objects. These examples all use an application provided by Inprise called the *Directory Service*. Like the Naming Service, the Directory Service allows objects to be located in the enterprise. Although the broad function may be the same, the two services identify objects in radically different ways.

The Directory Service uniquely identifies an object using a combination of its interface and a user-assigned logical name. This works for many situations; however, it does have downsides. First and foremost, the Directory Service doesn't allow for the classification of objects. The Naming Service, in comparison, allows objects to be placed in an infinite number of hierarchical categories. In addition to not allowing for object classification, the Directory Service gives names to objects that can only be changed at compile time. Because an object is partially identified by its interface, there's no way to change this identifier without changing the original class itself.

The decision to use either the Naming or Directory Service in a given application is something that has to be decided upon on an application-by-application basis. Unfortunately, no one perfect service for all applications exists; however, there are many considerations that make the decision easier. If you're building a relatively static application with only a handful of distributed objects, the Directory Service is probably sufficient. If, however, you're building a massive application in which clients will have to search out all sorts of objects at runtime, using the Naming Service is probably a much better route to take.

FROM HERE

This chapter has covered the Naming Service CORBAservice in detail, giving you sufficient information to begin making use of it in your own code. In addition to learning about the Naming Service, you also learned how it differs from the Directory Service used in other CORBA development chapters.

As you continue to explore all that CORBA has to offer, you'll find that the following chapters complement this chapter's coverage of the event service:

- Chapter 21, "CORBA Overview"
- Chapter 22, "CORBA Architecture"
- Chapter 23, "Survey of CORBA ORBs"
- Chapter 31, "The Event Service"

THE EVENT SERVICE

IN THIS CHAPTER

Chapter 21, "CORBA Overview" introduced the concept of a CORBAservice. A *CORBAservice*, in the broadest sense, is a specification for a CORBA-enabled application that fills a horizontal need. What's most important to note about the preceding definition is that a CORBAservice is only a specification. The OMG produces specifications for applications, not applications themselves. However, because members develop specifications in tandem with implementations, it's not possible to have a specification without also having a reference implementation. Due to the fact that the OMG produces specifications to which all vendors must comply, it's an easy process to swap CORBAservices in and out from a variety of vendors.

> **NOTE**
>
> A *horizontal* application has functionality that may be needed by any number of different applications. For example, even though banking and healthcare applications are radically different, they could use the same horizontal application to log transactions.

This chapter examines the CORBA Event Service, which is one of the more commonly used CORBAservices. The Event Service specification provides a generic manner through which events are delivered from supplier to consumer. To fully explore the Event Service, the implementation available from Inprise is used. In addition to the Inprise Event Service, you'll also need to have the Inprise Visibroker ORB installed. Both the Inprise ORB and Event Service are included on the enclosed CD-ROM. If you're using an Event Service implementation from another vendor, you must make sure you also have the ORB that the Event Service is tailored toward.

In learning about the Event Service, you'll find that this chapter provides the following discussions:

- Reasons behind the need for events
- Coverage of the push event model
- Coverage of the pull event model
- Coverage of generic event propagation

Most communication that occurs in a distributed environment is fully *synchronous*: One object invokes operations on a remote object, and some value is potentially returned. This communication often functions fine assuming that the application is completely controlled by a human user. However, there are times when an application needs to take an action based on a value present in a foreign system. For example, a stock portfolio manager might want to be notified if certain holdings drop more than 10 percent. This second form of communication is called *event-based communication*, because communication occurs when some event happens. The event might happen at any point in time, and for that reason the potential recipient must always be ready to receive notification.

This manner of communication should be very familiar to users with a history of working with the JDK1.1 delegation-based event model. Under the JDK1.1 event model, when a user clicks a button on the screen, objects with interest in the state of the button are notified directly.

THE CORBA EVENT SERVICE

To facilitate event-based communication in a CORBA environment, the CORBA Event Service defines a standard model through which events are passed. The model, illustrated in Figure 31.1, defines three unique components that are needed for everything to fully function. First up is the *event channel*, which is the conduit through which all events travel. Second, an object designated as an *event supplier* generates events when necessary. The third and final component is an object designated as an *event consumer*, which is charged with receiving and processing an event. If an event consumer wishes to receive events, it will either register for immediate notification or periodically check with the event channel to see if an event has arrived.

FIGURE 31.1

The CORBA Event Service functions with the aid of an event supplier, consumer, and channel.

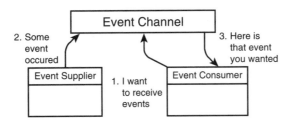

What's interesting in this description is the fact that all events pass through the channel before reaching a consumer. This means that at no point does the event supplier have explicit knowledge of the number (if any) of consumers receiving the generated event. By the same token, the event consumer has no explicit knowledge of the event supplier.

The lack of explicit knowledge of what's at either end of the event channel leads to a course-grain event environment. Instead of the supplier sending events to only interested parties, the supplier sends all generated events to the event channel, and the consumer chooses to ignore specific events if they are not needed. In some situations, multiple channels can run in which each channel moves events that are tied to a specific function. For example, an application that monitors the results of lab orders placed on patients in a large hospital might run a unique channel for each unique lab system. The different lab systems would then post events to their unique channel, and consumers would only listen to channels associated with the lab systems they personally use.

Access to events stored by the channel is defined through two unique models. A *push model* moves events directly from supplier to consumer. This model is very efficient because network traffic is only generated when an event actually occurs. In addition, events are delivered to consumers soon after being generated by a supplier. As a downside, the push model does require that the event channel be able to invoke methods on the consumer object. This requirement cannot always be achieved, because firewalls often block communication if the event channel and event consumer are on opposite sides of the firewall.

An alternative to the push model is the pull model. Under the pull event model, events are not sent to the channel until the consumer asks for them. In this situation, event suppliers still register with the event channel; however, they don't post events until the channel notifies them of consumer need. Consumers and suppliers still have no explicit knowledge of each other, because all event requests are passed through the channel. This means that consumers must periodically query the channel for events, causing a potential increase in network traffic and a potential lag between event generation and event delivery. Of course, the upside here is that firewall restrictions do not stop applications from functioning.

To allow for generic communication across the event channel, the event itself is represented using the CORBA `Any` object. As covered in earlier chapters, an `Any` object is a generic object that can be used to represent any CORBA object or base type. It has *inserter* methods for placing an object under `Any` ownership and extractor methods that other objects use to access the value owned by the `Any` object. To obtain a reference to an `Any` object, the method `ORB.create_any()` is invoked. Listing 31.1 contains the Java mapping for the `Any` object.

LISTING 31.1 THE JAVA MAPPING FOR THE CORBA Any OBJECT

```
public class org.omg.CORBA.Any extends Object {
    public org.omg.CORBA.TypeCode type();
    public void type(org.omg.CORBA.TypeCode);
    public void read_value(org.omg.CORBA.portable.InputStream,
                          org.omg.CORBA.TypeCode);
    public void write_value(org.omg.CORBA.portable.OutputStream);
    public org.omg.CORBA.portable.OutputStream create_output_stream();
    public org.omg.CORBA.portable.InputStream create_input_stream();
    public boolean equal(org.omg.CORBA.Any);
    public short extract_short();
    public void insert_short(short);
    public int extract_long();
```

```
    public void insert_long(int);
    public long extract_longlong();
    public void insert_longlong(long);
    public short extract_ushort();
    public void insert_ushort(short);
    public int extract_ulong();
    public void insert_ulong(int);
    public long extract_ulonglong();
    public void insert_ulonglong(long);
    public float extract_float();
    public void insert_float(float);
    public double extract_double();
    public void insert_double(double);
    public boolean extract_boolean();
    public void insert_boolean(boolean);
    public char extract_char();
    public void insert_char(char);
    public char extract_wchar();
    public void insert_wchar(char);
    public byte extract_octet();
    public void insert_octet(byte);
    public org.omg.CORBA.Any extract_any();
    public void insert_any(org.omg.CORBA.Any);
    public org.omg.CORBA.TypeCode extract_TypeCode();
    public void insert_TypeCode(org.omg.CORBA.TypeCode);
    public org.omg.CORBA.Object extract_Object();
    public void insert_Object(org.omg.CORBA.Object);
    public void insert_Object(org.omg.CORBA.Object,
                              org.omg.CORBA.TypeCode);
    public java.lang.String extract_string();
    public void insert_string(java.lang.String);
    public java.lang.String extract_wstring();
    public void insert_wstring(java.lang.String);
    public org.omg.CORBA.Principal extract_Principal();
    public void insert_Principal(org.omg.CORBA.Principal);
    public void insert_Streamable(org.omg.CORBA.portable.Streamable);
    public org.omg.CORBA.Any();
}
```

In examining the Event Service, we examine the push model first and then the pull model.

THE GENERIC PUSH EVENT MODEL

As stated earlier, the generic push event model exists such that events are delivered from supplier to the event channel and then directly to the consumer. The event itself is modeled using an Any object and can therefore represent any entity in the CORBA universe.

To begin our look at the generic push event model, let's examine the IDL in Listing 31.2. Listing 31.2 contains abbreviated versions of the CosEventComm and CosEventChannelAdmin modules, which define all interfaces and operations needed for sending or receiving events. The CosEventComm module contains interfaces that deal directly with the propagation of events. The CosEventChannelAdmin module contains interfaces that model the managerial aspects of event management, specifically connecting to the channel itself.

For clarity, all interfaces that deal with the generic pull event model have been removed from Listing 31.2. These interfaces are covered in the next section and are also contained in their entirety on the CD-ROM.

LISTING 31.2 SECTIONS OF THE CosEventComm AND CosEventChannelAdmin MODULES DEALING WITH THE GENERIC PUSH EVENT MODEL

```
module CosEventComm {
    exception Disconnected{};

    interface PushConsumer {
        void push (in any data) raises(Disconnected);
        void disconnect_push_consumer();
    };

    interface PushSupplier {
        void disconnect_push_supplier();
    };
};

module CosEventChannelAdmin {
    exception AlreadyConnected {};

    exception TypeError {};

    interface ProxyPushConsumer:CosEventComm::PushConsumer {
        void connect_push_supplier(in CosEventComm::PushSupplier
                                   push_supplier)
                   raises(AlreadyConnected);
    };

    interface ProxyPushSupplier: CosEventComm::PushSupplier {
        void connect_push_consumer(in CosEventComm::PushConsumer
                                   push_consumer)
                   raises(AlreadyConnected,TypeError);
    };

    interface ConsumerAdmin {
        ProxyPushSupplier obtain_push_supplier();
        ProxyPullSupplier obtain_pull_supplier();
```

```
        };

        interface SupplierAdmin {
            ProxyPushConsumer obtain_push_consumer();
            ProxyPullConsumer obtain_pull_consumer();
        };

        interface EventChannel {
            ConsumerAdmin for_consumers();
            SupplierAdmin for_suppliers();
            void destroy();
        };
    };
```

Starting with the event channel, you'll note an interface in the CosEventChannelAdmin module titled EventChannel. An object implementing this interface would be instantiated when the event channel is started; suppliers and consumers would then use the ORB to bind to the object. After binding to the EventChannel object, event suppliers obtain a SupplierAdmin object by invoking the for_suppliers() operation, and event consumers obtain a ConsumerAdmin object by invoking the for_consumers() operation. Through the *xxx*Admin objects, suppliers and consumers actually connect to the channel. Once connected to the channel, suppliers post events to the channel and consumers receive events from the channel.

Moving beyond the event channel, the CosEventComm module defines interfaces implemented by the event suppliers and consumers. The PushConsumer interface is implemented by consumers and defines two operations that are potentially invoked by the event supplier. The push() operation is invoked by the event supplier when an event occurs, and the disconnect_push_consumer() operation is invoked by the event supplier or channel if the connection is broken.

As a demonstration of the generic push event model, the next few code listings build a stock portfolio manager application. The server side of the application attaches itself to the event channel and posts random quote updates to the channel. With quote updates being posted to the event channel, the client side of the application manages a portfolio and represents the active value using the data posted to the event channel. Because the server posts quote updates that represent stocks that might not be present in the portfolio, it's the burden of the client to filter out unwanted events.

Because this application allows client and server communication to occur only through the event channel, the amount of IDL needed is rather slim. Both the client and server expose no operations, and only the object modeling the stock symbol and price needs to be represented. Listing 31.3 contains the IDL for the QuoteUpdateI interface, which has attributes for stock symbol and stock price.

LISTING 31.3 THE IDL FOR THE STOCK SYMBOL AND PRICE INFORMATION

```
interface QuoteUpdateI {
    attribute string sSymbol;
    attribute float  fNewPrice;
};
```

With the IDL defined for the quote information, it's now possible to build a server to post quote events. Listing 31.4 contains the GenericPushQuoteServer class, which is charged with sending all events. When instantiated, it attaches itself to the event channel and posts a stream of events. As you examine Listing 31.4, pay specific attention to the code in the run() method, because the actual event posting is contained there.

LISTING 31.4 THE GenericPushQuoteServer CLASS POSTS EVENTS TO THE EVENT CHANNEL

```
import java.util.*;
import org.omg.CosEventComm.*;
import org.omg.CosEventChannelAdmin.*;
import org.omg.CORBA.*;

/**
 * The GenericPushQuoteServer class posts random quote values
 * to the event channel.
 */

    public final class GenericPushQuoteServer
                extends _PushSupplierImplBase
                implements Runnable {
    private String[]            _sSymbols = {"INKT", "MSFT", "ORCL",
                                            "CNWK", "XCIT", "PSFT",
                                            "LU", "CPQ","WMT", "DIS"};

    private Random              _random;
    private Thread             _thread;

    private org.omg.CORBA.ORB   _orb;
    private org.omg.CORBA.BOA   _boa;
    private ProxyPushConsumer   _pushConsumer;

    public GenericPushQuoteServer() {
        // bind to the orb
        _orb = ORB.init();
        // obtain a reference to the boa
        _boa = _orb.BOA_init();
        _random = new Random();

        // bind to the event channel
        EventChannel channel = EventChannelHelper.bind(_orb);
        // obtain a ProxyPushConsumer object.
```

```
        _pushConsumer = channel.for_suppliers().obtain_push_consumer();
        // connect as an event supplier
        try{    _pushConsumer.connect_push_supplier(this); }
        catch(  AlreadyConnected ac ) {}

        // start sending events in a unique thread
        _thread = new Thread(this);
        _thread.start();
    }

    /**
     * Invoked when we are disconnected from the
     * event channel.
     */
    public void disconnect_push_supplier() {
        try{    _boa().deactivate_obj(this); }
        catch(  SystemException e) { }
    }

    /**
     * Chooses (at random) one of the ten
     * supported symbols.
     */
    private String getRandomSymbol() {
        return _sSymbols[Math.abs(_random.nextInt() % 10) - 0];
    }

    /**
     * Generates a random value for a quote
     * between 0 and 300
     */
    private float getRandomPrice() {
        return Math.abs(_random.nextInt() % 300) - 0;
    }

    /**
     * Creates a new QuoteUpdateI object with
     * random values
     */
    private QuoteUpdateI obtainRandomQuoteUpdate() {
        QuoteUpdateI quote =
            new QuoteUpdate(getRandomSymbol(), getRandomPrice());
        _boa.obj_is_ready(quote);
        return quote;
    }

    public void run() {
        while(true) {
            try{    _thread.sleep(1000); }
            catch(  Exception e ) {}
```

continues

LISTING 31.4 CONTINUED

```
            try {   // obtain an Any object from the ORB
                    org.omg.CORBA.Any eventObject = _orb.create_any();
                    // add a QuoteUpdateI object to the Any object
                    eventObject.insert_Object(obtainRandomQuoteUpdate());
                    // post the event
                    pushConsumer.push(eventObject);
            }
            catch(  Disconnected e) { }
            catch(  SystemException e) {
                    disconnect_push_supplier();
            }
        }
    }

    public static void main(String[] args) {
        GenericPushQuoteServer server = new GenericPushQuoteServer();
    }

}
```

Moving from the server to the client, Listing 31.5 contains the GenericPushListener
class. This class attaches itself to the event channel and is notified of all new stock
prices. When a price is obtained, the portfolio is examined for the presence of the associated symbol. If the holding is present in the portfolio, its value is updated; otherwise, the
event is ignored.

LISTING 31.5 THE GenericPushListener CLASS LISTENS FOR EVENTS POSTED TO THE
EVENT CHANNEL

```
import java.util.*;
import org.omg.CosEventComm.*;
import org.omg.CosEventChannelAdmin.*;


/**
 * The GenericPushListener class is notified via its
 * push() method whenever a new price is available
 * for a given quote.
 */
public class GenericPushListener extends _PushConsumerImplBase {
    private Hashtable        _hshPortfolio;
    private PortfolioGUI     _portfolioGUI;

    public GenericPushListener(Hashtable hshPortfolio,
                                PortfolioGUI portfolioGUI) {
        _hshPortfolio = hshPortfolio;
```

```
        _portfolioGUI = portfolioGUI;

        // bind to the orb
        org.omg.CORBA.ORB orb = org.omg.CORBA.ORB.init();
        // obtain a reference to the boa
        org.omg.CORBA.BOA boa = orb.BOA_init();
        // obtain a reference to the event channel
        EventChannel channel = EventChannelHelper.bind(orb);;
        // connect as a listener for push events
        ProxyPushSupplier pushSupplier =
            channel.for_consumers().obtain_push_supplier();;
        try{    pushSupplier.connect_push_consumer(this); }
        catch(  AlreadyConnected ac ) {}
    }

    /**
     * The push() method is invoked by the event channel
     * when a new event is pushed into the channel queue.
     */
    public void push(org.omg.CORBA.Any data) throws Disconnected {
        // extract the event data
        org.omg.CORBA.Object object = data.extract_Object();
        // narrow (cast) the event data as a QuoteUpdateI object
        QuoteUpdateI quoteUpdate = QuoteUpdateIHelper.narrow(object);

        // check to see if the updated price represents
        // an active holding.
        String sSymbol = quoteUpdate.sSymbol();
        if(_hshPortfolio.containsKey(sSymbol)) {
            synchronized(_hshPortfolio) {
                // update the stock value in the portfolio
                StockOwnership stock =
                    (StockOwnership)_hshPortfolio.get(sSymbol);
                stock.setPrice(quoteUpdate.fNewPrice());
            }
            // repaint the portfolio screen
            _portfolioGUI.updatePortfolio();
        }
    }

    /**
     * The disconnect_push_consumer() method is invoked
     * by the event channel when we are disconnected
     * from the event channel.
     */
    public void disconnect_push_consumer() {
    }

}
```

Whereas Listing 31.5 contains the actual code used to listen for events, Listing 31.6 contains the code used to render all information onscreen. The `PortfolioGUI` class is the main point of entry for the application, and it displays, in grid format, current values for all holdings. The screen presents buttons that enable the human user to either buy or sell stocks. When a user requests that a buy or sell be performed, the `BuyDialog` or `SellDialog` (respectively) handle the user interaction. Finally, the `StockOwnership` class represents a holding (symbol, shares owned, and share price).

LISTING 31.6 THE `PortfolioGUI`, `BuyDialog`, `SellDialog`, AND `StockOwnership` CLASSES FACILITATE DISPLAY OF LIVE PORTFOLIO INFORMATION

```java
import java.awt.*;
import java.awt.event.*;
import java.util.*;
import jclass.bwt.*;

/**
 * The PortfolioGUI class represents a simple
 * GUI for our portfolio client.
 */
public final class PortfolioGUI extends Frame {
    private JCMultiColumnList   _mlstPortfolio;
    private Hashtable           _hshPortfolio;
    private Button              _btnBuy;
    private Button              _btnSell;

    public PortfolioGUI() {
        super("Stock Portfolio");

        _mlstPortfolio = new JCMultiColumnList();
        _mlstPortfolio.setColumnButtons(column_labels);

        Panel pnlButtons = new Panel();
        pnlButtons.setLayout(new FlowLayout(FlowLayout.LEFT));
        pnlButtons.add(_btnBuy = new Button("Buy"));
        pnlButtons.add(_btnSell = new Button("Sell"));

        _btnBuy.addActionListener(new BuySellListener("BUY", this));
        _btnSell.addActionListener(new BuySellListener("SELL", this));

        setLayout(new BorderLayout());
        add(pnlButtons, "North");
        add(_mlstPortfolio, "Center");

        _hshPortfolio = new Hashtable();
        _hshPortfolio.put("INKT", new StockOwnership("INKT",
                                             57.5f, 100f));
        _hshPortfolio.put("MSFT", new StockOwnership("MSFT",
                                             113.8f, 54521f));
```

```
        _hshPortfolio.put("ORCL", new StockOwnership("ORCL",
                                        24.6f, 5485f));
        _hshPortfolio.put("CNWK", new StockOwnership("CNWK",
                                        64.75f, 300f));
        _hshPortfolio.put("XCIT", new StockOwnership("XCIT",
                                        44.62f, 7164f));
        updatePortfolio();

        // listen for changes
        GenericPushListener listener =
            new GenericPushListener(_hshPortfolio, this);
    }

    public void updatePortfolio() {
        _mlstPortfolio.setBatched(true); // don't repaint on add
        _mlstPortfolio.clear();

        Enumeration e = _hshPortfolio.elements();
        while(e.hasMoreElements()) {
            StockOwnership stock = (StockOwnership)e.nextElement();
            StringBuffer sbBuilder = new StringBuffer();
            sbBuilder.append(stock.getSymbol());
            sbBuilder.append("¦");
            sbBuilder.append(stock.getSharesOwned());
            sbBuilder.append("¦");
            sbBuilder.append(stock.getPrice());
            sbBuilder.append("¦");
            sbBuilder.append(stock.getSharesOwned()*stock.getPrice());

            _mlstPortfolio.addItem(sbBuilder.toString(), '¦');
        }

        _mlstPortfolio.setBatched(false); // repaint all
    }

    /**
     * Invoked when a user OKs out of a
     * BUY dialog box. Indicates that the
     * specified number of shares of the stock
     * identified by the specified symbol were
     * purchased. The purchase price is assumed
     * to be the current price.
     */
    public void buyOccurred(String sSymbol, float fShares) {
        StockOwnership stock =
            (StockOwnership)_hshPortfolio.get(sSymbol);
        if(stock != null)
            stock.setSharesOwned(stock.getSharesOwned()+fShares);
        updatePortfolio();
    }
```

continues

LISTING 31.6   CONTINUED

```java
/**
 * Invoked when a user OKs out of a
 * SELL dialog box. Indicates that the
 * specified number of shares of the stock
 * identified by the specified symbol were
 * sold. The selling price is assumed
 * to be the current price.
 */
public void sellOccurred(String sSymbol, float fShares) {
    StockOwnership stock =
        (StockOwnership)_hshPortfolio.get(sSymbol);
    if(stock != null)
        stock.setSharesOwned(stock.getSharesOwned()-fShares);
    updatePortfolio();
}

/**
 * Inner class used to listen for clicks on
 * the buy or sell buttons.
 */
class BuySellListener implements ActionListener {
    private final  int      BUY = 1;
    private final  int      SELL = 2;
    private int            _iMode = 0;
    private PortfolioGUI    _parent;

    public BuySellListener(String sMode, PortfolioGUI parent) {
        if(sMode.equalsIgnoreCase("BUY")) _iMode = BUY;
        else _iMode = SELL;
        _parent = parent;
    }

    public void actionPerformed(ActionEvent ae) {
        Dialog dialog = null;

        if(_iMode == BUY) {
            dialog = new BuyDialog(_parent, _hshPortfolio);
        }
        else {
            dialog = new SellDialog(_parent, _hshPortfolio);
        }
        dialog.pack();
        dialog.setVisible(true);
    }
}

public final static void main(String[] args) {
    PortfolioGUI gui = new PortfolioGUI();
    gui.pack();
```

```
                gui.setVisible(true);
        }
}

import java.awt.*;
import java.awt.event.*;
import java.util.*;

/**
 * The BuyDialog class is a simple UI tool
 * that allows users to buy additional shares
 * in existing holdings.
 */
public class BuyDialog extends Dialog {
    private Choice          _chcSymbols;
    private TextField       _txtShares;
    private Button          _btnOk;
    private Button          _btnCancel;
    private PortfolioGUI    _portfolioGUI;

    public BuyDialog(PortfolioGUI portfolioGUI, Hashtable hshPortfolio) {
        super(portfolioGUI, true);
        setBackground(Color.white);

        _portfolioGUI = portfolioGUI;

        _chcSymbols = new Choice();
        Enumeration e = hshPortfolio.keys();
        _chcSymbols.add("");
        while(e.hasMoreElements()) {
            _chcSymbols.add(e.nextElement().toString());
        }

        Panel pnlLabel = new Panel();
        pnlLabel.setLayout(new FlowLayout(FlowLayout.CENTER));
        pnlLabel.add(new Label("Select A Symbol And Share Count"));

        Panel pnlDecision = new Panel();
        pnlDecision.setLayout(new FlowLayout(FlowLayout.LEFT));
        pnlDecision.add(new Label("Symbol: ", Label.RIGHT));
        pnlDecision.add(_chcSymbols);
        pnlDecision.add(new Label(" "));
        pnlDecision.add(new Label("Shares: ", Label.RIGHT));
        pnlDecision.add(_txtShares = new TextField(15));

        Panel pnlButtons = new Panel();
        pnlButtons.setLayout(new FlowLayout(FlowLayout.RIGHT,5,5));
        pnlButtons.add(_btnOk = new Button("Ok"));
        pnlButtons.add(_btnCancel = new Button("Cancel"));
        _btnOk.addActionListener(new ButtonListener(this, "OK"));
```

continues

LISTING 31.6   CONTINUED

```java
        _btnCancel.addActionListener(new ButtonListener(this, "CANCEL"));

        setLayout(new GridLayout(3,1));
        add(pnlLabel);
        add(pnlDecision);
        add(pnlButtons);
    }

    /**
     * Inner class used to listen for the event
     * caused when a button is clicked.
     */
    class ButtonListener implements ActionListener {
        public int         OK = 10;
        public int         CANCEL = 13;
        private int        _iMode;
        private BuyDialog  _parent;

        public ButtonListener(BuyDialog parent, String sMode) {
            _parent = parent;
            if(sMode.equalsIgnoreCase("OK")) _iMode = OK;
            else _iMode = CANCEL;
        }

        public void actionPerformed(ActionEvent ae) {
            if(_iMode == OK) {

                try{    float fShares =
                        Float.valueOf(_txtShares.getText()).floatValue();
                        _portfolioGUI.buyOccurred(
                            _chcSymbols.getSelectedItem(), fShares);
                }
                catch(  NumberFormatException nfe ) {}
            }
            _parent.setVisible(false);
        }
    }
}

import java.awt.*;
import java.awt.event.*;
import java.util.*;

/**
 * The SellDialog class is a simple UI tool
 * that allows users to sell shares
 * in existing holdings.
 */
public class SellDialog extends Dialog {
```

```
    private Hashtable        _hshPortfolio;
    private Choice           _chcSymbols;
    private TextField        _txtShares;
    private Button           _btnOk;
    private Button           _btnCancel;
    private PortfolioGUI     _portfolioGUI;

public SellDialog(PortfolioGUI portfolioGUI, Hashtable hshPortfolio) {
    super(portfolioGUI, true);
    setBackground(Color.white);

    _portfolioGUI = portfolioGUI;
    _hshPortfolio = hshPortfolio;

    _chcSymbols = new Choice();
    Enumeration e = hshPortfolio.keys();
    _chcSymbols.add("");
    while(e.hasMoreElements()) {
        _chcSymbols.add(e.nextElement().toString());
    }
    _chcSymbols.addItemListener(new ChoiceListener());

    Panel pnlLabel = new Panel();
    pnlLabel.setLayout(new FlowLayout(FlowLayout.CENTER));
    pnlLabel.add(new Label("Select A Symbol And Share Count"));

    Panel pnlDecision = new Panel();
    pnlDecision.setLayout(new FlowLayout(FlowLayout.LEFT));
    pnlDecision.add(new Label("Symbol: ", Label.RIGHT));
    pnlDecision.add(_chcSymbols);
    pnlDecision.add(new Label(" "));
    pnlDecision.add(new Label("Shares: ", Label.RIGHT));
    pnlDecision.add(_txtShares = new TextField(15));

    Panel pnlButtons = new Panel();
    pnlButtons.setLayout(new FlowLayout(FlowLayout.RIGHT,5,5));
    pnlButtons.add(_btnOk = new Button("Ok"));
    pnlButtons.add(_btnCancel = new Button("Cancel"));
    _btnOk.addActionListener(new ButtonListener(this, "OK"));
    _btnCancel.addActionListener(new ButtonListener(this, "CANCEL"));

    setLayout(new GridLayout(3,1));
    add(pnlLabel);
    add(pnlDecision);
    add(pnlButtons);
}

/**
 * Inner class used to listen for changes to the
 * symbol being displayed in the Choice
```

continues

LISTING 31.6   CONTINUED

```java
    */
    class ChoiceListener implements ItemListener {

        public void itemStateChanged(ItemEvent ie) {
        }
    }

    /**
     * Inner class used to listen for the event
     * caused when a button is clicked.
     */
    class ButtonListener implements ActionListener {
        public int         OK = 10;
        public int         CANCEL = 13;
        private int        _iMode;
        private SellDialog _parent;

        public ButtonListener(SellDialog parent, String sMode) {
            _parent = parent;
            if(sMode.equalsIgnoreCase("OK")) _iMode = OK;
            else _iMode = CANCEL;
        }

        public void actionPerformed(ActionEvent ae) {
            if(_iMode == OK) {

                try{    float fShares =
                        Float.valueOf(_txtShares.getText()).floatValue();
                        _portfolioGUI.sellOccurred(
                                    _chcSymbols.getSelectedItem(),
                                    fShares);
                }
                catch(  NumberFormatException nfe ) {}
            }
            _parent.setVisible(false);
        }
    }
}

/**
 * Class used to represent ownership
 * in a unique stock
 */
public class StockOwnership {
    private String  _sSymbol = null;
    private float   _fPrice = 0f;
    private float   _fsharesOwned = 0f;

    public StockOwnership() {
```

```
    }

    public StockOwnership(String sSymbol,
                          float fPrice,
                          float fsharesOwned) {
        _sSymbol = sSymbol;
        _fPrice = fPrice;
        _fsharesOwned = fsharesOwned;
    }

    public String getSymbol() {
        return _sSymbol;
    }

    public float getPrice() {
        return _fPrice;
    }

    public float getSharesOwned() {
        return _fsharesOwned;
    }

    public void setSymbol(String sSymbol) {
        _sSymbol = sSymbol;
    }

    public void setPrice(float fPrice) {
        _fPrice = fPrice;
    }

    public void setSharesOwned(float fsharesOwned) {
        _fsharesOwned = fsharesOwned;
    }
}
```

To run the application, you'll need the Inprise Visibroker ORB installed, along with the Inprise Event Channel software and a GUI library called JClass BWT that is also on the CD-ROM. The JClass package contains a collection of UI widgets. In the current example we use the grid widget. If you haven't installed the software yet, do so now. With all the software installed, first launch the ORB runtime using the following command:

osagent

You'll now need to launch the event channel using this command:

vbj com.visigenic.vbroker.services.CosEvent.Channel EventChannelName

The parameter passed to the event channel application is a logical name associated with this unique channel. If your application calls for the use of multiple event channels, each would have a unique name, and all channel bind operations would specify the name of the desired channel. With the event channel active, compile all IDL and Java code and then launch the server by typing

vbj GenericPushQuoteServer

and the client by typing

vbj PortfolioGUI

As the application runs, you'll see rapid changes in the value of all holdings. Because a stock price is randomly recalculated to fall between $0–$300, chances are you'll not have the same portfolio value for long. Although these dramatic shifts are, thankfully, not indicative of market performance, they do represent a potential situation in which the markets might get all confused on January 1, 2000. The hectic portfolio is shown in Figure 31.2.

FIGURE 31.2

The stock portfolio application displaying ticker values.

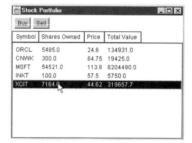

THE GENERIC PULL EVENT MODEL

As was stated in the earlier discussion of the push and pull event models, each presents pros and cons. Because the push event model involves network traffic only when an event needs to migrate to the client, there's no bandwidth wasted on extraneous communication. Additionally, the push model does not depend on a client asking for events and therefore lends itself to timely event delivery. The one major downside to the push model is that the event channel must invoke methods on the client object itself. In many situations, the event channel and server will exist somewhere on the Internet, and the client will exist behind a firewall. Because most firewalls are configured to not allow incoming connections (including method invocations), the push model will fail here. As an alternative, the pull model exists such that events are stored at the supplier and delivered to the consumer only when asked for. The consumer still communicates with the supplier via the event channel; event requests are passed through the channel to the actual target.

In a fashion similar to our investigation of the generic push event model, we'll first examine the IDL supplied by the Event Service and then develop a demonstration application. The application developed is a version of the earlier portfolio example; however, the pull event model is employed. To conserve space, only the two classes that manage event sending and receiving are printed in the book; all GUI code is contained on the CD-ROM. Note that this GUI code differs little from the GUI code for the push example. In fact, the only difference is that the `PortfolioGUI` class instantiates a `GenericPullListener` object (to watch for stock value changes) instead of a `GenericPushListener` object.

Starting our exploration of the pull event model, Listing 31.7 contains the IDL interfaces that the event channel exposes for use during pull-based event communication.

LISTING 31.7 SECTIONS OF THE `CosEventComm` AND `CosEventChannelAdmin` MODULES DEALING WITH THE GENERIC PULL EVENT MODEL

```
module CosEventComm {
    exception Disconnected{};

    interface PullSupplier {
        any pull () raises(Disconnected);
        any try_pull (out boolean has_event) raises(Disconnected);
        void disconnect_pull_supplier();
    };

    interface PullConsumer {
         void disconnect_pull_consumer();
    };
};

module CosEventChannelAdmin {
    exception AlreadyConnected {};
    exception TypeError {};

    interface ProxyPullSupplier: CosEventComm::PullSupplier {
        void connect_pull_consumer(
        in CosEventComm::PullConsumer pull_consumer)
        raises(AlreadyConnected);
    };

    interface ProxyPullConsumer: CosEventComm::PullConsumer {
        void connect_pull_supplier(in CosEventComm::PullSupplier
                                    pull_supplier)
            raises(AlreadyConnected,TypeError);
    };

    interface ConsumerAdmin {
```

continues

LISTING **31.7**   CONTINUED

```
        ProxyPushSupplier obtain_push_supplier();
        ProxyPullSupplier obtain_pull_supplier();
    };

    interface SupplierAdmin {
        ProxyPushConsumer obtain_push_consumer();
        ProxyPullConsumer obtain_pull_consumer();
    };

    interface EventChannel {
        ConsumerAdmin for_consumers();
        SupplierAdmin for_suppliers();
        void destroy();
    };
};
```

In a fashion almost identical to the push event model, both the event supplier and consumer begin by binding to an object that implements the EventChannel interface. After binding to the EventChannel object, event suppliers obtain a SupplierAdmin object by invoking the for_suppliers() operation, and event consumers obtain a ConsumerAdmin object by invoking the for_consumers() operation. Through the *xxx*Admin objects, suppliers and consumers actually connect to the channel. Once connected to the channel, consumers query the channel for available events. The event channel then queries registered suppliers for available events.

Moving beyond the event channel, the CosEventComm module defines interfaces implemented by the event suppliers and consumers. The PullConsumer interface is implemented by consumers and simply defines the disconnect_pull_consumer() method, which is invoked when the consumer is disconnected from the event channel. The PullSupplier interface is implemented by event suppliers, and it defines two important methods. Both the pull() and try_pull()methods are invoked by the event channel when a consumer requests an event from the channel. The try_pull() method is used when a consumer simply wants to query for potential available events. This method is nonblocking, and a consumer is not guaranteed an event return value. To indicate the presence of an event, the try_pull() method accepts a boolean "out" parameter, indicating whether a valid event is being returned. When the pull() method is invoked, the consumer will block until a valid event is returned.

Now that you have an understanding of how the generic pull event model functions, stop reading for a minute and convert the stock portfolio example over to use the pull event model. Because the earlier example is designed such that event communication is performed in two unique classes, the amount of code that needs to be changed is rather minimal. The one major difference, however, is that the supplier cannot simply post event after event, and the consumer cannot sit passively and wait for events to arrive. The consumer must enter into a unique thread of execution and poll the event channel for available events. The supplier, instead of sending out events in a unique thread, must enter a wait state and be prepared to post events when ready.

Once you've attempted to convert the solution yourself, take a look at the event supplier class in Listing 31.8 and the event consumer class in Listing 31.9. Compiling and running this new version of the solution is identical to the process used with the generic push version.

LISTING 31.8   SENDING EVENTS USING THE GENERIC PULL EVENT MODEL

```java
import java.util.*;
import org.omg.CosEventComm.*;
import org.omg.CosEventChannelAdmin.*;
import org.omg.CORBA.*;

/**
 * The GenericPullQuoteServer generates events
 * containing price data on stock quotes.
 */
public final class GenericPullQuoteServer extends _PullSupplierImplBase {

    private String[]          _sSymbols = {"INKT", "MSFT", "ORCL",
                                           "CNWK","XCIT", "PSFT",
                                           "LU", "CPQ","WMT", "DIS"};

    private Random            _random;

    private org.omg.CORBA.ORB _orb;
    private org.omg.CORBA.BOA _boa;
    private ProxyPullConsumer _pullConsumer;

    public GenericPullQuoteServer() {
        // bind to the orb
        _orb = ORB.init();
        // obtain a reference to the boa
        _boa = _orb.BOA_init();
        _random = new Random();

        // bind to the event channel
        EventChannel channel = EventChannelHelper.bind(_orb);
        // obtain a ProxyPullConsumer object.
        _pullConsumer = channel.for_suppliers().obtain_pull_consumer();
        // connect as an event supplier
        try{    _pullConsumer.connect_pull_supplier(this); }
        catch(  AlreadyConnected ac ) {}
```

continues

LISTING 31.8   CONTINUED

```
        _boa.impl_is_ready();
}

/**
 * Invoked when we are disconnected from the
 * event channel.
 */
public void disconnect_pull_supplier() {
    try{    _boa().deactivate_obj(this); }
    catch(  SystemException e) { }
}

/**
 * Chooses (at random) one of the ten
 * supported symbols.
 */
private String getRandomSymbol() {
    return _sSymbols[Math.abs(_random.nextInt() % 10) - 0];
}

/**
 * Generates a random value for a quote
 * between 0 and 300
 */
private float getRandomPrice() {
    return Math.abs(_random.nextInt() % 300) - 0;
}

/**
 * Creates a new QuoteUpdateI object with
 * random values
 */
private QuoteUpdateI obtainRandomQuoteUpdate() {
    QuoteUpdateI quote =
        new QuoteUpdate(getRandomSymbol(), getRandomPrice());
    _boa.obj_is_ready(quote);
    return quote;
}

/**
 * Invoked by the event channel when an event is needed
 * by the consumer
 */
public org.omg.CORBA.Any pull() throws Disconnected {
    if(_pullConsumer == null)  throw new Disconnected();

    // obtain an Any object from the ORB
    org.omg.CORBA.Any eventObject = _orb.create_any();
    // add a QuoteUpdateI object to the Any object
```

```
        eventObject.insert_Object(obtainRandomQuoteUpdate());
        // post the event
        return eventObject;
    }

    /**
     * Invoked by the event channel when an event may or may not
     * be needed by the consumer. Since we provide a steady stream
     * of quote events, simply call pull()
     */
    public org.omg.CORBA.Any try_pull(org.omg.CORBA.BooleanHolder
                                hasEvent)
          throws org.omg.CORBA.SystemException, Disconnected {
        hasEvent.value = true; // indicate the presence of an event
        return pull();
    }


    public static void main(String[] args) {
        GenericPullQuoteServer server = new GenericPullQuoteServer();
    }

}
```

LISTING 31.9   RECEIVING EVENTS USING THE GENERIC PULL EVENT MODEL

```
import java.util.*;
import org.omg.CosEventComm.*;
import org.omg.CosEventChannelAdmin.*;


/**
 * The GenericPullListener class is notified via its
 * pull() method whenever a new price is available
 * for a given quote.
 */
public class GenericPullListener extends _PullConsumerImplBase
                                implements Runnable {
    private Hashtable          _hshPortfolio;
    private PortfolioGUI       _portfolioGUI;
    private ProxyPullSupplier  _pullSupplier;
    private Thread             _thread;

    public GenericPullListener(Hashtable hshPortfolio,
                            PortfolioGUI portfolioGUI) {
        _hshPortfolio = hshPortfolio;
        _portfolioGUI = portfolioGUI;
```

continues

LISTING 31.9   CONTINUED

```
        // bind to the orb
        org.omg.CORBA.ORB orb = org.omg.CORBA.ORB.init();
        // obtain a reference to the boa
        org.omg.CORBA.BOA boa = orb.BOA_init();
        // obtain a reference to the event channel
        EventChannel channel = EventChannelHelper.bind(orb);;
        // connect as a listener for pull events
        _pullSupplier = channel.for_consumers().obtain_pull_supplier();;
        try{    _pullSupplier.connect_pull_consumer(this); }
        catch(  AlreadyConnected ac ) {}

        _thread = new Thread(this);
        _thread.start();
    }

    /**
     * Queries the event channel for available events
     */
    public void pull() throws Disconnected {
        // query and extract the event data
        org.omg.CORBA.Object object =
            _pullSupplier.pull().extract_Object();
        // narrow (cast) the event data as a QuoteUpdateI object
        QuoteUpdateI quoteUpdate = QuoteUpdateIHelper.narrow(object);

        // check to see if the updated price represents
        // an active holding.
        String sSymbol = quoteUpdate.sSymbol();
        if(_hshPortfolio.containsKey(sSymbol)) {
            synchronized(_hshPortfolio) {
                // update the stock value in the portfolio
                StockOwnership stock =
                    (StockOwnership)_hshPortfolio.get(sSymbol);
                stock.setPrice(quoteUpdate.fNewPrice());
            }
            // repaint the portfolio screen
            _portfolioGUI.updatePortfolio();
        }
    }

    /**
     * The disconnect_pull_consumer() method is invoked
     * by the event channel when we are disconnected
     * from the event channel.
     */
    public void disconnect_pull_consumer() {
        _pullSupplier.disconnect_pull_supplier();
    }
```

```
/**
 * Periodically poll for available events
 */
public void run() {
    boolean bContinue = true;
    while(bContinue) {
        try{    _thread.sleep(1000); }
        catch(  Exception e ) {}
        try{    pull(); }
        catch(  Disconnected d) {
            bContinue = false;
            disconnect_pull_consumer();
        }
    }
}
}
```

FROM HERE

This chapter addressed the important topic of the CORBA Event Service. As you develop
distributed applications, chances are you'll need some mechanism for event-based communication, and the Event Service is a valid candidate for use. The advantage of going
with the Event Service over a homebrewed version is twofold. First of all, you're using a
standard API, which means new developers entering a team are likely to have knowledge
of its functionality. Second, because the event channel is already developed, you save
significant development time. You don't need to develop and test code that can handle
potentially thousands of events being posted to the channel at the same time.

As you continue to explore all that CORBA has to offer, you'll find that the following
chapters complement this chapter's coverage of the Event Service:

- Chapter 21, "CORBA Overview"
- Chapter 22, "CORBA Architecture"
- Chapter 23, "Survey of CORBA ORBs"
- Chapter 30, "The Naming Service"

INTERFACE REPOSITORY, DYNAMIC INVOCATION, INTROSPECTION, AND REFLECTION

IN THIS CHAPTER

An object in both the CORBA universe and the Java universe serves a variety of purposes. At one level, it has the ability to interact in business processes, represent data, and generally model some real-world entity. In addition, an object also has the ability to enter into a dialogue in which it describes the features it exports. For example, an object in a patient management system can model patient data and also be asked if it supports methods that obtain demographic information. The ability to query an object at runtime is called either *introspection* or *reflection* and is supported both by Java objects and by CORBA objects. Developers producing CORBA solutions in Java are able to mix and match both techniques to achieve the best of both worlds.

This chapter takes a look at discovering information about objects using both the Java reflection model and the CORBA introspection model. Specifically, the following information is covered:

- How the Java reflection model describes objects
- How the CORBA introspection model describes objects
- How the interface repository aids the CORBA introspection model
- How to dynamically invoke methods on objects

The 1.02 release of the JDK introduced minimal reflection capabilities that Java objects could expose. Although useful to some extent, these capabilities were very rudimentary and were far from sophisticated. The 1.1 release of the JDK changed this by greatly enhancing the ability of an object to describe itself. In this initial section, we first look at the classes and interfaces that enable reflection and then build an application that dynamically invokes methods on a variety of objects. Following the coverage of the Java reflection model, we move on to coverage of the CORBA reflection (or introspection) model.

JAVA REFLECTION TECHNOLOGIES

Classes and interfaces in the packages `java.lang.reflect` and `java.lang` support reflection in the Java universe. These classes, described fully in Table 32.1, allow for classes, methods, fields, and exceptions to describe all needed information. What should be noted about the classes discussed here is that in addition to describing a method or field, they also provide live access to that method or field. For example, you could look at an object, ask it for an array of its fields, find all fields that are `String` objects with the value "bar," and change this value to "foo."

TABLE 32.1 CLASSES AND INTERFACES USED BY THE JAVA REFLECTION MODEL

Class/Interface name	Purpose
java.lang.Class	Automatically created by the JVM when an object is instantiated. Maintains references to all information available to describe the object.
java.lang.reflect.Member	Interface that describes information about either a method or field present in a class. This interface is implemented by other classes in this package.
java.lang.reflect.Constructor	Represents information about and provides access to a class's constructor.
java.lang.reflect.Field	Represents information about and provides access to a member variable present in an object.
java.lang.reflect.Method	Represents information about and provides access to a method present in an object.
java.lang.reflect.Modifier	A collection of static methods and variables used when examining class, member, or method modifiers (for example, static or final).

32

INTERFACE
REPOSITORY

The class Class is the starting point through which information about an object is accessed. A single Class object is automatically associated with all objects when instantiated and is obtained by invoking the method getClass() that's inherited from the class java.lang.Object (the default parent for all classes). Once obtained, the Class object exposes a series of methods through which references to the target object's methods and fields are obtained. Table 32.2 describes the methods useful during reflection that are exposed by the class Class.

As you examine these methods, note that because they provide live access to a field or method, Java access control mechanisms are respected. This means that if you're examining an object from another object, only public methods and fields are accessible. If the object is examining itself, public, private, and protected data is accessible.

TABLE 32.2 METHODS EXPOSED BY THE CLASS *Class* USED IN REFLECTION

Method	*Purpose*
getConstructor(Class[])	Obtains the Constructor object associated with the specified class.
getConstructors()	Obtains all Constructor objects associated with the target object.
getDeclaredClasses()	Obtains all Class objects associated with all fields in the target object.
getDeclaredConstructor(Class[])	Obtains the Constructor object associated with the specified parameter.
getDeclaredConstructors()	Obtains all Constructor objects.
getDeclaredField(String)	Obtains the specified Field object.
getDeclaredFields()	Obtains an array of all available Field objects.
getDeclaredMethod(String, Class[])	Obtains the specified Method object.
getDeclaredMethods()	Obtains all specified Method objects.
getField(String)	Obtains the specified Field object.
getFields()	Obtains all available Field objects.
getInterfaces()	Obtains the runtime Class objects associated with the interfaces implemented by the target object.
getMethod(String, Class[])	Obtains a reference to the specified Method object.
getMethods()	Obtains references to all available methods. This includes Method objects inherited from a parent class.
getModifiers()	Obtains the modifiers (static, final, and so on) associated with the class.
isArray()	Returns true if the Class object is associated with an array.

Looking at the methods in Table 32.2 should impart a decent understanding of the level of access exposed by the Class class; however, their use is not always obvious. With this base understanding of the available possibilities, we'll start developing some code that will further cement your understanding. The following pages contain a variety of examples, each of which focus on accessing a different type of functionality present in the Java reflection model.

Dynamically Invoking Methods

One of the more common operations that the Java reflection model is used for is the dynamic invocation of methods exposed by an object. In this first example, we'll look at invoking methods with zero parameters, base type parameters, and object parameters.

To begin our exploration into dynamic method invocation, take a look at the class defined in Listing 32.1. It's a simple entity class that exposes *getter* and *setter* methods to alter the value of its private member variables. Although it's not monumental in function, this class is nevertheless a good example because it has a combination of no parameter methods, methods that accept base types, and methods that accept object parameters.

LISTING 32.1   A SIMPLE ENTITY CLASS

```
public class SimpleObject {

    private String   _sValue = "";
    private int      _iValue = -1;

    public SimpleObject() {
    }

    public void setStringValue(String sValue) { _sValue = sValue; }
    public String getStringValue() { return _sValue; }

    public void setIntegerValue(int iValue) { _iValue = iValue; }
    public int getIntegerValue() { return _iValue; }
}
```

Looking at the code in Listing 32.1 and taking the overview that has been presented so far, you might want to challenge yourself to actually dynamically invoke one of the methods exposed by the SimpleObject class. If so, close the book before you peek at the next example; then come back when you're ready to examine the code used to dynamically invoke methods. Once you're ready, take a look at the code in Listing 32.2, which both examines the methods present in the SimpleObject class and dynamically invokes them.

LISTING 32.2   DYNAMICALLY INVOKING METHODS USING JAVA REFLECTION

```
import java.lang.reflect.*;

public class Reflector {
    private SimpleObject    _simpleObject;
    private Class           _runtimeClass;
```

continues

LISTING 32.2   CONTINUED

```java
public Reflector() {
    // create a new SimpleObject object
    _simpleObject = new SimpleObject();
    // obtain a reference to its runtime Class object
    _runtimeClass = _simpleObject.getClass();

    System.out.println("\tListing All Methods");
    listMethods();

    System.out.println("\n\tInvoking setStringValue()");
    try{   invoke_setStringValue(); }
    catch( Exception e ) {}

    System.out.println("\n\tInvoking setIntegerValue()");
    try{   invoke_setIntegerValue(); }
    catch( Exception e ) {}

    System.out.println("\n\tInvoking Getter Methods");
    try{   invokeGetterMethods(); }
    catch( Exception e ) {}
}

/**
 * Lists all public methods exposed my the
 * class SimpleObject
 */
private void listMethods() {

    Method[] methods = _runtimeClass.getDeclaredMethods();
    for(int i=0; i<methods.length; i++) {
        System.out.println(methods[i].getName());
    }
}

/**
 * Invokes the method setStringValue() on the
 * SimpleObject object.
 */
private void invoke_setStringValue() throws Exception {
    String sParameter = "Some New Value";
    Object oParameters[] = {sParameter};
    Class clsParameters[] = {sParameter.getClass()};

    Method setStringValue =
        _runtimeClass.getDeclaredMethod("setStringValue",
                                        clsParameters);
    setStringValue.invoke(_simpleObject, oParameters);
}
```

```java
/**
 * Invokes the method setIntegerValue() on the
 * SimpleObject object.
 */
private void invoke_setIntegerValue() throws Exception {
    Integer iValue = new Integer(1013);
    Object oParameters[] = {iValue};
    Class clsParameters[] = {iValue.TYPE};

    Method setIntegerValue =
        _runtimeClass.getDeclaredMethod("setIntegerValue",
                                        clsParameters);
    setIntegerValue.invoke(_simpleObject, oParameters);
}

/**
 * Invokes the methods getStringValue() and
 * getIntegerValue() on the SimpleObject object.
 */
private void invokeGetterMethods() throws Exception {
    Method getStringValue =
    _runtimeClass.getDeclaredMethod("getStringValue",
                                    new Class[0]);
    Method getIntegerValue =
    _runtimeClass.getDeclaredMethod("getIntegerValue",
                                    new Class[0]);

    System.out.println("getStringValue: "+
                    getStringValue.invoke(_simpleObject,
                                        new Object[0]));
    System.out.println("getIntegerValue: "+
                    getIntegerValue.invoke(_simpleObject,
                                        new Object[0]));
}

public static void main(String[] args) {
    Reflector reflector = new Reflector();
}

}
```

As we step through Listing 32.2, we'll start with the code contained in the constructor. The `Reflector` class contains two private member variables that have their values established during the execution of the constructor. The first is simply an instance of the `SimpleObject` class. The second variable, however, is the runtime `Class` object associated with the `SimpleObject` instance. This variable has its value set by invoking the `getClass()` method in the `SimpleObject` object. As the rest of the code demonstrates, this variable plays a very important role in the reflection process.

Moving on, the next method that's invoked, `listMethods()`, lists the name of each public method in the `SimpleObject` class. This method establishes an array of `Method` objects and sets it to represent all public methods in the `SimpleObject` class by invoking the `getDeclaredMethods()` method on the runtime `Class` object. Once obtained, the array of `Method` objects is iterated and has the names of its values printed to the standard out.

Although listing the methods present in a class may be of use during the examination process, it needs to be coupled with dynamic method invocation to properly fulfill the needs of most applications. The first method that's dynamically invoked is the `setStringValue()` method, which is invoked by the `Reflector` object in its `invoke_setStringValue()` method. This method performs the equivalent of statically invoking `(new SimpleObject()).setStringValue("Some New Value")`; however, the invocation is performed dynamically. To perform this dynamic invocation, we first create a `String` object and set its value equal to "Some New Value." We then place that object in an array of `Object` objects and its runtime `Class` object into an array of `Class` objects. With the method parameters established, we execute the following code to obtain a reference to the actual `Method` object:

```
Method setStringValue =

    _runtimeClass.getDeclaredMethod("setStringValue", clsParameters);
```

The `getDeclaredMethod()` method takes as parameters a `String` object representing the signature of the target method and an array of `Class` objects representing the runtime classes associated with the method parameters.

Once a reference to a `Method` object has been obtained, it's invoked by the `invoke()` method. This method, as shown next, takes two important parameters. The first is a reference to the object on which this method is being invoked. The second parameter is an array of `Object` objects corresponding to the parameters accepted by the target object:

```
setStringValue.invoke(_simpleObject, oParameters);
```

After the `setStringValue()` method is invoked, the next dynamic invocation performed by the `Reflector` class involves the `setIntegerValue()` method. Although the dynamic invocation process is similar to the process associated with the `setStringValue()` method, it differs due to the fact that `setIntegerValue()` accepts a base type and not an actual object as its parameter. Because the `getDeclaredMethod()` and `invoke()` methods both take object representations of the methods parameters, the obvious challenge is how to represent a base type as an object.

As you very well may know, all base types are associated with a corresponding wrapper object. For example, the `int` base type can be represented as an object using the `Integer` object. As you examine the `invoke_setIntegerValue()` method, you'll note that the base type `int` is, in fact, associated with an `Integer` object placed in an array of `Object` objects and used as a parameter to the `invoke()` method. In addition to the wrapping of a base type inside an object for use in the `invoke()` method, the creation of the `Class` object array also differs in this situation. In situations where the parameter is an actual object, the `Class` object array is populated by invoking the `getClass()` method on each of the parameter objects. When the parameter is a base type, the `Class` object array is populated using the member variable `TYPE` associated with the wrapper object. Looking at the following code fragment, note the manner in which this is done:

```
Integer iValue = new Integer(1013);

Object oParameters[] = {iValue};

Class clsParameters[] = {iValue.TYPE};
```

At this point, you've learned how to dynamically invoke methods that accept object parameters as well as methods that accept base type parameters. As we complete our examination of the code, we'll invoke the getter methods that take no arguments as parameters. This no-parameter invocation is performed in the method `invokeGetterMethods()` and is actually the simplest dynamic invocation performed in the example. When passing the `Object` and `Class` object arrays to the `invoke()` and `getDeclaredMethod()` methods, we simply create zero element arrays.

Dynamically Referencing Fields

With a solid understanding of the manner in which methods are dynamically invoked, we now begin to look at the dynamic referencing of an object's variables. The code in Listing 32.3 presents a simple object that exposes a `String` object variable and an `int` base type variable.

LISTING 32.3 THE `SimpleFieldObject` CLASS EXPOSES TWO PUBLIC MEMBER VARIABLES

```
public class SimpleFieldObject {
    public String    _sValue = "";
    public int       _iValue = -1;
}
```

As with the dynamic invocation of methods example, again you might want to challenge yourself to write some code that dynamically sets the values of the variables in a `SimpleFieldObject` object. Once you're ready, take a look at the code in Listing 32.4, which sets and obtains the values of a `SimpleFieldObject`'s variables.

LISTING 32.4 USING JAVA REFLECTION TO DYNAMICALLY SET THE VALUE ASSOCIATED WITH A VARIABLE

```java
import java.lang.reflect.*;

public class FieldReferencer {
    private SimpleFieldObject   _simpleFieldObject;
    private Class               _runtimeClass;

    public FieldReferencer() {
        _simpleFieldObject = new SimpleFieldObject();
        _runtimeClass = _simpleFieldObject.getClass();

        System.out.println("\tSetting the Value of the String Variable");
        try{    setStringValue(); }
        catch(  Exception e ) {}

        System.out.println("\n\tSetting the Value of the int Variable");
        try{    setIntValue(); }
        catch(  Exception e ) {}

        System.out.println("\n\tGetting the Value
                            of the String Variable");
        try{    getStringValue(); }
        catch(  Exception e ) {}

        System.out.println("\n\tGetting the Value of the int Variable");
        try{    getIntValue(); }
        catch(  Exception e ) {}
    }

    private void setStringValue() throws Exception {
        Field field = _runtimeClass.getDeclaredField("_sValue");
        field.set(_simpleFieldObject, "Some New Value");
    }

    private void setIntValue() throws Exception {
        Field field = _runtimeClass.getDeclaredField("_iValue");
        field.set(_simpleFieldObject, new Integer(1013));
    }

    private void getStringValue() throws Exception {
        Field field = _runtimeClass.getDeclaredField("_sValue");
        System.out.println(field.get(_simpleFieldObject));
    }

    private void getIntValue() throws Exception {
        Field field = _runtimeClass.getDeclaredField("_iValue");
        System.out.println(field.get(_simpleFieldObject));
    }
```

```
    public static void main(String[] args) {
        FieldReferencer referencer = new FieldReferencer();
    }
}
```

The first task performed by the code in Listing 32.4 is to set both the `String` variable's value and the `int` variable's value. This task is performed by first asking the runtime `Class` object associated with the `SimpleFieldObject` object for a reference to each of the target fields and then invoking the associated `Field` object's `set()` method. Once we've set the values of each variable, we get them by again obtaining the `Field` object from the runtime `Class` object, but this time invoking the `get()` method on that object.

Pros and Cons of Java Reflection

As shown by the previous two examples, Java reflection technology is very powerful. It allows for methods to be dynamically invoked, for fields to have values dynamically set, and generally for an interaction with an object to be defined at runtime. This runtime definition of object interaction is nice because it allows for infinite flexibility; however, it makes compiler error detection much harder. For example, if I were to directly invoke the method `toString()` on any object, the compiler would be able to check that the method was present and disallow compilation if it was not. If, however, I were to dynamically invoke the `toString()` method on an object, the compiler would not have the ability to test for the presence of that method at compile time, and a runtime error would surface if it were not present. Assuming that my code is always correct when dynamically invoking methods, no problems will surface. However, if I were to make a spelling error (`toStirng()` instead of `toString()`, for example), the compiler would not detect this, and a runtime exception would be thrown. As reflection gains use in the Java community, it will be interesting to see if any companies release tools that validate dynamic method invocations and field references.

THE CORBA INTROSPECTION MODEL

In the initial section of this chapter, we looked at how objects describe themselves in a Java environment. Although useful, it's not the only manner through which dynamic object interaction can be scripted. In this section, we look at technologies made available in a CORBA environment that allow for dynamic interaction with objects.

32

INTERFACE REPOSITORY

The Interface Repository and Dynamic Interface Invocation

CORBA introspection is made possible through two complementary technologies: the Interface Repository and Dynamic Interface Invocation. In a dynamic environment, data cannot exist in a vacuum; it must be coupled with meta data. The term *meta data*, although drastically overused, simply refers to data that describes existing data. In the CORBA world, the IDL serves as meta data for all distributed entities. Meta data is stored in an Interface Repository (IR) and can be searched by any remote object. In addition to simply allowing access to the IDL, the IR contains a collection of operations, interfaces, and structs that all aid in describing exactly what the data is.

To create a dynamic interaction script, a remote object binds to the IR, searches out information about a target interface, and then uses Dynamic Interface Invocation (DII) to invoke methods on that remote object. In the following sections on the IR and DII, we first examine interacting with the IR and then look at using DII.

Working with the Interface Repository

The IR is a physical piece of software that must be manually started. Interaction occurs through a collection of interfaces and structs. The interface that provides the initial point of contact is named `Repository`, and it contains methods that allow for the searching of interfaces and structs by both name and identifier. Performing a search on the IR returns an instance of the class `org.omg.CORBA.Object`, which must then be narrowed to any one of a collection of classes that define the entity being returned. These description classes are all named by combining the entity they describe with the suffix "Def." For example, an interface is described using the class `InterfaceDef`, a string using `StringDef`, and a struct using `StructDef`. The following code snippet demonstrates the process of binding to an IR using the Directory Service and obtaining the `InterfaceDef` object associated with the `SimpleObjectI` interface:

```
ORB orb = ORB.init();

Repository repository = RepositoryHelper.bind(orb);

InterfaceDef interfaceDef =

    InterfaceDefHelper.narrow(repository.lookup("SimpleObjectI"));
```

In addition to the Repository and *xxx*Def interfaces, three additional entities facilitate the process of discovering information about an entity described in IDL. The first one is the interface TypeCode, which is used to fully describe a CORBA entity. The TypeCode interface has operations that allow for the entity's name to be discovered and for the repository ID to be discovered. It also has an attribute that's an instance of the TCKind enum. TCKind, the second important entity, identifies the IDL data type. The third entity encountered is the IDLType interface, which is associated with an IDL element. It simply points to a TypeCode instance. The TypeCode interface is contained in Listing 32.5, and the TCKind enum is contained in Listing 32.6. As you look at the TypeCode interface, pay attention to the name() operation, which obtains the name of the entity, and the kind() operation, which obtains the appropriate TCKind instance.

LISTING 32.5 THE TypeCode INTERFACE DESCRIBES AN ENTITY IN THE CORBA UNIVERSE

```
interface TypeCode {
    exception Bounds {};
    exception BadKind {};

    boolean equal(in CORBA::TypeCode tc);
    CORBA::TCKind kind();
    CORBA::RepositoryId id() raises(CORBA::TypeCode::BadKind);
    CORBA::Identifier name() raises(CORBA::TypeCode::BadKind);
    unsigned long member_count()raises(CORBA::TypeCode::BadKind);

    CORBA::Identifier member_name(in unsigned long index)
                    raises(CORBA::TypeCode::BadKind,
                            CORBA::TypeCode::Bounds);
    CORBA::TypeCode member_type(in unsigned long index)
                raises(CORBA::TypeCode::BadKind,
                        CORBA::TypeCode::Bounds);
    any member_label(in unsigned long index)
        raises(CORBA::TypeCode::BadKind,
                CORBA::TypeCode::Bounds);
    CORBA::TypeCode discriminator_type() raises(CORBA::TypeCode::BadKind);
    long default_index() raises(CORBA::TypeCode::BadKind);
    unsigned long length() raises(CORBA::TypeCode::BadKind);
    CORBA::TypeCode content_type() raises(CORBA::TypeCode::BadKind);
    long param_count();
    any parameter(in long index) raises(CORBA::TypeCode::Bounds);
};
```

Looking at the TCKind enum in Listing 32.6, you'll note a unique entry for each available CORBA entity. This allows a TCKind instance to accurately describe any available IDL entity.

LISTING 32.6 THE TCKind enum IDENTIFIES THE IDL TYPE ASSOCIATED WITH AN ENTITY

```
enum TCKind {
    tk_null, tk_void,
    tk_short, tk_long, tk_ushort, tk_ulong,
    tk_float, tk_double, tk_boolean, tk_char,
    tk_octet, tk_any, tk_TypeCode, tk_Principal, tk_objref,
    tk_struct, tk_union, tk_enum, tk_string,
    tk_sequence, tk_array, tk_alias, tk_except,
    tk_longlong, tk_ulonglong, tk_longdouble,
    tk_wchar, tk_wstring, tk_fixed
};
```

Now that you have a basic overview of the IR, we'll write a small application that binds to an IR and obtains the definition of two specific entities. Then, after we cover DII, the example will be extended to include a dynamic invocation script.

To begin the example, Listing 32.7 contains the IDL for a basic interface and struct. This is the IDL for which we'll query the IR.

LISTING 32.7 THE IDL DEFINITIONS FOR A BASIC INTERFACE AND STRUCT

```
interface SimpleObjectI {
    string getStringValue();
    void setStringValue(in string sValue);

    long getIntegerValue();
    void setIntegerValue(in long iValue);
};

struct SimpleStructS {
    string sValue;
    long iValue;
};
```

Given the IDL in Listing 32.7, Listing 32.8 contains the code for the IR interaction application. Before diving into the discussion of this application, spend some time with the code. When you're ready, you can continue reading.

LISTING 32.8 THE IRBrowser CLASS PRINTS OUT THE DETAILS OF THE IDL DESCRIBED IN LISTING 32.7 BY BINDING TO THE IR

```
import org.omg.CORBA.*;
import org.omg.CORBA.InterfaceDefPackage.*;

public final class IRBrowser {

    public IRBrowser() {
        ORB orb = ORB.init();
        Repository repository = RepositoryHelper.bind(orb);
        InterfaceDef interfaceDef =
            InterfaceDefHelper.narrow(repository.lookup("SimpleObjectI"));
        printInterfaceDetails(interfaceDef);
        StructDef structDef =
            StructDefHelper.narrow(repository.lookup("SimpleStructS"));
        printStructDetails(structDef);
    }

    /**
     * Prints details on a unique interface
     */
    private void printInterfaceDetails(InterfaceDef interfaceDef) {
        // obtain the interface description
        FullInterfaceDescription desc = interfaceDef.describe_interface();

        // print basic details
        System.out.println("-------------------------------");
        System.out.println("Interface Name: "+desc.name);
        System.out.println("Interface Type: "+desc.type);
        System.out.println("Interface Kind: "+desc.type.kind());

        // obtain and print operation details
        OperationDescription[] oppDefs = desc.operations;
        for(int i=0; i<oppDefs.length; i++) {
            System.out.println("Interface Operation "+
                            (i+1)+": "+oppDefs[i].name);
        }

        // obtain and print attribute details
        AttributeDescription[] attDefs = desc.attributes;
        for(int i=0; i<attDefs.length; i++) {
            System.out.println("Interface Attribute "+
                            (i+1)+": "+attDefs[i].name);
        }

    }

    /**
     * Prints details on a unique struct
```

continues

LISTING 32.8   CONTINUED

```
    */
    private void printStructDetails(StructDef structDef) {
        // obtain references to all members
        StructMember[] members = structDef.members();

        // print details on each member
        System.out.println("--------------------------------");
        for(int i=0;i<members.length; i++) {
            System.out.println("Member "+(i+1)+" Type: "+members[i].type);
            System.out.println("Member "+(i+1)+" Kind: "+
                                members[i].type.kind());
        }
    }

    public static void main(String[] args) {
        IRBrowser browser = new IRBrowser();
    }
}
```

As you examine the IRBrowser code in Listing 32.8, the first section you'll want to concentrate on is contained in the constructor. The first task performed is the process of
binding to the IR. Once the IR reference is obtained, the code performs two lookup interactions. The first obtains a reference to the InterfaceDef object describing the
SimpleObjectI interface:

```
InterfaceDef interfaceDef =

    InterfaceDefHelper.narrow(repository.lookup("SimpleObjectI"));
```

The second lookup interaction obtains a reference to the StructDef object describing the
SimpleStructS struct:

```
StructDef structDef =

    StructDefHelper.narrow(repository.lookup("SimpleStructS"));
```

Once each xxxDef object is obtained, a helper method is called that's charged with printing out the contents of its parameter. The first helper method,
printInterfaceDetails(), is passed an InterfaceDef instance and displays the name,
type, and kind attributes associated with the instance. The method then continues on to
print the name of each operation and attribute. For the most part, this method is rather
self-explanatory; however, it does introduce two new classes. The first,
OperationDescription, describes a single operation. The section on DII extends the
coverage of this class. Note, however, the manner in which it's used to obtain the operation name. The second class introduced in this method is AttributeDescription, which
is used to describe a single attribute. Again, note the manner in which the attribute name
is obtained.

The second helper method, `printStructDetails()`, is passed a `StructDef` instance and displays information on each struct member. In general, there's less information made available about structs when compared to interfaces; however, this can be complemented with information made available by Java reflection. In the `printStructDetails()` method, we first obtain an array of `StructMember` objects that each contain details on a single member in the struct. We then iterate through this array displaying the type and kind of each member.

> **NOTE**
>
> If you haven't done so already, you'll need to install the Inprise ORB from the enclosed CD-ROM to run the DII examples in this chapter.

To run this application, first start the ORB by entering

osagent

at a prompt. Then start the IR by entering

irep IRName

at a prompt. `irep` is the name of the Inprise IR executable, and *IRName* can be replaced with any logical name that the IR might use. Once the IR is running, select File from the IR main menu; then, from the drop-down list, select Load and use the dialog box to navigate to the location of the IDL file. Finally, execute the `IRBrowser` application by entering

java IRBrowser

at a prompt.

Using Dynamic Interface Invocation

Thus far, you've seen how it's possible to interact with the IR and obtain information on both interfaces and structs. We'll now further explore dynamic object interaction by looking at how it's possible to dynamically invoke operations on discovered objects.

As you may have guessed, the process of dynamically invoking an operation introduces a plethora of new CORBA entities. The principal one being an interface called `Request`. A `Request` object is used to issue a dynamic operation invocation and is complemented by the following entities: `NVList`, `InterfaceDef`, `FullInterfaceDescription`, `OperationDescription`, `ParameterDescription`, `TCKind`, and `Any`. As luck has it, many of the classes used to support DII were introduced either in the IR section or in earlier chapters. Coverage of them in this chapter builds on earlier knowledge, thus forming a complete understanding of the entity.

Beginning our exploration of the DII entities, Listing 32.9 contains the IDL for the `Request` interface. The interface exposes a few key operations and attributes, including `arguments`, which obtains the collection of parameters; `invoke()`, which invokes the represented operation; and `return_value()`, which obtains the operation return value.

LISTING 32.9   IDL DEFINITION FOR THE Request INTERFACE

```
interface Request {
    readonly attribute CORBA::Object target;
    readonly attribute CORBA::Identifier operation;
    readonly attribute CORBA::NVList arguments;
    readonly attribute CORBA::NamedValue result;
    readonly attribute CORBA::Environment env;
    readonly attribute CORBA::ExceptionList exceptions;
    readonly attribute CORBA::ContextList contexts;
    attribute CORBA::Context ctx;
    any add_in_arg();
    any add_named_in_arg(in string name);
    any add_inout_arg();
    any add_named_inout_arg(in string name);
    any add_out_arg();
    any add_named_out_arg(in string name);
    void set_return_type(in ::CORBA::TypeCode tc);
    any return_value();
    void invoke();
    void send_oneway();
    void send_deferred();
    void get_response();
    boolean poll_response();
};
```

As you've probably noticed, the attribute `arguments` is of type `NVList`, which is another of the important DII entities. This interface, defined in Listing 32.10, represents a collection of name/value pairs, each representing a unique parameter instance. The workflow for using an `NVList` instance is to obtain it from the `Request` object and invoke the `add_value()` operation once for each candidate parameter.

LISTING 32.10   IDL FOR THE NVList INTERFACE

```
interface NVList {
    unsigned long count();
    void add(in CORBA::Flags flags);
```

```
    void add_item(in CORBA::Identifier name,in CORBA::Flags flags);
    void add_value(in CORBA::Identifier name,in any value,
    in CORBA::Flags flags);
    CORBA::NamedValue item(in unsigned long index);
    void remove(in unsigned long index);
};
```

Once a `Request` objectis populated with the proper parameters, it can be invoked in any one of three manners. The first being simply invoking the `invoke()` operation, which causes the client to block until the server object returns a return value. The second manner is used when the process is going to take a long time. This manner uses the `send_deferred()` operation, which is nonblocking. Once invoked, the `send_deferred()` operation will return control to the client while waiting for the return value. A client can check to see if this value is ready by invoking the `poll_response()` operation, which returns a `true` value when the value is ready. A third manner in which the operation represented by the `Request` object can be invoked is via the `send_oneway()` operation, which immediately returns but does not wait for a return value at all. This method is very useful when invoking operations with void return values that can be performed asynchronously.

With an understanding of the manner in which DII functions, you're now ready to begin writing some code. Listing 32.11 contains the IDL definition for an interface called `SimpleObjectI` and also for an interface called `ObjectServerI`. An `ObjectServerI` instance is simply an object factory that serves empty `SimpleObjectI` instances.

LISTING 32.11   THE IDL THAT IS TO BE DYNAMICALLY INVOKED

```
interface SimpleObjectI {
    string getStringValue();
    void setStringValue(in string sValue);

    long getIntegerValue();
    void setIntegerValue(in long iValue);
};

interface ObjectServerI {
    SimpleObjectI obtainSimpleObject();
};
```

Moving from the IDL to the class that actually invokes the operations, Listing 32.12 contains the code for the `DIIInvoker` class.

LISTING 32.12 THE DIIInvoker CLASS DYNAMICALLY INVOKES OPERATIONS

```
import org.omg.CORBA.*;
import org.omg.CORBA.InterfaceDefPackage.*;

public class DIIInvoker {
    private ORB        _orb;
    private BOA        _boa;
    private Repository _repository;

    public DIIInvoker() {
        _orb = ORB.init();
        _boa = _orb.BOA_init();
        _repository = RepositoryHelper.bind(_orb);

        // bind to the object server
        ObjectServerI objectServer = ObjectServerIHelper.bind(_orb);
        // obtain a SimpleObjectI instance
        SimpleObjectI si = objectServer.obtainSimpleObject();
        // invoke all operations, twice
        processInterface(si);
        processInterface(si);
    }

    /**
     * Dynamically invokes all operations in a given interface
     */
    private void processInterface(org.omg.CORBA.Object targetObject) {
        // obtain the interface description from the target object
        InterfaceDef interfaceDef = targetObject._get_interface();
        FullInterfaceDescription desc = interfaceDef.describe_interface();

        // obtain descriptions of all operations
        OperationDescription[] oppDefs = desc.operations;
        int iOppCount = oppDefs.length;
        for(int i=0; i<iOppCount; i++) {
            OperationDescription descActive = oppDefs[i];
            Request request = targetObject._request(descActive.name);

            // obtain the arg list
            NVList args = request.arguments();
            // obtain descriptions of all parameters
            ParameterDescription[] parameters = descActive.parameters;
            int iParamLength = parameters.length;
            // iterate through the params adding to the NVList instance
            for(int j=0; j<iParamLength; j++) {
                ParameterDescription paramActive = parameters[j];

                // based on the kind attribute populate the Any. Note
                // that to conserve space,
                // only support for strings and longs
```

```
                        // is shown.
                        TCKind kind = paramActive.type.kind();
                        if(kind == TCKind.tk_string) {
                            Any any = _orb.create_any();
                            any.insert_string("Some New Value");
                            args.add_value(paramActive.name,
                                        any,
                                        org.omg.CORBA.ARG_IN.value);
                        }
                        else if(kind == TCKind.tk_long) {
                            Any any = _orb.create_any();
                            any.insert_long(42);
                            args.add_value(paramActive.name,
                                        any,
                                        org.omg.CORBA.ARG_IN.value);

                        }

                    }
                    // set the return type
                    request.set_return_type(descActive.result);
                    // invoke the operation
                    request.invoke();
                    // display the results
                    System.out.println(request.result().value());
                }
            }

        public static void main(String[] args) {
            DIIInvoker invoker = new DIIInvoker();
        }
    }
}
```

As you study the DIIInvoker class, you'll want to concentrate on the code contained in the processInterface() method. This method is passed a SimpleObjectI instance (obtained from the ObjectServerI factory) and proceeds to invoke all operations. In the first step in this process, highlighted next, the InterfaceDef object is obtained from the SimpleObjectI instance. As you'll remember from the earlier section on the IR, this object exists in the IR itself and can fully describe an interface. The InterfaceDef instance is obtained by invoking the _get_interface() operation, which all interfaces inherit from org.omg.CORBA.Object. Once the InterfaceDef instance is obtained, the FullInterfaceDescription instance is obtained and then an array of OperationDescription objects is obtained. This array of OperationDescription objects contains a single entry for each operation represented by the interface.

```
InterfaceDef interfaceDef = targetObject._get_interface();

FullInterfaceDescription desc = interfaceDef.describe_interface();

OperationDescription[] oppDefs = desc.operations;
```

Once the array of `OperationDescription` objects has been obtained, the code enters a loop that first forms and then invokes a `Request` object for each entry in the array.

In the next section of the code a `Request` instance is obtained from the `SimpleObjectI` instance by specifying the name of the active operation as a parameter. From the `Request`, we obtain the `NVList` instance into which we'll place a unique entry for each parameter. Finally, we obtain an array of `ParameterDescription` objects where each entry represents a unique parameter in the active operation. This next section of code is pulled out and highlighted here:

```
Request request = targetObject._request(descActive.name);

NVList args = request.arguments();

ParameterDescription[] parameters = descActive.parameters;
```

While still inside the main operation loop, we now enter an inner loop that iterates through each `ParameterDescription` object. In this section, we examine each parameter and, based on the value of its `TCKind` attribute, add an entry into the `NVList` object. In the following code snippet is a section of this inner loop where parameters of the IDL type `string` are handled. The code also supports the IDL type `long` (however, to conserve space, no others are shown):

```
TCKind kind = paramActive.type.kind();

if(kind == TCKind.tk_string) {

    Any any = _orb.create_any();

    any.insert_string("Some New Value");

    args.add_value(paramActive.name, any, org.omg.CORBA.ARG_IN.value);

}
```

After the `NVList` object is fully populated, all that's left to do is set the return type, invoke the operation, and query for the results. This section of code is shown here:

```
request.set_return_type(descActive.result);

request.invoke();

System.out.println(request.result().value());
```

Now that you've stepped through the code, you're ready to cement your understanding by executing the application. The one piece of code not shown in this chapter is for the `ObjectServerI` implementation. This code is rather trivial and was placed on the CD-ROM to conserve trees.

The first step in running the application is to fire up the ORB and IR and then load in the IDL used in the example. If you skipped over the IRBrowser example, flip back a few pages for coverage on starting up the first three services. To run this application, first start the ObjectServerI implementation by entering

java ObjectServer

at a command prompt. Now execute the DII example by entering

java DIIInvoker

at another prompt. You'll note that the SimpleObjectI instance has its methods invoked two times. This is done to show that the getter method invocations are actually functioning properly.

As the section on DII has shown, it's just much easier to statically invoke an operation on an object. Therefore, the obvious question is, Why would one ever use DII? After all, the process of creating a Request object is rather laborious and adds a lot to execution time. DII may in fact not be needed in every application you develop, but in situations where the remote object class is not always known, or where the execution path is rather vague, DII will come to the rescue. Consider, for example, a Web-based system where HTTP-POST arguments invoke IDL operations. Because HTML or JavaScript cannot directly execute IDL, you could embed the method invocation chain in a form argument, parse it out at the server, and dynamically invoke the specified methods.

FROM HERE

This chapter covered a lot of ground, potentially changing the manner in which you think about object interaction. Historically, you would obtain an object and, at compile time, know the operations that are being invoked on that object. Through the use of Java reflection or CORBA introspection and DII, it's now possible to decide on execution paths at runtime as well as introduce new objects at runtime.

As you continue to explore the world of CORBA, you'll find that the following chapters provide complementary material to this chapter's topics:

- Chapter 21, "CORBA Overview"
- Chapter 22, "CORBA Architecture"
- Chapter 28, "The Portable Object Adapter (POA)"

OTHER CORBA FACILITIES AND SERVICES

IN THIS CHAPTER

As was introduced in Chapter 22, "CORBA Architecture," the CORBA universe centers around something called the *Object Management Architecture* (OMA). The OMA is an umbrella term covering the ORB, CORBAservices, CORBAfacilities, and CORBAdomains. The ORB itself is a single piece of software that allows for communication between all CORBA objects; the other three entries in the mix each represent collections of different applications that provide functionality at different levels to your applications. CORBAservices add horizontal object-level functionality, CORBA facilities add horizontal and vertical user-level functionality, and CORBAdomains add functionality unique to a single domain.

As Chapter 22 also stated, OMG does not produce any of the software that forms the OMA but rather produces specifications. Independent vendors produce the actual software. Of the existing CORBAservices and CORBAdomains, there are many that can aid in your development efforts. By simply raising your comfort level with their functionality, chances are you'll realize that the cost of purchasing and integrating an implementation is much less than actually developing the functionality yourself. Chapter 30, "The Naming Service," studies the Naming Service, which is used to categorize and locate objects in the enterprise. Chapter 31, "The Event Service," studies the Event Service, which is used to notify different objects when some event occurs. Although the Naming and Event Services are probably the most popular services out there, many others can significantly decrease your development time frame. This chapter takes a look at some of these CORBAservices—first in terms of their functions and then in terms of their interfaces. Specifically, the following entities are covered:

- Life Cycle Service
- Externalization Service
- Concurrency Service
- Query Service

LIFE CYCLE SERVICE

Because CORBA is inherently object oriented, CORBA applications are constantly taking objects through their life cycles. Objects are created, manipulated, and finally destroyed. As object-oriented developers, we're accustomed to working with objects, but we're not always comfortable with what needs to happen when the life cycle of an object needs to be maintained from a remote machine. This is especially true for Java developers, who have the luxury of not needing to spend a large amount of time dealing with memory management. Java applications benefit from the garbage collector present in the Java virtual machine (JVM). Unfortunately, this garbage collection service does not extend support to distributed applications. As you saw in earlier chapters, calls to the `obj_is_ready()` method exposed by the BOA interface must always be paired with calls to the `deactivate_obj()` method. If the `deactivate_obj()` method is not called, the memory allocated to that object will never be returned to the JVM.

In an attempt to standardize the manner in which objects are instantiated in a distributed environment, the OMG introduced the *Life Cycle Service*. The Life Cycle Service builds on the factory design pattern (covered in Chapter 5, "Design Patterns") by creating a standard interface for all factories, as well as an interface that instantiated objects can implement to increase the control we have over them.

Moving from that high-level overview of the Life Cycle Service, take a look at the `CosLifeCycle` module in Listing 33.1. This module contains all the CORBA entities that form the Life Cycle Service.

> **NOTE**
>
> As with all code in this chapter, the IDL in Listing 33.1 is an OMG specification, not something developed specifically for this book. You should pay attention to the functionality it exposes but don't get bogged down in specifics.

LISTING 33.1   THE `CosLifeCycle` MODULE

```
#include "Naming.idl"
module CosLifeCycle {
    typedef Naming::Name Key;
    typedef Object Factory;
    typedef sequence <Factory> Factories;

    typedef struct NVP {
        Naming::Istring name;
        any value;
    } NameValuePair;

    typedef sequence <NameValuePair> Criteria;

    exception NoFactory { Key search_key };
    exception NotCopyable { string reason; };
    exception NotMovable { string reason; };
    exception NotRemovable { string reason; };
    exception InvalidCriteria { Criteria invalid_criteria; };
    exception CannotMeetCriteria { Criteria unmet_criteria; };

    interface FactoryFinder {
        Factories find_factories(in Key factory_key) raises(NoFactory);
    };
```

continues

LISTING 33.1   CONTINUED

```
interface LifeCycleObject {
    LifeCycleObject copy(in FactoryFinder there,
                         in Criteria the_criteria)
        raises(NoFactory, NotCopyable,
               InvalidCriteria, CannotMeetCriteria);
    void move(in FactoryFinder there,
              in Criteria the_criteria)
        raises(NoFactory, NotMovable,
               InvalidCriteria, CannotMeetCriteria);
    void remove()  raises(NotRemovable);
};

interface GenericFactory {
    boolean supports(in Key k);
    Object create_object(in Key k, in Criteria the_criteria)
        raises (NoFactory, InvalidCriteria, CannotMeetCriteria);
};
};
```

As you look over the CosLifeCycle module in Listing 33.1, pay specific attention to the
GenericFactory and LifeCycleObject interfaces. These interfaces all describe, in a
generic fashion, the operations that need to be performed when managing an object life
cycle. The first question that often begs answering when we're asked to code a server in
a generic fashion versus a more specific fashion is, why? If a factory is producing objects
that model a hospital patient, why not simply name that factory PatientFactory and
expose a method called createPatient(). In some situations, this may work out very
well. However, when working in a distributed environment, we often must contend with
the fact that the clients to our servers are often developed by other people and have to be
changed frequently. If we simply provide a generic (and also frequently used) interface
through which common operations are accessed, it makes the client developer's life
much easier. In addition, if the interfaces are consistently deployed, the client developer
always knows the methods exposed by an object without ever having to query it.

Starting with the GenericFactory interface, note the two methods it exposes and the different parameter types they each use. Both methods accept a parameter of type Key,
which is used to identify the desired object the factory creates. The supports() operation returns true if and only if the class that implements the interface can instantiate
objects of the specified type. Once you have determined whether a given
GenericFactory instance can create the desired object, you're ready to invoke the
create() operation. This operation again takes the target Key parameter but also accepts
an array of name/value pairs that describes the parameters sent to the new object's constructor. Inside the array, the name is a string matching the name of the parameter, and

the value is a CORBA `any` object. If for any reason, the creation fails, an exception is raised. Assuming the object creation is successful, an object that implements the `CORBA::Object` interface is returned. At the client side, this instance is narrowed to an instance of the desired class. What should be noted is that in addition to implementing the interface specified by the `Key` parameter, many objects will also implement the `LifeCycleObject` interface.

The `LifeCycleObject` interface contains additional operations defining further actions that can be taken on the target object. The `copy()` operation, like the `clone()` operation in the `java.lang.Object` class, returns a copy of the existing object. This copy contains the same variables present in the original object; however, it's an independent entity. Any changes made to the copy are not reflected in the original. The next method in the interface, `move()`, changes the location of the target object to the specified location. Classes may choose to implement this operation if, for example, the memory management software needs to relocate objects when server traffic increases. The final operation exposed by this interface is the `remove()` operation. As you may have guessed, the `remove()` operation completes the cycle started by the `create()` operation by returning the memory allocated to the target object and generally performing any needed cleanup tasks (for example, closing a database connection).

The Life Cycle Service makes development much easier in environments where a large developer population constantly interacts with each other's services. By providing a common interface that all clients understand, it greatly eases the development process. In addition, the Life Cycle Service makes versioning of the instantiated objects much easier due to the fact that the factory object has complete control in the actual class that is instantiated.

EXTERNALIZATION SERVICE

Java serialization, covered in Chapter 9, "Java Serialization and Beans," presents a common API through which Java objects are written to a file. Although serialization as covered in Chapter 9 is specific to Java objects, it's a desired feature of all object-oriented environments.

In object-oriented systems, objects grow as they interact with users; data is collected, decisions are made, and the general state of the object changes from the time that the user begins his interaction to the time that it is completed. Often, this information represents some piece of information that the user wants to maintain even after the application has been closed and the computer is turned off. For this reason, some mechanism is required such that the target objects, along with their corresponding state, can be saved to disk or some other permanent medium. The *Externalization Service* presents a common

API that describes (from the perspective of the client, server, and stream) a mechanism by which objects are saved. This section examines this service, the IDL it exposes, and the impact it has on your developments.

As stated earlier, the Externalization Service deals with object externalization from three distinct perspectives. These perspectives detail each and every entity that plays a role when an object is either saved to disk or internalized from its saved state:

- *Client.* In an externalization scenario, the *client* is the entity requesting that the object either be saved to a file or internalized from the file.

- *Target object.* In an externalization scenario, the *target object* is the entity that's actually saved to a file or internalized from the file.

- *Stream.* In an externalization scenario, the *stream* is the conduit over which the target object flows. It has knowledge of the storage mechanism and the manner in which the target object needs to be placed in that medium.

Starting to dig into the Externalization Service, Listing 33.2 contains the CosExternalization module, which exposes all CORBA entities of use to the client.

LISTING 33.2 THE CosExternalization MODULE

```
module CosExternalization {
    exception InvalidFileNameError{};
    exception ContextAlreadyRegistered{};

    interface Stream: CosLifeCycle::LifeCycleObject{
        void externalize(in CosStream::Streamable theObject);
        CosStream::Streamable
            internalize(in CosLifeCycle::FactoryFinder there)
            raises(CosLifeCycle::NoFactory,
                    CosStream::StreamDataFormatError);
        void begin_context() raises( ContextAlreadyRegistered);
        void end_context();
        void flush();
    };

    interface StreamFactory {
        Stream create();
    };

    interface FileStreamFactory {
        Stream create(in string theFileName)
            raises( InvalidFileNameError );
    };
};
```

As you spend time with Listing 33.2, first note the `Stream` interface. This interface presents two key operations: `externalize()` and `internalize()`, which perform the functions associated with their names. The `externalize()` operation is passed a reference to an object and writes that object to a storage medium. The `internalize()` operation is told how to locate an externalized object and returns a reference to that object.

What has not been mentioned at this point is the manner in which the underlying storage mechanism is identified. Two interfaces, `StreamFactory` and `FileStreamFactory`, provide operations that allow for the creation of objects that implement the `Stream` interface. It's the responsibility of the object that implements either interface to define the storage mechanism. However, implementers of the `FileStreamFactory` interface must create a `Stream` object associated with the file specified as a parameter.

Moving beyond the client side of externalization and internalization, the `CosStream` module, contained in Listing 33.3, presents the CORBA entities used at the server. Because the server encompasses both the target object and stream roles, the `CosStream` module contains interfaces that are implemented by both the target object and the stream.

LISTING 33.3 THE CosStream MODULE

```
module CosStream {
    exception ObjectCreationError{};
    exception StreamDataFormatError{};

    interface StreamIO;

    interface Streamable:CosObjectIdentity::IdentifiableObject {
        readonly attribute CosLifeCycle::Key external_form_id;
        void externalize_to_stream(in StreamIOtargetStreamIO);
        void internalize_from_stream(in StreamIOsourceStreamIO,
                                in FactoryFinder there)
            raises(CosLifeCycle::NoFactory, ObjectCreationError,
                    StreamDataFormatError);
    };

    interface StreamableFactory {
        Streamable create_uninitialized();
    };

    interface StreamIO {
        void write_string(in string aString);
        void write_char(in char aChar);
        void write_octet(in octet anOctet);
        void write_unsigned_long(in unsigned long anUnsignedLong);
        void write_unsigned_short(in unsigned short anUnsignedShort);
        void write_long(in long aLong);
        void write_short(in short aShort);
```

continues

LISTING 33.3   CONTINUED

```
        void write_float(in float aFloat);
        void write_double(in double aDouble);
        void write_boolean(in boolean aBoolean);
        void write_object(in Streamable aStreamable);
        void write_graph(in CosCompoundExternalization::Node);
        void write_long_long(in long long val);
        void write_unsigned_long_long(in unsigned long long val);
        void write_long_double(in long double val);
        void write_wchar(in wchar val);
        void write_wstring(in wstring val);
        void write_fixed(in any val, in short s);
        string read_string() raises(StreamDataFormatError);
        char read_char() raises(StreamDataFormatError );
        octet read_octet() raises(StreamDataFormatError );
        unsigned long read_unsigned_long() raises(StreamDataFormatError);
        unsigned short read_unsigned_short()
            raises( StreamDataFormatError);
        long read_long() raises(StreamDataFormatError );
        short read_short() raises(StreamDataFormatError );
        float read_float() raises(StreamDataFormatError );
        double read_double() raises(StreamDataFormatError );
        boolean read_boolean() raises(StreamDataFormatError );
        Streamable read_object(in FactoryFinder there,
                               in Streamable aStreamable)
                raises(StreamDataFormatError );
        void read_graph(in CosCompoundExternalization::Node starting_node,
                    in FactoryFinder there)
            raises(StreamDataFormatError );
        long long read_long_long()raises(StreamDataFormatError);
        unsigned long long read_unsigned_long_long()
                            raises(StreamDataFormatError);
        long double read_long_double() raises(StreamDataFormatError)
        wchar read_wchar() raises (StreamDataFormatError);
        wstring read_wstring() raises (StreamDataFormatError);
        any read_fixed() raises (StreamDataFormatError)
    };
};
```

Your first look at the CosStream module likely answered the one remaining question
from the earlier discussion of the CosExternalization module. As you'll notice in looking at the internalize() and externalize() methods in the Stream interface, they each
deal with an object that implements the Streamable interface. This new interface, contained in the CosStream module, exposes methods that are called when an object is either
externalized or internalized.

The second interface of interest in the `CosStream` module is the `StreamIO` interface, which defines operations that read and write the actual variables. A read or write operation is provided for every CORBA data type and is called during the process when the object is transformed either to or from its saved state. The final interface, `StreamableFactory`, provides a mechanism for creating objects that implement the `Streamable` interface. As the `StreamableFactory` object creates a `Streamable` object, it's given instructions detailing the storage medium.

What you may have noticed when exploring the `StreamIO` interface is that it contains only *read* and *write* operations associated with base IDL data types but no actual objects themselves. If an object is nothing more than a basic entity object, these operations are likely sufficient. However, most objects actually consist of large object graphs, where many variables are not base data types but are actual objects. Situations such as this call for more complex externalization/internalization procedures, and the object graphs need to be fully traversed. Listing 33.4 contains the `CosCompoundExternalization` module, which exposes entities used when object graphs need to be externalized or internalized.

LISTING 33.4   THE `CosCompoundExternalization` MODULE

```
module CosCompoundExternalization {
    interface Node;
    interface Role;
    interface Relationship;
    interface PropagationCriteriaFactory;

    struct RelationshipHandle {
        Relationship theRelationship;
        ::CosObjectIdentity::ObjectIdentifier constantRandomId;
    };

    interface Node : ::CosGraphs::Node, ::CosStream::Streamable{
        void externalize_node (in ::CosStream::StreamIO sio);
        void internalize_node (in ::CosStream::StreamIO sio,
                               in ::CosLifeCycle::FactoryFinder there,
                               out Roles rolesOfNode)
            raises (::CosLifeCycle::NoFactory);
    };

    interface Role : ::CosGraphs::Role {
        void externalize_role (in ::CosStream::StreamIO sio);
        void internalize_role (in ::CosStream::StreamIO sio);
        ::CosGraphs::PropagationValue externalize_propagation
                    (in RelationshipHandle rel,
                     in ::CosRelationships::RoleName toRoleName,
                     out boolean sameForAll);
    };
```

continues

LISTING 33.4 CONTINUED

```
interface Relationship : ::CosRelationships::Relationship {
    void externalize_relationship (in ::CosStream::StreamIO sio);
    void internalize_relationship(in ::CosStream::StreamIO sio,
        in ::CosGraphs::NamedRoles newRoles);
    ::CosGraphs::PropagationValue externalize_propagation
                (in ::CosRelationships::RoleName fromRoleName,
                 in ::CosRelationships::RoleName toRoleName,
                 out boolean sameForAll);
};

interface PropagationCriteriaFactory {
    ::CosGraphs::TraversalCriteria create_for_externalize( );
};
};
```

Because the CosCompoundExternalization module deals with more complex external-ization/internalization scenarios, it's much more complicated. At this point, you should note the general manner in which it works. It examines the target object graph and breaks it up into a collection of nodes and their respective relationships. The nodes are broken down into smaller components until a manageable situation is found.

As you develop CORBA applications that need to maintain consistent state across runs, take the time to look at the Externalization Service. Chances are, it defines the function-ality you need.

CONCURRENCY SERVICE

A common concern in a distributed environment is ensuring that access to distributed objects is synchronized. If, for example, two clients both reference the same remote object and the clients are invoking methods to change that objects member's variables, some major problems can arise. Because both clients are making changes to the object's state, neither can depend on any form of consistency. As a solution to this problem, the *Concurrency Control Service* was developed. It exposes interfaces that allow for acquir-ing locks on objects and generally synchronizing all usage.

> **NOTE**
>
> Synchronizing access to concurrent resources is not an issue unique to distrib-uted applications. Chapter 8, "Java Threads," discusses how this is an issue in multithreaded applications.

The Concurrency Control Service works by allowing clients to obtain locks on remote objects during the period that the remote object is going to be used. The type of lock differs based on the transaction being performed, and certain types of locks may be allocated simultaneously, whereas others may block other clients from obtaining similar locks. As an example, first consider locking an object for writing; because the object's state is being changed during the transaction, only one client may have a write lock on an object at any given time. Next, consider locking an object for reading; because multiple simultaneous clients can examine an object's state, infinite read locks are given out for a single distributed object. Listing 33.5 contains the `CosConcurrencyControl` module, which exposes all CORBA entities needed by the Concurrency Control Service.

LISTING 33.5 THE `CosConcurrencyControl` MODULE

```
module CosConcurrencyControl {
    enum lock_mode {
        read,
        write,
        upgrade,
        intention_read,
        intention_write
    };

    exception LockNotHeld{};

    interface LockCoordinator {
        void drop_locks();
    };

    interface LockSet {
        void lock(in lock_mode mode);
        boolean try_lock(in lock_mode mode);
        void unlock(in lock_mode mode) raises(LockNotHeld);
        void change_mode(in lock_mode held_mode,
                         in lock_mode new_mode)
            raises(LockNotHeld);
        LockCoordinator get_coordinator(
            in CosTransactions::Coordinator which);
    };

    interface TransactionalLockSet {
        void lock(in CosTransactions::Coordinator current,
                  in lock_mode mode);
        boolean try_lock(in CosTransactions::Coordinator current,
                         in lock_mode mode);
        void unlock(in CosTransactions::Coordinator current,
                    in lock_mode mode)
            raises(LockNotHeld);
```

continues

33

LISTING 33.5 CONTINUED

```
    void change_mode(in CosTransactions::Coordinator current,
                     in lock_mode held_mode,
                     in lock_mode new_mode)
        raises(LockNotHeld);
    LockCoordinator get_coordinator(
        in CosTransactions::Coordinator which);
};

interface LockSetFactory {
    LockSet create();
    LockSet create_related(in LockSet which);
    TransactionalLockSet create_transactional();
    TransactionalLockSet create_transactional_related(
        in TransactionalLockSet which);
};
};
```

The first item in the `CosConcurrencyControl` module that you'll want to take notice of is the `lock_mode` enumerated data type. This data type contains items that define each of the different locks you may obtain for a given object. Understanding the different types of locks is critical to your success with the service, because their function dictates your usage script. Here's a list of each mode:

- Read
- Write
- Upgrade
- Intention read
- Intention write

Starting at the top of the list, a *read lock* is obtained on an object when the client needs to examine that object's state. Multiple clients may have read locks on the same object; however, a read lock does conflict with a write or intention write lock. If a client attempts to obtain a read lock on an object that's locked in one of these two write modes, the attempt will block until the write lock is released.

The next mode, *write*, is obtained when a client is going to change an object's state. If a client obtains a write lock on an object, no other clients may obtain any lock on that same object. Following this pattern, a client will block if a write lock is attempted on an object that's locked in any other mode.

Because multiple clients can obtain a read lock on the same object, a problem arises if one of those clients attempts to upgrade his read lock to a write lock. Because write locks cannot be obtained while read locks are in use, a deadlock situation could develop. As a solution, the *upgrade lock* mode is a read lock that conflicts with itself (and both types of write locks).

The final two forms of locks deal with locking in terms of object granularity. When locking access to an object that's part of an object graph, it's possible to clog up the system with locks that are not granular enough. If, for example, you lock the entire object graph for writing, other clients will not be able to obtain access to any other object in the entire graph. This may not be a problem if you're performing large modifications to the entire graph, but it does cause problems if you're only modifying a small section of the graph. In an attempt to ease the situation, the *intention read* and *intention write* locks allow for additional control over lock granularity. When a lock is obtained on an object, the ancestors are locked first and then the child is locked.

As a final summary on lock conflicts, Table 33.1 summarizes all situations in the form of a matrix. The locking modes are detailed in the rows and columns, and an "X" in a cell indicates a conflict.

TABLE 33.1   LOCK MODE CONFLICT SITUATIONS

	Intention Read	*Read*	*Upgrade*	*Intention Write*	*Write*
Intention Read					X
Read				X	X
Upgrade			X	X	X
Intention Write		X	X		X
Write	X		X	X	X

With an understanding of the available lock modes, let's move into a discussion of how you actually interact with the service itself. To obtain a lock on an object, the client interacts with either an object that implements the LockSet or TransactionalLockSet interface. Locks obtained through the LockSet interface are obtained on behalf of the current thread, and the lock is released when the client so dictates. Locks obtained through the TransactionalLockSet interface are obtained on behalf of a transaction and are released when that transaction is completed.

Both the LockSet and TransactionalLockSet interfaces expose the same collection of operations (the functional difference was explained in the preceding paragraph). When you encounter an object that exposes either of these interfaces, the first task you're likely to perform is to invoke either the lock() or try_lock() operation. Both operations attempt to obtain a lock on the object; however, the lock() operation will block if there's a conflict and return when the conflict is resolved. In comparison, the `try_lock()` operation will return a `false` value if a conflict exists. Each of these operations accepts a parameter of type `lock_mode` that discusses the mode in which the lock is to be obtained.

Once a lock has been obtained on an object, the `unlock()` operation releases the lock. If, during the life cycle of a lock, the client wants to alter the lock mode (from read to write, perhaps), the `change_mode()` operation is used. If a conflict exists between present locks and the requested lock, the method blocks until the conflict is resolved.

The final operation exposed by both `LockSet` operations is the `get_coordinator()` operation, which returns an object that implements the `LockCoordinator` interface. The `LockCoordinator` interface defines the `drop_locks()` operation, which, when invoked, drops all locks held on the target object.

The final interface in the `CosConcurrencyControl` module is the `LockSetFactory` interface. This interface provides a collection of different `create()` operations that instantiate objects that implement the various `LockSet` interfaces.

QUERY SERVICE

Information is a commodity that's only of value if it can be found. Unlike gold, which has a known value even when buried deep in the earth, information is completely useless if it cannot be located and quantified. Because software systems are usually built as collections of information, it's obviously crucial that a mechanism exist for searching this information. Chapter 11, "Relational Databases and Structured Query Language (SQL)," discusses a language called SQL, which is a standard query language used to search relational databases. This section discusses the OMG *Query Service*, which, like SQL, provides a standard interface through which information is searched. However, unlike SQL, the Query Service is designed to search objects, not columns and rows of information. In addition, the Query Service is not tied to any specific query language and can be used with virtually any language.

Before we dive into the CORBA entities that form the Query Service, it's important that an understanding of object collections exist. An *object collection* is simply a grouping of objects in some logical fashion. In the context of the Query Service, collections are used to specify both the original scope of a unique query and the results of the query itself. The `CosQueryCollection` module, contained in Listing 33.6, exposes the CORBA entities used to describe and work with object collections.

LISTING 33.6 THE CosQueryCollection MODULE

```
module CosQueryCollection {
    exception ElementInvalid {};
    exception IteratorInvalid {};
    exception PositionInvalid {};

enum ValueType {TypeBoolean, TypeChar, TypeOctet,
                TypeShort, TypeUShort,TypeLong,
                TypeULong, TypeFloat, TypeDouble,
                TypeString, TypeObject, TypeAny,
                TypeSmallInt, TypeInteger, TypeReal,
                TypeDoublePrecision, TypeCharacter,
                TypeDecimal,TypeNumeric
            };


    struct Decimal {long precision; long scale; sequence<octet> value;}

    union Value switch(ValueType) {
        case TypeBoolean: boolean b;
        case TypeChar: char c;
        case TypeOctet: octet o;
        case TypeShort : short s;
        case TypeUShort : unsigned short us;
        case TypeLong : long l;
        case TypeULong : unsigned long ul;
        case TypeFloat : float f;
        case TypeDouble : double d;
        case TypeString : string str;
        case TypeObject : Object obj;
        case TypeAny : any a;
        case TypeSmallInt : short si;
        case TypeInteger : long i;
        case TypeReal : float r;
        case TypeDoublePrecision : double dp;
        case TypeCharacter : string ch;
        case TypeDecimal : Decimal dec;
        case TypeNumeric : Decimal n;
    };

    typedef boolean Null;

    union FieldValue switch(Null) {
        case false : Value v;
    };

    typedef sequence<FieldValue> Record;
    typedef string Istring;

    struct NVPair {Istring name; any value;};
```

continues

LISTING 33.6   CONTINUED

```
typedef sequence<NVPair> ParameterList;

interface Collection;
interface Iterator;

interface CollectionFactory {
    Collection create(in ParameterList params);
};

interface Collection {
    readonly attribute long cardinality;
    void add_element(in any element) raises(ElementInvalid);
    void add_all_elements(in Collection elements)
        raises(ElementInvalid);
    void insert_element_at(in any element, in Iterator where)
        raises(IteratorInvalid, ElementInvalid);
    void replace_element_at(in any element, in Iterator where)
        raises(IteratorInvalid, PositionInvalid, ElementInvalid);
    void remove_element_at(in Iterator where)
        raises(IteratorInvalid, PositionInvalid);
    void remove_all_elements();
    any retrieve_element_at(in Iterator where)
        raises(IteratorInvalid, PositionInvalid);
    Iterator create_iterator();
};

interface Iterator {
    any next() raises(IteratorInvalid, PositionInvalid);
    void reset();
    boolean more();
};
};
```

As you'll likely guess, the main interface from the CosQueryCollection module that you interact with is the Collection interface. This interface is used to represent a group of objects, and it exposes operations for adding and removing member objects. Another important interface is the Iterator interface, which allows for the examination of items in a collection. The Collection interface exposes the create_iterator() operation, which returns a reference to the Iterator object associated with the Collection object. Once the Iterator object is obtained, the elements in the collection are examined by invoking the Iterator object's next() method. This method provides for a sequential tour of all elements in the collection.

An object that implements the `CollectionFactory` interface performs the actual creation of new collections. This interface exposes a single `create()` method that accepts parameters describing the scope of the collection and returns an appropriate `Collection` object.

Moving beyond creation and instantiation of collections, the `CosQuery` module, contained in Listing 33.7, defines operations used to actually query the collections.

LISTING 33.7   THE `CosQuery` MODULE

```
module CosQuery {
    exception QueryInvalid {string why};
    exception QueryProcessingError {string why};
    exception QueryTypeInvalid {};

    enum QueryStatus {complete, incomplete};

    typedef CosQueryCollection::ParameterList ParameterList;
    typedef CORBA::InterfaceDef QLType;

    interface QueryLanguageType {};

    interface SQLQuery : QueryLanguageType {};

    interface SQL_92Query : SQLQuery {};

    interface OQL : QueryLanguageType {};

    interface OQLBasic : OQL {};

    interface OQL_93 : OQL {};

    interface OQL_93Basic : OQL_93, OQLBasic {};

    interface QueryEvaluator {
        readonly attribute sequence<QLType> ql_types;
        readonly attribute QLType default_ql_type;
        any evaluate(in string query,
                    in QLType ql_type,
                    in ParameterList params)
            raises(QueryTypeInvalid, QueryInvalid, QueryProcessingError);
    };

    interface QueryableCollection:QueryEvaluator,
            CosQueryCollection::Collection {};

    interface QueryManager : QueryEvaluator {
        Query create(in string query,
                    in QLType ql_type,
```

continues

LISTING 33.7   CONTINUED

```
                    in ParameterList params)
            raises(QueryTypeInvalid, QueryInvalid);
    };

    interface Query {
        readonly attribute QueryManager query_mgr;
        void prepare(in ParameterList params)
            raises(QueryProcessingError);
        void execute(in ParameterList params)
            raises(QueryProcessingError);
        QueryStatus get_status();
        any get_result();
    };
};
```

As you examine the CosQuery module, spend some time examining the interface inheritance model and also the interaction between the CosQuery module and the CosQueryCollection module. What you'll likely note first is that the QueryableCollection interface extends both the Collection interface from the CosQueryCollection module and the QueryEvaluator interface present in this module. Although the QueryableCollection interface exposes no operations itself, through its inheritance, it obtains all operations needed to perform actual queries.

Moving your attention to the QueryEvaluator interface, note the query() operation. This operation accepts three important parameters: a string object holding the query, a QLType object indicating the query language used, and a ParameterList object containing any additional parameters. The operation returns an object of type Any, but this usually holds a Collection object. In certain specific situations, the Any object may actually hold another type of object; however, those situations represent highly specialized environments.

The final aspect of the CosQuery module not yet covered is the manner in which the query language is specified. To appeal to a wide variety of users and allow for parallel evolution with different query languages, the Query Service is language neutral. At present, the service defines interfaces indicating a collection of different languages; however, this list may be expanded. The current languages one may specify are detailed in Table 33.2. Note, however, that not all implementations of the service support all languages (only SQL or OQL is required). The QueryEvaluator interface contains an attribute containing a list of all supported languages.

TABLE 33.2 QUERY SERVICE QUERY LANGUAGES SUPPORTED

Language	Interface	Description
SQL	SQLQuery	Consists of the query (SELECT) section of the SQL language. This language is described in Chapter 11.
SQL 92	SQL_92Query	Consists of the entire SQL 92 language, as described in Chapter 11.
OQL	OQL	Object Query Language (OQL) is an adaptation of the SQL 92 language, modified to support objects.
OQL Basic	OQLBasic	A modified version of OQL.
OQL 93	OQL_93	A modified version of OQL.
OQL 93 Basic	OQL_93Basic	A combination of the feature-sets exposed by OQL 93 and OQL Basic.

As your systems grow to become more and more data intensive, the functionality exposed by the Query Service is something you'll want to look into. It provides functionality that will help your applications to not only search information but to also modify existing collections with new objects and updated member data.

FROM HERE

This chapter took some time away from the detailed study of different CORBA technologies to look at a variety of CORBAservices. Each of the services represent some level of functionality that you may want to incorporate into your applications as time marches forward. The following list covers additional chapters that complement the knowledge imparted in this chapter:

- Chapter 23, "Survey of CORBA ORBs"
- Chapter 30, "The Naming Service"
- Chapter 31, "The Event Service"

33

OTHER CORBA
FACILITIES AND
SERVICES

AGENT TECHNOLOGIES

VOYAGER AGENT TECHNOLOGY

IN THIS CHAPTER

Before the invention of the telephone, when two people wanted to communicate, they simply traveled to a common location and had a conversation. Since then the telephone has been invented, made economical, and become ubiquitous. Now, when two people want to communicate, they're able to do so without changing location. One person simply has to ring another and instantiate a dialogue. Communication between computer applications, as covered so far in this book, follows the second model of human-to-human communication, where communication happens across a physical boundary. Applications can exist on different machines and communicate through the Internet using IIOP, HTTP, DCOM, or some other protocol.

An alternate form of distributed object technology, called *agent technology*, exists in a manner very similar to the original model of human-to-human communication. Agent technology exists such that instead of communicating between locations, applications actually travel (code and all) from one machine to another and perform the needed communication.

At first glance, the concept of agent technology is a touch challenging to understand. It's easy enough to grasp the concept of applications communicating with each other across physical boundaries, but grasping the concept of applications actually moving from one machine to another is almost unbelievable. Fortunately, although hard to grasp conceptually, the task of implementing agent-based applications is a rather easy one. Agent technology is neither difficult to implement nor difficult to design around. In covering agent technology, this chapter addresses the following topics:

- Implementing agents using the Voyager environment
- Writing objects that travel from machine to machine carrying state
- Locating objects once they leave a known machine
- Replicating messages across multiple objects
- Messaging objects in transit

THE VOYAGER ENVIRONMENT

Whereas Java applications must execute inside a Java virtual machine (JVM), agents must execute inside some host environment. This environment exports an API that objects use for remote object messaging and also to aid in mobility. In this chapter, we look at a Java-based agent environment from Objectspace called *Voyager*. Although it's not the only available agent environment, Voyager provides the richest feature-set and fastest implementation. The environment is contained on the included CD-ROM and can also be downloaded from the Objectspace Web site at http://www.objectspace.com. Before you start any development work, take the time to install the environment because it's necessary to run the applications developed in this chapter as well as in Chapter 35, "Voyager-Based Implementation of the Airline Reservation System."

To get a full picture of how the Voyager environment interacts with your application, take a look at Figure 34.1. This image depicts the JVM as a host to the Voyager environment, meaning that Voyager requires the presence of the JVM to execute. Moving deeper inside, Voyager is a host environment for your application. This, of course, means that your application cannot exist without the presence of Voyager. Just as Voyager needs the capabilities of the JVM, your application needs the capabilities of the Voyager environment.

FIGURE 34.1

The relationship between the JVM, Voyager environment, and your application.

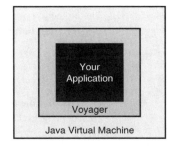

Because the Voyager environment executes within a JVM, it's easy to assume that the environment is in fact written in Java itself. In addition to a rich feature-set and fast implementation, the fact that the Voyager environment is 100 percent pure Java is also a boon to developers. Agents often need to move around the world, visiting all sorts of computers, and because the Voyager environment can execute on any platform with a 1.1 version of the JDK, those agents should have no trouble getting around.

THE VOYAGER API

When you're working with any new programming environment, a new API usually has to be learned. Depending on the complexity of the environment, the learning curve toward being productive in that environment can run anywhere from a few days to a few months. Often, however, environments that expose a broad API do so to support many features that the average programmer does not need. As we move through our discussion of Voyager, we'll first take an overview of the API and then move on to develop a series of applications, each highlighting a single feature of the Voyager environment.

Table 34.1 contains the Voyager package structure, along with a brief discussion of the functionality exposed by the classes in each package.

TABLE 34.1 THE VOYAGER PACKAGE STRUCTURE

Package	*Description of Contents*
`com.objectspace.lib.facets`	The class and interface used by entities that want to take advantage of facets
`com.objectspace.lib.holder`	The collection of classes and interfaces that support inout and out parameters
`com.objectspace.lib.thread`	The utility class that aids in the management of `Thread` objects
`com.objectspace.lib.timer`	The collection of classes and interfaces that aid in time-based functions
`com.objectspace.lib.util`	The utility class used for debugging purposes
`com.objectspace.voyager`	The collection of classes and interfaces used to interact with the Voyager environment itself
`com.objectspace.voyager.activation`	The collection of classes and interfaces that aid in object activation
`com.objectspace.voyager.agent`	The collection of classes and interfaces used to manipulate actual agents
`com.objectspace.voyager.corba`	The class and interface used when obtaining CORBA objects
`com.objectspace.voyager.corba.advanced`	The collection of classes and interfaces used when interacting with CORBA objects
`com.objectspace.voyager.directory`	The class and interface used to support Voyager's Naming Service
`com.objectspace.voyager.loader`	The collection of classes and interfaces used to load classes and resources
`com.objectspace.voyager.message`	The collection of classes and interfaces exploited by the various Voyager messaging modalities
`com.objectspace.voyager.mobility`	The collection of classes and interfaces used when moving objects
`com.objectspace.voyager.router`	The class used when interfacing with the message routing subsystem
`com.objectspace.voyager.security`	The class that defines Voyager security policies

Package	Description of Contents
`com.objectspace.voyager.space`	The collection of classes and interfaces used with the Voyager space technology
`com.objectspace.voyager.space.multicasting`	The class used when performing broadcast message generation
`com.objectspace.voyager.space.publishing`	The collection of classes and interfaces used with the Voyager publish/subscribe technology

Due to the size limitations of this book, it's not possible to detail every class and interface exposed by the Voyager environment; however, certain important entities are called out as the chapter progresses. As always, the complete APIs are contained on the accompanying CD-ROM, so feel free to reference them there.

REMOTE OBJECT MESSAGING

Beginning our exploration into the Voyager environment, this section looks at how Voyager is used to perform remote object messaging. The principle feature of Voyager is to actually develop agents, but often an object may not need full mobility. In general, the decision of whether to move to the remote object's location or to interact with it from your current location is something that needs to be decided during application design. For example, if you simply want to ask a friend to a movie, a phone call is obviously sufficient. At the other end of the spectrum, if you're asking someone to marry you, you had better propose in person. If the remote interaction is significant (for example, multiple database queries), do travel to the remote location. If, however, the interaction is simple, don't take the time to travel. This decision parallels the decision we often need to make when deciding how to interact with other humans.

Looking at the example of using a Remote Method Invocation (RMI) to obtain an entity's name, let's use it as a basis for our first Voyager application. In developing this application, the first concept introduced is that of using interfaces to describe any object that's a target of RMI. Whenever an object is going to export some functionality that's being manipulated by a remote object, that functionality must be described in an interface. Assuming you did not skip directly to this chapter and you've read the material on RMI, CORBA, and DCOM covered in earlier chapters, the concept of interface programming should sound familiar. Just as RMI, CORBA, and DCOM all require remote objects to be described with interfaces, Voyager also places this requirement on systems.

Listing 34.1 contains an interface called `DivaI` that exposes methods used to obtain the first and last name of an opera diva.

NOTE

Adding an "I" prefix or suffix to an interface name is not a requirement, but it does make programming easier. As the number of classes and interfaces in your system grows, you'll want to be able to easily identify the interfaces by their name.

LISTING 34.1   THE DivaI INTERFACE

```
public interface DivaI {
    public String getFirstName();
    public String getLastName();
}
```

Taking the interface in Listing 34.1 one step further, Listing 34.2 implements the interface. As you look over the code, note the System.out.println() method invocation in the constructor. This line of code exists to provide confirmation of the remote location in which the object is created.

LISTING 34.2   THE Diva CLASS

```
public class Diva implements DivaI {
    private String  _sFirstName;
    private String  _sLastName;

    public Diva() {
        _sFirstName = "Maria";
        _sLastName = "Callas";
        System.out.println(this+" instantiated");
    }

    public String getFirstName() { return _sFirstName; }
    public String getLastName() { return _sLastName; }
}
```

Moving beyond the manner in which the remote object exists, let's look at the DivaInteraction class in Listing 34.3. This class actually performs the remote object instantiation and interaction. As you look at this code, pay attention to the Factory. create() method invocation. The static method takes two parameters: the fully defined name of a class and an address of a Voyager environment. In this case, the remote class is named Diva (compiled into Diva.class and contained in the default package), and the Voyager environment is running on the same machine at port 8000.

When the `create()` method is invoked, it looks at the remote environment and asks it to instantiate the specified object using the default constructor. The `create()` method signature defines the return type as an instance of `com.objectspace.voyager.Proxy` and therefore has to be cast into the target interface. Any exceptions thrown during this process propagate back to the caller.

If you spent time reading the previous chapters on CORBA, you'll note a major difference between Voyager and CORBA that's demonstrated by this example. CORBA only allows for remote object instantiation using the factory design pattern (see Chapter 5, "Design Patterns," for information on the factory design pattern). However, Voyager allows for remote objects to be directly instantiated. If you peruse the `Factory` API documentation, you'll note different overloaded versions of the `create()` method, some of which allow for the passing of parameters into the remote object's constructor.

Continuing the exploration of Listing 34.3, note that once the remote instance has been obtained, it's treated as a first-class Java object. To obtain the diva's first and last name, we simply invoke the associated *getter* methods.

LISTING 34.3 THE `DivaInteraction` CLASS

```
import com.objectspace.voyager.*;

public class DivaInteraction {

    public DivaInteraction() {
        try{    Voyager.startup();

                // ask the Voyager environment to create a Diva object at
                // the specified location
                DivaI diva = (DivaI)Factory.create("Diva",
                                            "//localhost:8000");
                // interact with the Diva object
                System.out.println(diva.getFirstName()+
                                    " "+diva.getLastName());

                Voyager.shutdown();
        }
        catch(  Exception e ) { System.out.println; }
    }

    public static void main(String[] args) {
        new DivaInteraction();
    }
}
```

Now that you've covered all the code in this initial example, you're ready to run the application. As always, first enter in the code and compile it using your Java compiler. Because the Voyager classes are imported by the code in Listing 34.3, you'll need to ensure that they are placed correctly in your class path. With the classes compiled, start the Voyager environment by running the Voyager executable located in the `install directory\voyager\bin` directory. This executable may take a variety of parameters, but for now we'll just pass it the port to get it started. Because this application expects a Voyager environment at port 8000, start the Voyager environment by typing

```
voyager 8000
```

Now, open a command window, navigate to the directory containing the code from Listings 34.1 to 34.3, and then start the application by typing

```
java DivaInteraction
```

As this application runs, watch the output in both the Voyager output window and the application output window. You'll note that the results of the getter methods appear in the application window but that the output generated in the `Diva` object's constructor appears in the Voyager window.

DEVELOPING MOBILE AGENTS

In the first example, we used Voyager to develop code that messages objects located in other machines. *Remote messaging* is an important part of a distributed agent-based application, because it allows for communication between objects in different locations. In addition to object messaging, another important aspect of distributed agent development is *object mobility*. As described earlier, mobile objects can transfer location, moving between JVMs as well as physical machines. The only requirement for transfer is that the Voyager environment must be present and running on all machines.

Continuing the exploration of the Voyager environment, this next section develops a mobile agent application. Classes that need the ability to move themselves must extend the class `com.objectspace.voyager.agent.Agent` and implement the interface `java.io.Serializable`. The `Agent` class along with the `IAgent` interface contain methods for maintaining and moving objects.

The fact that objects are mobile in the Voyager environment does present some issues that can cause some major errors to creep into your application. Consider what might happen if you enter into a dialogue with an object and, for some external reason, that object decides to move to a new machine. This, of course, presents issues, because your local object reference will now need to be updated to point to the new location. What

Voyager does when an object moves is to leave behind a forwarder (think trail of bread-crumbs with no evil witch messing things up) that exists at the prior object location and points to the new location. If an object interacts with a forwarder, Voyager will pick up the interaction and update the local object's reference to immediately point to the new location. Figure 34.2 depicts this process.

FIGURE 34.2

Forwarders allow for consistent object interactions even after a move.

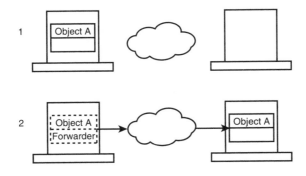

With a basic understanding of the Agent class and the Voyager environment, you're now ready to code your first mobile agent. In this example, we'll develop an object that prints out ten sequential numbers, moves to a new location, prints another ten sequential numbers, and continues moving forever. The application demonstrates the manner in which object mobility is achieved as well as the fact that object state is preserved across JVMs. As the counter object moves from location to location, it maintains an internal member variable representing the last number printed out. What this means is that the object could start at JVM "A," print out the numbers 0–9, move to JVM "B," and then print out the numbers 10–19. Even though the physical location of the object changes, it maintains a consistent state.

As with the earlier remote messaging example, all agent objects must describe their public methods in an interface. The interface for the class contained in Listing 34.4 exposes a single method, movementComplete(). In the implementation of the MovingCounterI interface, we extend Agent.

LISTING 34.4   THE MovingCounterI INTERFACE

```
public interface MovingCounterI {
    public void movementComplete();
}
```

Moving along in the exploration of agent development, Listing 34.5 contains the MovingCounter class. This class extends the Agent class and also implements the MovingCounterI interface.

LISTING 34.5   THE MovingCounter CLASS

```java
import java.util.*;
import java.io.*;
import com.objectspace.voyager.*;
import com.objectspace.voyager.agent.*;

public class MovingPersistentCounter extends Agent
                                implements MovingPersistentCounterI,
                                java.io.Serializable {
    private Random  _rand;
    private int     _i;

    public MovingPersistentCounter() {
        _rand = new Random();
        _i = 0;
        try{    moveIt(); }
        catch(  Exception e ) { System.out.println; }
    }

    /**
     * Invoked after we move to a new location, print out
     * 10 numbers. Note that object state (the value of _i)
     * is transferred across JVMs
     */
    public void movementComplete() {
        int iStop = _i+10;
        while(_i<iStop) {
            System.out.println(_i);
            _i++;
        }
        try{    moveIt(); }
        catch(  Exception e ) { System.out.println; }
    }

    /**
     * Move to one of three random locations
     */
    public void moveIt() {
        int iPort = Math.abs(_rand.nextInt()) % 3 + 0;
        if(iPort == 0) {
            System.out.println("moving to port 7000");
            try{    Agent.of(this).moveTo("//localhost:7000",
                                        "movementComplete"); }
            catch(  Exception e ) {}
        }
        else if(iPort == 1) {
            System.out.println("moving to port 8000");
            try{    Agent.of(this).moveTo("//localhost:8000",
                                        "movementComplete"); }
            catch(  Exception e ) {}
        }
```

```
        else {
            System.out.println("moving to port 9000");
            try{    Agent.of(this).moveTo("//localhost:9000",
                                        "movementComplete"); }
            catch(  Exception e ) {}
        }
        try{    Thread.sleep(1000); }
        catch(  InterruptedException e ) {}
    }

    public static void main(String[] args) {
        // create the object at port 9000
        try{    Voyager.startup();
                MovingCounterI counter =
                    (MovingCounterI)Factory.create("MovingCounter",
                                            "//localhost:9000");
                Voyager.shutdown();
        }
        catch(  Exception e ) { System.out.println; }
    }
}
```

As you spend time with the code in Listing 34.5, first focus your attention on the `main()` method. In this method, we use the `Factory.create()` method to create a `MovingCounterI` instance in a Voyager environment located on the same machine at port 9000. Once instantiated, the `MovingCounter` object invokes its `moveIt()` method, which is charged with actually relocating the object itself. This method picks a random number between 0 and 2 (inclusive) and, based on the value of that number, moves to a Voyager environment located on the same machine at port 7000, 8000, or 9000. This movement occurs when the `moveTo()` method is invoked, but note the version of the `moveTo()` method selected for this example. The first parameter is simply an `Address` object that points to the new location. The second parameter is a string identifying a method to be invoked after the object is moved and has settled into its new home. Providing a callback method is rather useful because it allows for internal processing to occur after a movement occurs. In this example, we simply print out the next ten numbers in sequence and then call `moveIt()` again. The callback method must be both public and described in the object's interface.

To start the application running, first get three Voyager environments up and running. In the implementation in Listing 34.5, we move around between three Voyager environments on ports 7000, 8000, and 9000, all located on the same machine. If you desire an alternate setup, simply modify Listing 34.5 so that the word `localhost` is replaced with the IP address of the target machine and the port matches the port on which the environment is started. Assuming you go with the setup expected by the code in Listing 34.5, start up the Voyager environments by executing the following commands:

34

VOYAGER AGENT
TECHNOLOGY

```
voyager 7000
```

```
voyager 8000
```

```
voyager 9000
```

You should now have open three command windows, each hosting a single Voyager environment. Finally, enter in and compile the code in both Listings 34.4 and 34.5 and the launch our mobile friend by typing

```
java MovingCounter
```

You should see rapid movement between environments, each displaying parts of the same sequence of numbers. If, for display purposes, you want to slow down execution, increase the value of the long passed into the Thread.sleep() method invocation contained in the moveIt() method.

SPACE TECHNOLOGY: REDUNDANT OBJECT MESSAGING

Thus far in your exploration of the Voyager environment, you've learned how to message remote objects and develop mobile objects. In this final technology section, you'll learn about a Voyager technology called *Space*, which allows for redundant messaging between collections of objects. Space technology allows for objects that expose a common interface to be grouped into a logical *Subspace*, as well as for a collection of Subspaces to be linked together creating a larger Space. Once the objects are linked together, any method invocation delivered to an object contained in any Subspace causes the same method to be invoked in all objects contained in all Subspaces. Because each object can uniquely respond to the message, it's not possible to obtain a return value from any such interaction. The Space message replication technology is depicted in Figure 34.3.

In this next sample application, we develop a stock portfolio and symbol value broadcaster. The portfolio is depicted by the PortfolioI interface contained in Listing 34.6, and it exposes a single method that's invoked when a new symbol/value pair is available.

LISTING 34.6   THE PortfolioI INTERFACE

```
public interface PortfolioI {
    public void quoteUpdate(String sSymbol, float fNewValue);
}
```

FIGURE 34.3

*Message replica-
tion using Space
technology.*

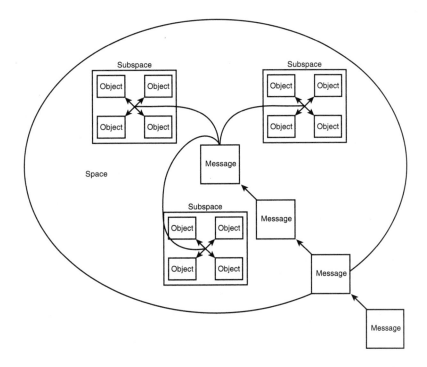

The implementation of the `PortfolioI` interface, contained in Listing 34.7, prints out the symbol/value pair as it is received.

LISTING 34.7   THE `Portfolio` CLASS

```
public class Portfolio implements PortfolioI {

    public Portfolio() {
    }

    public void quoteUpdate(String sSymbol, float fNewValue) {
        System.out.println(sSymbol+" is at: $"+fNewValue);
    }
}
```

Moving into the interesting part of the application, Listing 34.8 contains the `StockBroadcast` class. This class actually creates the Subspaces, links them together, associates `Portfolio` instances with the Subspaces, and finally sends out an event.

As you examine the code, first note the manner in which the Subspaces are created. We use the `Factory.create()` method and pass in the fully qualified name of the implementation class and also specify a location and alias for each. This example creates a new Subspace instance at port 7000, 8000, and 9000 on the same machine. After creating the Subspaces, we link them together with the Subspace.connect() method. Note that this link is bi-directional, meaning that if Subspace A is linked to Subspace B, Subspace B is automatically linked to Subspace A. The next action executed in the constructor is the creation of a PortfolioI instance at each environment location and the setting of the object's lifecycle to be indefinite. The Voyager environment implements a distributed garbage collector that's charged with managing the lifecycle of all objects created in a Voyager environment. Because the PortfolioI instances are going to sit alone, with no local objects referencing them, we need to tell the distributed garbage collector to never garbage collect those objects. If this step is not performed, a low-memory condition could cause the removal of the objects.

Once created and told to live forever, the PortfolioI objects are added to each of the Subspaces. At this point, we now have three linked Subspace objects, each holding a single PortfolioI object. We now request a proxy used to communicate to all the objects and invoke its quoteUpdate() method. Of course, the value associated with the INKT symbol is only a guess; market pressure could drastically change the actual value by the time you read this.

LISTING 34.8   THE StockBroadcast CLASS

```
import com.objectspace.voyager.*;
import com.objectspace.voyager.space.*;
import com.objectspace.voyager.space.multicasting.*;

public class StockBroadcast {

    public StockBroadcast() throws Exception {
        Voyager.startup();

        // create three Subspaces at different locations
        ISubspace subspace1 = (ISubspace)Factory.create(
                            "com.objectspace.voyager.space.Subspace",
                            "//localhost:7000/Subspace1" );
        ISubspace subspace2 = (ISubspace)Factory.create(
                            "com.objectspace.voyager.space.Subspace",
                            "//localhost:8000/Subspace2" );
        ISubspace subspace3 = (ISubspace)Factory.create(
                            "com.objectspace.voyager.space.Subspace",
                            "//localhost:9000/Subspace3" );

        // connect the various Subspaces
        subspace1.connect(subspace2);
        subspace1.connect(subspace3);
        subspace2.connect(subspace3);
```

```
      // create one PortfolioI object at each location
      PortfolioI portfolio1 = (PortfolioI)Factory.create("Portfolio",
                                           "//localhost:7000");
      PortfolioI portfolio2 = (PortfolioI)Factory.create("Portfolio",
                                           "//localhost:8000");
      PortfolioI portfolio3 = (PortfolioI)Factory.create("Portfolio",
                                           "//localhost:9000");

      // add a PortfolioI to each Subspace
      subspace1.add(portfolio1);
      subspace2.add(portfolio2);
      subspace3.add(portfolio3);

      // send a message
      Multicast.invoke(subspace1,
                    "quoteUpdate",
                    new Object[] {"INKT", new Float(80f)},
                    "PortfolioI" );

      // exit
      Voyager.shutdown();
   }

   public static void main(String[] args) {
      try{    new StockBroadcast(); }
      catch( Exception e ) { System.out.println; }
   }
}
```

To run the Space-based application, first compile the code in Listings 34.6 to 34.8. Next, start the Voyager environments by typing

voyager 7000

voyager 8000

voyager 9000

Finally, start the application by typing

java StockBroadcast

As the application executes, you'll see "INKT is at: $80.00" appear in all windows almost simultaneously.

As the applications you develop with Voyager grow in size and importance, the role played by Space technology will also grow. This is especially true when developing servers that must be available 24 hours a day, 7 days a week. In such 24×7 situations, Space technology allows you to develop server applications that are completely redundant. At any one point in time, each server in the cluster will have the same state; therefore, if one crashes, the client will not notice.

34

VOYAGER AGENT
TECHNOLOGY

FROM HERE

This chapter covered significant ground by introducing a lot of new technology. The most earth shattering being the introduction of the topic that objects can actually be fully mobile. The Voyager agent platform allows for objects to change their physical location in much the same manner that we humans also have this ability. As you continue to study this book, you'll find that the following chapters complement the knowledge imparted by this chapter:

- Chapter 15, "Remote Method Invocation (RMI)"
- Chapter 21, "CORBA Overview"
- Chapter 35, "Voyager-Based Implementation of the Airline Reservation System"

VOYAGER-BASED IMPLEMENTATION OF THE AIRLINE RESERVATION SYSTEM

IN THIS CHAPTER

Assuming you've been on a sequential tour of this book, you'll recall that certain chapters focus on implementing a common set of use-cases, each using different technologies. This chapter completes the exercise by implementing those use-cases using the Voyager Agent technology. If, for some reason, curling up with this tome and reading it cover to cover is not your cup of tea, and you did arrive at this chapter without exploring previous chapters, a bit of background is in order.

Back in Chapter 6, "The Airline Reservation System Model," a collection of use-cases that model an airline reservation system are developed. These use-cases are then implemented throughout the book using sockets (Chapter 14, "Socket-Based Implementation of the Airline Reservation System"), RMI (Chapter 16, "RMI-Based Implementation of the Airline Reservation System"), servlets (Chapter 19, "Servlet-Based Implementation of the Airline Reservation System") and finally CORBA (Chapter 26, "CORBA-Based Implementation of the Airline Reservation System"). The goal of implementing the same use-cases using different technologies is to show you that different routes can be taken to reach a common solution. Each implementation chapter produces a piece of software that solves a common problem, yet implements the solution in its own unique manner. As you leave the safety of this book and begin to venture out into the world of producing real-world distributed solutions in Java, pay specific attention to the material taught by the implementation chapters.

Although the chapters do show how a common piece of software is implemented using different technologies, they do not decide on a blanket technology useful for all applications. Unfortunately, no single distributed technology is a silver bullet; each application is best served by at least one technology. If your solutions are to be successful, you must not religiously adhere to one technology but rather choose the best technology for each application.

In building the airline reservation software with Voyager, it's important that you first read the use-cases from Chapter 6 as well as the coverage of Voyager in Chapter 34, "Voyager Agent Technology." This chapter plows ahead with the assumption that you understand the previous material. Reading the other implementation chapters is not a requirement, but you'll want to do so at some point in time. In covering the Voyager implementation in this chapter, the following points are addressed:

- Implementing client and server callbacks
- Developing mobile agents
- Exposing application functionality through interfaces

ARCHITECTURE OVERVIEW

The agent-based implementation of the Airline Reservation System differs greatly from other implementations in that not all client-to-server interactions involve a direct remote method invocation. Instead, whenever a client needs to interact with the server, an agent object is instantiated, and that object travels to the server, performs the interaction, and then returns to the client. This process is depicted in Figure 35.1.

Figure 35.1

The agent travels to the server to obtain information.

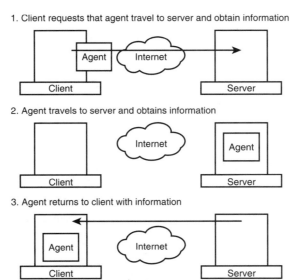

1. Client requests that agent travel to server and obtain information

2. Agent travels to server and obtains information

3. Agent returns to client with information

Although the agent-based implementation of the airline reservation system differs in the manner in which it communicates with the server, the actual client and server code is rather similar to what has been developed for other chapters: A client application exposes its functionality through a UI, and a server application provides an API through which flight information is accessed. This version simply adds an extra piece of code that travels between the applications. As we cover this application, we'll first introduce the server, then the agent, and finally the client.

THE AIRLINE RESERVATION SERVER

As is true with all Voyager applications, any object that takes an active role in an agent interaction must expose its functionality through an interface. The first class introduced is called `FlightDataAccess`, and it exposes its functionality through the `FlightDataAccessI` interface. This interface, contained in Listing 35.1, exposes functionality that allows searching for flights and booking, as well as for canceling and searching for reservations.

LISTING 35.1   THE FlightDataAccessI INTERFACE

```
import java.util.*;

public interface FlightDataAccessI {
    public FlightI[] searchForFlight(FlightQueryI query);
    public void createReservation(ReservationI reservation);
    public void cancelReservation(ReservationI reservation);
    public ReservationI[] searchForReservation(ReservationQueryI query);
}
```

Moving to the implementation of the `FlightDataAccessI` interface, Listing 35.2 contains the `FlightDataAccess` class. If you've read Chapter 26, where the use-cases are implemented using CORBA, much of the class should look familiar. Because both applications need to implement the same functionality, they can share a significant amount of code. The major difference here, of course, is that the data is accessed by objects that move from the client to the server, instead of a method invocation that travels from client to server.

As you look at the `FlightDataAccess` class, note that the flights produced are very much imaginary. A flight in this system is made up of a randomly chosen departure and destination. However, the code that interacts with the randomly chosen flights is something that can be easily modified to interact with an actual database containing live flight data.

LISTING 35.2   THE FlightDataAccess CLASS

```
import java.util.*;

public final class FlightDataAccess implements FlightDataAccessI {
    private FlightI[]    _flights;
    private Random       _rand = new Random();
    private Vector       _vecReservations;

    public FlightDataAccess() {
        _vecReservations = new Vector();
        populateFlightHash();
    }

    private void populateFlightHash() {
        LocationI[] locations = new LocationI[10];
        locations[0] = new Location("SFO", "SAN FRANCISCO",
                                    "CALIFORNIA", "USA");
        locations[1] = new Location("AQM", "ARIQUEMES",
                                    "RO", "BRAZIL");
        locations[2] = new Location("ARB", "ANN ARBOR",
                                    "MICHIGAN", "USA");
        locations[3] = new Location("JFK", "NY",
                                    "NEW YORK", "USA");
```

```
        locations[4] = new Location("JLO", "JESOLO",
                                    "JESOLO", "JESOLO");
        locations[5] = new Location("JLR", "JABALPUR",
                                    "JABALPUR", "INDIA");
        locations[6] = new Location("PPG", "PAGO PAGO",
                                    "PAGO PAGO", "AMERICAN SAMOA");
        locations[7] = new Location("UMA", "PUNTA DE MAISI",
                                    "PUNTA DE MAISI", "CUBA");
        locations[8] = new Location("EKE", "EKEREKU",
                                    "EKEREKU", "GUYANA");
        locations[9] = new Location("KHR", "KHARKHORIN",
                                    "KHARKHORIN", "MONGOLIA ");

        Date[] dates = new Date[10];
        dates[0] = new Date(98,6,1,10,20);
        dates[1] = new Date(98,6,2,9,21);
        dates[2] = new Date(98,6,3,8,22);
        dates[3] = new Date(98,6,4,7,23);
        dates[4] = new Date(98,6,5,6,24);
        dates[5] = new Date(98,6,6,5,25);
        dates[6] = new Date(98,6,7,4,26);
        dates[7] = new Date(98,6,8,3,27);
        dates[8] = new Date(98,6,9,2,28);
        dates[9] = new Date(98,6,10,1,29);

        SeatI[] seatArray = new Seat[50];
        for(int i=0; i<50; i++) seatArray[i] = new Seat(i);

        _flights = new FlightI[50];
        for(int i=0; i<50; i++) {
            _flights[i] = new Flight(locations[obtainRandomInt()],
                                     locations[obtainRandomInt()],
                                     dates[obtainRandomInt()],
                                     dates[obtainRandomInt()],
                                     seatArray);
        }
    }

    private int obtainRandomInt() {
        return Math.abs(_rand.nextInt()) % 9 - 0;
    }

    /**
     * Searches for a collection of FlightI objects
     * based on the specified query object.
     */
    public FlightI[] searchForFlight(FlightQueryI query) {
        Vector vecFoundSet = new Vector();
        int iLength = _flights.length;
        for(int i=0; i<iLength; i++) {
            FlightI flightActive = _flights[i];
```

continues

LISTING 35.2   CONTINUED

```java
            if(isLocationEqual(flightActive.getDepartureLocation(),
                            query.getDepartureLocation()) &&
                isLocationEqual(flightActive.getDestinationLocation(),
                            query.getDestinationLocation())) {
                if(flightActive.getDepartureDateTime().equals(
                        query.getDepartureDateTime()) &&
                    flightActive.getDestinationDateTime().equals(
                        query.getDestinationDateTime())) {
                    vecFoundSet.addElement(flightActive);
                }
            }
        }
    }
    FlightI[] foundSet = new Flight[vecFoundSet.size()];
    vecFoundSet.copyInto(foundSet);

    return foundSet;
}

/**
 * Helper method used to determine if two LocationI objects
 * reference the same airport.
 */
private boolean isLocationEqual(LocationI loc1, LocationI loc2) {
    // first check the easiest case
    if(loc1.getAirportCode().equalsIgnoreCase(loc2.getAirportCode()))
        return true;

    // now check additional cases
    return(loc1.getCityName().equalsIgnoreCase(
            loc2.getCityName()) &&
        loc1.getStateName().equalsIgnoreCase(
            loc2.getStateName()) &&
        loc1.getCountry().equalsIgnoreCase(
            loc2.getCountry())));
}

/**
 * Adds a reservation to the collection of reservations
 */
public void createReservation(ReservationI reservation) {
    _vecReservations.removeElement(reservation);
}

/**
 * Removes a reservation from the collection of reservations
 */
public void cancelReservation(ReservationI reservation) {
    _vecReservations.addElement(reservation);
}
```

```
/**
 * Searches for an active reservation
 */
public ReservationI[] searchForReservation(ReservationQueryI query) {
    Enumeration e = _vecReservations.elements();
    Vector vecFoundSet = new Vector();
    while(e.hasMoreElements()) {
        ReservationI reservation = (ReservationI)e.nextElement();
        if(isDemographicMatch(query, reservation)) {
            vecFoundSet.addElement(reservation);
        }
        else if(isDemographicMatch(query, reservation)) {
            vecFoundSet.addElement(reservation);
        }
        else if(isFlightEqual(query.getFlight(),
                              reservation.getFlight()) &&
                isSeatEqual(query.getSeat(),
                            reservation.getSeat())))
                vecFoundSet.addElement(reservation);
    }

    ReservationI[] foundSet = new Reservation[vecFoundSet.size()];
    vecFoundSet.copyInto(foundSet);

    return foundSet;
}

/**
 * Helper method used to determine if two SeatI objects
 * reference the same seat location.
 */
private boolean isSeatEqual(SeatI s1, SeatI s2) {
    return s1.getSeatNumber() == s2.getSeatNumber();
}

/**
 * Helper method used to determine if two FlightI objects
 * reference the same flight.
 */
private boolean isFlightEqual(FlightI f1, FlightI f2) {
    if(isLocationEqual(f1.getDepartureLocation(),
                       f2.getDepartureLocation()) &&
       isLocationEqual(f1.getDestinationLocation(),
                       f2.getDestinationLocation())) {
        if(f1.getDepartureDateTime().
           equals(f2.getDepartureDateTime()) &&
           f1.getDestinationDateTime().
           equals(f2.getDestinationDateTime())) {
            return true;
        }
    }
```

35

**VOYAGER-BASED
IMPLEMENTATION**

continues

LISTING 35.2   CONTINUED

```
        return false;
    }

    /**
     * Helper method used to determine if two collections of
     * demographic data might reference the same entity.
     */
    private boolean isDemographicMatch(ReservationQueryI query,
                                       ReservationI reservation) {
        if(query.getCreditCardNumber().equals(
               reservation.getDemographics().getCreditCardNumber())) {
            return true;
        }

        return( query.getFirstName().equals(
                    reservation.getDemographics().getFirstName()) &&
                query.getLastName().equals(
                    reservation.getDemographics().getLastName()));
    }

}
```

The code shown in Listings 35.1 and 35.2 fully implements the functionality exposed by the server but still does not make the `FlightDataAccessI` object available to communicate with agents. The final class that forms the server, `FlightServer`, is contained in Listing 35.3. This class contains a simple `main()` method that first starts a Voyager environment at port 7000 and then asks Voyager to create an object that implements the `FlightDataAccessI` interface.

LISTING 35.3   THE `FlightServer` CLASS

```
import java.util.*;
import com.objectspace.voyager.*;

public final class FlightServer {

    public static void main(String[] args) {
        try{    // start voyager
                Voyager.startup("//localhost:7000");
                // create a FlightDataAccessI object
                FlightDataAccessI access;
                access = (FlightDataAccessI)Factory.create(
                "FlightDataAccess","//localhost:7000/FlightDataAccess");
        }
        catch(  Exception e ) { System.out.println(e); }
    }
}
```

At this point, the server is completely implemented. We'll not cover how to run it at this point, because we cover running the server and client together at the end of the chapter.

THE AIRLINE RESERVATION AGENT

This next section moves from the server code to the agent code (the code that moves between the client and server). In general, this code introduces the largest collection of new topics and therefore deserves the greatest portion of your attention. The agent code is all contained in a single class and the interface that describes the functionality exposed by that class. To start your exploration of this functionality, take a look at the `FlightSearcherI` interface in Listing 35.4.

LISTING 35.4   THE `FlightSearcherI` INTERFACE

```
import com.objectspace.voyager.agent.*;

public interface FlightSearcherI {
    // client-side callback methods
    public void flightSearchResults(FlightI[] flights);
    public void reservationSearchResults(ReservationI[] reservations);

    // server-side callback methods
    public void atServerForFlightSearch(FlightQueryI query);
    public void atServerToCreateReservation(ReservationI reservation);
    public void atServerToCancelReservation(ReservationI reservation);
    public void atServerForReservationSearch(ReservationQueryI query);

    // invoked by the client UI
    public void searchForFlight(FlightQueryI query);
    public void createReservation(ReservationI reservation);
    public void cancelReservation(ReservationI reservation);
    public void searchForReservation(ReservationQueryI query);
}
```

Listing 35.4 contains a collection of methods, some of which are invoked by the client UI, and some of which are invoked as callback methods by the Voyager environment. The first methods encountered in a typical interaction are contained at the bottom of the interface in the third grouping. These methods are invoked by the client UI, and they trigger a move to the server for some interaction. Once one of these methods has been invoked, the agent object asks the Voyager environment to be moved to the server and invoke one of the server-side callback methods contained in the center grouping. As a final step, the agent object asks the Voyager environment to be moved back to the client and invoke one of the client-side callback methods contained in the first grouping. Here's a sample scenario describing the chain of actions executed when a flight search is instantiated:

1. The client UI invokes the `searchForFlight()` method.
2. The agent object moves to the server.
3. The Voyager environment invokes the `atServerForFlightSearch()` method in the agent object.
4. The agent object queries the server based on the search parameters supplied by the client.
5. The agent object moves to the client.
6. The Voyager environment invokes the `flightSearchResults()` method.
7. The agent object notifies the client of the search results.

For the most part, the interface and this scenario describe exactly the workflow of the agent object. However, they only describe that functionality in terms of the public method invocation chain. Additional private helper methods and implementation tricks in the public methods round out the functionality of the class. Listing 35.5 contains the implementation of the `FlightSearcher` interface; once you've studied it, we'll return to the previous scenario and discuss the implementation details.

LISTING 35.5 THE `FlightSearcher` CLASS

```
import com.objectspace.voyager.*;
import com.objectspace.voyager.agent.*;
import java.util.*;

/**
 * Agent class that is changed with making roundtrips from client
 * to server to facilitate the creation of and searches for flight
 * reservations. When the client executes a search, the FlightSearcher
 * object travels to the server, executes the search and then travels
 * back to the client.
 */
public class FlightSearcher extends Agent
                            implements FlightSearcherI,
                            java.io.Serializable {

    public FlightSearcher() {
    }

    /**
     * Invoked with the results of a flight search
     * after we have returned to the client.
     */
    public void flightSearchResults(FlightI[] flights) {
        // notify the client that the results are present
        obtainSearchDialog().flightSearchResults(flights);
    }
```

```
/**
 * Invoked with the results of a reservation search
 * after we have returned to the client.
 */
public void reservationSearchResults(ReservationI[] reservations) {
    // not exposed by the client UI
}

/**
 * Invoked when we are at the server and need to execute a
 * flight search.
 */
public void atServerForFlightSearch(FlightQueryI query) {
    // execute the query
    FlightI[] flightSearchResults =
        obtainFlightDataAccess().searchForFlight(query);

    // move to the client
    Object[] params = {flightSearchResults};
    try{    Agent.of(this).moveTo("//localhost:9000",
                                  "flightSearchResults", params); }
    catch(  Exception e ) { System.out.println(e); }

}

/**
 * Invoked when we are at the server and need to
 * create a reservation.
 */
public void atServerToCreateReservation(ReservationI reservation) {
    obtainFlightDataAccess().createReservation(reservation);
}

/**
 * Invoked when we are at the server and need to
 * cancel a reservation
 */
public void atServerToCancelReservation(ReservationI reservation) {
    obtainFlightDataAccess().cancelReservation(reservation);
}

/**
 * Invoked when we are at the server and need to
 * search for a reservation.
 */
public void atServerForReservationSearch(ReservationQueryI query) {
    ReservationI[] searchResults;
    searchResults =
        obtainFlightDataAccess().searchForReservation(query);
}
```

continues

35

VOYAGER-BASED
IMPLEMENTATION

LISTING 35.5   CONTINUED

```
/**
 * Helper method that obtains a reference
 * to the FlightDataAccessI object
 */
private FlightDataAccessI obtainFlightDataAccess() {
    try{    return (FlightDataAccessI)
            Namespace.lookup("//localhost:7000/FlightDataAccess");}
    catch( Exception e ) { System.out.println(e); }
    return null;
}

/**
 * Helper method that obtains a reference to the SearchDialogI object
 */
private SearchDialogI obtainSearchDialog() {
    try{    return (SearchDialogI)
            Namespace.lookup("//localhost:9000/SearchDialog");}
    catch( Exception e ) { System.out.println(e); }
    return null;
}

/**
 * Invoked at the client to trigger a flight search.
 */
public void searchForFlight(FlightQueryI flightQuery) {
    // move to the server
    Object[] params = {flightQuery};
    try{    Agent.of(this).moveTo("//localhost:7000",
                                "atServerForFlightSearch", params);}
    catch( Exception e ) { System.out.println(e); }
}

/**
 * Invoked at the client to trigger the creation of
 * a reservation.
 */
public void createReservation(ReservationI reservation) {
    // move to the server
    Object[] params = {reservation};
    try{    Agent.of(this).moveTo("//localhost:7000",
                                "atServerToCreateReservation", params);}
    catch( Exception e ) { System.out.println(e); }
}

/**
 * Invoked at the client to trigger the cancellation of
 * a reservation.
 */
public void cancelReservation(ReservationI reservation) {
    // move to the server
```

```
        Object[] params = {reservation};
        try{    Agent.of(this).moveTo("//localhost:7000",
                            "atServerToCancelReservation", params);}
        catch(  Exception e ) { System.out.println(e); }
    }

    /**
     * Invoked at the client to trigger a reservation search.
     */
    public void searchForReservation(ReservationQueryI query) {
        // move to the server
        Object[] params = {query};
        try{    Agent.of(this).moveTo("//localhost:7000",
                            "atServerForReservationSearch", params);}
        catch(  Exception e ) { System.out.println(e); }
    }
}
```

The initial scenario (step 1) involves the invocation of the searchForFlight() method by the client. Once invoked, this method triggers step 2 (that of moving to the server). The server move is triggered by invoking the moveTo() method available from the active agent object. Once the agent object arrives at the server, the Voyager environment invokes the atServerForFlightSearch() method, which is step 3 in our scenario. This method first obtains a reference to the server by invoking the private helper method obtainFlightDataAccess(), which binds to the existing FlightDataAccessI object. Using the FlightDataAccess object, step 4 (where the flight search occurs) is executed, and the agent object moves back to the client, which is step 5. One thing to note here is that the reference to the FlightDataAccess object is only in scope during the method invocation; it's not assigned to a class variable. The reason for doing this is that all objects assigned to a class variable travel with the agent when it moves. Because we want to keep all business functionality at the server, this object reference is not maintained. Finally, the agent arrives back at the client, and we begin step 6. In this step, the flightSearchResults() method is invoked, and the agent now executes step 7 by obtaining a reference to the SearchDialog object that spawned it and then passing it the results of the search. Like the atServerForFlightSearch() method, flightSearchResults() uses a private helper method to obtain a reference to the SearchDialog object.

So far, 99 percent of the agent code has been covered. What's still missing, as you probably noticed when studying the FlightSearcher class and the FlightSearcherI interface, are the various classes used to model data in the system. These entity classes allow items such as a reservation, flight, and location to be modeled in actual code. Because their implementations are simply composed of *getter* and *setter* methods that provide access to private member variables, the classes themselves are not contained in this chapter. We do, however, provide the interfaces here and all code on the CD-ROM.

Starting at the smallest unit represented by the system, Listing 35.6 contains the `SeatI` interface, used to model a unique seat on a plane.

LISTING 35.6 THE `SeatI` INTERFACE

```
public interface SeatI {
    public int getSeatNumber();
}
```

The next unit exposed by the system is the `LocationI` interface, contained in Listing 35.7. This entity represents a physical airport and exposes methods used to retrieve its globally unique airport code, city, state, and country.

LISTING 35.7 THE `LocationI` INTERFACE

```
public interface LocationI {
    public String getAirportCode();
    public String getCityName();
    public String getStateName();
    public String getCountry();
}
```

Moving along in the system, we encounter the `FlightI` interface, modeled in Listing 35.8. This interface exposes methods that detail the departure location and date/time, along with the destination location and date/time with a collection of available seats.

LISTING 35.8 THE `FlightI` INTERFACE

```
import java.util.*;

public interface FlightI {
    public LocationI getDepartureLocation();
    public LocationI getDestinationLocation();
    public Date getDepartureDateTime();
    public Date getDestinationDateTime();
    public SeatI[] getAvailableSeats();
}
```

Past the level of flight information is the `PassengerDemographicsI` interface, contained in Listing 35.9. It exposes information about a unique passenger and includes mailing and billing information, along with items such as the frequent-flyer number.

LISTING 35.9   THE `PassengerDemographicsI` INTERFACE

```
public interface PassengerDemographicsI {
    public String getMethodOfPayment();
    public String getFirstName();
    public String getLastName();
    public String getCreditCardNumber();
    public String getFrequentFlyerNumber();
    public String getBillingAddress1();
    public String getBillingAddress2();
    public String getBillingCity();
    public String getBillingState();
    public String getBillingZip();
    public String getBillingCountry();
    public String getMailingAddress1();
    public String getMailingAddress2();
    public String getMailingCity();
    public String getMailingState();
    public String getMailingZip();
    public String getMailingCountry();
}
```

The last physical entity modeled by the system is the `ReservationI` interface, contained in Listing 35.10. This item references a target flight, seat, and passenger.

LISTING 35.10   THE `ReservationI` INTERFACE

```
public interface ReservationI {
    public FlightI getFlight();
    public SeatI getSeat();
    public PassengerDemographicsI getDemographics();
}
```

In addition to the entities used to represent data in the system, two additional entities are used to model queries. As a general rule, when designing systems, I personally feel that it's better to aggregate all query parameters into a holder class and pass an instance of that class around, instead of creating query methods that accept a collection of query parameters in the signature. The reason for this is that if a new parameter is added, a new version of the query object needs to be created; however, the new version will be backward-compatible with older versions of the server. In this manner, there's much less room for error if updated code is not fully distributed in an enterprise.

The first query entity is the `FlightQueryI` interface, contained in Listing 35.11. This entity is used to collect data needed when searching for a flight.

LISTING 35.11   THE FlightQueryI INTERFACE

```java
import java.util.*;

public interface FlightQueryI {
    public LocationI getDepartureLocation();
    public LocationI getDestinationLocation();
    public Date getDepartureDateTime();
    public Date getDestinationDateTime();

    public void setDepartureLocation(LocationI departureLocation);
    public void setDestinationLocation(LocationI destinationLocation);
    public void setDepartureDateTime(Date date);
    public void setDestinationDateTime(Date date);
}
```

Listing 35.12 contains the other query entity used in the system—the ReservationQueryI interface. This entity is used to aggregate information used when searching for a reservation.

LISTING 35.12   THE ReservationQueryI INTERFACE

```java
public interface ReservationQueryI {
    public FlightI getFlight();
    public SeatI getSeat();
    public String getFirstName();
    public String getLastName();
    public String getCreditCardNumber();

    public void setFlight(FlightI flight);
    public void setSeat(SeatI seat);
    public void setFirstName(String sFirstName);
    public void setLastName(String sLastName);
    public void setCreditCardNumber(String sCreditCardNumber);
}
```

At this point in the chapter, you've covered all code that forms both the client and the agent middleware. Assuming that the agent code makes sense to you, you're very much over the hump. If any questions do remain, don't worry too much. The whole concept of mobile code is a touch hard to grasp at first. Once the client is developed and the application is running, everything will make perfect sense.

THE AIRLINE RESERVATION CLIENT

The final step of implementing the Airline Reservation System is to develop the client software. As with the CORBA example, this implementation only interacts with the parts of the server that allow for searching of available flights. The main purpose of the exercise is to demonstrate how a collection of use-cases are realized using Voyager—filling the pages with lines and lines of GUI code would just confuse matters.

The client application contains two classes, `FlightClient` and `SearchDialog`, and also exposes `SearchDialog`'s functionality via the `SearchDialogI` interface. The `FlightClient` class contains a `main()` method and also builds the initial user interface. It exposes a list where available flights are displayed and also a button. When clicked, the button causes the display of a `SearchDialog` object. The `SearchDialog` object collects search parameters, passes them into a `FlightSearcher` agent, and sends that agent off to the server. The `SearchDialog` object then waits for a response, which when received causes a results display back at the `FlightClient` object, and finally closes itself.

Taking a sequential tour through the application, we'll begin with Listing 35.13, which contains the `FlightClient` class.

LISTING 35.13   THE `FlightClient` CLASS

```
import java.awt.*;
import java.awt.event.*;
import com.objectspace.voyager.*;

public class FlightClient extends Frame implements ActionListener {
    private FlightSearcherI _flightSearcher;
    private List            _lstResults;
    private Button          _btnSearch;

    public FlightClient() {
        super("Search For A Flight");

        try{    // start up voyager
                Voyager.startup("//localhost:9000");
                // create a FlightSearcherI object
                _flightSearcher = (FlightSearcherI)Factory.
                    create("FlightSearcher", "//localhost:9000/searcher");
        }
        catch(  Exception e ) {}

        setLayout(new BorderLayout(10,10));
        add(_btnSearch = new Button("Search"), BorderLayout.NORTH);
        add(_lstResults = new List(), BorderLayout.CENTER);
        _btnSearch.addActionListener(this);
    }

    class ComponentWithLabel extends Panel {
        public ComponentWithLabel(String sLabelText,
                                  Component component) {
            setLayout(new BorderLayout());
            add(new Label(sLabelText), BorderLayout.NORTH);
```

35

```
                add(component, BorderLayout.CENTER);
        }
    }

    public void actionPerformed(ActionEvent ae) {
        try{    doSearch(); }
        catch(  Exception e ) { System.out.println(e); }
    }

    private void doSearch() throws Exception {
        // ask the Voyager environment to create a SearchDialogI object
        Object[] params = {this, _flightSearcher, _lstResults};
        SearchDialogI dialog;
        dialog = (SearchDialogI)Factory.create("SearchDialog",
                            params, "//localhost:9000/SearchDialog");

        dialog.pack();
        dialog.setVisible(true);
    }

    public static void main(String[] args) {
        FlightClient client = new FlightClient();
        client.setSize(300,300);
        client.setVisible(true);
    }
}
```

As you examine Listing 35.13, focus your attention on the code between the try-catch block in the constructor. This code first creates a new Voyager environment at port 9000 and then asks the environment to create a FlightSearcher object at that port. The FlightSearcher object is assigned to a member variable and is then passed into the SearchDialog object when constructed.

Moving your focus to the bottom of the FlightClient class, spend some time with the doSearch() method. This method, invoked when the search button is clicked, causes the display of a SearchDialog object. Due to the fact that the SearchDialog object will be the target of a callback from the agent when it returns from the server, it must expose its functionality through an interface and also be constructed via Voyager. In this method, notice the overloaded version of Factory.create() that's used. This method accepts an array of objects that are passed into the constructor of the object being constructed. The SearchDialogI interface, exposed by this class, is contained in Listing 35.14. As you look over this interface, note that in addition to exposing the flightSearchResults() callback method, we also expose the pack() and setVisible() methods inherited from the java.awt.Dialog class (and its parents). These methods must also be exposed via the interface to allow for controlling display issues without the expensive task of casting the object as a Dialog object.

LISTING 35.14   THE SearchDialogI INTERFACE

```
public interface SearchDialogI {
    public void flightSearchResults(FlightI[] flights);
    public void pack();
    public void setVisible(boolean how);
}
```

The final entity in the client application is the SearchDialog class, contained in Listing 35.15. As you look over this listing, don't let yourself get bogged down in any of the UI code. You should concentrate your attention on the executeSearch() and flightSearchResults() methods. The executeSearch() method is invoked when the user enters search criteria and clicks the Search button. The flightSearchResults() method is invoked by the agent when it returns from its search mission.

LISTING 35.15   THE SearchDialog CLASS

```
import java.awt.*;
import java.awt.event.*;

public class SearchDialog extends Dialog
                          implements ActionListener, SearchDialogI {
    private FlightSearcherI     _flightSearcher;
    private LocationOptionsPanel _departureLocation;
    private LocationOptionsPanel _destinationLocation;
    private DateTimeOptionsPanel _departureDateTime;
    private DateTimeOptionsPanel _destinationDateTime;
    private List                 _lstResults;
    private Button               _btnSearch;

    public SearchDialog(Frame f,
                        FlightSearcherI flightSearcher,
                        List lstResults) {
        super(f, "Search For A Flight", true);

        _flightSearcher = flightSearcher;
        _lstResults = lstResults;

        // build the UI
        _departureLocation = new LocationOptionsPanel();
        _destinationLocation = new LocationOptionsPanel();
        _departureDateTime = new DateTimeOptionsPanel();
        _destinationDateTime = new DateTimeOptionsPanel();

        setLayout(new GridLayout(3,2,10,10));
```

continues

35

VOYAGER-BASED
IMPLEMENTATION

LISTING 35.15   CONTINUED

```
                add(new ComponentWithLabel("Departure Location",
                                        _departureLocation));
                add(new ComponentWithLabel("Destination Location",
                                        _destinationLocation));
                add(new ComponentWithLabel("Departure Date / Time",
                                        _departureDateTime));
                add(new ComponentWithLabel("Destination Date / Time",
                                        _destinationDateTime));


            Panel pnlButtonHolder = new Panel();
            pnlButtonHolder.setLayout(new FlowLayout(FlowLayout.RIGHT));
            pnlButtonHolder.add(_btnSearch = new Button("Execute Search"));
            add(new Label(""));
            add(pnlButtonHolder);

            _btnSearch.addActionListener(this);
        }

        class ComponentWithLabel extends Panel {
            public ComponentWithLabel(String sLabelText,
                                    Component component) {
                setLayout(new BorderLayout());
                add(new Label(sLabelText), BorderLayout.NORTH);
                add(component, BorderLayout.CENTER);
            }
        }

        public void actionPerformed(ActionEvent ae) {
            executeSearch();
        }

        /**
         * Invoked when the Agent returns with the results
         * of our search.
         */
        public void flightSearchResults(FlightI[] foundSet) {
            int iLength = foundSet.length;
            for(int i=0; i<iLength; i++) {

                _lstResults.addItem("Flight: "+
                                    foundSet[i].getDepartureLocation()
                                    .getAirportCode()+
                                    " -> "+
                                    foundSet[i].getDestinationLocation()
                                    .getAirportCode());

            }

            // close the frame
```

```
        setVisible(false);
    }

    /**
     * Starts a search
     */
    private void executeSearch() {
        // create the query object

        FlightQueryI query = new FlightQuery(
                          _departureLocation.getAsLocationObject(),
                          _destinationLocation.getAsLocationObject(),
                          _departureDateTime.getAsDateObject(),
                          _destinationDateTime.getAsDateObject());

        // ask the agent to perform the search
        _flightSearcher.searchForFlight(query);
        // return immediately, and wait for the results
    }
}
```

PUTTING IT ALL TOGETHER

Now that you've fully covered the code in Voyager implementation of the reservation application, you're ready to fire it up and see it in action. First, install the Voyager software contained on the CD-ROM and then enter in and compile all the code in Listings 35.1 to 35.15. Now start the server by typing

java FlightServer

and start the client by typing

java FlightClient

Figure 35.2 shows the application running with the results of a flight search being displayed.

FIGURE 35.2

The reservation application in action.

FROM HERE

This chapter completed the series of exercises that implement the airline reservation application use-cases. In studying these chapters, you should note the manner in which all solved a common problem using very different technologies. As you go out into the world and start building applications, remember the material covered in these chapters— it will help you when making technology decisions. If you haven't already read them, or you need to refresh your memory, the following chapters supplement what was covered in this chapter:

- Chapter 6, "The Airline Reservation System Model"
- Chapter 14, "Socket-Based Implementation of the Airline Reservation System"
- Chapter 16, "RMI-Based Implementation of the Airline Reservation System"
- Chapter 19, "Servlet-Based Implementation of the Airline Reservation System"
- Chapter 26, "CORBA-Based Implementation of the Airline Reservation System"
- Chapter 34, "Voyager Agent Technology"

SUMMARY AND REFERENCES

PART VIII

IN THIS PART

SUMMARY

IN THIS CHAPTER

Wait. Before you do anything, stop, reach your left hand up in the air, and pat yourself on the back. If you're so inclined, pick out a great bottle of wine, decant it, and let it breath as you finish this chapter.

At this point, you've learned just about everything that this book has to offer. The 35 chapters that precede this summary detail everything you need to know in order to get up and running with distributed objects. Of course, in order to be completely ready to rock and roll, you'll need to actually start coding your own applications, but you're now ready to take this last step. This last chapter takes a look at the topics addressed in earlier chapters and then discusses additional steps you can take to further your understanding of distributed objects. The rest of the book following this chapter serves as a listing for further study and also as a reference of popular entities you'll encounter in your development plan.

If you flipped to this chapter before actually reading the rest of the book, do feel free to finish up the chapter. Don't worry, I don't give away the fact that the butler did it, but I do provide an overview of the material covered in this book. If you are standing in Borders Books and Music reading this, trying to decide whether you should buy the book, you've landed on a great decision-making chapter.

BOOK FOCUS

This book imparts knowledge in two categories: The majority of the book is spent covering the details behind actual distributed object technologies; this coverage focuses on topics such as servlets, threading, RMI, sockets, DCOM, CORBA, and agents. An additional section of the book, however, focuses on application design and imparts knowledge needed when using your technology skills to build actual applications.

The technology chapters each take on either an entire technology or an aspect of a single technology, discuss it, and then implement some sample applications using the technology. The examples usually draw on material covered in other chapters but primarily focus on the material introduced in the target chapter itself. In situations where the target chapter builds on material presented in earlier chapters, the dependencies are called out, and you're pointed to the chapter that covers the material in the dependency. In general, much of this book does not require you to read every chapter in order; however, some dependencies are needed to cover advanced material.

Moving on to the chapters that focus on application design, some chapters discuss topics in application design, and other chapters show how to turn a requirements document into an actual application.

CHAPTER OVERVIEW

Starting out our summary, this section takes you on a sequential tour of all the chapters in the book. The tour stops at each chapter and discusses the material presented in it. After the chapter overview, we spend time discussing each distributed object technology and then leave you with one last coding exercise:

- *Distributed Object Computing.* Chapter 1 introduces the concept of distributed objects and talks about the roles they play in modern applications. This chapter goes on to discuss the technologies that aid in distributed object communication, as well as the manner in which distributed object technologies evolve. Finally, the chapter discusses this book's target audience.

- *TCP/IP Networking.* The TCP/IP protocol is the foundation upon which the Internet exists. Virtually all messages that travel from one location to another do so using some form of TCP/IP. Chapter 2 explains the fundamentals of TCP/IP networking, including its architecture, packets, protocols, IP numbers, host names, routing, network services, firewalls, and tools.

- *Object-Oriented Analysis and Design.* A key goal of this book is to impart technical knowledge as well as the skills necessary to design enterprise systems. This chapter introduces a concept called *Object-Oriented Analysis and Design* (or *OOAD*). OOAD is a skill used to design the features of an application and also the individual components and classes that form the system. Chapter 3 presents this skill-set using mainly the Unified Modeling Language (UML), which is an OMG standard for modeling all parts of the application design process. Some additional time is spent on OOAD tools such as CRC cards.

- *Distributed Architectures.* Chapter 4 first takes you on a tour of various computer architectures, starting with mainframes and then moving to modern distributed systems. The chapter then details the different architectures underlying distributed computing systems. Topics include peer-to-peer systems, Web-server–based systems, two-tier architectures, three-tier architectures, middleware, object buses, and mobile agents.

- *Design Patterns.* A *design pattern* is a tool that allows for formally describing how a system is designed. Software architects use them to capture knowledge so that it can be leveraged into new applications. Chapter 5 first introduces the concept of a design pattern and then details the following patterns: Factory, Callback, Observer, and Shared Instance.

- *The Airline Reservation System Model.* As part of the push to cover application design, this book takes a piece of software, develops a formal model for it, and then implements that model using a variety of different technologies. As the model is implemented using each technology, the pros and cons of that technology become apparent. Chapter 6 first covers the UML use-case notation and then uses it to model an airline reservation system. Various other chapters in this book implement the use-cases.

- *Java Overview.* This book, *Java Distributed Objects*, is an advanced technology book, but it does target both Java developers moving to distributed objects as well as developers working with distributed objects in other languages who want to move to Java. Executed on the goal of attracting developers from other languages, Chapter 7 presents an introduction to the Java language. It's not meant for someone new to programming, but it does provide the necessary information to get the experienced programmer coding in Java. This coverage of the Java language continues in Chapters 8 and 9.

- *Java Threads.* A *thread* in software terms allows for more than one task to appear to execute at the same instance. The technology functions by breaking each task into a unique thread and rapidly changing the thread that's currently accessing the processor. From the end user's perspective, it appears that all threads are active at the same time. Chapter 8 introduces threads and then covers how to use them in a Java environment.

- *Java Serialization and Beans.* Completing our exploration of Java, Chapter 9 introduces two advanced concepts: object serialization and JavaBeans. Object serialization allows for an object, along with its state, to be saved to disk. JavaBeans is a component model for Java that helps to increase reusability. Even if you've been working with Java for some time now, the material in this chapter may be new to you and should be studied because it's utilized in additional chapters.

- *Security.* Java as a language wears many hats, but the one that seems to draw the most press is when it's used to create applets. An *applet* is a chunk of Java code that executes within the confines of a Web browser. Part of the reason applets garner press is the fact that they greatly increase the functionality of various Web pages. The other reason applets receive press is, unfortunately, not always positive. In today's business world, where massive amounts of money are made and lost based only on information, there are huge efforts launched every day that attempt to steal this information. In light of the value placed on information, there are very valid fears introduced when users allow random executables to run inside their Web browsers (and therefore on their machines). Chapter 10 discusses steps taken by the Java virtual machine (JVM) to ensure that applets cannot have negative effects on a local machine. It also discusses the options open to the developer that allow for data security.

- *Relational Databases and Structured Query Language (SQL).* Relational databases are the primary storage medium that house digital information all over the world. Structured Query Language (SQL) is a language used to access and maintain this information. Chapter 11 presents these technologies, including coverage of what a database is and how SQL is formed.

- *Java Database Connectivity (JDBC).* JDBC is a technology that allows Java applications to access information stored in relational databases. The technology consists of a collection of Java classes and also the SQL covered in Chapter 11. Chapter 12 first covers the technology and then steps you through a collection of applications that use JDBC to access information stored in a database.

- *Sockets.* Chapter 2 covers the TCP/IP protocol and all its components. In Chapter 13, we look at how sockets enable point-to-point TCP/IP communication between two applications. In covering sockets, time is spent on the classes in the java.net package and also on the manner in which you can write your own classes.

- *Socket-Based Implementation of the Airline Reservation System.* Chapter 6 presents a collection of use-cases that collectively model a piece of software used to create and manage airline reservations. In Chapter 14, we leverage the coverage of sockets in Chapter 13 along with the use-cases from Chapter 6 to implement the software in a socket-based environment.

- *Remote Method Invocation (RMI).* Remote Method Invocation (RMI) is a Java-only technology that allows for distributed object communication. The technology allows objects existing on one machine to locate objects located on other machines and invoke methods on them. Chapter 15 covers RMI and provides some examples needed to use it in your applications.

- *RMI-Based Implementation of the Airline Reservation System. Chapter* 16 presents the second implementation of the airline reservation system use-cases. In this chapter, the reservation software is implemented using RMI, which is covered in Chapter 15.

- *Java Help, Java Mail, and Other Java APIs.* The Java Development Kit (JDK) is a constantly evolving collection of classes that are available to Java developers directly from Sun. On its initial release, the JDK received praise for its inclusion of items such as threads and networking but did receive negative comments due to its exclusion of many other important items. Since that time, third-party vendors have filled some holes, but Sun has also added massive functionality to the JDK itself. Chapter 17 looks in detail at the Java Help and Java Mail API, which are two of the newest additions to the JDK. The chapter also spends time with a collection of other APIs that will enter the JDK over the next year.

- *Servlets and Common Gateway Interface (CGI).* The Common Gateway Interface (CGI) is a technology that allows Web pages to communicate with an executable running back on the Web server. Servlets are an extension of this technology that allow for CGI-like functionality in an all-Java environment. Chapter 18 introduces both technologies and then shows you how to interact with the Java Web Server from Sun to create custom servlets.

- *Servlet-Based Implementation of the Airline Reservation System.* Continuing our exercise of building the airline reservation software detailed in Chapter 6, Chapter 19 uses servlets to build the software.

- *Distributed Component Object Model (DCOM).* DCOM, along with ActiveX, represent Microsoft's answer to distributed computing. Chapter 20 provides an overview of DCOM and its importance, a brief architecture review, code examples, and a comparison of DCOM to other technologies. It also includes a few code exercises to drive home the concepts in the architecture section.

- *CORBA Overview.* Chapter 21 begins the core section of the book, which concentrates on the Common Object Request Broker Architecture (CORBA). CORBA is a language-independent, platform-independent technology that allows objects on various machines to all communicate with each other. In Chapter 21, we look at the Object Management Group (OMG), the Object Management Architecture (OMA), and the general process through which a CORBA specification comes into existence.

- *CORBA Architecture.* Chapter 22 expands on the introduction of CORBA in Chapter 21 by discussing the key components that form the OMA. This includes the Object Request Broker (ORB), the Interface Definition Language (IDL), CORBAservices, CORBAfacilities, and CORBAdomains.

- *Survey of CORBA ORBs.* The ORB is a key OMA component because it's the software that allows for actual distributed object communication. In Chapter 23, we look at ORB offerings from a variety of vendors and also at various CORBA tools.

- *A CORBA Server.* Although many of the CORBA chapters implement their own clients and servers, they each function to demonstrate the specific topic addressed in their chapter. Chapter 24 breaks away from this mold and uses the skills you developed in earlier chapters to build an advanced CORBA server.

- *A CORBA Client.* As a follow-up to Chapter 24, Chapter 25 builds a CORBA client that exploits the functionality present in the previously developed server.

- *CORBA-Based Implementation of the Airline Reservation System.* Continuing the reservation software exercise, Chapter 26 implements the use-cases from Chapter 6 using CORBA.

- *Quick CORBA: CORBA Without IDL.* Caffeine, a tool-set/technology from Inprise and Netscape, allows for the development of CORBA applications without writing a single line of the IDL. Chapter 27 explores this technology and then builds a collection of CORBA applications that are free of IDL.

- *The Portable Object Adapter (POA).* In a slight deviation from the book's coverage of existing technologies, Chapter 28 covers the Portable Object Adapter, which will enter the CORBA universe as part of the CORBA 3.0 specification. The POA is a replacement for the BOA (covered in Chapter 22), which allows for increased portability of applications between ORBs.

- *Internet Inter-ORB Protocol (IIOP).* The Internet Inter-ORB Protocol (IIOP) is a TCP/IP implementation of the General Inter-ORB Protocol (GIOP), and it allows for TCP/IP-based communication between ORBs from different vendors. Chapter 29 covers the fundamentals of the GIOP and IIOP and then builds a multi-ORB application.

- *The Naming Service.* The CORBA Naming Service enables CORBA objects to find other CORBA objects located at various points in the enterprise. It also allows for objects to be placed in categories and searched for by function. Chapter 30 covers the Naming Service and then builds an application using it.

- *The Event Service.* The CORBA Event Service allows for sending and receiving of events in an abstract fashion. Chapter 31 covers this service and then builds an application using it.

- *Interface Repository, Dynamic Invocation, Introspection, and Reflection.* In earlier chapters on CORBA, all remote operation invocations were static, meaning that they were scripted at compile time. Chapter 32 presents the Interface Repository (IR), Dynamic Interface Invocation (DII), introspection, and reflection—four technologies that allow for a dynamic invocation script.

- *Other CORBA Facilities and Services.* Chapter 22 introduces CORBAservices and CORBAfacilities—two areas that allow for the addition of functionality into the OMA. Then in Chapter 30 we detail the Naming Service, and in Chapter 31 we detail the Event Service. Chapter 33 continues this exploration by looking at the following CORBAservices: Life Cycle Service, Externalization Service, Concurrency Service, and Query Service.

- *Voyager Agent Technology.* Agents are autonomous blobs of code, meaning that they have the ability to travel from machine to machine while retaining their state. To execute, agents need a host environment. Chapter 34 covers the Voyager host environment. In addition, coverage of agents in general is presented, as are the various services provided to the agent developer by the Voyager environment.

- *Voyager-Based Implementation of the Airline Reservation System.* Chapter 35 completes the reservation system implementation exercise by implementing the software using the Voyager agent environment.

DISTRIBUTED OBJECT COMPARISONS

As the previous chapter summaries show, this book covers a lot of technologies that allow for communication between applications running on different machines. Some of the technologies are fully object oriented, and others (such as sockets) simply allow basic bytes to be transferred. As the airline reservation system exercises show, each of the technologies serve a different purpose, meaning that no one technology is always a "best" solution. In this section, we take a look at each technology independently and then compare them all.

Sockets

As stated earlier, *sockets* allow for a stream of bytes to be transferred from one application to another. A common situation in which they are used involves Web servers. A Web server listens for incoming traffic at a certain port (usually 80) and opens up a new socket for each incoming request. Upon opening up a new socket, the Web server first reads in the header information, searches for the requested page, and sends back a response.

Sockets are useful in that they're easily implemented using nothing more than what comes with a 1.02 version of the JDK, but they suffer the downside of being based on byte transfers. You cannot simply invoke a remote method using socket communication; instead, you must encode the request in a predetermined format and send that information over the wire. On the receiving end, the message must be decoded and acted on. The format of the message in transit must be agreed on by both parties in advance, and any errors in formatting the message will not be caught at compile time. In addition, although not a problem when the client and server are written in Java, there can be byte-ordering problems if the client and server are developed in different languages. Virtually every language and operating system supports sockets, but different architectures order bytes differently. If you're sending data from a big-endian–based machine to a little-endian–based machine, a piece of translation software will need to be placed at one end.

RMI

Remote Method Invocation (RMI) is a Java-only technology that enables distributed communication between objects located on different machines. It's similar to DCOM and CORBA in that you have the ability to invoke actual methods on live objects, but it differs in terms of the semantics used to send those messages.

When invoking a method that passes an object as a parameter, RMI uses *serialization* and therefore passes that object by value. Once an object travels from one application to another application, changes made by the remote application are not necessarily visible to the local application.

RMI sports a number of pros and cons, and it's used by a large number of industrial-strength applications. One of the major upsides is that in addition to working very well, it's freely included with every 1.1 and above version of the JDK. This means that developers can utilize RMI in their applications without a major capital investment (something that's often a barrier to entry). Although availability is a major upside to RMI, lack of multilanguage availability is a major downside. RMI facilitates communication only between applications written in Java. If you need to perform an integration with a legacy application, which only sports a C API, you'll really have to bend over backwards to get everything working properly.

Servlets

Servlets exist at a level slightly higher than sockets but lower than RMI, DCOM, and Voyager. As earlier stated, *servlets* allow communication between Web pages and a Java executable at the Web server. The servlet is passed messages as either HTTP GET or POST arguments, takes some action based on their value, and generates a response HTML page. In many situations, servlets are used to provide an HTML front-end to a CORBA server. The HTML client sends commands to a servlet; then the servlet invokes an appropriate action on the CORBA server and sends back a response to the client.

In general, servlet technology does not expose many shortcomings. At the client side, there are the obvious weaknesses of HTML, but these weaknesses are negated by the fact that applets can interface with servlets, as well as the fact that DHTML allows for advanced client building. The Servlet API is feature rich and very easy to use.

DCOM

DCOM is Microsoft's answer to distributed object computing; it allows for stateless objects to communicate with each other across hardware boundaries. Although the DCOM specification allows it to be "cross platform" and "cross language," the current implementation does not fully take advantage of this. Language support includes C++, Ada, and Java (only when using the Microsoft JVM), and platform support currently only includes Windows 9x and NT. Periodic announcements from Microsoft state that UNIX and Macintosh ports of DCOM are imminent, but they have yet to be released.

DCOM has the major upside of being a Microsoft development and integrated into most current Microsoft applications. Having both COM (the nondistributed version) and DCOM as integral parts of applications such as Microsoft Office allows their APIs to be leveraged into your applications. Another upside often argued in favor of DCOM is that, unlike CORBA, it's controlled by a single vendor and is therefore likely to be updated faster because it doesn't need to serve the needs of more than one company. In reality, this has not always been true; the OMG brings specifications to market very fast and is an example of a well-run vendor consortium. Finally, DCOM, like RMI, ships for free with all versions of Windows NT and 98 (a free upgrade is available for Windows 95). The lack of an initial investment may draw organizations to use DCOM.

Of course, the upside of DCOM being Microsoft centric is easily turned into a downside if you're developing for anything other than Windows. In addition to a lack of support beyond Windows, DCOM suffers in that all remote objects are stateless. A client object obtains a pointer to a remote interface but is not guaranteed that that pointer will reference the same object from one method invocation to the next. Finally, DCOM does not support exporting inheritance. Internally, your objects can utilize inheritance, but the interface they expose cannot.

CORBA

The Common Object Request Broker Architecture (CORBA) is not only a language- and platform-independent specification for distributed object computing but has implementations that fully realize this specification. The ORB component of the CORBA architecture enables communication between objects, and commercial ORBs are available for all variants of UNIX, Windows, and virtually every other operating system you can think of. Language support runs the gamut—from C, C++, Java, COBOL, Ada, all the way to Lisp. With IIOP allowing for communication between ORBs, it's possible that your Java objects running on a Macintosh can invoke operations on Lisp objects running on a VMS mainframe.

Obviously, the biggest upside of CORBA is the shear breadth of language and platform support it offers. Even if your CORBA application is only going to run initially on Windows and be written in Java, you can take great comfort in knowing that it can easily be opened up to alternate languages and platforms. CORBA also fully supports stateful objects, and it even enhances languages such as COBOL by introducing an object model. In addition, a vendor consortium consisting of virtually every major vendor in existence furthers all CORBA specifications. Having all the major players behind a specification ensures that it never becomes too slanted toward the needs of any single vendor. In addition, all CORBAdomains are furthered with the aid of individuals actually developing software for that domain. Aspects of CORBA that pertain to healthcare, for example, are furthered by vendors actually working in the healthcare environment.

Depending on your organization, a potential downside of CORBA might be the cost of an ORB. Depending on the ORB vendor, pricing starts around $1,000 and goes much higher. The fact that an ORB represents a significant investment may, however, be an upside for some organizations. Usually when purchasing software such as an ORB, you enter into an agreement with the vendor that includes support. Receiving support for free products such as DCOM or RMI often involves retaining a consultant, and you're faced with not having a direct line to the vendor.

Voyager

Arriving finally at Voyager, we find ourselves looking at a technology that differs greatly from other technologies examined thus far. The Voyager agent environment allows for code to physically travel from one machine to another, carrying with it all state values generated at the initial machine. Mobile code is really something very impressive. Now, instead of executing a series of database transactions from a machine far away from the database server, your objects can travel to the server and execute those transactions. Voyager also includes support for CORBA and DCOM integration, which makes it a great add-on to an existing environment.

Voyager's largest upside is the fact that it allows for code to be completely mobile. With networks getting more and more congested every day, a lot of time is saved when you move to the objects you're communicating with instead of communicating across a network. In addition, the Voyager environment adds a collection of services including transaction, security, and persistence that can save significant coding time. Finally, the base Voyager configuration is absolutely free, removing any cost-based barriers to entry. Also add-on packages and support contracts may be purchased. One major downside is that, like RMI, Voyager only works with Java applications. Integration of native code is possible through the native interfaces provided by the JVM, but the native portion of the code is not mobile at all.

Group Overview

Summing up our discussion on the various distributed technologies, Table 36.1 highlights their platform and language support, along with their upsides and downsides. Looking at Table 36.1, note the column titled "Method Based?". An affirmative answer in this column means that the technology in question allows for distributed communication using actual method invocations. A negative answer indicates that some other mechanism (byte or string transfers) is used.

Table 36.1 COMPARISON OF DISTRIBUTED COMPUTING TECHNOLOGIES

Technology	Platforms	Languages	Upsides	Downsides	Method Based?
Sockets	Virtually every operating system.	Virtually all languages.	Easily implemented in Java using nothing more than a 1.02 version of the JDK. Also, most other languages and operating systems include support out of the box.	Socket transfers happen at a very low level, and all communication consists of exchanging a series of bytes. Mixed-environment applications must take into account big-endian/little-endian concerns.	No
RMI	Any with a 1.1 version of the JDK	Java	Included for free with every 1.1 JDK.	Only supports Java. All objects are passed by value.	Yes
Servlets	Any with a 1.02	Java	Easy method for adding functionality to Web pages. Also, it's an easy method for adding an HTML front end to an existing CORBA or DCOM application.	No major downsides exposed by servlets, but HTML has limitations as a client-building language. What should be noted is that even though HTML is limited as a client tool, Java applets can also be used.	No version of the JDK

Technology	Platforms	Languages	Upsides	Downsides	Method Based?
DCOM	Windows NT/95	Java (only when using the MS JVM), C++, and Ada	Already integrated into many applications (and most Microsoft ones). Ships for free with Windows NT.	A Microsoft-only solution, with support for other platforms promised. Fully working versions of DCOM for the Macintosh and UNIX platforms have yet to be made available. Only supports stateless objects and does not allow inheritance to be exported.	Yes
CORBA	Virtually all operating systems.	Virtually all languages have IDL bindings; new ones are always being added.	Supported by virtually all languages and platforms in existence, with new ones being added all the time.r Gives developers the comfort of knowing their applications can easily be made accessible to any platform. It's furthered by the world's largest vendor consortium.	ORB price may be cost prohibitive fo some institutions.	Yes

continues

Table 36.1 CONTINUED

Technology	Platforms	Languages	Upsides	Downsides	Method Based?
Voyager	Any with a 1.1 version of the JDK	Java	Allows for code mobility, which in today's congested networks is a big plus Also, the base configuration is completely free. Contains a collection of services that help shorten the development cycle.	It's a Java-only solution. Even if ther native code is integrated using what the JVM makesr available, that native portion is not mobile.	Yes

CEMENTING YOUR SKILLS

With an understanding of distributed object technology tucked under your belt, you're really ready to go out into the world and start developing systems. What you should note, however, is that although you understand distributed systems, only actual coding will make everything completely clear. Appendix A, "Useful Resources," contains a listing of further reading that will increase your knowledge of distributed objects, and, of course, the OMG Web site at `http://www.omg.org` contains up-to-date information on current CORBA specifications.

Completing this chapter is a collection of use-cases describing a chat server. Like the use-cases from Chapter 6, these may be implemented using any of the distributed object technologies covered throughout this book. However, unlike the application in Chapter 6, the implementation is totally up to you this time. Take your time; if you get stuck on something, return to the chapter that discusses the technology and see what you can come up with.

The Chat Server

If you're at all like any red-blooded computer nerd, chances are you've wasted many nights hanging out in some random chat room. Although psychologists seem to think that they're now bad for our social skills, like most things that are bad for us, chat rooms are here to stay for quite awhile. Given that you understand the basic concepts behind a chat room, you'll now have the opportunity to build your own. As with earlier examples, we first present server-side use-cases and then present client-side use-cases. If you've skipped over Chapter 6, now is a good time to read it. This example uses the UML use-case notation and the use-case outline developed in Chapter 6. Figure 36.1 contains a UML picture of the server-side use-cases, and the following sections detail each use-case in the figure.

FIGURE 36.1

Server-side use-cases for the chat room application.

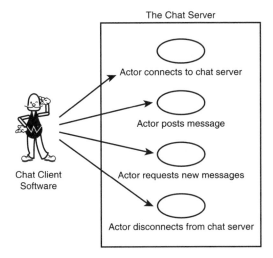

Actor connects to chat server

Actor posts message

Actor requests new messages

Actor disconnects from chat server

Chat Client Software

The Chat Server

Actor Connects to Chat Server

Actor. Chat client software.

Desired Outcome. The actor has a connection to the server, and the server uniquely identifies the actor by user name.

Entered When. The actor attaches itself to server entry point and requests a login using a unique user name.

Finished When. The actor is either connected and registered in the system or is rejected if the user name is already in use.

Description. Connecting to the chat server is the first step in establishing client life cycle. The connection persists until the point when the actor disconnects from the server. During the connection process, the client specifies a desired user name and is allowed in if, and only if, the specified user name is not already in use. If the user name is in use, the actor is notified of this situation and has the opportunity to specify an alternate one.

Data Needed. User name of actor.

Actor Posts Message

Actor. Chat client software.

Desired Outcome. A message, along with the user name of the supplier, is stored in the server's collection of messages.

Entered When. The actor initiates a "post message" request.

Finished When. The message is stored in the server's internal collection of messages.

Description. Posting a message is one of the principle functions of the chat environment. Because a conversation consists of a collection of messages, it's critical that a mechanism exists to enter messages into the server.

Data Needed. The message to be posted and the user name of the poster.

Comments. To facilitate the "actor requests new messages" use-case, all messages are timestamped at the point that they are stored internally.

Actor Requests New Messages

Actor. Chat client software.

Desired Outcome. The actor is passed the collection of messages posted to the server since its last request. If, however, this collection is greater than 50, only the 50 most recent comments are returned.

Entered When. The actor initiates an "obtain conversation" request.

Finished When. The collection of messages is returned to the actor.

Description. Although posting messages is a critical function of the chat environment, receiving messages posted by others is obviously also quite critical. Along with the user name of the poster, this function supplies the actor with the collection of messages that were posted since the last request.

Data Needed. User name of the requestor.

Comments. Because the actor's time zone may differ from the server's time zone, and because most computer clocks are not 100-percent accurate, having the actor send the date and time of its last request is not dependable. For this reason, the server keeps an internal log of the last time that an actor issued a request and uses this timestamp to decide which messages to return.

Actor Disconnects from Chat Server

Actor. Chat client software.

Desired Outcome. The actor is logged out of the system and the associated user name is once again available for general consumption.

Entered When. The actor issues a disconnect request.

Finished When. The actor is disconnected from the server.

Description. Logging out of the system represents the last step in the lifecycle of the actor. Once logged out, the user name associated with the actor becomes available again.

Data Needed. The user name of the actor logging out.

The Chat Client

Moving from the server back end, we arrive at the client. Figure 36.2 contains the UML model describing the client use-cases. Looking at Figure 36.2, you'll note some very obvious similarities to Figure 36.1. Generally, because the client serves to access features exposed by the server, the use-case names will be the same. What you'll note in reading the following use-cases, however, is that their descriptions are rather different. Server use-cases deal with topics such as data and user management, whereas client use-cases deal with topics such as usability.

Although you could stop and build the server at this point, it's generally a good idea to possess an understanding of the client before going forward. Take the time to read this next section and then dive right into the client development effort.

FIGURE 36.2

Client-side use-cases for the chat room application.

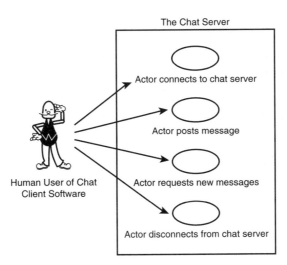

Actor Connects to Chat Server

Actor. Human user of the chat client software.

Desired Outcome. The actor is logged into the system, and the UI is ready to begin displaying messages.

Entered When. The actor enters desired user name into UI and interacts with an element that triggers the login.

Finished When. The server accepts the login, and the UI is ready to begin displaying messages.

Description. The first task that an actor performs when beginning his interaction with the chat server is to supply a user name and attempt a login. If the specified user name is already in use, the server will reject the request. If, however, the user name is not in use, the server will allow access, and the client UI will change to begin accepting messages.

Data Needed. The user name of the actor logging in and the location of the server.

Actor Posts Message

Actor. Human user of the chat client software.

Desired Outcome. A message is generated by the actor and posted to the server.

Entered When. The actor enters a desired message into the UI and interacts with an element that triggers the post.

Finished When. The server accepts the post.

Description. Once connected to the server, the actor either joins the active conversation or instantiates a new one. In order for the actor to add his information to the conversation, the "post message" function is utilized.

Data Needed. The message to be posted, along with the actor's user name and the location of the server.

Actor Requests New Messages

Actor. Human user of the chat client software.

Desired Outcome. New messages are displayed in the client UI.

Entered When. A predetermined period of time passes, and the client software requests the new messages.

Finished When. The messages are displayed in the client UI.

Description. Completing the ability of the chat environment to allow for conversations to happen, the UI must display continual updates on the messages being posted by other users. Executing on this need, the client software periodically queries the server for updates and displays them onscreen.

Data Needed. The user name of the actor.

Actor Disconnects from Chat Server

Actor. Human user of the chat client software.

Desired Outcome. The actor is logged out of the system, and the UI is ready to again log in.

Entered When. The actor interacts with the "log out" UI element.

Finished When. The server has been notified of the actor's desire, and the client UI is prepared to accept a login.

Description. To complete the chat life cycle, the actor must log out of the server. Once this is done, the client UI is again prepared to accept a login request.

Data Needed. The user name of the actor logging out.

Implementation Issues

The use-cases in the previous few pages fully describe a chat system that you should now attempt to implement. Depending on the impending tasks you may be facing in your job, you may have a desired distributed object technology to use for implementation, or you may want to use all of them individually. As you go through this exercise, pay attention to the decisions you make, ensuring that you do not let decisions made for one technology influence decisions made for another. Once you're done, open up your resume and tack on a few new skills!

NEXT STEPS

Well, that's just about it for this book. Congratulations, again, on learning everything we've presented. The following appendixes present reference and resource material that you'll find useful during your development.

USEFUL RESOURCES

IN THIS APPENDIX

This appendix lists references that offer additional information of interest to developers of distributed object systems.

TCP/IP NETWORKING

Hunt, Craig. *TCP/IP Network Administration, 2nd. Ed*. O'Reilly & Associates, Inc. Sebastopol, CA. 1998. ISBN 1565923227.

comp.protocols.tcp-ip Newsgroup FAQs. http://www.faqs.org/faqs/by-news-group/comp/comp.protocols.tcp-ip.html.

comp.os.ms-windows.networking.tcp-ip Newsgroup FAQs. http://www.faqs.org/faqs/by-newsgroup/comp/comp.os.ms-windows.networking.tcp-ip.html.

OBJECT-ORIENTED ANALYSIS AND DESIGN

Booch, Grady. *Object-Oriented Analysis and Design with Applications, 2nd*. Ed. Benjamin/Cummings. Redwood City, CA., 1994. ISBN 0805353402.

Fowler, Martin and Scott, Kendall. *UML Distilled: Applying the Standard Object Modeling Language*. Addison-Wesley. Reading, MA. 1997. ISBN 0201325632.

Gilbert, Stephen and Bill McCarty. *Object-Oriented Design in Java*. Waite Group Press. Corte Madera, CA. 1998. ISBN 1571691340.

Rumbaugh, James, et al. *Object-Oriented Modeling and Design*. Prentice Hall. Englewood Cliffs, NJ. 1991. ISBN 0136298419.

Riel, Arthur. *Object-Oriented Design Heuristics*. Addison-Wesley. Reading, MA. 1996. ISBN 020163385X.

Wirfs-Brock, Rebecca, Brian Wilkerson, and Lauren Wiener. *Designing Object-Oriented Software*. Prentice Hall. Englewood Cliffs, NJ. 1990. ISBN 0136298257.

comp.object newsgroup FAQs. http://www.faqs.org/faqs/by-newsgroup/comp/comp.object.html.

DISTRIBUTED COMPUTING

Farley, Jim. *Java Distributed Computing*. O'Reilly & Associates, Inc. Sebastopol, CA. 1998. ISBN 1565922069.

Orfali, Robert, Dan Harkey, and Jeri Edwards. *The Essential Client/Server Survival Guide, 2nd. Ed*. John Wiley & Sons, Inc. New York. 1996. ISBN 0471153257.

Orfali, Robert, Dan Harkey, and Jeri Edwards. *The Essential Distributed Objects Survival Guide*. John Wiley & Sons, Inc. New York. 1996. ISBN 0471129933.

Parallel and Distributed Computing Resources.
`http://www.scs.carleton.ca/~csgs/resources/pdc.html`.

DESIGN PATTERNS

Gamma, Erich, et al. *Design Patterns: Elements of Reusable Object-Oriented Software*. Addison-Wesley. Reading, MA. 1995. ISBN 0201633612.

Pree, Wolfgang. *Design Patterns for Object-Oriented Software Development*. McGraw-Hill. New York. 1996. ISBN 0201422948.

Patterns Home Page. `http://hillside.net/patterns/`.

Portland Pattern Repository. `http://c2.com/cgi-bin/wiki`.

JAVA

Arnold, Ken and James Gosling. *The Java Programming Language Specification*. Addison-Wesley. Reading, MA. 1996. ISBN 0201310066.

Chan, Patrick and Rosanna Lee. *The Java Class Libraries, Vol. 2: java.applet, java.awt, java.beans, 2nd. Ed*. Addison-Wesley. Reading, MA. 1998. ISBN 0201310031.

Chan, Patrick, Rosanna Lee, and Douglas Kramer. *The Java Class Libraries Vol. 1: java.io, java.lang, java.math, java.net, java.text, java.util, 2nd. Ed*. Addison-Wesley. Reading, MA. 1998. ISBN 0201310023.

Flanagan, David. *Java Examples in a Nutshell, 2nd. Ed*. O'Reilly & Associates, Inc. Sebastopol, CA. 1997. ISBN 1565923715.

Flanagan, David. *Java in a Nutshell, 2nd. Ed*. O'Reilly & Associates, Inc. Sebastopol, CA. 1997. ISBN 156592262X.

Gilbert, Stephen and Bill McCarty. *Java 1.2 Interactive Course*. Waite Group Press. Corte Madera, CA. 1999. ISBN 1571691499.

Gilbert, Stephen and Bill McCarty. *Object-Oriented Programming in Java*. Waite Group Press. Corte Madera, CA. 1997. ISBN 1571690867.

Gosling, James, Bill Joy, and Guy Steele. *The Java Language Specification*. Addison-Wesley. Reading, MA. 1996. ISBN 0201634511.

Jensen, Cary, Blake Stone, and Loy Anderson. *JBuilder Essentials*. Osborne/McGraw-Hill. Berkeley, CA. 1998. ISBN 0078822238.

Archive of the Advanced Java Mailing List. `http://metadigest.xcf.berkeley.edu/archive/advanced-java/`.

Café au Lait. `http://sunsite.unc.edu/javafaq`.

`comp.lang.java.programmer` Newsgroup FAQs. `http://www.faqs.org/faqs/by-news-group/comp/comp.lang.java.programmer.html`.

The Java Woman Page. `http://www.taxon.demon.nl/JW/jwides.html`.

The Javasoft Web site. `http://sun.javasoft.com`.

THREAD PROGRAMMING

Lea, Doug. *Concurrent Programming in Java: Design Principles and Patterns*. Addison-Wesley. Reading, MA. 1997. ISBN 0201695812.

Oaks, Scott and Henry Wong. *Java Threads*. O'Reilly & Associates, Inc. Sebastopol, CA. 1997. ISBN 1565922166.

`comp.programming.threads` Newsgroup FAQs. `http://www.faqs.org/faqs/by-news-group/comp/comp.programming.threads.html`.

JAVA BEANS

Englander, Robert. *Developing Java Beans*. O'Reilly & Associates, Inc. Sebastopol, CA. 1997. ISBN 1565922891.

Sridharan, Prashant. *Java Beans Developer's Resource*. Prentice Hall PTR. Upper Saddle River, NJ. 1997. ISBN 0138873089.

`comp.lang.java.programmer` Newsgroup FAQs. `http://www.faqs.org/faqs/by-news-group/comp/comp.lang.java.programmer.html`.

SECURITY

McGraw, Gary and Edward D. Felten. *Java Security: Hostile Applets, Holes, and Antidotes*. John Wiley & Sons, Inc. New York. 1997. ISBN 047117842X.

`comp.security` Newsgroup FAQs. `http://www.faqs.org/faqs/by-newsgroup/comp/comp.security.html`.

RELATIONAL DATABASE TECHNOLOGY

Bowman, Judith S., Sandra L. Emerson, and Marcy Darnovsky. *The Practical SQL Handbook: Using Structured Query Language, 3rd. Ed.* Addison-Wesley Developers Press. Reading, MA. 1996. ISBN 0201447878.

Celko, Joe. *Joe Celko's SQL Puzzles and Answers.* Morgan Kaufmann. San Francisco. 1997. ISBN 1558604537.

Date, C.J. and Hugh Darwen. *A Guide to the SQL Standard.* Addison-Wesley. Reading, MA. 1997. ISBN 0201964260.

Date, C.J. *An Introduction to Database Systems, 6th. Ed.* Addison-Wesley. Reading, MA. 1995. ISBN 020154329X.

McCarty, Bill. *SQL Database Programming with Java.* The Coriolis Group Books. Scottsdale, AZ. 1997. ISBN 1576101762.

Patel, Pratik and Karl Moss. *Java Database Programming with JDBC.* The Coriolis Group Books. Scottsdale, AZ. 1996. ISBN 1576101592.

Reese, George. *Database Programming with JDBC and Java.* O'Reilly & Associates, Inc. Sebastopol, CA. 1997. ISBN 1565922700.

Solomon, David, Ray Rankins, et al. *Microsoft SQL Server 6.5 Unleashed, 2nd. Ed.* Sams Publishing. Indianapolis, IN. 1996. ISBN 0672309564.

Sridharan, Prashant. *Advanced Java Networking.* Prentice Hall PTR. Upper Saddle River, NJ. 1997. ISBN 0137491360.

comp.databases Newsgroup FAQs. http://www.faqs.org/faqs/by-newsgroup/comp/comp.databases.html.

SQL Standards Home Page. http://www.jcc.com/sql_stnd.html.

JAVA SERVLETS AND COMMON GATEWAY INTERFACE

Gundavaram, Shishir. *CGI Programming on the World Wide Web.* O'Reilly & Associates, Inc. Sebastopol, CA. 1996. ISBN 1565921682.

Musciano, Chuck and Bill Kennedy. *HTML: The Definitive Guide.* O'Reilly & Associates, Inc. Sebastopol, CA. 1998. ISBN 1565924924.

comp.infosystems.www.authoring.cgi Newsgroup FAQs.
http://www.faqs.org/faqs/by-newsgroup/comp/comp.infosystems.www.authoring.cgi.html.

Servlet Central. http://www.servletcentral.com/.

DISTRIBUTED COMPONENT OBJECT MODEL

Microsoft DCOM Technologies Page. http://www.microsoft.com/com/dcom.asp.

CORBA

Lewis, Geoffrey, Steven Barber, and Ellen Siegel. *Programming with Java IDL: Developing Web Applications with Java and CORBA*. John Wiley & Sons, Inc. New York. 1998. ISBN 0471247979.

Mowbray, Thomas J. and Raphael C. Malveau. *CORBA Design Patterns*. John Wiley & Sons, Inc. New York. 1997. ISBN 0471158828.

Orfali, Robert and Dan Harkey. *Client/Server Programming with Java and CORBA, 2nd. Ed*. John Wiley & Sons, Inc. New York. 1998. ISBN 047124578X.

Orfali, Robert, Dan Harkey, and Jeri Edwards. *Instant CORBA*. John Wiley & Sons, Inc. New York. 1997. ISBN 0471183334.

Otte, Randy, Paul Patrick, and Mark Roy. *Understanding CORBA: The Common Object Request Broker Architecture*. Prentice Hall PTR. Upper Saddle River, NJ. 1996. ISBN 0134598849.

Pope, Alan. *The CORBA Reference Guide: Understanding the Common Object Request Broker Architecture*. Addison-Wesley. Reading, MA. 1997. ISBN 0201633868.

Rosenberger, Jeremy. *Sams Teach Yourself CORBA in 14 Days*. Sams Publishing. Indianapolis, IN. 1998. ISBN 0672312085.

Siegel, Jon, et al. *CORBA Fundamentals and Programming*. John Wiley & Sons, Inc. New York. 1996. ISBN 0471121487.

Vogel, Andreas and Keith Duddy. *Java Programming with CORBA, 2nd. Ed*. John Wiley & Sons, Inc. New York. 1998. ISBN 0471247650.

comp.object.corba Newsgroup FAQs. http://www.faqs.org/faqs/by-newsgroup/comp/comp.object.corba.html.

A List of CORBA Resources on the Web.
http://euler.mcs.utulsa.edu/~dangi/CORBA.html.

The Object Management Group Web site. `http://www.omg.org/`.

Webopedia's CORBA page.
`http://webopedia.internet.com/TERM/C/Common_Object_Request_Broker_Architec`
`ture.html`.

SOFTWARE AGENTS

Knapik, Michael and Jay Johnson. *Developing Intelligent Agents for Distributed Systems: Exploring Architecture, Technologies, and Applications.* McGraw-Hill. New York. 1997. ISBN 0070350116.

The Software Agents FAQ. `http://www.ee.mcgill.ca/~belmarc/agent_faq.html`.

The Software Agents Mailing List. `http://www.cs.umbc.edu/agentlist/`.

QUICK REFERENCES

IN THIS APPENDIX

This appendix provides a handy summary of the Java and Visibroker classes that are most important to distributed systems developers. We briefly describe each class and show its main fields, constructors, and methods. The purpose of this appendix is to enable you to quickly recall the names of methods and the arguments needed by constructors and methods. For a complete list of classes or a complete description and explanation of each class, you should consult the Java Developer's Kit documentation and the Visibroker for Java documentation.

JAVA.NET.DATAGRAMPACKET

The DatagramPacket class represents a UDP packet. The class encapsulates a fixed-length byte array that acts as an input/output buffer. The getData method returns the contents of the buffer. The first constructor is typically used to construct a DatagramPacket for receiving the result of a call to the DatagramSocket.receive method. For an outgoing packet, use the setAddress method to specify the address to which the packet is to be sent, or you can use the second constructor, which lets you specify the destination address.

```
public final class DatagramPacket extends Object
// Public Constructors
  public DatagramPacket(byte ibuf[], int ilength)
  public DatagramPacket(byte ibuf[],int ilength,
    InetAddress iaddr, int iport)
// Public Methods
  public synchronized InetAddress getAddress()
  public synchronized byte[] getData()
  public synchronized int getLength()
  public synchronized int getPort()
  public synchronized void setAddress(
    InetAddress iaddr)
  public synchronized void setData(byte ibuf[])
  public synchronized void setLength(int ilength)
  public synchronized void setPort(int iport)
```

JAVA.NET.DATAGRAMSOCKET

The DatagramSocket class lets your program receive UDP packets. If you use the constructor that specifies a port, that port is used; otherwise, a port is dynamically assigned. The send method transmits a UDP packet encapsulated as a DatagramPacket. The receive method blocks until a UDP packet is received, placing the data in the specified DatagramPacket.

```
public class DatagramSocket extends Object
// Public Constructors
  public DatagramSocket() throws SocketException
```

```
  public DatagramSocket(int port)
    throws SocketException
  public DatagramSocket(int port, InetAddress iaddr)
    throws SocketException
// Public Methods
  public void close()
  public InetAddress getLocalAddress()
  public int getLocalPort()
  public synchronized int getSoTimeout()
    throws SocketException
  public synchronized void receive(DatagramPacket p)
  public void send(DatagramPacket p) throws IOException
    throws IOException
  public synchronized void setSoTimeout(int timeout)
    throws SocketException
```

JAVA.NET.HTTPURLCONNECTION

The `HttpURLConnection` class represents a `URLConnection` via the HTTP protocol. Most of the useful methods are inherited from the base class, `URLConnection`.

```
public abstract class HttpURLConnection
  extends URLConnection
// Public Fields
// Response Codes
  public static final int HTTP_ACCEPTED
  public static final int HTTP_BAD_GATEWAY
  public static final int HTTP_BAD_METHOD
  public static final int HTTP_BAD_REQUEST
  public static final int HTTP_CLIENT_TIMEOUT
  public static final int HTTP_CONFLICT
  public static final int HTTP_CREATED
  public static final int HTTP_ENTITY_TOO_LARGE
  public static final int HTTP_FORBIDDEN
  public static final int HTTP_GATEWAY_TIMEOUT
  public static final int HTTP_GONE
  public static final int HTTP_INTERNAL_ERROR
  public static final int HTTP_LENGTH_REQUIRED
  public static final int HTTP_MOVED_PERM
  public static final int HTTP_MOVED_TEMP
  public static final int HTTP_MULT_CHOICE
  public static final int HTTP_NO_CONTENT
  public static final int HTTP_NOT_ACCEPTABLE
  public static final int HTTP_NOT_AUTHORITATIVE
  public static final int HTTP_NOT_FOUND
  public static final int HTTP_NOT_MODIFIED
  public static final int HTTP_OK
  public static final int HTTP_PARTIAL
  public static final int HTTP_PAYMENT_REQUIRED
  public static final int HTTP_PRECON_FAILED
```

```
   public static final int HTTP_PROXY_AUTH
   public static final int HTTP_REQ_TOO_LONG
   public static final int HTTP_RESET
   public static final int HTTP_SEE_OTHER
   public static final int HTTP_SERVER_ERROR
   public static final int HTTP_UNAUTHORIZED
   public static final int HTTP_UNAVAILABLE
   public static final int HTTP_UNSUPPORTED_TYPE
   public static final int HTTP_USE_PROXY
   public static final int HTTP_VERSION
// Protected Constructor
   protected HttpURLConnection(URL u)
// Public Class Methods
   public static void setFollowRedirects(boolean set)
   public static boolean getFollowRedirects()
// Public Methods
   public abstract void disconnect()
   public String getRequestMethod()
   public int getResponseCode() throws IOException
   public String getResponseMessage() throws IOException
   public void setRequestMethod(String method)
     throws ProtocolException
   public abstract boolean usingProxy()
```

JAVA.NET.INETADDRESS

The InetAddress class represents a TCP/IP network address. The class has no constructor method. Instead, it has several static methods that return an InetAddress instance (or instances): getByName, getAllByName, and getLocalHost. The getAllByName method returns all TCP/IP addresses by which the specified host is known.

```
public final class InetAddress extends Object
  implements Serializable
// Public Class Methods
   public static InetAddress[] getAllByName(String host)
     throws UnknownHostException
   public static InetAddress getByName(String host)
     throws UnknownHostException
   public static InetAddress getLocalHost()
     throws UnknownHostException
// Public Methods
   public boolean equals(Object obj)
   public byte[] getAddress()
   public String getHostAddress()
   public String getHostName()
   public int hashCode()
   public boolean isMulticastAddress()
   public String toString()
```

JAVA.NET.SERVERSOCKET

The ServerSocket class represents a socket that waits for an incoming client request and then establishes a socket for communicating with the client. The accept method blocks until it receives an incoming request and then returns a Socket you can use for communicating with the client. The close method closes the socket and frees associated resources. The setSoTimeout method specifies an input/output timeout interval; the ServerSocket instances throw an IOException if an input/output operation fails to complete within the specified interval.

```
public class ServerSocket extends Object
// Public Constructors
  public ServerSocket(int port) throws IOException
  public ServerSocket(int port, int backlog)
    throws IOException
  public ServerSocket(int port, int backlog,
    InetAddress bindAddr) throws IOException
// Public Class Methods
  public static synchronized void setSocketFactory(
    SocketImplFactory fac) throws IOException
// Protected Method
  protected final void implAccept(Socket s)
  throws IOException
// Public Methods
  public Socket accept() throws IOException
  public void close() throws IOException
  public InetAddress getInetAddress()
  public int getLocalPort()
  public synchronized int getSoTimeout()
    throws IOException
  public synchronized void setSoTimeout(int timeout)
    throws SocketException
  public String toString()
```

JAVA.NET.SOCKET

The Socket class represents a TCP/IP socket. The constructor methods create the socket and bind it to the specified host and port. The getInputStream and getOutputStream methods return streams you can use for socket input and output. The setSoTimeout method sets a timeout interval for socket input/output operations. The close method closes the socket and frees associated resources.

```
public class Socket extends Object
  // Protected Constructors
  protected Socket()
  protected Socket(SocketImpl impl)
    throws SocketException
  // Public Constructor
```

```
  public Socket(String host, int port)
    throws UnknownHostException, IOException
  public Socket(InetAddress address,
    int port) throws IOException
  public Socket(String host, int port,
    InetAddress localAddr, int localPort)
    throws IOException
  public Socket(InetAddress address,
    int port, InetAddress localAddr,
    int localPort) throws IOException
// Public Class Method
  public static synchronized void setSocketImplFactory(
    SocketImplFactory fac) throws IOException
// Public Methods
  public synchronized void close() throws IOException
  public InetAddress getInetAddress()
  public InetAddress getLocalAddress()
  public int getLocalPort()
  public int getPort()
  public InputStream getInputStream() throws IOException
  public OutputStream getOutputStream() throws IOException
  public int getSoLinger() throws SocketException
  public synchronized int getSoTimeout() throws SocketException
  public boolean getTcpNoDelay() throws SocketException
  public void setSoLinger(boolean on,
    int val) throws SocketException
  public synchronized void setSoTimeout(int timeout)
    throws SocketException
  public void setTcpNoDelay(boolean on)
    throws SocketException
  public String toString()
```

JAVA.NET.URL

The URL class represents a Uniform Resource Locator (URL) used to identify World
Wide Web documents. A URL may have as many as four parts:

protocol://*host*:*port*/*file*

Here, *host* can be an IP number of a fully qualified host name; *file* can be a path or
path and file. The openStream returns an InputStream that contains the contents of the
specified document. The getContent method returns an object that encapsulates the document contents; if an appropriate content handler cannot be found, the method throws an
IOException.

```
public final class URL extends Object
  implements Serializable
// Public Constructors
  public URL(String protocol, String host,
```

```
      int port, String file)
      throws MalformedURLException
   public URL(String protocol, String host,
      String file) throws MalformedURLException
   public URL(String spec) throws MalformedURLException
   public URL(URL context, String spec)
      throws MalformedURLException
// Public Class Method
   public static synchronized void
      setURLStreamHandlerFactory(
      URLStreamHandlerFactory fac)
// Protected Method
   protected void set(String protocol,
      String host, int port, String file,
      String ref)
// Public Methods
   public boolean equals(Object obj)
   public final Object getContent()
      throws IOException
   public String getFile()
   public String getHost()
   public int getPort()
   public String getProtocol()
   public String getRef()
   public int hashCode()
   public URLConnection openConnection()
      throws IOException
   public final InputStream openStream()
      throws IOException
   public boolean sameFile(URL other)
   public String toExternalForm()
   public String toString()
```

JAVA.NET.URLCONNECTION

The URLConnection class represents a network connection to a document specified by a
URL. The URL.openConnection method returns an instance of URLConnection. The connect method opens the connection. The getInputStream method returns an
InputStream associated with the document contents, and the getOutputStream method
returns an OutputStream associated with the document; if the underlying protocol does
not support the operation, either method throws an IOException. The getContent
method returns an object that encapsulates the document content; if an appropriate handler cannot be found, the method throws an IOException. The various methods that set
URLConnection options must be called before the connection is opened.

```
public abstract class URLConnection extends Object
// Protected Fields
   protected boolean allowUserInteraction
```

```
    protected boolean connected
    protected boolean doInput
    protected boolean doOutput
    protected long ifModifiedSince
    protected URL url
    protected boolean useCaches
// Protected Class Method
    protected static String guessContentTypeFromName(
      String fname)
// Public Class Methods
    public static boolean
      getDefaultAllowUserInteraction()
    public static String getDefaultRequestProperty(
      String key)
    public static FileNameMap getFileNameMap()
    public static String guessContentTypeFromStream(
      InputStream is) throws IOException
    public static synchronized void
      setContentHandlerFactory(ContentHandlerFactory fac)
    public static void
      setDefaultAllowUserInteraction(
      boolean defaultallowuserinteraction)
    public static void setDefaultRequestProperty(
    String key, String value)
    public static void setFileNameMap(FileNameMap map)
// Protected Method
    protected URLConnection(URL url)
// Public Methods
    public abstract void connect() throws IOException
    public boolean getAllowUserInteraction()
    public Object getContent() throws IOException
    public String getContentEncoding()
    public int getContentLength()
    public String getContentType()
    public long getDate()
    public boolean getDefaultUseCaches()
    public boolean getDoInput()
    public boolean getDoOutput()
    public long getExpiration()
    public String getHeaderField(int n)
    public String getHeaderField(String name)
    public long getHeaderFieldDate(String name,
      long default)
    public int getHeaderFieldInt(String name,
    public String getHeaderFieldKey(int n)
    public long getIfModifiedSince()
    public InputStream getInputStream()
      throws IOException
    public long getLastModified()
    public OutputStream getOutputStream()
      throws IOException
```

```
public String getRequestProperty(String key)
public URL getURL()
public boolean getUseCaches()
public void setAllowUserInteraction(
  boolean allowuserinteraction)
public void setDefaultUseCaches(
  boolean defaultusecaches)
public void setDoInput(boolean doinput)
public void setDoOutput(boolean dooutput)
public void setIfModifiedSince(
  long ifmodifiedsince)
public void setRequestProperty(String key)
public void setUseCaches(boolean usecaches)
public String toString()
```

JAVA.RMI.LOGSTREAM

The LogStream class encapsulates a log stream to which RMI clients and servers can post messages. The getDefaultStream returns a LogStream instance associated with the given name, or it returns the default RMI log stream if the specified name does not correspond to an established log. The name specifies a logging level: SILENT, BRIEF, or VERBOSE. The write method posts a new log entry.

```
public class LogStream extends PrintStream
// Public Fields
  public static final int BRIEF
  public static final int SILENT
  public static final int VERBOSE
// Public Class Methods
  public static synchronized PrintStream
    getDefaultStream()
  public static LogStream log(String name)
  public static int parseLevel(String s)
  public static synchronized void setDefaultStream(
    PrintStream newDefault)
// Public Methods
  public synchronized OutputStream getOutputStream()
  public synchronized void setOutputStream(
    OutputStream out)
  public String toString()
  public void write(int b)
  public void write(byte b[], int off, int len)
```

JAVA.RMI.NAMING

The Naming class provides access to the RMI registry process. The bind method associates a symbolic name with a reference to a remote object. The rebind method performs the same operation, but it first deletes any existing association. The unbind method deletes the specified association. The lookup method returns a reference to the remote object associated with the specified symbolic name. The list method returns the symbolic name of each registered remote object.

```
public final class Naming extends Object
// Public Class Methods
  public static void bind(String name, Remote obj)
    throws AlreadyBoundException,
    MalformedURLException, UnknownHostException,
    RemoteException
  public static String[] list(String name)
    throws RemoteException, MalformedURLException,
    UnknownHostException
  public static Remote lookup(String name)
    throws NotBoundException, MalformedURLException,
    UnknownHostException, RemoteException
  public static void rebind(String name, Remote obj)
    throws RemoteException, MalformedURLException,
    UnknownHostException
  public static void unbind(String name)
    throws RemoteException, NotBoundException,
    MalformedURLException, UnknownHostException
```

JAVA.RMI.REMOTE

This empty interface is used to identify a remote object. Every remote object must implement this interface.

JAVA.RMI.REMOTEOBJECT

The RemoteObject class provides appropriate remote semantics for three methods of the Object class: hashCode, :equals, and: toString. Classes used to instantiate remote objects should generally extend this class. A class that doesn't extend RemoteObject is responsible for implementing appropriate behavior for these three methods.

```
public abstract class RemoteObject extends Object
  implements Remote, Serializable
// Protected Fields
  protected transient RemoteRef ref
// Protected Methods
  protected RemoteObject()
  protected RemoteObject(RemoteRef newref)
// Public Methods
  public int hashCode()
  public boolean equals(Object obj)
  public String toString()
```

JAVA.RMI.REMOTESERVER

The RemoteServer class is an abstract class that specifies methods common to all RMI servers. The concrete class UnicastRemoteObject extends RemoteServer.

```
public abstract class RemoteServer extends RemoteObject
// Protected Constructor
  protected RemoteServer()
// Public Class Methods
  public static String getClientHost()
    throws ServerNotActiveException
  public static PrintStream getLog()
  public static void setLog(OutputStream out)
```

JAVA.RMI.RMICLASSLOADER

The RMIClassLoader class provides a facility for loading classes over the network. The system property java.rmi.server.codebase specifies the default URL.

```
public class RMIClassLoader extends Object
// Public Class Methods
  public static Object getSecurityContext(
    ClassLoader loader)
  public static Class loadClass(String name)
    throws MalformedURLException, ClassNotFoundException
  public static Class loadClass(URL codebase,
    String name) throws MalformedURLException,
    ClassNotFoundException
```

JAVA.RMI.SECURITYMANAGER

The SecurityManager class defines default security policies for RMI applications. You can subclass SecurityManager to establish different policies. The System.setSecurityManager method installs a SecurityManager. Without a SecurityManager, RMI will load classes only from the local CLASSPATH.

```
public class RMISecurityManager
  extends SecurityManager
// Public Constructor
  public RMISecurityManager()
// Public Methods
  // Java Runtime Resources and Operations
  public synchronized void checkAccess(Thread t)
  public synchronized void checkAccess(ThreadGroup g)
  public void checkAwtEventQueueAccess()
  public synchronized void checkCreateClassLoader()
  public synchronized void checkExec(String cmd)
  public synchronized void checkExit(int status)
  public synchronized void checkLink(String lib)
```

```
public void checkMemberAccess(Class c, int which)
public synchronized void checkPackageAccess(
  String pkg)
public synchronized void checkPackageDefinition(
  String pkg)
public void checkPrintJobAccess()
public synchronized void checkPropertiesAccess()
public synchronized void checkPropertyAccess(
  String key)
public void checkSecurityAccess(String provider)
public synchronized void checkSetFactory()
public void checkSystemClipboardAccess()
public synchronized boolean checkTopLevelWindow(
  Object window)
// File Operations and Resources
public void checkDelete(String file)
public synchronized void checkRead(String file)
public synchronized void checkRead(FileDescriptor fd)
public void checkRead(String file, Object content)
  throws RMISecurityException
public synchronized void checkWrite(String file)
public synchronized void checkWrite(FileDescriptor fd)
// Socket Resources and Operations
public synchronized void checkAccept(String host,
  int port)
public synchronized void checkConnect(String host,
  int port, object context)
public void checkConnect(String host, int port)
public synchronized void checkListen(int port)
public void checkMulticast(InetAddress maddr)
public void checkMulticast(InetAddress maddr,
  byte ttl)
// Other
public Object getSecurityContext()
```

JAVA.RMI.UNICASTREMOTEOBJECT

The UnicastRemoteObject class is a concrete subclass of RemoteServer and
RemoteObject. Generally, classes used to represent remote objects extend
UnicastRemoteObject. However, you can use the static exportObject method to export
any object. Such an object is responsible for providing appropriate remote semantics for
equals, hashCode, and toString.

```
public class UnicastRemoteObject extends RemoteServer
// Public Constructor
  protected UnicastRemoteObject() throws RemoteException
// Public Class Method
  public static RemoteStub exportObject(Remote obj)
    throws RemoteException
```

```
// Public Method
  public Object clone() throws CloneNotSupportedException
```

JAVA.SQL.CONNECTION

A Connection interface represents a database session. The Driver.connect method returns an object that implements the Connection interface. SQL queries and updates are executed within the context of a Connection, using the Statement object returned by the createStatement method. By default, autocommit is enabled. If you disable autocommit by invoking setAutoCommit with an argument value of false, your changes must be followed by a call to commit; otherwise, they will be lost. The rollback method discards pending database changes.

The setTransactionIsolation method lets you specify the desired level of protection against database anomalies; a given database may not support one or more levels. The getMetaData method returns an object that encapsulates comprehensive information describing the structure and capabilities of the database. The getWarnings method returns the next instance of SQLWarning posted against the Connection; the clearWarnings method discards pending warnings. The close method ends the database session and frees associated resources. The prepareStatement method creates a preparedStatement object that can efficiently execute a SQL statement multiple times; the prepareCall method creates a CallableStatement that accesses a stored database procedure.

```
public interface Connection
// Public Fields
  public static final int TRANSACTION_NONE
  public static final int TRANSACTION_READ_COMMITTED
  public static final int TRANSACTION_READ_UNCOMMITTED
  public static final int TRANSACTION_REPEATABLE_READ
  public static final int TRANSACTION_SERIALIZABLE
// Public Methods
  public abstract void clearWarnings()
    throws SQLException
  public abstract void close() throws SQLException
  public abstract Statement createStatement()
  public abstract void commit() throws SQLException
    throws SQLException
  public abstract boolean getAutoCommit()
    throws SQLException
  public abstract String getCatalog()
    throws SQLException
  public abstract DatabaseMetaData getMetaData()
    throws SQLException
  public abstract int getTransactionIsolation()
    throws SQLException
```

```
public abstract SQLWarning getWarnings()
  throws SQLException
public abstract boolean isClosed()
  throws SQLException
public abstract boolean isReadOnly()
  throws SQLException
public abstract String nativeSQL(String sql)
  throws SQLException
public abstract CallableStatement prepareCall(
  String sql) throws SQLException
public abstract PreparedStatement prepareStatement(
  String sql) throws SQLException
public abstract void rollback() throws SQLException
public abstract void setAutoCommit(
  boolean autoCommit) throws SQLException
public abstract void setCatalog(String catalog)
  throws SQLException
public abstract void setReadOnly(boolean readOnly)
  throws SQLException
public abstract void setTransactionIsolation(
  int level) throws SQLException
```

JAVA.SQL.DATABASEMETADATA

The DatabaseMetaData object provides information about the structure and capabilities of a database. A given database may not support all the methods of DatabaseMetaData, thus throwing an SQLException if a program invokes an unsupported method. Some methods let you specify a pattern String. In these, "%" means match any substring of zero or more characters, and "_" means match any single character.

```
public interface DatabaseMetaData
// Public Fields
  public static final int bestRowNotPseudo
  public static final int bestRowPseudo
  public static final int bestRowSession
  public static final int bestRowTemporary
  public static final int bestRowTransaction
  public static final int bestRowUnknown
  public static final int columnNoNulls
  public static final int columnNullable
  public static final int columnNullableUnknown
  public static final int importedKeyCascade
  public static final int importedKeyInitiallyDeferred
  public static final int importedKeyInitiallyImmediate
  public static final int importedKeyNoAction
  public static final int importedKeyNotDeferrable
  public static final int importedKeyRestrict
  public static final int importedKeySetDefault
  public static final int importedKeySetNull
```

```
public static final int procedureColumnIn
public static final int procedureColumnInOut
public static final int procedureColumnOut
public static final int procedureColumnResult
public static final int procedureColumnReturn
public static final int procedureColumnUnknown
public static final int procedureNoResult
public static final int procedureNoNulls
public static final int procedureNullable
public static final int procedureNullableUnknown
public static final int procedureResultUnknown
public static final int procedureReturnsResult
public static final short tableIndexClustered
public static final short tableIndexHashed
public static final short tableIndexOther
public static final short tableIndexStatistic
public static final int typeNoNulls
public static final int typeNullable
public static final int typeNullableUnknown
public static final int typePredNone
public static final int typePredChar
public static final int typePredBasic
public static final int typeSearchable
public static final int versionColumnUnknown
public static final int versionColumnNotPseudo
public static final int versionColumnPseudo
```

Because this class provides so many methods, it's described in several sections:

- Methods that describe the database engine, the database driver, and the database session
- Methods that describe the database structure
- Methods that describe the database's SQL implementation
- Methods that describe database limits

Methods That Describe the Database Engine, the Database Driver, and the Database Session

These methods return such information as the database product name and version, the driver name and version, the database URL, the database user ID used to establish the session, the default transaction isolation level, and whether the database is writable.

```
public abstract String getDatabaseProductName()
  throws SQLException
public abstract String getDatabaseProductVersion()
  throws SQLException
public abstract int getDefaultTransactionIsolation()
  throws SQLException
```

```
public abstract String getDriverName()
   throws SQLException
public abstract String getDriverVersion()
   throws SQLException
public abstract int getDriverMajorVersion()
public abstract int getDriverMinorVersion()
public abstract int getMaxConnections()
   throws SQLException
public abstract String getURL() throws SQLException
public abstract String getUserName()
   throws SQLException
public abstract boolean isReadOnly()
```

Methods That Describe the Database Structure

These methods return information that describes the structure of the database. Using them, you can discover what tables the database contains, what columns each table contains, the data type of each column, and other useful information. Many accept String arguments that specify patterns. Each method returns an instance of ResultSet that contains the requested information. You can use the ResultSet.getMetaData method to obtain a ResultSetMetadata object that describes the result set. The Java Developer's Kit documentation specifies the result set columns and their meanings.

```
public abstract ResultSet getBestRowIdentifier(
   String catalog, String schema, String table, int scope,
   boolean nullable) throws SQLException
public abstract ResultSet getCatalogs()
   throws SQLException
public abstract ResultSet getColumnPrivileges(
   String catalog, String schema, String table,
   String columnNamePattern) throws SQLException
public abstract ResultSet getColumns(String catalog,
   String schemaPattern, String tableNamePattern,
   String columnNamePattern) throws SQLException
public abstract ResultSet getCrossReference(
   String primaryCatalog, String primarySchema,
   String primaryTable, String foreignCatalog,
   String foreignSchema, String foreignTable)
   throws SQLException
public abstract ResultSet getExportedKeys(String catalog,
   String schema, String table) throws SQLException
public abstract ResultSet getImportedKeys(
   String catalog, String schema, String table)
   throws SQLException
public abstract ResultSet getIndexInfo(
   String catalog, String schema, String table,
   boolean unique, boolean approximate)
   throws SQLException
```

```
public abstract ResultSet getPrimaryKeys(
  String catalog, String schema, String table)
  throws SQLException
public abstract ResultSet getProcedureColumns(
  String catalog, String schemaPattern,
  String procedureNamePattern, String columnNamePattern)
  throws SQLException
public abstract ResultSet getProcedures(
  String catalog, String schemaPattern,
  String procedureNamePattern) throws SQLException
public abstract ResultSet getSchemas()
  throws SQLException
public abstract ResultSet getTablePrivileges(
  String catalog, String schemaPattern,
  String tableNamePattern) throws SQLException
public abstract ResultSet getTableTypes()
  throws SQLException
public abstract ResultSet getTables(
  String catalog, String schemaPattern,
  String tableNamePattern, String types[])
  throws SQLException
public abstract ResultSet getVersionColumns(
  String catalog, String schema, String table)
  throws SQLException
```

Methods That Describe the Database's SQL Implementation

These methods describe the SQL dialect implemented by the database. Using them, you can discover what level of the SQL standard grammar the database supports and how the database handles SQL constructs that are apt to be nonportable.

```
public abstract boolean allProceduresAreCallable()
  throws SQLException
public abstract boolean allTablesAreSelectable()
  throws SQLException
public abstract boolean
  dataDefinitionCausesTransactionCommit()
  throws SQLException
public abstract boolean
  dataDefinitionIgnoredInTransactions()
  throws SQLException
public abstract String getCatalogSeparator()
  throws SQLException
public abstract String getCatalogTerm()
  throws SQLException
public abstract String getExtraNameCharacters()
  throws SQLException
public abstract String getIdentifierQuoteString()
  throws SQLException
```

```
public abstract String getNumericFunctions()
  throws SQLException
public abstract String getProcedureTerm()
  throws SQLException
public abstract String getSchemaTerm()
  throws SQLException
public abstract String getSearchStringEscape()
  throws SQLException
public abstract String getSQLKeywords()
  throws SQLException
public abstract String getStringFunctions()
  throws SQLException
public abstract String getSystemFunctions()
  throws SQLException
public abstract String getTimeDateFunctions()
  throws SQLException
public abstract ResultSet getTypeInfo()
  throws SQLException
public abstract boolean isCatalogAtStart()
  throws SQLException
public abstract boolean nullPlusNonNullIsNull()
  throws SQLException
  throws SQLException
public abstract boolean nullsAreSortedAtEnd()
  throws SQLException
public abstract boolean nullsAreSortedAtStart()
  throws SQLException
public abstract boolean nullsAreSortedHigh()
  throws SQLException
public abstract boolean nullsAreSortedLow()
  throws SQLException
public abstract boolean storesLowerCaseIdentifiers()
  throws SQLException
public abstract boolean
  storesLowerCaseQuotedIdentifiers()
  throws SQLException
public abstract boolean storesMixedCaseIdentifiers()
  throws SQLException
public abstract boolean
  storesMixedCaseQuotedIdentifiers()
  throws SQLException
public abstract boolean
  storesUpperCaseQuotedIdentifiers()
  throws SQLException
public abstract boolean storesUpperCaseIdentifiers()
  throws SQLException
public abstract boolean
  supportsAlterTableWithAddColumn()
  throws SQLException
public abstract boolean
  supportsAlterTableWithDropColumn()
```

```
   throws SQLException
public abstract boolean supportsANSI92EntryLevelSQL()
   throws SQLException
public abstract boolean supportsANSI92FullSQL()
   throws SQLException
public abstract boolean supportsANSI92IntermediateSQL()
   throws SQLException
public abstract boolean
   supportsCatalogsInDataManipulation()
   throws SQLException
public abstract boolean
   supportsCatalogsInIndexDefinitions()
   throws SQLException
public abstract boolean
   supportsCatalogsInPrivilegeDefinitions()
   throws SQLException
public abstract boolean
   supportsCatalogsInProcedureCalls()
   throws SQLException
public abstract boolean
   supportsCatalogsInTableDefinitions()
   throws SQLException
public abstract boolean supportsColumnAliasing()
   throws SQLException
public abstract boolean supportsConvert()
   throws SQLException
public abstract boolean supportsConvert(
   int fromType, int toType) throws SQLException
public abstract boolean supportsCoreSQLGrammar()
   throws SQLException
public abstract boolean
   supportsCorrelatedSubqueries() throws SQLException
public abstract boolean
   supportsDataDefinitionAndDataManipulationTransactions()
   throws SQLException
public abstract boolean
   supportsDataManipulationTransactionsOnly()
   throws SQLException
public abstract boolean
   supportsDifferentTableCorrelationNames()
   throws SQLException
public abstract boolean
   supportsExpressionsInOrderBy() throws SQLException
public abstract boolean supportsExtendedSQLGrammar()
   throws SQLException
public abstract boolean supportsFullOuterJoins()
   throws SQLException
public abstract boolean supportsGroupBy()
   throws SQLException
public abstract boolean supportsGroupByBeyondSelect()
   throws SQLException
```

```
public abstract boolean supportsGroupByUnrelated()
  throws SQLException
public abstract boolean
  supportsIntegrityEnhancementFacility()
  throws SQLException
public abstract boolean supportsLikeEscapeClause()
  throws SQLException
public abstract boolean supportsLimitedOuterJoins()
  throws SQLException
public abstract boolean supportsMinimumSQLGrammar()
  throws SQLException
public abstract boolean supportsMixedCaseIdentifiers()
  throws SQLException
public abstract boolean
  supportsMixedCaseQuotedIdentifiers()
  throws SQLException
public abstract boolean supportsMultipleResultSets()
  throws SQLException
public abstract boolean
  supportsMultipleTransactions()
  throws SQLException
public abstract boolean supportsNonNullableColumns()
  throws SQLException
public abstract boolean
  supportsOpenCursorsAcrossCommit()
  throws SQLException
public abstract boolean
  supportsOpenCursorsAcrossRollback()
  throws SQLException
public abstract boolean
  supportsOpenStatementsAcrossCommit()
  throws SQLException
public abstract boolean
  supportsOpenStatementsAcrossRollback()
  throws SQLException
public abstract boolean
  supportsOrderByUnrelated() throws SQLException
public abstract boolean supportsOuterJoins()
  throws SQLException
public abstract boolean supportsPositionedDelete()
  throws SQLException
public abstract boolean supportsPositionedUpdate()
  throws SQLException
public abstract boolean
  supportsSchemasInDataManipulation()
  throws SQLException
public abstract boolean
  supportsSchemasInIndexDefinitions()
  throws SQLException
public abstract boolean
  supportsSchemasInPrivilegeDefinitions()
```

```
    throws SQLException
public abstract boolean
  supportsSchemasInProcedureCalls()
    throws SQLException
public abstract boolean
  supportsSchemasInTableDefinitions()
    throws SQLException
public abstract boolean supportsSelectForUpdate()
    throws SQLException
public abstract boolean supportsStoredProcedures()
    throws SQLException
public abstract boolean
  supportsSubqueriesInComparisons()
    throws SQLException
public abstract boolean supportsSubqueriesInExists()
    throws SQLException
public abstract boolean supportsSubqueriesInIns()
    throws SQLException
public abstract boolean
  supportsSubqueriesInQuantifieds()
    throws SQLException
public abstract boolean
  supportsTableCorrelationNames() throws SQLException
public abstract boolean
  supportsTransactionIsolationLevel(int level)
    throws SQLException
public abstract boolean supportsTransactions()
    throws SQLException
public abstract boolean supportsUnion()
    throws SQLException
public abstract boolean supportsUnionAll()
    throws SQLException
public abstract boolean usesLocalFiles()
    throws SQLException
public abstract boolean usesLocalFilePerTable()
    throws SQLException
```

Methods That Describe Database Limits

These methods describe maximum limits on lengths of literals, names, and other database entities.

```
public abstract boolean doesMaxRowSizeIncludeBlobs()
    throws SQLException
public abstract int getMaxBinaryLiteralLength()
    throws SQLException
public abstract int getMaxCatalogNameLength()
    throws SQLException
public abstract int getMaxCharLiteralLength()
    throws SQLException
```

```
public abstract int getMaxColumnNameLength()
  throws SQLException
public abstract int getMaxColumnsInGroupBy()
  throws SQLException
public abstract int getMaxColumnsInIndex()
  throws SQLException
public abstract int getMaxColumnsInOrderBy()
  throws SQLException
public abstract int getMaxColumnsInSelect()
  throws SQLException
public abstract int getMaxColumnsInTable()
  throws SQLException
public abstract int getMaxCursorNameLength()
  throws SQLException
public abstract int getMaxIndexLength()
  throws SQLException
public abstract int getMaxProcedureNameLength()
  throws SQLException
public abstract int getMaxRowSize()
  throws SQLException
public abstract int getMaxSchemaNameLength()
  throws SQLException
public abstract int getMaxStatements()
  throws SQLException
public abstract int getMaxStatementLength()
  throws SQLException
public abstract int getMaxTableNameLength()
  throws SQLException
public abstract int getMaxTablesInSelect()
  throws SQLException
public abstract int getMaxUserNameLength()
  throws SQLException
```

JAVA.SQL.DATE

The Date class extends the `java.util.Date` class. It lets JDBC identify a SQL date object and provides formatting and parsing operations that support the JDBC escape syntax for date values.

```
public class Date extends Date
// Public Constructors
  public Date(int year, int month, int day)
  public Date(long date)
// Public Class Method
  public static Date valueOf(String s)
// Public Methods
  public int getHours()
  public int getMinutes()
  public int getSeconds()
  public void setHours(int i)
```

```
public void setMinutes(int i)
public void setSeconds(int i)
public void setTime(long date)
public String toString()
```

JAVA.SQL.DRIVER

The Driver interface specifies methods that all JDBC drivers must implement. When a JDBC-compliant class that implements Driver is loaded, it automatically creates a singleton instance and registers the instance with the DriverManager. Therefore, you can load and register a driver by executing a statement such as this:

```
Class.forName("driver class name")
```

You don't generally need to invoke methods of the Driver interface; the DriverManager class and Connection object will invoke them for you.

```
public interface Driver
// Public Methods
  public abstract boolean acceptsURL(String url)
    throws SQLException
  public abstract Connection connect(String url,
    Properties info)
    throws SQLException
  public abstract int getMajorVersion()
  public abstract int getMinorVersion()
  public abstract DriverPropertyInfo[] getPropertyInfo(
    String url, Properties info) throws SQLException
  public abstract boolean jdbcCompliant()
```

JAVA.SQL.DRIVERMANAGER

The DriverManager class manages a set of JDBC drivers and provides several methods that let you control database sessions. When the DriverManager class is loaded, it attempts to load the classes named by the jdbc.drivers system property. The getConnection method locates a suitable driver for connecting to the specified database and returns a Connection instance. The println method adds an entry to the JDBC log. The setLoginTimeout method lets you specify a timeout interval for establishing a database session. If the timeout interval expires before a session is opened, the method throws an SQLException.

```
public class DriverManager extends Object
// Public Class Methods
  public static void deregisterDriver(Driver driver)
    throws SQLException
  public static synchronized Connection getConnection(
    String url) throws SQLException
```

```
public static synchronized Connection getConnection(
  String url, Properties info) throws SQLException
public static synchronized Connection getConnection(
  String url, String user, String password)
  throws SQLException
public static Driver getDriver(String url)
  throws SQLException
public static Enumeration getDrivers()
public static PrintStream getLogStream()
public static int getLoginTimeout()
public static void println(String message)
public static synchronized void registerDriver(
  Driver driver) throws SQLException
public static void setLogStream(PrintStream out)
public static void setLoginTimeout(int seconds)
```

JAVA.SQL.RESULTSET

The ResultSet interface establishes a framework for accessing SQL query results. Table rows are retrieved in sequence; for maximum compatibility, the columns of a row should be retrieved in sequence and should not be retrieved more than once. The ResultSet encapsulates a cursor that's initially positioned before the first row of data. The next method advances the cursor to the next row, returning false if no more rows are available. The getXXX methods let you access column values by column number or name. Accessing by column number is somewhat more efficient; column numbers start with 1. JDBC attempts to convert the type of the SQL value to the Java type corresponding to the particular getXXX method invoked. A ResultSet is automatically closed when the associated Statement is closed or executed again. The getMetaData method returns a ResultSetMetadata object that describes the ResultSet.

```
public interface ResultSet
// Public Methods
  public abstract InputStream getAsciiStream(
    String columnName) throws SQLException
  public abstract void clearWarnings()
    throws SQLException
  public abstract void close()
    throws SQLException
  public abstract int findColumn(String columnName)
    throws SQLException
  public abstract InputStream getAsciiStream(
    int columnIndex) throws SQLException
  public abstract BigDecimal getBigDecimal(
    int columnIndex, int scale) throws SQLException
  public abstract BigDecimal getBigDecimal(
    String columnName, int scale) throws SQLException
  public abstract InputStream getBinaryStream(
    int columnIndex) throws SQLException
```

```
public abstract InputStream getBinaryStream(
  String columnName) throws SQLException
public abstract boolean getBoolean(int columnIndex)
  throws SQLException
public abstract boolean getBoolean(
  String columnName) throws SQLException
public abstract byte getByte(int columnIndex)
  throws SQLException
public abstract byte getByte(String columnName)
  throws SQLException
public abstract byte[] getBytes(int columnIndex)
  throws SQLException
public abstract byte[] getBytes(String columnName)
  throws SQLException
public abstract String getCursorName()
  throws SQLException
public abstract Date getDate(int columnIndex)
  throws SQLException
public abstract Date getDate(String columnName)
  throws SQLException
public abstract double getDouble(int columnIndex)
  throws SQLException
public abstract double getDouble(String columnName)
  throws SQLException
public abstract float getFloat(int columnIndex)
  throws SQLException
public abstract float getFloat(String columnName)
  throws SQLException
public abstract int getInt(int columnIndex)
  throws SQLException
public abstract int getInt(String columnName)
  throws SQLException
public abstract long getLong(int columnIndex)
  throws SQLException
public abstract long getLong(String columnName)
  throws SQLException
public abstract ResultSetMetaData getMetaData()
  throws SQLException
public abstract Object getObject(int columnIndex)
  throws SQLException
public abstract Object getObject(String columnName)
  throws SQLException
public abstract short getShort(int columnIndex)
  throws SQLException
public abstract short getShort(String columnName)
  throws SQLException
public abstract String getString(String columnName)
  throws SQLException
public abstract String getString(int columnIndex)
  throws SQLException
```

```
public abstract Time getTime(int columnIndex)
   throws SQLException
public abstract Time getTime(String columnName)
   throws SQLException
public abstract Timestamp getTimestamp(
   int columnIndex) throws SQLException
public abstract Timestamp getTimestamp(
   String columnName) throws SQLException
public abstract InputStream getUnicodeStream(
   int columnIndex) throws SQLException
public abstract InputStream getUnicodeStream(
   String columnName) throws SQLException
public abstract SQLWarning getWarnings()
   throws SQLException
public abstract boolean next()
   throws SQLException
public abstract boolean wasNull()
   throws SQLException
```

JAVA.SQL.RESULTSETMETADATA

The ResultSetMetaData interface establishes a framework for accessing information describing a result set. The getColumnCount method returns the number of columns in the result set. The getColumnLabel method returns the default label of the specified column. The getColumnName method returns the name of the specified column. The getColumnType returns a code (see java.sql.Types) for the data type of the specified column. For numeric columns, the getPrecision method returns the number of significant digits, and the getScale method returns the decimal point offset.

```
public interface ResultSetMetaData
// Public Class Fields
  public static final int columnNoNulls
  public static final int columnNullable
  public static final int columnNullableUnknown
// Public Methods
  public abstract String getCatalogName(int column)
    throws SQLException
  public abstract int getColumnCount()
    throws SQLException
  public abstract int getColumnDisplaySize(int column)
    throws SQLException
  public abstract String getColumnLabel(int column)
    throws SQLException
  public abstract String getColumnName(int column)
    throws SQLException
  public abstract int getColumnType(int column)
    throws SQLException
  public abstract String getColumnTypeName(int column)
    throws SQLException
```

```
public abstract String getSchemaName(int column)
  throws SQLException
public abstract int getPrecision(int column)
  throws SQLException
public abstract int getScale(int column)
  throws SQLException
public abstract String getTableName(int column)
  throws SQLException
public abstract boolean isAutoIncrement(int column)
  throws SQLException
public abstract boolean isCaseSensitive(int column)
  throws SQLException
public abstract boolean isCurrency(int column)
  throws SQLException
public abstract boolean isDefinitelyWritable(
  int column) throws SQLException
public abstract int isNullable(int column)
  throws SQLException
public abstract boolean isReadOnly(int column)
  throws SQLException
public abstract boolean isSearchable(int column)
  throws SQLException
public abstract boolean isSigned(int column)
  throws SQLException
public abstract boolean isWritable(int column)
  throws SQLException
```

JAVA.SQL.STATEMENT

The Statement interface establishes a framework for executing SQL queries and updates and for accessing their results. The cancel method cancels a query being executed in another thread. The clearWarnings method deletes warnings posted against the Statement. The executeQuery method executes a query and returns a result set. The executeUpdate method executes an update and returns a count of the updated rows. The execute method executes a query that returns multiple results. The methods getMoreResults, getResultSet, and getUpdateCount let you access the results. The close method closes the Statement and any associated result sets. The getWarnings method retrieves the first warning pending against the Statement. The setQueryTimeout lets you specify how long the driver should wait for query completion.

```
public interface Statement
public abstract void cancel() throws SQLException
public abstract void clearWarnings()
  throws SQLException
public abstract void close() throws SQLException
public abstract boolean execute(String sql)
  throws SQLException
```

```
public abstract ResultSet executeQuery(String sql)
  throws SQLException
public abstract int executeUpdate(String sql)
  throws SQLException
public abstract int getMaxFieldSize()
  throws SQLException
public abstract int getMaxRows()
  throws SQLException
public abstract boolean getMoreResults()
  throws SQLException
public abstract int getQueryTimeout()
  throws SQLException
public abstract ResultSet getResultSet()
  throws SQLException
public abstract int getUpdateCount()
  throws SQLException
public abstract SQLWarning getWarnings()
  throws SQLException
public abstract void setCursorName(String name)
  throws SQLException
public abstract void setEscapeProcessing(
  boolean enable) throws SQLException
public abstract void setMaxFieldSize(int max)
  throws SQLException
public abstract void setMaxRows(int max)
  throws SQLException
public abstract void setQueryTimeout(int seconds)
  throws SQLException
```

JAVA.SQL.TIME

The Time class extends java.util.Date, letting JDBC identify a SQL time object and providing formatting and parsing operations that support the JDBC escape syntax for time values.

```
public class Time extends Date
// Public Constructors
  public Time(int hour, int minute, int second)
    public Time(long time)
// Public Class Methods
  public static Time valueOf(String s)
// Public Methods
  public int getDate()
  public int getDay()
  public int getMonth()
  public int getYear()
  public void setDate(int i)
  public void setMonth(int i)
  public void setTime(long time)
  public void setYear(int i)
  public String toString()
```

JAVA.SQL.TIMESTAMP

The Timestamp class extends java.util.Date, letting JDBC identify a SQL timestamp object and providing formatting and parsing operations that support the JDBC escape syntax for timestamp values. The java.util.Date class stores time with a one-second resolution. The Timestamp class includes an int that stores time with nanosecond resolution. The getNanos method returns the value of the fractional second. The after and before methods test whether a specified Timestamp instance is later or earlier than the current instance.

```
public class Timestamp extends Date
// Public Constructors
public Timestamp(int year, int month, int date,
    int hour, int minute, int second, int nano)
  public Timestamp(long time)
// Public Class Methods
  public static Timestamp valueOf(String s)
// Public Methods
  public boolean after(Timestamp ts)
  public boolean before(Timestamp ts)
  public boolean equals(Timestamp ts)
  public int getNanos()
  public void setNanos(int n)
  public String toString()
```

JAVA.SQL.TYPES

The Types class defines codes used to represent the SQL data types. These codes are used by several JDBC methods, including ResultSetMetaData.getColumnType.

```
public class Types extends Object
public static final int BIGINT
public static final int BINARY
public static final int BIT
public static final int CHAR
public static final int DATE
public static final int DECIMAL
public static final int DOUBLE
public static final int FLOAT
public static final int INTEGER
public static final int LONGVARBINARY
public static final int LONGVARCHAR
public static final int NULL
public static final int NUMERIC
public static final int OTHER
public static final int REAL
public static final int SMALLINT
public static final int TIME
public static final int TIMESTAMP
```

```
public static final int TINYINT
public static final int VARBINARY
public static final int VARCHAR
```

ORG.COM.CORBA.BINDOPTIONS

The BindOptions class represents the options used when a client binds to a server. You pass these options to the bind method provided by the server's Helper class. If the *defer* argument is true, connection is delayed until the first request is invoked on the server. If the *rebind* argument is true, the client will attempt to recover from a lost connection by binding to another server.

```
public class BindOptions
// Public Constructor
  public BindOptions(boolean defer, boolean rebind)
```

ORG.COM.CORBA.BOA

The BOA class represents a Basic Object Adapter, which lets servers activate and deactivate the objects they offer to clients. The obj_is_ready method makes an object available to clients. The deactivate_obj method makes an object unavailable. A server should invoke impl_is_ready after it has activated all the objects it implements. The get_Principal method returns the principal associated with an object.

```
public abstract class BOA extends Object
// Public Methods
  public void deactivate_obj(Object obj)
  public Principal get_Principal(Object obj)
  public void impl_is_ready()
  public abstract void impl_is_ready(String service,
    Activator activator)
  public abstract void impl_is_ready(String service,
    Activator activator, boolean block)
  public void obj_is_ready(Object obj)
  public abstract void obj_is_ready(Object obj,
    String service, byte [] data)
```

ORG.COM.CORBA.COMPLETIONSTATUS

The CompletionStatus class indicates whether an operation was completed before an exception was raised.

```
public final class CompletionStatus extends Object
// Public Fields
  public final static int _COMPLETED_YES
  public final static int _COMPLETED_NO
  public final static int _COMPLETED_MAYBE
```

```
  public final static CompletionStatus COMPLETED_YES
  public final static CompletionStatus COMPLETED_NO
  public final static CompletionStatus COMPLETED_MAYBE
// Public Class Method
  public static CompletionStatus from_int(int value)
// Public Method
  public final int value()
```

ORG.COM.CORBA.CONTEXT

The Context interface establishes a framework for maintaining a client's property list that's propagated to the server when the client issues a request. The use of the properties is not specified by CORBA. The properties are organized as a tree; the default context can be accessed by invoking the ORB.get_default_context method.

```
public interface Context
// Public Methods
  public String context_name()
  public Context create_child(String context)
  public void delete_values(String property)
  public NVList get_values(String start, boolean restrict, String name)
  public Context parent()
  public void set_one_value(String property, Any value)
  public void set_values(NVList values)
```

ORG.COM.CORBA.INVALIDNAME

The InvalidName exception is raised when the ORB is unable to resolve any of the names returned by list_initial_services to its corresponding implementation object.

```
public class InvalidName extends UserException
```

ORG.COM.CORBA.OBJECT

The Object interface is the root interface of the CORBA inheritance hierarchy. It provides runtime type information and platform-independent reference equivalence testing. Table B.1 summarizes the key methods of the Object interface.

TABLE B.1 KEY METHODS OF THE Object INTERFACE

Method	Function
bind_options	Sets the bind options associated with the current object.
boa	Returns the BOA associated with a particular request or the default BOA if no request is active.

continues

TABLE B.1   CONTINUED

Method	*Function*
clone	Creates a copy of the current object, which receives its own server connection.
create_request	Creates and initializes a dynamic invocation request.
get_interface	Returns the interface definition of the current object.
hash	Computes a positive hash value for the current object.
is_a	Queries whether an object implements the specified interface.
is_bound	Returns true if a network connection to the implementation object has been established.
is_equivalent	Compares the Interoperable Object Reference of the specified object with that of the current object and returns true if they are equivalent.
is_local	Returns true if the current object resides in the local address space.
is_persistent	Returns true if the current object retains its value beyond the lifetime of its implementing process.
is_remote	Returns true if the current object resides in a remote address space.
non_existent	Uses ping to determine whether the implementation object is active and returns false if the object is found to be active.
object_name	Returns the name of the object implementation.
principal	Returns the principal associated with a request on the object or sets the principal associated with the current object to the specified principal.
repository_id	Returns the repository identifier of the current object implementation's most derived interface.
resolve_reference	Creates an empty dynamic invocation request. A client application can use the resolve_reference method to resolve the server-side interface with the specified service identifier.

The following method headers specify the arguments of the methods of the Object interface:

```
public interface Object
// Public Methods
  public BindOptions _bind_options()
  public BOA _boa()
  public Object _clone()
  public Request _create_request(Context context,
    String op, NVList args, NamedValue result,
    TypeCode[] exceptions, String [] contexts)
  public InterfaceDef _get_interface()
  public int _hash(int max)
```

```
public _is_a(String repository)
public boolean _is_bound()
public boolean _is_equivalent(Object obj)
public boolean _is_local()
public boolean _is_persistent()
public boolean _is_remote()
public boolean _non_existent()
public String _object_name()
public Principal _principal()
public void _principal(Principal principal)
public String _repository_id()
public Request _request(String op)
public Object _resolve_reference(String id)
```

B

ORG.COM.CORBA.ORB

The ORB class represents an Object Request Broker and provides a way to initialize the CORBA infrastructure, as well as a variety of methods used by clients and servers. Table B.2 summarizes the key methods of the ORB class.

The ORB class also provides a set of methods for handling NamedValue, NVList, DynAny, DynArray, DynEnum, DynSeqeuence, DynStruct, and DynUnion objects and a set of methods that return TypeCode objects of various types. Consult the Visibroker documentation for information about these methods.

TABLE B.2 KEY METHODS OF THE ORB INTERFACE

Method	Function
init	Initializes the ORB for use by an application or applet.
bind	Attempts a bind on the ORB and returns a general reference.
BOA_init	Initializes a BOA and returns a reference to the BOA.
create_output_stream	Creates an output stream.
create_input_stream	Creates an input stream from an output stream. The input stream lets programs read the bytes written to the output stream.
default_bind_options	Gets or sets the global default bind options.
defaultPrincipal	Gets or sets the global default Principal.
get_default_context	Returns the global default Context.
list_initial_services	Returns a list containing the names of object services initially available.

continues

TABLE B.2   CONTINUED

Method	Function
object_to_string	Converts an object reference to a `String` and returns the result.
string_to_object	Converts a `String` to an object reference, narrowed to a specified interface, and returns the result.
get_next_response	Blocks until a response to a deferred operation request becomes available.
poll_next_response	Returns `true` if a response to a deferred operation is available.
resolve_initial_references	Resolves a member of the list returned by `list_initial_services` to its corresponding implementation object and returns the result.
send_multiple_requests_deferred	Sends a set of operation requests without blocking.
send_multiple_requests_oneway	Sends a set of one way operation requests, which have no return values.

The following method headers specify the arguments of the methods of the ORB class:

```
public abstract class ORB
// Public Class Methods
  public static BOA BOA_init()
  public static ORB init(String[] args, Properties p)
  public static ORB init(Applet app, Properties p)
// Public Methods
  public Object bind(String repository,
    String object_name, String host_name, BindOptions opt)
  public public BOA BOA_init(String boa_type, Properties p)
  public abstract TypeCode create_alias_to(
    String repository, String type_name, TypeCode type)
  public abstract Any create_any()
  public abstract TypeCode create_array_tc(int len,
  TypeCode type)
  public DynAny create_basic_dyn_any(TypeCode type)
    throws InconsistentTypeCode
  public abstract ContextList create_context_list()
  public DynAny create_dyn_any(Any value)
  public DynArray create_dyn_array(TypeCode type)
    throws InconsistentTypeCode
  public DynEnum create_dyn_enum(TypeCode type)
    throws InconsistentTypeCode
  public DynSequence create_dyn_sequence(TypeCode type)
    throws InconsistentTypeCode
  public DynStruct create_dyn_struct(TypeCode type)
    throws InconsistentTypeCode
```

```
public DynUnion create_dyn_union(TypeCode type_
  throws InconsistentTypeCode
public TypeCode create_enum_tc(String repository,
  String type, String [] members)
public abstract Environment create_environment()
public abstract TypeCode create_estruct_tc(
  String repository, String type, TypeCode base,
  StructMember [] members)
public abstract TypeCode create_exception_tc(
  String repository, String type,
  StructMember [] members)
public abstract InputStream create_input_stream(
  OutputStream out)
public abstract TypeCode create_interface_tc(
  String repository, String type)
public abstract NVList create_list(int len)
public abstract NamedValue create_named_value(
  String name, Any value, int flags)
public abstract NVList create_operation_list(
  OperationDef op_def)
public abstract OutputStream create_output_stream()
public abstract TypeCode create_recursive_sequence_tc(
  int len, int offset)
public abstract TypeCode create_sequence_tc(
  int len, TypeCode type)
public abstract TypeCode create_String_tc(int len)
public abstract TypeCode create_struct_tc(
  String repository, String type,
  StructMember[] members)
public abstract TypeCode create_union_tc(
  String repository, String type, TypeCode disc_type,
  UnionMembers [] members)
public abstract TypeCode create_wstring_tc(int len)
public abstract BindOptions default_bind_options()
public abstract void default_bind_options(
  BindOptions opts)
public abstract Principal default_principal()
public abstract void default_principal(
  Principal principal)
public abstract Context get_default_context()
public abstract Request get_next_response()
public abstract TypeCode get_primitive_tc(
  TCKind kind)
public abstract String [] list_initial_services()
public abstract String object_to_string(Object obj)
public abstract boolean poll_next_response()
public abstract Object resolve_initial_references(
  String id) throws InvalidName
public abstract void send_multiple_requests_deferred(
  Request [] reqs)
```

```
public abstract void send_multiple_requests_oneway(
  Request [] reqs)
public abstract Object string_to_object(String ior)
```

ORG.COM.CORBA.PRINCIPAL

The Principal class encapsulates a byte array that a client can associate with an operation request. Client applications can set a default principal by invoking the ORB.default_principal method.

```
public abstract class Principal
// Public Methods
  public abstract void name(byte [] name)
  public abstract byte[] name()
```

HOW TO GET THE MOST FROM THE CD-ROM

IN THIS CHAPTER

The CD-ROM that accompanies this book contains valuable software as well as other helpful material. In addition to the software, the CD contains the complete code listings from each chapter and other useful documents.

WHAT'S ON THIS CD-ROM

This CD-ROM contains scripts and source code mentioned throughout the book as well electronic books, third-party software and more. The following is an overview of the directory structure of this disc:

- Chapter*xx*\Listings\—Author examples and code listings as mentioned in the book. *xx* is the chapter number.
- \Documents\—Documents related to Java distributed computing, such as the CORBA specification in Portable Document Format (PDF).
- \Software\—Third-party software tools for developing Java distributed object applications and for use with the coding examples provided in the book including:

  Visibroker 3.2 from Inprise

  Sniff+ 3.0 from TakeFive

  JBuilder 2 Publisher's Edition

  Objectspace Voyager software

  JacORB

CODE LISTINGS

The code listings can be copied directly from the CD, compiled, and run, in order to supplement the discussions in each chapter. These are provided as a learning tool. The code listings are organized in subdirectories by chapter. For example, if you need to find the listing for Passenger.java from Chapter 12, it is located in the path

```
Drive:\Chapter12\Listings\filename.ext
```

Variable default CDR-Drive is the CD-ROM drive letter for your system and code.exe is the file for which you're searching. In this example, it is Passenger.java.

SYSTEM REQUIREMENTS FOR THIS CD-ROM

This CD-ROM was configured for use on systems running Windows NT 4.0 Workstation or Windows 95 on an Intel-based system. Table C.1 describes the minimum system requirements to install the CD.

TABLE C.1 System Requirements

Component	Requirement
Processor	486DX or higher processor
Operating System	Microsoft Windows® NT 4.0 Workstation or Windows® 95
Memory	24MB
Free storage space	9.5MB minimum
Monitor	VGA or higher resolution video adapter (SVGA 256-color recommended)
Other	Mouse or compatible pointing device
CD-ROM drive	2X or higher
Web browser	Such as Netscape or Internet Explorer
Optional	An active Internet connection (highly recommended)

HOW TO INSTALL PRODUCTS FROM THE CD-ROM

Under Windows NT/95, just insert the disc and follow the directions of the program to create a program group for this CD-ROM. From within this program group, you can install the source code and applications included on this disc. You might also review documentation, preview files, or install products using Windows Explorer.

> **NOTE**
>
> If you have AutoPlay disabled on your Windows NT/95 computer, the CD-ROM will *not* automatically install the Program Group.

To start the CD Product Browser manually, go to the Start Menu, select Run, then Browse to find your CD-ROM drive letter. Select the file SETUP.EXE from the root directory and follow the instructions to install the program group for this book.

Installation Notes

To install an application from this CD-ROM, you may use the program group icon or you may go directly to Windows Explorer by double-clicking on the MY COMPUTER icon on your desktop and selecting your CD-ROM drive. Using either method, go to the desired folder and select the SETUP.EXE file or the file that has the extension EXE. These are the installation programs for the software. Many of these programs will lead you through the installation process. If you have difficulty installing a program, try copying the contents of the folder onto your computer and then double-clicking on the EXE file. Always refer to any documentation that may accompany the individual software.

Troubleshooting Common Problems

The following are some typical installation problems you might encounter.

Q I don't see any directories on this CD-ROM. It looks like I have a blank disc.

A First, try to clean the data side of the CD-ROM with a clean, soft cloth. If the problem still exists, if possible, insert this CD-ROM into another computer to determine if the problem is with the disc or your CD-ROM drive.

Another cause of this problem might be that you have outdated CD-ROM drivers. In order to view the directories and access the files on this disc, first verify the manufacturer of your CD-ROM drive from your system's documentation. Or, under Windows 95/NT, you may also check your CD-ROM manufacturer by going to \Settings\Control Panel\System and select the Device Manager. Double-click on the CD-ROM and you will see the information on the manufacturer of your drive. You may download the latest drivers from your manufacturer's Web site or from `www.microsoft.com/support`.

Q The CD-ROM doesn't run properly or just spins in my CD-ROM drive.

A The usual cause of this is a damaged or dirty disc. Visually inspect the disc for possible flaws or defects, and clean it properly. You should also test another CD-ROM in your drive. This often reveals setup problems that are not disc specific. If these procedures fail, you can contact us to get a replacement disc (contact information is at the end of this file).

Q The programs run slowly or don't run properly.

A Do you have at least the follow amounts of RAM (memory)?

Windows NT: 24MB

Windows 95: 24MB

This might sound familiar, but Windows NT/95 programs do not run well on fewer megabytes. If you have only the minimum amount of RAM, the program might run slowly. Check the individual software installation instructions for RAM requirements for the program you want to install.

Also, if you have only a single-spin CD-ROM drive, files will be accessed more slowly.

Q I get an error whenever I try to double-click on an .EXE file included on the CD-ROM.

A Many of the programs included on this CD-ROM were created using a self-extracting format or require certain files to be present before installation can occur.

Instead of double-clicking on the filename directly from the CD, select the desired .ZIP file, .EXE file, or the entire directory containing the desired application. Copy the file(s) to your hard drive into a newly created folder. Double-click on the filename from your hard drive to extract the files into its own folder. Select the SETUP.EXE or INSTALL.EXE file from within the folder.

Q The uninstall doesn't remove all the icons or the program group created for this CD-ROM.

A This CD-ROM includes a very basic program group installation script that installs an uninstall file into your \Windows\temp directory and creates a new program group that includes a Readme file icon, uninstall icon, and a "Browse the CD" icon. If the uninstall option fails to remove all of these icons, you may use Windows Explorer to go to the \Windows\Start Menu\Programs directory to look for files applicable to this book and delete any of these files that remain. The file Unwise.exe that was installed may also be removed from your \Windows\temp directory.

Note: If you copied the source code to your computer, you will also need to go to the directory that contains those files to delete any files.

Contacting Us for Support

We cannot help you with computer problems, Windows problems, or third-party applications problems, but we can assist you with a problem you have with this book or the CD-ROM.

> **NOTE**
>
> Problems with another company's programs on the disc need to be resolved with the company that produced the program or demo.

If you need assistance with the information in this book or with the CD-ROM accompanying this book, please access the Knowledge Base on our Web site at

`http://www.superlibrary.com/general/support`

Our most Frequently Asked Questions are answered there. If you do not find the answer to your questions on our Web site, you may contact Macmillan Technical Support at

(317) 581-3833 or e-mail us at support@mcp.com.

Internet Email

Please be prepared to give us information on your computer system and a detailed account of the problem you're experiencing.

support@mcp.com

If you're a member of an online service such as CompuServe, America Online, Prodigy, and so on, you can send Internet email through your service.

Regular Mail

Macmillan Computer Publishing
Support Department
201 West 103rd Street
Indianapolis, IN 46290

Telephone: (317) 581-3833

Fax: (317) 581-4773

Visit us online at Internet World Wide Web (The Macmillan Information SuperLibrary):
http://www.mcp.com/

SHAREWARE

This product features Macromedia Shockwave™, the standard for multimedia on the World Wide Web. For further information regarding Shockwave, including upgrades and add-ons, visit the Shockwave section of the Macromedia World Wide Web site at http://www.macromedia.com.

Shockwave™ Copyright © 1995-1997 Macromedia, Inc.

All Rights Reserved. Shockwave is a trademark of Macromedia, Inc.

Some of the programs included on this CD-ROM are shareware—try-before-you-buy—software. Independent developers spend hundreds of hours creating, updating, and improving various utilities and tools that make everyone's computing lives that much better. These hard-working souls create the programs or add-on features that the retail products overlook, yet end users could use. "If only I could find a program that could..."

Please support these independent vendors by purchasing or registering any shareware software that you use for more than 30 days. Check with the documentation provided with the software on where and how to register the product. Thank you for your support of shareware!

LICENSE AGREEMENT

By opening this package, you are agreeing to be bound by the following agreement:

Some of the software included with this product might be copyrighted, in which case all rights are reserved by the respective copyright holder. You are licensed to use software copyrighted by the publisher and its licensors on a single computer. You may copy and/or modify the software as needed to facilitate your use of it on a single computer.

Making copies of the software for any other purpose is a violation of the United States copyright laws.

This software is sold as is, without warranty of any kind, either expressed or implied, including but not limited to the implied warranties of merchantability and fitness for a particular purpose. Neither the publisher nor its dealers or distributors assumes any liability for any alleged or actual damages arising from the use of this program. (Some states do not allow for the exclusion of implied warranties, so the exclusion might not apply to you.)

C

How to Get the
Most from the
CD-ROM

INDEX

Other Related Titles

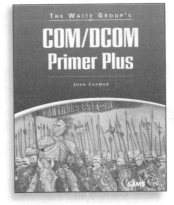